STATISTICS
FOR THE SOCIAL
AND BEHAVIORAL
SCIENCES:
UNIVARIATE, BIVARIATE,
MULTIVARIATE

STATISTICS
FOR THE SOCIAL AND BEHAVIORAL SCIENCES:
UNIVARIATE, BIVARIATE, MULTIVARIATE

GEORGE DIEKHOFF

MIDWESTERN STATE UNIVERSITY

Wm. C. Brown Publishers

Book Team

Editor *Michael Lange*
Developmental Editor *Sheralee Connors*
Production Editor *Daniel Rapp*
Art Editor *Carla Goldhammer*
Visuals Processor *Joyce E. Watters*
Visuals/Design Freelance Specialist *Barbara J. Hodgson*

Wm. C. Brown Publishers

President *G. Franklin Lewis*
Vice President, Publisher *Thomas E. Doran*
Vice President, Operations and Production *Beverly Kolz*
National Sales Manager *Virginia S. Moffat*
Group Sales Manager *Eric Ziegler*
Executive Editor *Edgar J. Laube*
Director of Marketing *Kathy Law Laube*
Marketing Manager *Carla Aspelmeier*
Managing Editor, Production *Colleen A. Yonda*
Manager of Visuals and Design *Faye M. Schilling*
Production Editorial Manager *Julie A. Kennedy*
Production Editorial Manager *Ann Fuerste*
Publishing Services Manager *Karen J. Slaght*

WCB Group

President and Chief Executive Officer *Mark C. Falb*
Chairman of the Board *Wm. C. Brown*

Cover and interior design by Elaine Allen

Library of Congress Catalog Card Number: 91–77493

ISBN 0–697–12116–X

Printed in the United States of America by Wm. C. Brown Publishers, 2460 Kerper Boulevard, Dubuque, IA 52001

10 9 8 7 6 5 4 3 2

DEDICATION

This is for Beverly,

without whose support and encouragement this book would never have been completed and whose insights are reflected in its pages

and Ben,

whose curious eyes provide a daily reminder of the joy of discovery.

CONTENTS

CHAPTER 3 DESCRIPTIVE STATISTICS 36

CHAPTER 4 STANDARD SCORES, THE NORMAL DISTRIBUTION, AND THE STANDARD NORMAL DISTRIBUTION 64

CHAPTER 5 SAMPLING DISTRIBUTIONS AND INTERVAL ESTIMATION 85

CHAPTER 6 SIGNIFICANT DIFFERENCES: ONE-SAMPLE TESTS 112

CHAPTER 7 SIGNIFICANT DIFFERENCES: TWO-SAMPLE TESTS 136

CHAPTER 16 FACTOR ANALYSIS 331

CHAPTER 17 CLUSTER ANALYSIS 360

CHAPTER 18 MULTIDIMENSIONAL SCALING 376

APPENDICES: STATISTICAL TABLES

REFERENCES AND RECOMMENDED READINGS 410

PREFACE

Statistics for the Social and Behavioral Sciences was written for graduate students in psychology, sociology, social work, and education. It is intended for use in the first graduate course in statistics or by students whose training includes only one graduate level statistics course. The goal of this text is to prepare students to be knowledgeable and competent users of statistical analysis in conducting both basic and applied research in the social and behavioral sciences.

Chapters 1 through 11 provide a review of univariate and bivariate statistics. Although most students using this text will have completed an undergraduate course in statistics, it is common to find that much has been forgotten since the completion of the undergraduate course, and that even more was not really understood in the first place. Even the best-prepared students will benefit considerably from the opportunity afforded by the early chapters of this text to review, solidify, and expand their already good foundations.

Chapters 12 through 18 cover multivariate statistical analysis. Unlike most treatments, this coverage is accomplished without resort to matrix algebra or calculus.

Throughout Statistics for the Social and Behavioral Sciences, the usual equations, derivations, and proofs have been replaced with a conceptual, sometimes intuitive approach, with plenty of diagrams and lots of concrete data-to-conclusions examples. Where mathematical expressions are used, they are backed up with verbal explanations. This approach ensures that students will both understand statistical ideas and be able to use statistical procedures.

The boxes included in most chapters serve to illustrate the statistical principles and procedures discussed in the main body of the text. Students may prefer to read the whole chapter and then return to the boxes, or the boxes may be read along with those sections of the text which they illustrate. Regardless, it is important not only that the boxes be read, but that students also work through the examples that are presented there. These examples will enhance understanding only if they are followed. In the initial chapters, a hand calculator is sufficient for this purpose; in later chapters, any of the widely used statistical software packages will be needed.

All examples included in the text are based on contrived data to ensure that the principles or procedures under consideration will be illustrated without ambiguity. Too, these data sets are sufficiently small that students can easily perform their own analyses and compare their results with those provided in the text.

It is assumed that training in the use of computers to handle data analysis is included in the course for which this text has been selected. Although software considerations are not covered in the text, an accompanying manual has been prepared that illustrates the use of the SPSS-X and SPSS-PC statistical software packages in accomplishing the procedures presented in the text.

Many people have contributed importantly to this text and the accompanying computing manual. I particularly want to thank Dr. Ludy T. Benjamin, who has been an inspiration to me throughout my student and professional years. I also want to thank Michael Lange at Wm. C. Brown for the encouragement he provided in the early stages of this project and Dorian Ring who picked up where Michael left off. Many thanks are also due Ann Shaffer, whose thoughtful advice and hard work are much appreciated. Dan Rapp is to be credited for skillfully guiding the book through the choppy waters of production. The book was also shaped by several reviewers whose comments contributed importantly, namely, Charles Mindel, University of Texas–Arlington; Michele Paludi, Hunter College, City University of New York; Ruth Ellen Proudfoot, City College, City University of New York; Matt L. Riggs, California State University–San Bernardino; Billy L. Smith, University of Central Arkansas; Eric Ward, Western Illinois University, and by Dr. Ellen Susman who class-tested an early manuscript. Thanks, too, go to my wife, Beverly, for many hours in front of the typewriter and encouragement from start to finish.

I am grateful to the literary executor of the late Sir Ronald A. Fisher, F. R. S.; to Dr. Frank Yates, F. R. S.; and to Longman Group Ltd., London for permission to reprint Tables III and VII from their book Statistical Tables for Biological, Agricultural, and Medical Research (6th edition 1974).

The study of statistical analysis need not be a mind grinding rite of passage through graduate study. It is my sincere hope that readers of Statistics for the Social and Behavioral Sciences will often experience the joy of discovery and the exhilaration of ideas connecting. I hope too that readers will let me know if that has happened and how I can make it happen more often.

George Diekhoff
Midwestern State University

STATISTICS

FOR THE SOCIAL AND BEHAVIORAL SCIENCES:

UNIVARIATE, BIVARIATE, MULTIVARIATE

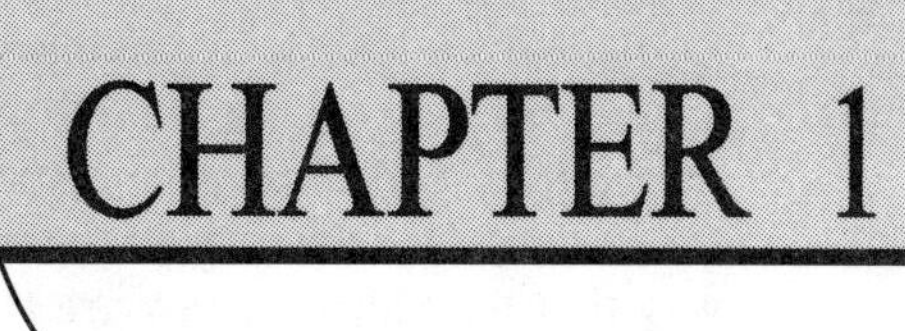

CHAPTER 1

STATISTICS, DATA, AND RESEARCH DESIGN

WHY STATISTICS?

Statistical analysis is so fundamental to the social and behavioral sciences that we can scarcely open a book or journal in these subjects without finding significance tests, correlations, and statistical summary tables. This is not surprising, for statistics are the tools of the social and behavioral scientist in much the same way that hammer and saw are the tools of the carpenter. With these statistical tools it is possible to accomplish goals as lofty as building a theory that more eloquently explains the whys and wherefores of human action, or as mundane as building an objective case for continued funding of a social service program.

Without statistics we would quickly become lost in a sea of facts and figures. The mind, after all, is scarcely able to apprehend more than about seven pieces of information at any one time, about the equivalent of a telephone number. Researchers in the social and behavioral sciences must routinely handle reams of information. **Statistics** are a means of organizing, condensing, and analyzing numerical data in ways that find order in chaos.

The importance of developing a working knowledge of statistics becomes not less important, but even more critical as computer programs for statistical analysis become more widespread. The researcher with a powerful statistical package, and no understanding of how the statistics work, can give witness to the maxim that a little knowledge is a dangerous thing! A computer program will take whatever data are provided and produce an output, but only a knowledgeable researcher can evaluate the meaning of that output, or, more importantly, the potential meaninglessness of the output. As one reviewer of this text commented, "Computing is no more statistics than word processing is writing."

Certainly, computers have changed the kind of statistical instruction that is needed by today's students. Things are different now that a factor analysis is accomplished in a matter of seconds, rather than weeks. Although computers have eliminated much of the need for an understanding of the mechanics of statistical analysis, computers still cannot choose the right statistical procedure for a given set of circumstances, nor can computers answer research questions. The answers are not in the printouts. They must be provided by the researcher. In short, the effective user of statistics needs a conceptual understanding of statistical analysis.

DATA

Statistics were defined earlier as procedures by which numerical data are organized, condensed, and analyzed. In a sense, the remainder of this book is an elaboration upon this definition, but one element of the definition, data, requires additional comment here.

The **data** to which statistical analyses are applied consist of numerical facts about cases. A **case** may be defined as the basic unit of observation. Students' test scores are data that provide numerical information about the students' level of mastery of some body of material. In this example, each student is a case, since the individual student is the unit of observation. As another example, a sociologist interested in comparing 10 cities' crime rates might rank order the cities so that the city with the highest crime rate is ranked 1, and the city with the lowest crime rate is ranked 10. Here, the ranks are the data, because they give numerical information about each city, and each city is a case.

We can see from these examples that all sorts of numerically expressed facts can serve as data for statistical analysis, and just about any imaginable entity can be a case. We will examine more fully here the various types of data used in the social and behavioral sciences, since the type of data will influence the choice of statistical analysis.

Data, the numerically expressed facts that provide the grist for statistical analysis, are the result of **measurement.** Measurement is the application of any rule by which numbers are assigned to cases in order to represent the presence or absence or quantity of some attribute possessed by each case. Simple examples of measurement abound. Reading the number adjacent to the top of a column of mercury is the rule used in measuring temperature. Counting the number of miles traveled in an hour gives a rule for measuring velocity.

Measurement in the social and behavioral sciences is seldom as simple as these examples, though, since the attributes of the cases we study are seldom as concrete as temperature or velocity. Intelligence, mood, attitude, organizational climate, and other such intangibles are at the core of most of our research. Measuring abstractions like these poses a special challenge, and ingenuity is needed for finding ways of tapping the attributes that are of interest in the social and behavioral sciences. All of these measures, though, can be placed into one of four basic categories, each called a **scale** or **level of measurement,** which are described next.

Nominal Scales of Measurement

The simplest form of measurement involves categorizing cases according to the presence or absence of some attribute. When people, rats, cities, or other cases are placed into one of a set of mutually exclusive categories according to their characteristics, a **nominal scale** of measurement is in use.

Simply categorizing cases, though, does not yield *numerical* information of the sort that is required by our definition of measurement. Measurement at the nominal level requires not only that cases be categorized, but also that they be assigned numerical scores that reflect their category assignments. These scores are arbitrarily selected numerical codes that refer to the various categories of the nominal scale variable. In the case of the nominal variable Gender, males might be assigned the score 0, and females might be scored 1. As another example, cases might be scored as follows on the nominal variable Religious Preference: 1 = Protestant, 2 = Catholic, 3 = Jewish, and 4 = Other. Of course, entirely different numbers might have been used as category codes.

Nominal scales are the "lowest" form of measurement because the numerical scores of a nominal scale variable indicate nothing about the *magnitude* or *quantity* of the attribute being measured. Cases scored 4 on the variable Religious Preference described above, for example, do not have more religious preference than do cases scored 1. Different scores indicate *qualitative* differences, not *quantitative* differences. Because of this, the mathematical manipulations that can be applied to nominal data are very limited, and even the most basic statistics, like the mean, are meaningless (pardon me!) when computed from most nominal scale data.

Dichotomously Scored Nominal Variables. There is an exception to this rule, however. The arithmetic limitations of nominal scale variables just described do not apply to dichotomously scored nominal variables, that is, variables that have only two categories, scored 0 and 1. Take the variable Gender, scored 0 = male and 1 = female, and read the data on this variable listed in Table 1.1.

TABLE 1.1 Scores on the Variable Gender

Case	Gender (0 = males; 1 = females)
Pat	0
Melissa	1
Mario	0
Kent	0
Susan	1

The mean of these scores may be computed as .4. What does this mean tell us? Does it say that the average gender in this group is .4? No. What it does show is the *proportion* of cases who received scores of 1 (females). The mean computed from data on any dichotomous nominal scale variable scored 0 or 1 describes the average makeup of the sample by giving the proportions of individuals that fall into each of the two categories of the variable. We will see in later chapters that other statistics can be computed from dichotomously scored nominal scale variables, making these variables preferable to multicategory nominal scale variables.

Dummy Variable Coding. Dichotomously scored nominal scale variables may be arithmetically manipulated in a meaningful fashion. In order to capitalize on this advantage, multicategory nominal variables are often converted to a set of several dichotomously scored nominal variables prior to statistical analysis in a process called **dummy variable coding.** Here, each category of the original multicategory variable forms a variable, and each case is scored 1 if it falls within that category and 0 if it does not. Thus, dummy variable coding creates as many new, dichotomously scored **dummy variables** as there are categories in the original variable.

Table 1.2 shows the process of dummy variable coding as it might be applied to data on the variable Religious Preference. The first case listed, a Protestant, receives four scores, one on each of the dummy variables. This case is scored 1 on the dummy variable "Protestant," because the case is a Protestant. Scores for this case on all remaining dummy variables are zeros because the case does not fall into any of the categories represented by these dummy variables. Similarly, the second case is scored 0 on the dummy variables "Protestant," "Jewish," and "Other" because this case does not fall into any of these categories. The case, a Catholic, receives a score of 1 on the dummy variable "Catholic."

TABLE 1.2 An Example of Dummy Variable Coding

Case	Religious Preference	Dummy Variables			
		Protestant	*Catholic*	*Jewish*	*Other*
Pat	1	1	0	0	0
Carla	2	0	1	0	0
Audrey	1	1	0	0	0
Melissa	4	0	0	0	1
Kent	3	0	0	1	0

Scores for five cases on a multicategory nominal scale variable, Religious Preference, are coded as follows: 1 = Protestant, 2 = Catholic, 3 = Jewish, and 4= Other. Also listed are scores on the four dummy variables that replace this multicategory nominal variable. A score of 0 on a dummy variable means that the case is not a member of that category; a score of 1 says that the case is a member of that category.

We can compute means for each of the dummy variables listed in Table 1.2 to further illustrate the advantages of dummy variable coding. These means are .4, .2, .2, and .2. They show the proportion of cases in the sample that fall into each of the different categories of the variable Religious Preference.

Ordinal Scales of Measurement

Scores on nominal scale variables convey no information about quantitative differences between cases. Scores on these variables show only qualitative differences. In contrast, scores on variables measured at the **ordinal level** offer at least a rough indication of quantitative differences.

Figure 1.1

Ordinal, interval, and ratio scales of measurement of the variable "intelligence." The horizontal line represents actual intelligence and a case's location along that line reflects the intelligence possessed by that case.

(a) In an ordinal scale, scores reflect the ordering of cases along the attribute dimension measured, but equal score differences do not necessarily reflect equal differences in the amount of the attribute possessed.

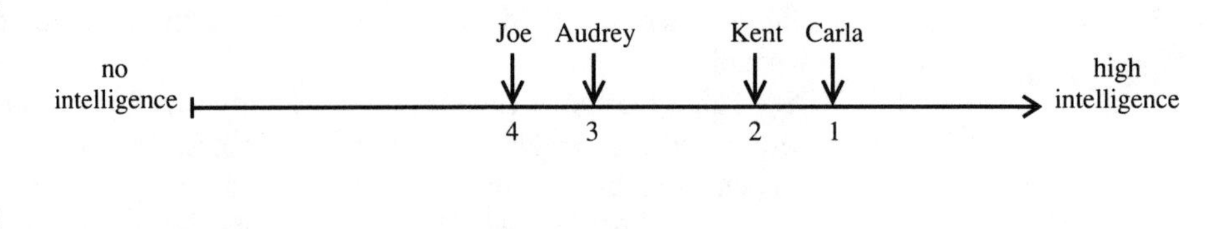

(b) In an interval scale, a case's score is equal to the number of fixed-sized units of the attribute that each case possesses. The zero point is arbitrary; it does not necessarily reflect an absence of the attribute.

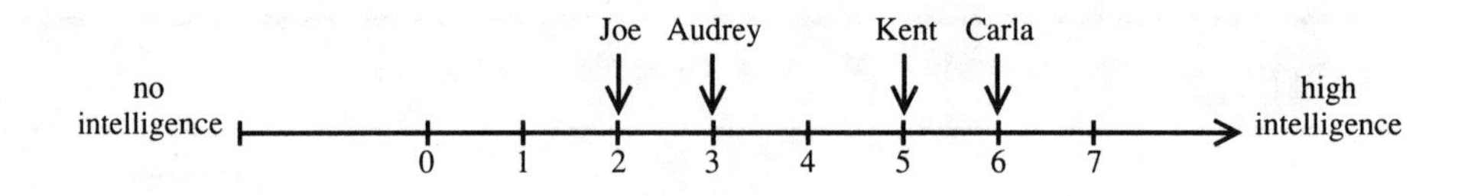

(c) In a ratio scale, each case's score is equal to the number of fixed-sized units of the attribute that a case possesses. The zero point is nonarbitrary; it represents the complete absence of the attribute.

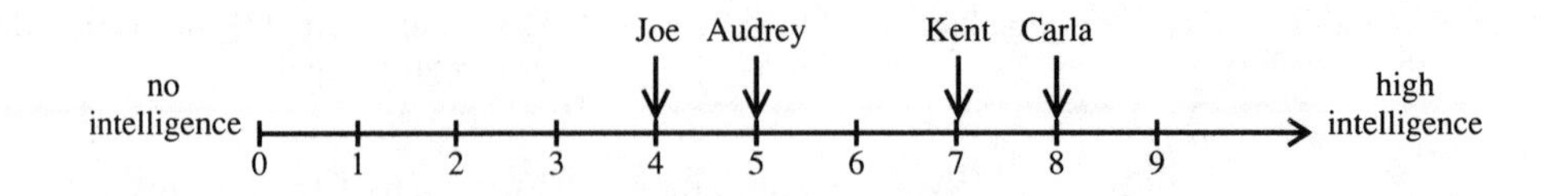

In Figure 1.1a, let the horizontal line represent an attribute, say intelligence, such that each case's location along the line shows how much intelligence that case possesses. At the far left end of the line, we find very low levels of intelligence including "no intelligence" at the extreme left. Moving toward the right we find higher levels of intelligence. If we were to rank order the cases in Figure 1.1a, Carla's "score" would be 1 (because Carla shows the highest intelligence), Kent would be scored 2 (as second highest), Audrey would be scored 3, and Joe would be ranked 4. These scores provide quantitative information about the relative amount of intelligence each case possesses. In other words, ordinal scale scores reflect the ordering of cases on the attribute being measured.

The most important defining feature of ordinal level measurement is that equal score differences do not necessarily reflect equal differences in the amount of the attribute being measured. In Figure 1.1a, for instance, Audrey's score of 3 differs from Kent's score of 2 by one point: $3 - 2 = 1$. Similarly, Kent's score of 2 differs from Carla's score of 1 by 1 point: $2 - 1 = 1$. We can see from the figure, though, that these equal score differences do not reflect equal differences in intelligence. Audrey and Kent show a greater difference in intelligence than do Kent and Carla, yet, from their scores alone, we might conclude that the difference between Audrey and Kent is equal to the difference between Kent and Carla.

This peculiarity of ordinal scales of measurement makes them about as handy as an elastic ruler! Imagine trying to measure an object with a ruler on which the distance between the 1 and 2 inch marks is different from the distance between the 2 and 3 inch marks! This is analogous to the situation that we face when using an ordinal scale of measurement.

Rank order variables provide limited opportunities for statistical analysis. Consider, for example, the following four rank order scores: 1, 2, 3, 4. The mean of these rank order scores is 2.5. What does this value tell us? Essentially nothing, since the mean of any set of rank order scores is determined not by the quantities of the attribute possessed by the cases, but by the number of cases. If there had been five cases, with ranks of 1, 2, 3, 4, and 5, the mean would have been 3. Six cases would yield a mean of 3.5. The fact that the mean of a set of rank order scores can be determined without knowing anything about the amount of the attribute that each case possesses suggests that the mean of the rank orders also tells nothing about the average amount of the attribute possessed by those cases.

Rank order scores are just one type of ordinal scale data. Rating scales are also often used to provide an ordinal level of measurement. Look at the following rating scale:

"Learning statistics is a little like having bees in your head."

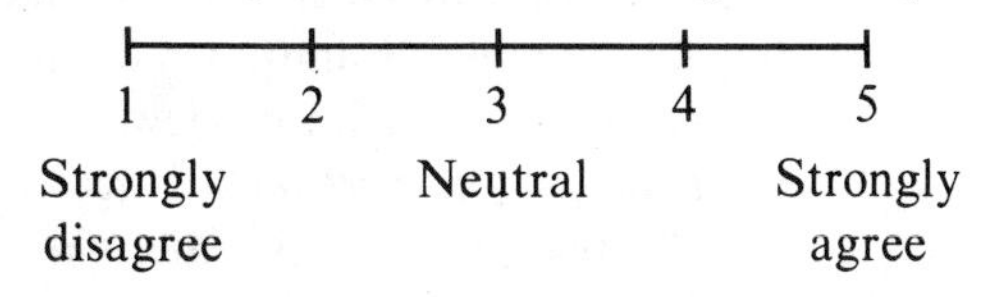

Scores obtained on this rating scale reflect magnitude of agreement with the sentiment expressed. Because there is no guarantee that equal score differences reflect equal attitudinal differences, rating scales provide an ordinal level of measurement. Although rating scales provide data that are technically ordinal, these data are often treated as interval scales, which is discussed next.

Interval Scales of Measurement

With variables measured at the **interval level** of measurement, equal score differences do reflect equal differences in the amount of the attribute being measured. This is a consequence of the fact that scores on an interval scale of measurement reflect the number of fixed-sized units of the attribute possessed by each case.

Read Figure 1.1b. Here, the dimension of intelligence has been marked off into units of equal size. If intelligence scores were assigned to the four cases now, Joe would score 2, being in possession of two of these units, Audrey would score 3, since she possesses three of the fixed-sized units, Kent would score 5, and Carla would score 6. These scores are at the interval level of measurement because (a) each case's score is equal to the number of fixed-sized units of intelligence that that case possesses; and (b) equal score differences reflect equal differences in the amount of intelligence possessed. Illustrating this second feature of the interval scale, notice in Figure 1.1b that Joe and Audrey's scores differ by the same amount (1 point) as do Kent and Carla's scores (also 1 point). Joe and Audrey differ in intelligence by the same amount as do Kent and Carla, as can be seen from the positions of these cases along the dimension representing intelligence.

The careful reader may have noticed an additional defining feature of the interval scale. The positioning of the zero point is entirely arbitrary. In Figure 1.1b, for example, a score of 0 does not indicate a complete lack of intelligence; it is simply an amount that is one unit less than the amount scored 1. A score of zero on an interval scale variable does not mean that the case presenting this score has none of the attribute being measured, but simply that the case possesses relatively little of the attribute, often an immeasurably small quantity.[1]

This feature of the interval scale leads to some complications. When working with interval scale data, it is inappropriate to make ratio statements of the sort, "Carla is twice as intelligent as Audrey." In Figure 1.1b it is evident that although Carla's score (6) is twice that of Audrey (3), Carla is less than twice as intelligent as Audrey. (If you are having trouble seeing this, measure the distance from the no-intelligence end of the line to Audrey's location and to Carla's location. Carla's distance from the no-intelligence point is *not* twice that of Audrey's.) Despite this limitation of interval scale variables, they are highly valuable from a statistical point of view, since these variables may be analyzed by using all of the most powerful statistical procedures.

The real problem with interval scales of measurement is finding out whether our data have reached this level. Imagine the task of constructing an intelligence test that yields interval level data. To make such a test, we might write a series of progressively more difficult test questions. Each question that is answered correctly would point to an increase in intelligence exactly equal to the increase indicated by a correct answer to the preceding question. Each case's score, then, would be set equal to the number of questions answered correctly. Although this seems simple enough on paper, stop to think for a minute. How would we ever know that each item measured the same fixed-sized unit of intelligence? There is no way to know. Social and behavioral scientists often assume that their data represent an interval scale of measurement when there is actually no way of knowing if this level has been achieved. It is not possible to know, for example, if the difference in intelligence between 100 and 110 IQ points is the same as the difference in intelligence between 90 and 100 IQ points, yet the psychologist analyzing intelligence test scores will undoubtedly make this assumption. Similarly, when working with rating scale data, there is no evidence that the scores represent an interval scale, but this is the assumption that is most commonly made.

Is this a risky assumption? What are the consequences of assuming data to be interval when, in fact, they are only ordinal? Let us use an example to answer this question. Figure 1.2a depicts the familiar inverted U-shaped relationship between arousal level and performance, the famous Yerkes-Dodson Law. In this diagram, both arousal and performance are measured in fixed-sized units; that is, at the interval level, and the inverted-U relationship is clearly apparent. In Figure 1.2b, both arousal and performance are measured at only the ordinal level, which means that equal score differences no longer necessarily reflect equal differences in the attributes being measured. How does this affect the plot depicting the relationship between arousal and performance? Not in any fundamental way. Arousal and performance still show an inverted-U shaped relationship. In other words, whether variables are actually measured at the ordinal or interval level matters little, since conclusions drawn about the relationships between these variables will be pretty much the same in either case. This being the case, we may as well assume that data that are not obviously ordinal (i.e., rank order data) are interval.

Figure 1.2

The inverted-*U* shaped relationship between arousal and performance is clear regardless of whether these variables are measured at the interval or ordinal levels.

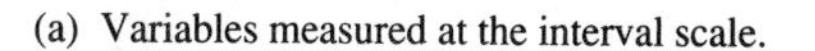
(a) Variables measured at the interval scale.

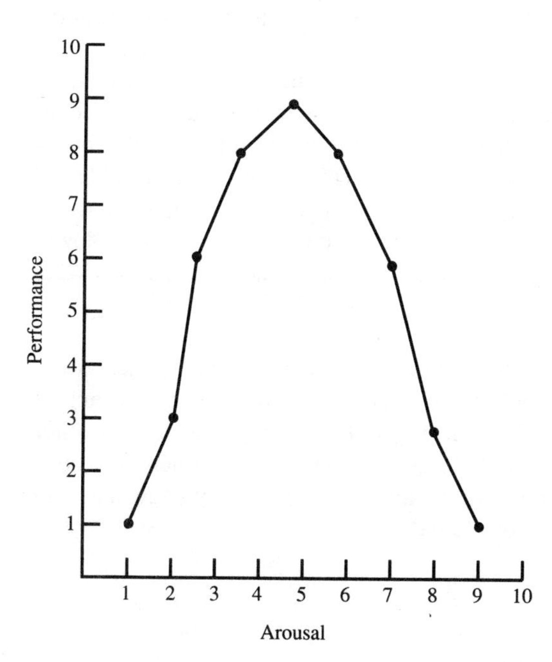

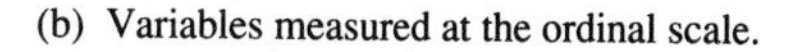
(b) Variables measured at the ordinal scale.

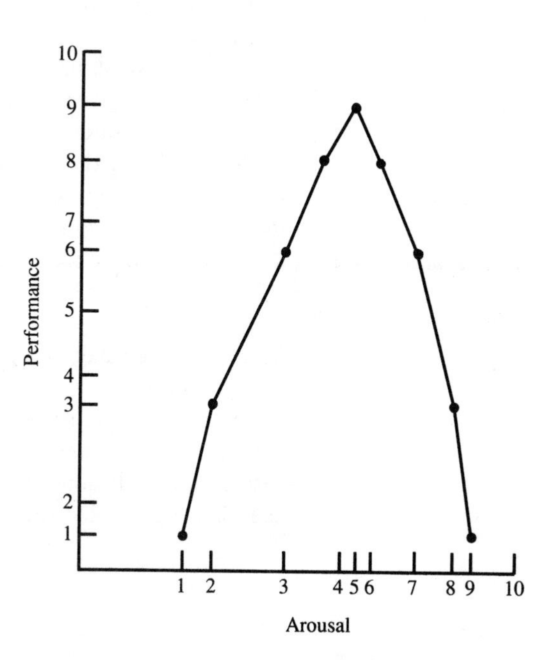

Ratio Scales of Measurement

Ratio scales of measurement possess all of the characteristics of interval scales, but have a nonarbitrary zero point. Thus, a case scored 0 on a ratio scale variable possesses none of the attribute being measured. This fact, combined with the use of fixed-sized units of measurement, means that ratio statements may now be made, for example, "Carla is twice as intelligent as Joe." To see why this is so, examine Figure 1.1c, which depicts a ratio scale of measurement. Note that a score of 0 represents the state of no intelligence. Combined with this, each case's score is equal to the number of fixed-sized units of intelligence possessed by that case. Carla has 8 units, Joe has 4. It can correctly be said that Carla has twice as much intelligence as does Joe, as their scores suggest.

Scaling Down

By now it may be apparent that some variables may be measured at any chosen level of measurement. In fact, a variable that can be measured at one level can also be measured at all lower levels. Take the variable of age as an example. Measured in years, age is a ratio scale variable. The zero point is nonarbitrary because it indicates no age, and a case's age is equal to the number of fixed-sized years that a case has accumulated. Age can be scaled down, though, to an interval level. For example, age might be represented as the number of years since a case graduated from high school. In this event, a score of 0 would be assigned to a case at the time of graduation, an obviously arbitrary zero point, but years would still serve as a fixed-sized unit of measure. Continuing the process of scaling down the age variable, cases might be rank ordered by age, with the oldest case ranked 1, the second oldest ranked 2, and so on. Finally, age categories might be established and coded numerically to create an age variable measured at the nominal level.

Notice two things about scaling down. First, although we can always scale down from any given level of measurement, it is not possible to scale up. Second, scaling down results in a loss of specificity of information about the variable being measured. With these things in mind, it makes sense to measure variables of interest at the highest possible scale of measurement. If the statistical analyses to be performed require data at a lower level, it is a simple matter to scale down.

RESEARCH DESIGN

The adage "garbage in, garbage out" is thoroughly relevant to statistical analysis, because no amount of statistical manipulation can compensate for lack of logic and common sense in the collection of the data being analyzed. In other words, a good **research design,** or plan for collecting data, is fundamental to good research. Conclusions drawn from statistical analyses will be only as good as was the plan that guided the collection of the data.

Relatively little will be said about research design in this book, but you will learn quite a bit about this topic indirectly. This is because the methods by which data are collected are constrained by the statistical analyses that are subsequently used in handling those data. There is little point in collecting data that cannot be analyzed.

To some extent, then, learning about statistics *is* learning about research design. The researcher's statistical arsenal serves as a filter through which he or she perceives research problems. The researcher who depends heavily upon tests of significance of difference (e.g., t-tests, analysis of variance) will tend to see research problems in terms of independent and dependent variables, experimental groups and control groups. The researcher with a more correlational orientation will be more attuned to survey research and the analysis of archival data, and will define problems in terms of identifying relationships between variables. It follows that the broader one's statistical knowledge, the more flexible one will be in the design of research.

SUMMARY

Statistics are defined in this chapter as procedures by which numerical facts (i.e., data) can be organized, condensed, and analyzed. Through statistical analysis we are able to make sense out of what would otherwise be incomprehensible mountains of numbers. A conceptual understanding of statistics is critically important in the age of computerized data analysis to ensure that the correct analysis will be selected and the results of this analysis will be interpreted correctly. The data for statistical analysis are obtained through measurement, defined as any rule by which each case (unit of observation) is assigned a number to reflect the presence or absence or quantity of an attribute possessed by that case. Numerical data fall into four categories, based on which of four levels of measurement is used in obtaining these data. Nominal scale measurement provides information only about qualitative differences between cases. Ordinal scale measurement gives a rough indication of quantitative differences between cases. Interval and ratio scale measurement provides even more specificity about quantitative differences. Data measured at the interval and ratio levels are used in the most powerful statistical analyses. A knowledge of statistical analysis is essential to the effective design of research since constraints on how data can be analyzed impose constraints on how those data are collected.

NOTE

1. A score of zero on an interval scale need not necessarily indicate an immeasurably low quantity of the measured attribute. For instance, the Celsius temperature scale is an interval scale on which 0 is assigned arbitrarily to the temperature at which water freezes. This score does not reflect an absence of temperature, nor is it unusual or difficult to measure temperatures below 0 degrees Celsius. These temperatures are simply expressed as negative values.

CHAPTER 2

DISTRIBUTIONS AND GRAPHING

In one way or another, all statistical procedures help to describe data and the cases that are represented by those data. A first step in this descriptive process is the organization of otherwise disorganized information and the condensation of otherwise unmanageably large quantities of information. Tabular distributions and graphs based on these distributions can be most useful in achieving these goals. Distributions, tabular or graphic, often reveal important characteristics of the data in a more direct manner than is possible using any of the more sophisticated statistical analyses.

In this chapter we will look first at how data may be organized and condensed with tables. Then we will study how these tables may be represented as graphs.

DISTRIBUTIONS

Data may be organized using several different types of distributions, each of which provides a different view of the data. We will discuss four types of distributions: frequency, percentage, cumulative frequency, and cumulative percentage. Each of these distributions may be either ungrouped or grouped. We will begin with ungrouped distributions.

Ungrouped Frequency Distributions

Look at the data in Table 2.1. The values listed are interval scale scores on the Phrenological Aptitude Test from 50 students enrolled in Phrenology 101 at Rocky Bottom State University. These scores are not arranged in a particular order, making it difficult to see clearly how well students performed as a group, how variable the scores are from one student to the next, or other features of the data.

TABLE 2.1 Scores on the Phrenological Aptitude Test from 50 Students

76	82	78	78	79	73	65	77	87	90	81	80	80	78
65	76	79	80	82	83	88	72	76	78	78	79	79	93
88	73	84	76	90	77	82	77	80	78	83	79	78	82
81	78	80	79	80	79	65	82						

Next, look at Table 2.2, an **ungrouped distribution,** which organizes these same data. Here, test scores are arranged in order from lowest to highest in the column labeled X, and frequencies are listed for each score in the column labeled f to show how many students received each listed score. With the data organized in this way, we can see at a glance that scores ranged from a low of 65 to a high of 93, that the students scoring 65 were exceptionally low scorers in this class, and that the typical score fell somewhere in the upper 70s.

The first two columns of Table 2.2, those listing scores (X) and frequencies (f), make up a tabular **ungrouped frequency distribution.** Ungrouped frequency distributions begin the process of organizing the data into a meaningful form.

TABLE 2.2 Ungrouped Distributions of Scores on the Phrenological Aptitude Test

X	f	%	f_c	$\%_c$
65	3	6	3	6
66	0	0	3	6
67	0	0	3	6
68	0	0	3	6
69	0	0	3	6
70	0	0	3	6
71	0	0	3	6
72	1	2	4	8
73	2	4	6	12
74	0	0	6	12
75	0	0	6	12
76	4	8	10	20
77	3	6	13	26
78	8	16	21	42
79	7	14	28	56
80	6	12	34	68
81	2	4	36	72
82	5	10	41	82
83	2	4	43	86
84	1	2	44	88
85	0	0	44	88
86	0	0	44	88
87	1	2	45	90
88	2	4	47	94
89	0	0	47	94
90	2	4	49	98
91	0	0	49	98
92	0	0	49	98
93	1	2	50	100
	N = 50			

Ungrouped frequency (f), percentage (%), cumulative frequency (f_c), and cumulative percentage ($\%_c$) distributions for scores (X) obtained from 50 (N) students.

Two questions may arise at this point about the construction of ungrouped frequency distributions. First, does it matter if scores are arranged in ascending or descending order? Second, should we bother listing scores that have a zero frequency of occurrence? When answering these questions remember that the purpose of constructing a distribution is to better understand the data. Do whatever works in accomplishing this. So, in answer to the first question, it does not matter if scores are arranged in ascending or descending order, provided that we begin organizing the data by ordering them in one way or the other. As far as including scores with zero frequencies, that procedure can add to the information conveyed by the table. For example, large gaps between obtained scores are more apparent if we include all potential scores, even those with zero frequencies. On the other hand, this practice clearly adds to the effort of constructing the table, as well as to the complexity and sheer size of the table. Remember that we generally construct frequency distributions *for ourselves* (such tables are seldom included in published papers or reports). We should be flexible in using whatever approach helps us to best understand the data. If we need to know about the presence of **outliers** (those isolated cases that are separated from the majority of cases by virtue of their unusually high or low scores), or need information about the relative continuity or discontinuity of scores in the distribution, then including zero frequency scores may be helpful. If this information is not important, we may decide to list only those scores that have actually occurred.

Ungrouped Percentage Distributions

An **ungrouped percentage distribution** lists the percentage of cases that obtained each score. This information is in Table 2.2 under the column headed with a percent (%) sign. These percentages are computed using Equation 2.1.

EQUATION 2.1

$$\% = \frac{f}{N} \times 100$$

where,

f = each score's frequency of occurrence
N = the total number of scores in the distribution

A percentage distribution addresses the same questions as a frequency distribution: What is the range of scores? Where are scores clustered? Are there outliers? However, percentage distributions have one advantage over frequency distributions. It is often easier to compare two or more percentage distributions than it is to compare frequency distributions. This is particularly true in those instances in which the distributions are based on data from samples of very different sizes.

This situation is illustrated in Table 2.3 where frequency and percentage distributions are given for two samples of sizes $N = 18$ and $N = 813$. Compare the frequency columns of these two tables. Despite the very different frequencies that are listed, we can see that the two frequency distributions follow the same general pattern. Next, compare the two samples' percentage distributions. Not only do the samples follow the same general pattern, we now see that their distributions are identical! The similarity in the distributions of the two samples is made much clearer through a comparison of the percentage distributions than through comparing their frequency distributions. Had the samples' distributions differed, these

TABLE 2.3 **Frequency (*f*) and percentage (%) distributions**

Sample 1 ($N_1 = 18$)			Sample 2 ($N_2 = 813$)		
X	f	%	X	f	%
1	3	16.7	1	136	16.7
2	5	27.8	2	226	27.8
3	2	11.1	3	90	11.1
4	6	33.3	4	271	33.3
5	2	11.1	5	90	11.1
	$N_1 = 18$			$N_2 = 813$	

Percentage distributions are more directly comparable than are frequency distributions when sample sizes differ.

differences would also have been seen more clearly in their percentage distributions than in their frequency distributions. It is generally true that percentage distributions convey the same information as do frequency distributions, but percentage distributions are superior to frequency distributions for directly comparing two or more sets of scores.

Ungrouped Cumulative Frequency Distributions

An **ungrouped cumulative frequency distribution** lists the number (frequency) of cases scoring at and below each listed score. Cumulative frequencies, which are determined by adding the frequency listed for a given score and frequencies listed for lower scores, are in Table 2.2 under the column labeled f_c. Cumulative frequency distributions offer little information that is of direct value, but cumulative frequency information is needed for computing cumulative percentages.

Ungrouped Cumulative Percentage (Percentile) Distributions

An **ungrouped cumulative percentage distribution** lists the percentage of cases scoring at and below each score. Cumulative percentages are given in Table 2.2 under the column headed $\%_c$. The cumulative percentage for any given score is computed using Equation 2.2.

EQUATION 2.2

$$\%_c = \frac{f_c}{N} \times 100$$

where,

f_c = the cumulative frequency listed for a score
N = the total number of scores in the distribution

Another label for cumulative percentage is **percentile.** The cumulative percentage or percentile for each score gives information that is useful for locating that score within the distribution. Thus, a score's percentile tells us how high or low, how good or bad a given score is by locating this score relative to the other scores that were obtained. This is information that a raw score does not reveal.

Imagine that Ima Odwon has just been notified that her score on the Phrenological Aptitude Test is 88. What does this mean? Unless Ima is familiar with the test and the usual distribution of scores that are obtained on this test, the raw score will tell her little. If she is told, though, that the cumulative percentage (percentile) for her score is 94%, she knows immediately that the score is a relatively high one. Ninety-four percent of the cases reported in Table 2.2 scored at and below 88. Only 6% scored higher.

A cumulative percentage or percentile distribution, then, is useful for determining quickly the relative locations of individual scores. This type of distribution can also help to identify scores that mark off specified regions of the distribution of scores, such as the lower and upper 33%. This type of information is often needed for identifying cases with low or high scores on some variable prior to a comparison of these cases on another variable.

Percentiles and Reference Groups. A percentile provides information about how good or bad, high or low, a score is. It should be emphasized, though, that this information is all relative to the particular reference group (i.e, distribution) with which the score is being compared. In Ima Odwon's case, her score of 88 on the Phrenological Aptitude Test is high, *when compared with scores of the 50 students in Phrenology 101,* and this fact is reflected in the high percentile associated with her score (94%). However, if Ima's score were compared with scores of a different reference group, say, practicing phrenologists, we would undoubtedly find her score associated with a lower percentile. Thus, percentiles must be interpreted within the context of the specific reference group being used in computing those percentiles.

Percentiles as Ordinal Scale Scores. Putting aside for the moment the relativity of the information provided by percentiles, we might still argue that percentiles are more useful than are raw scores. After all, a raw score provides no information about its location in the distribution; a percentile locates the score precisely. Why not, then, use percentiles more often? Why do we not routinely convert raw scores to percentiles and perform subsequent analyses on these percentile scores?

The reason is that the percentiles corresponding to raw scores measured at the interval or ratio levels give only an ordinal level of measurement. Look at Table 2.2 and assume that the raw scores listed there represent an interval scale of measurement. Remember from the preceding chapter that interval scales are defined by the fact that equal score differences reflect equal differences in the amount of the attribute being measured. Thus, the difference seen in Table 2.2

between scores of 65 and 76 (11 points) reflects a considerably greater real difference than is reflected by the difference between scores of 78 and 79 (1 point). If we compare the percentiles associated with these scores, though, it appears that the differences are of the same magnitude:

Raw scores	Raw score differences	Percentiles	Percentile differences
65 vs. 76	11 points	6% vs. 20%	14%
78 vs. 79	1 point	42% vs. 56%	14%

Thus, we see that equal differences in percentiles do not reflect equal differences in the amount of the attribute being measured. Remember that this characteristic defines the ordinal scale of measurement. It is generally the case that a raw score difference of a given size in the middle (average) range of a variable will be accompanied by a larger percentile difference than will the same raw score difference in the high or low ranges of the variable.

In sum, raw scores and percentile scores each provide a slightly different view of the data. These views are not equivalent, though, and each is more appropriate to some purposes than to others. Percentiles are useful for finding the relative location of a score in the distribution. Raw scores show the amount of the attribute that is possessed by each case.

Grouped Distributions

Grouped distributions are of the same four types previously described: frequency, percentage, cumulative frequency, and cumulative percentage. However, rather than listing frequencies, percentages, cumulative frequencies, and cumulative percentages for each score, grouped distributions list these values for each of several score ranges or **intervals.** As an example of grouped distributions, the data described by the ungrouped distributions of Table 2.2 are given again in Table 2.4, this time in the form of grouped distributions. Tables 2.4a through 2.4c differ only in the widths of their score ranges, called **interval widths,** and abbreviated with the letter *i.* Each score interval in Table 2.4a includes two potential scores. Thus, this grouped distribution has an interval width of $i = 2$. Table 2.4b includes five potential scores in each interval, to give an interval width of $i = 5$. Finally, Table 2.4c has an interval width of $i = 10$, because each interval includes 10 potential scores.

Several lessons about grouped distributions may be learned by comparing Tables 2.2 and 2.4. First, grouped distributions provide a simpler, more economical description of the data than do ungrouped distributions. By combining several scores into one score interval, grouped distributions reduce the total amount of information that must be digested by someone inspecting the table. Second, this information condensation becomes greater as the interval width grows larger. Notice in Table 2.4 how the distributions retain less and less information as we move from an interval width of 2 (Table 2.4a) to an interval width of 10 (Table 2.4c). Third, a price is paid for the data simplification that is achieved using grouped distributions. Information is not just simplified by a grouped distribution, it is lost. In the ungrouped distribution given as Table 2.2 we can see *exactly*

TABLE 2.4 **Grouped Distributions of Scores on the Phrenological Aptitude Test**

(a) Grouped distributions with interval width (i) of 2.

X (i = 2)	f	%	f_c	$\%_c$
65–66	3	6	3	6
67–68	0	0	3	6
69–70	0	0	3	6
71–72	1	2	4	8
73–74	2	4	6	12
75–76	4	8	10	20
77–78	11	22	21	42
79–80	13	26	34	68
81–82	7	14	41	82
83–84	3	6	44	88
85–86	0	0	44	88
87–88	3	6	47	94
89–90	2	4	49	98
91–92	0	0	49	98
93–94	1	2	50	100
	N = 50			

(b) Grouped distributions with interval width (i) of 5.

X (i = 5)	f	%	f_c	$\%_c$
65–69	3	6	3	6
70–74	3	6	6	12
75–79	22	44	28	56
80–84	16	32	44	88
85–89	3	6	47	94
90–94	3	6	50	100
	N = 50			

(c) Grouped distributions with interval width (i) of 10.

X (i = 10)	f	%	f_c	$\%_c$
65–74	6	12	6	12
75–84	38	76	44	88
85–94	6	12	50	100
	N = 50			

Grouped frequency (f), percentage (%), cumulative frequency (f_c), and cumulative percentage ($\%_c$) distributions for scores (X) from 50 (N) students.

how many cases received *exactly* which scores. In the grouped distributions of Table 2.4, however, this specificity of information is no longer available to us. From Table 2.4c (i = 10) we can see that six cases scored in the range 65–74, but we do not know *exactly* what their scores were. Did all six cases in this score interval obtain scores of 65? Perhaps three cases fell at 67, two at 72, and one at 74? There is no way of knowing. In contrast, Table 2.4b (i = 5) gives us somewhat greater specificity about how scores were distributed, and Table 2.4a ($i = 2$) tells us even more. Only the ungrouped distribution of Table 2.2, though, tells us exactly how the scores were distributed.

In short, grouped distributions can help simplify overly complex ungrouped distributions in which more information is maintained than may be needed. However, too broad an interval width can interfere with our attempt to understand the data by eliminating too much information. The trick is to find an interval width that keeps essential information, yet eliminates superfluous data.

Finding this happy compromise is mostly a matter of trial and error. Generally speaking, we should use a large enough interval width so there are few if any score intervals with frequencies of zero. Second, the interval width selected should point out the average score in the distribution. That is, one or two intervals will normally stand out as containing more cases than the surrounding intervals. Third, in grouping scores into intervals, we should generally avoid using intervals of differing widths; that is, all scores intervals in a given table should be of the same width. A failure to adhere to this rule can distort the picture provided by the distribution. However, when there are relatively few high or low scores spread out over a wide range of values, we may wish to make the bottom and/or top interval(s) open-ended, that is, "scores of X and higher," "scores of X and lower." Finally, no score intervals should include impossible scores. Suppose, for example, that we wished to use an interval width of 10 in forming a grouped distribution of scores from a test on which the top possible score was 100. Would these intervals work?

$X(i = 10)$
65–74
75–84
85–94
95–104

No. Although each score interval is of the same width as the others ($i = 10$), the top interval (95–104) includes several impossible scores (101–104). The only scores that could actually fall into this top interval are those from 95–100. In fact, the top interval really has a width of only 6, not 10. A better choice would be

$X\ (i = 10)$
61–70
71–80
81–90
91–100

All of these intervals are of equal width ($i = 10$) and none contains impossible values. Aside from these guidelines, there are no hard and fast rules on the construction of grouped distributions. Although statistical purists provide formulas for determining the "correct" interval width and worry a lot about the distinction between the "real" and "apparent" limits of each score interval, these are false concerns.

Distributions of Nominal and Ordinal Scale Data

Distributions are not just for organizing interval and ratio scale data. They can also be used with ordinal and nominal scale variables. Table 2.5 is an example of a tabular frequency and percentage distribution for the nominal scale variable of political affiliation. The frequency column, labeled *f*, provides a count of the number of cases falling into each category of the variable. The percentage column, labeled % (computed as in Equation 2.1), lists the percentage of cases falling into each category.

TABLE 2.5 Frequency (*f*) and Percentage (%) Distributions for the Variable Political Affiliation

Political affiliation	*f*	%
Republican	510	34.0
Democrat	625	41.7
Independent	200	13.3
Libertarian	165	11.0
	$N = 1500$	

Notice that cumulative frequency (f_c) and cumulative percentage ($\%_c$) columns are not included in Table 2.5. This is because these concepts are meaningless within the context of nominal scale measurement. Cumulative frequency is the number of cases scoring at and below a certain point, and cumulative percentage is the percentage of cases scoring at and below a certain point. With a nominal scale of measurement, though, there is no "below" or "above." Republicans are not considered to be "below" Democrats (except perhaps by some Democrats!), nor are Libertarians "above" Independents. Each category is simply different from the others.

This feature of nominal scale variables also makes grouped distributions inappropriate for nominal scale data. The grouped distributions in Table 2.4 were formed by combining scores that were adjacent on a continuous scale. There is no continuity among the discrete categories of a nominal scale variable. Although it made sense to form intervals of scores 65–69, 70–74, 75–79, and so on in Table 2.4b, it makes no sense to combine the categories of political affiliation that are in Table 2.5.[1]

Some types of ordinal data are meaningfully organized using distributions, but other types are not. It makes little sense, for instance, to try to organize rank order data using a frequency or percentage distribution, since, except for the occasional tied rank, each rank will occur only once. Thus, a frequency distribution of rank order data will consist of a list of as many ranks as there are cases, each with a frequency of 1. This is hardly illuminating!

TABLE 2.6 **Distributions of Rating Scale Responses**

X	f	%	f_c	$\%_c$
1 (strongly disagree)	1	5	1	5
2 (disagree)	2	10	3	15
3 (neutral or no opinion)	3	15	6	30
4 (agree)	10	50	16	80
5 (strongly agree)	4	20	20	100
	$N = 20$			

Frequency (f), percentage (%), cumulative frequency (f_c), and cumulative percentage ($\%_c$) distributions summarizing rating scale responses (X) of 20 (N) students to the statement, "Learning statistics is a little like having bees in your head."

Other types of ordinal data, such as scores obtained from rating scales, can be meaningfully organized into distributions. Table 2.6 illustrates how rating scale responses may be organized into frequency, percentage, cumulative frequency, and cumulative percentage distributions. This table summarizes data that were collected when 20 graduate students were asked to rate their level of agreement with the statement, "Learning statistics is a little like having bees in your head."

GRAPHING

Imagine that you are shown a small patch of canvas spotted with red and yellow paint. Next you are handed a piece of blue, followed by several pieces spattered with green and orange paint. Your task is to examine these painted shreds of canvas and identify the painting from which they came. What are the chances of your success? Probably pretty poor. The painting is more than individual scraps of colored paint; it is the configuration of parts that makes the painting. Examining one part, followed sequentially by the next and the next does not allow seeing the critical relationships between parts. We need to see all of the pieces simultaneously.

Making sense of data can be much like trying to identify a painting from its pieces. Numbers present information sequentially, one piece followed by the next. As in identifying the painting, we need to see the pieces together. This is made possible with graphs.

Graphs, like tabular distributions, are often neglected by researchers in the social and behavioral sciences. A graph's nonmathematical simplicity can make it look like the runt of the statistical litter. There is simply more glamour in a sophisticated statistical procedure. Nonetheless, to reshape an old adage, one graph is worth a thousand statistics. Graphs provide a unique view (literally) of our data and graphing should always precede glitzy statistical analyses.

Graphs may be used for exploring relationships between variables, differences between groups, the results of various treatments and treatment combinations, and patterns of similarity and difference between cases. These uses of graphs will be addressed in the appropriate chapters. In this chapter we will examine graphs of data distributions. Only the graphing of frequency and percentage distributions will be discussed here because there is seldom any reason to graph cumulative frequency or cumulative percentage distributions.

The type of graph most useful in plotting frequency or percentage distributions depends on the scale of measurement of the data under consideration. Only the two most widely useful graphing techniques will be studied here: bar graphs and frequency polygons.

Bar Graphs

Bar graphs are usually reserved for use with nominal scale data. Figure 2.1 uses a bar graph to display the frequency data pertaining to political affiliation that were given in Table 2.5. A bar graph depicting percentages of cases in each category would require only relabeling the graph, replacing frequencies with percentages.

Several points about bar graphs are illustrated by Figure 2.1. First, both axes of the graph are clearly labeled, with categories (levels) of the nominal variable represented along the horizontal axis (called the ***X* axis** or **abscissa**), and frequencies (or percentages) represented along the vertical axis (called the ***Y* axis** or **ordinate**). Second, bar height is used to indicate the frequency (or percentage) of cases falling within each level of the nominal scale variable. Third, the visual separation between the bars of the graph corresponds to the discrete, discontinuous nature of the categories of the nominal variable.

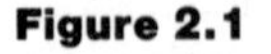

Figure 2.1

A bar graph depicting frequency data for the variable "political affiliation."

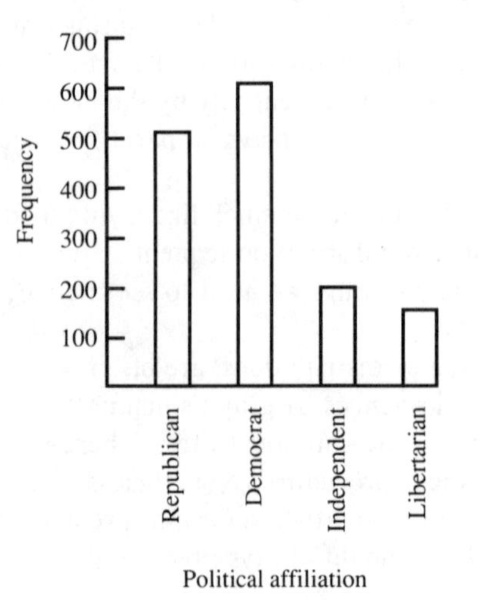

Frequency Polygons

Distributions of ordinal, interval, and ratio scale data are usually summarized using graphs called **frequency polygons.** (Although these graphs are called *frequency* polygons, they may also be used to depict *percentage* distributions.) A frequency polygon depicting the ungrouped tabular frequency distribution of Table 2.2 is presented in Figure 2.2.

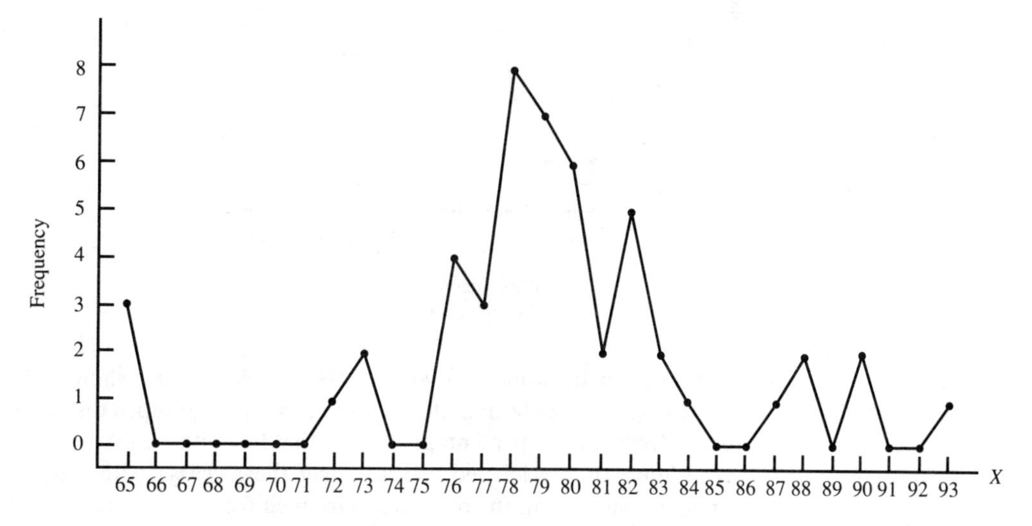

Figure 2.2

Ungrouped frequency polygon depicting the frequency of occurrence of test scores (X) on the Phrenological Aptitude Test.

You may notice several things about the graph in Figure 2.2. First, as should be the case with graphs of any sort, both axes are clearly labeled, with scores (X) listed along the abscissa, and frequencies arranged along the ordinate. Second, the frequency of cases falling at each score point is given by the altitude of a dot above that score. Third, these dots are connected with straight lines. (However, these straight lines may be replaced with a smooth curve that connects the dots, and the dots themselves may be eliminated. Look ahead to Figure 2.4 for an example of this.) This connectivity gives a visual continuity to the graph that mirrors the continuity of scores on variables measured at the ordinal, interval, and ratio levels. Finally, the complexity apparent in Table 2.2 is reflected in Figure 2.2 by the jagged angularity of the ungrouped frequency polygon. The important features of the data are difficult to identify in this graph, obscured by the graph's excessive detail.

Grouped distributions may also be graphed to assist us in better identifying the important features of the data. Figure 2.3 shows a frequency polygon for the grouped (i = 5) frequency distribution presented first in tabular form in Table 2.4b. As always, this graph is completely and clearly labeled. Unlike graphs of

Figure 2.3

Grouped frequency polygon (interval width = 5) depicting the frequency of occurrence of test scores (X) on the Phrenological Aptitude Test.

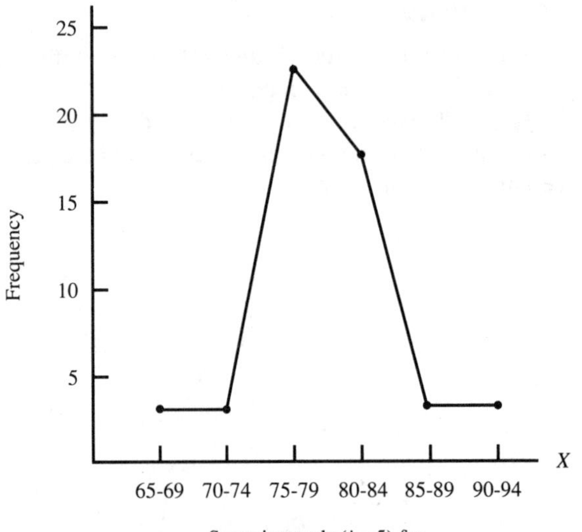

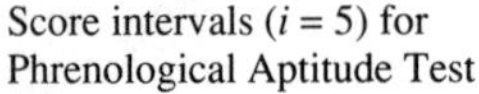

ungrouped distributions, in which dots over each *score* show the frequency or percentage of cases falling at that score, graphs of grouped distributions use dots for the frequency or percentage of cases that fall within each *score interval.* These score intervals are labeled clearly along the abscissa with frequencies or percentages listed along the ordinate.[2] Grouped frequency polygons sacrifice exactitude for greater economy and interpretability. The characteristics of the data are considerably clearer in Figure 2.3 than in the ungrouped frequency polygon of Figure 2.2.

WHAT TO LOOK FOR IN GRAPHED DISTRIBUTIONS

Let us consider next exactly what we should look for in graphed distributions. How do we "read" these graphs? Several important features of our data are apparent in the graphs of their distributions: central tendency, variability, kurtosis, skewness, and modality characteristics.

Central Tendency

The **central tendency** of the data refers to the typical or average score. Central tendency information is used when one is interested in describing a group as a whole, without regard to variability from one case to the next. For example, "The average starting salary for lawyers is $32,500." "The average cost of a new home in this area is $88,000." "The average score on the Phrenological Aptitude Test is 73." As seen in Figure 2.4, the central tendency of a graphed distribution of scores can be identified as that score or range of scores located toward the center of the distribution. There will generally be a frequency "peak" directly over the central tendency.

Figure 2.4

Central tendency refers to the typical or average score, usually located toward the center of the frequency distribution.

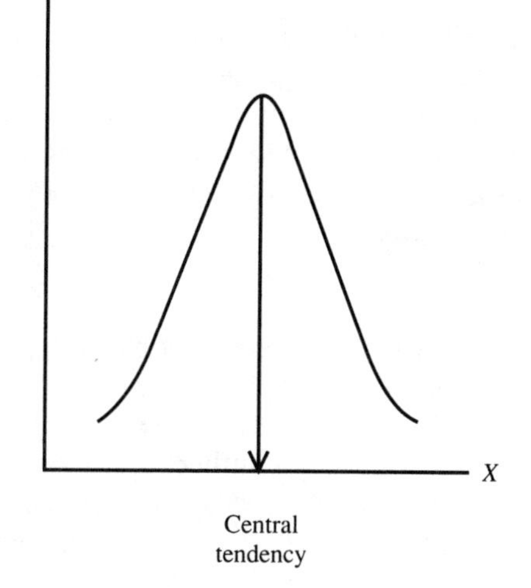

Variability

In assessing the **variability** or **dispersion** of scores, we are interested in knowing whether the cases all tend to score at about the same point (indicating low variability), or if the scores are widely scattered (indicating high variability). It is often as important to know about the variability of scores as it is to know about their central tendency. In a study of the effectiveness of an antidepressant drug, for instance, it is as important to know about the variability of the drug's effects from one patient to the next as it is to know the drug's average effectiveness.

Score variability is shown in a graphed distribution by the width of the frequency polygon. The two distributions depicted in Figure 2.5 show equivalent central tendencies, but differ in variability.

Figure 2.5

Variability refers to the dispersion or spread of scores, reflected in the width of the frequency distribution. The two distributions shown here differ only in variability; they show equivalent central tendencies. The wider graph depicts high variability; the narrower graph depicts less variability.

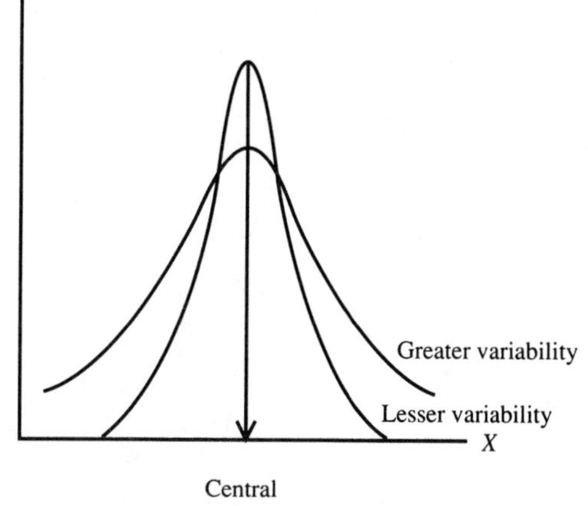

Kurtosis

The **kurtosis** of a distribution describes the relative flatness or peakedness of a distribution. (It does not refer to any olfactory unpleasantness of the data!) **Platykurtic** distributions are exceptionally flat, **leptokurtic** distributions are unusually peaked, and **mesokurtic** distributions are between these extremes. Because kurtosis is so strongly related to data variability, little more need be said about this feature of the distribution.

Skewness

Skewness is the symmetry vs. lopsidedness of our data, as shown in Figure 2.6. When most scores are relatively low, but there are a few unusually high scores (outliers), the data are said to be **positively skewed** (Figure 2.6a). When the majority of cases score high, but a few outliers score low, the data are **negatively skewed** (Figure 2.6b). Finally, when the data are symmetrically distributed, with high and low scores in approximately equal balance, there is no skewness at all (Figure 2.6c).

It is important to identify skewness in the data for several reasons. For one thing, we may wish to examine more closely those cases with extreme scores, the outliers. What about these cases accounts for their unusual scores? Second, skewed data can distort the outcomes of many commonly used statistical procedures. Even such a simple statistic as the mean (chapter 3) gives an inaccurate indication of the average score when the data are skewed. We will have more to say about skewed data in subsequent chapters. Let it suffice to say for now, however, that identifying skewness in our data is important and this is most easily accomplished by looking at a graph of the distribution.

Figure 2.6

Frequency distributions showing varying degrees of skewness.

(a) A positively skewed distribution.

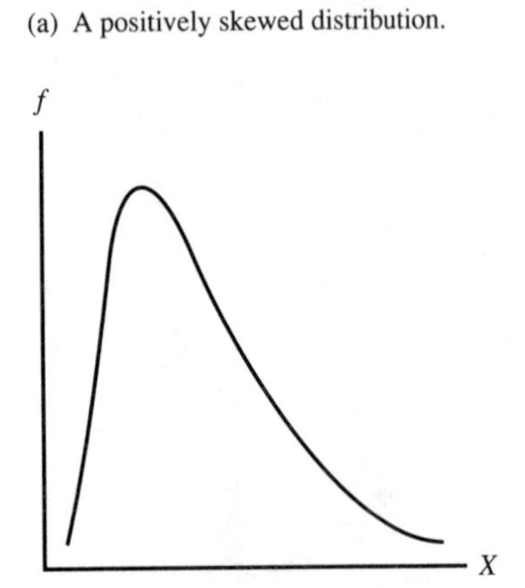

(b) A negatively skewed distribution.

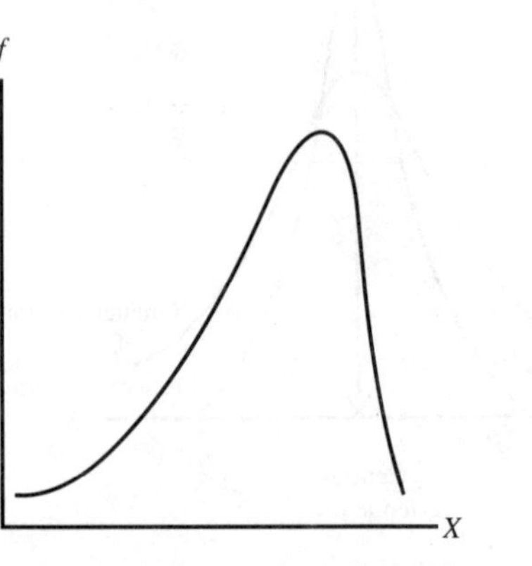

(c) A distribution with no skew.

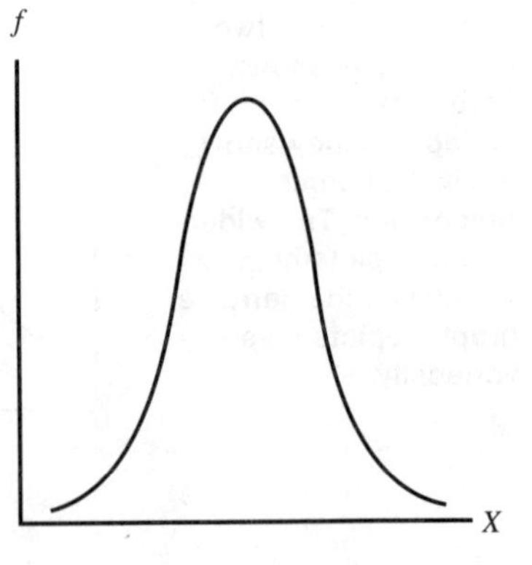

Figure 2.7

Frequency distributions showing various modality characteristics.

(a) A unimodal distribution.

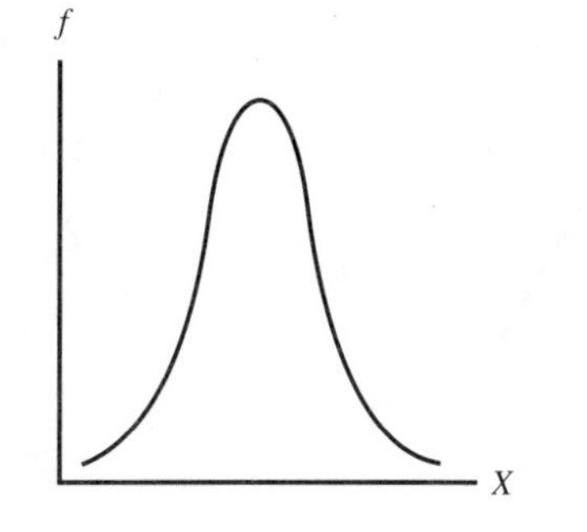

(b) A bimodal distribution.

f

X

(c) A multimodal distribution.

f

X

(d) A rectangular distribution.

f

X

Modality Characteristics

Frequency distributions also vary in their **modality characteristics** as illustrated in Figure 2.7. Distributions may be **unimodal** (Figure 2.7a), having a single frequency peak (mode), **bimodal** (Figure 2.7b), having two distinct frequency peaks, or **multimodal** (Figure 2.7c), having three or more frequency peaks. Sometimes data will show an equal distribution of scores across all scores or score intervals. These are called **rectangular** distributions (Figure 2.7d) and have no mode.

An example may be instructive in explaining how a distribution comes to have more than one mode and why this matters. Figure 2.8a depicts test scores from a section of Introduction to Common Knowledge that is heavily attended by t.v. junkies. Notice that the scores of students in this section are relatively low, with a frequency peak over the score range 66–70. Test scores for an honors section of students are in Figure 2.8b. Scores from this section tend to be somewhat higher, with a frequency peak over the score interval 86–90. In Figure 2.8c, data from these two classes have been combined into a single distribution. The result

Figure 2.8

Combining data from two distinct, relatively homogeneous subgroups results in a frequency distribution that is bimodal. These distributions present tests scores from two sections of Introduction to Common Knowledge (X).

(a) Frequency distribution of test scores for T.V. junkies section.

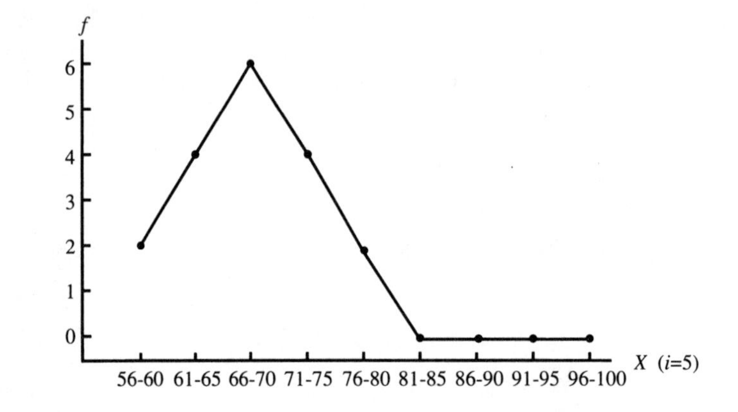

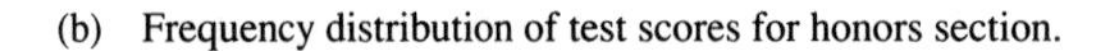
(b) Frequency distribution of test scores for honors section.

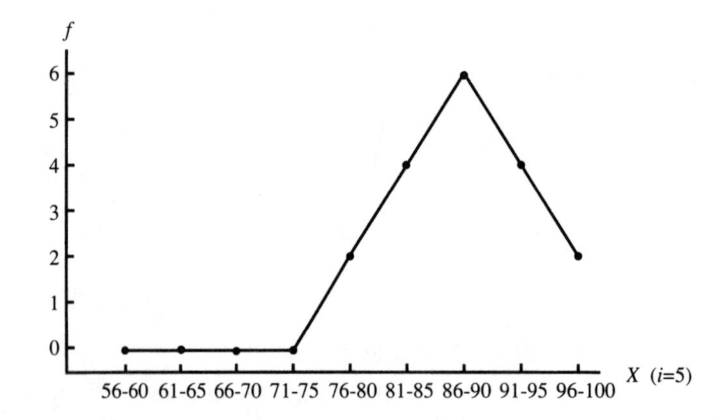

(c) Combined frequency distribution.

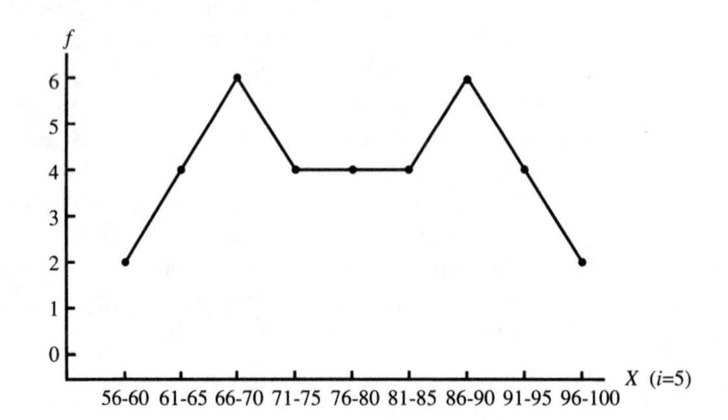

is a bimodal frequency distribution in which the lower frequency peak represents the t.v. junkies and the upper frequency peak represents the honors students. This bimodal distribution is the one that would have been obtained if, instead of dividing the students into two separate sections of Introduction to Common Knowledge, there had been a single, mixed class.

In general, the presence of more than one frequency peak (mode) in a distribution means that the data represent several relatively homogeneous subgroups within the larger sample being studied. Each mode represents one of these subgroups. Examining a frequency distribution for its modality characteristics, then, gives us important information about the composition of the sample under investigation.

SUMMARY

Tabular distributions and graphs of these distributions organize and condense what would otherwise be an incomprehensible mass of numerical information. Frequency distributions show the number of cases that received each score (in the case of ungrouped distributions) or fell into each of several score intervals (in the case of grouped distributions). Other distributions may also be grouped or ungrouped. Percentage distributions denote the percentage of cases scoring at each score or in each score interval. Cumulative frequency distributions list the number of cases falling at and below each score or score interval. Cumulative percentage distributions list the percentage of cases falling at and below each score or score interval. Cumulative percentages are also called percentiles and are good for locating a score relative to other scores in the distribution. Both grouped and ungrouped distributions have advantages and disadvantages. Ungrouped distributions preserve the maximum possible amount of information, but are often excessively complex. Grouped distributions are simpler, but at the expense of lost information. Graphs of frequency and percentage distributions are particularly useful, since these visual displays provide a direct means of assessing certain important characteristics of the data. Bar graphs are most often used to depict distributions of nominal scale data. Frequency polygons are used with ordinal, interval, and ratio scale data. Central tendency is the average or typical score in the distribution, indicated by scores toward the center of the distribution. Variability refers to how spread out the scores are from one case to the next, reflected in the width of the distribution. Kurtosis is strongly related to variability and refers to the peakedness vs. flatness of the distribution. Skewness exists when the distribution is lopsided. This happens when there are either a handful of extremely high scores (called positive skew) or a few extremely low scores (called negative skew). Finally, modality characteristics refer to how many frequency peaks or modes are seen in the distribution. Distributions with two (bimodal) or more (multimodal) modes suggest the presence of two or more relatively homogeneous subgroups within the sample being examined. Rectangular distributions show no frequency peak.

NOTES

1. It is generally true that because the categories of nominal scale variables are discontinuous, they cannot be meaningfully combined. However, we can imagine circumstances in which meaningful combinations might be formed on the basis of semantic relationships. In the present example, the categories Republican and Democrat might be combined and labeled "Traditional Affiliations." Similarly, the categories Independent and Libertarian might be combined and labeled "Nontraditional Affiliations." Using another example, take the variable of religion, with categories Baptist, Methodist, Lutheran, and Catholic. Since the first three categories are all Protestant denominations, they might be combined into a single category labeled "Protestant."
2. Graphs of grouped distributions often list only midpoints of score intervals along the abscissa. Were this practice to be followed in Figure 2.3, points along the abscissa would be labeled 67, 72, 77, 82, 87, and 92, and the abscissa would be labeled "Score Interval Midpoints."

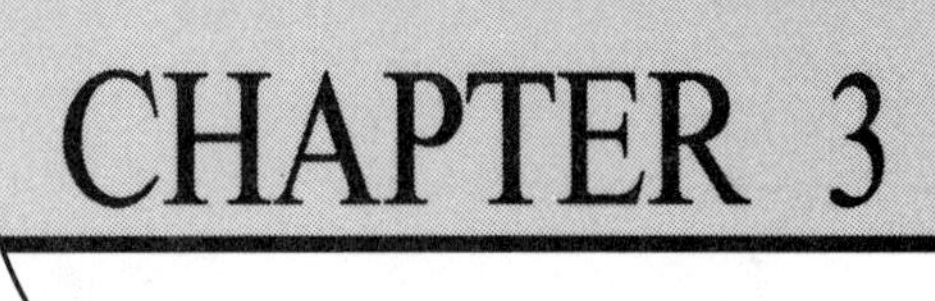

CHAPTER 3

DESCRIPTIVE STATISTICS

We learned in chapter 2 that central tendency, variability, and other important characteristics of our data can be explored using frequency distributions. Graphs of these distributions were particularly useful in getting acquainted with the data. Although there is no substitute for graphing in the initial stages of data analysis, graphs can provide only general information about the data, not specifics.

The greater precision that we seek is provided by **descriptive statistics.** Statistics may be defined as numbers computed from data that tell us something about those data. *Descriptive* statistics are numbers computed from data that describe the data's central tendency, variability, and other characteristics.

CENTRAL TENDENCY

Three statistics are commonly used to describe the typical or average score in a distribution, that is, the central tendency. These are the mean, median, and mode.

Mean

The **mean** is far and away the most frequently used measure of central tendency. The mean's popularity stems from its computational ease and from the fact that the mean is a component used in many other statistical procedures.

The mean of a variable X is commonly represented by the symbol $\overline{X}$. The mean of a variable Y is represented by $\overline{Y}$, and so on. Subscripts can be used to specify the means of various different groups. Thus, $\overline{X}_1$ is the mean of Group 1 on variable X; $\overline{Y}_2$ is the mean of Group 2 on variable Y. The mean of a population, as opposed to a sample, is represented by the Greek letter mu, μ.

Computation of the Mean. The mean may be computed in a variety of ways, depending on the nature of the data that are available. These computational methods are illustrated in Box 3.1 and are discussed here.

When working with raw scores, the mean of a variable is computed according to Equation 3.1.

EQUATION 3.1

$$\overline{X} = \frac{\Sigma X}{N}$$

where,

X = scores on the variable X
N = the total number of cases

In words, we add the values of the variable X and divide by the number of those values.

Means may also be computed from ungrouped frequency distributions. Since these distributions preserve all of the information that is present in the raw scores, means computed from raw scores and from ungrouped frequency distributions will be identical. Equation 3.2 is used in computing the mean from an ungrouped frequency distribution.

EQUATION 3.2

$$\overline{X} = \frac{\Sigma fX}{N}$$

where,

f = the frequency associated with each value of the variable X
X = values of the variable X
N = the total number of cases

In words, each value of X is multiplied by its frequency of occurrence, these products are summed, and this sum is divided by N.

Means can be estimated, but not computed exactly, from grouped frequency distributions according to Equation 3.3.

EQUATION 3.3

$$\overline{X} = \frac{\Sigma fm}{N}$$

where,

f = the frequency associated with each score interval
m = the midpoint of each score interval (i.e., the value exactly halfway between the upper and lower limits of the score interval)
N = the total number of cases

In words, the midpoint of each interval is multiplied by the frequency listed for that interval, these products are summed, and this sum is divided by N.

Means can only be *estimated* from grouped frequency distributions because, as we saw in the previous chapter, some information about scores is lost when scores are grouped into intervals. Generally, the wider the interval, the more error we can expect when estimating the mean from a grouped distribution.

Finally, there are occasions when we wish to combine means of two or more groups to obtain an overall mean, called a **grand mean** ($\overline{X}_G$) or **weighted mean.** The weighted or grand mean is computed using Equation 3.4.

EQUATION 3.4

$$\overline{X}_G = \frac{\Sigma n\overline{X}}{N}$$

where,

n = samples sizes
$\overline{X}$ = sample means
N = the total number of cases (Σn)

To illustrate, say we have obtained means on the Kierkegaard Angst Inventory from 20 psychology students ($\overline{X}_1 = 24$), 15 social work students ($\overline{X}_2 = 20$), and 30 sociology students ($\overline{X}_3 = 15$). In order to determine the mean level of angst for the entire group of 65 students, we weight the group means by their sample sizes, sum these weighted means, and divide by the total number of cases:

$$\begin{aligned}\bar{X}_G &= \frac{\Sigma n\bar{X}}{N} \\ &= \frac{20(24) + 15(20) + 30(15)}{65} \\ &= 18.92\end{aligned}$$

This procedure ensures that the grand mean will be influenced more by large samples than by small samples.

Characteristics of the Mean. The mean may be described in several ways. First, it is the most commonly used indicator of the average score in a distribution. When the word "average" is used, it can refer to any indicator of central tendency, but usually refers to the mean.

Second, the mean may be defined as that point in a distribution around which the deviations sum to zero:

$$\Sigma(X - \bar{X}) = 0$$

In other words, the mean is a sort of mathematical balancing point in the distribution, such that the sum of deviations of scores falling above the mean exactly equals the sum of deviations of scores falling below the mean. To illustrate this point, think about the following values of the variable X.

$$X = 2, 3, 8, 10, 17$$

The mean of these values is $\bar{X} = 8$. Scores below the mean show negative deviations from the mean:

$$\begin{aligned}2 - 8 &= -6 \\ 3 - 8 &= -5\end{aligned}$$

Scores above the mean show positive deviations from the mean:

$$\begin{aligned}10 - 8 &= +2 \\ 17 - 8 &= +9\end{aligned}$$

The score exactly at the mean shows a zero deviation from the mean:

$$8 - 8 = 0$$

The sum of these deviations is zero:

$$-6 + -5 + 2 + 9 + 0 = 0$$

Third, the sum of the squared deviations of scores around the mean is smaller than the sum of squared deviations around any other value:

$$\Sigma(X - \bar{X})^2 = \text{minimized}$$

Take the same values of X listed just above, subtract the mean from each, square each of these "deviations around the mean," and sum these squares:

X	$X - \bar{X}$	$(X - \bar{X})^2$
2	$2 - 8 = -6$	$-6^2 = 36$
3	$3 - 8 = -5$	$-5^2 = 25$
8	$8 - 8 = 0$	$0^2 = 0$
10	$10 - 8 = 2$	$2^2 = 4$
17	$17 - 8 = 9$	$9^2 = 81$
		$\Sigma(X - \bar{X})^2 = 146$

The value 146 is smaller than the sum of squared deviations around any other value, a fact that readers may wish to demonstrate for themselves. It is sometimes said that the mean meets the "least squares criterion," meaning simply that the mean is chosen so that $\Sigma(X - \bar{X})^2$ is minimized. This is a feature of the mean to which we will refer again in the context of regression analysis (chapter 11).

A final characteristic of the mean, and the feature that is of greatest importance from an applied standpoint, is that the mean is strongly influenced by extreme scores. Specifically, the mean is pulled toward these outliers in an exaggerated fashion. This instability of the mean makes it an inappropriate measure of central tendency when the distribution is skewed by outliers. To illustrate this point, consider the salaries at Capitalistic Exploitations, Inc., shown in Table 3.1. The mean annual salary at this company, computed according to Equation 3.1, is $\bar{X} = \$28,272.73$. This value hardly represents the typical salary at Capitalistic Exploitations. Only 2 of the 11 employees listed make this much money. What has happened is that the mean has been pulled excessively in the direction of the outlier, that is, the President's $150,000 annual salary.

TABLE 3.1 Salary Data for Employees of Capitalistic Exploitations, Inc.

	Salaries	
Employees (N = 11)	*Annual*	*Monthly*
President and Supreme Ruler	$150,000	$12,500
Vice-President for Bowing and Scraping	30,000	2,500
Chief Yes Man	25,000	2,083
Coordinator of Blind Obedience	22,000	1,833
Common Peasant, First Class	15,000	1,250
Common Peasant, First Class	15,000	1,250
Common Peasant, Second Class	12,000	1,000
Common Peasant, Second Class	12,000	1,000
Common Peasant, No Class	10,000	833
Common Peasant, No Class	10,000	833
Common Peasant, No Class	10,000	833

The location of the mean in skewed and nonskewed distributions is shown in Figure 3.1. Only in nonskewed, unimodal distributions (Figure 3.1a) is the mean an accurate indicator of the typical or average score. In positively skewed distributions (Figure 3.1b), the mean is too high to represent the central tendency accurately. In negatively skewed distributions (Figure 3.1c), the mean is too low to give a good indication of central tendency.

Figure 3.1

The location of the mean in skewed and nonskewed distributions.

(a) The mean of a unimodal, nonskewed distribution.

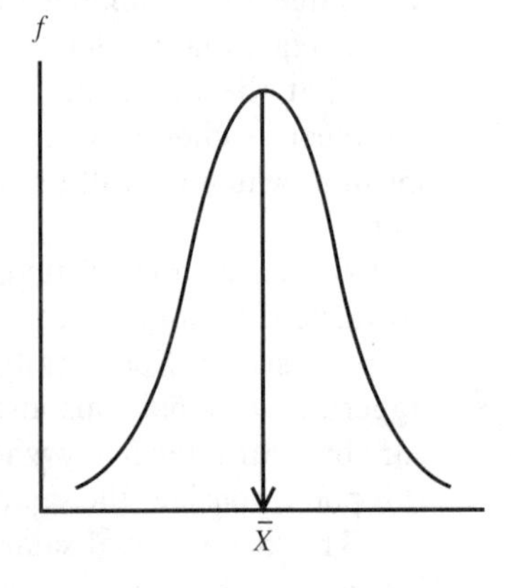

(b) The mean of a positively skewed distribution.

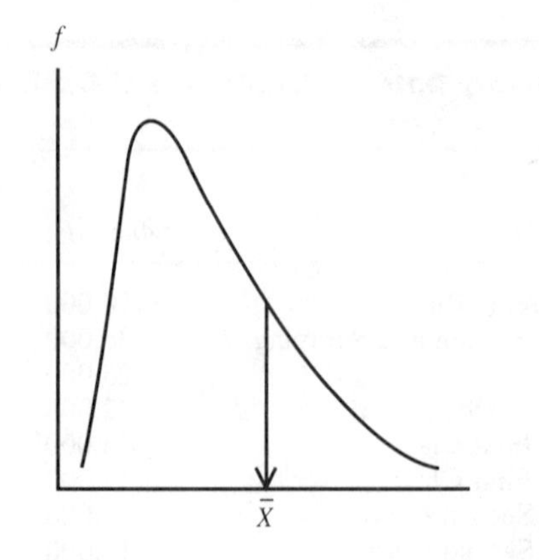

(c) The mean of a negatively skewed distribution.

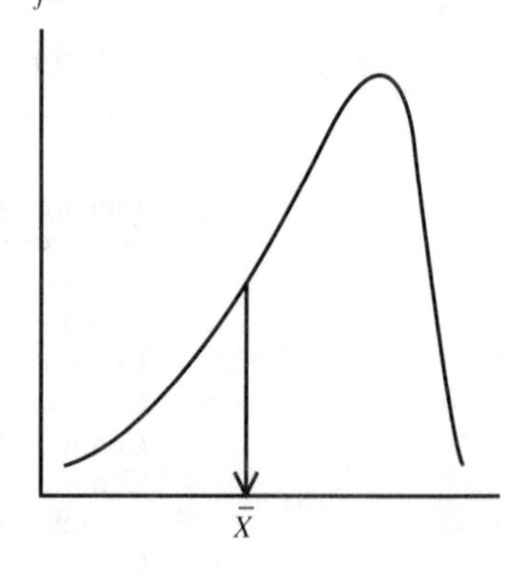

Another time when the mean gives a misleading indication of central tendency is when the scores form a bimodal distribution. Figure 3.2 illustrates this point. The mean in a bimodal distribution is located at a point where very few cases fall; the vast majority of cases score either higher or lower than the mean. Thus, whenever scores deviate from a unimodal distribution, the mean is suspect as an indicator of the typical or average score.

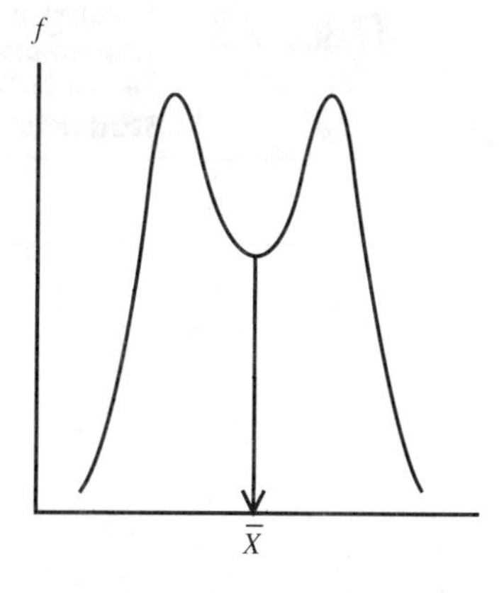

Figure 3.2
The location of the mean in a bimodal distribution.

Median

The **median,** abbreviated **Md,** is used less often than the mean as an indicator of central tendency. The median is more difficult to compute and is a component in relatively few other statistical procedures.

Computation of the Median. Like the mean, the median may be computed in a variety of ways, depending on the nature of the data that are available. These computational methods are illustrated in Box 3.2 and are discussed here.

The median of a collection of raw scores is computed according to Equation 3.5.

EQUATION 3.5

$$\text{Md} = \frac{N + 1}{2}\text{th score in an ordered array}$$

where,

$$N = \text{the total number of cases}$$

The first step in computing the median is to arrange scores in either ascending or descending order, thus forming an **ordered array.** It is this first step that can make computing a median from unorganized raw data very tedious. Once the scores are ordered, the median is determined by simply counting. The median is the score at the $(N + 1)/2$th position, counting either from the top score of the ordered array or the bottom score. In other words, the median is the score at the exact middle of the ordered array; an equal number of scores fall on each side.

BOX 3.1

COMPUTATION OF THE MEAN

Scores from 50 Rocky Bottom State University students on the Phrenological Aptitude Test, first seen in chapter 2, are given again in Table 3.2.

TABLE 3.2 Scores on the Phrenological Aptitude Test from $N = 50$ Students

76	82	78	78	79	73	65
65	76	79	80	82	83	88
88	73	84	76	90	77	82
81	78	80	79	80	79	65
77	87	90	81	80	80	78
72	76	78	78	79	79	93
77	80	78	83	79	78	82
82						

Computing the Mean Using Raw Scores

The mean of the raw scores in Table 3.2 is computed according to Equation 3.1.

$$\bar{X} = \frac{\Sigma X}{N}$$

$$= \frac{76 + 82 + 78 + \ldots + 82}{50}$$

$$= \frac{3963}{50}$$

$$= 79.26$$

This value shows that the average or typical student taking the test received a score of 79.26. This is consistent with the central tendency seen in Figure 2.2 in chapter 2.

TABLE 3.3 Frequency Distribution for Scores on the Phrenological Aptitude Test from $N = 50$ Students

X	f
65	3
72	1
73	2
76	4
77	3
78	8
79	7
80	6
81	2
82	5
83	2
84	1
87	1
88	2
90	2
93	1

Computing the Mean from an Ungrouped Frequency Distribution

Table 3.3 organizes the data from Table 3.2 into an ungrouped frequency distribution.

Medians are easily computed from ungrouped frequency distributions because scores have already been arranged into an ordered array in these distributions. We find the median in an ungrouped frequency distribution by counting frequencies. As before, the median is the score at the $(N + 1)/2$th position, counting either from the top score or the bottom score.

BOX 3.1—*continued*

The mean of these data is computed according to Equation 3.2.

$$\bar{X} = \frac{\Sigma fX}{N}$$

$$= \frac{3(65) + 1(72) + 2(73) + \ldots + 1(93)}{50}$$

$$= 79.26$$

Because an ungrouped frequency distribution retains all of the information present in the ungrouped raw scores, the mean computed here is exactly equal to the mean computed above using Equation 3.1.

Computation of the Mean from a Grouped Frequency Distribution

Table 3.4 lists the data from Table 3.2 in the form of a grouped frequency distribution ($i = 5$). The mean of this grouped frequency distribution is computed according to Equation 3.3.

$$\bar{X} = \frac{\Sigma fm}{N}$$

$$= \frac{3(67) + 3(72) + \ldots + 3(92)}{50}$$

$$= 79.20$$

TABLE 3.4 Grouped Frequency Distribution ($i = 5$) for Scores on the Phrenological Aptitude Test from $N = 50$ Students

X ($i = 5$)	m	f
65–69	67	3
70–74	72	3
75–79	77	22
80–84	82	16
85–89	87	3
90–94	92	3

Midpoints (m) are indicated for each score interval.

This value differs slightly from the values computed previously ($\bar{X} = 79.26$) because information needed to compute the true value of the mean is lost when scores are grouped into intervals in forming the grouped frequency distribution.

Medians may be estimated, but not computed exactly, from grouped frequency distributions. The median may be estimated as the midpoint of the score interval containing the $(N + 1)/2$th score. More elaborate procedures are available for use in estimating the median from grouped data (e.g., Shavelson, 1988), but these procedures add very little to the accuracy of the much simpler procedure recommended here.[1]

Finally, it is sometimes said that the median is the score at the 50th percentile. This is not exactly true. It is also said that the median is the score above and below which 50% of the scores fall. This is also not true. Consider the following values of the variable X:

$$X = 10, 20, 30, 40, 50$$

The median here is 30. This score, though, has a percentile of 60%, not 50%. Moreover, two scores fall above 30 and two fall below 30. Two scores do not constitute half of the scores in this set. Despite all this, in a large distribution of scores, the score at the 50th percentile provides a very good estimate of the median, and almost half of the scores will fall above and below the median.

Characteristics of the Median. Like the mean, the median is a sort of balancing point in a distribution. The median, though, is not a mathematical balancing point so much as it is a geometric balancing point. Specifically, the median is the point above and below which an equal number of scores fall.

The most distinguishing feature of the median is its stability in the face of outliers. The median, unlike the mean, accurately reports a distribution's central tendency regardless of whether the distribution is skewed because the median is much less affected by extreme scores than is the mean. This fact can be illustrated by looking back at the salary data in Table 3.1. Although the mean ($\bar{X}$ = $28,272.73) gave a misleading indication of the true average annual income in this set of salaries, the median gives us a true picture of central tendency. Computed according to Equation 3.5, the median annual salary in Table 3.1 is Md = $15,000. This value is close to the salaries received by the vast majority of employees.

In general, if our purpose is to describe the central tendency of a set of scores, the median is preferable to the mean. This is because the median gives an undistorted picture of central tendency whether the data are skewed or not. That is, there are fewer conditions that must be met in order for the median to be used. The relationship between skewness, the mean, and the median is summarized in Figure 3.3. As shown in Figure 3.3a when the data are unskewed, the mean and the median are equal and both are an accurate measure of central tendency. When the data are either positively skewed (Figure 3.3b) or negatively skewed (Figure 3.3c), though, the median is a more accurate indicator of central tendency.

This is not to say that the median is universally applicable. Neither the mean nor the median is resistant to the distorting influence of bimodal data. As seen in Figure 3.4, the mean and the median in a bimodal distribution both fall at a location that is far from typical for the vast majority of cases, who score either higher or lower than the mean or median.

Mode

The **mode** is a third measure of central tendency. It is technically defined as that score (or scores) in a distribution having the greatest frequency of occurrence.

Figure 3.3

The relative locations of the mean and median in nonskewed and skewed distributions.

(a) The mean and median are located at the same point in a nonskewed distribution.

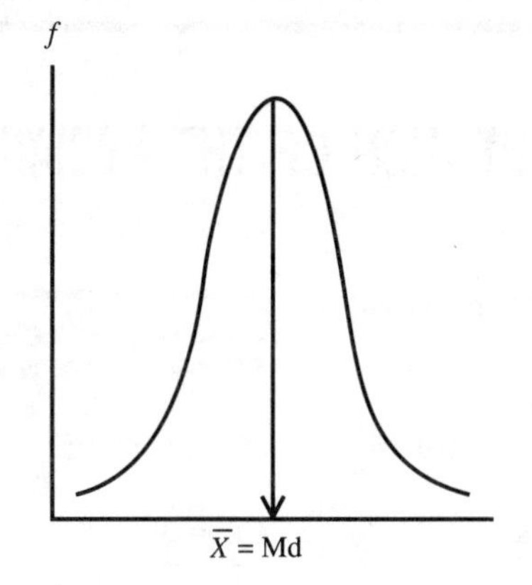

(b) The median provides a better indication of the typical score in a positively skewed distribution; the mean is too high.

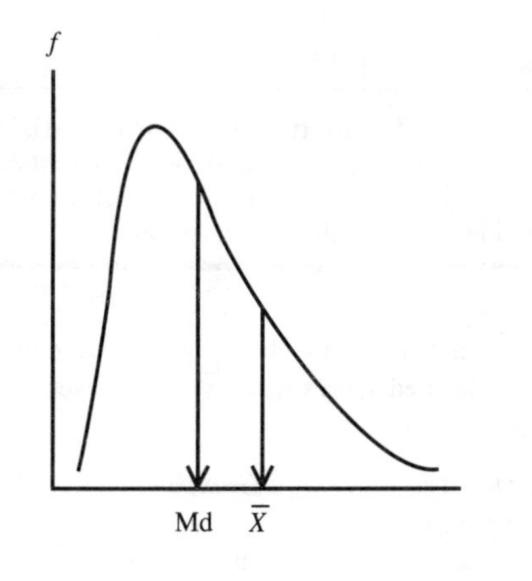

(c) The median provides a better indication of the typical score in a negatively skewed distribution; the mean is too low.

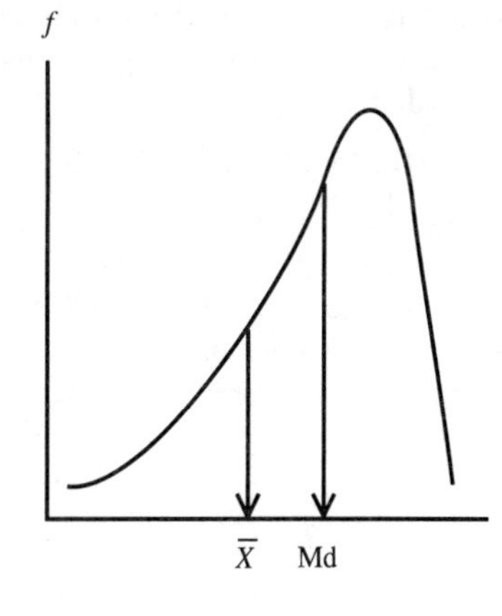

Figure 3.4

The locations of the mean and the median in a bimodal distribution. Neither provides a good indication of the typical score.

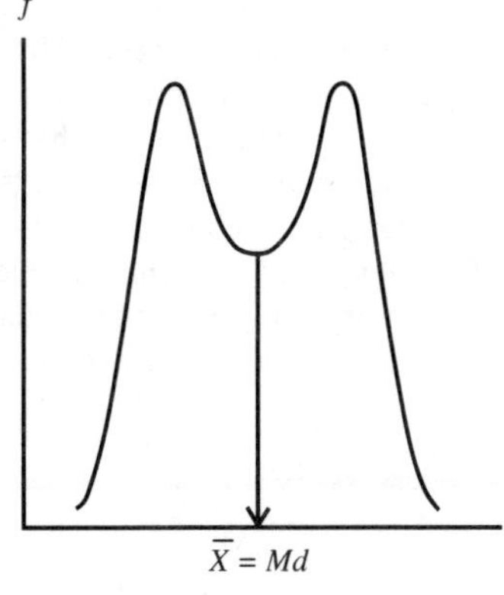

BOX 3.2

COMPUTATION OF THE MEDIAN

This box demonstrates the computation of the median from raw data and grouped frequency distributions.

Computation of the Median Using Raw Scores
According to Equation 3.5, the median is computed as

$$\text{Md} = \frac{N+1}{2}\text{th score in an ordered array}$$

Thus, the computation of the median must begin with arranging the scores in either ascending or descending order to form an ordered array. The following scores on the Kierkegaard Angst Inventory (X) provide such an ordered array. Each score is listed along with its position in the ordered array.

X = 10, 15, 22, 22, 25, 28, 30
Positions: 1, 2, 3, 4, 5, 6, 7

Since there are seven scores, $N = 7$, and the $(N + 1)/2$th score occupies the $(7 + 1)/2 = 4$th position. Thus, the median is the score of 22.

Think about the next set of scores, again ordered and listed with positions.

X = 15, 15, 24, 28, 31, 34
Positions: 1, 2, 3, 4, 5, 6

Now there are only six scores. Since $N = 6$, the median is located at the $(6 + 1)/2 = 3.5$th position. The score at the third position is 24; the score at the fourth position is 28. The 3.5th score is the value exactly halfway between these two values: $(24 + 28)/2 = 26$, which is the median for this distribution of scores.

Notice two things from these examples. First, each and every occurrence of a score is counted in finding the score at the $(N + 1)/2$th position. We do not count a duplicated score value only once. Second, the median will correspond to an obtained value if there are an odd number of scores; it will be a value halfway between two obtained scores if there are an even number of scores.

TABLE 3.5 Grouped Frequency Distribution for Student Absences

X (i = 3)	m	f
0–2	1	8
3–5	4	12
6–8	7	6
9–11	10	2
12–14	13	1

Grouped frequency distribution ($i = 3$) summarizing numbers of absences (X) accumulated by students in Introduction to Common Knowledge 101. Midpoints (m) are provided with each score interval.

Computing the Median from a Grouped Frequency Distribution
Table 3.5 gives a grouped frequency distribution ($i = 3$), which summarizes the number of absences (X) accumulated by students enrolled in Introduction to Common Knowledge 101. The median number of absences can be estimated as equal to the midpoint of the interval containing the $(N + 1)/2$th score in this ordered array. Since $N = 29$, $(N + 1)/2$ = the 15th score. This score would be found in the second score interval (3−5), which includes scores in positions 9 through 20. Thus, the median number of absences is estimated as 4, the midpoint of the interval.

Computation of the Mode. Identifying the mode(s) is as simple as counting. For scores of 1, 2, 3, 3, 4, and 5, the mode is 3. For scores of 1, 2, 2, 3, 3, 4, and 5, the modes are 2 and 3. When all scores occur with equal frequency, as with scores of 1, 2, 3, 4, and 5, there is said to be no mode. You may recall from the preceding chapter that this type of distribution is called a rectangular distribution in reference to the shape of the distribution's frequency polygon.

In the case of grouped frequency distributions, the mode(s) may be estimated as equal to the midpoint(s) of the score interval(s) showing the highest frequency. Of course, this value is only an estimate of the true mode of the distribution. We cannot compute the true mode from grouped data because information is lost when scores are combined into score intervals.

When using the terms bimodal or multimodal to describe a distribution, the technical definition of the mode is generally relaxed. Two or more scores (or score intervals or nominal categories) need not have exactly the same high frequencies for us to describe the distribution as bimodal or multimodal. Instead, these terms may be used appropriately any time there are two or more noticeable frequency peaks, even though these high frequencies may not be exactly equal.

Characteristics of the Mode. The mode is seldom used to describe the central tendency of interval or ratio scale variables. For one thing, the mode is not used as a component in other statistical procedures, so computing it leads us to a statistical dead end. In addition, the mode is extremely unstable; that is, it can change dramatically in response to relatively minor changes in the scores of a distribution. To illustrate this point look at the following values of the variable X:

$$X = 65, 70, 70, 82, 85, 90, 95, 99$$

The mode of these scores is 70. If we added another score of 95, though, we would have two modes, 70 and 95. If we deleted one score of 70 and added one score of 95, the mode would shift to 95. In sum, changing one or two values in a distribution can have a disproportionate effect on the value of the mode(s), making the mode a less than fully desirable indicator of central tendency.

Despite this, there are occasions when the mode is the best measure of central tendency. In Figure 3.5, the modes give a better indication of the average or typical score than does either the mean or the median when the distribution is bimodal (Figure 3.5a). When the data are unimodal and nonskewed (Figure 3.5b), the mean, median, and mode are equal and provide an equivalent view of central tendency. When the data are skewed (Figure 3.5c and Figure 3.5d), both the median and the mode are a better sign of the central tendency than the mean.

Scales of Measurement and Measures of Central Tendency

Scales of Measurement and the Mean. We saw in chapter 1 that data at the interval and ratio levels of measurement can be manipulated arithmetically in ways that are meaningful, making the mean appropriate for describing data at these levels. The mean is also useful in summarizing rating scale data because

(a) In a bimodal distribution, the modes give a better indication of the typical scores than either the mean or median.

f

Mode $\overline{X}$ = Md Mode

(b) In a unimodal distribution, the mode, mean, and median are equal.

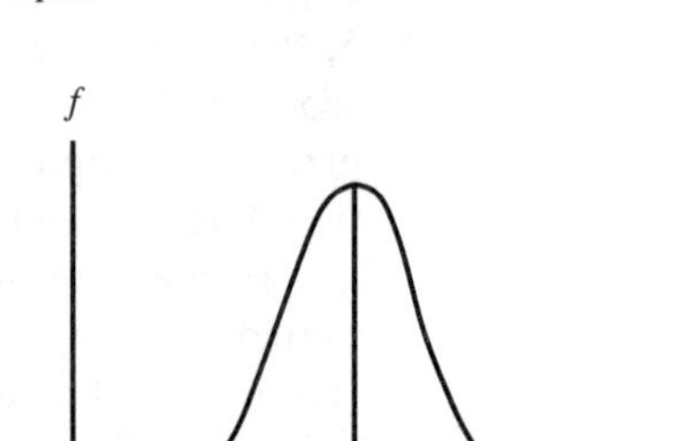

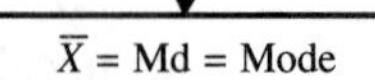

(c) In a positively skewed distribution, the mode and median provide a better indication of central tendency than does the mean.

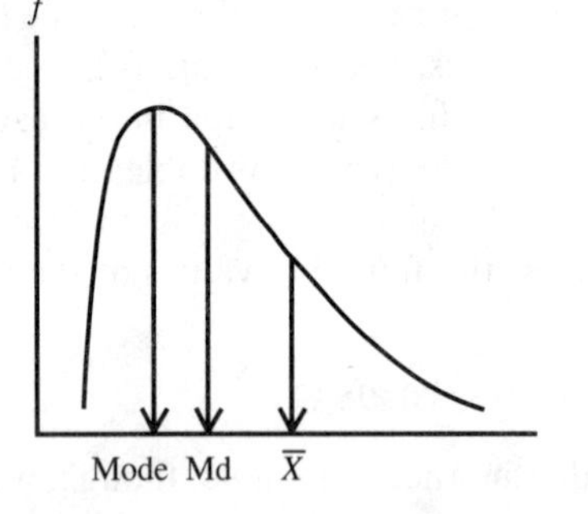

(d) In a negatively skewed distribution, the mode and median provide a better indication of central tendency than does the mean.

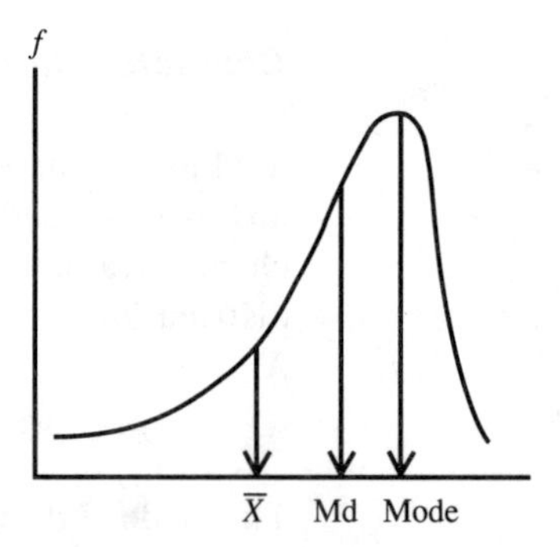

Figure 3.5

The relative locations of the mode, median, and mean in distributions of different shapes.

these data, though perhaps not fully interval, provide at least a close approximation to interval data. The mean of a set of rating scale scores gives us a good idea of the average or typical rating.

Rank order data, though, cannot be summarized using the mean, as a moment's reflection will make clear. The mean of a set of ranks is totally dependent on how many cases were ranked. If there are three cases, the mean of their ranks will equal 2, regardless of how much attribute is possessed by the typical case. If there are 10 cases, the mean of their 10 ranks will equal 5.5, again regardless of how much attribute is possessed by the typical case. In other words, the mean of a set of ranks reveals nothing about the amount of the attribute possessed by the typical or average case. The mean of such data reflects only how many cases were ranked.

Finally, the mean is inappropriate for summarizing data on a multicategory nominal scale variable. We saw in chapter 1 that data at this level of measurement have no mathematical meaning. The numbers are just convenient codes to represent the discrete levels of the nominal scale variable, so it makes no sense to manipulate those numbers mathematically. It may also be recalled, though, that data from dichotomously scored nominal scales (i.e., nominal variables with two categories, scored 0 and 1) can be arithmetically manipulated in a meaningful fashion. The mean of data like these is interpreted as the proportion of cases that received a score of 1 on the variable. Consider the following 10 cases, each scored 0 for male and 1 for female:

$$X = 0, 1, 1, 0, 1, 1, 0, 0, 1, 1$$

The mean is

$$\bar{X} = \frac{\Sigma X}{N}$$

$$= .6$$

This value is fully interpretable. It tells us that 60% of the cases are females.

Scales of Measurement and the Median. The median is useful in describing central tendency in data measured at the interval or ratio scales only. (This includes the approximation to interval scale data provided by rating scales.)

The median is inappropriate for use with fully ordinal rank order scores. The median of such data tells only how many cases were ranked. No information is given about how much of the attribute being measured was possessed by the average or typical case.

No type of nominal scale data may be measured for typicality using the median. We have seen before that the numbers associated with multicategory nominal scale variables have no quantitative meaning, making a quantitative summary statistic like the median meaningless. An example will demonstrate why the median also is inappropriate for use with dichotomously scored nominal scale variables.

Think about the following scores on the dichotomous variable sex, where 0 = male and 1 = female:

$$X = 0, 0, 0, 0, 1, 1, 1, 1, 1, 1$$

In this case there are six females and four males. The mean of these scores ($\bar{X} = .6$) reflects this division, but the median does not. The score in the $(N + 1)/2$th position is 1. It might be argued that this median value *does* represent the typical case, since six out of 10 cases are female. Look at the next set of scores on the sex variable:

$$X = 0, 1, 1, 1, 1, 1, 1, 1, 1, 1$$

There is only one male here and nine females. The mean ($\bar{X} = .9$) changes to reflect this fact, but the median remains unchanged from its former value (Md = 1). Clearly, the median does not offer the kind of sensitivity that we need in assessing typicality in dichotomous nominal variables.

Scales of Measurement and the Mode. The mode is appropriately used in describing the central tendency of interval and ratio scale distributions. (Again, the approximation to the interval scale that is provided by rating scales is included here.) When used with these scales of measurement, the mode tells how much of the attribute being measured is possessed by the average case.

The mode is also the only appropriate indicator of central tendency for multicategory nominal scale variables. In the case of a nominal scale variable, the "modal category" is the category that occurs with the highest frequency. Of course, there can be more than one modal category if two or more categories have equally high frequencies.

The mode is not useful in summarizing rank order data. With the exception of the occasional tied rank, rank order data show no mode, since each rank occurs only once.

VARIABILITY

We learned in chapter 2 that the variability of our data may be as important or more important than central tendency. In essence, variability limits our certainty. If the effects of a drug are highly variable, for example, we are less certain how that drug will affect any given individual than we would be if the drug's effects were less variable. Variability also limits the degree to which any of the descriptors of central tendency can serve to describe the cases as a group. Data that cluster tightly around the mean make the mean a good descriptor of the entire set of scores. Highly variable data, though, which are widely dispersed around the mean, make the mean a less effective descriptor of the cases as a group.

Just as central tendency statistics enable us to be precise in describing the typical or average case in the distribution, so too, descriptors of variability make it possible to describe this characteristic of the data with some degree of precision. Six measures of variability are the range, semi-interquartile range, variance, sum of squares, standard deviation, and coefficient of variation.

Range

The simplest index of variability is the **range.** Computed as the highest score minus the lowest score in the distribution, the range is also the least stable, and therefore, the least desirable statistic of variability. The range is not just influenced by extreme scores, it is completely determined by these outliers. Look at the following test scores:

$$X = 76, 82, 85, 87, 90, 92, 95, 96$$

The range of these scores is $96 - 76 = 20$. Simply changing the bottom score from 76 to 56, though, doubles the value of the range. We should certainly hesitate to describe an entire set of scores on the basis of the two weirdest scores in the distribution, yet that is exactly what the range does.

The range, though not a useful statistic, is a useful concept. That is, it is often helpful to state that our data *ranged* from some low value to some high value. Thus, the preceding data might be described as "ranging from a low of 76 to a high of 96." A statement of this sort reveals more information than is given by the simple arithmetic difference between the highest and lowest values.

Semi-Interquartile Range

The disadvantage of finding the range using the most extreme scores in the distribution is partially overcome by the related **semi-interquartile range.** This value is defined as the difference between the scores at the 75th and 25th percentiles. Since the semi-interquartile range is based upon the middle 50% of the scores, it is not influenced by outliers. However, the semi-interquartile range requires that there *be* scores at the 75th and 25th percentiles, which may not be the case in small distributions. Looking back at Table 2.2, for example, we find scores at the 72nd and 26th percentiles, but nothing exactly at the 75th and 25th percentiles. The semi-interquartile range is generally used in describing large distributions of standardized test scores where this is not a problem.

Variance

The **variance** of a sample of scores is represented by the symbol s^2. Where more than one variable or sample is involved, a subscript may be used to represent the variable or sample whose variance is being described. Thus, s_X^2 is the variance of the variable X; s_Y^2 is the variance of the variable Y; s_1^2 is the variance of Group 1; s_2^2 is the variance of Group 2 and so on. The variance of a population, as opposed to that of a sample, is represented by the lower case Greek letter sigma squared: σ^2.

Computation of the Variance. The variance may be defined as the average squared deviation of scores around the mean. This verbal definition is reflected in the formula for the variance.[2]

EQUATION 3.6

$$s_X^2 = \frac{\Sigma(X - \overline{X})^2}{N}$$

where,

X = values of the variable X
$\overline{X}$ = the mean of X
N = the number of cases

The computation of the variance is illustrated in Box 3.3.

As a descriptive statistic for variability, the variance changes in value as a function of the amount of variability seen in the data. When all scores are identical (and thus, fall exactly at the mean), such that there is no variability, $s^2 = 0$. As scores become more and more dispersed around the mean, this increased variability is reflected in ever increasing values of s^2.

BOX 3.3

COMPUTATION OF THE VARIANCE

A researcher in the Air Quality Division of the Environmental Protection Agency is interested in evaluating claims from three manufacturers of canine breath mints for the effectiveness of their products. Data are collected from five dogs after being given either Brand X, Brand Y, or Brand Z breath mints. Shown in Table 3.6 are scores from these pooches on the Whewie Canine Halitosis Scale.

TABLE 3.6 Scores on the Whewie Canine Halitosis Scale

Brand X	Brand Y	Brand Z
45	30	10
60	50	90
40	70	30
50	40	70
55	60	50

Scores for dogs given Brand X, Y, or Z canine breath mints.

A casual inspection of the scores reveals that, though the average effectiveness of the breath mints is equal ($\overline{X} = 50$ for all three mints), the mints differ in the variability of the data that are associated with each. Brand X scores cluster quite closely around the mean; Brand Y scores are somewhat more dispersed; and Brand Z scores show the greatest variability.

The variability of breath mint effectiveness can be described more precisely by computing the variance of each of the data sets according to Equation 3.6. For breath mint X:

$$s_X^2 = \frac{\Sigma(X - \overline{X})^2}{N}$$

$$= \frac{(45 - 50)^2 + (60 - 50)^2 + \ldots + (55 - 50)^2}{5}$$

$$= 50$$

For breath mint Y:

$$s_Y^2 = \frac{\Sigma(Y - \overline{Y})^2}{N}$$

$$= \frac{(30 - 50)^2 + (50 - 50)^2 + \ldots + (60 - 50)^2}{5}$$

$$= 200$$

Finally, for breath mint Z:

$$s_Z^2 = \frac{\Sigma(Z - \overline{Z})^2}{N}$$

$$= \frac{(10 - 50)^2 + (90 - 50)^2 + \ldots + (50 - 50)^2}{5}$$

$$= 800$$

These values confirm the observation made before that the breath mints differ in the variability of their effectiveness. Breath mint X gives the most predictable effects; mint Z effects are the least predictable.

Estimating the Population Variance. The variance computed according to Equation 3.6 is a sample variance. It tells us the average squared deviation of scores around the mean in a sample drawn from some larger population. The sample variance, though, is a biased estimate of the variance of the population from which the sample was drawn. That is, s^2 will usually be somewhat smaller than σ^2. It is easy enough to understand why this is the case. A population consists of far more cases than are found in a sample drawn from that population, and it is likely that any given sample will not include some of the more extreme or deviant cases that are included in the population. These extreme cases add to the population's variance, but, not being included in the sample, do not influence sample variance.

There are occasions when we wish to estimate a population variance from a sample drawn from that population, but we know that s^2 tends to give a low estimate of σ^2. The way around this dilemma is to compute what is called a **corrected variance,** abbreviated with the symbol $\hat{s}^2$. Subscripts, as always, may be used to signify precisely the variables or groups being referred to. The corrected variance is computed according to Equation 3.7.[3]

EQUATION 3.7

$$\hat{s}^2 = \frac{\Sigma(X - \overline{X})^2}{N - 1}$$

where,

X = values of the variable X
$\overline{X}$ = the mean of X
N = the number of cases

As you can see, $\hat{s}^2$ is inflated slightly, relative to s^2, by using a denominator of $N - 1$ rather than N. This inflation brings $\hat{s}^2$ closer into line with the larger population variance, σ^2.

You may wonder at this point just how important the distinction is between s^2 and $\hat{s}^2$. Is this something that really need concern us? The answer to this question depends upon the size of the sample with which we are dealing. Large samples show little difference between s^2 and $\hat{s}^2$ values because the difference between N and $N - 1$ is insignificant when N is large. On the other hand, when N is small, the difference between N and $N - 1$ is proportionally much larger, and the difference between s^2 and $\hat{s}^2$ becomes quite noticeable. In actual practice, sample sizes in the social and behavioral sciences are usually of sufficient size that the distinction between s^2 and $\hat{s}^2$ becomes quite unimportant. In fact, most statistical software packages compute only the corrected value and use this value in all subsequent computations.

Sum of Squares

The **sum of squares,** abbreviated SS, is a measure of variability that is used most often within the context of analysis of variance (see chapters 8 and 9). The sum of squares refers to the sum of the squared deviations around the mean of the distribution. This value was seen previously as the numerator of Equation 3.6: $\Sigma(X - \overline{X})^2$.

The sum of squares increases as score variability increases, but is also strongly influenced by the number of scores in the distribution. With variability held constant, as the number of cases (N) increases, the sum of squares increases too. The advantage of the variance over the sum of squares lies chiefly in the fact that the variance formula (Equation 3.6) provides a correction for this influence of sample size by dividing the numerator (SS) by N.

Standard Deviation

Although the variance is a very useful measure of variability in certain applications, its value as a descriptive statistic is limited somewhat by the difficulty most people have in thinking about squared deviations. For example, if you were told that a squared error of 9 points had been made in computing your last exam grade, you would probably wonder why the error's *squared* value was reported instead of the *actual* error. Taking the square root of this squared error of 9 would tell you immediately that the actual error was 3 points. Similarly, when we are told that the variance of a set of scores is 9, we know that this is the average squared deviation of scores around the mean. By computing the square root of the variance, we can express this variability in terms of the original score values, that is, 3 points. This square root of the variance is called the **standard deviation** and is approximately equal to the average absolute deviation of scores around the mean. Because the standard deviation is more readily interpreted than the variance, it is more often used than the variance to describe data variability. As with the variance, the value of the standard deviation reflects the amount of dispersion of scores around the mean, ranging from a low of zero, when there is no variability, to infinity at the upper extreme.

Computing the Standard Deviation. The standard deviation of a set of scores is represented by the lower case letter s. As with the variance, subscripts may be used to specify to which variable or which group of cases a given standard deviation value refers (e.g., s_X, s_Y, s_1, s_2). The symbol for a *population* standard deviation is the lower case Greek letter sigma: σ. The standard deviation is easily computed once the variance has been computed.

EQUATION 3.8

$$s = \sqrt{s^2}$$

Estimating the Population Standard Deviation. Just as the sample variance provides a low estimate of the population variance, so too, the sample standard deviation gives a low estimate of the population standard deviation. Equation 3.9 is the formula for the *corrected standard deviation* ($\hat{s}$) used in estimating the population standard deviation from sample data.

EQUATION 3.9

$$\hat{s} = \sqrt{\hat{s}^2}$$

Coefficient of Variation

Although the variance and standard deviation are the most widely used descriptors of variability, they suffer from one weakness. These statistics are influenced not just by the variability of the data, but by the magnitude of the scores as well.

That is, scores obtained using measuring procedures that yield high values will give higher variances and standard deviations than will scores obtained using measuring procedures that yield low values, even when the actual variability of the scores is the same.

Consider again the data in Table 3.1 where we find annual and monthly salaries listed for employees of Capitalistic Exploitations. It is intuitively obvious that these two measures of income contain the same variability, since each measure is a direct transformation of the other: Monthly Salary = 1/12 × Annual Salary; Annual Salary = 12 × Monthly Salary. If we compute the standard deviation of the annual salary figures, we obtain a value of s = \$39,027.01. The standard deviation of the corresponding monthly salaries is much smaller: s = \$3252.30. These standard deviations suggest greater variability in the annual salary figures than in the monthly figures, but we know that the variability is the same in the two sets of scores.

What is happening here is that the standard deviation (and variance) are not pure measures of variability; they are influenced by score magnitude. In this example, because annual salary figures are higher than monthly salaries, the annual salaries produce a standard deviation (and variance) that are higher as well.

There are occasions when we wish to compare the variability of two sets of scores that have been obtained using different measuring procedures. As we have just seen, though, we cannot directly compare the distributions' variances or standard deviations if the different measuring procedures yield scores of different magnitudes. The solution to this problem is to use the **coefficient of variation,** abbreviated V, and computed in Equation 3.10.

EQUATION 3.10

$$V = \frac{s}{\text{Md}}$$

where,

s = the standard deviation of the distribution
Md = the median of the distribution

In dividing the standard deviation by the median of the distribution, the coefficient of variation rescales the distribution's standard deviation according to the magnitude of the average score, as measured by Md.

When we apply Equation 3.10 to the annual and monthly salary standard deviations computed above, we find a coefficient of variation for annual salaries equal to $V = 39{,}027.01/15{,}000 = 2.60$. The corresponding value for monthly salaries is $V = 3252.30/1250 = 2.60$. The coefficient of variation provides us with a way of comparing the standard deviations of distributions which differ in the magnitude of scores.

Scales of Measurement and Measures of Variability

All of the measures of variability described in this chapter are applicable to interval and ratio scale variables. This includes rating scale data that approximate the interval level of measurement.

Rank order data cannot be described using any of the measures of variability. Only the number of cases, not their dispersion, will be reflected in the values of the computed variability statistics.

Finally, multicategory nominal scale variables produce data that possess no mathematical qualities, making the statistics described here inappropriate. The variability of dichotomously scored nominal scale variables, though, *can* be described with the variance and statistics that are related to the variance, that is, the sum of squares and standard deviation. Let us consider an example that will illustrate this usage of the variance.

Shown below are 10 scores on the variable sex, with 0 = male and 1 = female:

$$X = 0, 0, 0, 0, 0, 0, 0, 0, 0, 0$$

There is no variability here, since all cases are males. This is reflected in the computed value of the variance.[4]

$$s^2 = \frac{\Sigma(X - \bar{X})^2}{N}$$

$$= 0$$

Let us now introduce a little more variability into the data:

$$X = 0, 0, 0, 0, 0, 0, 0, 0, 0, 1$$

The variance now becomes $s^2 = .09$, an increase in value that reflects the increased variability in the variable sex. In the next set of scores, there are equal numbers of males and females, such that variability on the sex variable is maximized (i.e., there is the maximum possible amount of uncertainty in predicting whether a case drawn at random will be male or female):

$$X = 0, 1, 0, 1, 0, 1, 0, 1, 0, 1$$

The variance of these scores is $s^2 = .25$, the highest possible value of the variance when dealing with dichotomously scored nominal scale data. In sum, as variability (i.e., uncertainty) increases to its maximum level, the variance increases to its maximum value.

SKEWNESS

As described in chapter 2, skewness pertains to the lopsidedness or symmetry of a distribution. Relatively complex descriptive statistics exist that describe and quantify skewness, but none has the computational simplicity or conceptual clarity of the statistic Sk.[5]

EQUATION 3.11

$$\text{Sk} = \frac{\bar{X} - \text{Md}}{\text{Md}}$$

where,

$$\bar{X} = \text{the mean of the distribution}$$
$$\text{Md} = \text{the median of the distribution}$$

This measure of skewness is based on the relative positions of the mean and median in skewed and nonskewed distributions as pictured in Figure 3.3. When a distribution is negatively skewed, the mean is smaller than the median, yielding a negative value of Sk. A positively skewed distribution is accompanied by a mean that is larger than the median, resulting in a positive value of Sk. In a symmetrical distribution, the mean and median are equal, and Sk = 0. The *direction* of skewness, then, is reflected in the *sign* of Sk. The *degree* of skewness is reflected by the *magnitude* of Sk. The greater the skew, the greater the difference between the mean and median.

Equation 3.11 divides the mean − median difference by the median to control for the influence of score magnitude on Sk. This enables us to compare Sk values across distributions that differ in score magnitude. Since Sk is computed from the mean and median of a distribution, it is applicable only to those data that are meaningfully described by these statistics: interval and ratio scale data.

To illustrate the use of the skewness statistic, we will use Equation 3.11 to compute the skewness of the annual salary data in Table 3.1.

$$\begin{aligned}\text{Sk} &= \frac{\bar{X} - \text{Md}}{\text{Md}} \\ &= \frac{28{,}273.73 - 15{,}000}{15{,}000} \\ &= +.88\end{aligned}$$

The positive sign of Sk tells us that the annual salaries are positively skewed; the value (.88) of Sk shows the magnitude of the skew if we wished to compare the skewness of this distribution against that of some other distribution.

KURTOSIS

Karl Pearson developed the most commonly used index of kurtosis, Kur.

EQUATION 3.12

$$\text{Kur} = \frac{\left(\dfrac{\Sigma(X - \overline{X})^4}{N}\right)}{(s^2)^2}$$

where,

X = values of the variable X
$\overline{X}$ = the mean of X
N = the number of cases
s^2 = the variance of X

Platykurtic distributions produce values of Kur that are less than 3. Leptokurtic distributions produce values of Kur that are greater than 3. A mesokurtic distribution will produce a value of Kur = 3.

To demonstrate the use of this kurtosis statistic, we will use Equation 3.12 in computing the kurtosis of the distribution of Phrenological Aptitude Test scores in Table 3.2.

$$\text{Kur} = \frac{\left(\dfrac{\Sigma(X - \overline{X})^4}{N}\right)}{(s^2)^2}$$

$$= \frac{\dfrac{(76 - 79.26)^4 + (82 - 79.26)^4 + \ .\ .\ .\ + (82 - 79.26)^4}{N}}{30.83^2}$$

$$= \frac{\dfrac{209158.41}{50}}{950.49}$$

$$= 4.40$$

This greater than 3.0 value of Kur indicates a leptokurtic distribution, that is, one which is somewhat more peaked than normal (see Figure 2.2). We will consider the shape of the normal distribution more fully in the next chapter. There we will also learn what difference it makes whether or not a distribution is normally distributed.

Since Kur is computed using the mean and variance, it follows that Kur is applicable only to those data meaningfully described by these statistics: interval and ratio scale data. Kur is not applicable to dichotomously scored nominal data, even though the mean and variance are useful for describing these types of data. This is because kurtosis refers to the degree to which a distribution approximates a normal shape; a two-category nominal scale variable obviously cannot come even close to producing a frequency distribution that has a normal shape.

SUMMARY

Descriptive statistics are defined as numbers computed from data that describe those data. As such, descriptive statistics enable us to describe precisely the central tendency, variability, skewness, and kurtosis characteristics of data. The mean, median, and mode measure central tendency. The mean, often called the average, is the most widely used indicator of the typical score, but is unstable in the presence of outliers. This characteristic makes the mean unsuitable for use with skewed distributions. The median, defined as the middle score in the distribution, is resistant to outliers. It is therefore superior to the mean as a descriptor of central tendency in skewed distributions. The mode, the most frequently occurring score(s) in the distribution, is the only measure of typicality that is useful with multicategory nominal scale data. The mode is also often used to describe the shape of frequency distributions, for example, unimodal, bimodal, and multimodal. Measures of data variability include the range, semi-interquartile range, variance, sum of squares, standard deviation, and coefficient of variability. Computed as the difference between the highest and lowest scores in the distribution, the range is a highly unstable measure of variability. The semi-interquartile range resists the influence of outliers by eliminating the top and bottom 25% of the scores before computing the range. The sum of squares, defined as the sum of squared deviations of scores around the mean, and the variance, defined as the average squared deviation around the mean, are useful measures of variability in other contexts, but they are difficult to interpret directly as descriptive statistics of variability. The square root of the variance, called the standard deviation, provides a more directly interpretable measure of variability for descriptive purposes. The standard deviation approximates the average absolute deviation of scores around the mean. Finally, the coefficient of variation corrects the standard deviation for the influence of score magnitude, thus enabling us to compare the variabilities of distributions which differ in score magnitude. Although they are not widely used, measures of skewness and kurtosis are examined, since they are commonly reported as part of the output from statistical software packages.

NOTES

1. Interpolation procedures for estimating the median from grouped distributions (e.g., Shavelson, 1988) rest on the assumption that scores within an interval are distributed evenly throughout that interval. This is an unfounded assumption that becomes increasingly untenable as interval width increases and sample size decreases. It is the author's position that, all other things being equal, simple procedures are better than complicated procedures. Thus, the use of interpolation in estimating medians is left for those with a taste for complexity for complexity's sake.

2. The variance may be computed more easily using the following computational formula:

$$s^2 = \frac{\Sigma X^2 - \dfrac{(\Sigma X)^2}{N}}{N}$$

where,

X = scores on the variable X
N = the number of cases

Although this formula may appear more complicated than Equation 3.6, it requires far fewer individual calculations when the variance is being computed by hand.

3. The computational formula for the corrected sample variance is identical to the formula given in Note 2, except that the denominator is $N - 1$ rather than N.

4. The variance of a dichotomously scored nominal scale variable may be more easily computed as

$$s^2 = pq$$

where,

p = the proportion of cases scoring 0
q = the proportion of cases scoring 1

5. The most widely used measure of skewness was developed by Karl Pearson.

$$\text{Sk} = \frac{\left(\frac{\Sigma(X - \bar{X})^3}{N}\right)}{s^2(s)}$$

where,

X = scores on the variable X
N = the number of cases
s^2 = the variance of the variable X
s = the standard deviation of the variable X

A symmetrical distribution results in Sk = 0, positive skew is reflected by a positive value of Sk, and negative skew results in a negative value of Sk. The advantage of this formula over that given as Equation 3.11 is that Pearson's formula allows us to compare the skewness of distributions that may differ in variability.

CHAPTER 4

STANDARD SCORES, THE NORMAL DISTRIBUTION, AND THE STANDARD NORMAL DISTRIBUTION

Three central concepts will be presented in this chapter: standard scores, the normal distribution, and the standard normal distribution. The standard normal distribution, in particular, is useful in applied statistics. However, in order to understand the standard normal distribution, we will first need to consider the building block concepts of standard scores (which are quite useful in and of themselves) and the normal distribution (which is not directly applicable by itself, but which is fundamental to an understanding of how many other statistical tools work). We will begin with standard scores.

STANDARD SCORES

Standard scores are also called **z-scores** because the lowercase letter z is the symbol for standard scores. Standard scores are transformations of raw scores that specify each score's amount and direction of deviation from the mean, as measured in standard deviations. As we saw in chapter 3, every score in a distribution shows some deviation from the mean—positive, negative, or zero. These deviations can be measured by how many score points fall between each score and the mean, or, as with standard scores, the deviations can be measured using the distribution's standard deviation as the unit of measure. Thus, a z-score tells us how many standard deviations fall between a raw score and the mean. This is expressed mathematically in Equation 4.1.

EQUATION 4.1

$$z_X = \frac{X - \overline{X}}{s}$$

where,

z_X = the standard score corresponding to the raw score X
X = a raw score
$\overline{X}$ = the mean of the distribution of raw scores
s = the standard deviation of the distribution of raw scores

We can see from this equation that a z-score tells us two things. First, the sign (positive or negative) shows the direction of the score's deviation from the mean. Scores above the mean result in positive z-score values, scores below the mean result in negative z-score values, and scores at the mean have a z-score of zero. Second, the absolute magnitude of the z-scores tells us how many standard deviations fall between a score and the mean. Thus, a z-score of -1 represents a raw score located 1 standard deviation below the mean. A z-score of $+1.5$ represents a score 1.5 standard deviations above the mean. As we have already seen, a z-score of 0 indicates a raw score falling exactly at the mean.

From this discussion you may have gained an increased appreciation for the standard deviation. It is not just an indicator of score variability, as we saw in the preceding chapter, but also serves as a sort of yardstick for measuring the distance of raw scores from the mean of their distribution. Box 4.1 demonstrates how raw scores may be transformed to z-scores using Equation 4.1.

BOX 4.1

COMPUTATION OF STANDARD SCORES

Scores on the Snideley Whiplash Empathy Inventory are listed in Table 4.1 under the column headed X for 19 Hellhole County social workers. The mean, variance, and standard deviation of these scores have also been computed as

$$\bar{X} = 5.0$$
$$s^2 = 5.26$$
$$s = 2.29$$

Standard scores have been computed for each raw score using Equation 4.1. As an example, the z-score corresponding to a raw score of 7 would be computed as

$$z_X = \frac{X - \bar{X}}{s}$$

$$z_7 = \frac{7 - 5.0}{2.29}$$

$$= +.87$$

Standard scores corresponding to each raw score are listed in Table 4.1 under the column headed z. Notice for future reference that these z-scores sum to 0, show a mean of 0, and have a variance and standard deviation of 1.0.

TABLE 4.1 Raw Scores (X) on the Snideley Whiplash Empathy Inventory and Corresponding Standard Scores (z) for 19 Hellhole County Social Workers

X	z
2	−1.31
7	.87
5	0
8	1.31
5	0
7	.87
3	− .87
3	− .87
2	−1.31
1	−1.75
7	.87
9	1.75
8	1.31
7	.87
3	− .87
5	0
3	− .87
5	0
5	0

Characteristics of Standard Scores

Any distribution of raw scores may be transformed into a distribution of standard scores using Equation 4.1. Any distribution of standard scores will always display three characteristics.

First, the mean of a distribution of z-scores ($\bar{X}_z$) will always equal zero. This is because the deviations of raw scores around the mean sum to zero, $\Sigma(X - \bar{X}) = 0$, so that z-scores, which represent these deviations, $z = \frac{X - \bar{X}}{s}$, must also sum to zero.[1]

A second characteristic of any distribution of standard scores is that it will always have a variance and standard deviation equal to 1. Why this is so is not as obvious, nor is the proof particularly enlightening or important.[2]

Third, and finally, standardizing a distribution does not alter the shape of that distribution. If the distribution of raw scores is negatively skewed, the distribution of z-scores will still be negatively skewed. If the distribution of raw scores is rectangular, the distribution of standard scores will be rectangular.

Uses of Standard Scores

Standard scores have a number of uses in the social and behavioral sciences, two of which will be considered at this point.

The Use of Standard Scores to Locate Scores in a Distribution. First, standard scores help to locate scores within their distributions much as do percentiles. That is, just as a percentile helps us learn how high or low a score is, relative to other scores in the distribution, so too, z-scores help us to locate a score relative to the mean of the distribution.

The advantage of z-scores over percentiles in locating scores in a distribution is that percentiles give only an ordinal level transformation of interval or ratio scale raw scores. Standard scores, in contrast, maintain an interval level of measurement. This is illustrated in Figure 4.1, which compares raw scores, z-scores, percentiles, T-scores, and stanine scores in a normal distribution of intelligence test scores having a mean of 100 and a standard deviation of 15. (We will study T-scores and stanines later in the chapter.) Notice first how the 15-point difference between raw scores of 70 and 85 corresponds to a z-score difference of 1 and a percentile difference of 14. Next, notice how another 15-point difference between raw scores of 85 and 100 again corresponds to a z-score difference of 1, but is accompanied by a percentile difference of 34. We saw in chapter 2 that a given raw score difference at the top or bottom of a distribution will produce a smaller percentile difference than will the same raw score difference in the center of the distribution. We see here that this distortion does not occur with standard scores.

The disadvantage of z-scores, relative to percentiles, is that z-scores are less easily interpreted. For example, unless we know through our familiarity with statistics that a z-score of $+2$ is quite high, this value does not suggest directly that the corresponding score is all that unusual. In contrast, the percentile rank of 98% at the same score point tells us immediately that the score is exceptional. Also, those not accustomed to working with numbers find the negative values and decimal values associated with standard scores to be confusing.

The Use of Standard Scores in Comparing Scores. Standard scores may be used in a second way. They provide a "common metric" for comparing scores obtained using different measuring procedures. In this way, standard scores help us answer such seemingly impossible questions as "Is it hotter or uglier in Hellhole County?" We need only determine the z-scores of Hellhole County on

Figure 4.1

Relationships between raw scores, *z*-scores, percentiles, *T*-scores, and stanine scores in a normal distribution having a mean of 100 and a standard deviation of 15. *Source:* Reprinted with permission of Macmillan Publishing Company from *Psychological Testing* by Anne Anastasi. Copyright © 1988 by Anne Anastasi.

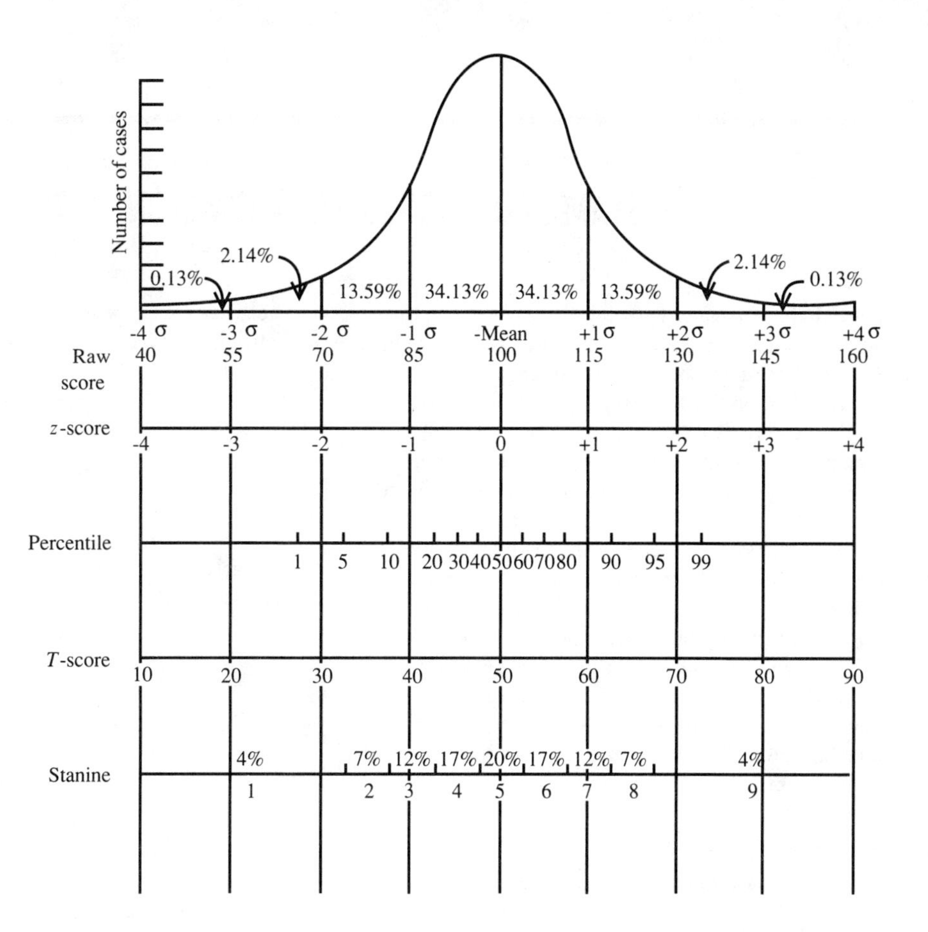

an environmental aesthetics scale and on the variable of average annual temperature to answer this question. These *z*-scores will tell us how hot and how ugly it is in Hellhole County in terms that are directly comparable. Standard scores provide us with a means of comparing apples and oranges. Box 4.2 illustrates this application of standard scores.

THE NORMAL DISTRIBUTION

The **normal distribution** is a frequency distribution that has a very specific shape.[3] It is a bell-shaped distribution in which 34.13% of the cases score between the mean and 1 standard deviation above (and below) the mean, 13.59% of the cases score between 1 and 2 standard deviations above (and below) the mean, 2.14% of the cases score between 2 and 3 standard deviations above (and below) the mean, and .13% of the cases score beyond 3 standard deviations above (and below) the mean. The distribution shown in Figure 4.1 is a normal distribution.

We can see from Figure 4.1 that the areas marked off under the normal curve correspond to the percentages or proportions of cases that have scored between

BOX 4.2

STANDARD SCORES AS A COMMON METRIC

Al LaMode, Personnel Director of Piece O' The Pie, Inc., is seeking someone to fill a mid-level management position. One applicant for the position, Cookie Crum, has scored 10 on the Management Aptitude Test. Another, Cherry Tart, scored 30 on the Test of Management Aptitude. Which applicant is better qualified? The two scores cannot be compared directly because they were obtained using different measuring instruments. What is needed is a "common metric" that will enable a direct comparison of the scores.

If Al assumes that both tests are equally good measures of management potential, that those taking each of the two tests were, on the whole, equally qualified individuals, and if he knows means and standard deviations for scores obtained on the two tests, he can use standard scores to provide the needed common metric.

Assume that Al has obtained the following descriptive statistics for scores on the two tests:

Management Aptitude Test	Test of Management Aptitude
$\overline{X} = 8$	$\overline{X} = 25$
$s = 2$	$s = 10$

Then, Cookie's raw score of 10 on the Management Aptitude Test has a z-score equivalent of

$$z_X = \frac{X - \overline{X}}{s}$$

$$z_{10} = \frac{10 - 8}{2}$$

$$= +1.0$$

Similarly, Cherry's raw score of 30 can be transformed to a z-score of

$$z_X = \frac{X - \overline{X}}{s}$$

$$z_{30} = \frac{30 - 25}{10}$$

$$= +.5$$

Thus, although both applicants have above-average management aptitude, Cookie has scored a full standard deviation above the mean of his distribution, while Cherry has scored only half a standard deviation above the mean of her distribution. In other words, Cookie's score is more outstanding than is Cherry's, even though Cherry's raw score is larger than Cookie's.

the specified score points. Thus, when we say, for instance, that 34.13% of the *area* under the normal curve falls between the mean and 1 standard deviation above the mean (i.e., $z = +1$), it is equivalent to saying that 34.13% of the *cases* scored between the mean and 1 standard deviation above the mean. This equivalence will become important to us later.

The normal distribution is a central concept in statistics because so many variables (e.g., height, weight, intelligence, personality traits, abilities) are distributed normally. Strictly speaking, though, the kinds of variables that concern social and behavioral scientists rarely show perfectly normal distributions. Any given sample, no matter how large, can be expected to deviate a bit from normalcy. Despite this, our distributions will often be close to normal and, in actual practice, any distribution that looks like the normal distribution can be assumed to be a close enough approximation so that the statistical conclusions based upon the assumption of a normal distribution will not be seriously incorrect.

THE STANDARD NORMAL DISTRIBUTION

We have now considered standard scores and the normal distribution. Putting the two concepts together we get the **standard normal distribution.** The standard normal distribution is any normal distribution of standard scores. In other words, a normal distribution of raw scores transformed to standard scores using Equation 4.1 will produce a normal distribution of standard scores, that is, a standard normal distribution.

Characteristics of the Standard Normal Distribution

The standard normal distribution has all of the combined characteristics of standard scores and the normal distribution. First, because this is a distribution of standard scores, the mean of the standard normal distribution is always 0 and the variance and standard deviation are always 1.0.

Second, because this is a normal distribution, the shape is exactly like that pictured in Figure 4.1: 34.13% of the cases score between the mean ($z = 0$) and 1 standard deviation above the mean ($z = +1.0$); 13.59% of the cases score between 1 standard deviation ($z = +1.0$) and 2 standard deviations ($z = +2.0$) above the mean; and so on. The proportion of cases falling between any two points of the standard normal distribution can be found in Appendix A: Table of Areas Under the Normal Curve. Let us see how this table is read. In Column A we see a listing of z-scores. Only positive values are listed, since the perfect symmetry of the standard normal distribution means that the proportions associated with the listed positive z-scores apply to the unlisted negative z-scores as well. Column B lists the proportion of area (and thus, the proportion of cases) that falls between the mean and each z-score. Finally, Column C lists the proportion of area (and thus, the proportion of cases) falling "beyond" each z-score. By "beyond," we mean to the right (higher) for positive z-scores, and to the left (lower) for negative z-scores. These areas are shown in Figure 4.2.

As an example of how the Table of Areas Under the Normal Curve is used, first find a z-score of $+.60$ in Column A. Now, in Column B we will see the proportion of area falling between $z = +.60$ and the mean ($z = 0$): .2257. Thus, 22.57% of the cases in a normal distribution score between the mean and .6 standard deviations above the mean. In Column C we are given the proportion of area that falls beyond (above) a z-score of $+.60$: .2743. Thus, 27.43% of the cases in a normal distribution score at or higher than the score located .6 standard deviations above the mean.

But what about proportions associated with the negative z-scores that are not listed? Suppose that we want to know the proportion of cases scoring between a z-score of -1.20 and the mean. Find the z-score of $+1.20$ in Column A. Listed in Column B is the proportion of cases between $z = +1.20$ and the mean: .3849.

Figure 4.2

Normal curves indicating the information provided in Appendix A, the Table of Areas Under the Normal Curve.

(a) For scores above the mean, Column A list positive z-scores, Column B indicates the area between the mean and z, and Column C indicates the area beyond z to the right.

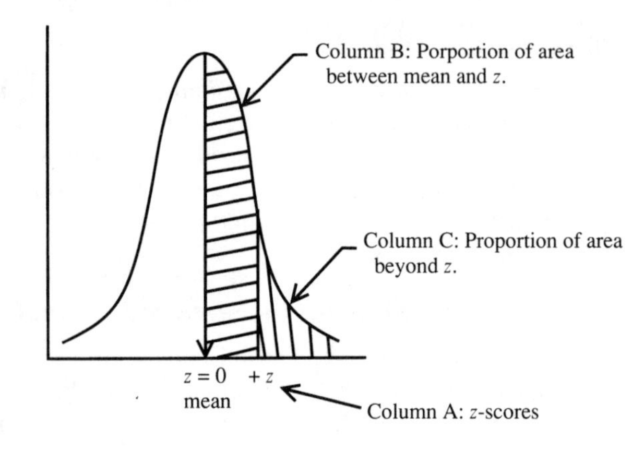

(b) For scores below the mean, Column A lists negative z-scores, Column B indicates the area between the mean and z, and Column C indicates the area beyond z to the left.

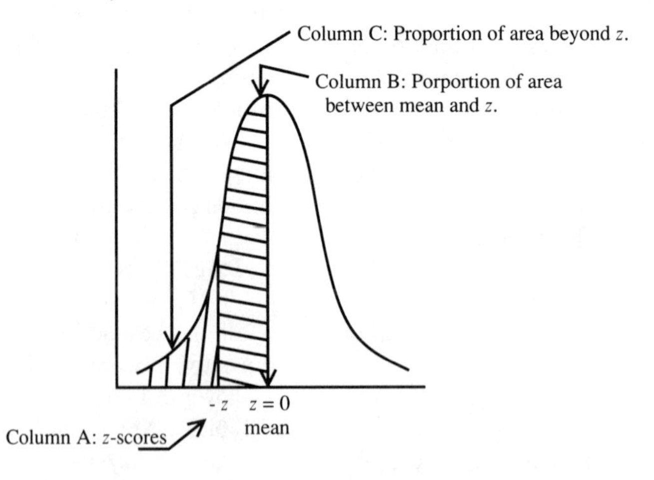

This is also the proportion of cases between $z = -1.20$ and the mean. Column C lists the proportion of cases that fall beyond (above) $z = +1.20$: .1151. This is also the proportion of cases that fall beyond (below) $z = -1.20$.

Certain other proportions that might be of interest are not given directly in Appendix A, but can be determined easily from the proportions that are presented. For example, what proportion of the cases in a normal distribution fall below $z = +1.50$? First, finding the z-score of 1.50 in Column A, we see from Column B that 43.32% (proportion = .4332) of the cases fall between $z = +1.50$ and the mean. But what proportion of the cases falls even lower than this? Ob-

(a) The area below $z = +1.50$ is equal to the sum of the area between the mean and z (Column B) and the area to the left of the mean (.5000).

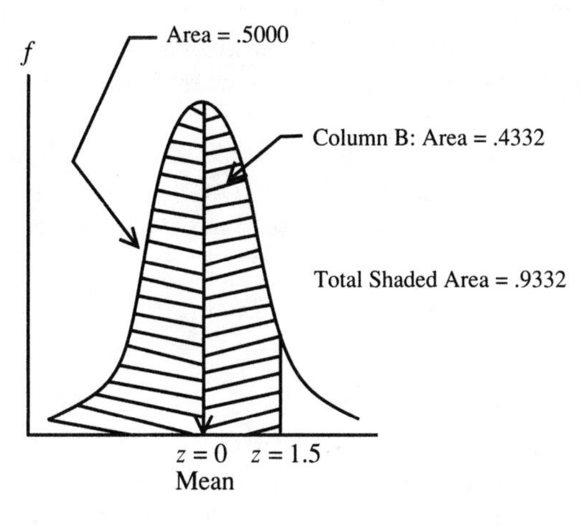

(b) The area above $z = -1$ is equal to the sum of the area between the mean and z, (Column B)and the area to the right of the mean (.5000).

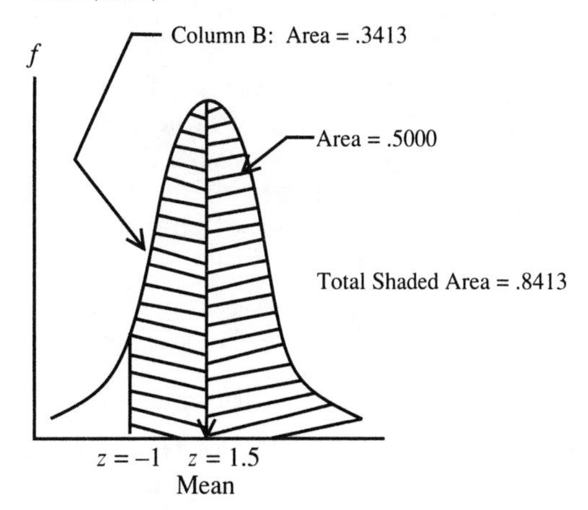

Figure 4.3

How to find areas under the normal curve by using the Table of Areas Under the Normal Curve.

(c) The area between z-scores of +1 and +1.7 is equal to the difference between the area beyond $z = +1$ (Column C) and the area beyond $z = +1.7$ (Column C).

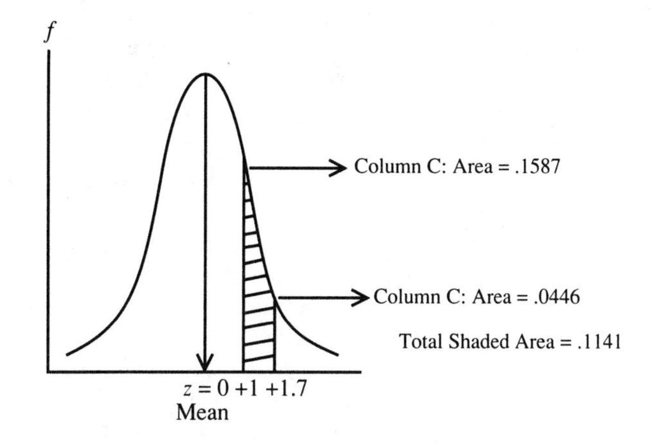

viously, half the cases do, or, .5000 or 50%. Thus, the total proportion of cases below $z = +1.50$ is $.4332 + .5000 = .9332$ or 93.32%. This example is illustrated in Figure 4.3a. As another example, suppose we want to know the proportion of cases scoring above a score of $z = -1.0$. Finding the z-score of $+1.0$ in Column A, we see from Column B that the proportion of cases between $z = +1$ (or $z = -1$) and the mean is .3413. In addition, the proportion of cases beyond the mean is .5000. Adding these values we get $.3413 + .5000 = .8413$, which is the proportion of cases above a z-score of -1.0. This example is illustrated in Figure 4.3b.

Finally, think about how the Table of Areas Under the Normal Curve would be used in finding the proportion of cases between any two specified scores. Say that we want to know the proportion of cases that scored between $z = +1.0$ and $z = +1.7$. The area corresponding to this proportion is shaded in Figure 4.3c. From the Table of Areas Under the Normal Curve we know that the proportion of area beyond $z = +1.0$ is .1587 (Column C). This proportion includes the shaded area in which we are interested, but also includes the area beyond $z = +1.7$. We can also tell from the table that the proportion of area beyond $z = +1.7$ is .0446 (Column C). If we subtract .0446 from .1587, we find the proportion of cases represented by the shaded area: .1141. Thus, 11.41% of the cases in a normal distribution fall between scores located at 1 and 1.7 standard deviations above (and below) the mean.

Applications of the Standard Normal Distribution

To the degree that the data approximate a normal distribution, the standard normal distribution can be a very useful tool in answering questions about those data. In the preceding discussion we saw that if a distribution of scores is normally distributed, we can find the proportion of cases falling between any two specified score points or beyond any specified single score. So what? Of what possible use might this be? In fact, there are several applications.

Estimating Percentiles. For one thing, the standard normal distribution can be used to estimate the percentile of any given score. This application is particularly useful in those situations in which we do not have available a complete frequency distribution (from which a cumulative percentage distribution might be formed), but we do have descriptive statistics for the distribution. Box 4.3 demonstrates how percentiles may be estimated for raw scores using the standard normal distribution.

Of course, percentiles estimated using the standard normal distribution are only estimates and will be inaccurate to the extent that the data deviate from a normal distribution. For example, look at the Phrenological Aptitude Test Scores in Table 4.2. Along with frequencies, this table lists cumulative percentages (percentiles) for each score. We learned in chapter 2 that these scores form a distribution that deviates somewhat from the normal shape (see Figure 2.2c). This being the case, percentiles estimated using the standard normal distribution will differ slightly from the true percentiles ($\%_c$) listed in Table 4.2. Take the score of 80 as a case in point. Given a mean of $\bar{X} = 79.26$ and a standard deviation of $s = 5.55$, this raw score has a z-score equivalent of

$$z_X = \frac{X - \bar{X}}{s}$$

$$z_{80} = \frac{80 - 79.26}{5.55}$$

$$= +.13$$

TABLE 4.2 Frequency and Cumulative Percentage (Percentile) Distributions for Scores on the Phrenological Aptitude Test

X	f	$\%_c$
65	3	6
72	1	8
73	2	12
76	4	20
77	3	26
78	8	42
79	7	56
80	6	68
81	2	72
82	5	82
83	2	86
84	1	88
87	1	90
88	2	94
90	2	98
93	1	100

If we use the Table of Areas Under the Normal Curve, we find that 55.17% of the cases *in a normal distribution* fall at or below a z-score of $+.13$. The problem is that our scores are not exactly normally distributed. Consequently, the estimated percentile of 55.17% differs somewhat from the true percentile of 68%. In general, the more our data deviate from the normal shape, the more error we can anticipate when estimating percentiles using standard scores and the standard normal distribution.

Estimating Raw Scores Corresponding to Percentiles. Sometimes we wish to know the raw score that corresponds to a specified percentile. Just as the standard normal distribution can be used to estimate percentiles from raw scores, it is also possible to work in the opposite direction, estimating raw scores for specified percentiles. If we have a percentile we can begin with the Table of Areas Under the Normal Curve by determining the z-score that marks off the appropriate proportion of cases. We then find the raw score that corresponds to this z-score by using Equation 4.1. This is the raw score that corresponds to the specified percentile. This procedure is illustrated in Box 4.4.

As always, however, raw scores estimated using this procedure are only estimates that are based on the assumption of normally distributed data. Because data are never exactly normally distributed, the estimates will always carry some error.

BOX 4.3

ESTIMATING PERCENTILES USING STANDARD SCORES

Ima Odwon has been informed that her score on the Jekyll and Hyde Multiple Personality Disorder Scale is 8,000. She knows that this is below the mean score of 10,000, but even so, 8,000 seems like a very big number and she is concerned. She wants to know just how high her score really is.

We can estimate the percentile rank corresponding to her score of 8,000 by transforming this raw score to a standard score. Given that the mean on the Jekyll and Hyde is 10,000 and the standard deviation is 5,000, Ima's z-score is computed according to Equation 4.1 as

$$z_X = \frac{X - \overline{X}}{s}$$

$$z_{8,000} = \frac{8,000 - 10,000}{5,000}$$

$$= -.40$$

Ima's percentile may now be estimated. Her z-score of $-.40$ is located in the standard normal distribution as shown in Figure 4.4. The shaded area to the left of $z = -.40$ represents the proportion of cases scoring at and below Ima's score. Finding this area will give us Ima's percentile. From the Table of Areas Under the Normal Curve (Appendix A), we see that the area beyond $z = -.40$ is .3446. Thus, Ima's score of 8,000 falls at the 34.46th percentile.

Figure 4.4

Using the standard normal curve to estimate percentiles. The area at and below a score represents that score's percentile.

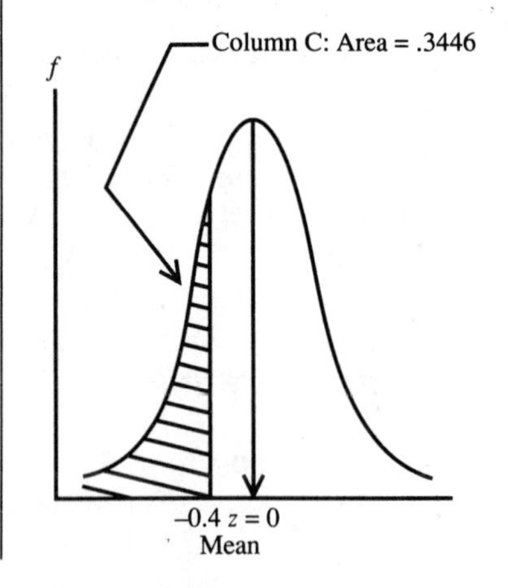

Assigning Cases to Groups. One final application of the standard normal distribution involves assigning cases to groups on the basis of their scores on some variable. In this application, the likelihood of a raw score occurring in each of two or more groups is determined by computing that raw score's z-score equivalent in each of the groups under consideration. The to-be-assigned case is placed into that group from whose mean the case shows the lowest deviation (i.e., smallest absolute z-score).

This application is relevant to tasks of diagnosis, job placement, or to any other situation in which a case presents a score on some variable and is to be assigned to the group in which that score is most likely to occur. An example of this application is in Box 4.5.

BOX 4.4

ESTIMATING RAW SCORES CORRESPONDING TO PERCENTILES

There is an opening for a pie taster at Piece O' The Pie, Inc. Al LaMode, Personnel Director, wishes to consider for this position only those applicants whose scores on the Porky Pig Gluttony Scale fall in the top third (i.e., 67th percentile or higher). He wants to know what raw score should be used as the cutoff as he examines applications for the job. This problem is diagrammed in Figure 4.5.

Given that the mean score on the test is $\bar{X} = 50$ and the standard deviation is $s = 5$, the cutoff score can be estimated as follows. Find the z-score at the 67th percentile by scanning Column B of the Table of Areas Under the Normal Curve for a listing of .1700. The z-score listed for this area is .44. This is the z-score that falls at the 67th percentile. But what is the corresponding raw score? This is computed using Equation 4.1.

$$z_X = \frac{X - \bar{X}}{s}$$

$$+.44 = \frac{X - 50}{5}$$

$$X - 50 = .44(5)$$

$$X - 50 = 2.20$$

$$X = 52.20$$

Figure 4.5

Using the standard normal curve to find the raw score corresponding to a specified percentile.

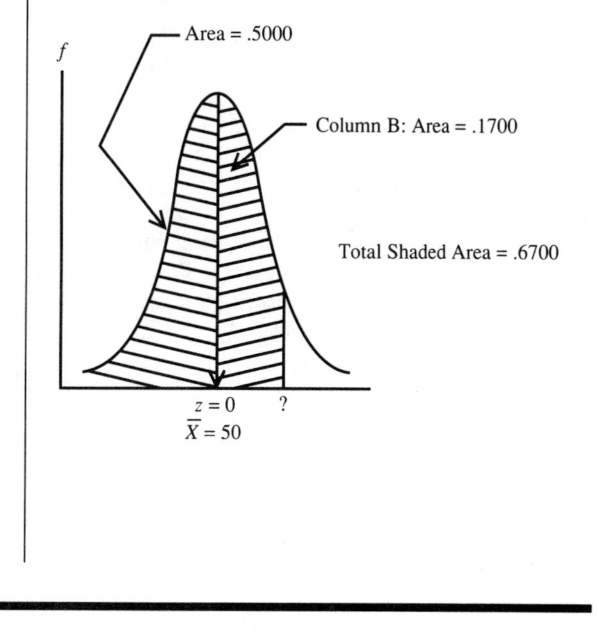

OTHER STANDARDIZED SCORES

Standardized scores come in many varieties in addition to the z-scores computed by Equation 4.1. These standardized scores accomplish various purposes that will be explained next.

Modified Standard Scores

Although z-scores are extremely useful, they have the disadvantage of requiring that we deal in negative values and values expressed in decimal form. Where we wish to avoid this, **modified standard scores** are useful. Modified standard scores can be created to form a distribution having any desired mean and standard deviation, and are computed according to Equation 4.2.

BOX 4.5

USING STANDARD SCORES TO ASSIGN CASES TO GROUPS

The publishers of the Snidely Whiplash Empathy Inventory have provided the following norms for social workers and professional wrestlers.

Social Workers	**Wrestlers**
$\overline{X} = 6.4$	$\overline{X} = 8.2$
$s = 2.5$	$s = 2.7$

Billy Bad has obtained a score of 7 on the Whiplash Inventory. On the basis of this score alone, would Billy be better advised to pursue a career as a social worker or a wrestler? That is, is a score of 7 more probable in the social workers' distribution or the wrestlers' distribution?

We can answer this question by determining Billy's location in each of the distributions as indicated by his z-scores. In the social workers' distribution, Billy's raw score of 7 corresponds to a z-score of

$$z_X = \frac{X - \overline{X}}{s}$$

$$z_7 = \frac{7 - 6.4}{2.5}$$

$$= +.24$$

In the wrestlers' distribution, Billy's score corresponds to a z-score of

$$z_X = \frac{X - \overline{X}}{s}$$

$$z_7 = \frac{7 - 8.2}{2.7}$$

$$= -.44$$

Billy's score falls closer to the mean of the social workers' distribution than to the mean of the wrestlers' distribution. In other words, Billy's score is more consistent with scores seen among social workers than among wrestlers, so we would advise him to pursue social work.

EQUATION 4.2

$$\text{Modified } z = s_{\text{desired}}(z) + \overline{X}_{\text{desired}}$$

where,

s_{desired} = the desired standard deviation

z = standard scores computed according to Equation 4.1

$\overline{X}_{\text{desired}}$ = the desired mean

In words, modified z-scores are computed by multiplying each original z-score by the desired standard deviation and adding the desired mean to this product.

Examples of modified standard scores abound. Scores on the College Board's Scholastic Aptitude Test (SAT) are modified standard scores with a mean set at 500 and a standard deviation set at 100. SAT scores are computed using Equation 4.2, substituting 100 for $s_{desired}$ and 500 for $\bar{X}_{desired}$.

$$\text{SAT} = 100(z) + 500$$

By multiplying z-scores by 100, we eliminate the decimal point. By then adding 500, we eliminate negative values. Take, for instance, the student whose z-score on the SAT is -1.52. Expressed as a modified z-score, the student's SAT score becomes

$$\begin{aligned}\text{SAT} &= s_{desired}(z) + \bar{X}_{desired} \\ &= 100(-1.52) + 500 \\ &= 348\end{aligned}$$

Scores on the subtests of the Wechsler Scales of Intelligence are commonly reported as modified z-scores with a mean set to 10 and a standard deviation set to 3. Of course, this is accomplished using Equation 4.2, substituting 3 for $s_{desired}$ and 10 for $\bar{X}_{desired}$.

Normalized Standard Scores

Standard scores, be they z-scores or modified z-scores, adjust the mean and standard deviation to more convenient values, but do nothing to alter the shape of the distribution. A normal distribution of raw scores will form a normal distribution of standard or modified standard scores. A non-normal distribution of raw scores remains non-normal following standardization.

We have seen, though, that a distribution having a normal shape is very desirable for certain purposes. The value of working with normally distributed scores will become even more apparent in subsequent chapters. Fortunately, it is possible to **normalize** a non-normal distribution of scores, that is, to rescale the original values to form a normal distribution.

In normalizing a distribution, the score that falls at the mean is assigned a **normalized *z*-score** of 0, since a z-score of 0 falls at the mean of a normal distribution. The score at the 16th percentile in the non-normal distribution is given a normalized z-score of -1, since, in a normal distribution, approximately 16% of the scores fall at and below a z-score of -1. The score at the 84th percentile in the non-normal distribution is given a normalized z-score of $+1$, since, in a normal distribution, approximately 84% of the scores fall at and below a z-score of $+1$. Similarly, each other score in the distribution of original scores is assigned a normalized z-score by finding the percentile rank of the raw score and identifying the z-score corresponding to this percentile in the Table of Areas Under the Normal Curve. The end result of these steps is a set of normalized z-scores that forms an approximately normal distribution, even though the original raw scores may not have been normal. Normalization is illustrated in Box 4.6.

BOX 4.6

NORMALIZING A DISTRIBUTION

In this box we will examine the process by which a non-normal distribution can be normalized. Raw (X) and standard (z) scores are listed in Table 4.3, and are plotted in Figure 4.6. Looking at Figure 4.6 we can see that the original distribution (drawn with a solid line) is somewhat positively skewed. We can create a more normal distribution by computing normalized z-scores.

TABLE 4.3 Frequency and Cumulative Percentage (Percentile) Distributions of Scores on the Variable *X*

X	f	$\%_c$	z	Normalized z
1	1	5.3	−1.57	−1.62
2	7	42.1	−.80	−.20
3	5	68.4	−.04	.48
4	3	84.2	.72	1.00
5	2	94.7	1.49	1.62
6	1	100.0	2.25	4.00

Raw Scores are listed under X, standard scores are labeled z, and normalized standard scores are labeled normalized z.

First, cumulative percentages (percentiles) are given for each raw score in Table 4.3 in the column headed $\%_c$. Next, using the Table of Areas Under the Normal Curve, we identify the z-scores listed for each percentile. These z-scores are the normalized z-scores listed in the last column of Table 4.3.

For example, the raw score of 1 has a percentile of 5.3%. This means that the area beyond (i.e., below) this score in the normal distribution is .0530. Looking in Column C in the Table of Areas Under the Normal Curve, we find a proportion close to this value (.0526) listed with a z-score of -1.62. As another example,

Figure 4.6

An illustration of the normalization of standard scores.

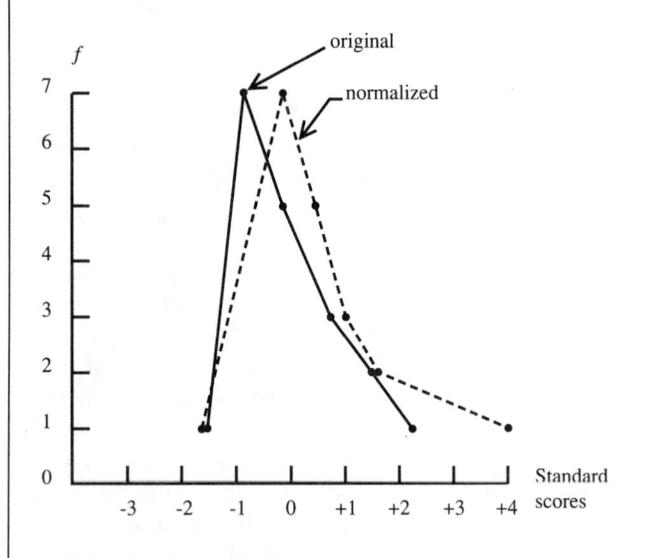

the raw score of 4 has a percentile of 84.2%. This means that the area beyond (above) this score will be $1.000 - .8420 = .1580$ in a normal distribution. We find a proportion close to this value (.1587) listed with a z-score of $+1.00$. Other normalized z-scores are determined in the same manner.

The normalized standard scores listed in Table 4.3 are plotted in Figure 4.6 as a dotted line. You can see that, excluding the top score, the distribution has been reshaped toward a more normal appearance.

Although the distribution of normalized z-scores shown in Figure 4.6 is closer to normal than is the distribution of original z-scores, the normalized distribution is not exactly normal. In general, the larger the distribution and the more continuous the distribution of scores, the closer the normalized distribution will come to being completely normal.

Normalization is generally recommended only in those situations in which deviations from the normal distribution can be attributed to a deficiency in the procedure used to measure the variable being studied. If the variable itself is distributed non-normally, our data should probably be allowed to reflect this fact. If the variable can be assumed to have a normal distribution, normalization is appropriate.

Normalization will move a non-normal distribution in the direction of increased normalcy, but will not achieve a perfect normal distribution. The more cases and the more continuous the distribution of scores, the closer the normalized distribution will come to a true normal distribution.

T-Scores

A commonly used modified standard score is called the ***T*-score.** *T*-scores, shown in Figure 4.1, are normalized standard scores that are modified using Equation 4.2 to have a mean of 50 and a standard deviation of 10. Once scores have been normalized (if they were not normally distributed to begin with), *T*-scores are computed by substituting in Equation 4.2 10 for s_{desired} and 50 for $\overline{X}_{\text{desired}}$.

Stanine Scores

Another commonly used standardized score is the "standard nine" or **stanine** score. Stanine scores are assigned to normally distributed raw scores (or to normalized *z*-scores) in accordance with Table 4.4. All raw scores in the bottom 4% of the distribution are assigned the stanine score of 1. The next 7% of the cases are assigned the stanine score of 2. The next 12% of the cases are assigned the stanine score of 3, and so on. As shown in Figure 4.1, stanines divide a normal distribution into nine equal divisions and a case's stanine score indicates the division of the distribution within which that case falls.

The advantages of stanine scores include the elimination of negative values and decimal scores, and the immediacy with which stanines give a case's relative location in the distribution. The obvious disadvantage of stanines is the loss of precision that results when we assign the same stanine score to several cases whose raw scores differ.

TABLE 4.4 Conversion to Stanine Scores

Location of Score in Distribution	Stanine
Bottom 4%	1
Next 7%	2
Next 12%	3
Next 17%	4
Middle 20%	5
Next 17%	6
Next 12%	7
Next 7%	8
Top 4%	9

SUMMARY

Standard scores, or z-scores, are transformations of raw scores that specify the direction and magnitude of the deviation between raw scores and the mean, measured in standard deviations. Standard scores have a mean of 0 and a standard deviation of 1. Standard scores are useful for locating cases within a distribution, much as percentiles locate cases, and provide a common metric that enables the comparison of scores obtained using different measuring procedures. The normal distribution is a frequency distribution having a very specific shape. This bell-shaped, symmetrical distribution is useful because so many variables of interest to researchers in the social and behavioral sciences are distributed normally. The standard normal distribution is a normal distribution of standard scores. As such, the standard normal distribution possesses the characteristics both of standard scores and of the normal distribution. The Table of Areas Under the Normal Curve is useful for finding the proportion of cases that falls between any specified standard scores in the standard normal distribution. This information can be applied in estimating percentiles, estimating scores corresponding to specified percentiles, and in assigning cases to groups on the basis of the relative likelihood of their scores occurring within those groups. Several additional types of standardized scores are described in this chapter. Modified standard scores are transformations of the familiar z-scores that set the mean and standard deviation equal to any desired values. Normalized standard scores are z-scores assigned to raw scores in such a manner as to normalize the shape of the distribution of scores. T-scores are normalized z-scores that have been modified to have a mean of 50 and a standard deviation of 10. Stanine scores range in value from 1 through 9, and locate cases within one of nine equal divisions of a normal distribution.

NOTES

1. It is easy to prove that the mean of a distribution of z-scores will always equal zero.

$$\bar{X}_z = \frac{\Sigma z}{N} \qquad \text{by definition of the mean}$$

$$= \frac{\Sigma\left(\frac{X - \bar{X}}{s}\right)}{N} \qquad \text{by substitution}$$

$$= \frac{0}{N} \qquad \text{because } \Sigma(X - \bar{X}) = 0$$

$$= 0$$

2. It can be shown that the variance and standard deviation of a distribution of z-scores will always equal 1.

$$s^2{}_Z = \frac{\Sigma(z - \bar{X}_z)^2}{N} \quad \text{by definition of the variance}$$

$$= \frac{\Sigma z^2}{N} \quad \text{because } \bar{X}_z = 0$$

$$= \frac{\Sigma\left[\frac{(X - \bar{X}}{s}\right]^2}{N} \quad \text{by substitution}$$

$$= \frac{\frac{\Sigma(X - \bar{X})^2}{s^2}}{N} \quad \text{by rearrangement}$$

$$= \frac{\Sigma\frac{1}{s^2}(X - \bar{X})^2}{N} \quad \text{by rearrangement}$$

$$= \frac{\frac{1}{s^2}\Sigma(X - \bar{X})^2}{N} \quad \text{by rearrangement}$$

$$= \frac{1}{s^2}(s^2) \quad \text{because } s^2 = \frac{\Sigma(X - \bar{X})^2}{N}$$

$$= 1$$

3. The normal distribution is described exactly by the function rule for the normal distribution.

$$y = \left(\frac{1}{\sigma\sqrt{2\pi}}\right)e^{-(X - \mu)^2/(2\sigma^2)}$$

where,

y = the height of the curve for any given value of X
σ = the standard deviation of the raw scores
π = approximately 3.1416
e = approximately 2.7183
X = a raw score on the variable X
μ = the mean of the raw scores

Once σ and μ are set, the only value that varies is X. For each value of X a different value of y can be computed that describes the shape of the normal distribution.

CHAPTER 5

SAMPLING DISTRIBUTIONS AND INTERVAL ESTIMATION

Sampling distributions are a central concept within statistics. Sampling distributions are fundamental to significance testing, discussed in later chapters, and to interval estimation, discussed in this chapter. We will begin with the general characteristics of sampling distributions. Sampling distributions will then be applied to the task of estimating population parameters from sample statistics.

SAMPLING DISTRIBUTIONS

The frequency distributions with which we dealt in previous chapters represented single samples. These distributions showed how many times various scores were obtained within a single sample. In contrast, **sampling distributions** may be defined as theoretical frequency distributions that depict the frequency of occurrence of values of some statistic computed for all possible samples of size N (or pairs, triplets, or other multi-sample sets) drawn from some population. Let us look more closely at this definition of sampling distributions.

First, sampling distributions are theoretical or imaginary entities. Although it is theoretically possible to draw all possible samples (or sets of two or more samples) from a population, to do so would be a practical impossibility, at least if the population is of any substantial size.

Second, sampling distributions do not display the frequency of occurrence of scores on some variable, but depict instead how often various values of some statistic are obtained as the statistic is computed for samples drawn from a population. For example, the **sampling distribution of the mean,** which we will consider in greater detail in a moment, would be formed by drawing all possible samples of size N from a population, computing the mean for each sample, and then plotting the frequency of occurrence of each of the various values of the mean obtained from one sample to the next. Other sampling distributions might involve computing a statistic other than the mean. We can imagine, for example, drawing all possible samples of size N from a population, computing the variance of each sample, and plotting the number of times different variance values occurred across the many samples. This would be the sampling distribution of the variance.

Third, sampling distributions are not always based on drawing all possible samples from a population. Some sampling distributions are created by drawing all possible pairs of samples, triplets of samples, quadruplets of samples, or other sets of several samples. Then, a statistic is computed for each pair, triplet, quadruplet, or other set of samples, and the frequency of occurrence of the various values of this statistic is plotted, forming the sampling distribution. In this chapter we will focus on sampling distributions based on sampling one sample at a time from a population. Later chapters will rely upon sampling distributions that involve sampling multi-sample sets from a population.

As we can see from this discussion, there are many sampling distributions. Each differs from the next by: (1) whether single samples or multi-sample sets are being drawn; (2) what statistic is being computed; and (3) sample size.

It is important to reiterate at this point that useful sampling distributions exist only in the imagination. No one would actually draw all possible samples from a population, compute a statistic on each, and plot the frequency of occurrence of the values obtained. It is not necessary to do this because we know what the sampling distributions look like even without actually forming them. We will come back to this point later. Now, though, we will turn to the first of several sampling distributions that will be examined in this book, the sampling distribution of the mean.

Sampling Distribution of the Mean

If we were to draw all possible samples of some size (N) from a population and compute the mean for each sample, we would find that the values of the means would vary somewhat from sample to sample. This variability should seem intuitively reasonable. Even though the samples were all drawn from the same population, we would not expect their means to be perfectly identical to each other. This variability in sample means seen from one sample to the next is due to **sampling error.** Because no sample is likely to match the population from which it was drawn in *every* way, the samples can be said to be "in error," thus the term sampling error. Because the means computed from one sample to the next vary, it is possible to count and plot the number of times each value of the mean occurs, forming the sampling distribution of the mean.

As stated earlier, the sampling distribution of the mean is usually a theoretical entity, existing only in the imagination. Nonetheless, if the population from which samples are being drawn is very small, it is possible to actually draw all possible samples of size N, compute the mean for each sample, and plot the frequencies associated with these mean values, thereby constructing a sampling distribution of the mean. For the sake of making the concept of the sampling distribution of the mean more concrete, we will construct one here.

Shown in Table 5.1 are IQ scores for the entire population of the small Hellhole County town of Wahoo. The frequency distribution of scores for this population of six cases is plotted in Figure 5.1. As we can see from Figure 5.1, the population shows a rectangular distribution with a mean of $\mu = 105$ and a standard deviation of $\sigma = 17.08$.

TABLE 5.1 IQ Scores for the Entire Population of Wahoo

Inhabitant	IQ
A	80
B	90
C	100
D	110
E	120
F	130

Figure 5.1

Frequency distribution of IQ scores for the population of Wahoo.

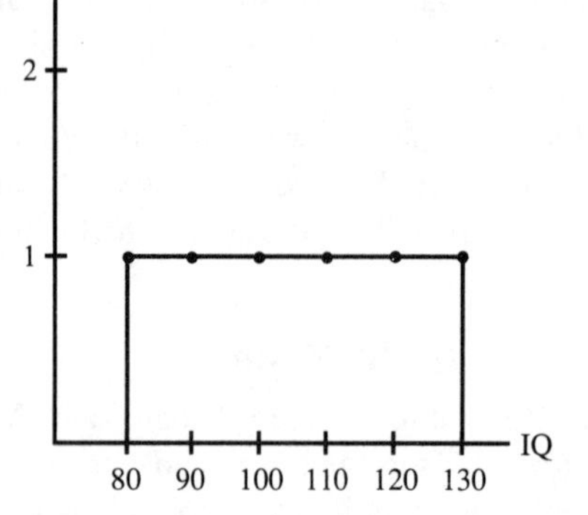

In order to construct the sampling distribution of the mean for samples of size $N = 2$, we would draw all possible samples of size 2 from this population, compute the mean for each, and plot the frequency of occurrence of each of the

TABLE 5.2 Sampling Distribution of the Mean Formed Using Sampling with Replacement

Samples	Scores	$\bar{X}$
A, A	80, 80	80
A, B	80, 90	85
A, C	80, 100	90
A, D	80, 110	95
A, E	80, 120	100
A, F	80, 130	105
B, B	90, 90	90
B, C	90, 100	95
B, D	90, 110	100
B, E	90, 120	105
B, F	90, 130	110
C, C	100, 100	100
C, D	100, 110	105
C, E	100, 120	110
C, F	100, 130	115
D, D	110, 110	110
D, E	110, 120	115
D, F	110, 130	120
E, E	120, 120	120
E, F	120, 130	125
F, F	130, 130	130

All possible samples (drawn with replacement) of size $N = 2$ from the population of six inhabitants of Wahoo. Listed with each sample are IQ scores and the sample mean ($\bar{X}$).

Figure 5.2

The sampling distribution of the mean for samples of size $N = 2$ drawn from the population of IQ scores for Wahoo.

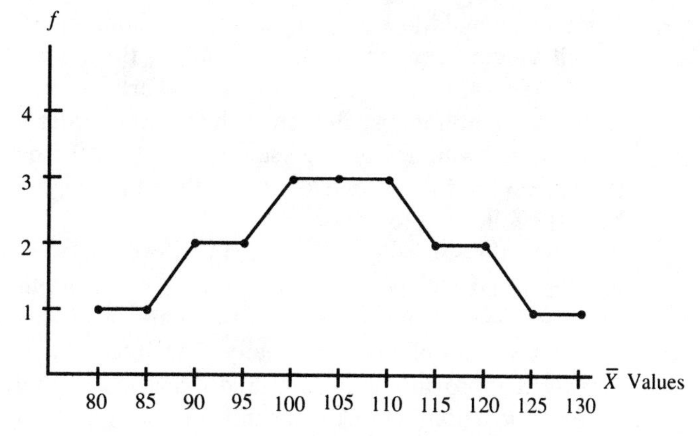

mean values. All possible samples of size $N = 2$ and their sample means are listed in Table 5.2. Plotting the frequency of occurrence of these sample means, as in Figure 5.2, we get the sampling distribution of the mean for samples of size $N = 2$ based on our population of six cases.

You may wonder why some of the samples in Table 5.2 list the same case twice (e.g., A, A; B, B). This is because sampling distributions are formed using **sampling with replacement.** Once a case is drawn from the population for inclusion in a sample, it is put back into the population, that is, "replaced." It is therefore possible that the same case may be drawn again for inclusion in the same sample. That statisticians have developed sampling distributions based upon the procedure of sampling with replacement is evidence of the discrepancy between pure and applied statistics. In research practice, **sampling without replacement** is the established procedure. Once a case has been selected for inclusion in a sample, it makes little sense to select that case again for the same sample! Using sampling with replacement, we could conceivably end up studying a sample of size $N = 100$ consisting of the same case drawn 100 times! Although this is mathematically acceptable, it is hardly acceptable from a practical standpoint! The fact that applied statistical procedures rely upon sampling without replacement, while statistical theory assumes sampling with replacement, is one of those things in statistics that we try not to worry too much about. In fact, there is little or no cause for concern, since the practice of sampling without replacement has no noticeable effect on the accuracy of the conclusions that are reached, provided we confine our attention to relatively large samples drawn from very large populations.

Characteristics of the Sampling Distribution of the Mean. Although we were able to construct an actual sampling distribution of the mean just above, it was only because the population in that example was unrealistically small and our samples were much tinier than would ever be the case in actual practice.

Normally, populations are very large, and the samples we study are of a fair size as well. Under these conditions, constructing the sampling distribution of the mean would be most tedious, to say the least. Fortunately, we need not actually construct the sampling distribution of the mean in order to know its characteristics. If we are drawing fairly large samples ($N \geq 50$) from a very large population, the **central limit theorem** tells us that the sampling distribution of the mean will have the following features.

First, the sampling distribution of the mean will be approximately normal in shape, and will become increasingly normal as the size of the samples increases. This is true regardless of the shape of the population's distribution, although if the population is normally distributed, the sampling distribution of the mean will approximate the normal distribution at smaller sample sizes. That the sampling distribution of the mean is normally distributed is important because this tells us about the relative likelihood of finding sample means that deviate by specified amounts from the mean of the sampling distribution of the mean. More will be made of this later.

This first characteristic of the sampling distribution of the mean, that is, its tendency to approximate a normal distribution, can be seen by comparing Figures 5.1 and 5.2. Although we started with a population distribution that was far from normal (Figure 5.1), and we drew tiny samples ($N = 2$) from the population, the sampling distribution of the mean (Figure 5.2) is already beginning to assume the classic symmetrical bell shape of the normal distribution.

A second feature of the sampling distribution of the mean is that the mean of this distribution (abbreviated with the symbol $\mu_{\overline{X}}$) will equal the population mean (μ). If we take a moment to compute the mean of the population described in Table 5.1, and the mean of the 21 sample means listed in Table 5.2, we will see that

$$\mu = \mu_{\overline{X}}$$
$$105 = 105$$

That $\mu = \mu_{\overline{X}}$ is also apparent from inspection of the plotted sampling distribution of the mean (Figure 5.2) in which the frequency peak is centered directly over the value $\overline{X} = 105$.

The third thing that we know about the sampling distribution of the mean from the central limit theorem is the variability of this distribution. The standard deviation of the sampling distribution of the mean, called the **standard error of the mean** (abbreviated with the symbol $\sigma_{\overline{X}}$), is computed in Equation 5.1.

EQUATION 5.1

$$\sigma_{\overline{X}} = \frac{\sigma}{\sqrt{N}} \text{ or } \frac{\hat{s}}{\sqrt{N}}$$

where,

σ = the population standard deviation
$\hat{s}$ = the corrected sample standard deviation
N = the size of the samples drawn from the population

For the sampling distribution of the mean depicted in Figure 5.2, Equation 5.1 gives us:

$$\sigma_{\overline{X}} = \frac{\sigma}{\sqrt{N}} \text{ or } \frac{\hat{s}}{\sqrt{N}}$$
$$= \frac{17.08}{\sqrt{2}}$$
$$= 12.08$$

We are already familiar with the standard deviation as a measure of variability (chapter 3). As the standard deviation of the sampling distribution of the mean, the standard error of the mean provides an approximate measure of the average absolute deviation of sample means around $\mu_{\overline{X}}$. When we say, then, that $\sigma_{\overline{X}} = 12.08$, we are saying that the average sample mean deviates from $\mu_{\overline{X}}$ by about 12 points.

The careful reader may have discovered something amiss at this point. If we will take the time to compute the standard deviation of the sample means listed in Table 5.2, we will discover that the value of the standard deviation computed using Equation 3.8 ($s = 12.91$) differs somewhat from the value computed using Equation 5.1 ($\sigma_{\overline{X}} = 12.08$). This is because Equation 5.1 describes the standard error of the mean accurately only when sample sizes are relatively large ($N \geq 50$). Thus, just as a sampling distribution of the mean based on small samples may not be exactly normal in shape, neither will the standard error of the mean be described exactly by Equation 5.1 when samples are small. As we can see, though, even with a population that deviates substantially from a normal distribution, and using very small samples, Equation 5.1 gives a close approximation to the actual standard deviation of the sample means.

Equation 5.1 reveals that the standard error of the mean will always be less than the standard deviation of the population distribution. This is because sample means are already the averages of all their constituent raw scores and can therefore never be as extreme as any single score. Further, the larger the samples (N) drawn from the population, the lower $\sigma_{\overline{X}}$ will be, since only rarely will the mean of a large sample deviate substantially from the mean of the population.

Sampling Distribution of the Proportion

Another useful sampling distribution is the **sampling distribution of the proportion.** Imagine a population in which some proportion of the cases possesses some characteristic (e.g., they are males or Republicans or make over $50,000 per year, or whatever). Let us use the symbol p_u to represent this proportion. (The p stands for proportion and the subscript $_u$ stands for "universe," synonymous with population.) Next, imagine drawing all possible samples of some size (N) from this population and determining the proportion of cases in each sample that possesses the characteristic under consideration. Let us use the lower case letter p to represent these sample proportions. From one sample to the next, we would expect the value of p to vary somewhat because of sampling error, the same cause to which variability in the sampling distribution of the mean was attributed. Finally,

TABLE 5.3 Data from the Entire Population of Wahoo

Inhabitant	County
A	1
B	0
C	0
D	1
E	1
F	0

A score of 0 indicates that the individual has never left the county; a score of 1 indicates that the individual has left the county at some time.

we can imagine plotting the frequency of occurrence of the various values of p obtained from one sample to the next. This frequency distribution would form the sampling distribution of the proportion.

Just as the sampling distribution of the mean is never actually constructed, neither is the sampling distribution of the proportion. To do so in the case of either sampling distribution is unnecessary, since the central limit theorem gives us the essential characteristics of these sampling distributions. Nonetheless, for the sake of a better understanding of the sampling distribution of the proportion, we will construct one here.

Shown in Table 5.3 are data from all six inhabitants of the Hellhole County town of Wahoo. For each case, a score of 1 is recorded if that individual has ever left the county and a score of 0 is recorded if the individual has never left the county. We can see that the proportion of people in this population who have been outside the county is $p_u = .50$.

In order to construct the sampling distribution of the proportion for samples of size $N = 2$, we would sample (with replacement) all possible samples of size $N = 2$ from this population, determine the proportion of cases in each sample that has been outside the county, and plot the frequency of occurrence of each of the sample proportions obtained in this manner. All possible samples of size $N = 2$, their scores, and their sample proportions are listed in Table 5.4. Plotting the frequency of occurrence of the sample proportions listed in Table 5.4 we get the sampling distribution of the proportion for samples of size $N = 2$ from the population of Wahoo shown in Figure 5.3.

Characteristics of the Sampling Distribution of the Proportion. We already know more about the sampling distribution of the proportion than we realize. This is because the sampling distribution of the proportion is exactly the same thing as the sampling distribution of the mean. This is so because, as we saw in chapter 3, a proportion is simply the mean of a distribution in which all

TABLE 5.4 Sampling Distribution of the Proportion Formed Using Sampling with Replacement

Samples	Scores	$\bar{X} = p$
A, A	1, 1	1
A, B	1, 0	.5
A, C	1, 0	.5
A, D	1, 1	1
A, E	1, 1	1
A, F	1, 0	.5
B, B	0, 0	0
B, C	0, 0	0
B, D	0, 1	.5
B, E	0, 1	.5
B, F	0, 0	0
C, C	0, 0	0
C, D	0, 1	.5
C, E	0, 1	.5
C, F	0, 0	0
D, D	1, 1	1
D, E	1, 1	1
D, F	1, 0	.5
E, E	1, 1	1
E, F	1, 0	.5
F, F	0, 0	0

Listed with each sample are scores indicating whether each inhabitant has (1) or has not (0) ever left the county. Also listed are sample means ($\bar{X}$), which indicate the proportion (p) of each sample that has left the county.

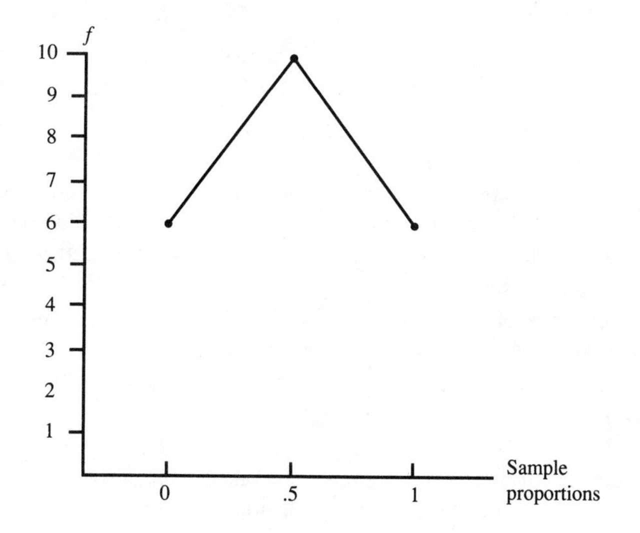

Figure 5.3

The sampling distribution of the proportion for samples of size $N = 2$ drawn from the population of Wahoo. These values indicate the proportion of each sample that has left the county.

scores are 0 or 1. Looking at Table 5.4 we can see that each sample proportion listed is equal to the mean of the two scores that form each sample. Thus, because a proportion is just a mean, the sampling distribution of the proportion is just a sampling distribution of the mean.

This means that all of the characteristics of the sampling distribution of the mean described above apply as well to the sampling distribution of the proportion. Provided that sample sizes are relatively large ($N \geq 50$), the sampling distribution of the proportion will assume a normal shape. Second, the mean of the sampling distribution of the proportion (μ_p) will equal the population proportion (i.e., $\mu_p = p_u$). Notice that the mean of the population described by Table 5.3 ($p_u = .5$) is equal to the mean of the sample proportions listed in Table 5.4 ($\mu_p = .5$). Finally, the standard deviation of the sampling distribution of the proportion (referred to more simply as the **standard error of the proportion,** and abbreviated by the symbol σ_p) may be computed exactly like the standard error of the mean in Equation 5.2.[1]

EQUATION 5.2

$$\sigma_p = \sigma_{\overline{X}} = \frac{\sigma}{\sqrt{N}} \text{ or } \frac{\hat{s}}{\sqrt{N}}$$

where,

σ = the population standard deviation
$\hat{s}$ = the corrected sample standard deviation
N = the size of the samples drawn from the population

Thus the standard error of the proportion for the sampling distribution of the proportion depicted in Figure 5.3 is

$$\sigma_p = \sigma_{\overline{X}} = \frac{\sigma}{\sqrt{N}} \text{ or } \frac{\hat{s}}{\sqrt{N}}$$

$$= \frac{.50}{\sqrt{2}}$$

$$= .35$$

Since a proportion is the same thing as a mean, and the sampling distribution of the proportion is the same thing as the sampling distribution of the mean, we can simplify matters considerably by forgetting that we ever heard of the sampling distribution of the proportion and the standard error of the proportion! Instead, remember when dealing with proportions that we are really working with means of dichotomously scored variables.

INTERVAL ESTIMATION

One recurring problem facing the researcher in the social and behavioral sciences is the task of describing population characteristics when only sample data are available. For example, a consultant might wish to know the mean reading grade level of the population of adults residing in Hellhole County, but has available only reading test scores for a sample of 100 adults from that county. Or, perhaps in order to qualify for special federal funds, Rocky Bottom State University must report the proportion of freshmen who have cranial calcification (i.e., bonehead syndrome). However, data are available from only 150 freshmen. Both of these situations call for an estimation of population characteristics from the available sample data.

There are two approaches to estimating population parameters from sample statistics—point estimation and interval estimation. **Point estimation** uses a sample-based statistic as the single value that best estimates the corresponding population parameter. Thus, the sample mean estimates the population mean, the sample proportion estimates the population proportion, and the corrected sample variance and standard deviation estimate the population variance and standard deviation. These sample-based statistics are called point estimators because they give a single value or point as the best possible estimate of a population parameter.

Interval estimation uses sample data to compute a range or "interval" of values which has a known probability of capturing the population parameter being estimated. This range of values, bounded by upper and lower **confidence limits,** is called a **confidence interval** because there is a known probability (i.e., level of "confidence") that the interval captures the population parameter being estimated. For example, consider Dan Blather's statement on the evening news that a telephone poll of 1000 households has shown that, "Sixty-one percent of Americans owning telephones support Porky Pig for president. This figure is subject to an error of plus or minus 5 percentage points."

Dan is citing a confidence interval. He has given a range of values, bounded by the confidence limits of 56% and 66%, within which the true population sentiment probably falls. Moreover, although Dan has not told us so, this confidence interval has some known probability (usually 95% or 99%) of capturing the population sentiment being estimated.

Confidence intervals are most commonly used to estimate population means and population proportions or percentages. We should remember in advance that our discussion of these two types of confidence intervals will be simplified by virtue of the fact that a proportion *is* a mean.

Confidence Interval for the Population Mean

Constructing a confidence interval for the population mean consists of finding a range of values that has a known probability of capturing the population mean. Let us consider how such an interval is constructed.

Imagine that we have drawn all possible samples of some relatively large size ($N \geq 50$) from the population in which we are interested.[2] Next, imagine that we have computed the mean for each sample on whatever variable it is that we are studying. Finally, imagine plotting the frequencies associated with these

(a) Ninety-five percent of the sample means fall within the shaded region between $\pm 1.96\sigma_{\overline{X}}$ from $\mu_{\overline{X}} = \mu$ in the normally distributed sampling distribution of the mean.

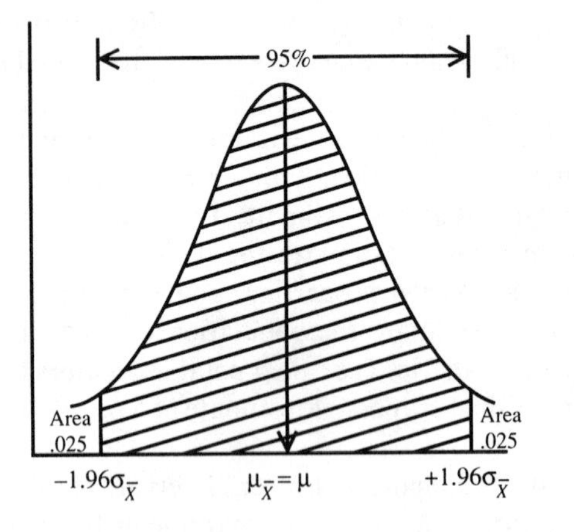

(b) A sample mean falling within the shaded region between $\pm 1.96\sigma_{\overline{X}}$ from $\mu_{\overline{X}} = \mu$, when surrounded by $1.96\sigma_{\overline{X}}$ points, will capture $\mu_{\overline{X}} = \mu$.

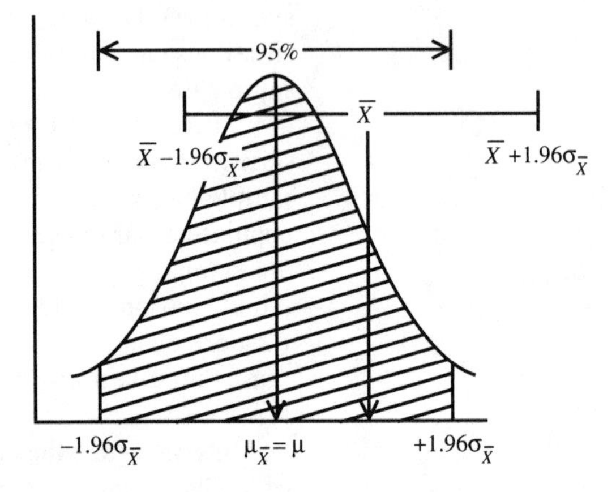

Figure 5.4

The sampling distribution of the mean used in the construction of the 95% confidence interval for the population mean.

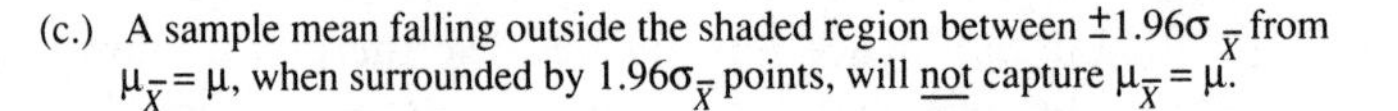

(c.) A sample mean falling outside the shaded region between $\pm 1.96\sigma_{\overline{X}}$ from $\mu_{\overline{X}} = \mu$, when surrounded by $1.96\sigma_{\overline{X}}$ points, will not capture $\mu_{\overline{X}} = \mu$.

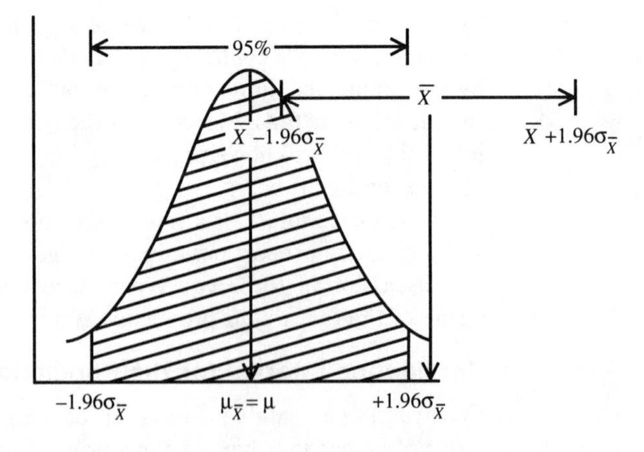

sample means to form the sampling distribution of the mean as shown in Figure 5.4. Because the sampling distribution of the mean is normally distributed (according to the central limit theorem), we can determine from the Table of Areas Under the Normal Curve (Appendix A) that 95% of the sample means fall between 1.96 standard deviations (i.e., standard errors of the mean) above and below the mean, $\mu_{\overline{X}} = \mu$, as shown in Figure 5.4a.

It follows that any given sample drawn from the population has a probability of .95 (95%) of falling within the shaded region of Figure 5.4a. If a sample mean *does* fall anywhere within this region, as shown in Figure 5.4b, surrounding the sample mean on both sides by 1.96 standard errors (i.e., $\overline{X} \pm 1.96\,\sigma_{\overline{X}}$) will give a range of values that captures μ, the population mean being estimated. This is because no sample mean falling within the shaded region of Figure 5.4 falls more than 1.96 $\sigma_{\overline{X}}$ points away from $\mu_{\overline{X}} = \mu$. The confidence limits provided by $\overline{X} \pm 1.96\,\sigma_{\overline{X}}$ define the 95% confidence interval, so called because the probability is 95% that this interval will capture the population mean.

Of course, there is some chance ($p = .05$ or 5%) that any given sample drawn from the population will fall outside the shaded region, as shown in Figure 5.4c. When this happens, surrounding the sample mean on both sides by 1.96 standard errors (i.e., $\overline{X} \pm 1.96\,\sigma_{\overline{X}}$) provides an interval that fails to capture the population mean, since all sample means outside the shaded region of Figure 5.4 fall more than 1.96 $\sigma_{\overline{X}}$ points from $\mu_{\overline{X}} = \mu$.

A numerical example of the construction of the 95% confidence interval is provided in Box 5.1.

One is not limited, of course, to 95% confidence intervals. Using the Table of Areas Under the Normal Curve it is possible to determine how many standard errors of the mean must surround a sample mean in order to construct a confidence interval having any desired level of confidence. The most commonly used confidence intervals are 90%, 95%, and 99%, defined by Equations 5.3 through 5.5, respectively.

EQUATION 5.3

$$\overline{X} \pm 1.65\,\sigma_{\overline{X}}$$

EQUATION 5.4

$$\overline{X} \pm 1.96\,\sigma_{\overline{X}}$$

EQUATION 5.5

$$\overline{X} \pm 2.58\,\sigma_{\overline{X}}$$

In the case of the 90% confidence interval, 90% of the sample means in a normally distributed sampling distribution of the mean will fall between 1.65 standard errors above and below $\mu_{\overline{X}} = \mu$. A sample mean that falls within this region, when surrounded by 1.65 standard errors (i.e., $\overline{X} \pm 1.65\,\sigma_{\overline{X}}$), will include a range of values that captures the population mean μ. Since the probability is .90 (90%) that any given sample mean will fall within 1.65 standard errors of $\mu_{\overline{X}} = \mu$, the range defined by $\overline{X} \pm 1.65\,\sigma_{\overline{X}}$ is called the 90% confidence interval.

The 99% confidence interval can be explained in the same manner. In a normally distributed sampling distribution of the mean, the probability is .99 (99%) that any given sample mean will fall within a region that ranges 2.58 standard errors on either side of $\mu_{\overline{X}} = \mu$. A mean located in this region, when surrounded on each side by 2.58 standard errors (i.e., $\overline{X} \pm 2.58\,\sigma_{\overline{X}}$), will capture the population mean μ.

BOX 5.1

CONSTRUCTION OF A CONFIDENCE INTERVAL FOR THE POPULATION MEAN

A consultant hired to estimate the mean reading grade level of adults residing in Hellhole County has tested a sample of $N = 100$ residents. Descriptive statistics from this sample follow:

$$\overline{X} = 8.5$$
$$\hat{s} = 3.0$$
$$N = 100$$

A 95% confidence interval for estimating the true population mean is constructed as follows. First, we know from the central limit theorem that the sampling distribution of the mean for samples of size $N = 100$ drawn from the population of Hellhole County is normally distributed, has a standard error of the mean ($\sigma_{\overline{X}}$) equal to $\hat{s} / \sqrt{N}$, and $\mu_{\overline{X}} = \mu$:

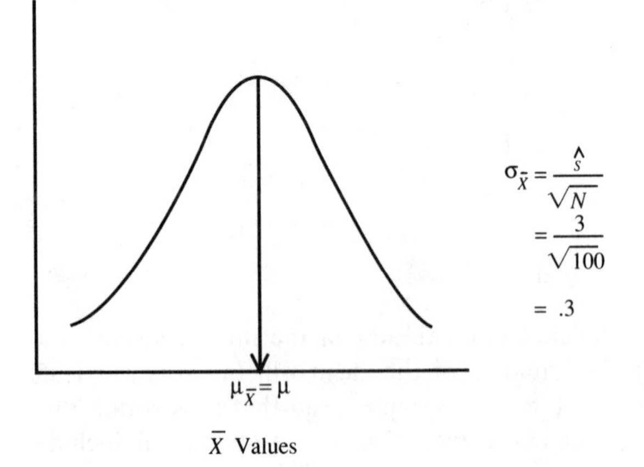

The sample that has been tested is one of the samples depicted in this sampling distribution. Because the sampling distribution is normally distributed, the probability is .95 (95%) that the sample falls within $\pm$ 1.96 $\sigma_{\overline{X}}$ above or below $\mu_{\overline{X}}$, that is, in the shaded region of the sampling distribution:

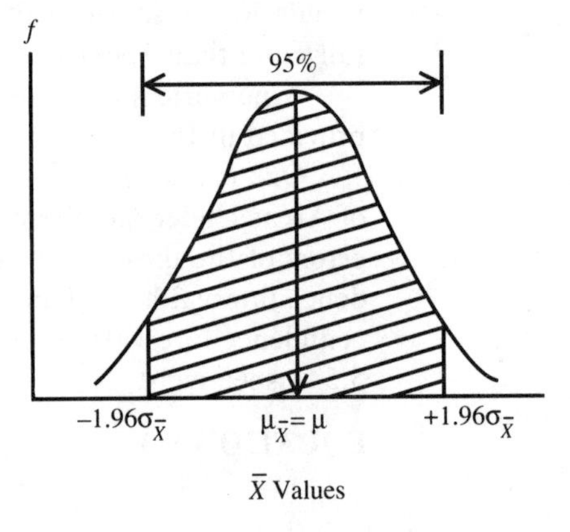

If the sample mean $\overline{X} = 8.5$ does fall anywhere within this region, it is no further from the population mean (μ) than 1.96 $\sigma_{\overline{X}}$ points. Thus, surrounding the sample mean on each side with 1.96 $\sigma_{\overline{X}}$ points will create a range of values that will capture $\mu_{\overline{X}} = \mu$. Thus, the 95% confidence interval for the population mean reading grade level is

$$\overline{X} \pm 1.96\,\sigma_{\overline{X}}$$
$$8.5 \pm 1.96(.3)$$
$$8.5 \pm .59$$

The probability is .95 (95%) that the mean reading grade level for adults residing in Hellhole County falls between 7.91 and 9.09. Of course, there is a probability of .05 (5%) that the true population mean falls outside this interval.

Confidence Interval for the Population Proportion

Confidence intervals are also used to estimate the proportion or percentage of cases in a population that possesses some attribute, holds some opinion, or expresses some attitude. The computations involved in constructing confidence intervals for population proportions are identical to those used in constructing confidence intervals for population means. This is because (for the last time!) a proportion *is* a mean. Box 5.2 provides an example of the construction of a confidence interval for a population proportion.

The Width of Confidence Intervals

It should be intuitively obvious that, all other things being equal, a narrow confidence interval is preferable to a wide confidence interval. For instance, it is more desirable to say:

"We are 95% certain that between 14% and 26% of freshman students are boneheads."

than it is to say:

"We are 95% certain that between 5% and 35% of freshman students are boneheads."

The first statement is preferable because it is more precise. The first confidence interval is only 12 percentage points wide; the second confidence interval is 30 percentage points wide.

In problems of interval estimation, then, we should strive to keep confidence intervals as narrow as possible. How can this be done? Three factors determine the width of the confidence interval: (1) level of confidence; (2) the amount of variability in the data; and (3) sample size. Each of these factors will be considered next.

Level of Confidence. All other things being equal, the higher the confidence level, the wider the confidence interval. Thus, a 99% confidence interval will be wider than a 90% confidence interval for the same data. This rule is one more example of getting what we pay for in statistics. If we want to be more confident that our confidence interval captures the true value of the population parameter, we must pay by accepting a wider interval. If we are willing to accept a lower level of confidence, the confidence interval will be narrower. Box 5.3 illustrates how confidence levels influence confidence interval widths.

BOX 5.2

CONSTRUCTION OF A CONFIDENCE INTERVAL FOR A POPULATION PROPORTION

The federal government has requested an estimate of the proportion of Rocky Bottom State University freshmen with cranial calcification. However, there are over a thousand freshman, and only 150 of them have been evaluated. Each student in this sample has been scored 0 if basically normal, and 1 if diagnosed as a bonehead. Data are summarized below in the form of a frequency distribution.

	X	f
normal	0	120
bonehead	1	30

The mean of these scores is computed according to Equation 3.2, revealing that 20% of the students in the sample are boneheads.

$$\overline{X} = \frac{\Sigma fX}{N} = \frac{30}{150} = .20$$

Next, the corrected sample variance and standard deviation are computed according to Equations 3.7 and 3.8.

$$\hat{s}^2 = \frac{\Sigma(X - \overline{X})^2}{N - 1} = .16$$

$$\hat{s} = \sqrt{\hat{s}^2} = .40$$

A 95% confidence interval for estimating the population proportion (i.e., mean) of boneheads is constructed as follows. It is known from the central limit theorem that the sampling distribution of the mean (i.e., proportion) for samples of size $N = 150$ drawn from the population of freshmen of Rocky Bottom State University is normally shaped, with $\mu_{\overline{X}} = \mu$ and $\sigma_{\overline{X}} = \hat{s} / \sqrt{N} = .40/\sqrt{150} = .03$.

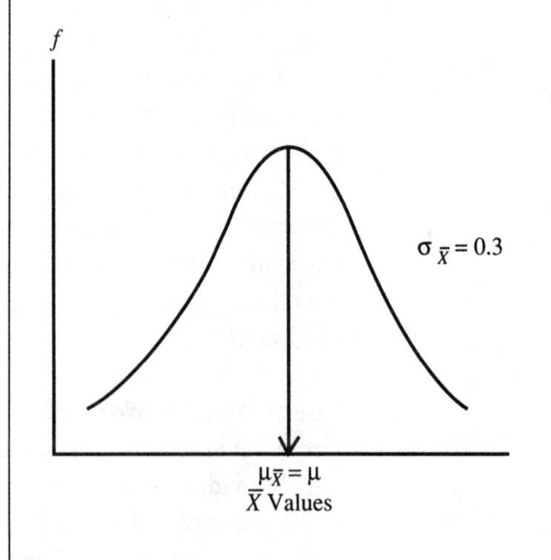

BOX 5.2—*continued*

The sample that has been examined is one of the samples depicted in this sampling distribution. Because the sampling distribution is normally distributed, the probability is .95 (95%) that the sample falls between 1.96 $\sigma_{\overline{X}}$ above and below $\mu_{\overline{X}} = \mu$, that is, in the shaded region of the sampling distribution shown next.

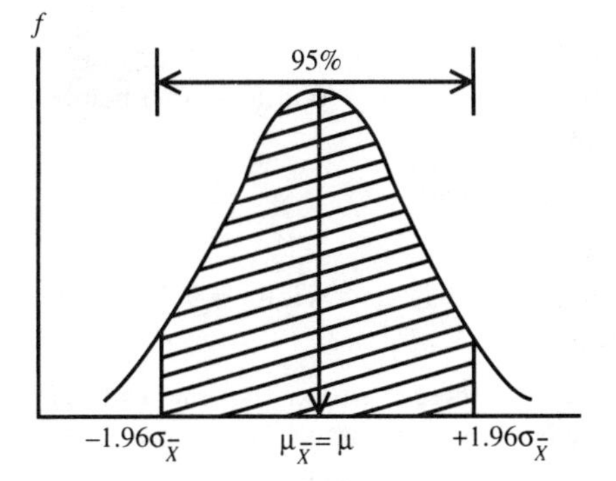

If the sample mean (proportion) $\overline{X} = .20$ does fall within this region, it can be no further from the population mean (proportion) than 1.96 $\sigma_{\overline{X}}$ points. Thus, surrounding the sample mean (proportion) on each side with 1.96 $\sigma_{\overline{X}}$ points will create a range of values that will capture $\mu_{\overline{X}} = \mu$. The 95% confidence interval for the mean (proportion) of boneheads in the freshman population is

$$\overline{X} \pm 1.96\,\sigma_{\overline{X}}$$
$$.20 \pm 1.96(.03)$$
$$.20 \pm .06$$

The probability is .95 (95%) that the population mean (proportion) being estimated falls between .14 (14%) and .26 (26%). The probability is .05 (5%) that the true population mean (proportion) falls outside these confidence limits.

BOX 5.3

CONFIDENCE INTERVAL WIDTH AND CONFIDENCE LEVEL

Computed below are confidence intervals for 50%, 60%, 70%, 80%, 90% and 99% levels of confidence. These intervals are based on the following sample descriptive statistics:

$$\bar{X} = 100$$
$$\hat{s} = 15$$
$$N = 100$$

For each confidence interval, the standard error of the mean is computed according to Equation 5.1 as

$$\sigma_{\bar{X}} = \hat{s} / \sqrt{N} = 15/\sqrt{100} = 1.5$$

50% Confidence Interval

$\bar{X} \pm .67\, \sigma_{\bar{X}}$
$100 \pm .67(1.5)$ Width = 2.02 points
100 ± 1.01

60% Confidence Interval

$\bar{X} \pm .84\, \sigma_{\bar{X}}$
$100 \pm .84(1.5)$ Width = 2.52 points
100 ± 1.76

70% Confidence Interval

$\bar{X} \pm 1.04\, \sigma_{\bar{X}}$
$100 \pm 1.04(1.5)$ Width = 3.12 points
100 ± 1.56

80% Confidence Interval

$\bar{X} \pm 1.28\, \sigma_{\bar{X}}$
$100 \pm 1.28(1.5)$ Width = 3.84 points
100 ± 1.92

90% Confidence Interval

$\bar{X} \pm 1.65\, \sigma_{\bar{X}}$
$100 \pm 1.65(1.5)$ Width = 4.96 points
100 ± 2.48

99% Confidence Interval

$\bar{X} \pm 2.58\, \sigma_{\bar{X}}$
$100 \pm 2.58(1.5)$ Width = 7.74 points
100 ± 3.87

We can see from these examples that the width of the confidence interval increases at an accelerating rate as level of confidence increases.

The widths of the confidence intervals computed in Box 5.3 are plotted as a function of levels of confidence in Figure 5.5. We can see that the relationship between confidence level and confidence interval width is curvilinear and positively accelerating. That is, we pay more dearly to move from a 90% to 95% confidence level than from an 80% to 85% confidence level.

How important is all of this? Not very. Since the most commonly cited confidence intervals in the social and behavioral sciences are the 95% and 99% confidence intervals, we are usually forced by tradition to select between these two.

Figure 5.5

Confidence interval widths as a function of levels of confidence (for $\overline{X} = 100$, $\hat{s} = 15$, and $N = 100$).

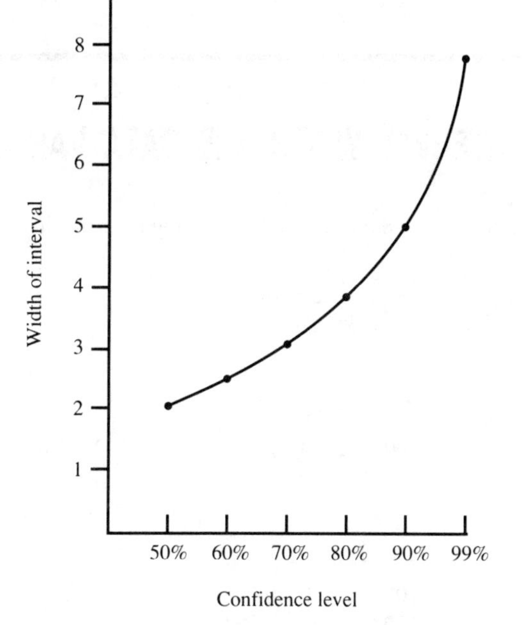

In making this selection, it is good practice to compute both intervals, compare their widths, and select between the two by balancing the advantages of higher confidence against the costs of greater interval widths.

Data Variability. All other things being equal, the more variable our data, the greater the standard error of the mean, and the wider the confidence interval. Thus, data that present a high standard deviation will produce a wider confidence interval than will data that have a lower standard deviation. Box 5.4 illustrates the relationship between the standard deviation of the data, the standard error of the mean, and the width of the confidence interval.

The widths of the confidence intervals computed in Box 5.4 are plotted as a function of data variability (standard deviation) in Figure 5.6. Figure 5.6 shows a linear relationship between the standard deviation of the data and the width of the confidence interval based on those data. It is clear from this diagram that anything we can do to reduce data variability will have the desirable effect of reducing the width of the confidence interval. Unfortunately, data variability is the one factor influencing confidence interval width over which we have the least

BOX 5.4

CONFIDENCE INTERVAL WIDTH AND DATA VARIABILITY

Computed below are 95% confidence intervals for data sets that differ only in variability ($\hat{s}$). All intervals are based on samples in which:

$$\bar{X} = 100$$
$$N = 100$$

For $\hat{s} = 5$

$\sigma_{\bar{X}} = \hat{s} / \sqrt{N}$	$\bar{X} \pm 1.96\, \sigma_{\bar{X}}$	
$= 5/\sqrt{100}$	$100 \pm 1.96(.5)$	Width = 1.96 points
$= .50$	$100 \pm .98$	

For $\hat{s} = 10$

$\sigma_{\bar{X}} = \hat{s} / \sqrt{N}$	$\bar{X} \pm 1.96\, \sigma_{\bar{X}}$	
$= 10/\sqrt{100}$	$100 \pm 1.96(1.0)$	Width = 3.92 points
$= 1.0$	100 ± 1.96	

For $\hat{s} = 15$

$\sigma_{\bar{X}} = \hat{s} / \sqrt{N}$	$\bar{X} \pm 1.96\, \sigma_{\bar{X}}$	
$= 15/\sqrt{100}$	$100 \pm 1.96(1.5)$	Width = 5.88 points
$= 1.5$	100 ± 2.94	

Figure 5.6

Confidence interval widths as a function of data variability ($\hat{s}$) (for $\bar{X}$ = 100, N = 100).

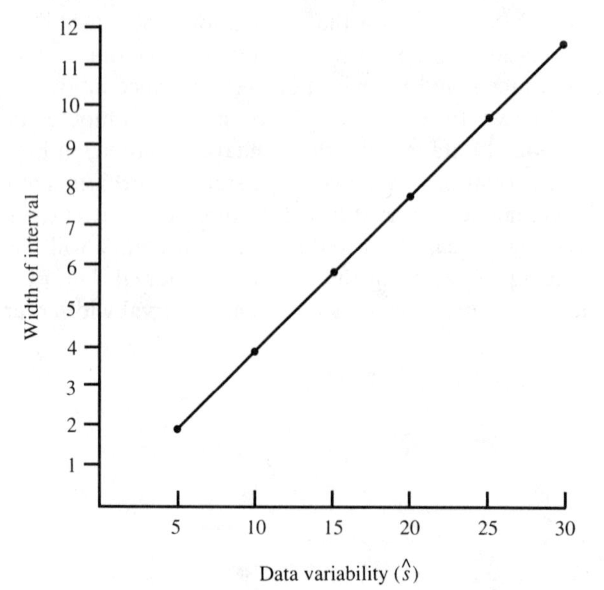

BOX 5.4—*continued*

For* $\hat{s}$ *= 20

$\sigma_{\overline{X}} = \hat{s} / \sqrt{N}$	$\overline{X} \pm 1.96\,\sigma_{\overline{X}}$	
$= 20/\sqrt{100}$	$100 \pm 1.96(2.0)$	Width = 7.84 points
$= 2.0$	100 ± 3.92	

For* $\hat{s}$ *= 25

$\sigma_{\overline{X}} = \hat{s} / \sqrt{N}$	$\overline{X} \pm 1.96\,\sigma_{\overline{X}}$	
$= 25/\sqrt{100}$	$100 \pm 1.96(2.5)$	Width = 9.8 points
$= 2.5$	100 ± 4.9	

For* $\hat{s}$ *= 30

$\sigma_{\overline{X}} = \hat{s} / \sqrt{N}$	$\overline{X} \pm 1.96\,\sigma_{\overline{X}}$	
$= 30/\sqrt{100}$	$100 \pm 1.96(3.0)$	Width = 11.76 points
$= 3.0$	100 ± 5.88	

As these examples show, as the variability of the data increases, the standard error of the mean increases as well, causing the width of the confidence intervals to increase.

---

control. About the only practical means we have of reducing data variability is to use measuring procedures and instruments that are as reliable as possible. In this way, some of the "measurement error" can be eliminated from the data that contributes to data variability, but does not reflect true variability in the attribute or trait being measured.

Sample Size. All other things being equal, the smaller the sample size, the greater the standard error of the mean, and the wider the confidence interval. Thus, a confidence interval based on data from 50 cases will be wider than one based on 150 cases. A narrower confidence interval may be purchased by gathering data from more cases. Box 5.5 illustrates the relationship between confidence interval width and sample size.

BOX 5.5

CONFIDENCE INTERVAL WIDTH AND SAMPLE SIZE

Computed below are 95% confidence intervals for data sets that differ only in sample size (N). All intervals are based on samples in which:

$$\bar{X} = 100$$
$$\hat{s} = 15$$

For N = 50

$\sigma_{\bar{X}} = \hat{s}/\sqrt{N}$	$\bar{X} \pm 1.96\,\sigma_{\bar{X}}$	
$= 15/\sqrt{50}$	$100 \pm 1.96(2.12)$	Width = 8.32 points
$= 2.12$	100 ± 4.6	

For N = 100

$\sigma_{\bar{X}} = \hat{s}/\sqrt{N}$	$\bar{X} \pm 1.96\,\sigma_{\bar{X}}$	
$= 15/\sqrt{100}$	$100 \pm 1.96(1.5)$	Width = 5.88 points
$= 1.5$	100 ± 2.94	

For N = 150

$\sigma_{\bar{X}} = \hat{s}/\sqrt{N}$	$\bar{X} \pm 1.96\,\sigma_{\bar{X}}$	
$= 15/\sqrt{150}$	$100 \pm 1.96(1.22)$	Width = 4.78 points
$= 1.22$	100 ± 2.39	

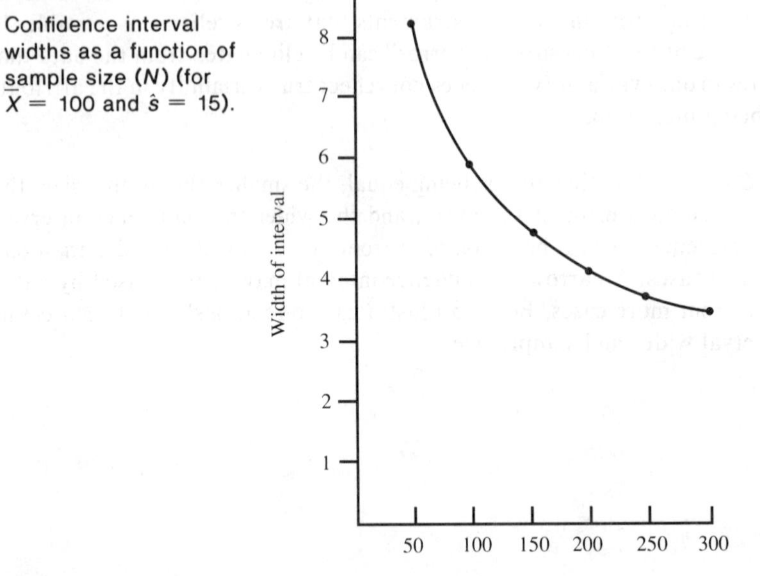

Figure 5.7

Confidence interval widths as a function of sample size (N) (for $\bar{X} = 100$ and $\hat{s} = 15$).

BOX 5.5—*continued*

For N = 200

$$\sigma_{\bar{X}} = \hat{s}/\sqrt{N} = 1.5/\sqrt{200} = 1.06$$

$$\bar{X} \pm 1.96\,\sigma_{\bar{X}}$$
$$100 \pm 1.96(1.06)$$
$$100 \pm 2.08$$

Width = 4.16 points

For N = 250

$$\sigma_{\bar{X}} = \hat{s}/\sqrt{N} = 15/\sqrt{250} = .95$$

$$\bar{X} \pm 1.96\,\sigma_{\bar{X}}$$
$$100 \pm 1.96(.95)$$
$$100 \pm 1.86$$

Width = 3.72 points

For N = 300

$$\sigma_{\bar{X}} = \hat{s}/\sqrt{N} = 15/\sqrt{300} = .87$$

$$\bar{X} \pm 1.96\,\sigma_{\bar{X}}$$
$$100 \pm 1.96(.87)$$
$$100 \pm 1.71$$

Width = 3.42 points

The widths of the confidence intervals computed in Box 5.5 are plotted as a function of sample sizes in Figure 5.7. We can see that an increase in sample size will buy a decrease in the width of the confidence interval, particularly when we are working with relatively small samples. However, there is a point of diminishing returns that occurs in the effort to achieve narrower confidence intervals by increasing sample sizes. In Figure 5.7 we see a substantial reduction in interval width when N increases from 50 to 100 cases. In contrast, little reduction in interval width is seen for an increase in N from 250 to 300 cases. In practice, then, it makes little sense to use sample size "overkill," but we should attempt to gather data from as large a sample as is practical.

If we know in advance (1) the desired level of confidence; (2) the acceptable width of the confidence interval; and (3) the approximate variability of the data that will be examined, it is possible to compute the size of the sample that will be required. This process is demonstrated in Box 5.6.

BOX 5.6

DETERMINING SAMPLE SIZE FOR A CONFIDENCE INTERVAL

In estimating the mean reading grade level of adults residing in Hellhole County, we (1) have decided upon a 95% confidence interval; (2) want this interval to be .5 points wide (i.e., .25 points on each side of the sample mean); and (3) have estimated from a pilot study that the standard deviation of reading test scores will be about $\hat{s} = 3.0$. In this box, we will determine how large a sample must be studied in order to construct the desired confidence interval.

First, recall the form of the 95% confidence interval as given in Equation 5.4:

$$\bar{X} \pm 1.96\,\sigma_{\bar{X}}$$

If the interval is to have a total width of .5 points, it follows that the sample mean ($\bar{X}$) will be surrounded on each side by .25 points. That is, the confidence interval will look like this,

$$\bar{X} \pm .25$$

Thus,

$$\bar{X} \pm 1.96\,\sigma_{\bar{X}} = \bar{X} \pm .25$$

Subtracting $\bar{X}$ from each side of the equation we get

$$1.96\,\sigma_{\bar{X}} = .25$$

By definition of $\sigma_{\bar{X}}$:

$$1.96(\hat{s}\,/\sqrt{N}) = .25$$

By substitution:

$$1.96(3/\sqrt{N}) = .25$$

By rearrangement:

$$3/\sqrt{N} = .25/1.96$$

By substitution:

$$3/\sqrt{N} = .128$$

By rearrangement:

$$.128\sqrt{N} = 3$$

Dividing both sides by .128:

$$\sqrt{N} = 3/.128$$

By substitution:

$$\sqrt{N} = 23.44$$

Squaring each side of the equation:

$$N = 549.43$$

Thus, it will be necessary to examine about 550 cases in order to construct a 95% confidence interval with a total width of .5 points, provided that the standard deviation has been estimated correctly at $\hat{s} = 3.0$.

SUMMARY

A sampling distribution is a theoretical frequency distribution that describes the frequency of occurrence of values of some statistic computed for all possible samples of size N (or multi-sample sets) drawn from a single population. Sampling distributions are central to significance testing, discussed in later chapters, and to interval estimation, the focus of this chapter. The sampling distribution of the mean is formed by drawing all possible samples of size N from a population and plotting the frequency of occurrence of the various values of the sample mean obtained in this manner. The central limit theorem states that, provided sample sizes are relatively large ($N \geq 50$), the sampling distribution of the mean will be normally distributed, with a mean ($\mu_{\bar{X}}$) equal to the mean of the population from which the samples came (μ), and a standard deviation, called the standard error of the mean ($\sigma_{\bar{X}}$), equal to $\sigma / \sqrt{N}$ or $\hat{s} / \sqrt{N}$. The sampling distribution of the proportion depicts the frequency of occurrence of values of the sample proportion obtained when all possible samples of size N are drawn from a population and the proportion of cases in each sample that shows some characteristic of interest is computed. Since proportions are means, it follows that the sampling distribution of the proportion is identical to the sampling distribution of the mean. Sampling distributions are used in constructing confidence intervals. A confidence interval is a range of values computed from sample data that has a known probability of capturing the population parameter being estimated. The population mean and population proportion are the population parameters most commonly estimated using confidence intervals. Three factors influence the width of confidence intervals: level of confidence, data variability, and sample size. These factors can be manipulated in producing a confidence interval of the desired width.

NOTES

1. Recall from chapter 3 that the standard deviation of a dichotomously scored variable may be computed as

$$s = \sqrt{pq}$$

where,

p = the proportion of cases scored 0
q = the proportion of cases scored 1

It follows that, when N is large, such that s and $\hat{s}$ do not differ appreciably, the standard error of the proportion may be computed more simply as

$$\sigma_p = \frac{\sqrt{p_u q_u}}{\sqrt{N}}$$

where,

p_u = the proportion of cases in the population that scored 1
q_u = the proportion of cases in the population that scored 0
N = sample size

2. Confidence intervals can be constructed using smaller samples than $N = 50$, but the sampling distribution of the mean becomes increasingly platykurtic as sample size decreases below this value. This being the case, confidence

intervals cannot be based on the normal distribution when sample sizes are small. The t-distribution (Appendix B: Critical Values of t) describes the sampling distribution of the mean when samples are small and can be used in constructing confidence intervals when working with these small samples (e.g., Comrey, Bott, and Lee, 1989; Runyon and Haber, 1988; Shavelson, 1988). Using this procedure, the 95% confidence interval is defined as

$$\overline{X} \pm t_{(.05,\ df)}\sigma_{\overline{X}}$$

where,

$t_{(.05,\ df)}$ = the critical value of t listed for $N - 1$ degrees of freedom at the .05 two-tail significance level

$\sigma_{\overline{X}}$ = the standard error of the mean computed according to Equation 5.1

The 99% confidence interval is defined as

$$\overline{X} \pm t_{(.01, df)}\sigma_{\overline{X}}$$

where,

$t_{(.01,\ df)}$ = the critical value of t listed for $N - 1$ degrees of freedom at the .01 two-tail significance level

$\sigma_{\overline{X}}$ = the standard error of the mean computed according to Equation 5.1

This procedure is widely used, but the author does not recommend it because small sample sizes generally produce confidence intervals that are unacceptably wide. The relationship between sample size and the width of confidence intervals is discussed near the end of chapter 5.

CHAPTER 6

SIGNIFICANT DIFFERENCES: ONE-SAMPLE TESTS

Significance testing is a staple of research in the social and behavioral sciences. When reading the literature of psychology, sociology, political science, and other disciplines, phrases such as "statistically significant difference," "significant correlation," "significant at the .05 level," and so on, are commonplace. What does it mean to say that a difference is statistically significant or that a relationship between variables is significant?

A complete understanding of this issue will have to wait until we have learned how the various tests of significance work, but at least a partial, intuitive explanation can be offered here. A statistically significant finding is a reliable finding. When a correlation is found to be statistically significant, it means simply that a similar correlation would likely be observed if the research were replicated with a completely new sample. When a difference between two or more groups is found to be statistically significant, it means only that a similar difference would be expected were the research replicated with new samples.

In discussing tests of statistical significance it is convenient to organize the presentation into two broad categories of tests: tests of significant differences and tests of the significance of correlations and other measures of relationship. As will become apparent, though, this division is artificial. For instance, when a significant difference test reveals that two groups' means *differ* significantly, it means that there is a reliable *relationship* between group membership and scores on the dependent variable. Or, looking at the problem from another angle, when the *relationship* between two variables is found to be statistically significant, it means that values of one variable *differ* reliably as a function of values on the other variable.

Having seen that tests of difference and tests of relationship are really the same thing, we will examine separately tests in these two categories. Difference tests will occupy our attention in this and the next three chapters. We will return to the testing of differences in chapters 14 and 15. Tests of the significance of correlations and other measures of relationship will be reserved for chapters 10 through 13.

TYPES OF DIFFERENCE TESTS

There are a multitude of significant difference tests, each designed to handle the requirements and restrictions of a different situation. Before we begin looking at these tests, it may be helpful to know some of the ways in which the tests of difference may be distinguished from each other.

First, the tests differ according to how many groups are being compared. At one extreme, we may wish to study the difference between a single group or sample and an entire population. As an example of a **one-sample significance test** of this sort, a researcher might wish to determine whether the average length of stay following the first admission to Red Tape State Hospital is significantly longer than the national average. We will focus in this chapter on these one-sample significance tests. In many other research settings, two groups are to be compared.

For example, do males and females show significantly different responses to television evangelists? Do depressed patients receiving an experimental antidepressant drug show significantly lower levels of depression than is seen among patients who receive a placebo? Do cities in the Northeast have significantly higher crime rates than those in the Midwest? All of these questions require a comparison of two groups to see if they differ significantly. These **two-sample significance tests** will be explored in chapter 7. Of course, there are more complicated research problems that lead us to comparisons of three or more groups. These tests will be explained in chapters 8 and 9.

Tests of the significance of difference may also be distinguished by the number of ways in which the groups being compared differ. That is, on how many different dimensions or **independent variables** do the groups vary? In a four-group comparison, for instance, there might be a single independent variable, say, drug dosage, with each group receiving a different dosage. Or, the four groups might differ on two independent variables—Sex (male vs. female) and Dosage (low vs. high). There is theoretically no limit to the number of independent variables that may be used in defining the groups to be compared. Chapter 9 will examine significant difference tests with two or more independent variables. This chapter and chapters 7 and 8 will explore just those situations in which the groups being compared differ on a single independent variable.

A third way of differentiating between the many tests of significant difference is to ask what kind of difference is being evaluated for statistical significance. We saw in chapter 3 that groups' frequency distributions may differ in central tendency, variability, and shape. Significant difference assessments may focus on any of these differences. In addition, because there are several indices of central tendency, variability, and shape, tests of significant difference may be distinguished by which of these indices is used in the comparison. Most often, significant difference tests include comparisons of central tendency as measured by the mean, but we will also examine methods of comparing central tendency without means and will consider the comparison of shapes of distributions.

The last way in which significant difference tests may be distinguished from each other is on the basis of how many **dependent variables** are involved in the comparison. So-called **univariate tests** look for differences on one dependent variable at a time. In contrast, **multivariate tests** look for differences between groups on a combination of several dependent variables. For example, a comparison of two groups' means on the Jeff and Abdul Depression Scale would be a univariate test because only one dependent variable is involved. However, there are times when we do not wish to rely upon a single measure of the trait being studied. Under these circumstances, a combination of several measures may be formed and the groups' difference on this combination measure can be evaluated. These multivariate comparisons will be the focus of chapters 14 and 15.

USES OF ONE-SAMPLE SIGNIFICANCE TESTS

As discussed previously, one-sample significance tests are used in those settings in which we wish to test the significance of a difference between a sample and a population. There are two research settings that call for this type of comparison. First, one-sample tests are often used to determine if a given sample is representative of some specified population. This question normally arises in research when we need to know if the study of a particular sample will produce results that may be generalized to some larger population. Say, for example, that we want to study the factors that contribute to student attrition from Rocky Bottom State University. We have obtained questionnaires from 25 freshmen that address this issue, but, before analyzing the data further, we want to make certain that our sample is representative of the population of 3000 freshmen at Rocky Bottom. In answering this question, we might see if our sample of freshmen differs significantly from the population of freshmen on age, grade point average, income, or any other dependent variable on which we have data. If our sample is found to differ significantly from the population on one or more of these dependent variables, it would be questionable to generalize other findings from the sample to the population. On the other hand, finding no significant differences between the sample and the population would suggest that the sample is representative of the population and generalization of sample findings to the population would be appropriate.

A second application of one-sample significant difference tests enables determining if a treatment administered to a sample has caused that sample to differ in some fashion from a specified larger population. As an example, therapists at Bubba's Mental Health Clinic have adopted a cognitive behavior modification approach to treating depression in which patients put empty pails over their heads and shout, "Every day in every way I'm getting better and better!" We are curious to see if, after a six-week course of treatment, the average patient in Bubba's clinic (the sample) shows a significantly better mood than is seen in the much larger population of depressed patients being treated in the state's mental health facilities. Finding a significant difference would support the conclusion that Bubba's method is more (or less) effective than conventional procedures.

THE ONE-SAMPLE *t*-TEST

The **one-sample *t*-test** compares a sample mean against a population mean. It is assumed in using this test that the dependent variable is a continuous variable measured at the interval or ratio scale and that the sample data are approximately normally distributed. The one-sample *t*-test, though, is quite robust with respect to minor violations of the assumption of normally distributed data when sample sizes are large ($N \geq 50$).

It will be instructive to examine how the one-sample t-test reveals if a significant difference exists since the same logic applies to the other significance tests as well. Box 6.1 provides a concrete example of the one-sample t-test to accompany the more general discussion that follows.

Sampling Distribution of *t*

The foundation of the one-sample t-test is the **sampling distribution of *t*.** Imagine drawing all possible samples of size N from a population and computing t for each sample, as in Equation 6.1.

EQUATION 6.1

$$t = \frac{\overline{X} - \mu}{\sigma_{\overline{X}}}$$

where,

$\overline{X}$ = the sample mean
μ = the population mean
$\sigma_{\overline{X}}$ = the standard error of the mean computed as $\sigma / \sqrt{N}$ or $\hat{s} / \sqrt{N}$

We can see from Equation 6.1 that the value of t computed for any given sample will reflect the size of the difference between that sample's mean and the mean of the population from which it was drawn ($\overline{X} - \mu$). The statistic t expresses this difference using the standard error of the mean ($\sigma_{\overline{X}}$) as the unit of measure. Because the value of t reflects the size of the difference being tested for significance, t is considered a **test statistic.** By definition, a test statistic is a statistic computed from data that varies in value as a function of the size of the difference (or relationship) being tested for significance. The t statistic meets this definition because as the difference between $\overline{X}$ and μ grows larger, the absolute value of t grows larger as well. We will give more consideration later to how the value of t is influenced by $\sigma_{\overline{X}}$ (which, in turn, is determined by sample size and the variability of the data).

In drawing all possible samples of size N from a population and computing t for each sample, the value of t that is computed will vary somewhat from one sample to the next due to sampling error. Thus, we could plot the frequency of occurrence of the various values of t that were obtained across the many samples. This distribution is called the **sampling distribution of *t*,** and is depicted in Figure 6.1. The single most likely value of t in the sampling distribution of t is 0, since the single most likely sample would have a mean equal to that of the population. Under these circumstances, where $\overline{X} = \mu$, $t = \overline{X} - \mu/\sigma_{\overline{X}} = 0$. Moving away from the center of the sampling distribution of t we encounter larger and larger values of t. Those to the left are negative, resulting from sample means smaller

Figure 6.1

The sampling distribution of t shown for samples of size $N = 10$ ($df = N - 1 = 9$), $N = 100$ ($df = N - 1 = 99$), and $N = \infty$.

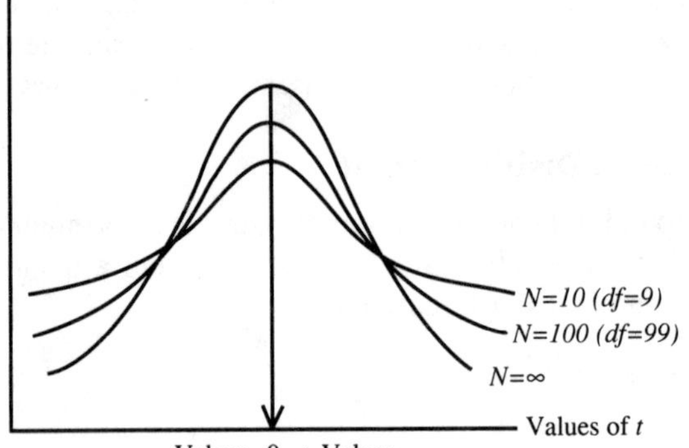

than the population mean; those to the right are positive, resulting from sample means that are greater than the population mean. Extremely high values, either positive or negative, are unlikely (but not impossible), because they occur only when $\bar{X} - \mu$ is very large, something that happens only rarely.

It should also be noted from Figure 6.1 that the shape of the sampling distribution of t changes, depending on the size of the samples being drawn (N). This should not come as a complete surprise, because in chapter 5 we saw that the sampling distribution of the mean also changes shape as a function of sample size, moving toward a normal distribution as sample sizes increase. In a similar fashion, once $N \geq 50$, the sampling distribution of t is approximately normal in shape (although, strictly speaking, the sampling distribution of t does not become exactly normal until $N = \infty$). However, with sample sizes below 50, a common situation in research in the social and behavioral sciences, the t distribution becomes flatter and flatter as sample sizes decrease.

The shape of the sampling distribution of t also varies as a function of the shape of the population distribution from which the samples are drawn. This effect is particularly pronounced when sample sizes are small. Thus, when $N < 50$, the sampling distribution of t will echo any deviations from normalcy that are evident in the population distribution. It is difficult enough to keep track of the shape of the sampling distribution of t as N varies, without also having to worry about distortions that are produced by a non-normal population distribution. This is why the t statistic and t distribution are only appropriately used when we can assume that the population from which our data have been drawn is at least approximately normal in shape.

With this assumption of normally distributed data in mind, Appendix B: Critical Values of t, describes the shape of the t distribution as it varies with sample size. Let us see how this table is used. The values in the main body of the table are those values of t called **critical values** that mark off the upper and lower tails of the t distribution, the so-called **critical regions.** The proportions of samples found within these tails (and thus, the relative probabilities of obtaining these samples) are given by the columns headed "level of significance." The column labeled "df" refers to **degrees of freedom,** a term that means essentially the same thing as sample size here, since, in the case of the one-sample t-test, $df = N - 1$.

An example should clarify how the table of t values is used. Refer to Figure 6.2a. This figure depicts the sampling distribution of t for the situation in which all possible samples of size $N = 20$ (i.e., $df = N - 1 = 19$) have been drawn from a population and t has been computed for each sample according to Equation 6.1. What is the critical value of t that marks off the upper 5% tail (or, a proportion of .05) of the distribution? First, find $df = 19$ in the left-hand column of the table of t values. Next, find the value .05 in the column labeled "level of significance for one-tail test." Scanning down that column until we reach the row marked by $df = 19$, we find the critical value of $t = 1.729$. This is the value of t that marks off the upper 5% tail of the distribution. Only 5% of the samples drawn from a population have larger t values than 1.729. Thus, samples yielding values of t that exceed 1.729, that is, values falling within the shaded critical region of Figure 6.2a, have a probability of occurring that is less than 5%, or, as this is commonly abbreviated, $p < .05$. What about the other end of the distribution? What is the critical value of t that marks the lower 5% tail? Because the t distribution is symmetrical (assuming a normal population distribution, that is) the critical value of t for $df = 19$ and a .05 level of significance is -1.729. Again, samples yielding t values that are more strongly negative than -1.729 have a probability of less than 5% ($p < .05$) of being drawn from a population.

There is one additional feature of the table of t values that needs to be mentioned here, the difference between one-tail and two-tail significance levels. We have just seen that values of t listed under the columns labeled "levels of significance for one-tail test" are the values of t that mark off critical regions at one end or the other end of the distribution (thus, the phrase "one-tail" significance test). In contrast, values of t listed under the column labeled "level of significance for two-tail test" are those values of t that mark off critical regions at both ends of the distribution, which combine to capture a specified total percentage of the samples. Consider Figure 6.2b. What values of t mark off upper and lower tails, which together contain 5% of the samples? As before, find $df = 19$. Now, find .05 in the columns for two-tail significance levels. Scanning down that column until we get to the row marked by $df = 19$, we find that the critical value of $t = 2.093$. This is the absolute value of t that marks off the two critical regions that total 5% of the samples—2.5% in the upper tail and 2.5% in the lower tail. More will be said later about one- versus two-tail significance tests.

Rationale of the One-Sample t-test

Having looked at the sampling distribution of t, we are prepared now to explore the logic of the one-sample t-test. How does the t-test answer the question of whether a difference between a sample mean and population mean is "statistically significant?" Once data have been collected that show a difference between $\bar{X}$ and μ, the process of assessing the significance of the difference may be dissected into three steps as described next.

Figure 6.2

Critical values and critical regions of the sampling distribution of t for $N = 20$ ($df = 19$).

(a) Critical value and critical region for one tail.

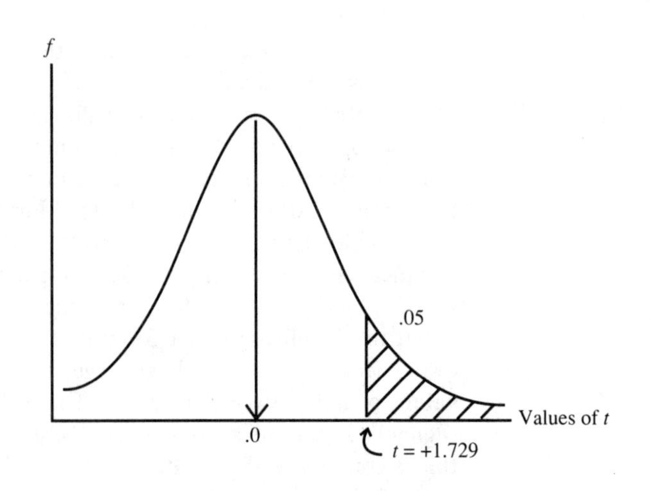

(b) Critical value and critical region for two tails.

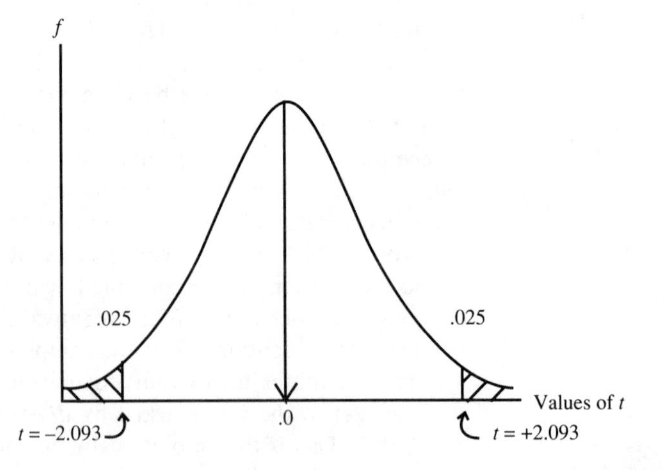

Step 1: The Null and Alternative Hypotheses. There are two possible explanations for the observed difference between sample mean and population mean, each referred to as a "hypothesis." The **null hypothesis** (symbolized H_0) explains the difference as being the simple result of sampling error. That is, the observed difference between $\bar{X}$ and μ is small enough to be expected when drawing samples from the population specified. The **alternative hypothesis** (symbolized H_1) sets forth a diametrically opposite explanation for the observed difference; i.e., the difference is too great to be attributed to sampling error. A difference this large between $\bar{X}$ and μ is highly improbable (although not totally impossible) when drawing samples from the specified population. Thus, the sample at hand prob-

ably did not come from this population and certainly is not representative of it. Perhaps the sample has been treated in some fashion that has caused it to differ from the population on the dependent variable being investigated.

Step 2: The Test Statistic. Next, a test statistic is computed. As we saw previously, this is a statistic computed from the data that varies in value as a function of the size of the difference being tested for significance. The t statistic, computed according to Equation 6.1, is the most commonly used test statistic for one-sample significance testing, although we will examine another test statistic, chi-square, later in this chapter that is also used in one-sample significance testing.

Step 3: Determining the Probability of the Test Statistic. The question now becomes, how probable is it that we would obtain a value of t of the size observed (i.e., a difference between $\bar{X}$ and μ of the obtained size) from a sample drawn from the specified population? As we have already seen, this is the question that the sampling distribution of t enables us to answer. If the probability of the obtained value of t is extremely low ("low" is traditionally defined as .05 or less), it follows that the sample which yielded that t value is highly unlikely to have come from the specified population. It is unrepresentative of the population and may have been treated in some fashion that made it different from the population. In other words, if the absolute value of the obtained t exceeds the critical value of t, we would reject the null hypothesis (which stated that the observed difference was small enough to attribute to sampling error) and accept the alternative hypothesis (which attributes the difference to factors other than sampling error.) Put simply, we would declare that a statistically significant difference exists.

On the other hand, if the probability of the obtained value of t is relatively high (greater than .05), it means the sample that yielded that value of t is likely to have been drawn from the specified population. It is representative of the population and was not treated in a manner that caused it to differ from the population. In other words, if the obtained value of t does not exceed the tabled critical value of t, we would accept the null hypothesis (which attributes the observed difference to sampling error) and reject the alternative hypothesis (which states that the difference is so large as not to be reasonably attributed to sampling error). Put simply, we would declare that no significant difference exists.

ONE- VS. TWO-TAIL TESTS

It is now time to address again the issue of one- versus two-tail significance tests. **One-tail significance tests** are used in those situations in which the researcher has predicted in advance the direction of the difference being tested for significance. Thus, if we have predicted before gathering any data that Bubba's pail therapy for depression will be more effective than conventional therapies (i.e., that Bubba's patients will show a higher mean mood score than will the population as a whole), we have essentially predicted that our obtained value of t will be positive. This being the case, the only critical value of t of interest to us is the one that marks off the upper 5% tail. This one-tail critical value is found in the Table of Critical Values of t listed under one-tail significance levels. Or, if we have predicted in advance that the difference would generate a negative value ($\bar{X} < \mu$), we have again specified the single tail that is of concern to us, the lower tail, and would again be correct in using the one-tail critical values of t.

What about the situation, though, in which we have not predicted in advance the direction of the difference, and thus, the sign of t? In this event, a **two-tail significance test** is appropriate. Perhaps, for example, we want to know if dropouts from Rocky Bottom State University (the sample) have grade point averages that differ significantly from the student body population as a whole. On the one hand, we reason, dropouts may have lower than average grades and are thereby discouraged and drop out. On the other hand, perhaps dropouts have higher than average grades and are dropping out because they are bored. In other words we believe that there may be a difference between our sample (dropouts) and the population as a whole, but we are unable to predict in advance the direction of that difference. In this case, either a large negative *or* positive t value would be of interest to us. Thus, we are concerned with critical regions on both ends of the t distribution and would use two-tail critical t values.

COMPARING ENTIRE DISTRIBUTIONS: THE CHI-SQUARE GOODNESS-OF-FIT TEST

The one-sample t-test is designed to test the significance of the difference between a sample mean and a population mean. Focused on central tendency as it is, the t-test is completely insensitive to any other differences that might exist between a sample and population. As seen in Figure 6.3, though, two distributions can have identical means (and thus, show no difference on a t-test) and yet differ radically in their other characteristics.

The **chi-square** (symbolized χ^2) **goodness-of-fit test** is commonly used to assess differences between a sample and population. Unlike the t-test, the χ^2 test will detect *any* type of difference between a sample and a population, be it a difference in central tendency, variability, or shape. Moreover, the χ^2 test can be used to compare sample and population frequency distributions on a nominal scale variable as well as on interval or ratio scale variables.

With all this working for the χ^2 test, we might wonder why the t-test is used at all! The answer is simply that, when the assumptions of the t-test are met, the t-test is a more powerful test of differences in central tendencies than is χ^2. In other words, if the difference between sample and population involves central tendency, the t-test will identify smaller differences as significant than will χ^2.

BOX 6.1

ONE SAMPLE *t*-TEST

In our quest to better understand why hordes of freshmen are dropping out of Rocky Bottom State University, we have persuaded a sample of 25 freshmen to complete a short questionnaire. Before analyzing their other responses to this questionnaire, however, we want to see if this sample is representative of the entire population of 3000 freshmen at Rocky Bottom. Specifically, we have decided to check the mean grade point average of our sample against that of the entire freshman class. Descriptive statistics for our sample are

$$\bar{X} = 1.40$$
$$\hat{s} = .75$$
$$N = 25$$

The mean grade point average for the entire freshman class is

$$\mu = 2.10$$

Step 1: ***The Null and Alternative Hypotheses***

H_0: The observed $\bar{X} - \mu$ difference is due to sampling error. That is, a sample with $\bar{X} = 1.40$ and $\hat{s} = .75$ is likely to have been drawn from a population with $\mu = 2.10$.

H_1: The observed $\bar{X} - \mu$ difference is too great to be attributed to sampling error. That is, a sample with $\bar{X} = 1.40$ and $\hat{s} = .75$ is unlikely to have been drawn from a population with $\mu = 2.10$ and is certainly not representative of that population.

Step 2: ***The Test Statistic***

The test statistic t is computed according to Equation 6.1.

$$t = \frac{\bar{X} - \mu}{\sigma_{\bar{X}}} = \frac{1.40 - 2.10}{.15} = -4.67 \qquad \text{where } \sigma_{\bar{X}} = \frac{\hat{s}}{\sqrt{N}} = \frac{.75}{\sqrt{25}} = .15$$

Step 3: ***Determining the Probability of the Test Statistic***

The obtained value of $t = -4.67$ is compared to the sampling distribution of t for $df = N - 1 = 24$ in order to determine its probability. From the Table of Critical Values of t (Appendix B), we find that the one-tail probability of a t of -4.67 is $p < .0005$; the two-tail probability is $p < .001$. If the direction of the difference between sample and population had been predicted in advance, the one-tail significance would be used; without a prediction of the direction of the difference, the two-tail significance level is appropriate. In either case, our obtained value of $t = -4.67$ exceeds the listed critical values and is highly unlikely to have been produced by a sample drawn from the specified population. Thus, we reject the null hypothesis and accept the alternative hypothesis. Grades of this sample of freshmen differ significantly from the population of freshmen and findings based on the sample should not be generalized to the population of freshmen as a whole.

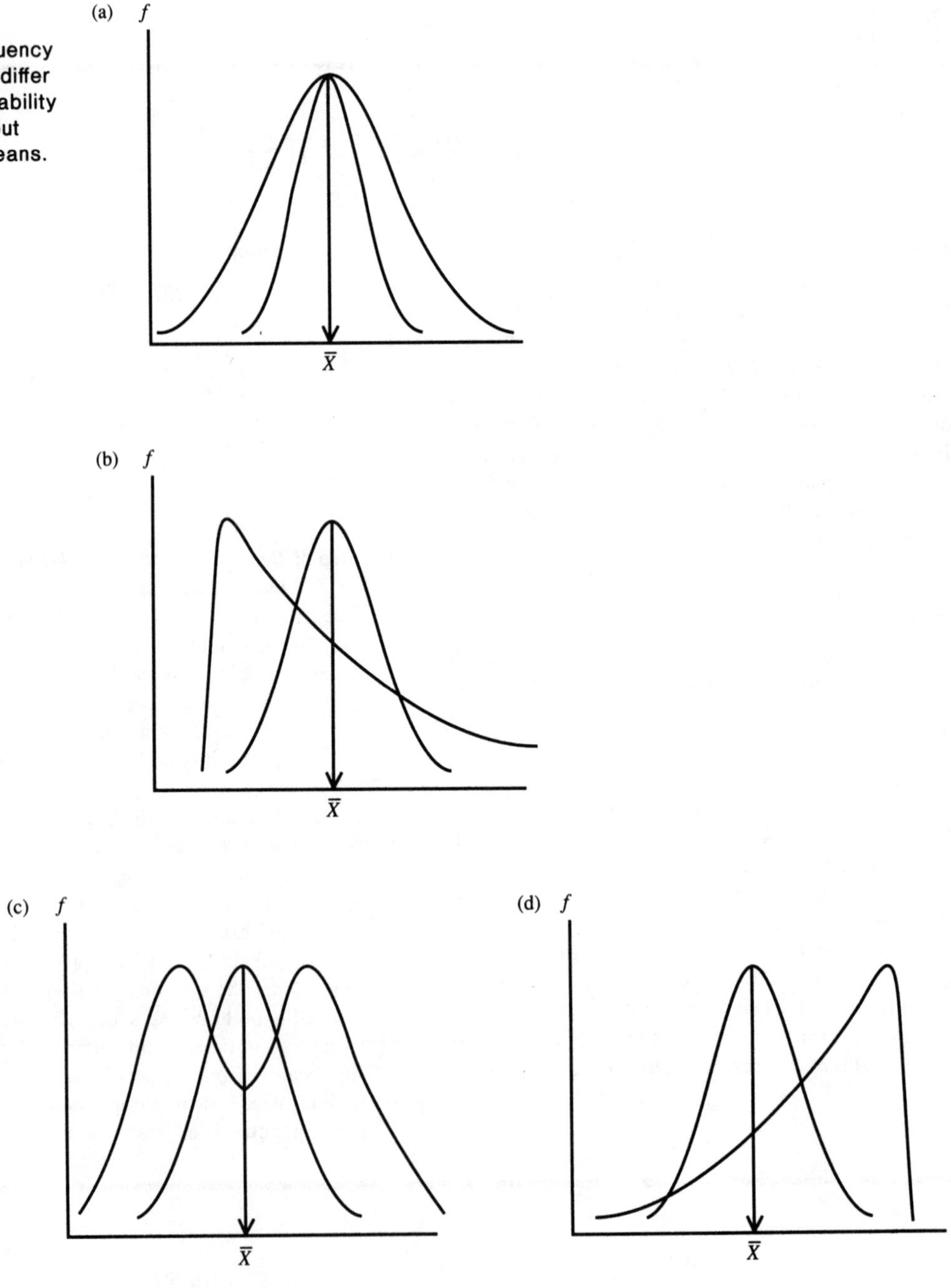

Figure 6.3

Examples of frequency distributions that differ in shape and variability characteristics, but show identical means.

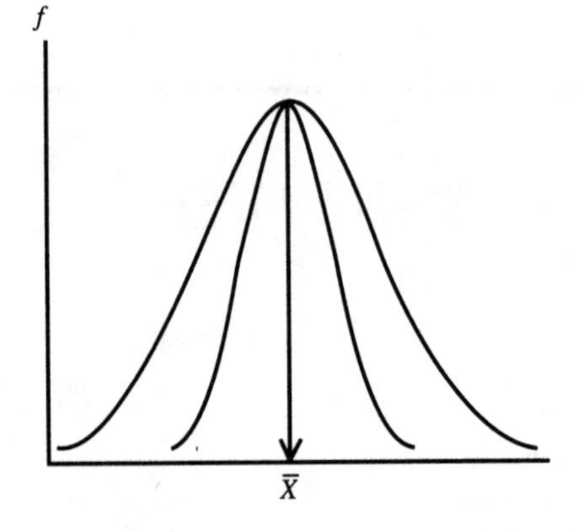

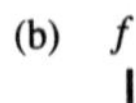
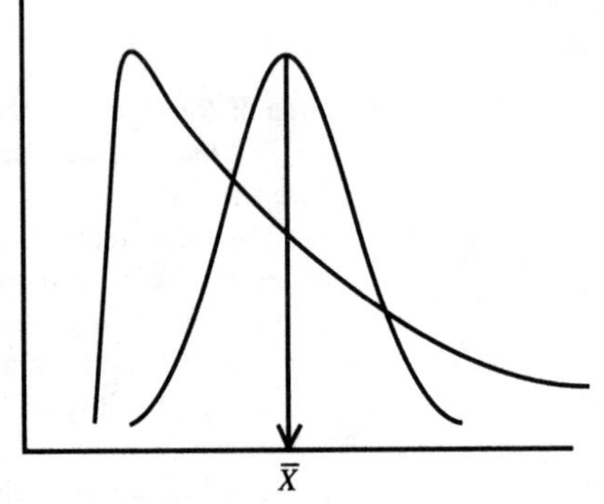

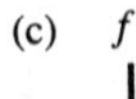
(c) f

$\bar{X}$

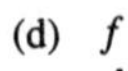
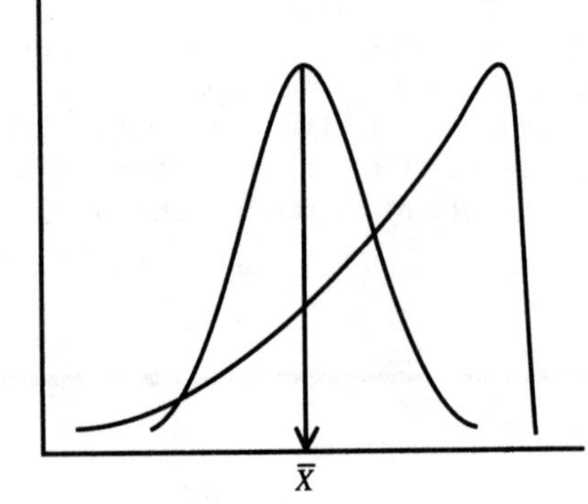

The Sampling Distribution of χ^2

It is necessary to consider the **sampling distribution of χ^2** before we can understand how the χ^2 goodness-of-fit test works in assessing differences between a sample distribution and a population distribution. First, imagine drawing all possible samples of size N from a population. Imagine further that the χ^2 statistic is computed for each sample as in Equation 6.2.

EQUATION 6.2

$$\chi^2 = \sum_{i=1}^{k} \frac{(f_{o_i} - f_{e_i})^2}{f_{e_i}}$$

where,

k = the number of different scores, score intervals, or nominal scale categories in the distributions being compared

f_o = **observed frequencies** for each of the k score intervals; i.e., the number of cases receiving each of k different scores in an ungrouped frequency distribution, falling within each of k score intervals in the case of a grouped frequency distribution, or found within each of k categories of a nominal scale variable

f_e = **expected frequencies** for each of k score intervals; i.e., the number of cases that would be *expected* to receive each of k different scores in an ungrouped frequency distribution, fall within each of k score intervals in the case of a grouped frequency distribution, or be found within each of k categories of a nominal scale variable *if the sample was distributed exactly like the population*

From one sample to the next drawn from a population, the computed value of χ^2 would be expected to vary somewhat because of sampling error. The χ^2 test statistic takes its minimum value of 0 when the sample is distributed exactly like the population, since, under these circumstances, $f_o = f_e$ for each score, score interval, or category. As the sample distribution deviates in any fashion from the population distribution, χ^2 becomes progressively larger. If one were to plot the frequency of occurrence of the various obtained values of χ^2, the result would be the sampling distribution of χ^2 as shown in Figure 6.4.

Two features of the sampling distribution of χ^2 that are apparent in Figure 6.4 require further explanation here. First, you can see that the sampling distribution of χ^2 changes shape as a function of degrees of freedom (df), computed as $df = k - 1$. It should not surprise you to discover that the χ^2 distribution's shape is not fixed; we saw earlier how the t distribution also varies as a function of degrees of freedom.

Figure 6.4

Shapes of the χ^2 sampling distribution as a function of degrees of freedom.

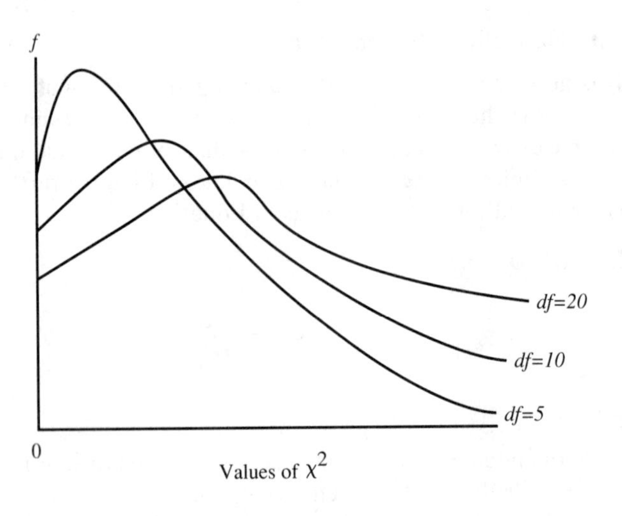

The second feature of the χ^2 distribution that deserves comment is the relatively low frequency of occurrence of χ^2 values of 0. At first thought one might expect 0 to be the single most common value of χ^2, just as 0 was the single most common value of *t*. After all, would not the single most frequently occurring sample drawn from a population be expected to have a frequency distribution matching that of the population? Yes. It is true that the single most frequently occurring value of $f_o - f_e$ will be 0. However, the single most frequently occurring value of χ^2 will be greater than 0 because, as you can see in Equation 6.2, χ^2 is computed using the *squared* difference between observed and expected frequencies: $\Sigma(f_o - f_e)^2$. There will be some samples in which $\Sigma(f_o - f_e)$ will be slightly negative. When squared, though, these negative values (and χ^2) will become positive. There will also be a few samples in which $\Sigma(f_o - f_e)$ will be slightly positive in value. When squared, these positive values (and χ^2) will also be positive. A few squared negative numerators of Equation 6.4 (yielding χ^2 values greater than 0) combined with a few squared positive numerators (also yielding χ^2 values greater than 0) will give more values of χ^2 that are greater than 0 than there are χ^2 values, which exactly equal 0. Thus, we get a sampling distribution of χ^2 in which the most frequent value of χ^2 is greater than 0. What exactly this most frequent value will be depends, as you can see from Figure 6.4, on *k*, the number of different scores, score intervals, or categories in the distributions being compared.

Appendix C: Critical Values of χ^2 provides more information about the χ^2 sampling distribution. As with the *t* distribution, the Table of Critical Values of χ^2 lists values of χ^2 that mark off selected critical regions in the tail of the χ^2 distribution. Unlike the *t* distribution, though, there are no negative values of χ^2. That is, the tabled values all refer to the right-hand tail of the χ^2 distribution. The χ^2 table is used in essentially the same manner as is the Table of Critical Values of *t*. Degrees of freedom (*df*) are listed in the left-hand column and significance levels are listed across the top of the table. For example, the value of χ^2 that marks off the upper 5% of the χ^2 sampling distribution for problems in which $df = 10$ (i.e., there are 11 score points, score intervals, or nominal scale categories in the distributions being compared) is 18.31. Only 5% of the samples drawn from a given population will yield χ^2 values greater than 18.31. Similarly, the value of χ^2 that marks off the upper 1% of the χ^2 sampling distribution for problems in which $df = 24$ is 42.98. Only 1% of the samples drawn from a population will yield χ^2 values larger than 42.98.

Rationale of the One-Sample χ^2 Goodness-of-Fit Test

The one-sample χ^2 goodness-of-fit test determines whether a given sample's frequency distribution deviates significantly from a specified population distribution. The logic of the χ^2 test can be dissected into the same three steps that we have already seen in examining the one-sample *t*-test. The discussion that follows is illustrated in Box 6.2 with an example.

Step 1: The Null and Alternative Hypotheses. A sample distribution may differ from a specified population distribution for either of two reasons. The null hypothesis (H_0) explains the difference as resulting from sampling error. That is, the difference is not so great as to be entirely unexpected. Chance events alone could have produced a sample that is this discrepant from the population, and thus, the sample can be considered fairly representative of the population. The alternative hypothesis (H_1) explains the difference as being more than just a result of sampling error. The difference observed is so large that it is highly improbable that the sample came from, or represents, the specified population. It may be that the sample has received some unique treatment that has caused its distribution to become different from that of the specified population.

Step 2: The Test Statistic. Next, a test statistic is computed. As with all test statistics, the value of χ^2, computed according to Equation 6.2, varies as a function of the size of the difference (or relationship) being tested for significance. In the case of χ^2, as we have seen, that difference includes differences in central tendency, variability, and/or shape characteristics of the distributions.

Step 3: Determining the Probability of the Test Statistic. Finally, how likely is it that a sample drawn from the specified population would yield the obtained value of χ^2? This question is answered by comparing the obtained value of χ^2 against the critical value of χ^2 listed for $df = k - 1$ in the Table of Critical Values of χ^2. If the obtained value exceeds this critical value, we know that the sample that produced it is highly unlikely to have come from the specified population: (1) it is unrepresentative of that population; (2) it may have been treated differently than the population; and (3) it differs significantly from the population. If, on the other hand, the obtained value of χ^2 is lower than the tabled critical value, we know that values of χ^2 of this size are not improbable in samples drawn from the specified population. That is, the sample that gave this χ^2 value is representative of the population; or, in the shorthand of statistical jargon, it does not differ significantly from the specified population. In short, in Step 3 we

BOX 6.2

ONE-SAMPLE χ^2 GOODNESS-OF-FIT TEST

In the population as a whole, it is assumed that scores on the Kierkegaard Angst Inventory are approximately normally distributed, with $\mu = 50$ and $\sigma = 10$. Thus, in the population, we would expect to observe the grouped percentage distribution shown in Table 6.1.

TABLE 6.1 Grouped Percentage Distribution ($i = 10$) for Scores on the Kierkegaard Angst Inventory. This Distribution Is Approximately Normally Distributed

X ($i = 10$)	%
21–30	2.15
31–40	13.59
41–50	34.13
51–60	34.13
61–70	13.59
71–80	2.15

TABLE 6.2 Grouped Frequency Distribution ($i = 10$) for Scores on the Kierkegaard Angst Inventory Obtained from a Sample of Size $N = 110$

X ($i = 10$)	f_o	f_e
21–30	2	2.3
31–40	18	15.0
41–50	40	37.5
51–60	35	37.5
61–70	10	15.0
71–80	5	2.3
	$N = 110$	

This inventory has been administered to a group of 110 psychology graduate students and the grouped frequency distribution shown in Table 6.2 has been obtained. Observed frequencies are listed in the column labeled f_o. Frequencies that would have been expected if the 110 cases forming the sample were

choose between the null and alternative hypotheses the one that is to be accepted as an explanation of any difference observed between the sample and the population distributions.

Small Expected Frequencies

The χ^2 statistic has one very disturbing characteristic. It is affected excessively by low values of f_e. Imagine a distribution consisting of six score intervals or nominal scale categories. In one of these categories, $f_o = 5$ and $f_e = 1$. We already know that χ^2 will be significant without knowing values of f_o or f_e for any of the other categories. For $df = 5$, the critical value of χ^2 at the .05 level of significance is 11.07. The contribution to χ^2 of the one known category is $(f_o - f_e)^2/f_e = (5 - 1)^2/1 = 16$. Regardless of the remainder of the distri-

BOX 6.2—*continued*

distributed in a manner proportional to the normally distributed population are listed under the column labeled f_e. We will use the χ^2 goodness-of-fit test to see if the distribution of the sample of graduate students differs significantly from the normally distributed population distribution.

Step 1: ***The Null and Alternative Hypotheses***

H_o: The observed difference between the distributions is due to sampling error. That is, a sample drawn from the specified population is quite likely to show a distribution this discrepant from that of the population.

H_1: The observed difference between the distributions is too great to attribute to sampling error. That is, a sample drawn from the specified population would be highly unlikely to show a frequency distribution this discrepant from that of the population.

Step 2: ***The Test Statistic***

Chi-square is used as the test statistic, computed according to Equation 6.2:

$$\chi^2 = \sum_{i=1}^{k} \frac{(f_{o_i} - f_{e_i})^2}{f_{e_i}}$$

$$= \frac{(2 - 2.3)^2}{2.3} + \frac{(18 - 15.0)^2}{15.0} + \ldots + \frac{(5 - 2.3)^2}{2.3}$$

$$= 5.81$$

Step 3: ***Determining the Probability of the Test Statistic***

The obtained χ^2 value of 5.81 is compared to the sampling distribution of χ^2 for $df = k - 1 = 5$. From the Table of Critical Values of χ^2 (Appendix C) you can see that, for $df = 5$, a χ^2 value of 11.07 marks off the 5% tail of the χ^2 distribution. Since the obtained value of $\chi^2 = 5.81$ is less than this critical value, we know the probability is relatively high ($p > .05$) that we would obtain a χ^2 value of this size had the sample come from the specified population. This sample distribution does not deviate significantly from the normally distributed population distribution.

bution, the outcome of the χ^2 test has been determined. Worse, χ^2 is significant because of a discrepancy of only four cases between observed and expected frequencies. If this makes you uncomfortable, good! It should.

Because of this feature of χ^2, it is recommended that where $k = 2$, both expected frequencies should be 5 or larger. Where $k > 2$, the χ^2 goodness-of-fit test should not be used if more than 20% of the expected frequencies are less than 5, or if any expected frequency is less than 1 (Siegel & Castellan, 1988). When expected frequencies are small, it is sometimes possible to combine or eliminate score intervals or categories to get expected frequencies that are sufficiently large. Of course, one may also add data from more cases to boost expected frequencies.

TYPE I AND TYPE II ERRORS

Significant difference tests, including the one-sample t-test and the χ^2 goodness-of-fit test, require that one choose between the null and alternative hypotheses on the basis of probabilities, not certainties. It is highly *unlikely* that a sample that yields a very high value of t or χ^2 would be drawn from the specified population, but it is not *impossible* that it came from that population. Conversely, a low value of t or χ^2 may lead us to conclude that a sample *probably* was not treated differently from some specified population, but it *may* have been. Two types of decision errors can result from the practice of making decisions on the basis of probabilities. Called **Type I** or "alpha" errors and **Type II** or "beta" errors, we will consider each in turn.

Type I Errors

A Type I error is mistakenly declaring a difference to be significant when most replications of the research would fail to find the difference observed. In other words, when an observed difference is explained as being too great to be due to sampling error, it is only because such a difference is highly *unlikely* to be the result of sampling error. Unlikely, though, is not the same thing as impossible. Even very large differences and the extreme test statistic values they create can be the result of sampling error. In such cases, a replication of the study will usually yield a very different set of results.

The probability of making a Type I error is always equal to whatever significance level one has adopted for the significance test. If one has chosen the traditional .05 level of significance, any test statistic value having a probability of less than .05 will be ruled statistically significant. However, using the .05 level of significance means that the probability is .05, or 5%, that the observed difference *is* due to sampling error. Adopting a more stringent significance level, such as the .01 level, reduces the likelihood of a Type I error to .01, but does not eliminate this type of error entirely.

Type II Errors

A Type II error occurs when a difference is declared nonsignificant that a replication of the research would have found to be significant. Here, luck has conspired against the researcher by giving data that are spuriously lacking in whatever difference is being tested. Perhaps you can imagine an investigation in which the unfortunate researcher has drawn that one peculiar sample, of all the possible samples that might have been drawn, which fails to respond to the treatment being evaluated, a treatment that almost any other sample would have responded to. Based on data from such a sample, it would be concluded that the treatment was ineffective, when a replication of the study with a new sample would almost surely reveal the truth about the treatment's effectiveness.

Discussions of Type II errors often use the term **power.** The power of a significance test is equal to one minus the probability of a Type II error. Thus, the lower the probability of a Type II error, the greater the power of the significance test. Determining the probability of a Type II error, and power, is not as easy as finding the probability of a Type I error, but the following guidelines can be offered (also, see Lipsey, 1989 and Runyon & Haber, 1988). First, Type I and Type II error probabilities are inversely related and may be played against each other. That is, the higher the Type I error rate, the lower the Type II error rate, and vice versa. Adopting a very stringent significance level will reduce Type I errors, but will boost Type II errors. Type II errors can be reduced by adopting a less stringent level of significance, but this boosts Type I errors. (You only get what you pay for in statistics.) Second, any steps we can take to decrease the size of the difference needed to be detected as significant will decrease the probability of Type II errors without increasing the likelihood of Type I errors. As was mentioned earlier in the chapter, more than just the size of the difference being tested for significance contributes to the value of our test statistic. These other contributing factors, discussed in the next section, can sometimes be manipulated in decreasing Type II error rates.

STATISTICAL VS. PRACTICAL SIGNIFICANCE

Over and above the size of the difference being tested for significance, two elements decide whether a given difference will be statistically significant: sample size and data variability. The workings of these two elements will be illustrated within the context of the familiar one-sample *t*-test, but we should remember that the principles involved apply to all significant difference tests.

Sample Size

Significance

All other things being equal, differences found in an examination of large samples are more likely to be found statistically significant than are differences observed in a study of smaller samples. Remember that a significant difference is a *reliable* difference, that is, a difference that one would expect to see again in a replication. Any finding that is observed in a study of many cases will be more trustworthy or reliable (significant) than a finding based on a small handful of cases. Thus, if even a small difference is observed in a study of many cases, the small difference is likely to be found statistically significant. In contrast, we must see much larger differences in studies of small samples before those differences are judged statistically significant. This is because with a smaller sample there is a greater chance that the findings are idiosyncratic to that specific sample and would not be replicated. Box 6.3 demonstrates how sample size influences the level of significance of a one-sample *t*-test. As N increases, two things happen

BOX 6.3

THE EFFECT OF SAMPLE SIZE ON LEVEL OF SIGNIFICANCE OF A ONE-SAMPLE *t*-TEST

Shown below are one-tail, one-sample t-tests based on the following data:

$$\overline{X} = 105 \qquad \mu = 100$$
$$\hat{s} = 15$$

The t-tests differ only in that sample sizes (N) increase from a starting value of $N = 10$ to end with $N = 50$. As N increases, the difference being tested for significance is first found not to be significant, but gradually becomes more and more highly significant.

***N* = 10 (*df* = 9)**

$$t = \frac{\overline{X} - \mu}{\sigma_{\overline{X}}} \qquad \sigma_{\overline{X}} = \frac{\hat{s}}{\sqrt{N}}$$
$$= 1.05 \qquad = 4.74$$

Critical value of t (.05 level) = 1.833. Obtained $t = 1.05$ is not significant, therefore, the sample is likely to have been drawn from a population in which $\mu = 100$.

***N* = 20 (*df* = 19)**

$$t = \frac{\overline{X} - \mu}{\sigma_{\overline{X}}} \qquad \sigma_{\overline{X}} = \frac{\hat{s}}{\sqrt{N}}$$
$$= 1.49 \qquad = 3.35$$

Critical value of t (.05 level) = 1.729. Obtained $t = 1.49$ is not significant, therefore, the sample is likely to have been drawn from a population in which $\mu = 100$.

***N* = 30 (*df* = 29)**

$$t = \frac{\overline{X} = \mu}{\sigma_{\overline{X}}} \qquad \sigma_{\overline{X}} = \frac{\hat{s}}{\sqrt{N}}$$
$$= 1.82 \qquad = 2.74$$

Critical value of t (.05 level) = 1.699. Obtained $t = 1.82$ is significant at .05 level, therefore, the sample is unlikely to have been drawn from a population in which $\mu = 100$.

***N* = 40 (*df* = 39)**

$$t = \frac{\overline{X} - \mu}{\sigma_{\overline{X}}} \qquad \sigma_{\overline{X}} = \frac{\hat{s}}{\sqrt{N}}$$
$$= 2.11 \qquad = 2.37$$

Critical value of t (.05 level) = 1.697. Obtained $t = 2.11$ is significant at .025 level, therefore, the sample is unlikely to have been drawn from a population in which $\mu = 100$.

that make it easier for a given difference to be found significant. First, $\sigma_{\overline{X}}$ decreases, causing t to increase. Second, degrees of freedom increase, reducing the critical values of t that must be reached for computed values of t to be significant. Figure 6.5 plots both critical t values and obtained values of t as a function of sample size.

The relationship between sample size and statistical significance means that statistically significant findings based on large samples may, in fact, be small, unimportant differences. Unfortunately, the statistical significance of a finding is much easier to determine than is the practical significance of that finding.

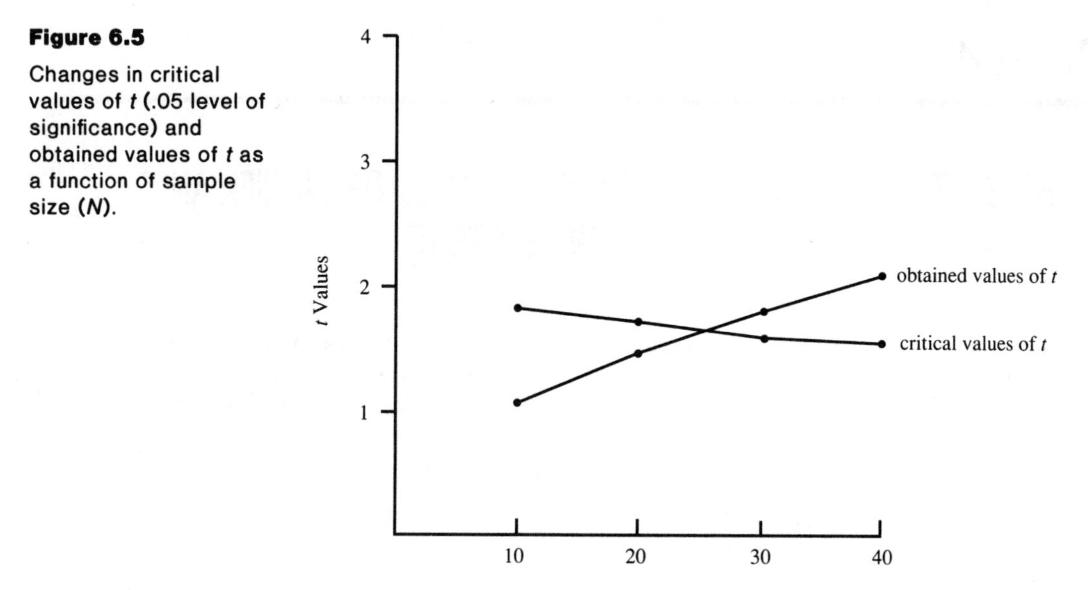

Figure 6.5

Changes in critical values of t (.05 level of significance) and obtained values of t as a function of sample size (N).

Data Variability

All other things being equal, differences found through an examination of data showing low variability are more likely to be found statistically significant than are differences found through a study of data showing higher variability. If our data are highly variable from case to case, those data are, in a sense, unreliable. Given such unreliable data, any differences that may be observed should be quite large before we trust them as stable, reliable, or replicable. On the other hand, if scores show little variability from one case to the next, the data are consistent and stable. Observed differences in this kind of data are just as stable or reliable as are the data, and relatively smaller differences can be trusted as reliable and replicable. Box 6.4 demonstrates the effect of data variability on significance levels of one-sample t-tests. Box 6.4 shows that as the stability of the data (measured inversely by $\hat{s}$) increases, the computed value of the test statistic t increases, even though the size of the difference being tested for significance remains constant. This relationship between data variability and computed t values is depicted graphically in Figure 6.6.

As you can see from Figure 6.6, anything that can be done to reduce data variability will increase our prospects of finding an observed difference to be statistically significant. As we saw in chapter 5, however, data variability is not as easily controlled as is sample size. Using reliable measuring instruments and standardized data collection procedures will reduce some of the "noise" or error variance that would otherwise appear in our data.

BOX 6.4

THE EFFECT OF DATA VARIABILITY ON LEVEL OF SIGNIFICANCE OF A ONE-SAMPLE *t*-TEST

Shown below are one-tail, one-sample t-tests based on the following data:

$$\overline{X} = 105 \qquad \mu = 100$$
$$N = 15$$

The t-tests differ because data variability ($\hat{s}$) increases from a starting value of $\hat{s} = 10$ to end with $\hat{s} = 25$. As variability increases, the difference being tested for significance gradually becomes less significant and is finally found to be nonsignificant.

$\hat{s} = 10$

$$t = \frac{\overline{X} - \mu}{\sigma_{\overline{X}}} = 1.94 \qquad \sigma_{\overline{X}} = \frac{\hat{s}}{\sqrt{N}} = 2.58$$

Critical value of t (.05 level) = 1.761. Obtained value of t = 1.94 is significant at .05 level, therefore, the sample is unlikely to have been drawn from a population in which $\mu = 100$.

$\hat{s} = 15$

$$t = \frac{\overline{X} - \mu}{\sigma_{\overline{X}}} = 1.29 \qquad \sigma_{\overline{X}} = \frac{\hat{s}}{\sqrt{N}} = 3.87$$

Critical value of t (.05 level) = 1.761. Obtained value of t = 1.29 is not significant, therefore, the sample is quite likely to have been drawn from a population in which $\mu = 100$.

$\hat{s} = 20$

$$t = \frac{\overline{X} - \mu}{\sigma_{\overline{X}}} = .97 \qquad \sigma_{\overline{X}} = \frac{\hat{s}}{\sqrt{N}} = 5.16$$

Critical value of t (.05 level) = 1.761. Obtained value of t = .97 is not significant, therefore, the sample is quite likely to have been drawn from a population in which $\mu = 100$.

$\hat{s} = 25$

$$t = \frac{\overline{X} - \mu}{\sigma_{\overline{X}}} = .78 \qquad \sigma_{\overline{X}} = \frac{\hat{s}}{\sqrt{N}} = 6.45$$

Critical value of t (.05 level) = 1.761. Obtained value of t = .78 is not significant, therefore, the sample is quite likely to have been drawn from a population in which $\mu = 100$.

Figure 6.6

Changes in obtained values of t as a function of data variability ($\hat{s}$).

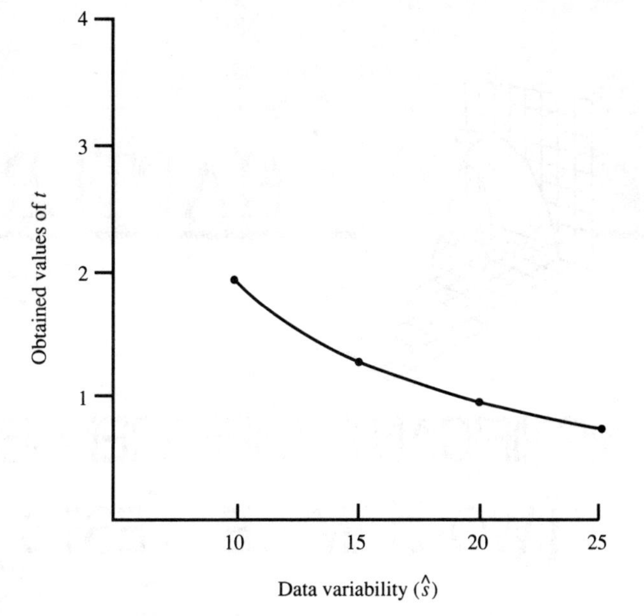

SUMMARY

This chapter introduces the concept of statistical significance. A difference or relationship is statistically significant if it is reliable or replicable. One-sample significant difference tests are used in assessing the significance (reliability) of differences found between a sample and a population. The one-sample t-test is useful in examining a difference observed between a sample mean and a population mean. The chi-square goodness-of-fit test compares the entire distributions of a sample and a population. Conclusions drawn from tests of the significance of differences are based on probabilities, and thus, are not error free. Either Type I or Type II errors may occur. Finally, it is noted that a statistically significant difference may not be a practically significant difference. Very small and unimportant differences can be found to be statistically significant under certain circumstances.

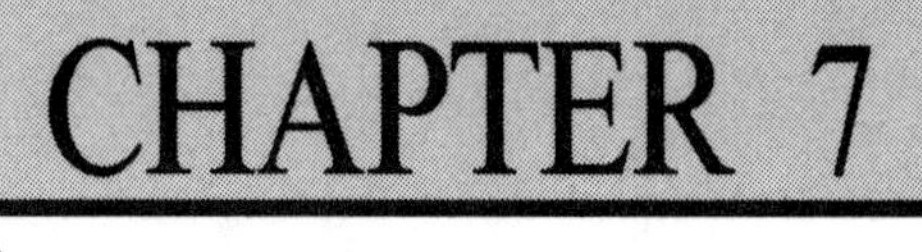

CHAPTER 7

SIGNIFICANT DIFFERENCES: TWO-SAMPLE TESTS

Comparisons between samples and populations, like those discussed in the preceding chapter, are limited in the kinds of questions they can address. Because one-sample designs lack control groups of any kind, it can be difficult or impossible to determine *why* a sample and population differ significantly. Suppose we were to find, for instance, that varsity soccer players at Rocky Bottom State University (the sample) show significantly lower grades than the student body as a whole (the population). Is it because soccer players' minds have become addled by bouncing too many balls off their heads? Perhaps soccer players practice soccer when they should be studying. A one-sample significance test may tell us that a sample differs from a population without enabling us to determine why this difference exists.

Adding a control group to the research design, though, makes it possible to see whether a particular factor is responsible for a difference observed between a sample and a population. To learn if soccer players' grades are lower because they bounce balls off their heads, we might equip one group of players with protective headgear (the experimental group) and compare their grades at the end of the semester with those of unprotected players (the control group). To find out if soccer players' grades are below the average for the university because the soccer players practice when they should be studying, we might compare the grades of soccer players who are required to skip every other practice to attend a supervised study session (the experimental group) against grades of players who are not provided with these extra study opportunities (the control group). The addition of a control group to the research design enables determining whether any particular factor is responsible for an observed sample-population difference. Not surprisingly, the literature of the social and behavioral sciences is replete with two-sample research designs.

This chapter will focus on two-sample tests of significant difference. In many instances the two samples compared using these tests represent different levels of some **independent variable** that is manipulated by the experimenter. Comparisons of experimental and control groups illustrate this application. In other instances, the two samples being compared represent two levels of an independent variable that varies naturally (i.e., outside the researcher's control). Examples of such independent variables include sex (with the levels male vs. female), year in school (with levels freshmen vs. seniors), religion (with levels Protestant vs. Catholic), and so on. Finally, levels of the independent variable in a two-sample comparison may differ quantitatively (e.g., samples given 10 vs. 50 mg. of some drug) or qualitatively (e.g., one sample provided with televised instruction vs. a second sample given live instruction).

Putting these differences aside, though, all two-sample comparisons seek to answer the same basic question. Is the difference between the samples on some dependent variable large enough to be considered reliable? If this question is answered in the affirmative, we may or may not be able to conclude that the independent variable has exerted a causal influence over the dependent variable. If the researcher has actively manipulated the independent variable in a true experiment and a significant difference on the dependent variable is subsequently observed, it is legitimate to describe the independent and dependent variables as being causally linked. If the independent variable varies naturally, though, outside the researcher's control, a significant difference between samples on the dependent variable justifies only the conclusion that the independent and dependent variables are related in the correlational sense. The conditions necessary to establishing causality will be examined more closely in chapter 10.

BETWEEN- AND WITHIN-SUBJECTS DESIGNS

Two-sample significance tests are of two types: **between-subjects tests** (sometimes called independent samples tests) and **within-subjects tests** (sometimes called dependent samples tests). Between-subjects tests compare two independent samples. By "independent" it is meant that each sample consists of a different set of cases and the composition of one sample is in no way influenced by the composition of the other sample. This is generally accomplished by random assignment of cases to groups. If 10 soccer players were randomly assigned to an experimental group to be issued helmets, and 10 were randomly assigned to a no-helmet control group, we would have a between-subjects designs.

In contrast, within-subjects designs involve comparing two sets of scores that are obtained either by measuring the same sample twice (called a **repeated-measures design**) or by comparing two samples which were created so as to be as similar as possible in one or more ways (called a **matched-samples design**). As an example of a repeated-measures design, we might compare soccer players' grades before and after a program of mandatory study sessions has been initiated. There is only one sample, but there are two sets of scores to be compared—those obtained *before* vs. *after* the program of study sessions. As an example of a matched-samples design, we might form two groups of soccer players matched on age, IQ, or some other variable(s), assign cases in one group to mandatory study sessions, and allow players in the other group to study as they wished. Here there are two samples, but the samples are not independent of each other. They are dependent in the sense that cases forming the second sample have been selected for inclusion in that sample so as to match cases forming the first sample. In other words, characteristics of cases in the second sample depend upon characteristics of cases forming the first sample, and vice versa.

Between-subjects and within-subjects designs each have advantages and disadvantages. As we will see later in this chapter, the chief advantage of within-subjects tests is their greater power. That is, a difference of a given size between two sample means is more likely to be found statistically significant using a within-subjects test than using a between-subjects test. Within-subjects designs, though, can present logistical problems that do not plague between-subjects designs. In matched-samples designs, for instance, it can be difficult to find cases that match exactly, especially when several matching variables are involved. Repeated-measures designs sidestep difficulties in finding matching cases, but present their own problems. In some situations, the first act of measuring a case influences the outcome of that case's second measurement. It would not be reasonable, for example, to compare the effectiveness of live vs. televised instruction by exposing students first to live instruction, then testing them, then giving them instruction over the same material via televised instruction, and testing them again. In short, reason and common sense must be exercised in selecting a between-subjects or within-subjects design. In those situations in which either type of design can be used, though, within-subjects designs are generally preferable because of their greater power.

THE BETWEEN-SUBJECTS *t*-TEST

The **between-subjects *t*-test** compares the means of two samples to determine if those means differ significantly. It is assumed in using this test that the dependent variable is measured on a continuous interval or ratio scale, that the samples show approximately equal variances, and that both samples are approximately normally distributed. When sample sizes are large (both samples are greater than or equal to 25) and are approximately equal, though, the between-subjects *t*-test is quite robust to violations of the assumptions of normalcy and homogeneous variances. It is for this reason that available tests of the assumption of homogeneous variances (Kirk, 1968) are seldom used. It is also for this reason that we should attempt to keep sample sizes approximately equal and as large as possible.

Like all significance tests, the between-subjects *t*-test is based on a sampling distribution. Let us examine next the characteristics of this sampling distribution of the difference between means.

The Sampling Distribution of the Difference between Means

Imagine drawing all possible pairs of samples of sizes N_1 and N_2 from a population of cases that have all been treated identically. Here, N_1 refers to the size of the first sample in every pair, and N_2 refers to the size of every second sample. These sample sizes may be the same ($N_1 = N_2$) or different ($N_1 \neq N_2$), but N_1 and N_2 will remain constant across pairs of samples. Each sample in each pair would have a mean ($\bar{X}_1$ and $\bar{X}_2$ respectively), and, as we might expect, the size of the $\bar{X}_1 - \bar{X}_2$ difference will vary somewhat from one pair of samples to the next. The frequency distribution of these $\bar{X}_1 - \bar{X}_2$ differences is called the **sampling distribution of the difference between means,** depicted in Figure 7.1.

As we would expect, given that both samples forming each pair have been treated identically the single most frequently occurring value of $\bar{X}_1 - \bar{X}_2$ in this sampling distribution, the mean of the sampling distribution ($\mu_{\bar{X}_1 - \bar{X}_2}$), is 0. In pairs in which $\bar{X}_1 < \bar{X}_2$, the difference will be negative; in pairs in which $\bar{X}_1 > \bar{X}_2$, the difference will be positive. It is intuitively obvious that, since samples are being drawn from a single population, large absolute values of $\bar{X}_1 - \bar{X}_2$ will occur less frequently than will smaller values; that is, most $\bar{X}_1 - \bar{X}_2$ values will cluster around $\mu_{\bar{X}_1 - \bar{X}_2} = 0$.

The variability seen in the sampling distribution of the difference between means is measured by the standard deviation of the $\bar{X}_1 - \bar{X}_2$ values. Called the **standard error of the difference,** symbolized $\sigma_{\bar{X}_1 - \bar{X}_2}$, this value is computed according to Equation 7.1.[1]

Figure 7.1

The sampling distribution of the difference between means shown as a function of varying sample sizes.

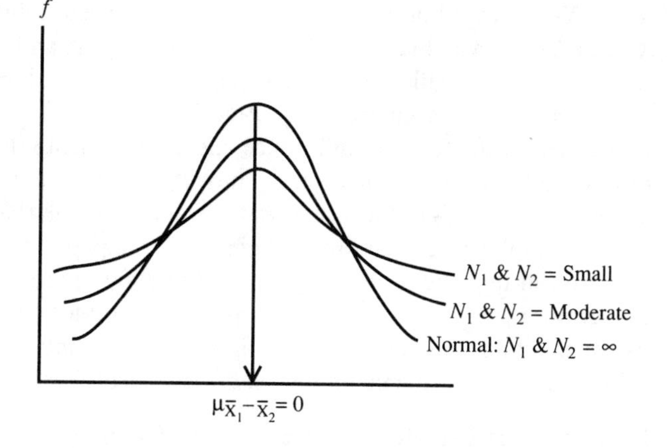

EQUATION 7.1

$$\sigma_{\bar{X}_1 - \bar{X}_2} = \sqrt{\left[\frac{(N_1 - 1)\hat{s}_1^2 + (N_2 - 1)\hat{s}_2^2}{N_1 + N_2 - 2}\right]\left[\frac{N_1 + N_2}{N_1 N_2}\right]}$$

where,

N_1 = the size of the first sample in each pair
N_2 = the size of the second sample in each pair
$\hat{s}_1^2$ = the corrected variance of the first sample
$\hat{s}_2^2$ = the corrected variance of the second sample

Finally, Figure 7.1 shows that the shape of the sampling distribution of the difference between means varies as a function of sample sizes (expressed as degrees of freedom, where df $= N_1 + N_2 - 2$). As sample sizes grow larger, the sampling distribution of the difference between means more closely approximates the normal distribution; smaller samples result in increasingly platykurtic distributions.

The Test Statistic $t_{\bar{X}_1 - \bar{X}_2}$

We use the test statistic $t_{\bar{X}_1 - \bar{X}_2}$ to find the relative likelihood of observing a given $\bar{X}_1 - \bar{X}_2$ difference under circumstances in which both samples have been drawn from the same population. This statistic is computed according to Equation 7.2.

EQUATION 7.2

$$t_{\bar{X}_1 - \bar{X}_2} = \frac{(\bar{X}_1 - \bar{X}_2) - \mu_{\bar{X}_1 - \bar{X}_2}}{\sigma_{\bar{X}_1 - \bar{X}_2}}$$

We can see that $t_{\bar{X}_1 - \bar{X}_2}$ meets our definition of a test statistic since it varies in value as a function of the size of the difference being tested for significance $(\bar{X}_1 - \bar{X}_2)$. Since $\mu_{\bar{X}_1 - \bar{X}_2} = 0$, the numerator of Equation 7.2 simplifies to

$\overline{X}_1 - \overline{X}_2$. Thus, all other things being equal, large absolute differences between $\overline{X}_1$ and $\overline{X}_2$ will yield large absolute values of $t_{\overline{X}_1 - \overline{X}_2}$ and smaller differences between $\overline{X}_1$ and $\overline{X}_2$ will yield correspondingly smaller values of $t_{\overline{X}_1 - \overline{X}_2}$.

It can also be seen from Equation 7.2 that $t_{\overline{X}_1 - \overline{X}_2}$ expresses the deviation between a given $\overline{X}_1 - \overline{X}_2$ difference and $\mu_{\overline{X}_1 - \overline{X}_2}$ using the standard error of the difference as the unit of measure. Thus, $t_{\overline{X}_1 - \overline{X}_2}$ tells how many standard errors any given $\overline{X}_1 - \overline{X}_2$ difference deviates from the value that would be most likely if both samples had been drawn from the same population.

We can find the probability of obtaining any given $t_{\overline{X}_1 - \overline{X}_2}$ value (and thus, any given $\overline{X}_1 - \overline{X}_2$ value) using Appendix B: Table of Critical Values of t. The use of this table was explained in chapter 6. The only change for the between-subjects t-test is in the computation of degrees of freedom: $df = N_1 + N_2 - 2$.

Rationale of the Between-Subjects *t*-Test

The same logic that underlies the one-sample significance tests discussed in the preceding chapter may be extended for understanding the two-sample between-subjects t-test. The discussion that follows is illustrated in Box 7.1.

Step 1: The Null and Alternative Hypotheses. When two sample means are found to differ, the observed difference may be explained in either of two ways. The null hypothesis (H_0) concludes that the difference is due to sampling error. That is, it is quite likely that a $\overline{X}_1 - \overline{X}_2$ difference of the observed magnitude would occur had both samples been drawn from a single population of identically treated cases. The alternative hypothesis (H_1) proposes that the observed difference is too large to be attributed reasonably to sampling error. It is highly unlikely that two sample means would differ this much if both samples had been drawn from a single population of identically treated cases. Instead, it is more likely that the samples were not drawn from such a population, but instead, were treated differently.

Step 2: The Test Statistic. Next, the test statistic $t_{\overline{X}_1 - \overline{X}_2}$ is computed according to Equation 7.2. This statistic reflects the size of the difference being tested for significance ($\overline{X}_1 - \overline{X}_2$) by measuring the deviation of the obtained value of $\overline{X}_1 - \overline{X}_2$ from that value which would be most likely in a pair of samples drawn from a single population ($\mu_{\overline{X}_1 - \overline{X}_2} = 0$).

Step 3: Determining the Probability of the Test Statistic. Finally, the probability of obtaining the observed value of $t_{\overline{X}_1 - \overline{X}_2}$ from identically treated samples is obtained from the Table of Critical Values of t. The table is entered using degrees of freedom ($df = N_1 + N_2 - 2$ for a between-subjects t-test). One-tail significance levels are used if the direction of the $\overline{X}_1 - \overline{X}_2$ difference was predicted in advance; two-tail levels are used if no direction was predicted. If the probability of the obtained value of $t_{\overline{X}_1 - \overline{X}_2}$ is low ("low" is traditionally defined as $p < .05$), we would conclude that it is improbable that such a value of $t_{\overline{X}_1 - \overline{X}_2}$ (and the $\overline{X}_1 - \overline{X}_2$ difference it reflects) would come from a pair of samples drawn from a single population of identically treated cases. That is, the

BOX 7.1

THE BETWEEN-SUBJECTS *t*-TEST

The grades of varsity soccer players at Rocky Bottom State University tend to be somewhat below average. Thinking that this might be due to subtle brain injuries resulting from soccer players' habit of bouncing balls off their heads, we have conducted an experiment. Twenty first-year soccer players are randomly assigned to an experimental group and are equipped with protective helmets. The control group consists of 20 randomly assigned first-year soccer players who are without this protective headgear. At the end of the school year, the players' grades reveal the following pattern:

Experimental group	Control group
$\overline{X}_1 = 2.50$	$\overline{X}_2 = 1.90$
$\hat{s}_1^2 = .25$	$\hat{s}_2^2 = .36$
$N_1 = 20$	$N_2 = 20$

A between-subjects *t*-test is used to evaluate the statistical significance of the observed difference between sample means.

Step 1: *The Null and Alternative Hypotheses*

H_0 : The observed difference is due to sampling error. These two samples do not differ more than would be expected if both came from a population of cases all treated identically.

H_1 : The observed difference is too large to be due to sampling error alone. It is highly unlikely that two samples drawn from a single population of identically treated cases would differ by this much. Therefore, the two samples probably have not been treated identically.

Step 2: *The Test Statistic*

In order to compute the test statistic $t_{\overline{X}_1 - \overline{X}_2}$, we must first compute $\sigma_{\overline{X}_1 - \overline{X}_2}$ according to Equation 7.1:

$$\sigma_{\overline{X}_1 - \overline{X}_2} = \sqrt{\left[\frac{(N_1 - 1)\hat{s}_1^2 + (N_2 - 1)\hat{s}_2^2}{N_1 + N_2 - 2}\right]\left[\frac{N_1 + N_2}{N_1 N_2}\right]}$$

$$= \sqrt{\left[\frac{(20 - 1).25 + (20 - 1).36}{20 + 20 - 2}\right]\left[\frac{20 + 20}{20(20)}\right]}$$

$$= \sqrt{(.305)(.10)}$$

$$= .175$$

Next, we compute $t_{\overline{X}_1 - \overline{X}_2}$ according to Equation 7.2:

$$t_{\overline{X}_1 - \overline{X}_2} = \frac{(\overline{X}_1 - \overline{X}_2) - \mu_{\overline{X}_1 - \overline{X}_2}}{\sigma_{\overline{X}_1 - \overline{X}_2}}$$

$$= \frac{(2.5 - 1.9) - 0}{.175}$$

$$= 3.43$$

Step 3: *Determining the Probability of the Test Statistic*

Because we have predicted in advance that helmeted players ($\overline{X}_1$) would show higher grades than unprotected players ($\overline{X}_2$), a one-tail significance test is appropriate. For $df = N_1 + N_2 - 2 = 38$, the critical value of t listed in the Table of Critical Values of t (Appendix C) for the .005 one-tail level of significance is $t = 2.750$ (Since there is no listing for 38 degrees of freedom, we use the next smaller listing, which is 30 in this example.) Since the obtained value of $t = 3.43$ exceeds this critical value, we may conclude that it is highly unlikely ($p < .005$) that two samples drawn from a single population of identically treated cases would yield a $t_{\overline{X}_1 - \overline{X}_2}$ of this magnitude. Thus, it is much more likely that the observed difference is a consequence of the two samples having not been treated identically. In other words, the difference is significant.

null hypothesis would be rejected. The alternative hypothesis would thus be accepted and we would declare the observed difference to be significant. On the other hand, if the probability of the obtained $t_{\bar{X}_1 - \bar{X}_2}$ value (and underlying $\bar{X}_1 - \bar{X}_2$ difference) is greater than .05, we would recognize that the value has a reasonably high probability of occurring in a pair of samples drawn from a single population. That is, the null hypothesis would be accepted, the alternative hypothesis would be rejected, and we would declare the observed $\bar{X}_1 - \bar{X}_2$ difference to be nonsignificant.

THE WITHIN-SUBJECTS *t*-TEST

A **within-subjects *t*-test** is used to compare two means either in the situation in which a single sample has been measured twice (conveniently called a **repeated-measures *t*-test**) or when two matched samples are to be compared (called a **matched-samples *t*-test**). It should be emphasized that the repeated-measures *t*-test and the matched-samples *t*-test are both within-subjects *t*-tests and are computationally identical. The different labels refer to differences in experimental designs.

In using the within-subjects *t*-test, it is assumed that the dependent variable is continuous, measured at the interval or ratio scale level, and that there are two levels of the independent variable that differ either qualitatively or quantitatively. It is also assumed that the two samples being compared show approximately equal variances and that both show approximately normal distributions.

We will first examine the repeated-measures *t*-test in order to better understand why a within-subjects test is more powerful than a between-subjects test. Next, we will see how the matched-samples test achieves this increased power.

The Repeated-Measures *t*-Test

The chief advantage of the within-subjects *t*-test is its increased power. By this it is meant simply that a given $\bar{X}_1 - \bar{X}_2$ difference is more likely to be found statistically significant using a within-subjects *t*-test than using a between-subjects *t*-test. Stated another way, the between-subjects *t*-test requires considerably larger sample sizes than the within-subjects *t*-test in order to find the same $\bar{X}_1 - \bar{X}_2$ difference significant. Let us see how the repeated-measures *t*-test achieves its increased power.

Consider again the sampling distribution of the difference between means that is obtained when all possible pairs of independent samples are drawn at random from a single population. As we have seen, values of the $\bar{X}_1 - \bar{X}_2$ difference will vary from one pair of samples to the next, this variability being reflected in the value of the standard error of the difference between means, $\sigma_{\bar{X}_1 - \bar{X}_2}$. We need to consider more carefully here exactly what causes this variability.

Measurement error causes some of the $\bar{X}_1 - \bar{X}_2$ differences. Imagine a population of cases who are all of exactly the same true intelligence. Despite their identical levels of intelligence, intelligence test scores for the cases would probably differ somewhat from case to case, simply because no test provides a perfect measure of intelligence. This is measurement error. Given that these cases' test scores vary because of measurement error, different samples drawn from that population would be expected to show slightly different means. It follows from this that different *pairs* of samples drawn from the population would yield different $\overline{X}_1 - \overline{X}_2$ values. Thus, we see that some of the variability in the sampling distribution of the difference between means is due to measurement error.

There is a second source of variability in $\overline{X}_1 - \overline{X}_2$ values that is more important for our purposes here. This is variability due to **individual difference characteristics.** Imagine that an intelligence-enhancing drug has been developed and that all of the cases in some population have been administered identical doses of the drug. Imagine, moreover, that we have an error-free measure of intelligence that is administered to each of the cases in this population. Will all subjects yield identical scores on the test? No. Because of such individual difference characteristics as intelligence prior to taking the drug, body weight, digestive system characteristics, and other individual difference factors, different cases would be expected to react differently to the drug and would yield different intelligence test scores. This is variability due to individual differences. Given that identically treated cases' scores will vary because of individual differences, we would expect that samples drawn from the population would show different means. It follows that different *pairs* of samples drawn from the population would show different $\overline{X}_1 - \overline{X}_2$ values. Thus, we see that individual differences contribute to the variability in values of $\overline{X}_1 - \overline{X}_2$ seen in the sampling distribution of the difference between means.

If we could somehow remove the variability from this sampling distribution that is due to individual differences, $\sigma_{\overline{X}_1 - \overline{X}_2}$ would be lowered, such that any given $\overline{X}_1 - \overline{X}_2$ difference would be associated with a higher value of $t_{\overline{X}_1 - \overline{X}_2}$ (see Equation 7.2). The repeated-measures design accomplishes just this reduction in the variability of the sampling distribution of the difference between means.

We have just seen that individual difference idiosyncrasies of each sample in each pair contribute to the variability of the sampling distribution of the difference between means. For one pair, the $\overline{X}_1 - \overline{X}_2$ difference may be rather low because the two samples in that pair just happen to be quite similar in their individual difference characteristics. For another pair, the $\overline{X}_1 - \overline{X}_2$ difference may be very large because the two samples forming that pair just happen to possess very different individual difference characteristics. Imagine what would happen to the sampling distribution of the difference between means if, instead of computing $\overline{X}_1 - \overline{X}_2$ for all possible randomly sampled pairs of samples, we instead computed $\overline{X}_1 - \overline{X}_2$ for all possible single samples, each measured twice. With single samples measured twice, a major source of variability in the sampling distribution of the difference between means, that is, sample idiosyncrasies, would be eliminated. Since the first sample in each pair would now consist of exactly the same cases as the second sample in each pair, the only reason the first sample mean ($\overline{X}_1$) would differ from the second sample mean ($\overline{X}_2$) would be measurement error.

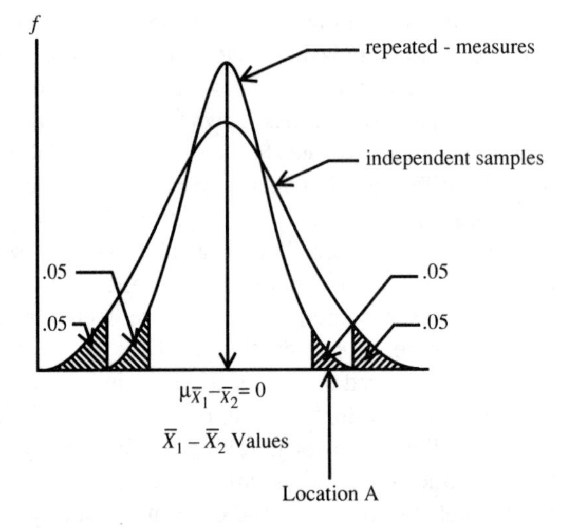

Figure 7.2

Sampling distributions of the difference between means for independent samples (the broader distribution) and repeated-measures (the narrower distribution). A $\overline{X}_1 - \overline{X}_2$ difference corresponding to the point identified as "Location A" would be significant if compared to the repeated-measures distribution, but does not reach the critical region of the independent samples distribution.

We can see, then, that by using a repeated-measures procedure we can reduce some of the variability of the sampling distribution of the difference between means, $\sigma_{\overline{X}_1 - \overline{X}_2}$. With $\sigma_{\overline{X}_1 - \overline{X}_2}$ reduced, any given $\overline{X}_1 - \overline{X}_2$ value will produce a higher value of $t_{\overline{X}_1 - \overline{X}_2}$, and this higher value of $t_{\overline{X}_1 - \overline{X}_2}$ will be more likely to reach statistical significance.

The effect of removing individual difference variability from the sampling distribution of the difference between means is depicted in Figure 7.2. Two sampling distributions are shown in that figure. The broader, more variable distribution represents $\overline{X}_1 - \overline{X}_2$ values obtained from pairs of independent samples drawn at random from a population. The narrower, less variable distribution represents $\overline{X}_1 - \overline{X}_2$ values obtained from single samples measured twice. Figure 7.2 also shows critical regions (upper and lower 5% tails) of both sampling distributions.

Figure 7.2 shows that a smaller absolute $\overline{X}_1 - \overline{X}_2$ difference will reach into the critical regions of the repeated measures distribution than is required to reach into the critical regions of the broader sampling distribution of independent samples. For example, a $\overline{X}_1 - \overline{X}_2$ difference corresponding to the point marked "Location A" in Figure 7.2 would be significant if this difference were obtained in a repeated-measures design; the same difference would be nonsignificant if it were obtained in a study of two independent samples.

The Matched-Samples *t*-Test

The increased power associated with the repeated-measures *t*-test results from the elimination of sample idiosyncrasies as a source of variability in the sampling distribution of the difference between means. This is accomplished by using the same sample to obtain both $\overline{X}_1$ and $\overline{X}_2$. Much the same reduction in $\overline{X}_1 - \overline{X}_2$ variability can be accomplished by using matched-samples.

In a matched-samples research design, two samples, rather than one, are involved in the comparison, but the second sample is selected so as to match the first on selected individual difference characteristics. Thus, the second sample, though consisting of different cases than the first, is a kind of repetition of the first sample. Data obtained from two matched samples are, in a sense, equivalent to the data obtained in a repeated-measures design.

In using a matched-samples design, we must decide which individual difference characteristic or characteristics of the first sample should be matched in forming the second sample. Selecting matching variables is a matter of identifying those individual difference characteristics that are most likely to contribute to variability in the dependent variable being examined. Of course, there is also the problem of finding cases for the second sample that match those in the first. This problem can be particularly thorny if cases are to be matched on several characteristics.

The matching process is otherwise very straightforward. Say, for example, that we have decided to match samples on the basis of high school grade point average and IQ in our study of soccer players because these variables are likely contributors to the variability in grades, the dependent variable. If the first case assigned to the experimental group has a high school grade point average of 2.9 and IQ of 105, the first case in the control group must be selected to have these same characteristics. Similarly, all other cases forming the experimental and control groups must match on high school grade point average and IQ.

Computations for the Within-Subjects *t*-Test

In addition to the conceptual differences between between-subjects and within-subjects *t*-tests just discussed, there are computational differences. First, we have seen that the standard error of the difference between means will be lower when we use a within-subjects design. This value, symbolized $\sigma_{\overline{D}}$, is computed as

EQUATION 7.3

$$\sigma_{\overline{D}} = \frac{\sqrt{\Sigma(D - \overline{D})^2/(n-1)}}{\sqrt{n}}$$

where,

D = differences between corresponding scores in the first and second samples; that is, difference scores
$\overline{D}$ = the mean of the difference scores
n = the number of *pairs* of scores

Second, the value of $t_{\overline{X}_1 - \overline{X}_2}$ for the within-subjects *t*-test is computed as before, substituting $\sigma_{\overline{D}}$ for $\sigma_{\overline{X}_1 - \overline{X}_2}$.[2]

EQUATION 7.4

$$t_{\overline{X}_1 - \overline{X}_2} = \frac{(\overline{X}_1 - \overline{X}_2) - \mu_{\overline{X}_1 - \overline{X}_2}}{\sigma_{\overline{D}}}$$

Since $\mu_{\overline{X}_1 - \overline{X}_2} = 0$, the numerator of Equation 7.4 simplifies to $\overline{X}_1 - \overline{X}_2$. A third computational difference between the between-subjects and within-subjects *t*-tests is in the computation of degrees of freedom. For within-subjects tests, $df = n - 1$, where n = the number of pairs of scores. This means that, given the same size data matrix (i.e., the same total number of scores), degrees of freedom for a within-subjects t-test will be smaller than for a between-subjects t-test. For example, in a between-subjects comparison of two samples of sizes $N_1 = 10$ and $N_2 = 10$, $df = N_1 + N_2 - 2 = 18$. In a within-subjects comparison of the same 10 *pairs* of scores, $df = n - 1 = 9$. Thus, some of the increased power of the within-subjects t-test that results from a reduction in the size of the standard error of the difference is offset by a reduction in degrees of freedom. Despite this, the gain in power that accompanies within-subjects designs more than compensates for the small loss in power associated with the reduced degrees of freedom.

Rationale of the Within-Subjects *t*-Test

Let us analyze the within-subjects t-test into the same three steps that should by now be familiar to you from previous discussions of significance testing. Box 7.2 provides an example of a within-subjects t-test that illustrates the following discussion.

Step 1: The Null and Alternative Hypotheses. A difference observed between the means of two dependent samples (obtained through either a repeated-measures design or a matched-samples design) may be explained in one of two ways. The null hypothesis (H_0) states that the $\bar{X}_1 - \bar{X}_2$ difference is no larger than we would reasonably expect to see from two matched samples or a single sample measured twice drawn from a single population of cases, all of whom have been treated identically. That is, the difference is due to sampling error. The alternative hypothesis (H_1) proposes that the observed difference is too great to be likely if both samples came from a population of identically treated cases. Instead, it is more likely that the difference has resulted from the samples being treated differently.

Step 2: The Test Statistic. Next, the test statistic $t_{\bar{X}_1 - \bar{X}_2}$ is computed according to Equation 7.4. This value increases as a function of the magnitude of the difference being tested for significance ($\bar{X}_1 - \bar{X}_2$) and indicates how much the observed difference deviates from the value $\mu_{\bar{X}_1 - \bar{X}_2} = 0$ that is most likely if both samples were treated identically.

Step 3: Determining the Probability of the Test Statistic. The Table of Critical Values of t is used in the usual fashion to find the probability of the obtained value of $t_{\bar{X}_1 - \bar{X}_2}$. Degrees of freedom are computed as $df = n - 1$, where $n =$ the number of pairs of scores. One- or two-tail significance levels are used, depending upon whether or not the direction of the difference between means was predicted in advance. If the obtained value of $t_{\bar{X}_1 - \bar{X}_2}$ is found to have a probability of less than .05, it means that a $t_{\bar{X}_1 - \bar{X}_2}$ of this size (and thus, a difference between $\bar{X}_1$ and $\bar{X}_2$ of the size that has been obtained) is unlikely to have occurred if both samples came from a population of identically treated cases. In this case, we reject the null hypothesis and declare a significant difference. On

BOX 7.2

THE WITHIN-SUBJECTS *t*-TEST

In this box we will use a within-subjects *t*-test to analyze matched-samples data pertaining to the effects of helmets on the grades of soccer players. Twenty soccer players have been randomly assigned to two matched samples of 10 players per group. Players have been matched on IQ and high school grade point average. Players in Group 1 have worn helmets all season, while players in Group 2 have not worn helmets. Grades for these two matched samples are shown in Table 7.1.

TABLE 7.1 Grades Obtained from Matched Samples of Soccer Players

Group 1	Group 2	D
3.4	2.8	.6
2.8	3.2	−.4
3.1	2.9	.2
3.0	3.2	−.2
2.8	2.8	0
3.1	3.4	−.3
3.6	2.6	1.0
3.1	2.0	1.1
3.0	2.4	.6
2.5	2.4	.1
$\overline{X}_1 = 3.04$	$\overline{X}_2 = 2.77$	

Group 1 players wore helmets throughout the season; Group 2 players did not wear helmets. Also shown are difference scores (D) and descriptive statistics.

Step 1: ***The Null and Alternative Hypotheses***

H_0 : The observed $\overline{X}_1 - \overline{X}_2$ difference is small enough to attribute to sampling error. A difference of this magnitude is quite likely to be seen in two sets of scores drawn from a population of cases that are all treated identically.

H_1 : The observed $\overline{X}_1 - \overline{X}_2$ difference is too large to be due to sampling error. A difference of this size is improbable for two sets of scores drawn from a single population of cases all treated identically.

Step 2: ***The Test Statistic***

In order to compute the test statistic $t_{\overline{X}_1 - \overline{X}_2}$ for matched-samples data, we must first compute $\sigma_{\overline{D}}$ according to Equation 7.3:

$$\begin{aligned}
\sigma_{\overline{D}} &= \frac{\sqrt{\Sigma(D - \overline{D})^2/(n - 1)}}{\sqrt{n}} \\
&= \frac{\sqrt{(.6 - .27)^2 + (-.4 - .27)^2 + \ldots + (.1 - .27)^2/(10 - 1)}}{\sqrt{10}} \\
&= \frac{\sqrt{2.54/9}}{\sqrt{10}} \\
&= .17
\end{aligned}$$

continued

BOX 7.2—*continued*

Next, we compute $t_{\bar{X}_1 - \bar{X}_2}$ according to Equation 7.4:

$$t_{\bar{X}_1 - \bar{X}_2} = \frac{(\bar{X}_1 - \bar{X}_2) - \mu_{\bar{X}_1 - \bar{X}_2}}{\sigma_{\bar{D}}}$$

$$= \frac{(3.04 - 2.77) - 0}{.17}$$

$$= 1.59$$

Step 3: ***Determining the Probability of the Test Statistic***

The obtained value of $t_{\bar{X}_1 - \bar{X}_2} = 1.59$ is compared to the sampling distribution of $t_{\bar{X}_1 - \bar{X}_2}$ for $df = n - 1 = 10 - 1 = 9$. Because the initial prediction was that Group 1 players would show higher grades than Group 2 players, one-tail significance levels may be used. The critical value of t marking the upper 5% of the sampling distribution is 1.833. As the obtained value of $t_{\bar{X}_1 - \bar{X}_2}$ has failed to reach this critical value, we can conclude that there is no significant difference between the means. That is, it is quite probable ($p > .05$) that a difference of the observed size would be obtained in two samples drawn from a single population of cases treated identically. Thus, we conclude that the observed difference can be attributed to sampling error.

the other hand, if the obtained $t_{\bar{X}_1 - \bar{X}_2}$ value has a high probability of occurring in a pair of samples drawn from a single population ($p > .05$), we would accept the null hypothesis and declare the difference to be nonsignificant.

SANDLER'S *A*

Directly related to the within-subjects *t*-test is **Sandler's *A*** statistic.[3] Sandler's *A* is useful in all of the same situations as the within-subjects *t*-test, that is, with repeated-measures or matched-samples designs. Its only advantage over the *t*-test is its computational ease. Sandler's *A* is computed in Equation 7.5.

EQUATION 7.5

$$A = \Sigma D^2 \,/\, (\Sigma D)^2$$

where,

D = differences between corresponding scores in the first and second samples; that is, difference scores

Critical values of the *A* statistic are listed in Appendix D: Critical Values of *A*. The table is entered using $n - 1$ degrees of freedom (where n = the number of pairs of scores), and the desired one- or two-tail significance level. In order for

BOX 7.3

SANDLER'S *A*

In this box we will use Sandler's A statistic to analyze the matched-samples data in Table 7.1 of Box 7.2. According to Equation 7.5, Sandler's A is computed as

$$\begin{aligned} A &= \Sigma D^2 \,/\, (\Sigma D)^2 \\ &= \frac{.6^2 - .4^2 + .2^2 + \ldots + .1^2}{(.6 - .4 + .2 + \ldots + .1)^2} \\ &= \frac{3.27}{7.29} \\ &= .45 \end{aligned}$$

For $n - 1 = 9$ degrees of freedom, the one-tail critical value of A for the .05 level of significance is listed in the Table of Critical Values of A (Appendix D) as .368. In order to be significant, the obtained value must be equal to or less than the tabled value. Since our obtained value of $A = .45$ exceeds the critical value, the difference is nonsignificant.

an obtained value of A to be statistically significant, it must be equal to or less than the tabled critical value. The use of Sandler's A is illustrated in Box 7.3.

MANN-WHITNEY *U*

The **Mann-Whitney *U*** is a useful nonparametric alternative to the between-subjects t-test. While the t-test assumes approximately homogeneous variances and normal distributions, the Mann-Whitney U places none of these restrictions on the characteristics (or "parameters") of the data. The Mann-Whitney U tests for differences between the central tendencies of two independent samples, like the t-test, but, because it makes fewer assumptions about the nature of the data, it can be used more widely. That the Mann-Whitney U is not more widely used is a result of its low power, relative to that of the t-test (especially when the assumptions of the t-test are satisfied), as well as the robustness of the t-test to violations of its assumptions (especially when sample sizes are large and equal). Nonetheless, where the parametric assumptions of the between-subjects t-test are strongly violated, the Mann-Whitney U can provide a useful, and often, more powerful alternative.

Data for the Mann-Whitney *U*

Interval or ratio scale data that fail to meet the assumptions of the between-subjects t-test may be rank-ordered and analyzed using the Mann-Whitney U. In rank-ordering the data for a Mann-Whitney U analysis, scores are ranked from lowest to highest (i.e., the lowest score is ranked 1, the next higher score is ranked 2, and so on). Notice that scores from the two groups are combined before being ranked; that is, the groups are *not* ranked separately. When two or more scores are tied, all tied scores receive the same rank, equal to the average of the positions of those scores in an ordered array. For example, look at the following scores and their ranks:

Raw scores	Position	Ranks
2	1	1
3	2	2
7	3	3.5
7	4	3.5
9	5	5

In this ordered array of scores, 7 is in the third and fourth positions. It would be inappropriate to rank these two scores 3 and 4, though, since they are equal. Instead, each is given a rank equal to the average of their positions: 3.5. Consider another example:

Raw scores	Position	Ranks
60	1	2
60	2	2
60	3	2
72	4	4
100	5	5

Here, the score 60 appears three times, in the first, second, and third positions in the ordered array. Therefore, each score of 60 is assigned the average rank of 2.

The *U* Test Statistic

All other things being equal, when scores from two groups are combined and rank-ordered, the sum of the ranks for one group will differ from the sum of the ranks for the other group to the degree that those groups differ on the dependent variable being ranked. Of course, if one group contains more cases than the other, the larger group may have a larger sum of ranks even though those ranks are all lower than those of the smaller size group. Or, the sum of ranks for the two groups could be equal, even though the two groups differ on the dependent variable under investigation, simply because the larger group had the smaller ranks. Obviously, two groups' sums of ranks cannot be compared directly. Some adjustment must be made to correct for effect of sample sizes. The Mann-Whitney U is a test statistic that reflects the difference between the sums of ranks of two groups, corrected for the influence of sample sizes.

EQUATION 7.6

$$U = N_1N_2 + \frac{N_1(N_1 + 1)}{2} - R_1$$

where,

N_1 = sample size of first sample
N_2 = sample size of second sample
R_1 = sum of ranks for the first sample

This test statistic may look a little peculiar at first glance, since ranks from the second sample do not seem to be involved in the computation of U. How can U, then, reflect the difference in ranks assigned to cases in the two groups? Realize first that the sum of ranks for the entire set of scores will be limited by the total number of cases. For example, if there are 10 cases in all, the largest rank will be 10. Thus, we know that the sum of the ranks must be $1 + 2 + 3 + \ldots + 10 = 55$. If we know the sizes of each sample, N_1 and N_2, and the sum of ranks for one sample, R_1, the sum of the ranks for the second sample, R_2, can also be determined. Extending the example begun above, if $N_1 = 5$ and $N_2 = 5$ such that the total sample is of size $N = 10$, the sum of all ranks, $R_1 + R_2$, must equal 55. If we know that $R_1 = 25$, for instance, it follows that $R_2 = 30$. Thus, although the sum of ranks for the second sample does not appear directly in Equation 7.7, it is represented by its relationship to values that do appear, that is, N_1, N_2, and R_1.

As the ranks assigned to two samples become more and more discrepant, U will become correspondingly smaller or larger, depending on the direction of the difference. When the first sample contains the smaller values of the dependent variable, and thus, the smaller ranks, R_1 will be small and U will be large. When the first sample contains the larger values of the dependent variable, and thus, the larger ranks, R_1 will be large and U will be small. When the two samples are approximately equal, R_1 and U will take on intermediate values. In this way, the value of U varies as a function of the magnitude of the difference between scores associated with the samples being compared.

The Sampling Distribution of *U*

The **sampling distribution of *U*** is the frequency distribution of values of U that are obtained when all possible pairs of samples of sizes N_1 and N_2 are drawn from a single population of identically treated cases and U is computed for each pair. The shape of this sampling distribution varies, depending upon N_1 and N_2, with critical values for one- and two-tail significance tests listed in Appendix E: Critical Values of U. In order for a given value of U to be found significant, it must fall outside the boundary values listed in the table.[4] Box 7.4 gives an example of how the Mann-Whitney U may be used to test the significance of a difference between two independent samples.

WILCOXON *T*-TEST

A nonparametric alternative to the within-subjects t-test is the **Wilcoxon *T*-test** (also known as the Wilcoxon matched-pairs signed-ranks test). The T statistic and its sampling distribution provide a test of the significance of an observed difference between two sets of scores obtained through either a repeated-measures or matched-samples design.

The *T*-Test Statistic

The Wilcoxon T statistic is computed by calculating a difference score for each case or pair of matched cases: $D = X_1 - X_2$. Next, ignoring the signs of the difference scores, they are rank-ordered from smallest to largest on the basis of

BOX 7.4

THE MANN-WHITNEY *U*

Shown in Table 7.2 are scores on the Jeff and Abdul Depression Scale for two groups of patients at Bubba's Mental Health Clinic. Group 1 subjects are new arrivals and have received no treatment. Group 2 subjects have received the full course of Bubba's cognitive behavior modification therapy. Twice each day for the last month, these patients have placed buckets over their heads and shouted "Every day in every way I'm getting better and better!" Because of substantial differences in the standard deviations of the two groups, we have decided to analyze these data using the Mann-Whitney U rather than a between-subjects t-test. We have predicted in advance of collecting these data that patients in Group 1 will show higher levels of depression than will Group 2 patients.

The first step in using the Mann-Whitney U is to rank order the scores as shown in Table 7.2. Notice that the smallest raw score has been ranked 1 and the largest has been ranked N (in this case, $N = 15$). Also notice how the score of 40, which appears twice, has been ranked. In an ordered array of all the scores, the score of 40 appears in the eighth and ninth positions. It would be inappropriate to rank these scores 8 and 9, however, since they are equal. Thus, each is assigned a rank equal to the average of their positions in the ordered array: 8.5.

TABLE 7.2 Scores on the Jeff and Abdul Depression Scale for Untreated (Group 1) and Treated (Group 2) Patients at Bubba's Mental Health Clinic

Group 1		Group 2	
Raw score	*Rank*	*Raw score*	*Rank*
40	8.5	10	2
47	11	75	15
35	5	40	8.5
37	6	32	4
51	13	25	3
38	7	62	14
42	10	5	1
49	12		
$N_1 = 8$		$N_2 = 7$	
$\overline{X}_1 = 42.38$		$\overline{X}_2 = 35.57$	
$\hat{s}_1 = 5.95$		$\hat{s}_2 = 25.77$	

Shown are raw scores and their descriptive statistics, as well as rank orders used in computing the Mann-Whitney U statistic.

absolute size, except for difference scores of 0, which are ignored. Then, each of the ranks is given a positive or negative sign to reflect the sign of the corresponding difference score. Finally, T is computed as in Equation 7.7.

EQUATION 7.7

T = the smaller of the two: (1) the absolute sum of the positive ranks or (2) the absolute sum of the negative ranks.

To the degree that the two sets of scores are equal, the sum of positive ranks and the sum of negative ranks will be approximately equal. As the two sets of scores grow more disparate, these two sums will become increasingly different. If scores on the dependent variable are greater in the first set of scores than in

Step 1: ***The Null and Alternative Hypotheses***

H_0 : The observed difference between the two groups is no greater than would be expected by chance. There is a reasonably high probability of obtaining a difference of this size between two groups drawn from a single population of cases treated identically.

H_1 : The observed difference between the two samples is too great to attribute to sampling error. It is highly improbable that two samples drawn from a single population of identically treated cases would show a difference this large. Thus, it is more likely that the two samples have received different treatments.

Step 2: ***The Test Statistic***

The Mann-Whitney U is computed according to Equation 7.6:

$$U = N_1N_2 + \frac{N_1(N_1 + 1)}{2} - R_1$$

$$= (8)(7) + \frac{8(8 + 1)}{2} - 72.5$$

$$= 19.5$$

Step 3: ***Determining the Probability of the Test Statistic***

In the Table of Critical Values of U (Appendix E), we find listed the critical boundary values of U for $N_1 = 8$ and $N_2 = 7$. For a one-tail test at the .05 significance level, these boundary values are 13 and 43. Because the obtained value of U falls within the listed critical boundaries of 13 and 43, it has a probability of greater than .05 of occurring in two samples drawn from a single population. Thus, the obtained value of U, and the between-group difference it reflects, is not statistically significant.

the second set, the sum of positive ranks will exceed the sum of negative ranks. If scores in the first set are generally lower than those of the second set, the sum of negative ranks will exceed the sum of positive ranks. Since the statistic T is equal to the smaller of either the sum of the positive ranks or the sum of the negative ranks, we can see that T will vary inversely with the magnitude of the difference between the two sets of scores; that is, T will become larger as the difference becomes smaller and vice versa.

The Sampling Distribution of the Wilcoxon T

The **sampling distribution of T** is the frequency distribution of values of T computed for all possible pairs of samples drawn from a single population of identically treated cases. Critical values for one- and two-tail significance levels for

BOX 7.5

THE WILCOXON T

In Box 7.2 we used a matched-samples t-test to analyze grades obtained by helmet-protected (Group 1) vs. unprotected (Group 2) soccer players. In this box, we will reanalyze these same data using the Wilcoxon T. Grades for the two groups are given in Table 7.3 below.

TABLE 7.3 Grades Obtained from Matched Samples of Soccer Players

Group 1	Group 2	D	Rank
3.4	2.8	.6	(+)6.5
2.8	3.2	− .4	(−)5
3.1	2.9	.2	(+)2.5
3.0	3.2	− .2	(−)2.5
2.8	2.8	0	—
3.1	3.4	− .3	(−)4
3.6	2.6	1.0	(+)8
3.1	2.0	1.1	(+)9
3.0	2.4	.6	(+)6.5
2.5	2.4	.1	(+)1

Group 1 players wore helmets throughout the season; Group 2 players did not wear helmets. Also shown are difference scores (D) and signed ranks.

First, a difference score (D) is computed for each pair of matched cases. Next, all nonzero difference scores are ranked from smallest to largest without regard to their signs. (Notice how ties are handled.) Finally, each rank is given a sign (+ or −) consistent with the sign of the corresponding difference score. Difference scores and signed ranks are in Table 7.3 along with grades.

Step 1: ***The Null and Alternative Hypotheses***

H_0 : The observed difference between the two sets of scores is small enough to be quite likely had the two sets been drawn from a single population of identically treated cases. That is, the difference is due to sampling error.

H_1 : The difference is too great to attribute to sampling error. It is unlikely that two sets of scores drawn from a single population of identically treated cases would differ this much. Thus, it is more likely that the two samples have not received identical treatment.

Step 2: ***The Test Statistic***

The Wilcoxon T statistic is computed according to Equation 7.7:

$T =$ the smaller of the two: (1) the absolute sum of the positive ranks or (2) the absolute sum of the negative ranks.

In the present example, the sum of the positive ranks is 33.5 and the sum of the negative ranks is 11.5. Thus, $T = 11.5$.

Step 3: ***Determining the Probability of the Test Statistic***

The Table of Critical Values of T (Appendix F) lists $T = 8$ as the critical value of T for $N = 9$ (there were only 9 nonzero difference scores) at the one-tail .05 level of significance. The obtained value of $T = 11.5$ is larger than this critical value and we therefore conclude that the difference between groups is nonsignificant. In other words, the probability is quite high ($p > .05$) that we would see a difference of this magnitude in two samples drawn from a single population of identically treated cases.

the T distribution are given in Appendix F: Critical Values of T.[5] These values are listed according to N, the number of ranked pairs of scores. Thus, any pair of scores showing a difference of 0 (which would not have been ranked) does not contribute to N. Box 7.5 demonstrates how the Wilcoxon T-test is used for testing the significance of a difference between two sets of dependent scores.

CHI-SQUARE TEST FOR TWO INDEPENDENT SAMPLES

Another nonparametric test of the significance of difference between two samples is the **chi-square test for two independent samples.** We saw in the preceding chapter how the chi-square goodness-of-fit test may be used in testing the significance of a difference between a sample distribution and a population distribution. The chi-square statistic may also be used to test the significance of a difference between two sample distributions. Because the χ^2 statistic is sensitive to any kind of difference between two distributions—central tendency, variability, or shape—no assumptions about these parameters of the data need be met in order for the test to be used appropriately. Too, the chi-square test for two independent samples may be used in comparing distributions on interval, ratio, or nominal scale dependent variables.

The Contingency Table

The chi-square test for two independent samples begins with a **contingency table** like the one shown in Table 7.4 of Box 7.6. The columns of the contingency table represent groups and each row represents one of the categories of the dependent variable. Recorded in each cell of the table is the number of cases in each group that falls into each category of the dependent variable. These frequencies are called **observed frequencies,** symbolized f_o. Also appearing in each cell are **expected frequencies,** symbolized f_e. These values represent the number of cases that would be expected to appear in each cell if there were no relationship between group membership and membership in the categories of the dependent variable, that is, no difference between the distributions of the groups being compared. Any discrepancy between observed and expected frequencies, then, is evidence that there is a difference between the distributions of the groups being compared.

The Chi-Square Test Statistic

The χ^2 test statistic is computed for a two-sample comparison just as it was for a one-sample test (Equation 6.2):

$$\chi^2 = \Sigma\frac{(f_o - f_e)^2}{f_e}$$

In words, in each cell of the contingency table, the expected frequency is subtracted from the observed frequency, this difference is squared, and this squared difference is divided by that cell's expected frequency. Finally, these values are

BOX 7.6

CHI-SQUARE TEST FOR INDEPENDENT SAMPLES

Ba-Ba-Lu's, the big night spot in Hellhole County, recently surveyed 265 of their patrons to determine which type of appetizers they would prefer. Responses from 150 male and 115 female Ba-Ba-Lusers are summarized in Table 7.4. Observed frequencies (f_o) shown in each cell indicate the number of patrons who expressed a preference for each type of appetizer. Row and column totals are the sums of these observed frequencies. Row percentages, also based on observed frequencies, indicate the percentage of patrons who expressed a preference for each type of appetizer.

Expected frequencies (f_e) shown in each cell give the number of patrons who would be expected to express a preference for each type of appetizer if males and females did not differ in their patterns of preferences. Consider how these expected frequencies were computed. We know that 29.4% of all patrons preferred nachos (see row %). If males and females have identical preferences, we would expect that 29.4% of the 150 males (i.e., 44.1) and 29.4% of the 115 females (i.e., 33.8) would prefer nachos. These are

TABLE 7.4 Contingency Table Summarizing Responses of Male and Female Patrons of Ba-Ba-Lu's When Asked About Their Preferred Type of Appetizers

Preferred Appetizer	Groups: Males	Groups: Females	**Row Totals**	**Row %**
Nachos	$f_o = 54$ $f_e = 44.1$	$f_o = 24$ $f_e = 33.8$	78	29.4%
Potato skins	$f_o = 45$ $f_e = 33.9$	$f_o = 15$ $f_e = 26.0$	60	22.6%
Fried cheese	$f_o = 38$ $f_e = 36.2$	$f_o = 18$ $f_e = 24.3$	56	21.1%
Veggie plate	$f_o = 13$ $f_e = 40.2$	$f_o = 58$ $f_e = 30.8$	71	26.8%
Column Totals	150	115	$N = 265$	

summed across all cells of the contingency table to yield χ^2. When two samples' distributions are identical, such that $f_o = f_e$ for all cells, $\chi^2 = 0$. As the two samples' distributions become more and more discrepant, the values of f_o and f_e will differ increasingly and the value of χ^2 will increase.

The Sampling Distribution of Chi-Square

The sampling distribution of χ^2 for the two-sample comparison is based on χ^2 values computed for all possible pairs of samples drawn from a single population. The shape of the chi-square sampling distribution, described more fully in chapter

BOX 7.6—*continued*

the expected frequencies for the first row of the contingency table. For the second row, we know that 22.6% of all patrons preferred potato skins. If males and females did not differ in their appetizer preferences, we would expect that 22.6% of the 150 males (i.e., 33.9) and 22.6% of the 115 females (i.e., 26.0) would prefer potato skins. These are the expected frequencies for the second row of the table. Similarly, expected frequencies may be computed for the remaining cells of the table by multiplying column totals by row percentages.

The fact that observed and expected frequencies do not match exactly indicates that males and females expressed different preferences for appetizers. The question that remains is whether this difference is large enough to be considered statistically significant.

Step 1: ***The Null and Alternative Hypotheses***

H_0 : The observed difference between the distributions of males and females can be attributed to sampling error. Two samples drawn from a single population of like-minded cases would have a reasonably high probability of showing this much difference in their distributions.

H_1 : The observed difference in the distributions of these two groups is too great to be attributed to sampling error. Two samples drawn from a single population of like-minded cases would be highly unlikely to show a difference this great. Thus, the two samples at hand probably do not represent such a single population and like-mindedness.

Step 2: ***The Test Statistic***

The χ^2 test for two independent samples is computed according to Equation 6.2:

$$\chi^2 = \Sigma\frac{(f_o - f_e)^2}{f_e}$$

$$= \frac{(54 - 44.1)^2}{44.1} + \frac{(24 - 33.8)^2}{33.8} + \ldots + \frac{(58 - 30.8)^2}{30.8}$$

$$= 57.50$$

Step 3: ***Determining the Probability of the Test Statistic***

For $df = (R - 1)(C - 1) = (4 - 1)(2 - 1) = 3$, the Table of Critical Values of χ^2 (Appendix C) lists $\chi^2 = 11.34$ as the critical value that marks the .01 level of significance. Because the obtained value of $\chi^2 = 57.50$ exceeds this critical value, we know that $p < .01$ that two samples that show frequency distributions this discrepant would be drawn from a single population of like-minded individuals. Thus, our samples of males and females can be concluded to differ significantly with respect to their appetizer preferences.

6, varies as a function of $(R - 1)(C - 1)$ degrees of freedom, where R = the number of rows in the contingency table and C = the number of columns in the table. Critical values of χ^2 are listed in Appendix C: Critical Values of χ^2. Box 7.6 demonstrates how the χ^2 test may be used to compare two sample distributions.

Small Expected Frequencies and Yates' Correction

We saw in the preceding chapter that the χ^2 goodness-of-fit test can be problematic in situations in which expected frequencies are small. This is because the χ^2

test statistic is influenced excessively by small expected frequencies. Small expected frequencies present a problem for the chi-square test for two independent samples as well.

Imagine a contingency table with two rows ($R = 2$) and two columns ($C = 2$). In one cell of this table, $f_o = 3$ and $f_e = 1$. Without knowing values of f_o or f_e for any of the other cells of the table, we know already that χ^2 will be significant. When $df = (R - 1)(C - 1) = 1$, the critical value of χ^2 at the .05 level of significance is 3.841. The contribution to χ^2 of the known cell of the contingency table is $(f_o - f_e)^2/f_e = (3 - 1)^2/1 = 4$. No matter what information appears in the other cells of the contingency table, the result of the χ^2 significance test has been determined. Here, χ^2 is significant because of a discrepancy of only two cases between observed and expected frequencies in one cell of the contingency table.

Because of this feature of χ^2, the χ^2 test for two independent samples is recommended only when all expected frequencies in a 2×2 contingency table are at least 5. For larger tables, at least 80% of the cells should contain expected frequencies of at least 5 and no cell should contain an expected frequency of less than 1. When expected frequencies are too small, we may sometimes combine categories of the dependent variable and/or increase the sample size to boost expected frequencies to an acceptable level.

As another alternative, used only with 2×2 contingency tables, χ^2 can be computed using **Yates' correction for continuity** as in Equation 7.8:

EQUATION 7.8

$$\chi^2 = \Sigma \frac{(|f_o - f_e|) - .5)^2}{f_e}$$

The numerator of Equation 7.8 directs that the absolute value of each cell's $f_o - f_e$ difference be reduced by .5 prior to squaring. If Yates' correction were applied to the preceding data, the offending cell would contribute only $(|3 - 1|) - .5)^2/1 = 2.25$ to the corrected χ^2 value and this cell alone would not cause χ^2 to be significant.

Although Yates' correction has been widely used in the past, use of the procedure appears to be in decline because it results in an overly conservative test. Many authors recommend against its use (Daniel, 1978; Siegel & Castellan, 1988).

STATISTICAL VS. PRACTICAL SIGNIFICANCE

We learned in the preceding chapter that the magnitude of the difference between a sample and a population is not the only factor that influences the outcome of tests of statistical significance. Sample size and data variability also play a role. The same is true in the case of two-sample significance tests, where, all other things being equal, larger sample sizes and lower data variability will increase the likelihood that an observed difference will be found to be statistically significant. Sample sizes and data variability figure into the computation of two-sample test statistics and sample sizes also determine degrees of freedom, and thus, critical values of the test statistics.

It follows that when sample sizes are large and data variability is low, even unimportant differences between two samples may be identified as statistically significant. The outcomes of two-sample significance tests must be interpreted with this fact in mind. The tests tell us only whether an observed difference is a reliable one, not whether it is an important one.

Omega-Square

Along with common sense, the statistic **omega-square** (ω^2) provides information useful for evaluating the practical significance of a statistically significant value of $t_{\overline{X}_1 - \overline{X}_2}$. In the context of the two-sample t-test (either between-subjects or within-subjects), ω^2 is computed in Equation 7.9.

EQUATION 7.9

$$\omega^2 = \frac{t^2 - 1}{t^2 + N_1 + N_2 - 1}$$

where,

t = the obtained value of $t_{\overline{X}_1 - \overline{X}_2}$
N_1 = the size of the first sample
N_2 = the size of the second sample

When a significant value of $t_{\overline{X}_1 - \overline{X}_2}$ reveals that two samples differ significantly, we can conclude that there is a reliable relationship between the independent and dependent variables being examined. For example, if Alzheimer's patients receiving 0 vs. 150 mg of an experimental drug (the independent variable) were found to differ significantly on a subsequent measure of cognitive functioning (the dependent variable), we would know that there is a reliable relationship between the drug and cognitive functioning. Knowing that the relationship is reliable, though, does not tell us directly how strong that relationship is. To continue the example begun above, we might like to know just how strong an effect the experimental drug exerts on cognitive functioning. This is information provided by ω^2.

Omega-square provides a standardized measure of relationship strength that ranges in value from 0 to 1, with 0 indicating no relationship between independent and dependent variables, and 1 indicating a perfect relationship. Omega-square is interpreted in the same manner as a squared correlation (chapter 10), in that it indicates the proportion of variance in the dependent variable that is explained by the independent variable.

Cramer's *V*

Useful in evaluating the practical significance of a statistically significant two-sample χ^2 is the statistic **Cramer's *V*.** Cramer's V can range from 0 to 1 and is analogous to omega-square for providing an index of the strength of the relationship or linkage between group membership and membership in the categories of a dependent variable. Cramer's V is computed in Equation 7.10.

EQUATION 7.10

$$V = \sqrt{\frac{\chi^2}{N(n-1)}}$$

where,

N = sample size
n = the number of rows or columns, whichever is smaller

When $\chi^2 = 0$, V will also equal 0, indicating no relationship between group membership and the dependent variable. As χ^2 increases, so will V.

SUMMARY

Two-sample comparisons are fundamental to research in the social and behavioral sciences. In this chapter, two-sample tests of significant difference are explored. All of these tests enable the researcher to assess the reliability or replicability of a difference observed between two samples. Between-subjects significance tests are useful in comparisons of two separate, independent samples that are exposed to either qualitatively or quantitatively different levels of an independent variable. Within-subjects significance tests are useful both in repeated-measures research designs, where the same cases are measured twice, and in matched-samples designs, where two separate, but matched samples are compared. Within-subjects tests have the advantage of greater statistical power than between-subjects tests. Within-subjects designs, though, present logistical problems that do not accompany between-subject designs. Between-subjects tests examined in this chapter include the between-subjects t-test, the Mann-Whitney U, and the chi-square test. Within-subjects tests examined include the within-subjects t-test and the Wilcoxon T. All of these tests enable us to determine the relative likelihood that an observed difference between samples is due to chance factors or is more likely the consequence of different independent variable treatments received by the samples. A statistically significant difference indicates that the independent and dependent variables are linked, but significant difference tests do not indicate directly how strong this linkage is, nor how important it is. The statistic omega-square provides a measure of relationship strength for two-sample t-tests. In a similar manner, Cramer's V gives an indication of the strength of the relationship between group membership and membership in the categories of a dependent variable in the two-sample χ^2 test. Common sense provides an answer to the question of practical significance.

NOTES

1. When sample sizes are equal ($N_1 = N_2$), the standard error of the difference between means is more simply computed as:

$$\sigma_{\bar{X}_1 - \bar{X}_2} = \sqrt{\frac{\hat{s}_1^2}{N_1} + \frac{\hat{s}_2^2}{N_2}}$$

where,

$\hat{s}_1^2$ = the corrected variance of the first sample
$\hat{s}_2^2$ = the corrected variance of the second sample
N_1 = the size of the first sample
N_2 = the size of the second sample

2. The within-subjects t-test may be computed more simply using the following computational formula:

$$t_{\overline{X}_1 - \overline{X}_2} = \frac{\Sigma D}{\sqrt{\dfrac{n\Sigma D^2 - (\Sigma D)^2}{n - 1}}}$$

where,

D = differences between corresponding scores in the first and second samples, i.e., difference scores
n = the number of pairs of scores

3. Sandler's A statistic is a direct transformation of the within-subjects $t_{\overline{X}_1 - \overline{X}_2}$ statistic:

$$A = \frac{n - 1}{nt^2} + \frac{1}{n}$$

where,

n = the number of *pairs* of scores

4. Table E: Critical Values of U provides critical values of the U statistic only for sample sizes up to $N = 20$. For larger samples, U can be transformed to z_U and Appendix A: The Table of Areas Under the Normal Curve can be used in assessing significance:

$$z_U = \frac{U - \dfrac{N_1 N_2}{2}}{\sqrt{\dfrac{N_1 N_2 (N_1 + N_2 + 1)}{12}}}$$

5. Table F: Critical Values of T provides critical values of the Wilcoxon T statistic up to $N = 50$. For larger values of N, T may be transformed to z_T and Appendix A: The Table of Areas Under the Normal Curve can be used in assessing its significance:

$$z_T = \frac{T - \dfrac{N(N + 1)}{4}}{\dfrac{N(N + 1)(2N + 1)}{24}}$$

CHAPTER 8

SIGNIFICANT DIFFERENCES: AN INTRODUCTION TO ANALYSIS OF VARIANCE

One-way analysis of variance (ANOVA) can be viewed as an extension of the two-sample *t*-test (chapter 7) because one-way ANOVA is useful in assessing the significance of differences between two *or more* group means. This ANOVA is called one-way because the two or more samples being compared in the analysis differ on a single independent variable. For example, we might use one-way ANOVA to compare levels of depression (the dependent variable) observed in groups receiving 50 mg, 100 mg, and 150 mg per day of an antidepressant drug. These groups differ on a single independent variable, drug dosage. As another example, we might use one-way ANOVA to compare levels of sexual knowledge (the dependent variable) observed in subjects from lower-, middle-, and upper-class backgrounds. These groups also differ on a single independent variable, socioeconomic background.

One-way ANOVA requires that the dependent variable be measured at the interval or ratio level. It is also assumed that the dependent variable is normally distributed in all groups involved in the comparison, and that the groups show approximately equal variances on the dependent variable. These are the same assumptions upon which the two-sample *t*-test is based. Provided samples sizes are approximately equal and reasonably large (at least 15 cases per group), though, the one-way ANOVA is fairly robust to violations of these later two assumptions.

TYPES OF ONE-WAY ANOVAS

The independent variable in a one-way ANOVA may include levels that differ quantitatively (e.g., drug dosage levels, levels of noise exposure) or qualitatively (e.g., religious preference, political affiliation). The independent variable may be one that varies naturally (e.g., gender, race) or may be a variable that is controlled and manipulated by the experimenter (e.g., schedule of reinforcement, drug dosage). The levels of the independent variable may have been selected as the only levels that are of interest to the researcher, called a **fixed-effects model,** or may have been randomly sampled to represent a broader assortment of levels, called a **random-effects model.** Finally, any given case may be exposed to only one level of the independent variable, a **completely randomized ANOVA** design, or each case may be exposed to all levels of the independent variable, a **repeated measures** or **randomized block** ANOVA. Because the purpose of this chapter is to introduce the fundamental concepts of ANOVA, our discussion of one-way ANOVA will be limited to the fixed-effects, completely randomized design. The curious reader may refer to Keppel (1983), Kirk (1968), or Lindman (1974) for more information about other design options. Nonparametric ANOVAs, which relax the assumptions about the characteristics of the dependent variable listed previously, are also available. The reader may consult Daniel (1978) or Siegel and Castellan (1988) for more information about these procedures.

ANOVA VS. MULTIPLE PAIRWISE COMPARISONS

We might wonder why the one-way ANOVA is even necessary. If several groups representing different levels of an independent variable show differences in their means on a dependent variable, why not just test the significance of these differences with a series of *t*-tests? Say, for instance, that four group means were to be compared: $\overline{X}_1$, $\overline{X}_2$, $\overline{X}_3$, and $\overline{X}_4$. Using a series of *t*-tests, we might examine differences among these four means by examining all possible pairwise combinations: $\overline{X}_1$ vs. $\overline{X}_2$, $\overline{X}_1$ vs. $\overline{X}_3$, $\overline{X}_1$ vs. $\overline{X}_4$, $\overline{X}_2$ vs. $\overline{X}_3$, $\overline{X}_2$ vs. $\overline{X}_4$, and $\overline{X}_3$ vs. $\overline{X}_4$. Or, a single one-way ANOVA can be computed that would simultaneously examine all of these differences in one significance test. We can immediately see one advantage of the one-way ANOVA: it is computationally less tedious. Even a few means can generate a substantial number of pairwise comparisons. If k = the number of means, the total number of pairwise comparisons is $(k^2 - k)/2$. As the number of groups grows, the number of pairwise comparisons increases at an accelerating rate.

Another advantage of one-way ANOVA over multiple pairwise comparisons is not so obvious, but is actually more important. Each significance test that is computed has some probability of leading to a Type I error (this probability being equal to the selected level of significance) as well as some often even larger probability of a Type II error. Thus, in a series of $(k^2 - k)/2$ pairwise comparisons called for by k sample means, a substantial number of errors can occur. In a series of 100 tests at the .05 level of significance, we would expect five Type I errors and possibly even more Type II errors, and this assumes that all of the tests are independent, which they probably are not.

To illustrate, if $\overline{X}_1$ is found to be significantly greater than $\overline{X}_2$, and $\overline{X}_2$ is greater than $\overline{X}_3$, we know that $\overline{X}_1$ must be significantly greater than $\overline{X}_3$. But, if the $\overline{X}_1$ vs. $\overline{X}_2$ comparison appeared significant only because $\overline{X}_1$ was spuriously high, the probability that the $\overline{X}_1$ vs. $\overline{X}_3$ comparison will produce a Type I error will be greater than .05. In short, because the outcomes of pairwise comparisons are seldom independent of each other, the rate of Type I and Type II errors in a series of such comparisons can be startlingly high. The one-way ANOVA, by simultaneously accomplishing all $(k^2 - k)/2$ comparisons with a single significance test, avoids the inflated error rates of multiple pairwise comparisons.

As we have seen before, though, there are no free statistical lunches. In the case of one-way ANOVA, we buy control over error rates only by sacrificing specificity of information about the source(s) of the statistical significance indicated by the ANOVA. Although the single significance test of the ANOVA indicates that a statistical difference exists somewhere among the sample means being compared, it does not indicate which specific means differ significantly. Perhaps only one pair of means differs; perhaps they all do. Teasing out the source of the significant ANOVA requires the use of post hoc and a priori comparison procedures, which are discussed later in this chapter.

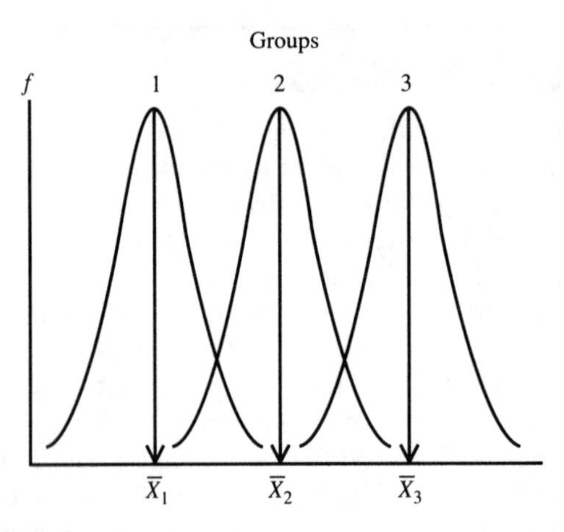

Figure 8.1

The data for a one-way ANOVA. Frequency distributions of three groups with means $\overline{X}_1$, $\overline{X}_2$, and $\overline{X}_3$.

WITHIN- AND BETWEEN-GROUP VARIANCE

Figure 8.1 depicts the type of data that are analyzed using one-way ANOVA. In this diagram we see three groups' frequency distributions with means $\overline{X}_1$, $\overline{X}_2$, and $\overline{X}_3$ as indicated. There are two types or "sources" of variability in the data depicted in this figure: **within-group variance,** and **between-group variance.** Expressed in another way, total variance = within-group variance + between-group variance.

Within-Group Variance

We are already familiar with what is now being called within-group variance. This is simply the variability observed within any given group's distribution. This variability is seen in Figure 8.1 as the dispersion or scattering shown in each group's frequency distribution.

Within-group variance is caused by two factors. First, although all cases within a group represent the same independent variable category or level, (i.e., all cases have been treated the same or are all members of the same naturally occurring group), they will show individual differences in their reactions to that treatment. These differences account for some of the variability in the dependent variable found within any given group. Subjects who all receive 50 mg of some drug, for example, will show some variability in their responses to that drug due to individual differences in body weight, age, and other factors. Subjects exposed to the same 10 db noise will react differently due to individual differences in personality, experience, hearing sensitivity, and so forth.

A second factor contributing to within-group variance is measurement error. Seldom in the social and behavioral sciences do we find a dependent variable that is measured without error, sometimes a substantial amount of error. Two individuals of exactly the same actual intelligence (whatever "intelligence" is) are unlikely to receive exactly the same score on an intelligence test. This is measurement error. Subjects who receive an identical dosage of a drug and who do happen to react identically may be recorded as having reacted differently. Mistakes do happen. This is also measurement error. Whatever its cause, measurement error can contribute substantially to the variability seen in the scores within any group, thus contributing to within-group variance.

Between-Group Variance

The second type of variance seen in Figure 8.1 is between-group variance. Notice that the means of the three samples differ or vary. This variability between means is referred to as between-group variance.

Between-group variance is caused by three factors. First, just as individual differences contribute to differences from one individual to the next within a group, these individual differences also contribute to the variability seen between groups. Second, the same measurement error that adds to the variability of scores within a group also adds to the variability of scores between groups. Finally, the fact that the groups have been exposed to different levels of the independent variable may contribute to the differences seen from one group to the next.

TREATMENT EFFECTS AND THE *F* STATISTIC

We have just seen that within-group variance is caused by (1) individual differences and (2) measurement error. Between-group variance is caused by (1) individual differences; (2) measurement error; and (3) the effects of the independent variable on the dependent variable. It follows that, to the extent that the independent variable affects the dependent variable, between-group variance will be greater than within-group variance. In other words, between-group variance will exceed within-group variance to the degree that there is a **treatment effect.** On the other hand, if the independent variable exerts no effect on the dependent variable (i.e., no treatment effect), between-group and within-group variances should be approximately equal, since both will be determined by the same two factors—individual differences and measurement error.

Figure 8.2 illustrates how between-group variance, but not within-group variance, is influenced by treatment effects of varying strengths. In Figure 8.2a, the frequency distributions show substantial separation of group means, relative to the variability seen within groups. This illustrates a strong treatment effect, where between-group variance exceeds within-group variance. In Figure 8.2b, the strength of the treatment effect is not as great. The separation of group means (i.e., between-group variance) is now reduced, relative to that seen in Figure 8.2a, while within-group variance remains the same. Finally, Figure 8.2c shows virtually no treatment effect. Here, the amount of variability between groups has decreased to the point that it is essentially equal to the variability seen within groups.

The ***F* statistic,** computed as the ratio of between-group variance to within-group variance (F = between-group variance/within-group variance) provides a numerical index that reflects the amount of separation between the groups' frequency distributions. Because the F statistic varies in value as a function of

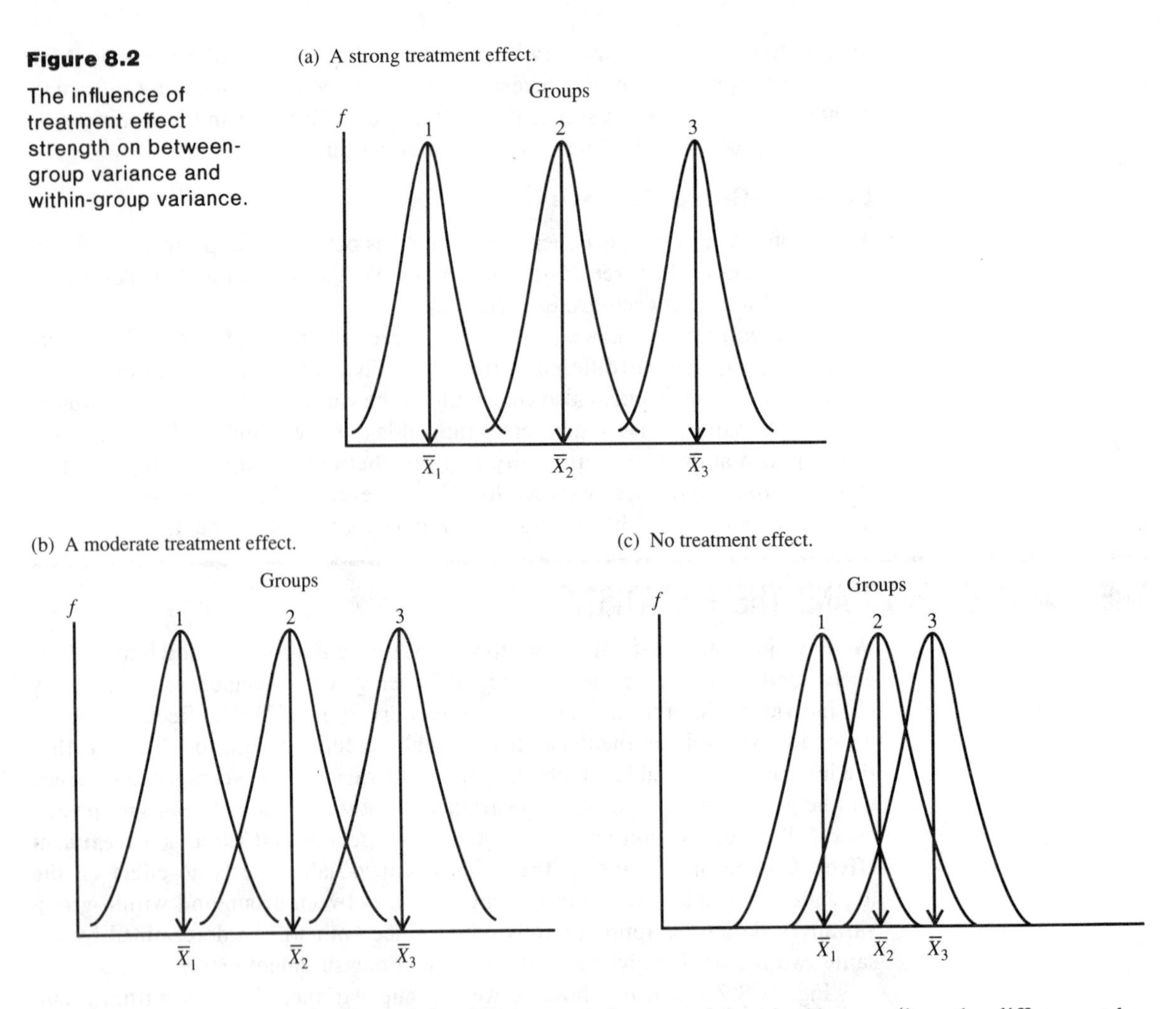

Figure 8.2

The influence of treatment effect strength on between-group variance and within-group variance.

the size of the differences being tested for significance (i.e., the differences between the group means), F can be considered a test statistic. The F test in the one-way ANOVA, then, tests the significance of between-group differences in means by comparing between-group variance against within-group variance.

Sums of Squares

We have seen that F is computed as the ratio of between-group variance to within-group variance. The question now becomes, how do we compute these two variances? They are represented by values called **sums of squares.**

Within-Group Sum of Squares. Within-group variability is reflected in a value called the **within-group sum of squares,** abbreviated SS_{within}. The within-group sum of squares is computed according to Equation 8.1:

EQUATION 8.1

$$SS_{within} = \sum_{i=1}^{n_1} (X_i - \bar{X}_1)^2 + \sum_{i=1}^{n_2} (X_i - \bar{X}_2)^2 + \ldots + \sum_{i=1}^{n_k} (X_i - \bar{X}_k)^2$$

where,

k = the number of groups
$n_1 - n_k$ = sample sizes of each of the k groups
$\bar{X}_1 - \bar{X}_k$ = means of each of the k groups

In words, SS_{within} is computed by subtracting a group's mean from each score in that group, squaring these differences, summing the squares, and summing these values across the several groups.

Between-Group Sum of Squares. The variability observed between the means of the groups being compared with an ANOVA is represented by the value of the **between-group sum of squares,** abbreviated $SS_{between}$. The between-group sum of squares is computed according to Equation 8.2:

EQUATION 8.2

$$SS_{between} = (\bar{X}_1 - \bar{X}_G)^2 (n_1) + (\bar{X}_2 - \bar{X}_G)^2 (n_2) + \ldots + (\bar{X}_k - \bar{X}_G)^2 (n_k)$$

where,

k = the number of groups
$n_1 - n_k$ = sample sizes of each of the k groups
$\bar{X}_1 - \bar{X}_k$ = means of each of the k groups
$\bar{X}_G$ = grand mean, the mean of all scores in the analysis

In words, $SS_{between}$ is computed by subtracting the grand mean from each group mean, squaring these differences, multiplying each squared difference by the size of the group, and summing these values across the groups.

Total Sum of Squares. There are only two sources of variability in the data collected in a one-way ANOVA design: within-group variability, reflected in SS_{within}, and between-group variability, reflected in $SS_{between}$. As a computational check on these two values, it should be confirmed that they sum to equal the **total sum of squares,** abbreviated SS_{total}, computed in Equation 8.3:

EQUATION 8.3

$$SS_{total} = \sum_{i=1}^{N} (X_i - \bar{X}_G)^2$$

where,

N = the number of scores in the analysis
$\bar{X}_G$ = the grand mean

In words, SS_{total} is computed by subtracting the grand mean from each score, squaring these differences, and summing the squares. SS_{total} represents the total variability in the data, which, as just described, can be partitioned into two sources represented by SS_{within} and $SS_{between}$. Thus, $SS_{total} = SS_{within} + SS_{between}$.

Mean Squares

Although SS_{within} and $SS_{between}$ represent the two sources of variability in the data of a one-way ANOVA, these values provide imperfect measures of variability, being influenced not only by variability, but also by the number of groups and number of scores within each group. All other things being equal, the more groups and scores, the higher will be the values of the sums of squares. This problem is overcome by dividing each sum of squares value by its corresponding **degrees of freedom** to yield average variability statistics called the **mean squares.**

Within-Group Mean Squares. The variability represented by SS_{within} is averaged by dividing SS_{within} by the **within-group degrees of freedom** (df_{within}), computed as $(n_1 - 1) + (n_2 - 1) + \ldots + (n_k - 1) = N - k$. The resulting within-group variability statistic is called the **within-group mean squares,** abbreviated MS_{within}.

EQUATION 8.4

$$MS_{within} = \frac{SS_{within}}{df_{within}}$$

By dividing SS_{within} by $(n_1 - 1) + (n_2 - 1) + \ldots + (n_k - 1) = N - k$ we are essentially dividing each group's sum of squares, $\Sigma(X - \bar{X})^2$, by one less than the number of cases in that group, $n - 1$, to obtain an average variability within each group. These values are then summed across all k groups to give us a measure of within-group variance, MS_{within}, that is free from the influence of sample sizes.

Between-Group Mean Squares. $SS_{between}$ is averaged by dividing it by the **between-group degrees of freedom** ($df_{between}$), computed as $k - 1$. The resulting value is called the **between-group mean squares,** abbreviated $MS_{between}$.

EQUATION 8.5

$$MS_{between} = \frac{SS_{between}}{df_{between}}$$

In this way, between-group variability seen from one group mean to the next is averaged by dividing this variability by one less than the total number of group means that are varying, (i.e., $k - 1$). This is consistent with the computation of any corrected variance (see chapter 3); that is, the sum of squared deviations of values around the mean of those values is divided by one less than the number of values. The between-group mean squares provides a measure of between-group variance that is unaffected by the number of samples.

Computing *F*

We saw earlier that the F statistic is computed as the ratio of between-group variance to within-group variance. Having now determined that between-group variance may be computed as $MS_{between}$ and within-group variance may be computed as MS_{within}, it follows that the F statistic may be computed as shown in Equation 8.6.

EQUATION 8.6

$$F = \frac{MS_{between}}{MS_{within}}$$

The ANOVA Summary Table

The computations associated with the one-way ANOVA are numerous and keeping them organized is important. The **ANOVA summary table** is commonly used for this purpose, and provides a standardized format within which the results of the ANOVA are presented. The ANOVA summary table lists computed values of the sums of squares, degrees of freedom, mean squares, and F. Look ahead to Table 8.2 in Box 8.1 for an example of an ANOVA summary table that organizes the computations required by the ANOVA.

THE SAMPLING DISTRIBUTION OF *F*

The **sampling distribution of *F*** is the frequency distribution of values of F computed for all possible pairs, triplets, quadruplets, quintuplets, or other sized sets of samples drawn from a single population of identically treated cases. Since each value of F in this distribution is based upon a set of samples that have been treated identically, the F distribution indicates the relative likelihood of seeing any particular value of F in a set of identically treated samples. The sampling distribution of F is depicted in Figure 8.3. As shown there, the values of F computed from one set of samples to the next vary somewhat. This is because of sampling error. Values as low as 0 occur when all sample means are identical, so that between-group variance ($MS_{between}$) is zero. The most frequently occurring value of F in the sampling distribution is 1, resulting from equal between- and within-group variances. This is just what one would expect, since the samples are being drawn from a population in which all cases have been treated identically. There are no treatment differences from one sample to the next to cause between-group variance to exceed within-group variance. Of course, high values of F become increasingly unlikely in the sampling distribution of F since these high values

Figure 8.3

The sampling distribution of *F*.

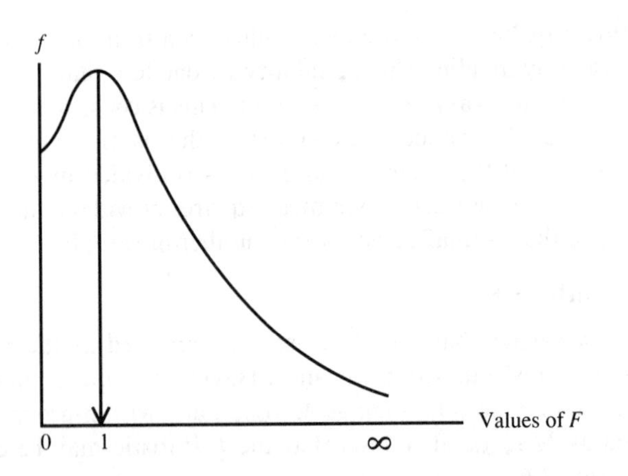

occur only when sample means differ substantially, an unlikely (but not impossible) event when all samples receive identical treatment.

Although Figure 8.3 portrays the general form of the *F* distribution, the specific shape will vary depending upon a number of factors, including sample sizes and the number of samples comprising each set. These variations in shape are described in Appendix G: Critical Values of *F*. Values found within this table mark off the upper 5% and 1% tails for significance tests involving the .05 and .01 levels of significance. The table is entered using between-group degrees of freedom (listed across the top of the table as "degrees of freedom for numerator") and within-group degrees of freedom (listed down the left-hand side of the table as "degrees of freedom for denominator"). For example, for $df_{\text{between}} = 2$ and $df_{within} = 27$, the tabled critical values of F are 3.35 (marking the upper 5% of the distribution) and 5.49 (marking the upper 1% tail).

RATIONALE OF THE ONE-WAY ANOVA

As a significance test, the one-way ANOVA follows the same logic that we have examined for other significance tests. Box 8.1 provides a concrete example of a one-way ANOVA to accompany the more general discussion that follows.

Step 1: The Null and Alternative Hypotheses

The null hypothesis (H_0) explains any differences observed between the means of two or more groups in a one-way ANOVA design as being due to sampling error. The differences are sufficiently small as to be fairly common when samples are drawn from a single population of identically treated cases. The alternative hypothesis (H_1) attributes the observed differences between group means to differences in treatments received by the groups. According to the alternative hypothesis, the differences observed between group means are too large to be likely if the groups were all treated identically. Instead, then, it is more likely that the groups received different treatments that produced the observed differences in means.

Step 2: The Test Statistic

The F statistic, computed according to Equations 8.1–8.6, serves as the test statistic in one-way ANOVA. As a test statistic for comparisons of two or more sample means, the value of F increases as treatment effects increase (i.e., as the differences between group means increase). The F statistic thus indicates how much the obtained between-group differences deviate from what would be expected if there were no treatment effects acting to separate the group means.

Step 3: Determining the Probability of the Test Statistic

The probability of a given value of F occurring when all samples have been drawn from a single population of identically treated cases is determined from the Table of Critical Values of F (Appendix G). If the obtained value of F meets or exceeds the tabled value, it means that the probability is less than .05 (or .01, depending upon which significance level has been selected) that an F of the obtained size would be obtained from a set of samples drawn from a single population. Under these circumstances, the null hypothesis would be rejected and the obtained F would be considered statistically significant. On the other hand, if the obtained value of F is less than the tabled critical value, it is concluded that the probability is fairly high ($p > .05$) that the obtained F would occur in a collection of samples drawn from a single population. That is, the observed differences in sample means have a relatively high probability of resulting from sampling error and should not be considered statistically significant.

INTERPRETING A SIGNIFICANT *F*

Finding a statistically significant F in an ANOVA tells us only that somewhere in the data there exists a statistically significant difference. This leaves some questions unanswered, though. First, which means differ? This is a question that is answered by data snooping with **post hoc** and a **priori comparison procedures.** Second, is the statistical significance that has been identified *practically* significant? How *strong* is the treatment effect?

Post Hoc Comparisons

Once a significant F has revealed the presence of one or more significant differences between the group means being compared, the usual next step is to identify which of these differences produced the significant F. This is often accomplished using post hoc comparisons, so named because these procedures are appropriate only after a significant F has been obtained. **Tukey's HSD** (Honestly Significant Difference) and the **Scheffé test** are two widely-used post hoc comparison procedures that will be presented here.[1]

Tukey's HSD. Tukey's HSD test is used in making all possible pairwise comparisons between group means after a significant F has indicated that one or more significant differences exist. A difference between any two means may be considered statistically significant at the selected level of significance if the obtained difference equals or exceeds HSD computed according to Equation 8.7.

BOX 8.1

ONE-WAY ANOVA

Shown in Table 8.1 are data from 30 patrons of Ba-Ba-Lu's. The management of Ba-Ba-Lu's has decided to see if the saltiness of their appetizers can be adjusted to increase the number of drinks purchased by Ba-Ba-Lusers during the course of an evening's revelry. Three sections of the club are targeted to receive appetizers that are of low, medium, or high saltiness, the three levels of the independent variable. The number of drinks ordered by 10 customers seated in each of these three areas is recorded as the dependent variable. A one-way ANOVA is used to evaluate the statistical significance of the observed differences in group means.

TABLE 8.1 Appetizer Saltiness and Number of Drinks Ordered

Group 1 (low salt)	Group 2 (medium salt)	Group 3 (high salt)
2	3	3
3	4	1
1	4	2
1	5	2
2	6	3
2	4	1
1	3	1
2	2	2
2	4	1
4	4	2

$n_1 = 10 \quad n_2 = 10 \quad n_3 = 10 \quad N = 30$

$\bar{X}_1 = 2.00 \quad \bar{X}_2 = 3.90 \quad \bar{X}_3 = 1.80 \quad \bar{X}_G = 2.57$

Number of drinks ordered by 30 patrons of Ba-Ba-Lu's who received either appetizres of low salt content (Group 1), medium salt content (Group 2), or high salt content (Group 3).

Step 1: ***The Null and Alternative Hypotheses***

H_0 : The observed between-group differences are small enough to attribute to sampling error. Three groups treated identically would be likely to show as much difference in their means as is seen here.

H_1 : The observed differences are too large to be attributed to sampling error. It is unlikely that three identically-treated groups would show differences this large. Thus, the three groups probably were not treated identically; that is, the treatments they received produced reliable differences in their means.

Step 2: ***The Test Statistic***

The test statistic F is computed according to Equations 8.1–8.6.

SS_{within}

EQUATION 8.1

$$SS_{within} = \sum_{i=1}^{n_1} (X_i - \bar{X}_1)^2 + \sum_{i=1}^{n_2} (X_i - \bar{X}_2)^2 + \ldots + \sum_{i=1}^{n_k} (X_i - \bar{X}_k)^2$$

$$= (2-2)^2 + (3-2)^2 + \ldots + (4-2)^2 + (3-3.9)^2 + (4-3.9)^2 + \ldots + (4-3.9)^2 + (3-1.8)^2 + (1-1.8)^2 + \ldots + (2-1.8)^2$$

$$= 24.5$$

BOX 8.1—*continued*

$SS_{between}$

EQUATION 8.2

$$SS_{between} = (\overline{X}_1 - \overline{X}_G)^2 (n_1) + (\overline{X}_2 - \overline{X}_G)^2 (n_2) + \ldots + (\overline{X}_k - \overline{X}_G)^2 (n_k)$$
$$= (2 - 2.57)^2 (10) + (3.9 - 2.57)^2 (10) + (1.8 - 2.57)^2 (10)$$
$$= 26.87$$

SS_{total}

EQUATION 8.3

$$SS_{total} = \sum_{i=1}^{N} (X_i - \overline{X}_G)^2$$
$$= (2 - 2.57)^2 + (3 - 2.57)^2 + \ldots + (2 - 2.57)^2$$
$$= 51.37$$

Notice, as a computational check, that SS_{total} computed according to Equation 8.3 equals SS_{total} computed as $SS_{within} + SS_{between} = 24.5 + 26.87 = 51.37$.

MS_{within}

EQUATION 8.4

$$MS_{within} = \frac{SS_{within}}{df_{within}}$$
$$\text{where, } df_{within} = N - k$$
$$= \frac{24.5}{30 - 3}$$
$$= .91$$

$MS_{between}$

EQUATION 8.5

$$MS_{between} = \frac{SS_{between}}{df_{between}}$$
$$\text{where, } df_{between} = k - 1$$
$$= \frac{26.87}{3 - 1}$$
$$= 13.44$$

F

EQUATION 8.6

$$F = \frac{MS_{between}}{MS_{within}}$$
$$= \frac{13.44}{.91}$$
$$= 14.77$$

These computations are organized in standard format in the ANOVA summary table presented as Table 8.2.

TABLE 8.2 ANOVA Summary Table

Source	*SS*	*df*	*MS*	*F*
Between-Group	26.87	2	13.44	14.77
Within-Group	24.50	27	.91	
Total	51.37	29		

Step 3: ***Determining the Probability of the Test Statistic***

For $df_{between} = 2$ and $df_{within} = 27$, the critical value of F marking the upper 1% of the sampling distribution of F is 5.49. Our obtained value of $F = 14.77$ exceeds this critical value, and thus, has a probability of less than .01 of occurring in samples that received identical treatment. It is most probable, then, that these three samples have not been treated identically. We reject the null hypothesis and declare our obtained value of F to be significant at the .01 level.

BOX 8.2

THE TUKEY HSD POST HOC COMPARISON

It was discovered from the one-way ANOVA computed in Box 8.1 that Ba-Ba-Lusers imbibed at significantly different levels depending on how salty their appetizers were. Here, we will use the Tukey HSD test to compare group means in determining which differences produced the significant F in our one-way ANOVA.

First, HSD is computed according to Equation 8.7:

$$HSD = q_{(\alpha,\ df_{within},\ k)} \sqrt{\frac{MS_{within}}{n}}$$

$$= q_{(.05,\ 27,\ 3)} \sqrt{\frac{MS_{within}}{n}}$$

$$= 3.53 \sqrt{\frac{.91}{10}}$$

$$= 1.06$$

The value of q in this equation was found in Appendix H: Percentage Points of the Studentized Range Statistic by entering the table with the values of α (the desired level of significance) = .05, df_{within} from the significant ANOVA = $N - k = 27$, and the number of groups in the significant ANOVA, $k = 3$. Any between-group differences that exceed HSD = 1.06 are significant at the .05 level of significance. These differences are listed below.

$$\overline{X}_1 \text{ vs. } \overline{X}_2 = 2.00 - 3.90 = 1.90^*$$
$$\overline{X}_1 \text{ vs. } \overline{X}_3 = 2.00 - 1.80 = .20$$
$$\overline{X}_2 \text{ vs. } \overline{X}_3 = 3.90 - 1.80 = 2.10^*$$
$$^*p < .05$$

We see from this series of comparisons that Group 2 (medium salt) consumed more drinks than either Group 1 (low salt) or Group 3 (high salt). Groups 1 and 3 did not differ significantly in the number of drinks consumed. This pattern of differences suggests that increasing the saltiness of appetizers slightly, to the medium saltiness level received by Group 2, can increase patrons' drink orders. Too much salt (Group 3), though, seems to be distasteful to patrons who leave in search of more flavorful appetizers to be found elsewhere.

EQUATION 8.7

$$HSD = q_{(\alpha,\ df_{within},\ k)} \sqrt{\frac{MS_{within}}{n}}$$

where,

q	= value obtained from Appendix H (Percentage Points of the Studentized Range Statistic)
α	= the desired significance level of the comparison
df_{within}	= within-group degrees of freedom from the ANOVA
k	= the number of groups in the significant ANOVA
MS_{within}	= within-group mean squares from the ANOVA
n	= the value of the smallest group in the ANOVA

Box 8.2 provides an example of how Tukey's HSD is used to explore data following a significant ANOVA.

Scheffé Test. The Scheffé test is another widely used post hoc comparison procedure. Though less powerful than the Tukey HSD test for pairwise comparisons, the Scheffé test is more generally useful. This is because the Scheffé test can be used in comparing not just pairs of means, but other combinations as well. For example, in a three-group study comparing groups given aspirin, acetaminophen, and an inert placebo, a researcher might wish to compare the combined (i.e., averaged) level of pain relief reported by the two groups given active drugs against that of the placebo control group. It would not be appropriate to use the Tukey HSD in this case, but the Scheffé test could be used.

The Scheffé test begins by computing the value C, the "comparison," as expressed in Equation 8.8.

EQUATION 8.8

$$C = w_1\bar{X}_1 + w_2\bar{X}_2 + \ldots + w_k\bar{X}_k$$

where,

k = the number of groups in the ANOVA
$w_1 - w_k$ = weights applied to the k group means
$\bar{X}_1 - \bar{X}_k$ = means of the k groups

In this equation, weights w_1 through w_k may take on any values as long as the sum of the weights is zero:

$$\sum_{i=1}^{k} w_i = 0$$

Thus, some means must receive positive weights while others receive negative weights. Those means not to be included in a given comparison are weighted zero. Those means that are to be grouped together are given weights of the same sign (positive or negative) and magnitude.

Returning to the example begun above, if we wished to compare the pain relief levels of the aspirin and acetaminophen groups combined ($\bar{X}_1$ and $\bar{X}_2$, respectively) against the pain relief levels reported by the placebo control group ($\bar{X}_3$), the comparison might take any of the following forms:

$$C = 1\bar{X}_1 + 1\bar{X}_2 - 2\bar{X}_3$$

or

$$C = .5\bar{X}_1 + .5\bar{X}_2 - 1\bar{X}_3$$

or

$$C = -4\bar{X}_1 - 4\bar{X}_2 + 8\bar{X}_3$$

Any other weights will do as well, so long as means to be combined have weights of the same sign (positive or negative) and magnitude, and the sum of the weights is zero.

If we wished to compare just the aspirin group ($\bar{X}_1$) against the placebo control group ($\bar{X}_3$) in a pairwise comparison, C could be computed in any of a variety of ways, including the following:

$$C = 1\bar{X}_1 + 0\bar{X}_2 - 1\bar{X}_3$$

or

$$C = -1\bar{X}_1 + 0\bar{X}_2 + 1\bar{X}_3$$

or

$$C = 10\bar{X}_1 + 0\bar{X}_2 - 10\bar{X}_3$$

In all of these comparisons, the group mean not involved ($\bar{X}_2$ in this example) is weighted zero, means in groups being compared are weighted by values having opposite signs, and the sum of the weights is zero.

Once the comparison, C, has been computed according to Equation 8.8, the Scheffé test is computed in Equation 8.9.

EQUATION 8.9

$$t_{obtained} = \frac{C}{\sqrt{MS_{within}\left(\frac{w_1^2}{n_1} + \frac{w_2^2}{n_2} + \ldots + \frac{w_k^2}{n_k}\right)}}$$

where,

C = the comparison value computed according to Equation 8.8
MS_{within} = within-group mean square value from the ANOVA
$w_1 - w_k$ = weights used in computing the comparison, C
$n_1 - n_k$ = samples sizes of the k groups in the ANOVA
k = the number of groups in the ANOVA

Finally, the critical value of t ($t_{critical}$), which the obtained value of t must meet or exceed in order for the comparison to be statistically significant, is computed in Equation 8.10.

EQUATION 8.10

$$t_{critical} = \sqrt{(k - 1)F_{critical\ (\alpha,\ df_{between},\ df_{within})}}$$

where,

k = the number of groups in the ANOVA
$F_{critical}$ = the tabled value of F for the selected significance level (α), $df_{between}$, and df_{within} from the ANOVA

If $t_{obtained}$ meets or exceeds $t_{critical}$, the Scheffé comparison is statistically significant. Box 8.3 illustrates the use of the Scheffé test in making post hoc comparisons.

Error Rates in Post Hoc Comparisons. You may have wondered why it is acceptable to compute a series of post hoc comparisons after a significant F has been obtained when, at the beginning of this chapter, it was explained that computing a series of comparisons is inadvisable because of the inflated error rates

BOX 8.3

THE SCHEFFÉ POST HOC COMPARISON

Differences between group means explored in Box 8.2 with the Tukey HSD test are examined again here to illustrate the use of the Scheffé test.

The computation of the comparison value (C) from Equation 8.8 depends upon the group means to be compared. Let us make the following two comparisons: $\bar{X}_1$ vs. $\bar{X}_3$ and ($\bar{X}_1$ & $\bar{X}_3$) vs. $\bar{X}_2$.

$\bar{X}_1$ *vs.* $\bar{X}_3$

First, we compute C according to Equation 8.8:

$$\begin{aligned} C &= w_1\bar{X}_1 + w_2\bar{X}_2 + \ . \ . \ . + w_k\bar{X}_k \\ &= 1(\bar{X}_1) + 0(\bar{X}_2) - 1(\bar{X}_3) \\ &= 1(2.0) + 0(3.9) - 1(1.8) \\ &= .2 \end{aligned}$$

Notice how the weights w_1 through w_3 sum to zero and how $\bar{X}_2$, which is excluded from the comparison, is weighted zero. Finally, notice how the means being compared ($\bar{X}_1$ and $\bar{X}_3$) are given weights of opposite signs.

Next, we compute $t_{obtained}$ according to Equation 8.9.

$$\begin{aligned} t_{obtained} &= \frac{C}{\sqrt{MS_{within}\left(\frac{w_1^2}{n_1} + \frac{w_2^2}{n_2} + \ . \ . \ . + \frac{w_k^2}{n_k}\right)}} \\ &= \frac{.2}{\sqrt{.91\left(\frac{1^2}{10} + \frac{0^2}{10} + \frac{-1^2}{10}\right)}} \\ &= .47 \end{aligned}$$

Finally, we compute $t_{critical}$ according to Equation 8.10.

$$\begin{aligned} t_{critical} &= \sqrt{(k - 1)F_{critical\ (\alpha,\ df_{between},\ df_{within})}} \\ &= \sqrt{(3 - 1)F_{critical\ (.05,\ 2,\ 27)}} \\ &= \sqrt{(2)3.35} \\ &= 2.59 \end{aligned}$$

Since, in this comparison, the absolute value of $t_{obtained} = .47$ fails to meet or exceed the value of $t_{critical} = 2.59$, the comparison is found to be nonsignificant.

($\bar{X}_1$ & $\bar{X}_3$) *vs.* $\bar{X}_2$)

In this second comparison we will compare the combined means of Groups 1 and 3 against the mean of Group 2. As above, we first compute C.

$$\begin{aligned} C &= w_1\bar{X}_1 + w_2\bar{X}_2 + \ . \ . \ . + w_k\bar{X}_k \\ &= .5(2.0) - 1(3.9) + .5(1.8) \\ &= -2.0 \end{aligned}$$

Notice how the weights sum to zero, how means being combined are given weights that are of the same sign, and how means being compared are given weights that are of opposite signs.

Next, $t_{obtained}$ is computed.

$$\begin{aligned} t_{obtained} &= \frac{C}{\sqrt{MS_{within}\left(\frac{w_1^2}{n_1} + \frac{w_2^2}{n_2} + \ . \ . \ . + \frac{w_k^2}{n_k}\right)}} \\ &= \frac{-2.0}{\sqrt{.91\left(\frac{.5^2}{10} + \frac{-1^2}{10} + \frac{.5^2}{10}\right)}} \\ &= -5.41 \end{aligned}$$

Finally, we need to know the value of $t_{critical}$. We will discover from an examination of Equation 8.10 that $t_{critical}$ does not vary as a function of which specific means or combinations of means are being compared. In a series of Scheffé comparisons, then, $t_{critical}$ only needs to be computed once; the same value is used for all comparisons. In the present example, $t_{critical}$ remains equal to 2.59.

Since, in this comparison, the absolute value of $t_{obtained} = 5.41$ exceeds $t_{critical} = 2.59$, the comparison is found to be statistically significant. The means of Groups 1 and 3, considered together, are significantly lower than the mean of Group 2 at the .05 level of significance. In other words, Ba-Ba-Lusers who received appetizers at low or high saltiness levels drank less, as a group, than did patrons who received appetizers of medium saltiness.

that result. The answer to this apparent contradiction is that while standard significance tests set the probability of Type I error at the desired level for each test (e.g., .05, .01), post hoc comparisons set the probability of Type I error at the chosen level for the entire set of post hoc comparisons.

A Priori (Planned) Comparisons

Although the post hoc comparison procedures described in the preceding section give us considerable flexibility in ferreting out the source of a significant F test, these procedures are not particularly powerful. A more powerful alternative method of evaluating differences between two or more means is the method of **a priori** or **planned comparisons.** The enhanced power that planned comparisons offer, though, must be purchased.

First, planned comparisons may be used only in testing differences that were predicted before the data were collected. They are not appropriate in after-the-fact data exploration. Planned comparisons are generally useful whenever there are strong theoretical and/or empirical reasons to anticipate that two or more means will differ. To return to an earlier example, we would anticipate that samples given aspirin or acetaminophen would both show reduced pain relative to a placebo control group. Planned comparisons between these groups would be justified by this a priori expectation.

The second restriction placed on planned comparisons is that only independent comparisons may be made. Each planned comparison must provide unique, nonoverlapping information. More will be said later about the independence of planned comparisons.

Computing Planned Comparisons. Planned comparisons begin with the computation of the value C, the comparison, exactly as described previously (Equation 8.8):

$$C = w_1\bar{X}_1 + w_2\bar{X}_2 + \ . \ . \ . \ + w_k\bar{X}_k$$

As before, weights $w_1 - w_k$ may take on any values as long as the sum of the weights is zero. Means that are not to be included in the comparison are weighted zero. Means that are to be combined are given weights of the same sign (positive or negative).

In addition, planned comparisons must be computed in a manner that makes each comparison independent of the next, such that the outcome of one comparison provides no information whatsoever concerning the outcome of other comparisons. In a one-way ANOVA design involving k means, there are $k - 1$ independent comparisons. Two comparisons are independent if the sum of the cross products of their corresponding weights is zero.

EQUATION 8.11

$$\sum_{i=1}^{k} w_{1i}w_{2i} = 0$$

where,

w_{1i} = weights assigned to each of k group means in forming the first comparison

w_{2i} = weights assigned to each of k group means in forming the second comparison

Take the following two comparisons as an example:

$$C_1 = 1\overline{X}_1 - .5\overline{X}_2 - .5\overline{X}_3$$
$$C_2 = 0\overline{X}_1 + 1\overline{X}_2 - 1\overline{X}_3$$

The first comparison, C_1 compares the combined means of Groups 2 and 3 against the mean of Group 1. The second, C_2, compares Groups 2 and 3. These comparisons are independent because the sum of the cross-products of the corresponding weights is equal to zero:

$$\sum_{i=1}^{k} w_{1i}w_{2i} = (1)(0) + (-.5)(1) + (-.5)(-1) = 0$$

The following two comparisons, though, are *not* independent:

$$C_1 = 1\overline{X}_1 + 0\overline{X}_2 - 1\overline{X}_3$$
$$C_2 = 0\overline{X}_1 + 1\overline{X}_2 - 1\overline{X}_3$$

The first comparison, C_1, compares Groups 1 and 3. The second, C_2, compares Groups 2 and 3. These comparisons are not independent because the sum of the corresponding cross-products does not equal zero:

$$\sum_{i=1}^{k} w_{1i}w_{2i} = (1)(0) + (0)(1) + (-1)(-1) = 1$$

Assessing the Statistical Significance of Planned Comparisons. Once a comparison, C, has been computed, it is tested for significance using the t statistic computed according to Equation 8.9. If $t_{obtained}$ meets or exceeds the critical value of t listed in Appendix B (Critical Values of t) for $df = N - k$ and the desired level of significance, the comparison is considered statistically significant. Notice that the significance test for planned comparisons is identical to the test for post hoc comparisons, except that planned comparisons do not require that $t_{critical}$ be computed.

Practical vs. Statistical Significance

We have seen before that statistical and practical significance are not always the same thing. In one-way ANOVA, the F test is influenced not only by the magnitude of the treatment effect, but also by sample sizes and data variability. If the sample sizes are large and variability within groups is low, even a minuscule treatment effect may be found to be statistically significant. While statistical significance can be assessed objectively, one must rely upon common sense to evaluate practical significance.

BOX 8.4

OMEGA-SQUARE

We found in Box 8.1 that the saltiness of appetizers had a statistically significant effect on the amount of libation consumed by the patrons of Ba-Ba-Lu's. In Boxes 8.2 and 8.3 we explored the sources of this significant one-way ANOVA with Tukey's HSD and Scheffé's post hoc comparison procedures. Here, we will compute the statistic omega-square (ω^2) to measure the strength of the relationship between appetizer saltiness and number of drinks consumed.

According to Equation 8.12:

$$\omega^2 = \frac{SS_{between} - (k-1)MS_{within}}{SS_{total} + MS_{within}}$$

$$= \frac{26.87 - (3-1)\,.91}{51.37 + .91}$$

$$= .48$$

In other words, 48% of the total variability in the number of drinks consumed by Ba-Ba-Lusers can be attributed to differences in the saltiness of the appetizers served. This means that 52% of the variability in drinking behavior is a consequence of other factors. We can conclude that appetizer saltiness exerts a fairly strong influence on drinking.

Assessing practical significance begins by examining the sizes of the differences between group means. Do the means differ enough to make a real difference? Or, are the differences observed insignificant in terms of practical consequences?

Omega-Square. It also helps in evaluating the practical significance of a statistically significant ANOVA to have some information about the strength of the treatment effect. The significant F indicates only that the observed pattern of differences between means would probably be seen again in a replication of the research. In other words, the F test tells us either that there is or there is not a treatment effect that is reliable, but F does not provide a directly interpretable indication of how strong the treatment effect is. Such a measure of treatment effect strength is given by the statistic **omega-square,** abbreviated ω^2, and computed according to Equation 8.12.

EQUATION 8.12

$$\omega^2 = \frac{SS_{between} - (k-1)MS_{within}}{SS_{total} + MS_{within}}$$

Omega-square, the computation of which is illustrated in Box 8.4, can vary in value from 0 to 1, with 0 indicating no treatment effect whatsoever, and 1 indicating that all of the variability in the scores can be attributed to the different levels of the independent variable being examined. Omega-square thus tells us about the strength of the relationship between an independent variable and dependent variable in much the same manner that the squared correlation (chapter 10) describes the strength of the relationship between two variables.

SUMMARY

This chapter introduces concepts fundamental to analysis of variance (ANOVA). One-way ANOVA is useful in comparing two or more group means on an interval or ratio scale dependent variable. These groups may have received treatments that differ qualitatively or quantitatively. Differences between group means are reflected in the test statistic *F,* computed as the ratio of between-group variance to within-group variance. Between-group variance refers to variability from one group mean to the next, and is the result of individual differences, measurement error, and the different treatments received by different groups (i.e., treatment effects). Between-group variance is measured by the sum of squares between groups and by the mean squares between groups. Within-group variance refers to variability in the data of any given group, and is the result of individual differences and measurement error. Within-group variance is measured by the sum of squares within groups and by the mean squares within groups. As treatment effects grow stronger, the ratio of between-group variance to within-group variance, *F,* grows larger. In evaluating the statistical significance of between-group differences, the obtained value of *F* is compared to the sampling distribution of *F.* This sampling distribution is a frequency distribution of values of the *F* statistic computed on all possible sets of two, three, or more samples drawn from a population of identically treated cases. Thus, the sampling distribution of *F* gives the probability of obtaining a given value of *F* under circumstances in which all samples in the set have received identical treatment. If an obtained value of *F* is found to occur infrequently in the sampling distribution of *F,* it follows that the obtained *F* was probably produced by a set of samples which were not treated identically. In such a case, a significant treatment effect is declared, that is, the sample means are seen as differing significantly. Once a significant *F* test reveals that two or more sample means differ significantly, post hoc comparison procedures like Tukey's HSD and Scheffé's test are used to identify the source or sources of that significance. Planned comparisons are also described, which enable us to assess the statistical significance of between-group differences that have been predicted in advance of data collection. Omega-square is a statistic used to obtain a clearer picture of the strength of the treatment effect that is revealed by a significant *F.*

NOTE

1. The Newman-Keuls and Duncan Multiple Range tests are two other widely used post hoc comparison procedures (Kirk, 1968). Less conservative than the Tukey or Scheffé procedures, Keppel (1982) states that "The collective evidence seems to support the conclusion that the Tukey test is preferred over (the Newman-Keuls and Duncan) tests" (p. 157).

CHAPTER 9

Significant Differences: Factorial Analysis of Variance

We learned in the preceding chapter how to use one-way ANOVA in testing the significance of differences between two or more groups that represent the different levels of a single independent variable. **Factorial analysis of variance** procedures enable us to assess the separate and combined effects of *two or more* independent variables on a dependent variable of interest. These procedures are often used in analyzing data gathered in laboratory settings where the researcher can actively manipulate several independent variables simultaneously. For instance, a researcher involved in evaluating treatments for Alzheimer's disease might be interested in assessing simultaneously the effects of two independent variables: chemotherapy (drug vs. no-drug) and memory enhancement training (training vs. no-training). A factorial ANOVA would answer three questions. First, is chemotherapy an effective treatment for Alzheimer's? Second, is memory enhancement training an effective treatment for Alzheimer's? Third, are some combinations of chemotherapy and memory enhancement training (e.g., drug + training or drug + no-training) more effective than other combinations (e.g., no-drug + training or no-drug + no-training)?

THE DATA FOR FACTORIAL ANOVA

In the simplest factorial experiments, the experimenter "fully crosses" all levels of two or more independent variables, called **factors** in the terminology of factorial ANOVA. That is, the experimenter sets up all possible combinations of levels of the two or more independent variables under consideration. The data obtained using such a design are often organized in a data matrix like the one represented in Table 9.1. In this table, rows represent the two levels (a_1 and a_2) of the first factor (Factor A), and columns represent the two levels (b_1 and b_2) of a second factor (Factor B). Each cell within the matrix represents a unique combination of the levels of the two factors. Notice the notation used in Table 9.1 to represent cell, row, and column means, and the grand mean.

Factorial ANOVA is based on many of the same assumptions that were listed for one-way ANOVA in the preceding chapter. The various levels of the factors in factorial ANOVA may differ either qualitatively (e.g., the variable of gender with levels of male and female) or quantitatively (e.g., several dosages of an experiment drug). Independent variables analyzed in the factorial design may include those that vary naturally (e.g., gender, religion), as well as those that are

TABLE 9.1 Data Matrix Used to Organize Data in a Factorial ANOVA Design

		Factor B		
		b_1	b_2	
Factor A	a_1	$\bar{X}_{a_1b_1}$	$\bar{X}_{a_1b_2}$	$\bar{X}_{a_1}$
	a_2	$\bar{X}_{a_2b_1}$	$\bar{X}_{a_2b_2}$	$\bar{X}_{a_2}$
		$\bar{X}_{b_1}$	$\bar{X}_{b_2}$	$\bar{X}_G$

controlled by the experimenter (e.g., drug dosage, level of noise exposure). The dependent variable in the factorial ANOVA must always be a continuous variable measured at the interval or ratio scale of measurement. It is also assumed that data from all groups (i.e., cells) are normally distributed and that the groups show approximately equal variances. Finally, if sample sizes in each cell of the factorial design are approximately equal and fairly large (at least 10 cases per cell), the factorial ANOVA is fairly resistant to violations of the assumptions of homogeneous variances and normal distributions.

TYPES OF FACTORIAL ANOVAS

Factorial designs are generally described according to how many factors are being investigated, and how many levels are included within each factor. A study in Alzheimer's patients of the effects of chemotherapy (drug vs. no-drug) and memory enhancement training (training vs. no-training) on cognitive functioning (the dependent variable) would be labeled a 2 × 2 ("two by two") factorial design. A study of the effects of number of years spent teaching (5, 10, 15, over 15), type of school (public vs. private), and gender (male vs. female) on emotional stability (the dependent variable) would be labeled a 4 × 2 × 2 factorial design.

Factorial ANOVAs are also labeled according to the number of different treatment combinations to which any given case is exposed. In a **completely randomized factorial** design, any given case appears in one and only one cell of the data matrix. Each case is exposed to only one treatment combination. It is also possible, though, for a case to be exposed to all levels of one or more factors. When a case appears in every cell of the matrix, the design is called a **repeated-measures** or **randomized block factorial** design. When a case is exposed to all levels of one or more factors, but only one level of one or more other factors, the design is called a **split-plot factorial.** Factorial designs are called **fixed effects** models if the levels of each factor represent all levels of interest to the experimenter. If these levels have been randomly sampled from a larger group of levels to which the experimenter intends to generalize his or her findings, the ANOVA is called a **random effects** model. If some factors include all levels of interest and other factors include only a random sampling of the levels of interest, we have a **mixed effects** model. Finally, there are nonparametric versions of the factorial ANOVAs that relax the assumptions made about the dependent variable.

It quickly becomes apparent that a limited treatment of factorial ANOVAs must exclude some material. In this chapter, we will examine the most basic factorial ANOVA, the completely randomized, two-factor, fixed effects model, with equal sample sizes. The principles underlying this ANOVA will provide a foundation for a broader understanding of factorial ANOVA. The reader who hopes to achieve this more complete understanding of factorial ANOVA designs, who intends to use one of the more complex designs, or whose data include different numbers of cases in each cell should consult one of the many good treatments of ANOVA designs (e.g., Keppel, 1983; Lindman, 1974; Kirk, 1968).

FACTORIAL ANOVA VS. MULTIPLE ONE-WAY ANOVAS

Given that the purpose of factorial ANOVA is to assess the effects of two or more factors on some dependent variable, the question becomes, why not just run two (or more) one-way ANOVAs, one for each factor? There are two compelling advantages of factorial ANOVA over multiple one-way ANOVAs. First, factorial ANOVA does not just help us to assess the effects of each of the factors considered singly, called **main effects.** Factorial ANOVA also lets us examine the unique effects of various treatment combinations. This is called the analysis of **interaction effects.** Second, factorial ANOVA allows us to statistically control error variance by including as a factor in the design any nuisance variables that contribute to variability in the dependent variable. These applications of factorial ANOVA are discussed next.

Interaction Effects

Factorial ANOVA not only determines if each factor considered singly affects the dependent variable (main effects), but also the degree to which the effects of one factor are conditional upon or mediated by the level of the other factor(s) under consideration. These conditional effects are the interaction effects referred to previously.

Interaction effects are most easily understood by examining graphs of the data matrix cell means. Figure 9.1 provides some examples of these graphs. In each graph, levels of Factor A are represented on the abscissa, the ordinate represents scores on the dependent variable, and each line in the graph represents one of the levels of Factor B. (It is equally acceptable to represent Factor B on the abscissa and Factor A as lines. We should prepare the graph in whatever way enhances its interpretability.) Plotted in each graph are means on the dependent variable for each treatment combination, or cell.

Figure 9.1

Graphs of cell means are useful in interpreting outcomes of factorial ANOVAs.

(a) A disordinal interaction effect between Factor A (type of employee; a_1= smoker, a_2= nonsmoker) and Factor B (organization's smoking policy; b_1= smoking allowed; b_2= no smoking allowed).

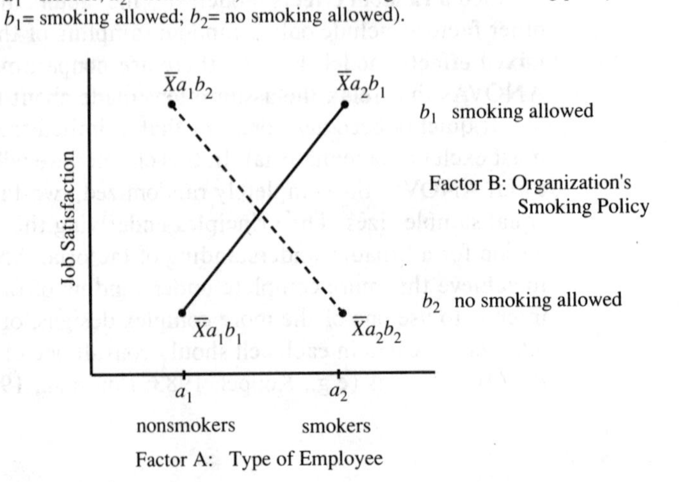

Figure 9.1—*continued*

(b) An ordinal interaction effect between Factor A (type of student; a_1= high anxiety; a_2= low anxiety) and Factor B (anxiety treatment; b_1= treated; b_2= no-treatment). This graph also shows main effects of Factor A and Factor B.

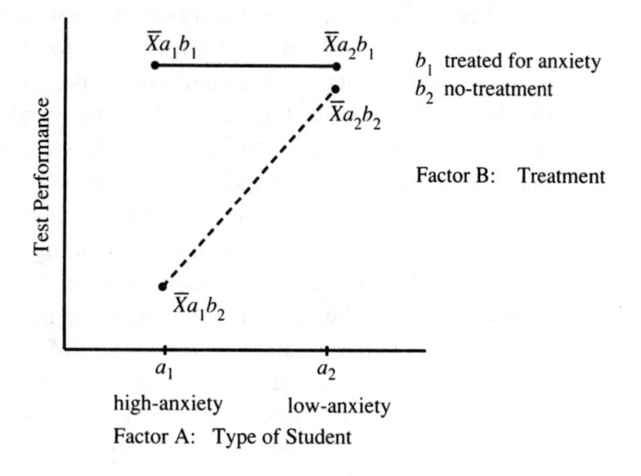

(c) No interaction effect. Both Factors A and B show main effects.

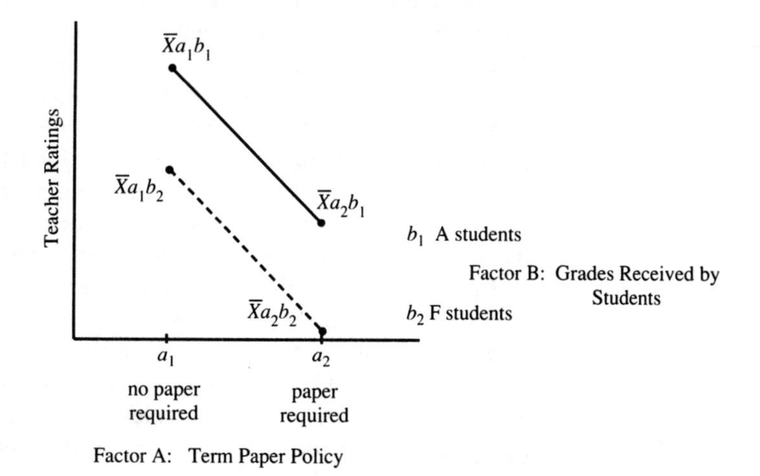

An interaction effect is suggested any time the lines in graphs like these are nonparallel. Figure 9.1a illustrates a **disordinal interaction,** one in which the lines cross. This type of interaction effect tells us that the effect of Factor A is reversed depending upon which level of Factor B is under consideration, and vice versa. In Figure 9.1a, the ordinate represents the dependent variable of job satisfaction. The abscissa represents Factor A, type of employee, with two levels: a_1 = non-smokers; a_2 = smokers. The two lines in the graph represent Factor B, the organization's smoking policy, with two levels: b_1 = smoking allowed; b_2 = no smoking allowed. This graph shows that the effect on job satisfaction of an organization's smoking policy depends on whether the employees are smokers or nonsmokers. Conversely, the job satisfaction levels of smokers and nonsmokers depend on the organization's smoking policy. Not surprisingly, smokers show higher levels of job satisfaction in organizations that allow smoking; nonsmokers show higher levels of job satisfaction in organizations that do not allow smoking.

Figure 9.1a also reveals that average levels of job satisfaction are approximately equal among smokers and nonsmokers if we combine the data across the two levels of Factor B. Put succinctly, this graph shows no main effect of Factor A, type of worker. Job satisfaction levels are also approximately equal in organizations that do allow smoking and in those that do not allow smoking when we combine the data across the two levels of Factor B. The graph shows no main effect of Factor B, the organization's smoking policy.

Figure 9.1b illustrates a second type of interaction effect, the **ordinal interaction,** in which the lines of the graph are nonparallel, but do not cross. From this graph we can see that the effectiveness of a treatment for test anxiety (Factor B) is conditional upon the type of student that receives this treatment (Factor A). Highly anxious students perform at higher levels when treated than when not treated. Students with low anxiety levels, though, are not affected by the treatment; they show equivalent levels of test performance whether treated or not.

Figure 9.1b also shows Factor A and B main effects. Average test performance is higher among low-anxiety than high-anxiety students. This is the Factor A main effect. Average test performance is higher among students who receive the treatment than among those who do not. This is the Factor B main effect.

In Figure 9.1c, the fact that the lines are parallel tells us that there is no interaction effect. However, both Factors A and B show main effects. Students rate teachers higher who do not require term papers—the Factor A main effect. Students who receive higher grades (A students) rate their teachers higher than do students who receive lower grades (F students)—the Facter B main effect.

In a factorial experiment, we can observe any combination of main and interaction effects. The graphs of Figure 9.1 illustrate only some of the possibilities. As more and more factors are added to the design, even interaction effects may be found to be conditional upon levels of some other factor. These **higher-order interactions** can become quite complex and can limit our ability to draw broad or general conclusions about the effects of the factors being investigated.

Control of Error Variance

In addition to enabling us to evaluate interaction effects, factorial ANOVAs have a second advantage over multiple one-way ANOVAs. By including as factors those nuisance variables that are known to influence the dependent variable, their influence on the dependent variable will be removed from the within-group variance (error variance) term. When within-group variance is reduced like this, the way is cleared for more powerful tests of the significance of factors that are of interest, since a smaller between-group variance term will be required to produce a significant *F* ratio when within-group variance is low.

PARTITIONING THE VARIANCE IN A FACTORIAL DESIGN

We saw in chapter 8 that the total variability in the data analyzed using one-way ANOVA is represented by the total sum of squares (SS_{total}). We partitioned or divided this total into two components: within-group variability, represented by the within-group sum of squares (SS_{within}), and between-group variability, represented by the between-group sum of squares ($SS_{between}$). The variability in data gathered in a factorial design may also be partitioned into several sources.

Total Sum of Squares

First, just as in one-way ANOVA, the total variability observed from one case to the next in the data of a factorial design is reflected in the total sum of squares (SS_{total}), computed according to Equation 9.1.

EQUATION 9.1

$$SS_{total} = \sum_{i=1}^{N} (X_i - \overline{X}_G)^2$$

where,

N = the total number of cases
X = scores on the dependent variable
$\overline{X}_G$ = the grand mean, or the mean of all the scores

In words, we subtract the grand mean from each score in the data matrix, square each difference, and sum these squared differences.

Within-Group Sum of Squares

Some of the total variability represented by SS_{total} is a result of measurement error and individual differences. This "error variability" as it is sometimes called can be estimated by examining the variability that occurs within the cells of the data matrix. Since every case within a cell has received the same treatment combination, the only explanation for variability seen from one case to the next within a cell is the action of measurement error and individual differences. We learned in chapter 8 that error variance is reflected in the value of the within-group sum of squares (SS_{within}). In the context of factorial ANOVA, SS_{within} is computed according to Equation 9.2.

EQUATION 9.2

$$\begin{aligned} SS_{within} = {} & \Sigma\,(X_{a_1b_1} - \overline{X}_{a_1b_1})^2 + \\ & \Sigma\,(X_{a_1b_2} - \overline{X}_{a_1b_2})^2 + \\ & \Sigma\,(X_{a_2b_1} - \overline{X}_{a_2b_1})^2 + \\ & \Sigma\,(X_{a_2b_2} - \overline{X}_{a_2b_2})^2 \end{aligned}$$

where,

$$X_{a_1b_1} - X_{a_2b_2} = \text{scores in cells } a_1b_1 \text{ through } a_2b_2$$
$$\overline{X}_{a_1b_1} - \overline{X}_{a_2b_2} = \text{cell means}$$

Expressed in words, Equation 9.2 directs us to subtract from each score in a given cell that cell's mean. Next we square these differences and sum them. Finally, we sum these sums across the cells of the data matrix to obtain SS_{within}.

Between-Group Sum of Squares

We saw in chapter 8 that variability from one group mean to the next is called between-group variability and that it reflects not only measurement error and individual differences, but also differences in the treatments received by the different groups. Between-group variability is also seen in factorial designs. Row means vary, column means vary, and cell means vary. This between-group variability is reflected in the between-group sum of squares ($SS_{between}$) computed according to Equation 9.3.

EQUATION 9.3

$$\begin{aligned} SS_{between} = {} & (\overline{X}_{a_1b_1} - \overline{X}_G)^2 N_{a_1b_1} + \\ & (\overline{X}_{a_1b_2} - \overline{X}_G)^2 N_{a_1b_2} + \\ & (\overline{X}_{a_2b_1} - \overline{X}_G)^2 N_{a_2b_1} + \\ & (\overline{X}_{a_2b_2} - \overline{X}_G)^2 N_{a_2b_2} \end{aligned}$$

where,

$$\overline{X}_{a_1b_1} - \overline{X}_{a_2b_2} = \text{cell means}$$
$$\overline{X}_G = \text{the grand mean}$$
$$N_{a_1b_1} - N_{a_2b_2} = \text{samples sizes within each cell}$$

In words, $SS_{between}$ is computed by subtracting the grand mean from each cell mean, squaring these differences, and multiplying each by the number of cases in the corresponding cell. Finally, these weighted squared differences are summed across the cells of the data matrix to yield $SS_{between}$.

Some of the between-group variability represented by $SS_{between}$ is a result of different groups (i.e., cells) receiving different levels of Factor A, some is due to their receiving different levels of Factor B, and some is due to their receiving different combinations of levels of Factors A and B. Our next step, then, is to partition $SS_{between}$ into these three sources.

Factor A Sum of Squares

The variability that occurs from one row mean to the next, or from one level of Factor A to the next, comprises one part of the overall between-group variability in the factorial ANOVA and is represented by the **Factor A sum of squares** (SS_A). This variability results from measurement error, individual differences, and differences in treatments received by cases occupying the different rows of the data matrix. We compute SS_A exactly as we computed $SS_{between}$ in chapter 8, using the data in the rows of the data matrix and ignoring the columns. Equation 9.4 summarizes this procedure.

EQUATION 9.4

$$SS_A = (\overline{X}_{a_1} - \overline{X}_G)^2 N_{a_1} + (\overline{X}_{a_2} - \overline{X}_G)^2 N_{a_2}$$

where,

$\overline{X}_{a_1}$ & $\overline{X}_{a_2}$ = row means for the first (a_1) and second (a_2) rows
$\overline{X}_G$ = the grand mean
N_{a_1} & N_{a_2} = number of cases occupying the first (a_1) and second (a_2) rows

In words, we subtract the grand mean from each row mean, square these differences, multiply each squared difference by the number of cases in the corresponding row, and sum these weighted squared differences to yield SS_A.

Factor B Sum of Squares

The variability that occurs from one column mean to the next, that is, from one level of Factor B to the next, comprises a second part of the overall between-group variability in a factorial design, and is represented by the **Factor B sum of squares** (SS_B). This variability results from measurement error, individual differences, and differences in treatments received by cases occupying different columns of the data matrix. SS_B is also computed exactly like $SS_{between}$ in chapter 8, using the data in the columns of the data matrix and ignoring the rows. Equation 9.5 summarizes this procedure.

EQUATION 9.5

$$SS_B = (\overline{X}_{b_1} - \overline{X}_G)^2 N_{b_1} + (\overline{X}_{b_2} - \overline{X}_G)^2 N_{b_2}$$

where,

$\overline{X}_{b_1}$ & $\overline{X}_{b_2}$ = column means for the first (b_1) and second (b_2) columns
$\overline{X}_G$ = the grand mean
N_{b_1} & N_{b_2} = number of cases occupying the first (b_1) and second (b_2) columns

In words, we subtract the grand mean from each column mean, square these differences, multiply each squared difference by the number of cases in the corresponding column, and sum these weighted squared differences to get SS_B.

Interaction Sum of Squares

The final source of between-group variability in the factorial ANOVA appears as differences from one cell mean to the next. The cell means differ because of

TABLE 9.2 Degrees of Freedom for the Completely Randomized Factorial Anova

df	**Computation**
between	(A − 1) + (B − 1) + (A − 1)(B − 1)
A	A − 1
B	B − 1
AB	(A − 1)(B − 1)
within	N − (A)(B) = $N - k$
total	$N - 1$

where,

A = number of levels of Factor A
B = number of levels of Factor B
N = total number of cases
k = the total number of cells in the data matrix

measurement error, individual differences, and the different treatment combinations represented by the different cells of the data matrix. This third source of overall between-group variability is reflected in the **interaction sum of squares** (SS_{AB}). This term is most easily computed using subtraction, remembering that overall between-group variability ($SS_{between}$) is composed of three parts: that due to different levels of Factor A (SS_A), that due to different levels of Factor B (SS_B), and that due to different combinations of Factors A and B (SS_{AB}). In other words, $SS_{between} = SS_A + SS_B + SS_{AB}$. This being the case, SS_{AB} is given as shown in Equation 9.6.

EQUATION 9.6

$$SS_{AB} = SS_{between} - SS_A - SS_B$$

MEAN SQUARES IN FACTORIAL ANOVA

We learned in chapter 8 that sums of squares do reflect data variability, but are also influenced by the number of groups and number of cases. All other things being equal, the more groups and the more cases, the larger the sums of squares become. We also learned in chapter 8 that the solution to this problem is to divide SS values by the appropriate number of degrees of freedom (df) to create mean square values. Degrees of freedom for the sources of variance in factorial ANOVA are listed in Table 9.2. Dividing each SS term by its corresponding df term, we obtain the mean squares for the completely randomized factorial ANOVA as summarized in Table 9.3.

F Tests in Factorial ANOVA

In addition to a test of overall significance, the factorial ANOVA provides a separate F test for each main effect and interaction effect. Each of these tests compares between-group variance, which is attributable to error variability plus some treatment or treatment combination, to within-group variance, which reflects only error variability.

TABLE 9.3 Computation of Mean Squares for the Completely Randomized Factorial ANOVA

MS	Computation
between	$SS_{between}/df_{between}$
A	SS_A/df_A
B	SS_B/df_B
AB	SS_{AB}/df_{AB}
within	SS_{within}/df_{within}

Test of Overall Significance

The first F test in a factorial ANOVA compares overall between-group variance ($MS_{between}$) to within-group variance (MS_{within}): $F_{overall} = MS_{between}/MS_{within}$. This test is called the **test of overall significance** because it determines if there are *any* treatment effects in the data.

$MS_{between}$ is influenced by measurement error, individual differences, and all treatment effects operating within the factorial experiment. MS_{within} is influenced only by measurement error and individual differences. If there are any significant treatment effects, then, be they one or more main effects and/or an interaction effect, $MS_{between}$ will take on a larger value than MS_{within} and the ratio of these terms, F, will grow correspondingly large.

The statistical significance of this obtained value of F is determined in the usual manner (see chapter 8), that is, by comparing the obtained value of F against the critical value of F listed in Appendix G: Critical Values of F for the desired significance level and appropriate degrees of freedom ($df_{between} = df$ for numerator; $df_{within} = df$ for denominator).

Finding the overall test significant, though, does not tell us *which* treatment, treatments, or treatment combinations are exerting an influence on the dependent variable. For this reason, the overall test of significance is often omitted from the factorial ANOVA.

Test of Factor A

Because MS_A measures variance due to Factor A, as well as measurement error and individual differences, the ratio $F_A = MS_A/MS_{within}$ grows increasingly larger as the effects of Factor A become more pronounced. The obtained value of F_A is evaluated for significance by comparing it to the tabled critical value of F for the desired level of significance and appropriate degrees of freedom ($df_A = df$ for numerator; $df_{within} = df$ for denominator).

Test of Factor B

Following the same logic, the main effect of Factor B is assessed with the F ratio computed as $F_B = MS_B/MS_{within}$. The obtained value is again evaluated for significance by comparing it to the tabled critical value for the desired level of significance and appropriate degrees of freedom ($df_B = df$ for numerator; $df_{within} = df$ for denominator).

Test of the Interaction Effect

Finally, the interaction between Factors A and B is assessed with the ratio $F_{AB} = MS_{AB}/MS_{within}$. As between-group variance due to treatment combinations increases, MS_{AB} grows larger than MS_{within} and the value of F_{AB} increases correspondingly. The obtained value of F_{AB} is evaluated for significance by comparing it against the tabled critical value of F listed for the desired significance level and appropriate degrees of freedom ($df_{AB} = df$ for numerator; $df_{within} = df$ for denominator).

FACTORIAL ANOVA SUMMARY TABLE

The computations required with the factorial ANOVA are not particularly difficult, but they are numerous and need to be kept organized. This purpose is served by the ANOVA summary table, an example of which can be seen by looking ahead to Table 9.5 in Box 9.1. This table provides a standardized format for presenting sums of squares, degrees of freedom, mean squares, and F ratios. Notice, as a computational check, that $SS_{between} = SS_A + SS_B + SS_{AB}$. In addition, $SS_{total} = SS_{between} + SS_{within}$. We should also check to make sure that $df_{between} = df_A + df_B + df_{AB}$, and that $df_{total} = df_{between} + df_{within}$.

RATIONALE OF THE *F* TESTS IN FACTORIAL ANOVA

The same logic that applies to all significance tests applies again to the tests included in the factorial ANOVA. In this section, we will analyze the factorial ANOVA into the same three steps that have become familiar in previous chapters. Box 9.1 provides a concrete example to accompany the more general discussion that follows.

Step 1: The Null and Alternative Hypotheses

There are three independent F tests in a two-factor ANOVA—A, B, and the AB interaction—and each has its own null and alternative hypotheses. For the main effect of Factor A, the null hypothesis (H_0) states that differences seen from one row mean to the next can be attributed to sampling error. That is, differences of this size would be quite likely to occur even if the samples had come from a single population of cases, all of which were treated in exactly the same manner. The alternative hypothesis (H_1) states that the differences observed between row means are too great to be reasonably attributed to sampling error. It is unlikely that samples treated identically would present means this different. It is more likely that the means differ because of the different treatments received by the groups represented by each row.

The null and alternative hypotheses associated with the main effect of Factor B follow the same pattern. The null hypothesis explains that differences between column means are due to sampling error; the alternative hypothesis attributes the differences to the different treatments received by groups representing each column.

The null hypothesis for the interaction effect explains differences between cell means (i.e., treatment combinations) as resulting from sampling error. That is, differences of the observed size are small enough that they would be expected even if the groups occupying each cell were drawn from a population of cases treated identically. The alternative hypothesis states that the observed differences in cell means are too great to be reasonably attributed to sampling error. Instead, it is more likely that the cell means differ because the groups represented in each cell received different treatment combinations.

Step 2: The Test Statistic

The F ratio serves as the test statistic in factorial ANOVA. As differences between row means increase, F_A increases. As differences between column means increase, F_B increases. As differences between cell means increase, F_{AB} increases. For each F test, then, the F statistic provides an indication of how much the obtained between-group differences deviate from what would be expected if the groups being compared had all been treated identically.

Step 3: Determining the Probability of the Test Statistic

The probability that a given value of F would be obtained if all samples involved in computing that F had been treated identically is given in Appendix G: Table of Critical Values of F. This table lists information about the sampling distribution of F. You will recall from chapter 8 that the sampling distribution of F is the frequency distribution of F values obtained when all possible sets of two or more samples are drawn from a single population in which all cases have been treated identically and F is computed on each set of samples. When an obtained value of F falls into the .01 or .05 critical region of this sampling distribution (i.e., meets or exceeds the tabled critical value) it means that the probability is very low that the samples being compared with that F test were treated identically. Only very infrequently do identically treated samples yield F values so large. In such a case, it is much more likely that the high obtained value of F is the result of the samples having been treated differently. In this case, we reject the null hypothesis and accept the alternative hypothesis.

On the other hand, if the obtained value of F falls outside the .05 or .01 critical regions of the sampling distribution of F (i.e., the obtained F is lower than the tabled critical value), it means that the probability is relatively high of seeing an F ratio of the obtained size in samples that were treated identically. In this case, we accept the null hypothesis and explain any between-group differences that are observed as resulting from sampling error.

INTERPRETING SIGNIFICANT *F* TESTS IN FACTORIAL ANOVA

When one or more of the F tests in a factorial ANOVA is found to be significant, we are faced with several problems of interpretation. First, if the interaction effect is significant, it may not be reasonable to place much emphasis on any main effects that are also found to be significant. Second, a significant F tells us that there is a significant difference somewhere between the means being compared

BOX 9.1

COMPLETELY RANDOMIZED FACTORIAL ANOVA

All is not well at the Home for Retired Statistics Teachers. The neighbors have begun to complain that the home's residents are disturbing the tranquility of the neighborhood by screaming obscenities at passersby. The home's director, Jerry Atric, has decided that the only solution is to attach voice-actuated shock generators to his charges (so to speak). These devices will deliver a mild shock when their wearers become too loud. Before investing in too many of the devices, though, Jerry has decided to test their effectiveness. He is particularly concerned about whether the shocks will be effective with longtime statistics teachers, since this group of residents has proven to be particularly incorrigible in the past.

A completely randomized 2 × 2 factorial ANOVA is used in the evaluation. Teaching experience is represented as Factor A with two levels: a_1 = under 20 years; a_2 = over 20 years. Factor B is the shock treatment factor, with two levels: b_1 = no-shock control group; b_2 = shock group. The dependent variable in the analysis is the number of outbursts recorded during the week-long experiment. Five residents of the home are assigned to each of the four cells in the design. Their scores are recorded in Table 9.4, along with cell, row, column, and grand means. Cell means are graphed in Figure 9.2.

Step 1: *The Null and Alternative Hypotheses*
In addition to the test of overall significance, there are three independent significance tests in a two-factor ANOVA: Factor A and Factor B main effects, and the A × B interaction effect. Each of these effects has its own null and alternative hypotheses.

Factor A Main Effect

H_0 : The observed difference in row means is small enough to attribute to sampling error. Two groups treated identically would be likely to show as much difference in their means as is seen between these two row means.

Figure 9.2

Graph of the cell means for 2 x 2 factorial ANOVA examination of the effects of teaching experience and shock treatment on number of outbursts.

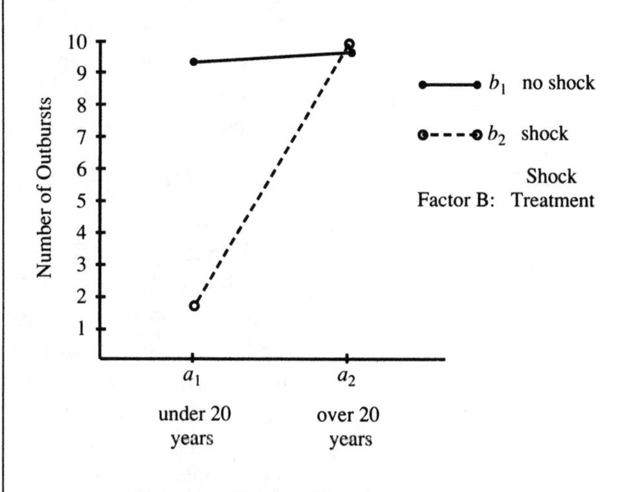

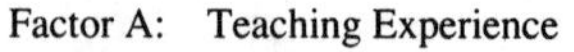

H_1 : The observed difference in row means is too great to be attributed to sampling error. It is unlikely that two identically treated groups would show means this different. It is more likely, then, that the observed difference between rows is due to the different levels of teaching experience of cases occupying the two rows.

Factor B Main Effect

H_0 : The observed difference in column means is small enough to attribute to sampling error. Two groups treated identically would be likely to show as much difference in their means as is seen between these two column means.

H_1 : The observed difference in column means is too great to attribute to sampling error. It is unlikely that two identically treated groups would show

TABLE 9.4 **2 × 2 Factorial ANOVA Data Matrix with Cell, Row, Column, and Grand Means**

		Factor B: Shock Treatment		
		b_1 (no-shock)	b_2 (shock)	
Factor A: Teaching Experience	a_1 (under 20 years)	9 10 8 9 11 $\overline{X}_{a_1b_1} = 9.4$	2 3 2 1 1 $\overline{X}_{a_1b_2} = 1.8$	$\overline{X}_{a_1} = 5.6$
	a_2 (over 20 years)	10 11 9 9 10 $\overline{X}_{a_2b_1} = 9.8$	9 12 10 9 10 $\overline{X}_{a_2b_2} = 10.0$	$\overline{X}_{a_2} = 9.9$
		$\overline{X}_{b_1} = 9.6$	$\overline{X}_{b_2} = 5.9$	$\overline{X}_G = 7.75$

means this different. It is more likely, then, that the observed difference between column means is due to the different treatments received by cases occupying the two columns of the data matrix, that is, shock vs. no-shock.

A × B Interaction Effect

H_0 : The observed differences in cell means are small enough to attribute to sampling error. Four groups treated identically would be likely to show as much difference between their means as is seen here.

H_1 : The observed differences in cell means are too great to attribute to sampling error. It is unlikely that four identically treated groups would show means this different. It is more likely, then, that the observed differences are due to the different treatment combinations received by cases occupying the four cells.

Step 2: *The Test Statistic*

Sums of squares for the two-factor ANOVA are computed according to Equations 9.1 through 9.6.

SS_{total}

$$SS_{total} = \sum_{i=1}^{N} (X_i - \overline{X}_G)^2$$
$$= (9 - 7.75)^2 + (10 - 7.75)^2 + \ldots + (10 - 7.75)^2$$
$$= 253.75$$

continued

SS_{within}

$$SS_{within} = \Sigma (X_{a_1b_1} - \overline{X}_{a_1b_1})^2 + \Sigma (X_{a_1b_2} - \overline{X}_{a_1b_2})^2 + \Sigma (X_{a_2b_1} - \overline{X}_{a_2b_1})^2 + \Sigma (X_{a_2b_2} - \overline{X}_{a_2b_2})^2$$

$$= (9 - 9.4)^2 + (10 - 9.4)^2 + \ldots + (11 - 9.4)^2 + (2 - 1.8)^2 + (3 - 1.8)^2 + \ldots + (1 - 1.8)^2 + (10 - 9.8)^2 + (11 - 9.8)^2 + \ldots + (10 - 9.8)^2 + (9 - 10.0)^2 + (12 - 10.0)^2 + \ldots + (10 - 10.0)^2$$

$$= 16.80$$

$SS_{between}$

$$SS_{between} = (\overline{X}_{a_1b_1} - \overline{X}_G)^2 N_{a_1b_1} + (\overline{X}_{a_1b_2} - \overline{X}_G)^2 N_{a_1b_2} + (\overline{X}_{a_2b_1} - \overline{X}_G)^2 N_{a_2b_1} + (\overline{X}_{a_2b_2} - \overline{X}_G)^2 N_{a_2b_2}$$

$$= (9.4 - 7.75)^2 5 + (1.8 - 7.75)^2 5 + (9.8 - 7.75)^2 5 + (10.0 - 7.75)^2 5$$

$$= 236.95$$

SS_A

$$SS_A = (\overline{X}_{a_1} - \overline{X}_G)^2 N_{a_1} + (\overline{X}_{a_2} - \overline{X}_G)^2 N_{a_2}$$
$$= (5.6 - 7.75)^2 10 + (9.9 - 7.75)^2 10$$
$$= 92.45$$

SS_B

$$SS_B = (\overline{X}_{b_1} - \overline{X}_G)^2 N_{b_1} + (\overline{X}_{b_2} - \overline{X}_G)^2 N_{b_2}$$
$$= (9.6 - 7.75)^2 10 + (5.9 - 7.75)^2 10$$
$$= 68.45$$

SS_{AB}

$$SS_{AB} = SS_{between} - SS_A - SS_B$$
$$= 236.95 - 92.45 - 68.45$$
$$= 76.05$$

Next, degrees of freedom are computed as described in Table 9.2.

$df_{between}$

$$df_{between} = (A - 1) + (B - 1) + (A - 1)(B - 1)$$
$$= (2 - 1) + (2 - 1) + (2 - 1)(2 - 1)$$
$$= 3$$

df_A

$$df_A = A - 1$$
$$= 2 - 1$$
$$= 1$$

with that F test, but which means differ must still be determined. Finally, the distinction between statistical and practical significance must be kept in mind when interpreting outcomes of factorial ANOVAs.

Significant Interaction Effects

A significant interaction effect tells us that the effects of the factors are conditional on each other. The effect of Factor A depends upon which level of Factor B is under consideration, and vice versa. The specific nature of this conditionality is best clarified by examining a graph of the cell means like those in Figure 9.1. But what if, in addition to a significant interaction effect, one or both main effects are found to be significant? Once it has been determined that the effects of the

BOX 9.1—*continued*

df_B

$$\begin{aligned} df_B &= B - 1 \\ &= 2 - 1 \\ &= 1 \end{aligned}$$

df_{AB}

$$\begin{aligned} df_{AB} &= (A - 1)(B - 1) \\ &= (2 - 1)(2 - 1) \\ &= 1 \end{aligned}$$

df_{within}

$$\begin{aligned} df_{within} &= N - (A)(B) \\ &= 20 - (2)(2) \\ &= 16 \end{aligned}$$

df_{total}

$$\begin{aligned} df_{total} &= N - 1 \\ &= 20 - 1 \\ &= 19 \end{aligned}$$

Mean squares are now computed by dividing each *SS* term by its corresponding *df* term.

$MS_{between}$

$$\begin{aligned} MS_{between} &= SS_{between}/df_{between} \\ &= 236.95/3 \\ &= 78.98 \end{aligned}$$

MS_A

$$\begin{aligned} MS_A &= SS_A/df_A \\ &= 92.45/1 \\ &= 92.45 \end{aligned}$$

MS_B

$$\begin{aligned} MS_B &= SS_B/df_B \\ &= 68.45/1 \\ &= 68.45 \end{aligned}$$

MS_{AB}

$$\begin{aligned} MS_{AB} &= SS_{AB}/df_{AB} \\ &= 76.05/1 \\ &= 76.05 \end{aligned}$$

MS_{within}

$$\begin{aligned} MS_{within} &= SS_{within}/df_{within} \\ &= 16.80/16 \\ &= 1.05 \end{aligned}$$

F tests are computed next by dividing each *MS* term by MS_{within}.

$F_{overall}$

$$\begin{aligned} F_{overall} &= MS_{between}/MS_{within} \\ &= 78.98/1.05 \\ &= 75.22 \end{aligned}$$

continued

factors are conditional, or that there is an interaction, it can be misleading to make the kinds of generalized, unconditional statements about the effects of the factors that significant main effects might suggest.

Figure 9.1b was used previously to illustrate the situation in which there are both main effects and an interaction effect. The Factor A main effect considered alone would lead to the conclusion that high-anxiety students show lower test performance than do low-anxiety students, but this is an oversimplification, a half-truth. The interaction effect tells us that only those high-anxiety students show lower performance who have not received treatment for their anxiety. When treatment is provided, the performance of high-anxiety students is just as high as it is for low-anxiety students. The Factor B main effect considered alone would

F_A

$$F_A = MS_A/MS_{within} = 92.45/1.05 = 88.05$$

F_B

$$F_B = MS_B/MS_{within} = 68.45/1.05 = 65.19$$

F_{AB}

$$F_{AB} = MS_{AB}/MS_{within} = 76.05/1.05 = 72.43$$

Finally, we organize the results of the analysis using an ANOVA summary table as shown in Table 9.5.

TABLE 9.5 Summary table for 2 × 2 factorial ANOVA

Source	*SS*	*df*	*MS*	*F*
Between-Group	236.95	3	78.98	75.22*
A	92.45	1	92.45	88.05*
B	68.45	1	68.45	65.19*
A × B	76.05	1	76.05	72.43*
Within-Group	16.80	16	1.05	
Total	253.75	19		

Factor A: Teaching Experience; Factor B: Shock Treatment.

$^*p < .01$

Step 3: *Determining the Probability of the Test Statistic*

The significance of each F test is evaluated by comparing the obtained values of F against the critical values of F listed in Appendix G: Table of Critical Values of F. For the test of overall significance, with 3 and 16 degrees of freedom, the critical value of F for the .01 level of significance is 5.29. Since the obtained $F_{overall} = 75.22$ exceeds this critical value, the overall F test is significant. This tells us that at least one of the independent F tests will be significant. For all three of these F tests, degrees of freedom are 1 (*df* for numerator) and 16 (*df* for denominator). The critical value of F at the .01 level for these tests is 8.53. All of the obtained values of F exceed this critical value. Thus, all F tests are significant. We can conclude from this that the patterns of differences between row, column, and cell means that were observed with these samples would be found again in a replication. The differences are reliable.

The significant main effect of Factor A (teaching experience) tells us that this factor is reliably associated with our dependent variable (number of outbursts). Those with fewer than 20 years teaching experience showed significantly fewer outbursts ($\overline{X}_{a_1} = 5.6$) than did those with over 20 years teaching experience ($\overline{X}_{a_2} = 9.9$). The significant main effect of Factor B tells us that the no-shock control group showed significantly more outbursts ($\overline{X}_{b_1} = 9.6$) than did subjects who received shocks ($\overline{X}_{b_2} = 5.9$).

However, the presence of a significant A × B interaction effect means that the effects of Factors A and B are conditional. In the context of this example, it makes greatest sense to describe the effectiveness of shock as conditional upon length of teaching experience. Looking at the graph of cell means in Figure 9.2, we can see that shock was quite effective in reducing the frequency of outbursts in teachers with fewer than 20 years experience. For those with over 20 years experience, though, shock had essentially no effect on this behavior.

lead us to conclude that providing treatment for test anxiety enhances performance on tests, but this is another overgeneralization. We know from the interaction effect that treating test anxiety has little or no beneficial effect for low-anxiety students. It is helpful only to those who experience high anxiety levels.

When there are both significant interaction effects and significant main effects, interaction effects should be given greater consideration in interpreting the results of the ANOVA. Interaction effects require that statements about the effects of the factors be made in conditional terms.

Post Hoc Comparisons

When there are no interaction effects, the interpretation of significant main effects is straightforward; a significant Factor A main effect tells us that the row means differ significantly and a significant Factor B main effect tells us that the column means differ significantly. If there are only two row means, the significant F_A tells us immediately that these two row means differ significantly. Similarly, when there are only two column means, the significant F_B tells us that these two column means differ significantly. However, when a factor includes three or more levels, a significant main effect for that factor tells us only that a significant difference exists somewhere among the means, but we do not know which means differ significantly. This same problem presents itself when we obtain a significant interaction effect. The interaction effect tells us that there is at least one significant difference between the cell means, but we must still determine which cell means differ.

Chapter 8 introduced post hoc comparisons as a method of exploring between-group differences once a significant F has revealed that significant differences exist. The Scheffé test is a particularly flexible procedure in the context of factorial ANOVA. It enables us to compare combinations of cell means in exploring main effects, or to explore interaction effects by making pairwise comparisons between cell means. A graph of cell means will show which means or combinations of means should be compared. In computing Scheffé comparisons in a factorial experiment, Equations 8.8 through 8.10 are again applicable. However, in a factorial design the value of k in these equations is equal to the total number of cells in the factorial data matrix.

Tukey's HSD test may also be used in data snooping in a factorial design. Because Tukey's test is more powerful than Scheffé's test in making pairwise comparisons, it is especially useful when we compare pairs of cell means. In computing Tukey's HSD, Equation 8.7 is applicable to both one-way and factorial ANOVAs, but in the factorial design, the value of k in Equation 8.7 is equal to the total number of cells in the factorial data matrix. Tukey's procedure is used in Box 9.2 to compare cell means in exploring an interaction effect.

A Priori (Planned) Comparisons

A priori or planned comparisons were introduced in chapter 8 as a method of assessing the statistical significance of between-group differences that have been predicted in advance of data collection. Planned comparisons are also useful within

BOX 9.2

TUKEY'S HSD FOLLOWING A FACTORIAL ANOVA

The significant interaction effect between Factor A (teaching experience) and Factor B (shock treatment) uncovered in Box 9.1 tells us that there are one or more significant differences between cell means, but only through some post hoc data snooping can we discover exactly which cells differ. We will use the Tukey HSD post hoc comparison procedure here to determine how large a difference must be in order to be considered significant.

We compute HSD using Equation 8.7 (with k = the number of cells in the factorial data matrix):

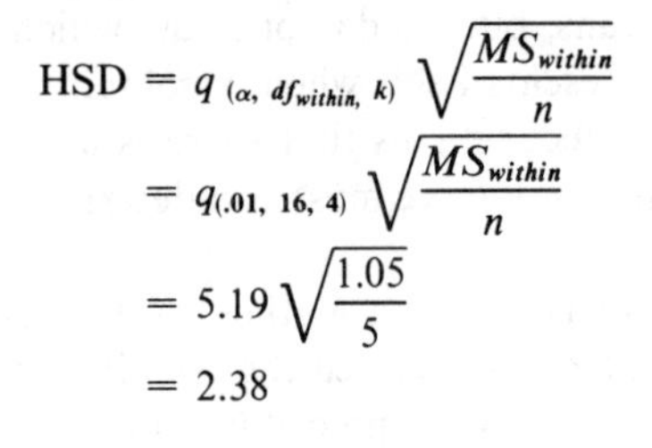

$$\begin{aligned} \text{HSD} &= q_{(\alpha,\ df_{within},\ k)} \sqrt{\frac{MS_{within}}{n}} \\ &= q_{(.01,\ 16,\ 4)} \sqrt{\frac{MS_{within}}{n}} \\ &= 5.19 \sqrt{\frac{1.05}{5}} \\ &= 2.38 \end{aligned}$$

Of the six possible pairwise comparisons that can be formed from the four cell means of Table 9.4, three meet or exceed this value of HSD:

$$\overline{X}_{a_1b_1} \text{ vs. } \overline{X}_{a_1b_2} = 7.6$$
$$\overline{X}_{a_1b_2} \text{ vs. } \overline{X}_{a_2b_1} = 8.0$$
$$\overline{X}_{a_1b_2} \text{ vs. } \overline{X}_{a_2b_2} = 8.2$$

These three differences are all significant at the .01 level. The first tells us that shock had a significant effect in reducing the frequency of outbursts in those with fewer than 20 years teaching experience. The second and third tell us that teachers with fewer than 20 years teaching experience who received shocks showed significantly fewer outbursts than did teachers with more than 20 years experience, regardless of whether or not these longtime teachers received shocks. In other words, Jerry's initial hunch was right. The shock devices will work well with the less experienced teachers, but longtime teachers seem to be completely out of control.

the context of factorial ANOVA in accomplishing this same purpose. The computational procedures described in chapter 8 may be applied directly to the factorial design, remembering that k = the number of cells in the factorial data matrix.

Practical vs. Statistical Significance

In factorial ANOVA, as in other significance tests, it is important to distinguish between practical and statistical significance, and to make sure that the evaluation of significance does not stop with the discovery of statistical significance. The F tests of the factorial ANOVA tell us if the pattern of between-group differences that has been obtained is likely to be seen again in a replication of the experiment. These tests do not tell us whether or not the observed pattern makes a practical difference. A little common sense is probably the best tool in evaluating practical significance.

BOX 9.3

OMEGA-SQUARE FOLLOWING A FACTORIAL ANOVA

Significant main effects of Factors A (teaching experience) and B (shock treatment), as well as a significant A × B interaction effect, were discovered in Box 9.1. The question to be answered here is how strong are these statistically significant effects? We can measure the strength of the effects observed using omega-square, computed according to Equations 9.7 through 9.9.

$$\omega^2_A = \frac{SS_A - (df_A)MS_{within}}{SS_{total} + MS_{within}} = \frac{92.45 - (1)\,1.05}{253.75 + 1.05} = .36$$

$$\omega^2_B = \frac{SS_B - (df_B)MS_{within}}{SS_{total} + MS_{within}} = \frac{68.45 - (1)\,1.05}{253.75 + 1.05} = .26$$

$$\omega^2_{AB} = \frac{SS_{AB} - (df_{AB})MS_{within}}{SS_{total} + MS_{within}} = \frac{76.05 - (1)\,1.05}{253.75 + 1.05} = .29$$

The first of these values, $\omega^2_A = .36$, tells us that 36% of the variability in frequency of outbursts can be attributed to Factor A: teaching experience. This factor appears to be the most powerful determinant of this behavior. The second value, $\omega^2_B = .26$, indicates that 26% of the variability in frequency of outbursts is attributed to the shock vs. no-shock conditions of Factor B. Finally, $\omega^2_{AB} = .29$, tells us that 29% of the variability in the data can be attributed to the different combinations of levels of Factors A and B represented by the four cells of Table 9.4.

Omega-Square. Omega-square (ω^2), introduced in chapter 7, is also useful in evaluating practical significance in factorial ANOVA designs. When sample sizes are large, even very weak treatment effects can be found to be statistically significant. In assessing practical significance, then, it is helpful to have some measure of the strength of the treatment effect. This measure is furnished by ω^2. Omega-square is computed differently, according to which treatment effect is being measured. Equations 9.7 through 9.9 summarize the computation of ω^2 for treatment effects associated with Factor A, Factor B, and the A × B interaction effect, respectively.

EQUATION 9.7

$$\omega^2_A = \frac{SS_A - (df_A)MS_{within}}{SS_{total} + MS_{within}}$$

EQUATION 9.8

$$\omega^2_B = \frac{SS_B - (df_B)MS_{within}}{SS_{total} + MS_{within}}$$

EQUATION 9.9

$$\omega^2_{AB} = \frac{SS_{AB} - (df_{AB})MS_{within}}{SS_{total} + MS_{within}}$$

The use of omega-square in the context of factorial ANOVA is demonstrated in Box 9.3.

SUMMARY

This chapter presents concepts fundamental to factorial ANOVA. Factorial ANOVA procedures are used in simultaneously evaluating the effects of two or more independent variables (called factors) on an interval or ratio scale dependent variable. Factorial ANOVAs enable us to analyze both main effects and interaction effects. A main effect is said to have occurred when a factor exerts a significant influence over the dependent variable. An interaction effect is said to have occurred when the effects of one factor are conditional upon the other factor. Factorial ANOVA partitions the total variability in the data into several components. First, within-group variability (MS_{within}) results from the random action of individual differences and measurement error, referred to collectively as "error variance." Second, variability between the means of the groups that received different levels of Factor A (MS_A) represents both error variance and the effect of Factor A. Third, variability between the means of groups that received different levels of Factor B (MS_B) represents both error variance and the effect of Factor B. Finally, variability between the means of groups that received different combinations of the levels of Factors A and B (MS_{AB}) represents both error variance and the effect of these different treatment combinations. A series of F tests are used in factorial ANOVA to provide independent evaluations of Factor A and B main effects and the A $\times$ B interaction effect. Each F test divides the appropriate between-group MS term by MS_{within}. Obtained values of F are evaluated for statistical significance by comparing them to the sampling distribution of F. This sampling distribution gives the probability of obtaining any given value of F from a set of samples that were treated identically, and thus also indicates the probability that the obtained differences were the result of the groups receiving different treatment combinations. Interpreting significant F tests from the factorial ANOVA can be facilitated by using the post hoc comparison procedures described in chapter 8. Planned comparisons, also introduced in chapter 8, enable us to assess the statistical significance of between-group differences that have been predicted in advance of data collection. Omega-square, also introduced previously, is useful in assessing the strength of the various treatment effects in factorial ANOVA.

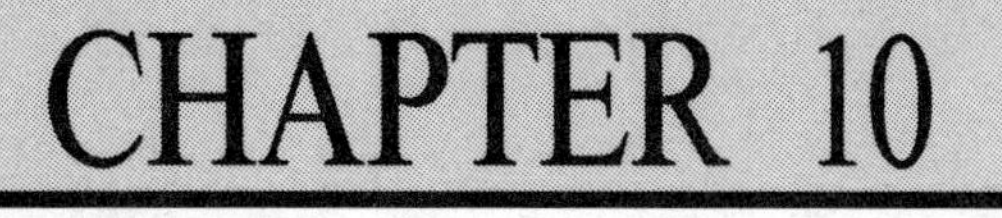

CHAPTER 10

BIVARIATE CORRELATION

This chapter will begin our examination of correlational statistics. All correlational procedures measure the strength of relationships between variables. That is, they all seek to quantify the degree to which variables "go together" or covary. Correlational procedures differ in how many variables are involved and at what level or scale these variables are measured. **Bivariate** correlational procedures, as the name suggests, assess the relationship between two variables, one called the *X*, or **predictor variable,** and the other called the *Y*, or **criterion variable.** These bivariate procedures will be the focus of this chapter. **Multivariate** correlational procedures deal with relationships between more than two variables and will be taken up in later chapters. Correlational procedures that involve normally distributed variables measured at the interval or ratio scales of measurement are called **parametric** procedures; those which involve ordinal or nominal scale variables and do not assume normal distributions are called **nonparametric.**

Much social and behavioral science research lends itself naturally to correlational analysis. How strongly related are such variables as teacher attractiveness and student ratings of teaching effectiveness? Number of hours in psychotherapy and amount of improvement in daily functioning? Attitudinal similarity and interpersonal attraction? Wind speed and spitting distance? Widely useful, we will discover that tradition, more than mathematical proscription, has circumscribed the circumstances in which correlational methods are generally applied.

PEARSON PRODUCT-MOMENT CORRELATION

Certainly the most widely used correlational statistic is the **Pearson product-moment correlation,** symbolized by the letter *r*. We will begin our consideration of correlational statistics with the Pearson correlation.

The Data for the Pearson Correlation

Data to which the Pearson *r* is appropriately applied consist of two normally distributed sets of interval or ratio scale scores (which will be referred to as variables *X* and *Y*) obtained from *N* cases, such that each case presents one score on *X* and one score on *Y*.[1] For instance, if spitting distance and wind speed were recorded for each of 10 contestants in this year's Olympic Wind Spitting competition, we would have data suitable to a Pearson correlational analysis.

The Scatterplot

We may depict the data of a correlational problem graphically using a **scatterplot.** Table 10.1 in Box 10.1 lists data from 10 contestants in this year's Olympic Wind Spitting competition. Figure 10.1 in that same box is a scatterplot that summarizes graphically the relationship between variable *X* (wind speed) and variable *Y* (spitting distance). Each point in a scatterplot represents one case's scores on the two variables represented by the two axes of the graph. A given case's point is located at the intersection of that case's values on each variable, where the horizontal axis (abscissa) represents *X* and the vertical axis (ordinate) represents *Y*.

BOX 10.1

THE SCATTERPLOT

In this year's Olympic Wind Spitting competition, contestants each took a turn spitting into the wind. As the data in Table 10.1 illustrate, both the wind and spitting distances were quite variable.

These data are summarized graphically in the scatterplot shown in Figure 10.1. In this scatterplot, each point represents one of the contestants, identified by number. Normally, no such identifying information is included in the scatterplot. It is done here for instructional purposes.

Figure 10.1

Data from the Olympic Wind Spitting competition depicted in the form of a scatterplot.

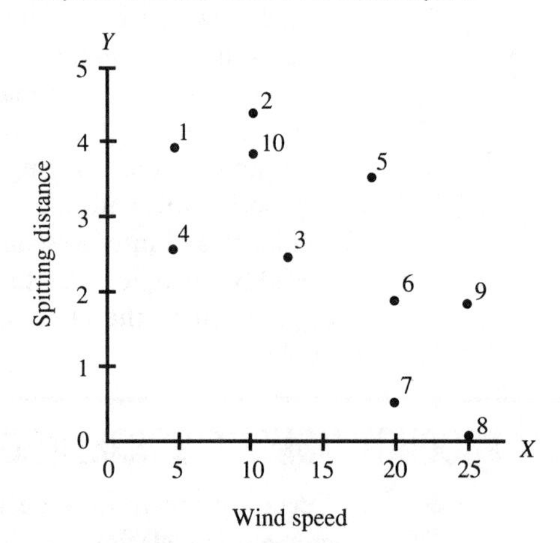

TABLE 10.1 **Data from the Olympic Wind Spitting Competition**

	X		Y	
Contestants	Wind Speed (in mph)	z_X	Spitting Distance (in meters)	z_Y
1	5	−1.41	4	1.00
2	10	− .71	4.5	1.35
3	13	− .29	2.5	− .06
4	5	−1.41	2.75	.12
5	18	.41	3.5	.65
6	20	.68	2	− .41
7	20	.68	.5	−1.46
8	25	1.38	0 (poor guy!)	−1.82
9	25	1.38	2	− .41
10	10	− .71	4	1.00
	$\overline{X} = 15.10$		$\overline{Y} = 2.58$	
	$s_X = 7.16$		$s_Y = 1.42$	

(a) A positive correlation.

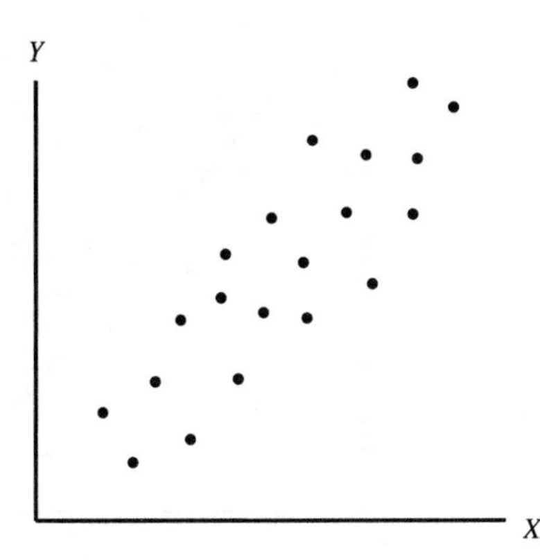

(b) A negative correlation.

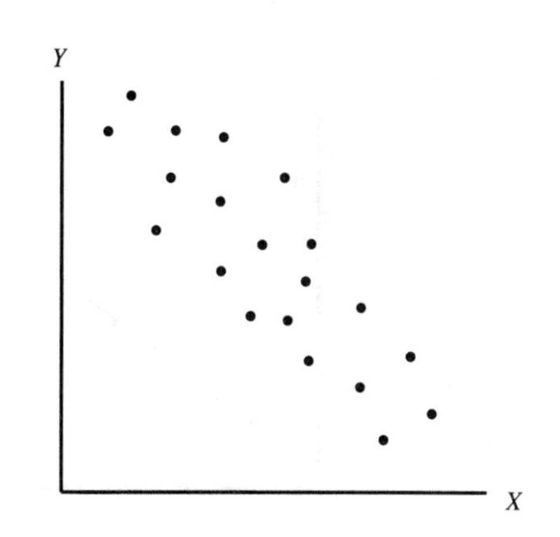

Figure 10.2

Scatterplots depicting (a) positive and (b) negative correlations.

Scatterplots, including the one in Box 10.1, provide several important pieces of information about the relationship between *X* and *Y*. In fact, scatterplots can often provide information about this relationship that is missed from a casual inspection of the statistics usually computed in connection with a correlational analysis. For this reason, a scatterplot should always be constructed as the first step in correlational analysis.

Direction of the Relationship. One piece of information provided by the scatterplot concerns the direction of the relationship between *X* and *Y*. **Positive correlations** exist when values on one variable increase and decrease along with values on the second variable. This is indicated by a scatterplot in which the points generally ascend as one moves from left to right. Examples of positive correlations would be the correlation between SAT scores and college grade point average, the correlation between height and weight, and the correlation between temperature and crime rate.

Two variables are **negatively correlated** when scores on those variables move together, but in opposite directions; as scores on *X* increase, scores on *Y* decrease. The scatterplot of Figure 10.1 in Box 10.1 depicts a negative relationship. As wind speed (*X*) increases, spitting distance (*Y*) decreases. Figure 10.2 provides additional examples of positive (Figure 10.2a) and negative (Figure 10.2b) correlations.

Strength of the Relationship. Another piece of information given by a scatterplot is the magnitude or strength of the relationship between *X* and *Y*. To what degree do values of *X* and *Y* vary together? To what degree are *X* and *Y* linked? Relationship strength is shown in a scatterplot by the amount of dispersion or scattering of the points. The strongest possible relationship (called a "perfect" relationship) is indicated by a scatterplot in which the points form a perfectly straight line. As the relationship between *X* and *Y* weakens, the points become increasingly dispersed around an imaginary straight line fitted through them. A

(a) A perfect relationship.

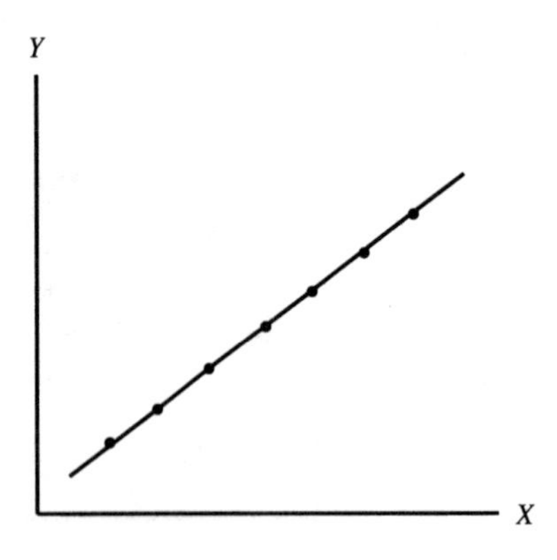

(b) A moderate relationship.

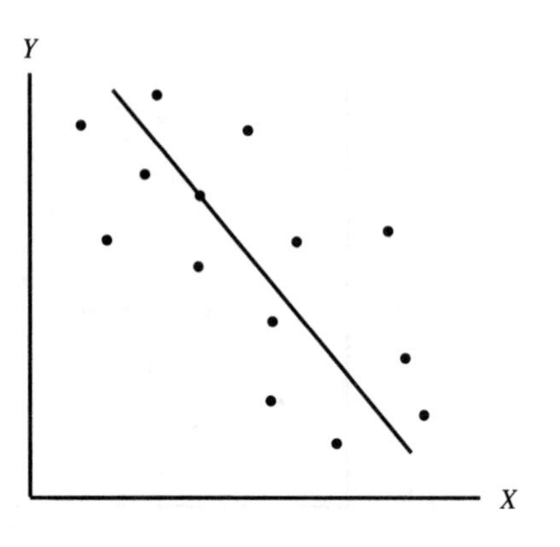

Figure 10.3
Relationship strength as depicted in scatterplots.

(c) No relationship.

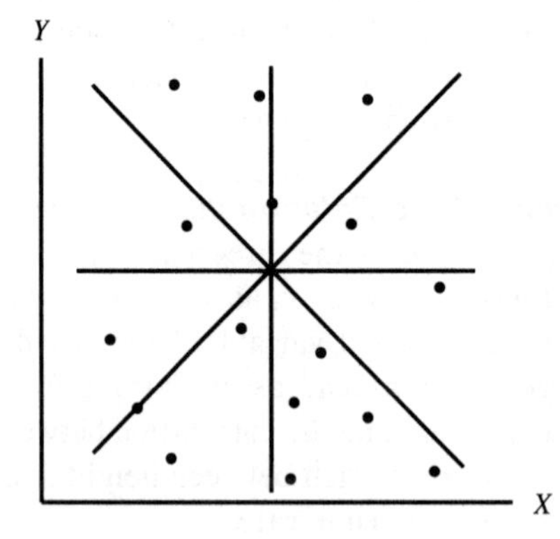

totally random arrangement of points depicts a lack of any relationship whatsoever. It is impossible to fit a line through such a scattered array of points; one "fit" is just as good (or bad) as the next. Figure 10.3 illustrates how relationship strength is reflected in the dispersion of points in a scatterplot. In Figure 10.3a, we find a perfect positive correlation; Figure 10.3b illustrates a negative correlation of moderate strength; Figure 10.3c shows the random arrangement of points that marks the absence of any relationship between X and Y.

There are two exceptions to the rule that points in a scatterplot that form a straight line represent a perfect relationship. When the points form a line that is either perfectly horizontal, as in Figure 10.4a, or perfectly vertical, as in Figure 10.4b, there is no relationship between X and Y. Why this is so should be clear after a moment's reflection. Two variables, X and Y, are said to be related or correlated to the extent that they go together or covary. Obviously, in order for X and Y to covary, each must vary. The scatterplots of Figure 10.4 each represent

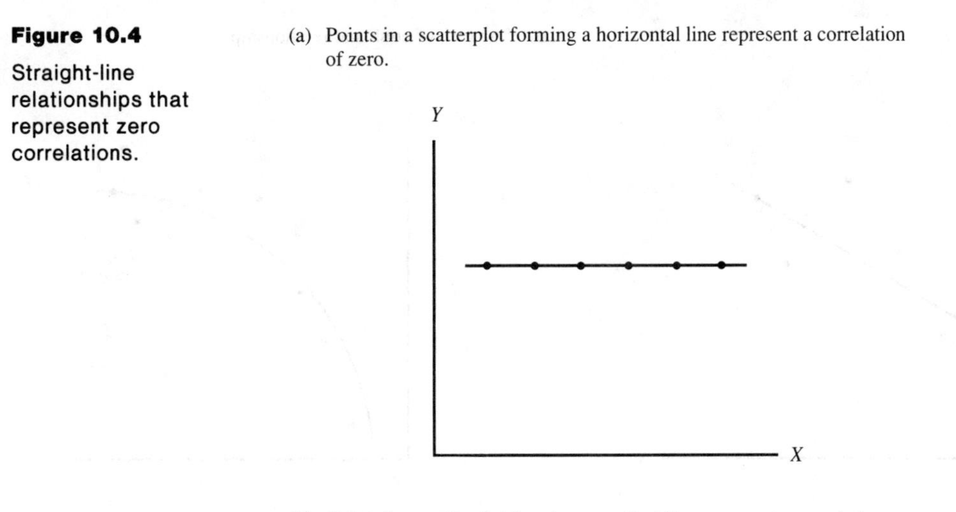

Figure 10.4

Straight-line relationships that represent zero correlations.

(a) Points in a scatterplot forming a horizontal line represent a correlation of zero.

(b) Points in a scatterplot forming a vertical line represent a correlation of zero.

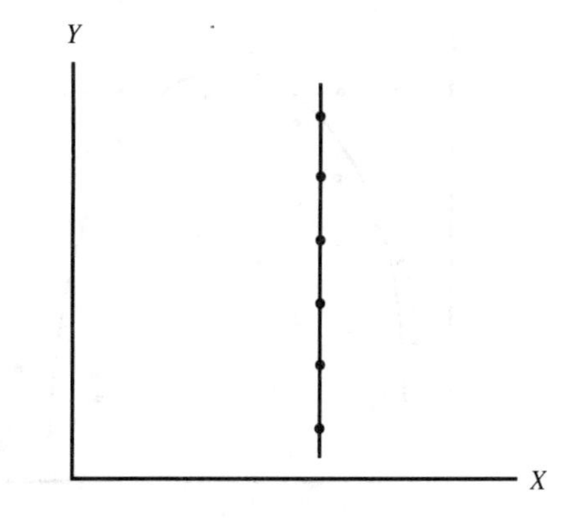

a situation in which scores on one variable do not vary from case to case. In Figure 10.4a, there is variance on X, but every case has taken the same value on Y. Figure 10.4b illustrates the situation in which cases vary on Y, but there is no X variance. In sum, then, a correlation requires that our data show variability on both variables involved in the correlation. Scatterplots reveal both the extent to which variables covary, and also the amount of variability found in each variable considered singly.

Deviations from Linearity. The Pearson product-moment correlation was described earlier as an index of the strength of the relationship between two variables. Strictly speaking, however, it describes the strength of the **linear relationship** between two variables. Many other, **nonlinear relationships** that may exist between X and Y are not measured by r.[2] As seen in Figure 10.5, a glance at a scatterplot can reveal more quickly than any other method the degree to which our data represent a linear vs. nonlinear relationship.

(a) A linear relationship.

(b) One type of nonlinear relationship.

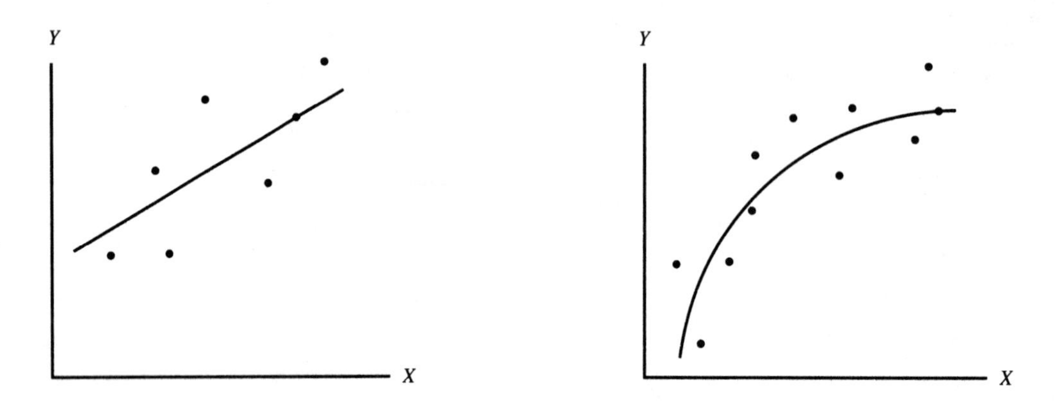

Figure 10.5

Scatterplots depicting (a) linear and (b, c) nonlinear relationships.

(c) A second nonlinear relationship: the inverted U-shaped relationship.

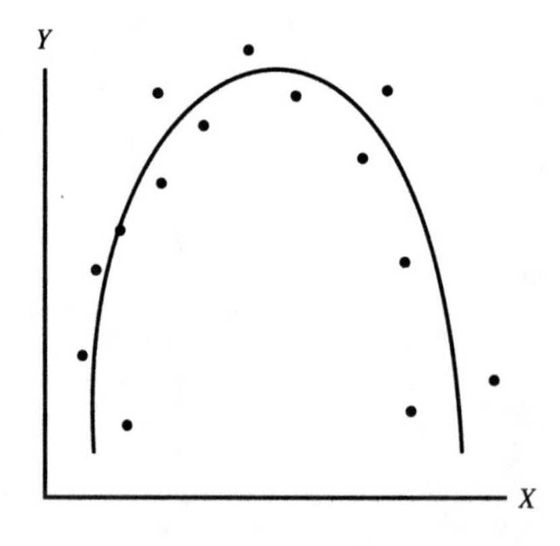

Figure 10.5a represents a positive linear relationship of moderate strength. Notice that the line best fitting these points is a straight line. Figures 10.5b and 10.5c show two commonly occurring forms of nonlinear relationship. In Figure 10.5b, the relationship between X and Y accelerates rapidly at relatively low values of X and Y, but flattens as we reach higher values. A straight line does not fit this scatterplot well; it is better described with the curve shown. As an example of this type of nonlinear relationship, take the relationship between the physical intensity of a stimulus (X) and the perceived intensity (brightness, loudness, sweetness, etc.) of that stimulus (Y). At lower levels of physical stimulus intensity, small increases produce marked increases in perceived intensity; at higher levels of physical intensity, the same amount of increase results in considerably less change in perceived intensity.

In Figure 10.5c we see an "inverted-U" shaped relationship between X and Y. Here again, the relationship is best described not with a straight line, but with a curve, this time one taking the form of an inverted U. The well known rela-

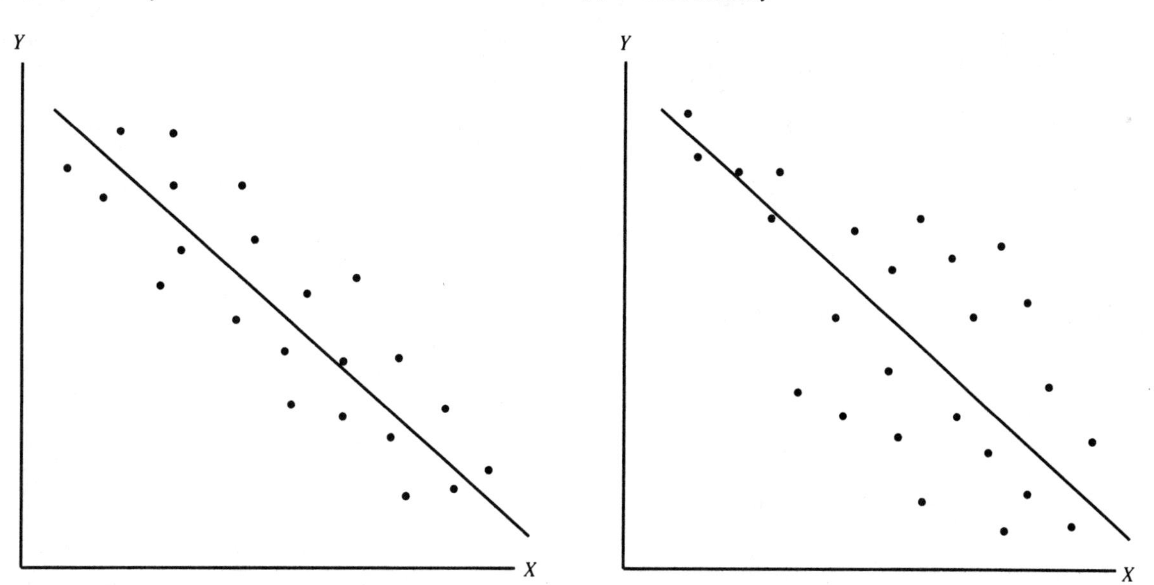

Figure 10.6
Homoscedasticity and heteroscedasticity as depicted in scatterplots.

tionship between arousal level (X) and task performance level (Y) is an example of an inverted-U shaped relationship. At extremely low levels of arousal, task performance tends to be quite low. As arousal increases, so does performance—up to a point. As arousal increases beyond this optimal level, performance deteriorates.

Deviations from linear relationship are not uncommon in the social sciences. The best way of identifying these nonlinear trends is to examine a scatterplot. As we saw in chapter 2, one graph can be worth a thousand statistics.

Homoscedasticity. One of the most delightful of all statistical terms must be **homoscedasticity!** Data display homoscedasticity to the extent that the relationship between X and Y is of equal strength across the whole range of both X and Y. The data lack homoscedasticity (i.e., show **heteroscedasticity**) if the relationship varies in strength from one range of values of X (or Y) to another. Homoscedasticity is clearly a desirable characteristic to find in our data, for it eliminates the need to qualify statements about the relationship between X and Y. For example, it is certainly preferable (at least simpler) to say "X and Y show a strong negative relationship" than to say "X and Y show a strong negative relationship at low values of X, but the relationship becomes weaker as X increases."

Figure 10.6a illustrates data that are fully homoscedastic. Notice how the points in this scatterplot are equally dispersed all along the length of an imaginary line fitted through them. In Figure 10.6b, in contrast, notice how the points are more dispersed at one end of the imaginary line than at the other. These data are **heteroscedastic.**

Figure 10.7

An outlier depicted in a scatterplot.

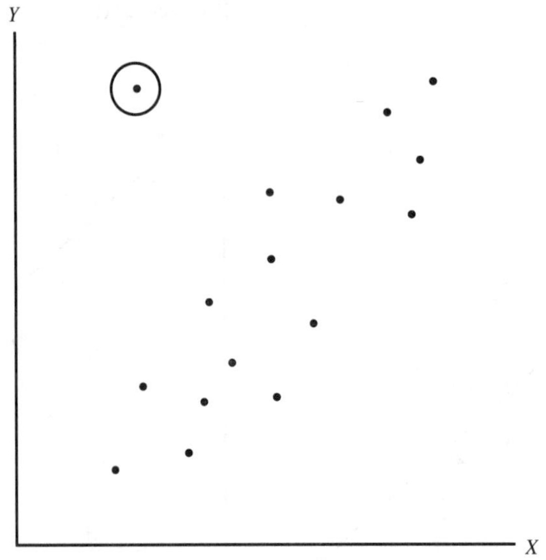

Heteroscedasticity is the result of relating two variables, one or both of which are skewed. If both variables are more or less normally distributed, the relationship between them will be more or less homoscedastic. Obviously, then, descriptive statistics measuring skewness can give a preliminary indication of the homoscedasticity of our data, but a scatterplot provides a much more immediate picture (literally) of this characteristic.

The Presence of Outliers. One last feature of the data to which we can be alerted by a scatterplot is the presence of **outliers.** An outlier is a case that is radically different from the majority of other cases in terms of its combined or joint values on X and Y. Although an outlier may show scores on X and Y that are each well within the normal ranges for those variables, the pair of scores may make the case quite deviant. Figure 10.7 illustrates what is meant by the term outlier.

The case circled in Figure 10.7 is an outlier. Identifying outliers can be important for several reasons. For one thing, an outlier may represent a case whose scores on X and/or Y have been recorded incorrectly. Second, outliers may show deviant combined scores on X and Y because they did not understand (or deliberately disobeyed) instructions given during data collection. Third, outliers represent, if nothing else, cases to which statements about the relationship between X and Y drawn from the majority of cases do not apply. Identifying these exceptions to the rule can initiate some interesting research. Finally, as we will see later, outliers exert a disproportionate effect on computed correlations, much as extreme scores have a disproportionate effect on the computed mean of those scores.

Computing the Pearson *r*

Just as descriptive statistics give a precise measure of characteristics that may be observed in graphed frequency distributions, it is also true that the Pearson correlation (r) gives a more precise indication of the linear relationship between X and Y than is available from inspection of a scatterplot. The Pearson r is computed in Equation 10.1.[3]

EQUATION 10.1

$$r = \frac{\Sigma(z_X z_Y)}{N}$$

where,

N = the number of cases; i.e., the number of score pairs
z_X = standard scores on the variable X
z_Y = standard scores on the variable Y

How r provides an index of the relationship between X and Y is apparent from an examination of Equation 10.1. Recall first that a standard score gives us the location of a score in the distribution by locating that score relative to the mean of the distribution. Thus, z_X tells us the location of a cases's score on the variable X and z_Y gives us the location of that case's scores on the variable Y. When cases with low scores on X (negative z_X values) present equally low scores on Y (negative z_Y values), and cases with high scores on X (positive z_X values) present equally high scores on Y (positive z_Y values), such that $z_X = z_Y$ for each case, $\Sigma\, z_X z_Y$ will be positive and equal to N. Under these circumstances, $r = +1$. Consider next what happens when cases with low scores on X present equally high scores on Y and vice versa. Here, each case would have identical absolute values of z_X and z_Y, but one value would be negative and the other positive. In this situation, $\Sigma\, z_X z_Y$ will be negative and equal to N, and $r = -1$. When X and Y are unrelated, we will observe some pairs of z-scores in which both values are positive, some pairs in which both are negative, and some pairs in which one z-score is positive while the other z-score is negative. In this case, $\Sigma z_X z_Y = 0$, and $r = 0$. The upshot of all this is that the absolute value of r gives us the average agreement between cases' locations on variables X and Y. Box 10.2 demonstrates the computation of r.

Interpreting *r*

The Pearson correlation reveals two things about the relationship between X and Y. First, the sign of r (positive or negative) indicates the direction of the relationship. Second, the absolute magnitude of r reflects the strength of the linear relationship between X and Y. Correlations can range in value from -1 (a perfect negative correlation) to 0 (no relationship) to $+1$ (a perfect positive correlation).

BOX 10.2

PEARSON *r*

Scores from the Olympic Wind Spitting competition are given in Table 10.1 in Box 10.1. The scatterplot of these scores (Figure 10.1) revealed a moderate, negative relationship between wind speed (X) and spitting distance (Y). This relationship can be quantified using the Pearson r computed according to Equation 10.1.

$$
\begin{aligned}
r &= \frac{\Sigma(z_X z_Y)}{N} \\
&= \frac{(-1.41)(1.00) + (-.71)(1.35) + \ldots + (-.71)(1.00)}{10} \\
&= \frac{-7.31}{10} \\
&= -.73
\end{aligned}
$$

What we had learned already from the scatterplot of Figure 10.1 has been confirmed and made more precise by this computed correlation ($r = -.73$). First, the negative sign of the correlation tells us that the relationship between X (wind speed) and Y (spitting distance into the wind) is negative; a positive sign would have indicated a positive relationship. Second, the absolute magnitude of the correlation reflects the moderate strength of the linear relationship between wind speed and spitting distance.

Even better than r, though, as a measure of relationship strength, is r^2, the squared correlation. The reason for this will be clearer after reading chapter 11. Briefly, though, r provides a nonlinear measure of relationship strength. This situation is shown in Figure 10.8a. As is also shown in Figure 10.8b, though, r^2 provides a linear measure of the strength of the relationship between X and Y. Thus, r^2 is a more readily interpreted value than is r. The Pearson correlation is best described as an ordinal scale indicator of relationship strength, since equal differences in r values do not reflect equal differences in the strength of the relationship between X and Y. The squared correlation, though, is a ratio scale indicator of relationship strength, since equal differences in r^2 do reflect equal differences in the strength of the relationship between X and Y, and $r^2 = 0$ indicates the complete absence of any linear relationship between X and Y.

There is more to know, though, about interpreting a correlation. As we will see next, a number of factors combine to create situations in which low values of r do not necessarily indicate a weak relationship, and high values of r do not necessarily indicate a strong relationship.

Truncated Variance. We have already seen that in order for two variables to be correlated, they must each show at least some variance. It is also true that

Figure 10.8

The (a) correlation and (b) squared correlation as measures of relationship strength.

(a) The correlation (r) provides a nonlinear measure of the strength of the linear relationship between variables X and Y.

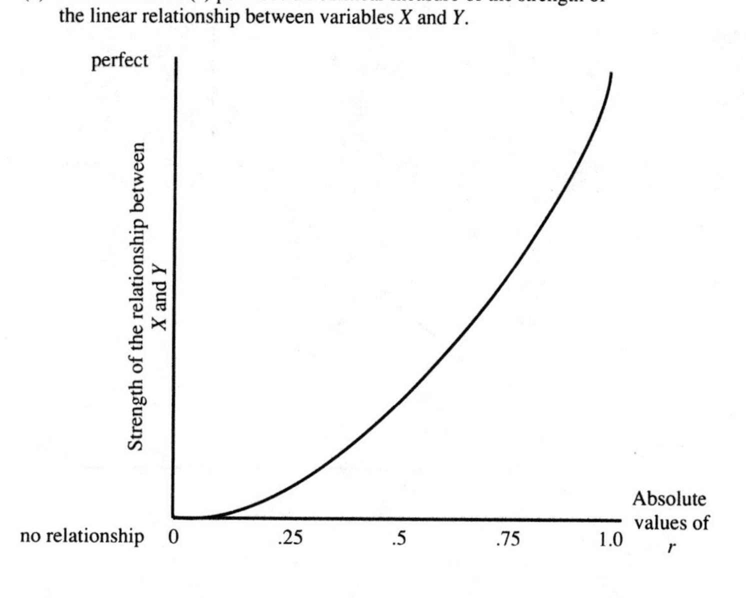

(b) The squared correlation (r^2) provides a linear measure of the strength of the linear relationship between variables X and Y.

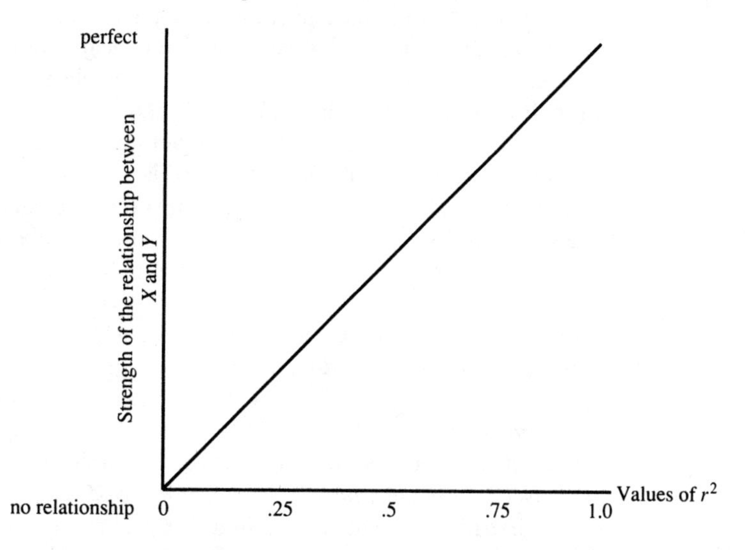

correlations computed between variables with restricted or truncated variance will tend to be somewhat attenuated. Figure 10.9 illustrates why this is the case.

When we consider the full range of scores on variables X and Y, Figure 10.9 reveals a moderately strong, positive, linear relationship between X and Y. There is some dispersion of points around an imaginary line fitted through these points, but the linear trend is still very clear. However, when the range of scores on X

Figure 10.9

The effect of truncated variance on the size of the correlation.

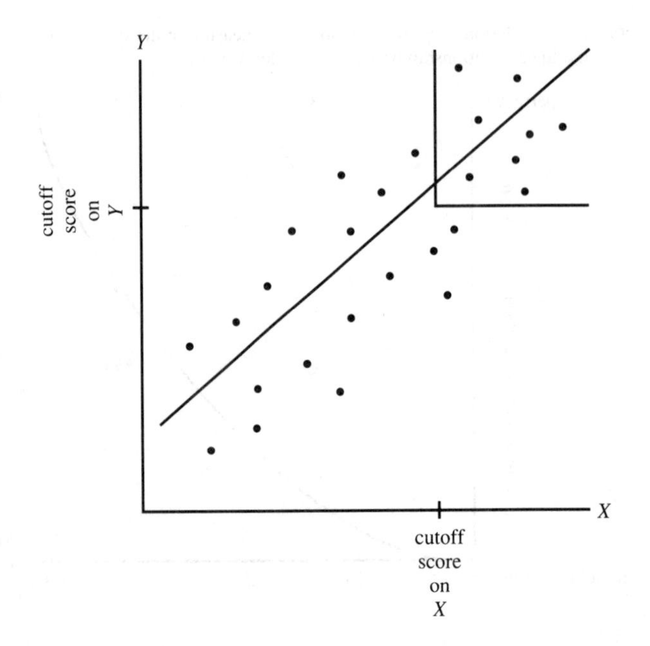

and Y is restricted so as to include only relatively high scores (above the cutoff points marked in Figure 10.9), the resulting scatterplot (the smaller scatterplot) shows no clear linear relationship and represents quite a low value of r. What happened? How could there be such a high correlation when considering the data in their entirety, and such a low correlation when the range (and, of course, the variance) of scores is truncated? Restricting the variability of one or both variables in a correlation will lower that correlation because in order for two variables to be correlated they must covary. Restricting the variance of either or both of the variables restricts the degree to which the variables can covary. What this all means, of course, is that a low correlation may be due to truncated variance, not to an absence of relationship between two variables. If one or both variables in a correlational analysis seems to show little variability or a restriction in range, interpret low correlations with this fact in mind.

Nonlinear Relationships. As we have seen, the Pearson correlation is sensitive only to linear relationships between variables.[4] A low correlation, then, may not always indicate that the variables involved are unrelated. It may mean instead that they are not related in a linear fashion. Look back at Figures 10.5b and 10.5c. Neither of these scatterplots (especially Figure 10.5c) would be well fitted with a straight line. Consequently, neither would produce an exceptionally strong correlation. Despite this, we can see from both scatterplots that X and Y are quite strongly related. In short, when a correlation is low, check the scatterplot to make sure that this is not just a result of a nonlinear relationship.

Lack of Homoscedasticity. Heteroscedastic data can produce a correlation that is both too low and too high to reflect the true strength of linear relationship.

(a) Without outliers, we see a perfect correlation.

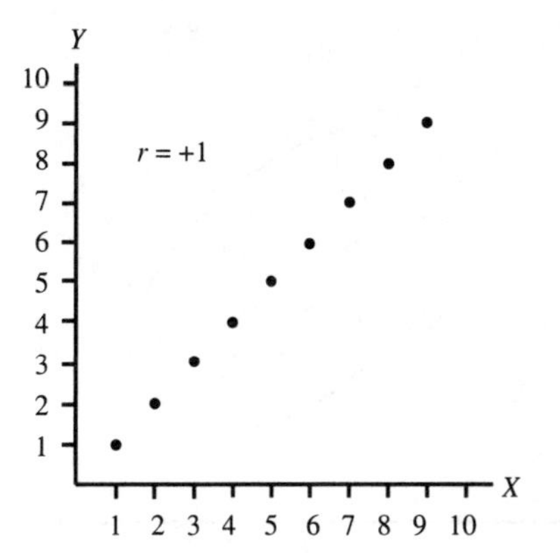

(b) Adding a single outlier reduces the perfect correlation severely.

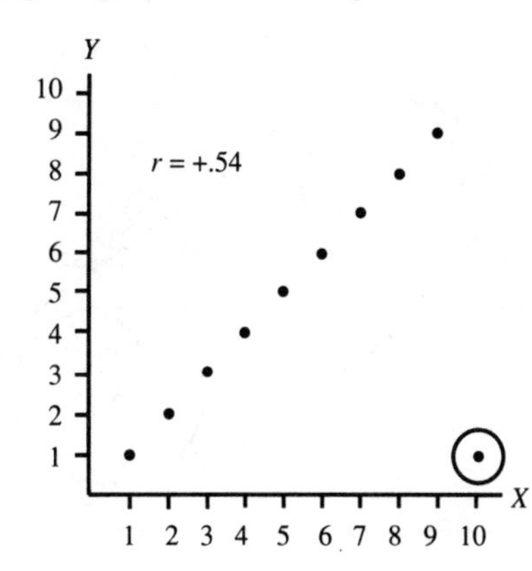

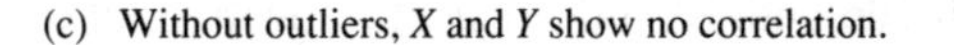
(c) Without outliers, X and Y show no correlation.

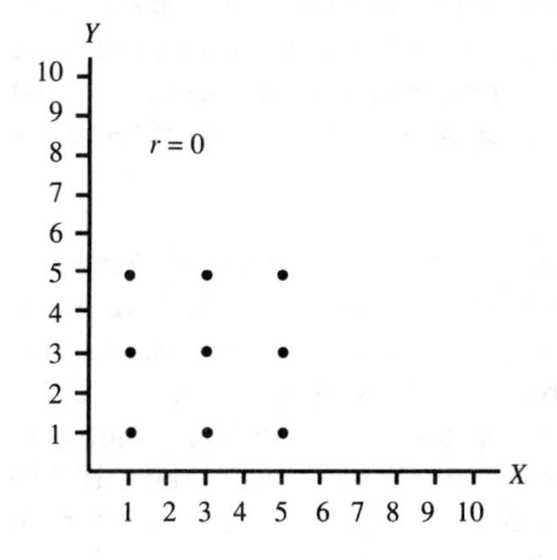

(d) Adding a single outlier creates a correlation in the moderate range.

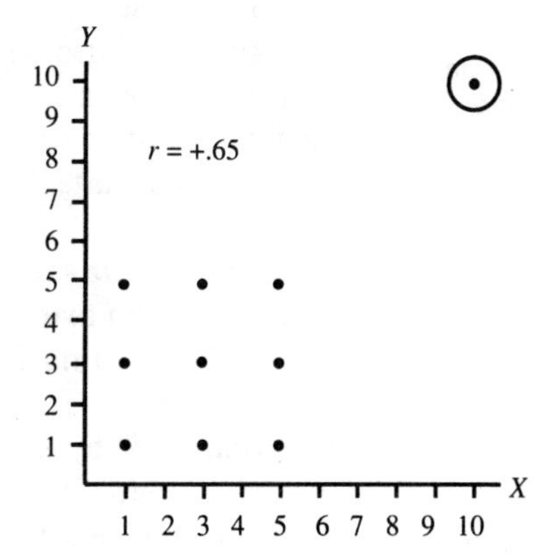

Figure 10.10

The disproportionate effects of outliers on the size of the computed correlation.

Examine Figure 10.6b. The correlation associated with this scatterplot would at once be too low to reflect the strong relationship between X and Y at low values of X, and too high to reflect the weak relationship between X and Y at high values of X. As described previously, the simplest way of assessing homoscedasticity in our data is to look at the scatterplot.

Outliers. Outliers, cases whose combined scores on X and Y mark them as deviant in comparison to the majority of cases, exert a disproportionate influence over the size of r. Correlations computed on data containing outliers may be either inflated or deflated by outliers. In either case, outliers cause the correlation to lose its accuracy as an indicator of the true strength of the relationship between X and Y.

Figure 10.10a depicts a perfect positive correlation between X and Y ($r = 1.0$). The addition of a single outlier, as shown in Figure 10.10b, lowers this correlation substantially to $r = .54$. Obviously, the relationship depicted in Figure 10.10b is stronger than this modest correlation would seem to suggest. Adding one deviant case severely attenuated the perfect correlation produced from the

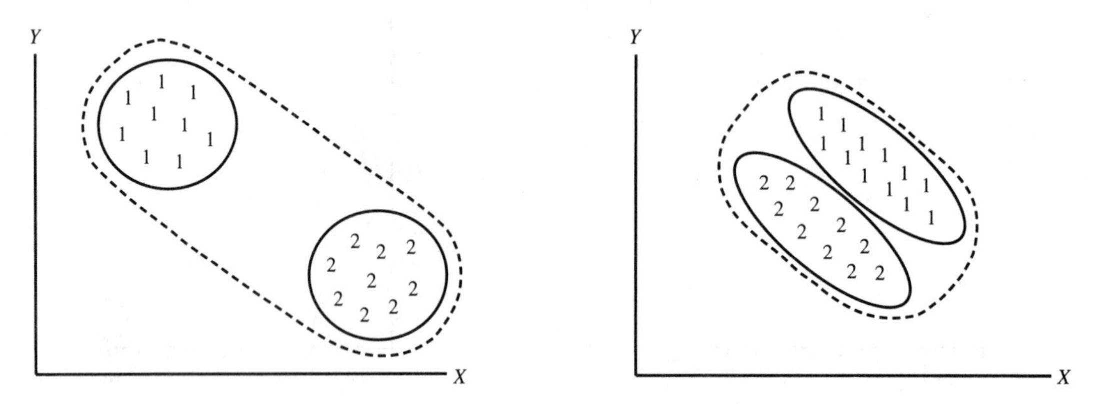
(a) Combining groups can create an artificially high correlation.
(b) Combining groups can create an artificially low correlation.
Y
X
1
2

Figure 10.11

The effects of combining group data on the size of the correlation.

data of the first nine cases. Figures 10.10c and 10.10d illustrate how a single outlier can also inflate a correlation. The scatterplot of Figure 10.10c shows no relationship whatsoever between X and Y ($r = 0$). Adding one outlier, in Figure 10.10d, gives us a correlation of $r = .65$! It is obvious from these examples that the interpretation of a computed correlation requires that we know if there are outliers in our data.

Correlations Based on Combined Group Data. A correlation computed using data from two or more groups whose means differ on one or both variables can also be either misleadingly high or low. Figure 10.11a illustrates the situation in which neither Group 1 data (indicated by 1's in the scatterplot) nor Group 2 data (indicated by 2's) alone would yield an appreciable correlation. Combined, though, the data from these groups show a substantial correlation. Figure 10.11b illustrates the situation in which both Group 1 and Group 2 show substantial correlations when considered alone. When the data are combined, though, the correlation disappears.

Statistical Significance of *r*

How large must a correlation be before it can be considered reliable? Is a correlation of $r = \pm.2$ sufficient for us to conclude that the relationship between X and Y is real and not just a spurious result of random error in the sample data? How about $r = \pm.4$? What about $r = \pm.7$? This is the problem of statistical significance as it applies to correlations. The significant difference tests examined in previous chapters revealed how large a difference had to be before that difference would be considered reliable, trustworthy, or, in the terminology of statistics, significant. Correlational statistics, including the Pearson r, may also be tested for statistical significance. These significance tests use much the same logic as did tests of difference. The discussion that follows is illustrated by an example in Box 10.3.

Step 1: The Null and Alternative Hypotheses. There are two possible explanations for a correlation found between X and Y. One, the null hypothesis (H_0), attributes the observed correlation to sampling error. A correlation of the observed size would be relatively likely even if the sample data were drawn from a population in which X and Y showed no correlation whatsoever. Sampling error alone has yielded a sample in which the correlation is greater than zero. The alternative hypothesis (H_1) proposes that the observed correlation is too large to attribute to sampling error. That is, it is unlikely that one would draw a sample yielding a correlation of the observed magnitude from a population in which $r = 0$. It is more likely that the sample which yielded the greater-than-zero correlation was drawn from a population in which X and Y are correlated. Thus, replicating the research would probably produce a similar correlation.

Step 2: The Test Statistic. In difference testing, the test statistic varies in value as a function of the magnitude of the difference being tested for significance. In significance tests for correlations, the test statistic varies in value as a function of the magnitude of the relationship being tested for significance. In testing the statistical significance of the Pearson r, a variety of test statistics may be used. The most obvious test statistic, though, and the one we will examine here, is r itself. The Pearson correlation qualifies as a test statistic for the significance of the linear relationship between two variables since, in keeping with our definition above, it varies in size according to the magnitude of the relationship that is being tested for significance.[5]

Step 3: Determining the Probability of the Test Statistic. Determining the probability that a given value of a test statistic may have occurred under conditions in which the null hypothesis is true requires that the obtained value be compared to values forming the sampling distribution of that test statistic. Let us consider here the nature of the sampling distribution of r.

Imagine drawing all possible samples of size N from a population in which X and Y are uncorrelated ($r = 0$). The Pearson correlation computed for each sample according to Equation 10.1 would, because of sampling error, produce a variety of values from sample to sample, but most would be close to zero. More extreme values, both positive and negative, would occur less and less frequently. The frequency distribution of these sample r values is the sampling distribution of r, the general form of which appears in Figure 10.12.

It should come as no surprise to you by now that the specific shape of the sampling distribution of r varies as a function of sample size. As samples grow smaller, the distribution becomes flatter, with high absolute values of r occurring more frequently than is true when samples are larger. These shape changes are reflected in Appendix I: Critical Values of the Pearson Product-Moment Correlation. This table lists absolute values of r that mark off the upper and lower tails of the sampling distribution of r. The table is entered using $df = N - 2$, where $N =$ the number of pairs of scores (i.e., the number of cases). Appendix

BOX 10.3

STATISTICAL SIGNIFICANCE OF PEARSON *r*

In Box 10.1 we plotted data from the Olympic Wind Spitting competition in a scatterplot. The correlation between wind speed and spitting distance was computed in Box 10.2. The question now becomes, is this correlation ($r = -.73$) sufficiently large to be considered statistically significant?

Step 1: *The Null and Alternative Hypotheses*

H_0 : The observed value of r has occurred because of sampling error. A correlation of this size would be relatively likely in a sample drawn from a population in which $r = 0$.

H_1 : The observed magnitude of r is too great to be a likely result of sampling error. It is highly improbable that a sample drawn from a population in which $r = 0$ would yield a correlation of this magnitude. Thus, the sample probably came from a population in which absolute $r > 0$ and a replication of the study would probably also show a greater-than-zero absolute correlation.

Step 2: *The Test Statistic*

The Pearson $r = -.73$ will itself serve as our test statistic.

Step 3: *Determining the Probability of the Test Statistic*

By comparing the obtained value of $r = -.73$ to the sampling distribution of r, we can determine its approximate probability of occurrence in samples drawn from a population in which $r = 0$. For $df = N - 2 = 8$, the critical value of r that marks off the lower 1% of the r values forming the sampling distribution of r is $-.7155$. Our obtained value exceeds this critical value, indicating that the probability is less than .01 that a sample drawn from a population in which $r = 0$ would have yielded a correlation as strong as the one obtained. We conclude, then, that the sample probably does not represent a population in which $r = 0$, but instead, has come from a population in which absolute $r > 0$. This being the case, the same correlation observed here would probably be observed again in a replication of the study. In other words, we reject H_0 and declare the correlation to be statistically significant.

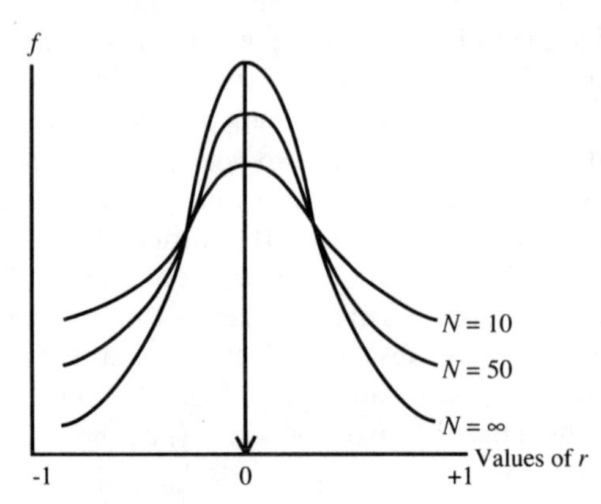

Figure 10.12

The shape of the sampling distribution of *r* varies as a function of sample size (*N*).

I helps us perform both one-tail and two-tail tests of the significance of r. One-tail significance levels are used when the direction of the correlation (positive or negative) has been predicted in advance; two-tail significance levels are used when the direction of the relationship has not been predicted. An observed value of r is statistically significant if it meets or exceeds the tabled critical value of r for $N - 2$ degrees of freedom and the selected significance level.

Statistical vs. Practical Significance of Correlations

The distinction between statistically significant and practically significant differences was discussed in previous chapters. We saw there that several factors, other than the size of the difference being tested for significance, influence whether a given difference will or will not be found to be statistically significant. A difference of no practical importance can, under the right circumstances, be found statistically significant.

Significance tests of correlations are also influenced by factors other than the magnitude of the correlation. Sample size is particularly important in this regard. Almost any correlation, no matter how small, will be found to be statistically significant if it is based on a large enough sample. Inspection of Appendix I, the Table of Critical Values of the Pearson Product-Moment Correlation, shows that a correlation as small as $r = \pm.1638$ is significant at the .05 level (one-tail) if it is obtained for a sample of size $N = 102$ ($df = 100$). In correlational research large samples are common. With samples larger than 100, correlations that approach zero are statistically significant! The magnitude of the correlation, or better yet, r^2, should always be considered when interpreting the meaning and importance of a statistically significant correlation.

Correlation and Causation

Beginning students in the social and behavioral sciences are invariably warned against drawing causal conclusions from correlations. Indeed, there are many obvious examples of situations in which doing so would be fallacious. For instance, say a researcher found a moderate correlation between the number of packs of cigarettes smoked in a year's time and the number of colds contracted during the same time. Would this evidence alone lead reasonably to the conclusion that cigarette smoking causes colds? Of course not. Instead, perhaps the more one smokes, the more trips must be made to the store to buy cigarettes, resulting in greater exposure to cold viruses. Or, perhaps the stress that predisposes some people to smoke also predisposes them to catch more colds. Simply observing that two variables are correlated does not provide the basis for drawing causal conclusions. However, a causal relationship between two variables will be reflected in a correlation and, under some circumstances, a correlation can provide the basis for drawing a causal conclusion.

Drawing causal conclusions depends on how the data are collected, not on how they are subsequently analyzed. We conclude that variable X (the independent variable) has exerted a causal influence on variable Y (the dependent variable) when we actively manipulate the independent variable (i.e., vary it from one case to the next or from one group to the next) and observe a subsequent, accompanying variability in the dependent variable. Imagine that you found a black box with a knob on the front panel and a light bulb on the top. Each time you turned the knob to the left, the light got dimmer; each time you turned it to the right, the light got brighter. After a time spent turning the knob and observing the changing intensity of the light, you would justifiably conclude that moving the knob caused the light's intensity to change. Causal conclusions in science depend upon the same kind of active manipulation of an independent variable (like turning the knob) and passive observation and measurement of a dependent variable (like observing the changing intensity of the light). This is called an **experiment.**

Traditionally, data collected in an experiment are analyzed using some type of significant difference test. For example, one group of depressed patients is given a placebo and a second group is given a daily dose of 50 mg of an experimental drug. The independent variable here is drug dosage (0 vs. 50 mg) and is clearly being manipulated by the experimenter. After some suitable period of time has elapsed, the two groups' levels of depression (the dependent variable) are measured in some way and are compared, perhaps with a two-sample t-test, to see if the groups now show different levels of depression. If they do, the drug, received by one group, but not the other, may be assumed to have caused the observed difference.

A correlational approach might just as easily have been used, though, in determining if the drug had a causal effect on level of depression. If different subjects were administered different doses of the drug, covering the full range of possible dosages, and subjects' depression levels were subsequently measured, a correlation between drug dosage (X) and depression (Y) could be taken as a measure of the strength of the causal relationship between the drug and depression. The key to drawing causal conclusions lies in collecting data in such a way that the independent variable is actively manipulated and the dependent variable is measured subsequent to this manipulation. Whether these data are analyzed using significant difference tests or correlations has no bearing on whether or not a causal conclusion can be drawn.

SPEARMAN RANK-ORDER CORRELATION

The Pearson product-moment correlation was described previously as applicable to interval and ratio scale data that are approximately normally distributed. Ordinal scale correlational data, or interval or ratio scale data that deviate substantially from normalcy, are traditionally analyzed using the **Spearman rank-order correlation,** sometimes called "rho." Since rho uses rank-orders, relationships that are nonlinear, but **monotonic** (as in Figure 10.5b), may also be evaluated with rho. A monotonic relationship is one in which scores on one variable show a continuous increase or decrease as scores increase or decrease on a second variable, even though the trend may not be linear. Like the Pearson correlation, rho varies from -1 to 0 to $+1$, with the sign and magnitude of rho being interpreted in a fashion identical to that discussed previously for the Pearson correlation.

Computing the Spearman Rank-Order Correlation

The first step in computing rho is to rank-order the values of X and Y, if they are not already in this form. Ties are treated as described in chapter 7. Next, rho may be computed according to Equation 10.2.

EQUATION 10.2

$$\text{rho} = 1 - \frac{6\Sigma D^2}{N(N^2 - 1)}$$

where,

D = differences between corresponding ranks of X and Y
N = the number of cases (i.e., pairs of scores)

Rho may also be computed using the formula for the Pearson correlation (Equation 10.1). When Equations 10.1 and 10.2 are applied to rank-ordered data in which there are no tied ranks, the results are identical. When there are many tied ranks, rho computed using Equation 10.2 will tend to be spuriously high, and it is actually better to use the Pearson correlation formula.

Statistical Significance of the Spearman Correlation

The logic of significance testing of the Spearman rank-order correlation is identical to that discussed previously for the Pearson correlation. The significance test answers the question, "What is the probability that a correlation of this size would have been obtained from a sample drawn from a population in which X and Y are uncorrelated?" A relatively high probability ($p > .05$) leads to the conclusion that the observed correlation is due to sampling error; a low probability ($p < .05$) is support for the alternative hypothesis that the correlation between X and Y is greater than zero in the population from which the sample was drawn.

In testing the statistical significance of rho, rho itself serves as the test statistic.[6] We may use Appendix I: Table of Critical Values of the Pearson Product-Moment Correlation for finding the probability of an obtained value of rho. As with the Pearson r, rho must meet or exceed the tabled critical value for $df = N - 2$ and the selected level of significance. Box 10.4 demonstrates how rho is computed and tested for significance.

CHI-SQUARE AND CRAMER'S *V* STATISTIC

Two statistics are used together to explore relationships between nominal scale variables: the chi-square (χ^2) statistic and Cramer's V statistic. As we will see, χ^2 provides a numerical index of the strength of association between two nominal scale variables and a test statistic for assessing the statistical significance of this relationship. Cramer's V rescales the value of χ^2 so that it falls between 0 and 1, making interpretation more convenient. Box 10.5 provides an example of the use of χ^2 and V in the analysis of relationships between nominal scale variables.

BOX 10.4

THE SPEARMAN RANK-ORDER CORRELATION

Professor Yogi Zen, Head of the Division of Metaphysical Sciences at Rocky Bottom State University, has observed that the productivity of faculty members in his division seems to be inversely related to their tendency to self-aggrandize. To explore this possibility further, he rank-ordered nine faculty members according to their self-aggrandizing tendencies (X) and professional productivity (Y). These rankings are listed in Table 10.2. Also listed in Table 10.2 are differences (D) between each case's ranks on X and Y.

Rho is computed from the data in Table 10.2 according to Equation 10.2:

$$\text{rho} = 1 - \frac{6 \Sigma D^2}{N(N^2 - 1)}$$
$$= 1 - \frac{1224}{9(9^2 - 1)}$$
$$= -.70$$

We can see from this value that there is a moderately strong, negative, monotonic relationship between the tendency to self-aggrandize and professional productivity.

In testing the statistical significance of rho, the obtained value (rho $= -.70$) is compared to the sampling distribution of the Pearson correlation in Appendix I. For $df = N - 2 = 7$, we find that our obtained value of rho is statistically significant at the .025 level of significance (one-tail) as it exceeds the tabled critical value of .6664.

TABLE 10.2 Rank-Order Data on Self-Aggrandizement and Professional Productivity

	Self-aggrandizement	Productivity	
Faculty members	X	Y	D
1	1	9	−8
2	3	8	−5
3	2	7	−5
4	6	2	4
5	7	3	4
6	8	1	7
7	4	4	0
8	9	6	3
9	5	5	0

The Contingency Table

The analysis of relationships between nominal scale variables begins with a **contingency table** like the one shown in Table 10.3 of Box 10.5. Each cell in this table represents one of the possible combinations of categories of the variables being investigated. Recorded in each cell is the number of cases that are observed to show that particular combination of categories on the two variables. These frequency counts are called *observed frequencies,* symbolized f_o. It is assumed that each case appears in one and only one cell of the contingency table and that each case is completely independent of the others. **Expected frequencies,** symbolized f_e, are also recorded in each cell of the contingency table. These are frequencies that would be expected if the variables being investigated were not related. Any discrepancy between observed and expected frequencies, then, is evidence that the variables are related. The absence of a relationship results in observed frequencies matching exactly the expected frequencies. The greater the discrepancy between observed and expected frequencies, the stronger the relationship between the variables.

The Chi-Square Statistic

The chi-square statistic provides a numerical index of the discrepancy between f_o and f_e found across the cells of the contingency table. Chi-square is computed just as it was for the χ^2 goodness-of-fit test (chapter 6) and the χ^2 test for two independent samples (chapter 7):

$$\chi^2 = \Sigma \frac{(f_o - f_e)^2}{f_e}$$

where,

f_o = observed frequencies; the number of cases falling in each cell of the contingency table
f_e = expected frequencies; the number of cases that would be expected to fall in each cell of the contingency table if there were no relationship between the variables being examined

In words, in each cell of the contingency table, the expected frequency is subtracted from the observed frequency, this difference is squared, and this squared difference is divided by that cell's expected frequency. Finally, all of these values are summed across the cells of the contingency table to yield χ^2. As the differences between observed and expected frequencies accumulate across the cells of the contingency table, χ^2 increases in value.

Cramer's *V* Statistic

The value of χ^2 is not a convenient measure of the strength of the relationship between nominal variables. This is because χ^2 is determined not just by the strength of the relationship, but by the number of cases being studied as well. Cramer's *V* Statistic, computed from χ^2, "corrects" χ^2 for the influence of sample size and provides a more easily interpreted measure of the strength of the relationship between two nominal variables. Cramer's *V*, first seen in chapter 7, is computed according to Equation 7.10.

$$V = \sqrt{\frac{\chi^2}{N(n - 1)}}$$

where,

N = the total number of cases
n = the number of rows or columns, whichever is smaller

Because χ^2 can never take on negative values, neither can *V*. Except for this, *V* is interpreted like a Pearson or Spearman correlation. When there is no relationship displayed in the contingency table (i.e., when $f_o = f_e$ for all cells of the table), χ^2 will equal 0, as will *V*. As the f_o vs. f_e discrepancies increase, χ^2 will increase, causing *V* to increase as well, up to a maximum value of 1.

BOX 10.5

CHI-SQUARE AND CRAMER'S *V*

Students in the social and behavioral sciences at Rocky Bottom State University have been appearing in record numbers this semester to receive psychological counseling in the campus clinic. Their complaints have been mostly psychosomatic in nature and appear to fall into one of the following categories: teeth gnashing, hair pulling, and sweating blood. You are curious to know if there is any relationship between presenting symptoms and students' majors: psychology, sociology, and social work.

The first step in analyzing data obtained from the 116 students is to construct the contingency table presented as Table 10.3. Recorded in this table are the numbers of students falling in each cell (f_o values). Also shown are column, row, and grand totals, along with row percentages. The table also contains expected frequencies (f_e) in each cell. An expected frequency is the number of cases that we would expect to see in a cell if the variables of college major and symptoms were unrelated. Since 33.6% of the entire sample gnash their teeth (see the first row percentage), one would expect that 33.6% of the psychology students ($n = 34$), 33.6% of the sociology students ($n = 40$), and 33.6% of the social work students ($n = 42$) would be teeth gnashers if major and symptom had no relationship. Thus, our expected frequencies for the first row are 33.6% × 34 = 11.42; 33.6% × 40 = 13.44; and 33.6% × 42 = 14.11. Similarly, we know that 42.2% of the sample pull their hair (see the second row of percentage). If major and symptom are unrelated, we would expect this percentage to apply equally to students in each major, yielding expected frequencies for the second row of the table of 42.2% × 34 = 14.35; 42.2% × 40 = 16.88; and 42.2% × 42 = 17.72. Finally, 24.1% of the sample sweat blood (see the third row percentage). If major and symptoms are unrelated, this percentage should apply to all majors, giving expected frequencies for the third row of the table of 24.1% × 34 = 8.19; 24.1% × 40 = 9.64; and 24.1% × 42 = 10.12.

Examining the contingency table, we see that expected frequencies (f_e) differ somewhat from frequencies that were actually observed (f_o). The magnitude of the discrepancies between f_o and f_e is directly related to the strength of the relationship between major and symptoms.

To quantify this relationship, χ^2 is computed according to Equation 6.2.

$$\begin{aligned}\chi^2 &= \Sigma \frac{(f_o - f_e)^2}{f_e} \\ &= \frac{(16 - 11.42)^2}{11.42} + \\ &\quad \frac{(12 - 13.44)^2}{13.44} + \ldots + \frac{(10 - 10.12)^2}{10.12} \\ &= 4.70\end{aligned}$$

It makes sense that *V* cannot take on any negative values. A negative correlation means that as values on *X* increase, values on *Y* decrease. When dealing with nominal scale variables, though, the terms "increase" and "decrease" have no meaning. It is meaningless to say, for example, that there is a positive or negative relationship between religious affiliation and political affiliation. There may be a relationship, but it cannot be described as either positive or negative.

Significance of χ^2

Chi-square serves as the test statistic in testing the statistical significance of the relationship quantified both by χ^2 and *V*. The logic of the χ^2 test of significance is consistent with that of the Pearson and Spearman significance tests. We determine the likelihood that a given χ^2 value would have occurred in a sample drawn from a population in which the variables under study are not related. This

BOX 10.5—*continued*

TABLE 10.3 Contingency Table for College Major and Psychosomatic Symptoms

		Majors				
		Psychology	*Sociology*	*Social Work*	*Row Totals*	*Row %*
	Teeth Gnashing	$f_o = 16$ $f_e = 11.42$	$f_o = 12$ $f_e = 13.44$	$f_o = 11$ $f_e = 14.11$	39	33.6
Symptoms	*Hair Pulling*	$f_o = 10$ $f_e = 14.35$	$f_o = 18$ $f_e = 16.88$	$f_o = 21$ $f_e = 17.72$	49	42.2
	Bloody Sweat	$f_o = 8$ $f_e = 8.19$	$f_o = 10$ $f_e = 9.64$	$f_o = 10$ $f_e = 10.12$	28	24.1
	Column Totals	34	40	42	$N = 116$	

Next, this χ^2 value is used in computing Cramer's V according to Equation 7.10.

$$V = \sqrt{\frac{\chi^2}{N(n-1)}} = \sqrt{\frac{4.70}{116(2)}} = .14$$

This low value of Cramer's V implies that there is only a very weak relationship between major and symptoms.

Finally, χ^2 is evaluated for statistical significance. For $df = (R - 1)(C - 1) = (3 - 1)(3 - 1) = 4$, the critical value of χ^2 for the .05 level of significance is 9.49. The obtained value of $\chi^2 = 4.70$ falls short of this critical value and is therefore not considered statistically significant. We conclude that there is no reliable relationship between college major and symptoms.

is accomplished by comparing the obtained χ^2 value to the sampling distribution of χ^2. Critical values of χ^2 are listed in Appendix C: Critical Values of Chi-Square.

The Table of Critical Values of Chi-Square is entered according to the selected level of significance and degrees of freedom (df). For the χ^2 test of significance of relationship between nominal variables, degrees of freedom are computed as $df = (R - 1)(C - 1)$, where R = the number of rows in the contingency table, and C = the number of columns. The obtained value of χ^2 is significant at the selected level of significance if it meets or exceeds the tabled critical value.

Small Expected Frequencies and Yates' Correction. We have seen previously (chapters 6 and 7) that the χ^2 statistic is affected excessively by low values of f_e. Because of this, it is recommended that the χ^2 test of association be used only when all expected frequencies in a 2 × 2 contingency table are at least 5. For larger tables, at least 80% of the cells should contain expected frequencies of at least 5 and no cell should contain an expected frequency of less than 1. When expected frequencies are too small, it is sometimes possible to combine or eliminate categories to get expected frequencies that are sufficiently large. Of course, we may also add data from more cases. As a third alternative, useful only with 2 × 2 contingency tables, χ^2 can be computed using Yates' correction for continuity, presented in chapter 7 as Equation 7.8.

SUMMARY

This chapter examines measures of association between two variables. These bivariate correlational statistics are available for interval and ratio scale data (the Pearson correlation), ordinal data (the Spearman rank-order correlation), and nominal scale data (chi-square and Cramer's *V* statistic). Interpreting correlational statistics is eased by examining graphs of the data, called scatterplots, and by an awareness of factors that can lead to misleadingly high or low computed correlational statistics. Evaluating the statistical significance of a correlation focuses on the issue of replicability. A significant correlation is one that is sufficiently large that it would most probably be observed again in a replication of the research. A statistically significant correlation may or may not help us to draw a causal conclusion about the relationship between the variables, depending on how the data were collected. Finally, the statistical significance of a correlation must not be equated automatically with practical significance of a relationship, since even very small correlations may be found to be statistically significant.

NOTES

1. The Pearson r may also be applied in assessing the relationship between one interval or ratio variable and a second variable, which is a dichotomously-scored nominal scale variable. In this situation, the correlation is commonly called a point-biserial correlation, but may be computed using Equation 10.1 or the computational formula for the Pearson r given in Note 3. Alternatively, the point-biserial correlation may be computed more conveniently using the following computational formula:

$$r = \frac{\overline{X}_0 - \overline{X}_1}{s_X} \sqrt{pq}$$

where,

$\overline{X}_0$ = mean on the continuous variable X of cases scored 0 on the dichotomous variable Y

$\overline{X}_1$ = mean on the continuous variable X of cases scored 1 on the dichotomous variable Y

s_X = standard deviation of the continuous variable X for all cases

p = the proportion of cases scored 0 on the dichotomous variable Y

q = the proportion of cases scored 1 on the dichotomous variable Y

The statistical significance of the point-biserial is evaluated exactly as is the Pearson correlation.

2. The **eta coefficient** or **correlation ratio** provides an index of association for variables that show a nonlinear relationship. Eta can range in value from 0 to +1, never taking on negative values. Aside from this, eta is interpreted just as the Pearson correlation. The computation of eta is relatively complicated. The interested reader should consult Hinkle, Wiersma, & Jurs (1988).
3. The Pearson correlation formula may be computed more conveniently using the following computational formula:

$$r = \frac{N\Sigma XY - (\Sigma X)(\Sigma Y)}{\sqrt{[N\Sigma X^2 - (\Sigma X)^2][N\Sigma Y^2 - (\Sigma Y)^2]}}$$

where,

N = the number of cases; i.e., the number of score pairs
X = scores on the variable X
Y = scores on the variable Y

4. See note 2.
5. The t statistic is often computed from r to serve as a test statistic for the significance of r with $df = N - 2$:

$$t = \frac{r\sqrt{N-2}}{\sqrt{1-r^2}}$$

where,

r = the correlation being tested for significance
N = the number of cases; i.e., the number of score pairs

6. The t statistic may also be used in testing the significance of the Spearman rank-order correlation, substituting rho for r in the equation given in Note 5.

CHAPTER 11

Bivariate Regression Analysis

Prediction is a goal common to all sciences, including the social and behavioral sciences. Meteorologists try to predict the weather, political scientists try to predict election outcomes, economists try to predict economic trends, and behavioral scientists try to predict behavior in its varied forms. All of these attempts at prediction are based on relationships between variables. It is the fact that crime rate and cost of living are correlated that enables us to predict crime rate from cost of living, or conversely, to predict cost of living from crime rate. Similarly, it is the correlation between SAT scores and college grade point average that helps us to predict a student's college grades from his or her SAT scores, or, though this seems rather pointless, to predict the student's SAT scores from his or her grades. In sum, the correlation between two variables sets the stage for predicting one variable from another.

One of the most powerful tools for translating correlations into predictions is **bivariate regression analysis.** It is through bivariate regression analysis that the correlation between two variables, *X* and *Y*, is used in predicting one variable, called the **criterion variable,** from the other variable, called the **predictor variable. Multiple regression,** to which we will turn in chapter 13, uses a combination of several predictor variables in predicting a criterion variable.

THE SCATTERPLOT AND REGRESSION LINE OF *Y* ON *X*

Given that regression analysis depends upon the correlation between variables *X* and *Y*, it is not surprising to find that the scatterplot, which is so useful in evaluating correlations, is also useful in understanding regression analysis. As we saw in the preceding chapter, the strength of the correlation between *X* and *Y* is represented in a scatterplot by the amount of dispersion of points around a straight line positioned through those points. The less scattering of points around the line, the stronger the correlation. Unnamed until now, this line is called the **regression line.** As we will see later in this chapter, there are actually two regression lines that may be fitted through the points forming the scatterplot. The first, used in predicting variable *Y* from variable *X*, is called the **regression line of *Y* on *X*.** The second, used in predicting *X* from *Y*, is called the **regression line of *X* on *Y*.** We will focus on the first of these lines here and will turn to the second regression line later in this chapter.

Consider Figure 11.1, a scatterplot depicting the relationship between *X*, the size of dogs measured in pounds, and *Y*, scores on the Whewie Canine Halitosis Scale. The line shown fitted through the data points of Figure 11.1 is the regression line of *Y* on *X*, positioned so as to minimize errors in predicting halitosis level from size.

The mechanics of using this regression line to predict breath quality from dog size are very straightforward. Suppose you are considering buying a 40-pound Chow, but are concerned that the dog's breath may be unbearable. Based on the scatterplot relating dog size and halitosis, you can predict the quality of a 40-pound dog's breath. First, locate 40 on the abscissa and draw a line vertically to the regression line. Next, draw a horizontal line from this point on the regression line to the ordinate. The value on the ordinate intersected by this horizontal

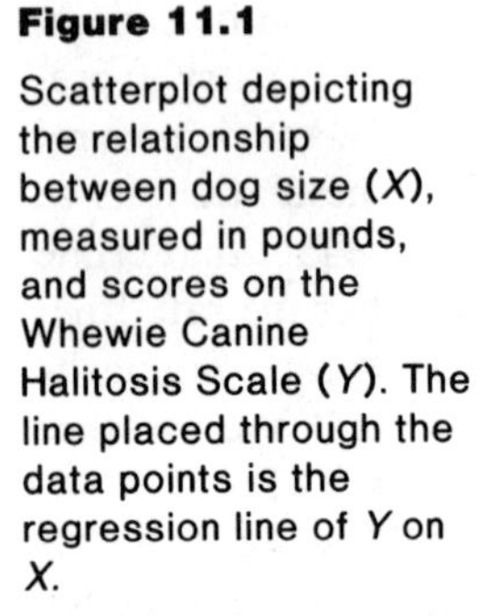

Figure 11.1
Scatterplot depicting the relationship between dog size (X), measured in pounds, and scores on the Whewie Canine Halitosis Scale (Y). The line placed through the data points is the regression line of Y on X.

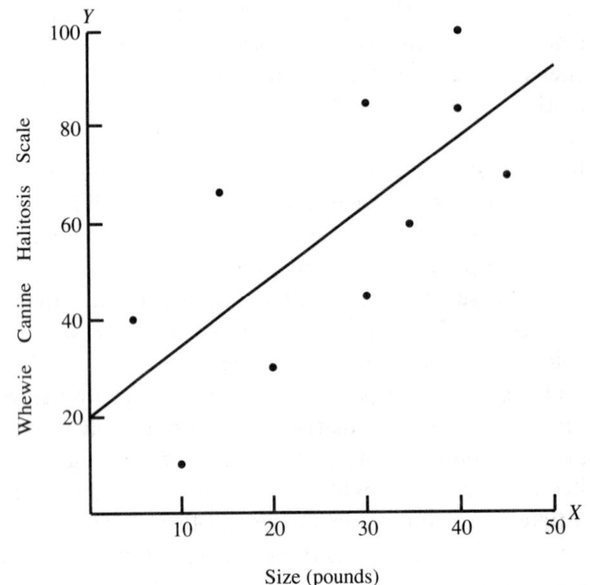

line represents the predicted value of halitosis. The regression line of Y on X thus predicts that a 40-pound dog will have a halitosis score of about 80.

Notice two things from this example. First, unless $r = \pm 1.0$, such that data points line up exactly along the regression line, we can expect some error in our predictions of Y from X. In Figure 11.1, for instance, we have predicted that a 40-pound dog would have a halitosis score of 80, yet the data that are summarized in this scatterplot include two 40-pound dogs whose halitosis scores were 100 and 85. We have underpredicted halitosis for dogs of 40 pounds. Looking at other locations along the regression line we can see that the regression line yields predictions that are sometimes a bit too high. The regression line predicts that a 20-pound dog will score around 50 on the halitosis scale, yet the scatterplot shows us that a dog actually weighing 20 pounds presented a score of 30. In sum, the regression line makes errors of both underprediction and overprediction, but errors of these two types are balanced. This is a point to which we will return later.

The second thing to notice from Figure 11.1 is that fitting a regression line through a scatterplot by eye is imprecise at best. As the correlation between X and Y grows smaller, the linear relationship between the variables become less obvious and it becomes more difficult to see exactly where the regression line should be placed in order to achieve the best possible fit. Fortunately, regression analysis can be, and normally is, accomplished much more precisely using the linear regression equation, which defines the regression line.

THE LINEAR REGRESSION EQUATION OF *Y* ON *X*

The regression line of Y on X is defined by the **linear regression equation of *Y* on *X*.**[1]

EQUATION 11.1

$$Y' = a_Y + b_Y X$$

where,

$$Y' = \text{values of } Y \text{ predicted for given values of } X$$

$$b_Y = r\left(\frac{s_Y}{s_X}\right)$$

$$a_Y = \overline{Y} - b_Y\overline{X}$$

$$X = \text{values of } X$$

Once values of b_Y and a_Y are computed, any given value of X can be substituted into Equation 11.1 to determine the corresponding value of Y'. Let us next consider the values of b_Y and a_Y.

The value b_Y is called the **regression coefficient of *Y* on *X*.** This value determines the slope of the regression line. Thus, positive values of b_Y (that result from positive correlations) produce regression lines which ascend as one moves to higher values of X; negative values of b_Y (that result from negative correlations) produce regression lines which descend as one moves to higher values of X. When $r = 0$ such that $b_Y = 0$, the regression line of Y on X is perfectly horizontal. Equation 11.1 shows that the regression coefficient determines how much change will occur in Y' for each unit (i.e., one-point) change in X. In Figure 11.1, notice that as weight increases 10 pounds from $X = 30$ to $X = 40$, Y' increases 14.6 points from $Y' = 63.4$ to 78. Thus, for every 1-pound increase in X, Y' increases about 1.46 points. The slope, b_Y, of the regression line for predicting halitosis from weight, then, is 1.46. As the absolute value of b_Y increases, the slope of the regression line becomes correspondingly steeper.

The value a_Y in Equation 11.1 is called the **regression constant of *Y* on *X*.** This value determines the altitude of the regression line of Y on X. The regression constant is sometimes called the ***Y-intercept*** because, as can be seen in Equation 11.1, it determines the value of Y' when $X = 0$. In Figure 11.1 we see that for $X = 0$, $Y' = 19.6$. Thus, the regression constant for the regression line of Y on X in Figure 11.1 is $a_Y = 19.6$. A moment's reflection will confirm that as the value of a_Y increases, the height or altitude of the regression line will increase; as the value a_Y decreases, the regression line will be lowered.

In summary, given data suitable to analysis using the Pearson product-moment correlation, one can compute Y' for any given value of X using Equation 11.1. Values of Y' computed from one value of X to the next will vary, defining the regression line of Y on X in the scatterplot depicting the correlation between X and Y. Box 11.1 provides an example of the use of the regression equation of Y on X.

BOX 11.1

THE REGRESSION OF *Y* ON *X*

TABLE 11.1 Data on Wall Street Sentiment (X), Number of Clients (Y), and Predicted Number of Clients(Y')

Day	Wall Street Sentiment	No. of Clients	Predicted No. of Clients
	(X)	(Y)	(Y')
1	6	8	8.3525
2	10	2	3.7185
3	4	6	10.6695
4	3	11	11.8280
5	2	14	12.9865
6	3	14	11.8280
7	5	12	9.5110
8	7	4	7.1940
9	8	10	6.0355
10	9	6	4.8770

Long a student of human nature, The Great Snatchaudollar has established a brisk fortune-telling business on Wall Street. Recently, he has noticed that the soothsaying business waxes and wanes in a manner that is inversely related to the mood on Wall Street. His clientele, mostly stockbrokers, flock in on days of down markets, and stay away in herds during bull markets.

An accomplished statistician, Snatchaudollar has decided to quantify the relationship between the mood on Wall Street and the volume of his business and to use regression analysis in predicting daily fluctuations in his business. As his predictor variable (X), the sentiment on Wall Street, he counts the number of brokers he sees laughing as he walks to work each morning. The criterion variable (Y), business volume, is the number of clients that he sees each day. Both of these variables are listed in Table 11.1.

First, descriptive statistics are computed for both variables:

$$\bar{X} = 5.70 \qquad \bar{Y} = 8.70$$
$$s_X^2 = 6.810 \qquad s_Y^2 = 15.610$$
$$s_X = 2.6096 \qquad s_Y = 3.9509$$

(Values are computed to beyond the usual number of decimal places to avoid rounding errors later on.)

Next, the correlation between sentiment and business volume is depicted as a scatterplot in Figure 11.2. This scatterplot indicates that the Great Snatchaudollar's hunch was right. Business volume and the mood on Wall Street show a moderate to strong negative linear relationship. The Pearson product-moment correlation between sentiment and business volume confirms this: $r = -.7652$.

In order to predict business volume from sentiment, we must compute values of the regression coefficient (b_Y) and the regression constant (a_Y) according to Equation 11.1.

$$b_Y = r\left(\frac{s_Y}{s_X}\right)$$
$$= -.7652\left(\frac{3.9509}{2.6096}\right)$$
$$= -1.1585$$

and

$$
\begin{aligned}
a_Y &= \overline{Y} - b_Y\overline{X} \\
&= 8.70 + 1.1585(5.70) \\
&= 15.3035
\end{aligned}
$$

With these values, we can compute Y' values for any given values of X using the regression equation for Y on X (Equation 11.1). For example:

for $X = 6$

$$
\begin{aligned}
Y' &= a_Y + b_YX \\
&= 15.3035 - 1.1585(6) \\
&= 8.3525
\end{aligned}
$$

for $X = 10$

$$
\begin{aligned}
Y' &= a_Y + b_YX \\
&= 15.3035 - 1.1585(10) \\
&= 3.7185
\end{aligned}
$$

for $X = 4$

$$
\begin{aligned}
Y' &= a_Y + b_YX \\
&= 15.3035 - 1.1585(4) \\
&= 10.6695
\end{aligned}
$$

In a similar fashion we can compute Y' values for each value of X listed in Table 11.1. These values are included in that table under the column headed Y' and are plotted in Figure 11.2 as asterisks. As you can see, Y' values computed using the regression equation of Y on X form a straight line, the regression line of Y on X.

Figure 11.2

Scatterplot depicting the relationship between Wall Street sentiment (X) and The Great Snatchaudollar's business volume (Y). Asterisks represent predicted values of Y (Y') for each value of X.

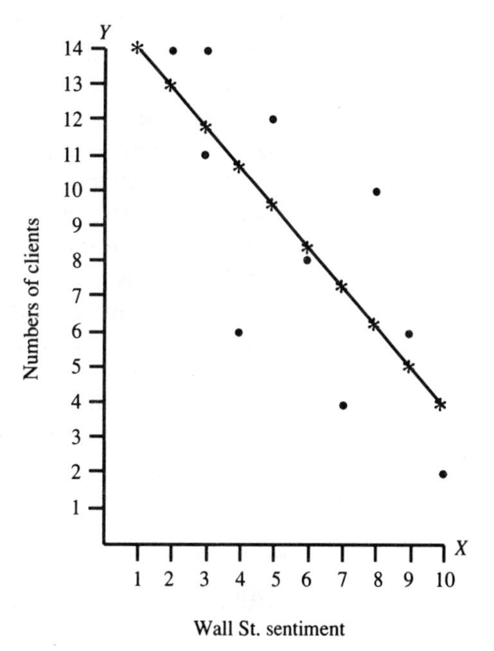

ERRORS OF PREDICTION: MEASURING PREDICTIVE ACCURACY

As we noted earlier, unless $r = \pm 1.0$, predicted Y' values will deviate somewhat from obtained Y values; there will be errors of prediction. We will now examine these errors more closely. Table 11.2 lists values of X, Y, and Y' corresponding to the scatterplot and regression line of Y on X depicted in Figure 11.1. Also listed are values of $Y - Y'$, the difference between Y and Y' values for each case. These $Y - Y'$ values reflect errors of prediction from one case to the next and are called **residual scores.**

Notice how the residual scores (i.e., prediction errors) include both errors of overprediction ($Y < Y'$) and errors of underprediction ($Y > Y'$). Too, if we take a moment to sum the residual scores, we will discover that they sum to zero, $\Sigma(Y - Y') = 0$, indicating that errors of overprediction are exactly balanced by errors of underprediction. This would not be true for any other placement of the regression line, that is, for any other values of the regression constant (a_Y) and regression coefficient (b_Y). It is also true that prediction errors represented by the residual scores are, on average, as low as they possibly can be. In other words, any other placement of the regression line would produce greater overall error than we see here. Finally, values of Y' computed using Equation 11.1 show the smallest possible sum of squared residual scores; that is, $\Sigma(Y - Y')^2$ is minimized. It is this fact that sometimes leads Equation 11.1 to be called the **least squares regression equation.** No other values of a_Y and b_Y would produce as low a sum of squared residuals.

Only when $r = \pm 1.0$, such that X and Y are perfectly linked, will Y and Y' values match perfectly. This seldom occurs in actual practice, making it necessary to find ways of describing and quantifying the amount of accuracy or inaccuracy that appears in the predictions produced through regression analysis. We will turn our attention next to this problem.

TABLE 11.2 Data on Dog Size (X), Canine Halitosis (Y), Predicted Halitosis (Y'), and Residuals ($Y - Y'$)

Size	Halitosis	Predicted Halitosis	Residuals
X	Y	Y′	Y − Y′
5	40	26.91	13.09
15	65	41.51	23.49
30	85	63.41	21.59
20	30	48.81	−18.81
40	100	78.01	21.99
35	60	70.71	−10.71
45	70	85.31	−15.31
30	45	63.41	−18.41
40	85	78.01	6.99
10	10	34.21	−24.21

Two procedures are normally followed in assessing the accuracy of predictions made through regression analysis. First, errors of postdiction serve as the best available estimate of errors of prediction that will occur if the regression equation is used in making predictions for a new set of cases. As we will see, this procedure means examining the residual scores produced by the regression equation and using them as an estimate of the prediction errors the equation would make if it were applied to new data.

If this initial assessment of the regression equation shows that levels of error are within an acceptable range, the predictive accuracy of the equation may be evaluated further through **cross-validation.** In this procedure, the regression equation developed for one sample is checked for accuracy on a second, cross-validation sample. As we will see in chapter 13, cross-validation is especially important in developing multiple regression equations. In this chapter, though, we will focus on the use of postdictive accuracy as an estimate of predictive accuracy. The general discussion of accuracy and error in regression analysis that follows is illustrated by a concrete example in Box 11.2.

Evaluating the postdictive accuracy of a regression equation includes comparing values of total variance, predicted variance, and residual variance, each of which is discussed in the sections that follow.

Total Variance

Total variance or **obtained variance** is the variance that is observed to occur in Y. Total variance is abbreviated s_Y^2 and is computed in Equation 11.2.

EQUATION 11.2

$$s_Y^2 = \frac{\Sigma(Y - \overline{Y})^2}{N}$$

The total variability seen in values of Y across cases is due to many factors. Some of this variability is the result of measurement error. Other variability results from individual differences. Some variability in Y may be linked (either causally or indirectly) to variability in X. Yet more variability is due to the influence of unknown factors.

Predicted Variance and the Coefficient of Determination

Predicted variance, symbolized $s_{Y'}^2$, can be defined in a number of ways. First, predicted variance is the variance of the Y' values. As such, it may be computed using the usual variance formula applied to Y' values.

EQUATION 11.3

$$s_{Y'}^2 = \frac{\Sigma(Y' - \overline{Y}')^2}{N}$$

where,

$\overline{Y}'$ = the mean of the Y' values

A second way of describing predicted variance is to note that it is that portion of the variability in Y that was predicted to occur by virtue of the relationship between X and Y. In other words, predicted variance is that portion of the total variance in Y that is linked to X. Sometimes predicted variance is called **explained variance** because it is variability in Y that is explained by the linkage between X and Y.

If $r < \pm 1.0$, it will always be true that $s^2_{Y'} < s^2_Y$. This is because only a portion of the variability in Y is linked to X when the correlation between X and Y is imperfect, this portion being $s^2_{Y'}$. The remaining variability in Y is due to factors other than X. On the other hand, if $r = \pm 1.0$, $s^2_Y = s^2_{Y'}$, because for every value of X, the obtained and predicted values of Y will be identical ($Y = Y'$).

Perhaps you have already anticipated that the accuracy of predictions in regression analysis will be reflected by the relationship between s^2_Y and $s^2_{Y'}$. When $r = \pm 1.0$, such that predictions are perfectly accurate, $s^2_{Y'} = s^2_Y$ and $s^2_{Y'}/s^2_Y = 1.0$. When $r = 0$, such that there is no basis for predicting Y from X, $s^2_{Y'} = 0$, and $s^2_{Y'}/s^2_Y = 0$. Accuracy of prediction between these two extremes is reflected in ratios of $s^2_{Y'}$ to s^2_Y between 0 and 1. The ratio of predicted variance to total variance ($s^2_{Y'}/s^2_Y$) is called the **coefficient of determination** and is a commonly used measure of predictive accuracy. The coefficient of determination may be defined as the proportion of the total variance in the criterion variable that has been predicted or explained by the regression equation. In other words, the coefficient of determination is the proportion of variance in the criterion variable that is linked to the predictor variable. Since the accuracy of prediction depends on the strength of the correlation between X and Y, it should come as no surprise to find that the coefficient of determination is determined entirely by the correlation.

EQUATION 11.4

$$\frac{s^2_{Y'}}{s^2_Y} = r^2$$

Since it represents the proportion of variance in Y that is explained by X, r^2 may be used in computing predicted variance.

EQUATION 11.5

$$s^2_{Y'} = r^2(s^2_Y)$$

In words, the predicted variance ($s^2_{Y'}$) will equal the proportion of variance that was predicted (r^2) times the total variance available to *be* predicted (s^2_Y).

Residual Variance and the Coefficient of Nondetermination

Residual variance, symbolized $s^2_{Y-Y'}$, can also be viewed from several perspectives. First, residual variance is the variance of the residual scores ($Y - Y'$) and can be computed as any variance:

EQUATION 11.6

$$s^2_{Y-Y'} = \frac{\Sigma[(Y - Y') - (\overline{Y - Y'})]^2}{N}$$

where,

$$(\overline{Y - Y'}) = \text{the mean of the residual scores} = 0$$

Since $\overline{Y - Y'} = 0$, Equation 11.6 is expressed more simply as:

EQUATION 11.7

$$s^2_{Y-Y'} = \frac{\Sigma(Y - Y')^2}{N}$$

Equation 11.7 makes clear a second definition of the residual variance. It is the average squared error of prediction (i.e., the average squared residual score). As such, the residual variance can be used to quantify prediction errors. As errors increase, the average squared error, or residual variance, will increase correspondingly.

Finally, the residual variance may be described as that portion of the total variance in Y that was not predicted by X.

EQUATION 11.8

$$s^2_{Y-Y'} = s^2_Y - s^2_{Y'}$$

As shown by Equation 11.8, the total variance in Y (s^2_Y) can be partitioned into two components. Some of the variance in Y is predicted or explained by variable X, the predicted variance ($s^2_{Y'}$). What remains, the residue so to speak, is the residual variance ($s^2_{Y-Y'}$). This is the variance in Y that is unexplained by X. Of course, as the relationship between X and Y grows stronger, more and more of the variance in Y will be explained by X and residual variance will grow correspondingly smaller. Conversely, as the relationship between X and Y grows weaker, less of the variance of Y will be explained by X, and residual variance will grow correspondingly larger.

This gives us yet another way of quantifying the accuracy of predictions. The ratio of residual variance to total variance, $s^2_{Y-Y'}/s^2_Y$, called the **coefficient of nondetermination,** is the proportion of the total variance in the criterion variable which is not explained by the predictor variable. As predictive accuracy grows, residual variance declines and the coefficient of nondetermination becomes smaller. Conversely, the coefficient of nondetermination grows larger as accuracy declines. Finally, just as we saw that the coefficient of determination was directly related to the correlation, so too is the coefficient of nondetermination.

EQUATION 11.9

$$\frac{s^2_{Y-Y'}}{s^2_Y} = 1 - r^2$$

Since $1 - r^2$ represents the proportion of variance in Y that is not explained by X, $1 - r^2$ may be used in computing the residual variance.

EQUATION 11.10

$$s^2_{Y-Y'} = (1 - r^2)s^2_Y$$

In words, the proportion of variance in Y not predicted by X $(1 - r^2)$ times the total variance in Y available to *be* predicted (s_Y^2) will equal the variance in Y that is not predicted ($s_{Y-Y'}^2$).

The Standard Error of the Estimate

We previously defined the residual variance as the average squared error of prediction. As such, residual variance can serve as a measure of prediction error, but it is an unwieldy measure. Would you rather be told that a *squared* error of 2.25 points was made in predicting your grade point average, or that an error of 1.5 points was made? Clearly, the later expression is more direct and easily understood. The **standard error of the estimate** ($s_{Y-Y'}$) provides this more direct expression. Computed as the square root of the residual variance, the standard error of the estimate gives an approximate indication of the average absolute error of prediction.

EQUATION 11.11

$$s_{Y-Y'} = \sqrt{s_{Y-Y'}^2}$$

r_{XY} and $r_{YY'}$

All measures of predictive accuracy describe, in one way or another, the degree to which obtained values match predicted values. Where we are predicting Y from X, high predictive accuracy means that Y and Y' values match closely; less predictive accuracy is reflected by larger discrepancies between Y and Y' values. One final measure of this match, and thus, predictive accuracy, is the correlation between obtained and predicted values of Y: $r_{YY'}$.

As described in chapter 10, the correlation is not just useful as a measure of linear relationship between two variables. It is also a useful measure of the similarity or match between any two sets of numbers. In the present context, $r_{YY'}$ gives us a measure of the match between values of Y and Y'.

We can compute $r_{YY'}$ using the usual Pearson product-moment correlation formula (Equation 10.1), but this is not necessary, since, in absolute terms, $r_{YY'} = r_{XY}$. The accuracy of our predictions, measured by $r_{YY'}$, is determined entirely by the strength of the relationship between X and Y, measured by r_{XY}. Looking at the problem in another way, remember that Y' is simply a transform of X: $Y' = a_Y + b_Y X$. Thus, we would expect that X and Y' would show the same pattern of variation from one case to the next. It follows that the pattern of covariation between X and Y (which determines r_{XY}) will be exactly the same as the pattern of covariation between Y' and Y (which determines $r_{YY'}$). Consequently, in absolute terms, $r_{YY'} = r_{XY}$.

REGRESSING *X* ON *Y*

It was noted earlier in this chapter that two regression lines may be fitted through the points of a scatterplot. We have examined only one of these lines thus far, the regression line of Y on X. This line, and the regression equation of Y on X (Equation 11.1), balances and minimizes the errors that occur when we predict Y from X, that is, $Y - Y'$.

BOX 11.2

EVALUATING PREDICTIVE ACCURACY

TABLE 11.3 Data on Wall Street Sentiment (X), Number of Clients (Y), Predicted Number of Clients (Y'), and Residuals ($Y - Y'$)

Day	Wall Street Sentiment	No. of Clients	Predicted No. of Clients	Residuals
	X	Y	Y'	$Y - Y'$
1	6	8	8.3525	− .3525
2	10	2	3.7185	−1.7185
3	4	6	10.6695	−4.6695
4	3	11	11.8280	− .8280
5	2	14	12.9865	1.0135
6	3	14	11.8280	2.1720
7	5	12	9.5110	2.4890
8	7	4	7.1940	−3.1940
9	8	10	6.0355	3.9645
10	9	6	4.8770	1.1230

The relationship between Wall Street sentiment (X) and activity level of The Great Snatchaudollar's fortune-telling business (Y) was established in Box 11.1. There we saw that, based on the correlation between X and Y ($r = -.7652$), we can predict how many clients Snatchaudollar will see (Y') for any specified level of Wall Street sentiment (X) using the regression equation of Y on X.

$$\begin{aligned} Y' &= a_Y + b_Y X \\ &= 15.3035 - 1.1585(X) \end{aligned}$$

Because $r < \pm 1.0$ in this problem, though, we can anticipate that predictions generated by this equation will be less than perfectly accurate. In this box, we will examine and quantify these prediction errors.

Listed in Table 11.3 are values of Wall Street sentiment (X), business volume (Y), and predicted values of business volume (Y'). Also listed in Table 11.3 are values of $Y - Y'$ (residual scores) for each value of X. These values reflect the amount of error made in predicting business volume from sentiment. (Strictly speaking, Y' values are postdictions, not predictions, and $Y - Y'$ values thus become errors of postdiction, not errors of prediction. Nonetheless, errors of postdiction can be used in estimating errors of true prediction.)

From one value of X to another, the amount of error varies, with some residual scores larger than others. Some errors are of overprediction ($Y < Y'$), while other errors are of underprediction ($Y > Y'$). Summing the residuals, though, we see that, allowing for rounding error, $\Sigma\,(Y - Y') = 0$. Thus, we know that the magnitude of the errors of overprediction is balanced by the magnitude of the errors of underprediction. It is also true that the sum of the squared residuals, $\Sigma\,(Y - Y')^2$, is as small as possible. In other words, any other values of the regression constant (a_Y) and the regression coefficient (b_Y) would

continued

yield a sum of squared errors larger than that seen here. Stated even more succinctly, the least squares regression equation of Y on X both balances and minimizes errors of prediction.

Total Variance
The variance observed in Y (s_Y^2) reflects the total amount of variability that is available to be predicted. Computed according to Equation 11.2, total variance is

$$s_Y^2 = \frac{\Sigma(Y - \overline{Y})^2}{N}$$
$$= 15.61$$

We will see next how much of this total variance was and how much was not predicted successfully.

Predicted Variance and the Coefficient of Determination
Predicted variance ($s_Y^{2\prime}$) may be defined first as the variance of the Y' values (Equation 11.3):

$$s_{Y'}^2 = \frac{\Sigma(Y' - \overline{Y'})^2}{N}$$
$$= \frac{(8.3525 - 8.70)^2 + (3.7185 - 8.70)^2 + \ldots + (4.8770 - 8.70)^2}{10}$$
$$= 9.14$$

The predicted variance is that portion of the total variance that is linked to or explained by X. In this example, the predicted variance ($s_{Y'}^2 = 9.14$) indicates how much of the total variability in The Great Snatchaudollar's business volume ($s_Y^2 = 15.61$) can be attributed (not necessarily in the causal sense) to fluctuations in the mood on Wall Street.

The ratio of predicted variance to total variance, called the coefficient of determination, is the proportion of variance in Y that is explained by X. In the present example

$$\frac{s_{Y'}^2}{s_Y^2} = \frac{9.14}{15.61} = .59$$

The coefficient of determination can be computed more easily as r^2 according to Equation 11.4:

$$\frac{s_{Y'}^2}{s_Y^2} = r^2$$
$$\frac{9.14}{15.61} = -.77^2$$
$$.59 = .59$$

Thus, we see that 59% of the variability in Snatchaudollar's fortune-telling business is linked to the mood on Wall Street.

The coefficient of determination, as the proportion of variance in Y that is explained by X, also provides a quick way of computing the predicted variance ($s_{Y'}^2$). According to Equation 11.5:

$$s_{Y'}^2 = r^2(s_Y^2)$$
$$= -.7652^2(15.61)$$
$$= 9.14$$

This value agrees with $s_{Y'}^2$ computed previously using Equation 11.3.

Residual Variance and the Coefficient of Nondetermination
Residual variance ($s_{Y-Y'}^2$) may be defined first as the variance of the residual scores, computed according to Equation 11.6:

$$s_{Y-Y'}^2 = \frac{\Sigma[(Y - Y') - (\overline{Y - Y'})]^2}{N}$$
$$= \frac{(-.3525 - 0)^2 + (-1.7185 - 0)^2 + \ldots + (1.1230 - 0)^2}{10}$$
$$= 6.47$$

BOX 11.2—*continued*

Because the mean of the residuals ($\overline{Y - Y'}$) is always equal to zero, Equation 11.6 is more simply expressed as Equation 11.7:

$$s^2_{Y-Y'} = \frac{\Sigma (Y - Y')^2}{N}$$

$$= \frac{(-.3525^2) + (-1.7185^2) + \ldots + (1.1230^2)}{10}$$

$$= 6.47$$

In the present example, then, the residual variance, the average squared error made in predicting business volume from Wall Street sentiment, is 6.47 clients.

The residual variance can be computed in another way. The residual variance is that portion of the total variance (s^2_Y) that is left over after predicted variance ($s^2_{Y'}$) has been partialled out or removed. Thus, according to Equation 11.8:

$$s^2_{Y-Y'} = s^2_Y - s^2_{Y'}$$
$$= 15.61 - 9.14$$
$$= 6.47$$

The ratio of residual variance to total variance, the coefficient of nondetermination, is the proportion of variance in Y that is not explained by X:

$$\frac{s^2_{Y-Y'}}{s^2_Y} = \frac{6.47}{15.61} = .41$$

The coefficient of nondetermination can be computed more easily as $1 - r^2$:

$$\frac{s^2_{Y-Y'}}{s^2_Y} = 1 - r^2$$

$$\frac{6.47}{15.61} = 1 - (-.7652^2)$$

$$.41 = .41$$

In the present example, then, we see that 41% of the variability in Snatchaudollar's business volume is not predicted by variations in the sentiment on Wall Street. You will recall that we determined in the preceding section that 59% of the variance in business volume was predicted by sentiment.

The coefficient of nondetermination, as the proportion of variance in Y not explained by X, provides us with a quick means of computing residual variance ($s^2_{Y-Y'}$). According to Equation 11.10:

$$s^2_{Y-Y'} = (1 - r^2)s^2_Y$$
$$= (.41)15.61$$
$$= 6.47$$

This value agrees with $s^2_{Y-Y'}$ computed previously using Equations 11.6, 11.7, and 11.8.

Standard Error of the Estimate

One of the most directly interpretable measures of predictive accuracy is the standard error of the estimate ($s_{Y-Y'}$). This is the square root of the residual variance, and indicates the average absolute error of prediction. According to Equation 11.11:

$$s_{Y-Y'} = \sqrt{s^2_{Y-Y'}}$$
$$= \sqrt{6.47}$$
$$= 2.54$$

In the present example, this value tells us that Snatchaudollar's predictions of business volume from sentiment will show an average error from one daily prediction to the next of about 2.54 clients.

r_{XY} and $r_{YY'}$

Finally, the correlation between obtained and predicted values of Y ($r_{YY'}$) serves as a sign of predictive accuracy by measuring the similarity of obtained (Y) and predicted (Y') values. This correlation, computed using the usual Pearson formula (Equation 10.1) is $r_{YY'} = +.765$. Notice that, in absolute terms, this value is identical to $r_{XY} = -.765$.

The second regression line, the regression line of X on Y, balances and minimizes the errors that occur when we predict X from Y, that is, $X - X'$. In research where one variable is clearly the predictor (e.g., SAT scores) and the second is clearly the criterion (e.g., grades), it is standard practice to label the predictor X and the criterion Y and to regress Y on X. However, in some research settings, either variable may be considered the predictor and either may be considered the criterion. The variables of crime rate and cost of living are one example of this. We might be as interested in predicting crime rate from cost of living as in predicting cost of living from crime rate. Under these circumstances, deciding which variable to label X and which to label Y is purely arbitrary and both regression lines are equally useful.

The regression line of X on Y is described by the **regression equation of X on Y.**

EQUATION 11.12

$$X' = a_X + b_X Y$$

where,

$$X' = \text{values of } X \text{ predicted for given values of } Y$$

$$b_X = \left(r \frac{s_X}{s_Y} \right)$$

$$a_X = \overline{X} - b_X \overline{Y}$$

$$Y = \text{values of } Y$$

In Equation 11.12, a_X is called the **regression constant of X on Y** or the **X-intercept** and b_X is called the **regression coefficient of X on Y.** We see, when comparing Equations 11.1 and 11.12, that where Equation 11.1 refers to variable X, Equation 11.12 refers to variable Y. Where Equation 11.1 refers to variable Y, Equation 11.12 refers to variable X.

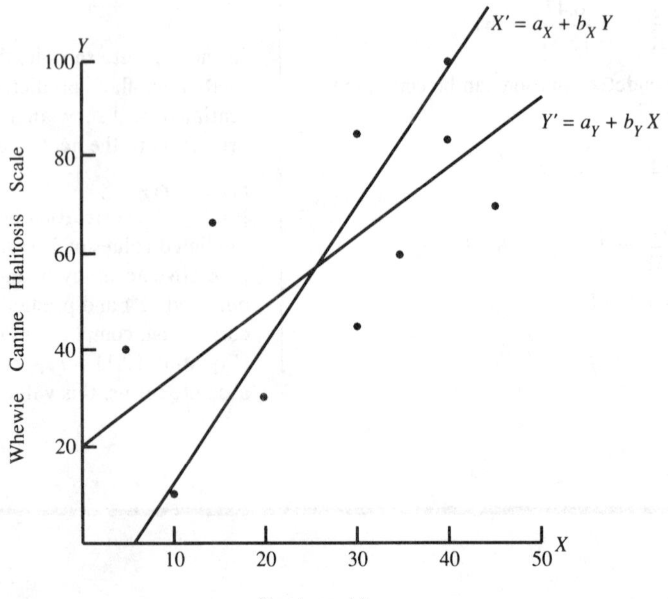

Figure 11.3

Scatterplot depicting the relationship between dog size (X), measured in pounds, and scores on the Whewie Canine Halitosis Scale (Y). Two regression lines have been placed as labeled: the regression line of Y on X, and the regression line of X on Y.

Figure 11.3 shows a scatterplot describing the relationship between dog size (X) and scores on the Whewie Canine Halitosis Scale (Y). Included in Figure 11.3 are both regression lines: Y on X, and X on Y. These two regression lines are similarly, but not identically, positioned because r is relatively strong. When $r = \pm 1.0$, the two regression lines will be identical. This is illustrated by Figure 11.4, which shows a perfect positive correlation (Figure 11.4a) and perfect negative correlation (Figure 11.4b). When the data points in a scatterplot form a straight line, as they do in Figure 11.4, there is only one place to position the regression line, whether it is the regression line of Y on X or X on Y.

Figure 11.4

The regression line of Y on X and the regression line of X on Y occupy the same position when the correlation between X and Y is perfect.

(a) A perfect positive correlation.

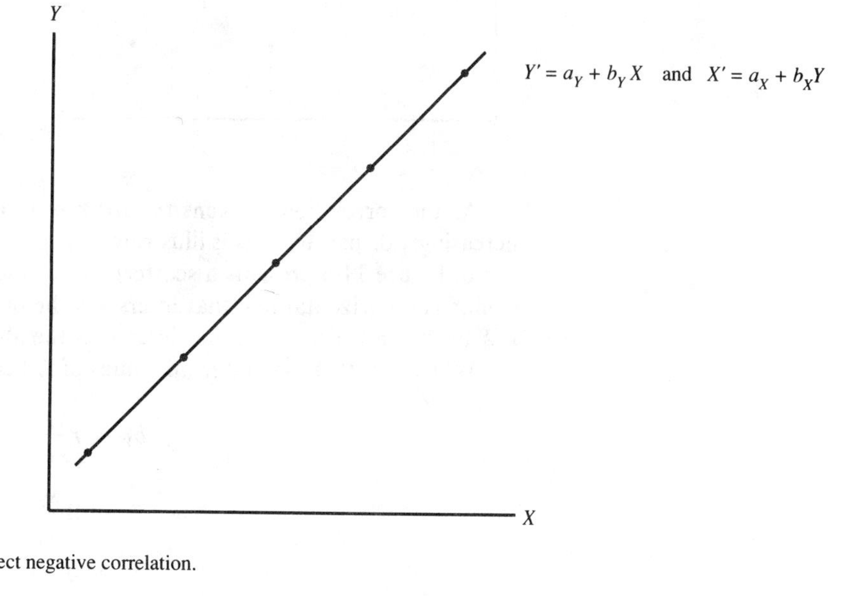

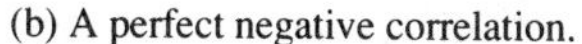

(b) A perfect negative correlation.

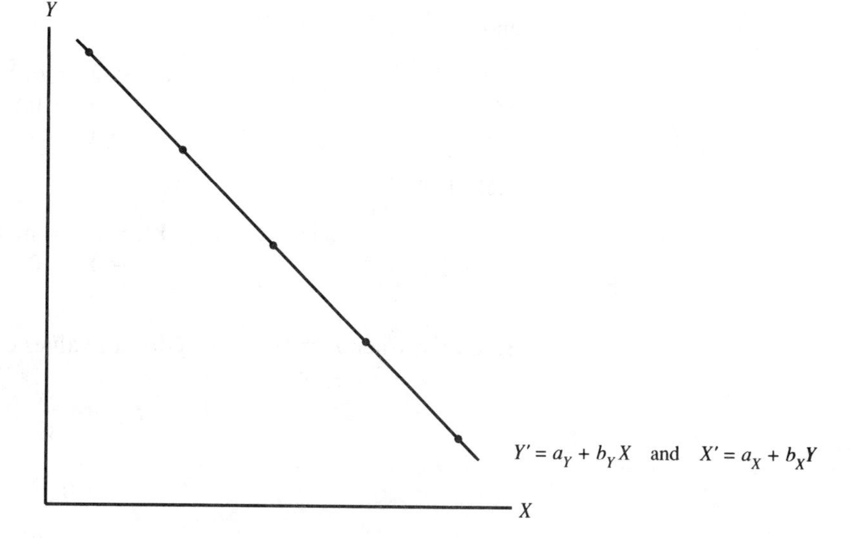

Figure 11.5

Placement of the regression lines of Y on X and X on Y when $r = 0$.

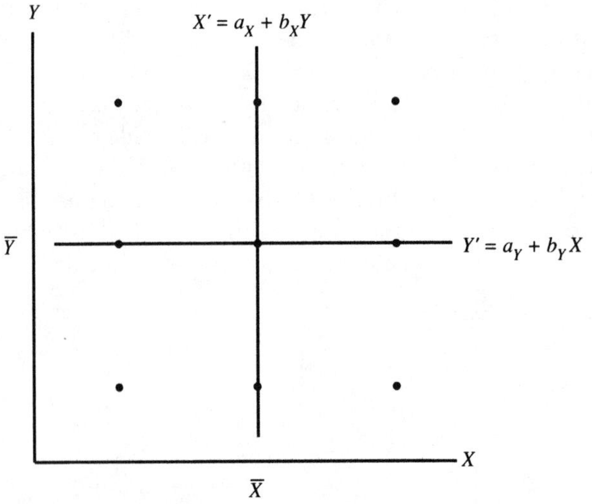

As the correlation weakens toward $r = 0$, the two regression lines become increasingly disparate. This is illustrated by considering the extreme case in which $r = 0$. Figure 11.5 presents a scatterplot in which $r = 0$. The regression line of Y on X is a horizontal line that intersects the ordinate at $\overline{Y}$. The regression line of X on Y is a vertical line that intersects the abscissa at $\overline{X}$.

When $r = 0$, $Y' = \overline{Y}$ for all values of X because:

$$\begin{aligned} b_Y &= r\frac{s_Y}{s_X} \\ &= 0\,\frac{s_Y}{s_X} \\ &= 0 \end{aligned}$$

and

$$\begin{aligned} a_Y &= \overline{Y} - b_Y\overline{X} \\ &= \overline{Y} - 0\overline{X} \\ &= \overline{Y} \end{aligned}$$

such that

$$\begin{aligned} Y' &= a_Y + b_YX \\ &= \overline{Y} + 0X \\ &= \overline{Y} \end{aligned}$$

Similarly, when $r = 0$, $X' = \overline{X}$ for all values of Y because:

$$\begin{aligned} b_X &= r\,\frac{s_X}{s_Y} \\ &= 0\,\frac{s_X}{s_Y} \\ &= 0 \end{aligned}$$

and

$$\begin{aligned} a_X &= \overline{X} - b_X\overline{Y} \\ &= \overline{X} - 0\overline{Y} \\ &= \overline{X} \end{aligned}$$

such that

$$\begin{aligned} X' &= a_X + b_X Y \\ &= \overline{X} + 0Y \\ &= \overline{X} \end{aligned}$$

Measuring Predictive Accuracy of the Regression Equation of *X* on *Y*

We examined previously several measures of predictive accuracy (or inaccuracy) of the regression equation of Y on X: predicted variance, residual variance, the standard error of the estimate, the coefficients of determination and nondetermination, and $r_{YY'}$. Corresponding values may be computed in quantifying the predictive accuracy of the regression equation of X on Y. In fact, several of these measures are identical for both regression equations.

The coefficient of determination, equal to r^2 (Equation 11.4), represents the proportion of variance in the criterion variable (be that Y or X) that is explained by the predictor variable (be that X or Y). Similarly, the coefficient of nondetermination, equal to $1 - r^2$ (Equation 11.9), measures the proportion of variance in the criterion variable that is left unexplained by the predictor, regardless of which variable is designated the predictor and which is designated the criterion. Finally, just as $r_{YY'} = r_{XY}$, so too, $r_{XX'} = r_{XY}$.

Only the predicted variance of X on Y ($s^2_{X'}$), the residual variance of X on Y ($s^2_{X-X'}$), and the standard error of the estimate of X on Y ($s_{X-X'}$) must be computed separately. This is easily accomplished using the equations presented previously, substituting values of X for Y and values of Y for X.

SUMMARY

Bivariate regression analysis uses the correlation between two variables as the basis for predicting values of one variable (the criterion) from values of the other variable (the predictor). The regression equation of Y on X uses Y as criterion and X as predictor. The regression equation of X on Y uses X as criterion and Y as predictor. Unless $r = \pm 1.0$, predictions in either direction will include some inaccuracies, but regression analysis minimizes these errors and balances errors of overprediction and errors of underprediction. Much of this chapter focuses on measures of predictive accuracy and inaccuracy. All of these measures are based directly or indirectly on the correlation between X and Y, since it is the strength of the correlation that ultimately determines predictive accuracy.

NOTE

1. Equation 11.1 defines the regression line of Y on X for raw score values of X and Y. When X and Y are expressed as standard (z) scores, the regression equation of Y on X is somewhat simpler:

$$z_{Y'} = rZ_x$$

where,

$$\begin{aligned} z_{Y'} &= \text{predicted values of } Y \text{ expressed as standard scores} \\ r &= \text{the correlation between } X \text{ and } Y \\ z_X &= \text{values of } X\text{, expressed as standard scores} \end{aligned}$$

In the standard score regression equation, the regression coefficient is equal to r. Since $b_Y = r\left(\frac{s_Y}{s_X}\right)$ and $s_Y = s_X = 1$, it follows that $b_Y = r$. The regression constant, a_Y, is eliminated from the standard score regression equation because it is equal to 0. Since the mean of the standard scores on variables X and Y are both zero, $a_Y = \overline{Y} - b_Y\overline{X} = 0 - r0 = 0$.

CHAPTER 12

PARTIAL AND SEMIPARTIAL CORRELATION

We saw in the last chapter that dog size, measured in pounds, is positively correlated with canine halitosis, indicating that, as dogs get larger, their breath becomes increasingly malodorous. Let us pause here to understand why this relationship prevails. In large part, it is surely because big dogs are less likely to receive routine dental care than are small dogs. It is one thing to brush the teeth of a Pekinese once a week, and an entirely different matter to corral Darth, the family Rottweiler, to administer a little dental hygiene. The relationship between dog size and dog breath, then, is at least partially mediated by the variable of dental hygiene.

Stated generally, the relationship between any two variables, X and Y, may be based upon a shared relationship to some third variable, A. This third variable is variously labeled a **mediating variable,** an **intervening variable,** a **covariate,** or, particularly when the variable interferes with our wish to examine the relationship between X and Y, a **nuisance variable.** The study of the mediating effects of third variables is commonplace in the social and behavioral sciences. The sports psychologist studying the relationship between athletes' compulsivity and injury rates would like to see how much of this relationship is mediated by the tendency of compulsive athletes to overtrain. The sociologist studying the relationship between socioeconomic status and educational achievement might wish to know if this relationship is a spurious result of the intervening variable of quality of education. We might wish to know if the relationship between dog size and dog halitosis is explained by the poorer dental hygiene received by most large dogs.

One of the beauties of laboratory research is the opportunity it affords for controlling nuisance variables, thus clarifying the nature of the relationship under investigation. In a laboratory study of the relationship between dog size and dog breath, we would control the dental care variable by seeing to it that all dogs, regardless of size, received the same amount of dental care. More generally, a laboratory investigation enables us to eliminate the effects of mediating variables, be these environmental or individual difference variables, by holding those variables constant across all cases.

The problem with highly controlled laboratory research, though, is that many important issues in the social and behavioral sciences do not lend themselves readily to the controlled environment of the laboratory. Social and behavioral scientists are not just interested in laboratory dogs, rats in mazes, or the artificial behavior of college freshmen coerced into participating in contrived experiments. We study people in complex, changing, and uncontrollable environments. We study case units like cities and countries that cannot be brought into the laboratory for controlled inspection. In the world outside the laboratory, mediating variables abound. Nuisance variables often exert effects on our designated dependent variables that are stronger than the effects of our designated independent variables. These variables are "nuisance" variables only because they obscure the particular relationship that we have chosen to study.

Must we choose, then, between precise, but often trivial laboratory research, or important, but impossibly clouded field research? No. Given data that are appropriate to analysis through the Pearson product-moment correlation (chapter

10), **partial** and **semipartial correlation** procedures enable us to exert *statistical* control over one or more mediating variables. Partial correlation statistically removes from both the dependent and independent variables the influence of one or more mediating variables, leaving data that are mathematically equivalent to those which might have been collected in an environment in which these variables were held constant. Semipartial correlation removes the effects of one or more nuisance variables from just one variable, often the dependent variable, thus again achieving statistically what would otherwise require laboratory-style control over these variables.

PARTIAL CORRELATION

The partial correlation between X and Y, controlling for variable A, is represented by the symbol $r_{XY.A}$. This partial correlation is simply a Pearson product-moment correlation between two sets of residual scores, or "partials" as they are sometimes called.

The first set of residuals comes from the regression of X on A, in which the nuisance variable A serves as the predictor and the variable X serves as the criterion variable.

EQUATION 12.1

$$X' = a_X + b_X A$$

where,

$$X' = \text{predicted values of } X \text{ for given values of } A$$

$$b_X = r_{AX}\left(\frac{s_X}{s_A}\right)$$

$$a_X = \overline{X} - b_X\overline{A}$$

$$A = \text{values of the nuisance variable } A$$

Once X' values are computed for each value of A, residuals $(X - X')$ may be computed. Consider what these residual scores represent. Since predicted values of X (X') represent variance in X that *is* explained by or linked to the nuisance variable A, the $X - X'$ residual scores must represent variability in X that is *not* linked to A. The $X - X'$ residuals thus represent X from which the effect of the nuisance variable A has been removed. Consistent with this, the correlation between the nuisance variable A and the residual scores $X - X'$ will always equal zero.

The second set of residuals used in the computation of $r_{XY.A}$ comes from the regression of Y on A. Here, the nuisance variable A again serves as the predictor, but now the variable Y serves as the criterion.

EQUATION 12.2

$$Y' = a_Y + b_Y A$$

where,

$$Y' = \text{predicted values of } Y \text{ for given values of } A$$

$$b_Y = r_{AY}\left(\frac{s_Y}{s_A}\right)$$

$$a_Y = \overline{Y} - b_Y\overline{A}$$

$$A = \text{values of the nuisance variable } A$$

Once Y' values are computed for each value of A, residuals $(Y - Y')$ are computed. These $Y - Y'$ residuals represent variability in Y that has not been predicted by the nuisance variable A. In other words, the $Y - Y'$ residuals represent the variable Y from which all effects of the variable A have been removed.

Once the two sets of residuals, $X - X'$ and $Y - Y'$, have been computed, they are correlated using the Pearson product-moment correlation (Equation 10.1) to yield $r_{XY.A}$.[1] Because neither set of residuals contains any variance linked to A, the correlation between the residuals, that is, the partial correlation, reflects the strength of the relationship between X and Y with any mediating effects of A removed or "partialled out." The partial correlation may also be viewed as an average of the simple correlations between X and Y that we would obtain if these simple correlations were computed at several levels or values along the nuisance variable. The partial correlation is interpreted exactly like a simple correlation in terms of sign and magnitude. Likewise, the squared partial correlation represents the proportion of variance in Y that is explained by X (or vice versa) when A is controlled. Box 12.1 illustrates the computation of a partial correlation.

Higher-Order Partial Correlation

The partial correlation between X and Y, controlling for A, is called a **first-order partial correlation.** Also possible, though, are **higher-order partial correlations,** which control for the effects of two or more mediating variables. The **second-order partial correlation** controls for two mediating variables, the **third-order partial correlation** controls for three variables, and so on.

Higher-order partial correlations remove from both X and Y the variance explained by all nuisance variables and then correlates these "purified" X and Y variables. This is accomplished through a straightforward extension of the procedure described previously for the first-order partial correlation.[2] In the case of the second-order partial correlation between X and Y, controlling for A and B $(r_{XY.AB})$, X and Y are regressed on A, the first nuisance variable, and residuals $X - X'$ and $Y - Y'$ are computed. These residuals represent X and Y from which all effects of the first nuisance variable, A, have been removed. Next, these residuals are regressed on the second nuisance variable, B, and the residuals from these analyses are computed. These residuals represent X and Y from which the effects of both the first and second nuisance variables have been removed. Finally, these residuals are correlated with the Pearson formula to yield $r_{XY.AB}$. Third- and higher-order partial correlations continue the process of removing the effects of successive nuisance variables from successive residuals of X and Y, finally correlating the last sets of X and Y residuals.

BOX 12.1

COMPUTING THE PARTIAL CORRELATION

Army psychologist Major Putdown has noticed a higher incidence of colds among soldiers who smoke than among nonsmokers. However, smokers also seem to experience more occupational stress than do nonsmokers, and this stress may be the cause of their poorer health. Major Putdown would like to explore the relationship between smoking and colds, but this relationship is obscured by stress. In a laboratory study of smoking and colds, the effects of stress might be eliminated by holding stress levels constant for all cases while manipulating smoking. But in the real world, this kind of control is not possible. Instead, Major Putdown has decided to use partial correlation analysis to exert statistical control over stress, thus enabling him to view the smoking-colds relationship more clearly.

Table 12.1 lists for each of 10 soldiers the number of cigarettes smoked per week (X), the number of colds contracted during the last year (Y), and relative levels of occupational stress (A), rated on a 1–5 scale, with 1 = very low stress and 5 = extremely high stress. Included in Table 12.1 are descriptive statistics for each variable along with simple correlations between the variables.

The simple correlations confirm Major Putdown's observations. Smoking and colds are positively correlated ($r_{XY} = .53$), but stress and colds are also positively correlated ($r_{AY} = .40$) and smoking and stress are linked ($r_{AX} = .29$) as well. The partial correlation between smoking and colds, controlling for stress ($r_{XY.A}$), will remove variability in both smoking and colds that is linked to stress, thus clarifying the relationship between smoking and colds.

The first step in computing this partial correlation is to remove the variance from X (smoking) that is linked to A (stress). This is accomplished by regressing X on A and computing $X - X'$ residuals. Equation 12.1 describes the regression of X on A:

$$X' = a_X + b_X A$$

TABLE 12.1 Data on Number of Cigarettes Smoked per Week (X), Number of Colds Contracted during the Preceding Year (Y), and Ratings of Occupational Stress (A)

Smoking	Colds	Stress
X	Y	A
70	2	4
105	6	3
35	1	2
105	4	3
0	2	2
70	7	3
35	3	1
140	6	5
0	4	5
140	4	3
$\overline{X} = 70$	$\overline{Y} = 3.9$	$\overline{A} = 3.10$
$s_X^2 = 2450.0$	$s_Y^2 = 3.49$	$s_A^2 = 1.49$
$s_X = 49.50$	$s_Y = 1.87$	$s_A = 1.22$

$r_{XY} = .53$
$r_{AY} = .40$
$r_{AX} = .29$

where,

$$b_X = r_{AX}\left(\frac{s_X}{s_A}\right) = .29\left(\frac{49.50}{1.22}\right) = 11.77$$

$$a_X = \overline{X} - b_X\overline{A} = 70 - 11.77(3.10) = 33.51$$

From the regression of X on A, X' values and $X - X'$ residuals are computed as listed in Table 12.2. The $X - X'$ residuals represent variability in X (smoking) that is unexplained by the nuisance variable A (stress).

continued

BOX 12.1—*continued*

TABLE 12.2 Number of Cigarettes Smoked (X), Occupational Stress (A), Number of Cigarettes Smoked Predicted from Occupational Stress (X'), and Residuals ($X - X'$) from the Regression of X on A.

Stress	Smoking	Predicted Cigarettes	Residuals
A	X	X'	$X - X'$
4	70	80.59	−10.59
3	105	68.82	36.18
2	35	57.05	−22.05
3	105	68.82	36.18
2	0	57.05	−57.05
3	70	68.82	1.18
1	35	45.28	−10.28
5	140	92.36	47.64
5	0	92.36	−92.36
3	140	68.82	71.18

In the next step of the analysis, variance is removed from Y (colds) that is linked to A (stress). This is accomplished by regressing Y on A and computing $Y - Y'$ residuals. Equation 12.2 describes the regression of Y on A:

$$Y' = a_Y + b_Y A$$

where,

$$b_Y = r_{AY}\left(\frac{s_Y}{s_A}\right) = .40\left(\frac{1.87}{1.22}\right) = .61$$

$$a_Y = \overline{Y} - b_Y\overline{A} = 3.9 - .61(3.10) = 2.01$$

From the regression of Y on A, Y' values and $Y - Y'$ residuals are computed, as listed in Table 12.3. The $Y - Y'$ residuals represent variability in Y (colds) that is unexplained by nuisance variable A (stress).

Statistical Significance of the Partial Correlation

Partial correlations may be assessed for statistical significance by applying the same logic that we used in chapter 10 in evaluating the significance of simple correlations. The discussion that follows is phrased in terms of the first-order partial correlation, $r_{XY.A}$, but the logic presented extends directly to higher-order partial correlations as well.

Step 1: The Null and Alternative Hypotheses. When a greater-than-zero partial correlation is found between X and Y, controlling for A, there are two possible explanations. The null hypothesis (H_0) states that the partial correlation

BOX 12.1—*continued*

TABLE 12.3 Number of Colds (Y), Occupational Stress (A), Number of Colds Predicted from Occupational Stress (Y'), and Residuals ($Y - Y'$) from the Regression of Y on A

Stress	Colds	Predicted Colds	Residuals
A	Y	Y'	$Y - Y'$
4	2	4.45	−2.45
3	6	3.84	2.16
2	1	3.23	−2.23
3	4	3.84	.16
2	2	3.23	−1.23
3	7	3.84	3.16
1	3	2.62	.38
5	6	5.06	.94
5	4	5.06	−1.06
3	4	3.84	.16

The last step of the partial correlation analysis is the computation of the Pearson correlation (Equation 10.1) between the $X - X'$ residuals and the $Y - Y'$ residuals: $r_{XY.A} = .47$. The fact that this partial correlation is positive means that colds (Y) increase as cigarette smoking (X) increases, even when the potentially mediating effects of occupational stress (A) are eliminated. The squared partial correlation $r^2_{XY.A} = .47^2 = .22$ indicates that 22% of the variance in colds is predicted by the number of cigarettes smoked, once stress level is controlled.

reflects sampling error. A sample of cases drawn from a population in which $r_{XY.A} = 0$ might show a greater-than-zero partial correlation simply because no single sample from the population will likely reflect exactly the true characteristics of the population. The alternative hypothesis (H_1) states that the obtained greater-than-zero partial correlation is too large to attribute to sampling error. A value this large would be highly unlikely to occur in a sample drawn from a population in which $r_{XY.A} = 0$. Instead, it is more likely that the sample partial correlation is greater than zero because the partial correlation in the population is also greater than zero. This being the case, a replication, using a new sample drawn from the population, would probably again produce a greater-than-zero partial correlation.

Step 2: The Test Statistic. If we were to draw all possible samples of size N from a population in which $r_{XY.A} = 0$, and compute $r_{XY.A}$ for each sample, the resulting values would vary somewhat from one sample to the next because of sampling error. Most often, $r_{XY.A}$ would equal zero, but higher positive and negative values would also occur, though less and less frequently as values approached $r_{XY.A} = \pm 1.0$. This frequency distribution of $r_{XY.A}$ values is the sampling distribution of the partial correlation of X and Y, controlling for A and $r_{XY.A}$ is the test statistic for the relationship between X and Y, controlling for A.

Step 3: Determining the Probability of the Test Statistic. The probability that a given sample was drawn from the population in which $r_{XY.A} = 0$ is equal to the probability of that sample's value of $r_{XY.A}$ occurring in the sampling distribution of $r_{XY.A}$. If that probability is very low ($p < .05$), we would conclude that the sample probably did not come from the population in which $r_{XY.A} = 0$, but instead, came from a population in which $r_{XY.A} > 0$. If the probability of the obtained value of $r_{XY.A}$ is relatively high ($p > .05$), it would be concluded that the sample value was probably the result of sampling error. Thus, on the basis of the probability of observing the obtained value of $r_{XY.A}$ in the sampling distribution of $r_{XY.A}$, we would choose between the null and alternative hypotheses.

We may use Appendix I: Critical Values of the Pearson Product-Moment Correlation for finding this probability.[3] However, degrees of freedom for the partial correlation are computed as $df = N - j$, where $N =$ the number of cases, and $j =$ the total number of variables in the analysis (including X, Y, and all nuisance variables). The Table of Critical Values of r provides critical values for both one- and two-tail significance tests. One-tail values are used when the direction of the partial correlation (positive or negative) was predicted in advance. Two-tail values are used when no prediction was made concerning the direction of the relationship. Significance testing of the partial correlation is demonstrated in Box 12.2.

THE SEMIPARTIAL CORRELATION

Partial correlation removes variance from X and Y that is due to some third variable before correlating X and Y. In contrast, semipartial correlation (sometimes called the **part correlation**) removes variance due to some third variable from only X or Y (usually Y) before correlating X and Y.[4]

Higher-Order Semipartial Correlation

In the case of the **first-order semipartial correlation,** Y is regressed on a single nuisance variable, A, and X is correlated with the resulting $Y - Y'$ residuals to get $r_{X(Y.A)}$, the semipartial correlation between X and Y, controlling for A.[5] In the case of the **second-order semipartial correlation,** Y is first regressed on the first nuisance variable, A, then the residuals from this analysis are regressed on the

BOX 12.2

TESTING THE SIGNIFICANCE OF THE PARTIAL CORRELATION

The partial correlation between cigarette smoking (X) and colds (Y), controlling for occupational stress (A), was computed in Box 12.1 as $r_{XY.A} = .47$. The question to be addressed here is whether this partial correlation is large enough to be considered reliable and replicable. In other words, is the partial correlation statistically significant?

Step 1: ***The Null and Alternative Hypotheses***

H_0 : The observed value of $r_{XY.A}$ is due to sampling error. A partial correlation of this size would be relatively likely to be found in a sample drawn from a population in which $r_{XY.A} = 0$.

H_1 : The observed value of $r_{XY.A}$ is too large to be a likely result of sampling error. It is highly improbable that a sample drawn from a population in which $r_{XY.A} = 0$ would yield a partial correlation this high. Thus, the sample probably came from a population in which $r_{XY.A} > 0$ and a replication of the study would probably also show a greater-than-zero partial correlation.

Step 2: ***The Test Statistic***

The partial correlation, $r_{XY.A} = .47$ serves as the test statistic for the relationship between X and Y, controlling for A.

Step 3: ***Determining the Probability of the Test Statistic***

By comparing the obtained value of $r_{XY.A} = .47$ to the sampling distribution of $r_{XY.A}$, we can determine the approximate probability that a sample yielding this partial correlation would have come from a population in which $r_{XY.A} = 0$. For $df = N - j = 10 - 3 = 7$ (where N = the number of cases and j = the total number of variables in the analysis), and a one-tail test, the critical value of r listed in Appendix I for the .05 level of significance is .5822. Since the obtained value of $r_{XY.A} = .47$ falls below this critical value, we conclude that the probability is greater than .05 that a sample drawn from a population in which $r_{XY.A} = 0$ would have yielded a partial correlation as high as $r_{XY.A} = .47$. Thus, our sample is quite likely to represent such a population. In other words, the relationship between smoking and colds is statistically nonsignificant when occupational stress level is controlled statistically.

---

second nuisance variable, B, and finally, the residuals from this second regression analysis are correlated with X to get $r_{X(Y.AB)}$. **Third- and higher-order semipartial correlations** proceed in a likewise fashion.

Statistical Significance of the Semipartial Correlation

Significance testing of the semipartial correlation follows the same logic used previously for the partial correlation. The semipartial correlation may be referred to Appendix I: Critical Values of the Pearson Product-Moment Correlation with $N - j$ degrees of freedom, where N = the number of cases and j = the total number of variables in the analysis (including X, Y, and all nuisance variables).[6] An example of the computation and significance testing of a semipartial correlation is in Box 12.3.

BOX 12.3

SEMIPARTIAL CORRELATION

Never content to accept the data at face value, you wonder if the positive correlation between dog size and halitosis might be largely mediated by the variable of dental hygiene. You reason that because it is more difficult to brush a large dog's teeth than the teeth of a small dog, large dogs may receive less dental care, resulting in their poorer breath quality.

In a laboratory investigation of the relationship between dog size and halitosis, the effects of dental hygiene would be eliminated by ensuring that all dogs, regardless of size, received the same amount of dental care. In the real world, though, canine dental hygiene is not a variable that can be controlled in this manner. Semipartial correlation can be used, though, to statistically eliminate the effect of dental hygiene on halitosis to achieve a clearer view of the relationship between dog size and halitosis.

Data pertinent to the analysis are in Table 12.4. Size (X) reflects dog size as measured in pounds. Halitosis (Y) is measured on the Whewie Canine Halitosis Scale. Finally, Dental Hygiene (A), the nuisance variable, is measured as the number of tooth brushings each dog received during a two-month interval. Sample descriptive statistics and simple correlations are also presented in Table 12.4.

These correlations show that larger dogs do suffer from greater halitosis than do small dogs ($r_{XY} = .79$). It is also clear, though, that large dogs receive less dental care than do smaller dogs ($r_{AX} = -.81$) and that halitosis is inversely related to dental care ($r_{AY} = -.72$). What remains to be determined by the semipartial correlation between size and breath, controlling for dental care, is if dog size and breath quality are still linked even when the effect of dental hygiene on halitosis is eliminated.

In order to remove variance in dog breath (Y), which is linked to dental hygiene (A), we regress Y on A according to Equation 12.2.

$$Y' = a_Y + b_Y A$$

TABLE 12.4 Data on Dog Size (X), Scores on the Whewie Canine Halitosis Scale (Y), and Dental Hygiene (A)

Size	Halitosis	Dental Hygiene
X	Y	A
5	2	3
10	4	6
15	3	5
20	4	4
25	7	3
30	6	4
35	5	3
40	8	2
45	6	3
50	8	2
55	10	0
60	6	1
$\overline{X} = 32.50$	$\overline{Y} = 5.75$	$\overline{A} = 3.00$
$s_X^2 = 297.92$	$s_Y^2 = 4.84$	$s_A^2 = 2.50$
$s_X = 17.26$	$s_Y = 2.20$	$s_A = 1.58$

$r_{XY} = .79$
$r_{AX} = -.81$
$r_{AY} = -.72$

where,

$$b_Y = r_{AY}\left(\frac{s_Y}{s_A}\right) = -.72\left(\frac{2.20}{1.58}\right) = -1.00$$

$$a_Y = \overline{Y} - b_Y\overline{A} = 5.75 + 1.00(3.0) = 8.75$$

Values of A, Y, Y' and the $Y - Y'$ residuals from this regression analysis are given in Table 12.5.

BOX 12.3—*continued*

TABLE 12.5 **Values of Dental Hygiene (A), Scores on the Canine Halitosis Scale (Y), Halitosis Predicted from Dental Hygiene (Y'), and Residuals ($Y-Y'$) from the Regression of Y on A**

Hygiene	Halitosis	Predicted Halitosis	Residuals
A	Y	Y'	$Y - Y'$
3	2	5.75	−3.75
6	4	2.75	1.25
5	3	3.75	− .75
4	4	4.75	− .75
3	7	5.75	1.25
4	6	4.75	1.25
3	5	5.75	− .75
2	8	6.75	1.25
3	6	5.75	.25
2	8	6.75	1.25
0	10	8.75	1.25
1	6	7.75	−1.75

Because the Y' values represent variability in Y (dog breath) that is explained by A (dental hygiene), the residuals ($Y - Y'$) represent the variability in dog breath that is not related to dental hygiene. In other words, we have partitioned out of the Y variable all variance linked to A.

The next (and last) step in the semipartial correlation analysis is to compute the Pearson product-moment correlation (Equation 10.1) between X (dog size) and the $Y - Y'$ residuals: $r_{X(Y.A)} = .31$. The positive sign of this partial correlation shows that dog halitosis (Y) increases with dog size (X), even when one controls for dental hygiene (A). The squared semipartial correlation $r^2_{X(Y.A)} = .31^2 = .10$ indicates, though, that only 10% of the variance in halitosis is explained by dog size, once dental hygiene is controlled. This figure may be contrasted with the squared simple correlation between dog size and halitosis, $r^2_{XY} = .79^2 = .62$, which suggested that 62% of the variance in halitosis could be explained by dog size. Although the originally observed relationship is not entirely spurious, it does seem to be largely mediated by dental hygiene.

The semipartial correlation may be evaluated for statistical significance by comparing it to the critical value listed in Appendix I: Critical Values of the Pearson Product-Moment Correlation. For $df = N - j = 12 - 3 = 9$ (where N = the number of cases and j = the total number of variables in the analysis), and a one-tail test, the critical value listed for the .05 significance level is .5214. Since the obtained value of $r_{X(Y.A)} = .31$ falls below this critical value, we may conclude that the semipartial correlation is nonsignificant. It is relatively likely that a sample drawn from a population in which $r_{X(Y.A)} = 0$ would yield a semipartial correlation of the magnitude observed in our sample.

CHOOSING BETWEEN PARTIAL AND SEMIPARTIAL CORRELATION

In research where the focus is on the relationship between variables X and Y, and there is a nuisance variable, A, we must choose between partial and semipartial correlation analysis. When is partial correlation appropriate and when should semipartial correlation be used? Choosing between these methods requires using whatever empirical evidence, theoretical insights, and intuitions are available in deciding whether the nuisance variable might likely affect both X and Y or only one of these variables.

Sometimes a nuisance variable can reasonably be expected to influence only one of the variables, X or Y. In this situation, semipartial correlation analysis is indicated, which removes the effect of the nuisance variable from just the affected variable. In a study of the relationship between dog size (X) and quality of dog breath (Y), for example, the amount of dental hygiene received by each dog is an important nuisance variable that should be controlled. Since this variable would be expected to influence dog breath, but would not be expected to influence dog size, a semipartial correlation would be indicated that would eliminate the effect of dental hygiene just from the breath quality variable.

In other situations, a nuisance variable can reasonably be expected to exert an influence over both the X and Y variables. It is this situation that calls for partial correlation, which eliminates the effect of the nuisance variable from both X and Y. In a study of the relationship between cigarette smoking (X) and incidence of colds (Y), for example, stress is a potentially important nuisance variable. Because it can be reasonably hypothesized that stress affects both cigarette smoking and the incidence of colds, partial correlation is called for to eliminate statistically the effects of stress from both smoking and the incidence of colds.

In sum, partial correlation analysis is called for when the nuisance variable can reasonably be expected to influence both X and Y. Semipartial correlation analysis is preferred when the nuisance variable can reasonably be expected to influence only X or Y.

SUMMARY

Correlations between two variables, X and Y, are often mediated by their mutual relationship to one or more other variables. Variously labeled mediating variables, intervening variables, covariates, or nuisance variables, these extraneous variables can interfere with our assessment of the direct relationship between X and Y. Partial correlation analysis provides a solution to this problem by removing from the X and Y variables variance that is explained by one or more nuisance variables, and then correlating these "purified" X and Y variables. The partial correlation gives statistical control over variance due to one or more nuisance variables as an alternative to the experimental control of nuisance variables that is achieved in the laboratory by holding the variables constant across cases. The semipartial correlation is similar to the partial correlation, but removes from only one variable, often the Y variable, that variance which is linked to one or more nuisance variables. Both types of correlations can be tested for statistical significance.

NOTES

1. The partial correlation between X and Y, controlling for A, may be computed more directly as

$$r_{XY.A} = \frac{r_{XY} - r_{AX}r_{AY}}{\sqrt{1 - r_{AX}^2}\sqrt{1 - r_{AY}^2}}$$

2. The second-order partial correlation between X and Y, controlling for A and B, may be computed more directly as

$$r_{XY.AB} = \frac{r_{XY.B} - r_{AX.B}r_{AY.B}}{\sqrt{1 - r_{AX.B}^2}\sqrt{1 - r_{AY.B}^2}}$$

3. Both partial and semipartial correlations may also be tested for significance using the t statistic:

$$t = \frac{r_p}{\sqrt{1 - r_p^2}}\sqrt{N - j}$$

where,

r_p = the partial or semipartial correlation
N = the number of cases
j = the total number of variables in the analysis, including X, Y, and all nuisance variables

The obtained value of t is evaluated for significance using Appendix B: Critical Values of t with $df = N - j$. One-tail significance levels are used if the direction of the correlation (positive or negative) was predicted in advance; two-tail significance levels are used if no direction was predicted.

4. In the case of true experiments, where the researcher actively manipulates one or more independent variables, statistical control of the effects of one or more nuisance variables is generally accomplished using the method of *analysis of covariance* (abbreviated ANCOVA). This hybrid of analysis of variance and semipartial correlation analysis includes the statistical removal from the dependent variable that variance which is linked to one or more nuisance variables. This is followed by an analysis of variance on the "purified" dependent variable. The reader interested in ANCOVA designs should consult Keppel (1982) or Kirk (1968).

5. The semipartial correlation between X and Y, controlling for A, may be computed more directly as

$$r_{X(Y.A)} = \frac{r_{XY} - r_{AX}r_{AY}}{\sqrt{1 - r_{AY}^2}}$$

6. See note 3.

CHAPTER 13

MULTIPLE CORRELATION AND REGRESSION

We saw in chapter 11 (Bivariate Regression) that the correlation between two variables, X and Y, sets the stage for predicting values of one variable from values of the other variable. In most applications of regression analysis, though, several potential predictor variables exist, and a combination of these predictors will explain more of the variability in the criterion variable than is explained by any one predictor alone. For example, a combination of high school grade point average and standardized scholastic aptitude test scores would be expected to provide a better estimate of college grade point average than would either of these predictors considered singly. Or, to continue an example from previous chapters, there is no reason to limit ourselves to dogs' sizes in predicting canine halitosis. Frequency of dental hygiene, dietary variables, age, breed, and other factors are undoubtedly also useful predictors.

The prediction of scores on a single criterion variable using a combination of several predictor variables is the goal of **multiple regression analysis.**[1] It is usually the case in such an analysis that all variables, predictors and criterion alike, are measured on a continuous ratio or interval scale. This is not necessary though, as dichotomously-scored nominal scale variables may serve in either the role of predictor or criterion.[2] Also it is assumed usually that relationships between variables are linear, but methods are available for use in those instances in which the predictor and criterion variables are related in a nonlinear fashion.

Just as bivariate regression is built upon the bivariate correlation, so too, multiple regression is built upon the **multiple correlation** (symbolized by the letter R). This is the correlation between a linear combination of k independent variables (predictors) and a single dependent variable (criterion). Therefore, we will begin this chapter by examining the logic of multiple correlation and will turn next to its application in multiple regression.

MULTIPLE CORRELATION

Figure 13.1 presents a Venn diagram, which illustrates the multiple correlation problem. In this figure, each circle represents a variable: Y, the criterion variable, and X_1 and X_2, two predictors. The area of each circle represents the variance of

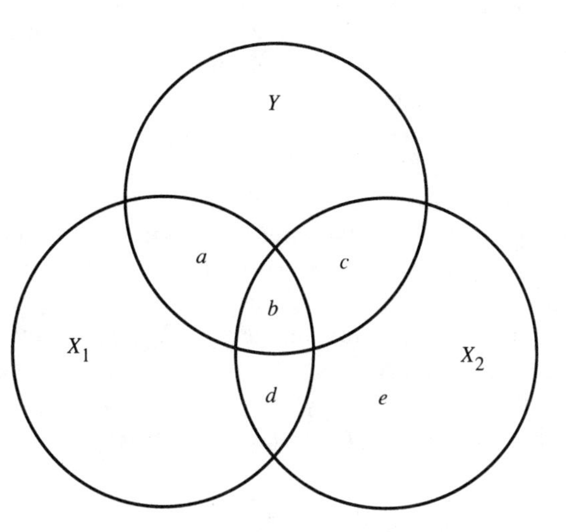

Figure 13.1

Venn diagram depicting the correlations between three variables, X_1, X_2, and Y. Each circle represents the variance of one variable. Areas of overlap represent variance shared between variables, that is, the squared correlations between variables.

each variable, and areas of overlap represent variance shared between variables. Thus, area *ab* represents the proportion of variance in Y that is explained by X_1 (i.e., $r^2_{X_1Y}$), *bc* is the proportion of variance in Y explained by X_2 (i.e., $r^2_{X_2Y}$), and *bd* is the proportion of variance in X_2 explained by X_1 (i.e., $r^2_{X_1X_2}$). Areas *a, c,* and *d* represent variance shared by only two variables, while area *b* represents variance that is common to all variables. In short, the situation depicted by Figure 13.1 is one in which two correlated predictors, X_1 and X_2, are both correlated with the to-be-predicted criterion variable, Y.

The goal of multiple correlation analysis is to determine area *abc,* which represents the proportion of variance in Y explained by variables X_1 and X_2 used jointly. This proportion is equal to $R^2_{Y.X_1X_2}$, the squared multiple correlation between Y and the two predictors. The square root of this value, $R_{Y.X_1X_2}$, is the sought-after multiple correlation. Area *abc* (R^2) is found by first determining area *ab* and by next adding area *c* to this value. How to do this is described next and Box 13.1 gives a concrete example of the procedure.

As a first step in finding area *abc,* we will focus on area *ab,* the proportion of variance in Y explained by X_1. This area is computed simply as the squared correlation between X_1 and Y: $r^2_{X_1Y}$.

Finding area *c* is not so straightforward. The squared correlation between X_2 and Y ($r^2_{X_2Y}$) gives us area *bc,* but area *b* was already included as part of area *ab.* How can we find just area *c?* We need to remove the variance from X_2 that is shared with X_1 (i.e., area *bd*). Then, the squared correlation between what is left of variable X_2 (area *ce*) and variable Y will give us area *c.* Thus, we see that area *c* is the squared semipartial correlation between Y and X_2, controlling for X_1: $r^2_{Y(X_2.X_1)}$. The computation of semipartial correlations was discussed in the preceding chapter. Briefly, though, $r^2_{Y(X_2.X_1)}$ is computed by regressing X_2 on X_1 and correlating the residuals from this analysis with Y.[3]

Having determined area *ab* as $r^2_{X_1Y}$, and area *c* as $r^2_{Y(X_2.X_1)}$, we may find area *abc* by summing these values. This area, $R^2_{Y.X_1X_2}$, represents the proportion of variance in Y that is explained by X_1 and X_2 used in combination. The square root of R^2 gives $R_{Y.X_1X_2}$, which is the multiple correlation between Y and the two predictors, X_1 and X_2. Note that the process of deriving R from R^2 precludes R from taking on negative values, even though some or all of the predictors may be negatively correlated with the criterion variable. Thus, R can range from 0, when none of the variance in Y is explained, to 1.0, when all of the variance is explained.

The same logic used in computing $R_{Y.X_1X_2}$ may be extended to include any number of predictor variables. Take, for instance, the situation in which there is one criterion variable, Y, and three predictors—X_1, X_2, and X_3. The squared simple correlation $r^2_{X_1Y}$ gives the proportion of variance in Y that is explained by X_1. The squared first-order semipartial correlation $r^2_{Y(X_2.X_1)}$ gives the proportion of variance in Y that is explained uniquely by X_2 and *not* by X_1. The squared second-order semipartial correlation $r^2_{Y(X_3.X_1X_2)}$ gives the proportion of variance in Y that is explained uniquely by X_3 and *not* by X_1 or X_2. The sum of these squared correlations is $R^2_{Y.X_1X_2X_3}$, the proportion of variance in Y that is explained by the combination of X_1, X_2, and X_3. Finally, the square root of R^2 gives us the multiple correlation, R. As you can well imagine, the complexity of the calculations required in a multiple correlation analysis involving several predictors quickly surpasses the motivation of the most dedicated researcher! Fortunately, the widespread availability of computerized multiple correlation programs provides a convenient solution to this spiritual weakness.

MULTIPLE REGRESSION

Bivariate regression analysis was described in chapter 11 as the fitting of a regression line through a scatterplot to achieve a "least-squares" criterion. The regression line of Y on X, which minimizes the average squared deviation of obtained values of Y from predicted values of Y, is described by the regression equation of Y on X:

$$Y' = a_Y + b_Y X$$

Multiple regression can also be depicted graphically, at least up to a point. Figure 13.2 illustrates the situation in which there are two predictors, X_1 and X_2, and a criterion variable, Y. In the three-dimensional space defined by X_1, X_2, and Y, the points forming the scatterplot are located according to their values on three variables, not just two as we are familiar with from previous chapters. Consequently, the scattered points forming the scatterplot are arranged in a three-dimensional configuration, rather than just two dimensions. The problem in multiple regression involving two predictors is to fit a two-dimensional **regression plane** through the three-dimensional scatterplot to a least-squares criterion. The points on the surface of the regression plane reflect predicted values of Y for any given pair of predictor scores, just as points on the regression line in bivariate

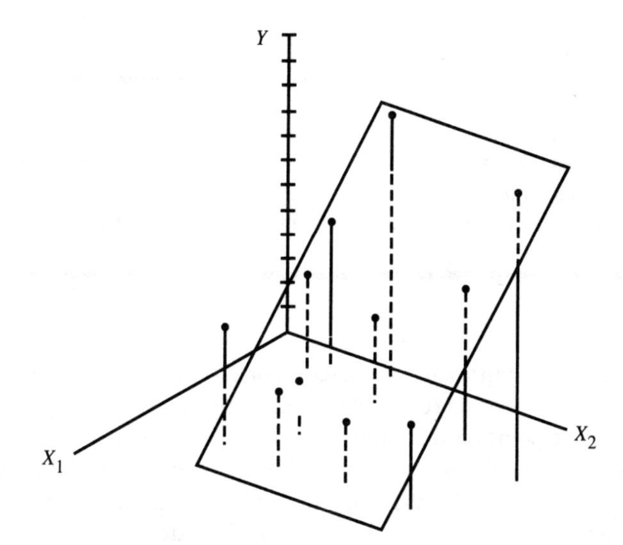

Figure 13.2

The regression plane for the situation in which there are two predictor variables, X_1 and X_2, and one criterion variable, Y.

BOX 13.1

MULTIPLE CORRELATION

Shown in Table 13.1 are data from 10 cases sampled at random from the files of Bubba's Mental Health Clinic. Listed for each case are: (1) rated severity of the disorder for which treatment was received (X_1), where 1 = extremely mild and 10 = extremely severe; (2) maximum allowable insurance coverage (X_2), expressed in thousands of dollars; and, (3) duration of the patient's treatment (Y), expressed as number of days. Also listed in Table 13.1 are descriptive statistics for each variable and simple correlations between variables.

The three variables in this problem show a pattern of correlations that is approximated by the Venn diagram in Figure 13.1. The task of the analysis given in this box is to find area *abc*, the squared multiple correlation: $R^2_{Y.X_1X_2}$.

TABLE 13.1 Data from 10 Patients of Bubba's Mental Health Clinic

Severity of Disorder	Insurance Coverage	Treatment Duration
X_1	X_2	Y
5	25	20
3	0	10
7	150	120
5	20	80
4	0	2
10	10	60
6	20	60
8	10	30
5	15	60
8	100	120
$\overline{X}_1 = 6.10$	$\overline{X}_2 = 35.00$	$\overline{Y} = 56.20$
$s_{X_1} = 2.02$	$s_{X_2} = 47.01$	$s_Y = 39.77$
	$r_{X_1Y} = .51$	
	$r_{X_2Y} = .83$	
	$r_{X_1X_2} = .33$	

Step 1: ***Find Area ab***

Area *ab* of Figure 13.1 represents the proportion of variance in duration of treatment (Y) that is explained by severity of disorder (X_1). This proportion is equal to the squared simple correlation between these two variables:

$$r^2_{X_1Y} = .51^2 = .27.$$

Step 2: ***Find Area c***

Next we need to find area *c* of Figure 13.1 to add this value to area *ab* in determining area *abc*. Area *c* represents the proportion of variance in duration of treatment (Y) that is uniquely explained by insurance coverage (X_2). In other words, it is the squared semipartial correlation between duration of treatment and insurance coverage, controlling for severity of

regression represent predicted values of Y for any given value of a single predictor. To use the regression plane in predicting Y from values of X_1 and X_2, first find the point on the "floor" of Figure 13.2, which is marked by the intersection of any two values of X_1 and X_2. Next, draw a vertical line from this point up to the regression plane. Finally, a horizontal line from this point on the regression plane to the Y-axis will indicate the Y' value corresponding to the selected values

BOX 13.1—*continued*

TABLE 13.2 Values of Insurance Coverage Predicted from Severity of Disorder (X_2') and Residual Scores from the Regression of Insurance Coverage on Severity of Disorder ($X_2 - X_2'$). Also Listed are Values of Treatment Duration (Y).

X_2'	$X_2 - X_2'$	Y
26.55	− 1.55	20
11.19	−11.19	10
41.91	108.09	120
26.55	− 6.55	80
18.87	−18.87	2
64.95	−54.95	60
34.23	−14.23	60
49.59	−39.59	30
26.55	−11.55	60
49.59	50.41	120

disorder: $r^2_{Y(X_2.X_1)}$. This semipartial correlation is computed by regressing X_2 on X_1 and correlating the residuals from this analysis with scores on Y.

The regression equation of X_2 on X_1 is

$$X_2' = a_{X_2} + b_{X_2}(X_1)$$

where,

$$b_{X_2} = r_{X_1X_2}\left(\frac{s_{X_2}}{s_{X_1}}\right) = .33\left(\frac{47.01}{2.02}\right) = 7.68$$

$$a_{X_2} = \overline{X}_2 - b_{X_2}\overline{X}_1 = 35.0 - 7.68(6.10) = -11.85$$

Using this regression equation of X_2 on X_1, we can compute predicted values of X_2 and residuals ($X_2 - X_2'$), which, along with values of Y, are listed in Table 13.2.

The semipartial correlation between duration of treatment (Y) and insurance coverage (X_2), controlling for severity of disorder (X_1) is computed as the correlation between the $X_2 - X_2'$ residuals and Y: $r_{Y(X_2.X_1)} = .70$. Squared, this semipartial correlation gives us the proportion of variance in Y that is uniquely explained by X_2: $r^2_{Y(X_2.X_1)} = .49$.

Step 3: *Find Area abc*

Having found area *ab* in Step 1 and area *c* in Step 2, we can now find area *abc* by summing these two values: .27 + .49 = .76. This is the proportion of variance in duration of treatment (Y) that is explained by the combination of severity of disorder (X_1) and insurance coverage (X_2), that is, the squared multiple correlation. The square root of this value gives us $R_{Y.X_1X_2} = .87$.

of X_1 and X_2. Because the regression plane is fitted to a least-squares criterion, the average squared deviation between obtained and predicted values of Y is minimized, and errors of overprediction are balanced by errors of underprediction.

When there are more than two predictors, we can no longer depict the multiple regression problem visually, as we run out of spatial dimensions to represent our variables. However, regardless of the number of predictors involved, the regression plane is described by the **multiple linear regression equation** given in Equation 13.1.[4]

EQUATION 13.1

$$Y' = a + b_1X_1 + b_2X_2 + \ldots + b_kX_k$$

where,

Y' = predicted values of Y
a = the regression constant
$b_1 - b_k$ = regression weights or coefficients
$X_1 - X_k$ = k predictor variables

In this equation, the regression constant (a) is the predicted value of Y when all predictor variables take on values of zero. The regression weights (b_1 through b_k) reflect the correlations between each predictor and the criterion variable, as well as the correlations between the predictors. Together, these weights determine the slope of the regression plane.

The multiple regression equation may be used in predicting Y for any given combination of values on the variables X_1 through X_k. First, though, values of the regression constant (a) and the regression weights ($b_1 - b_k$) must be determined. This is a tedious task when done by hand, the mechanics of which requires a familiarity with matrix algebra that is beyond the scope of this text. Let it suffice to say that the solution of multiple regression equations is best left to one of the many available computer programs. Those readers who are interested in the mathematical details of multiple regression analysis should consult Edwards (1984), Harris (1985), or Tabachnick and Fidell (1983).

Regression Methods

Although the computational specifics of multiple regression are beyond the scope of this text, the fundamental concepts of this analytic technique are fairly straightforward. Several approaches to multiple correlation and regression have been developed, which we will discuss next.

Direct Regression. When all available predictors are included as terms in the regression equation, the analysis is called a **direct solution.** A direct solution is called for when, for theoretical or other reasons, we wish to examine the relationship between a whole set of predictors and a criterion. The multiple correlation (R) generated by the multiple regression analysis quantifies this relationship.

Forward Regression. Another approach to multiple regression is called **forward regression.** In a forward solution, the multiple regression equation is built one step at a time by sequentially adding predictors to the equation. On the first step of the analysis, that predictor which explains the greatest amount of variance in the criterion variable is included in the equation. This first predictor will be that variable (call it X_1) which shows the highest squared simple correlation to Y: $r^2_{X_1Y}$. At the end of the first step, the regression equation includes only one predictor and takes a form familiar to us from Equation 11.1:

$$Y' = a + b_1X_1$$

On the second step of the analysis, that predictor (call it X_2) is added to the equation which, of all predictors not yet included, adds the most additional explained variance (i.e., raises R^2 the most), giving us:

$$Y' = a + b_1X_1 + b_2X_2$$

This second predictor will be that variable which shows the highest squared first-order semipartial correlation to Y, controlling for X_1: $r^2_{Y(X_2 \cdot X_1)}$. In a similar fashion, additional predictors are included at subsequent steps. At each step, that predictor which provides the greatest increase in R^2 is added. This will be the predictor that shows the largest squared semipartial correlation to Y when all previously selected predictors are controlled. The inclusion of additional predictors generally is halted when the inclusion fails to provide a significant increase in R^2. An example of a forward regression analysis appears in Box 13.2.

Backward Regression. An alternative to forward regression, called **backward regression,** includes all predictor variables in the regression equation, as in a direct solution, and then removes them in a stepwise fashion. At each step, that variable is removed which results in the smallest reduction of R^2. The removal of predictors stops just before that removal results in a significant reduction in R^2.

Stepwise Regression. Yet another procedure, called **stepwise regression,** combines the forward and backward approaches. As in the forward solution, at each step that predictor is included in the regression equation which adds the most to R^2. As in the backward solution, at each step a variable already in the equation may be eliminated if doing so would not result in a significant loss of predictive power. When predictors are correlated, it can easily happen that a variable selected at an early step will be largely predicted by two or more variables selected on later steps. This being the case, it is uneconomical to keep all the variables, and any predictor that is well predicted by other predictors will be eliminated.

Choosing a Solution. A direct regression analysis enables us to assess the relationship between all predictors and the criterion variable in those situations in which we have a good theoretical reason for doing this. However, the stepwise procedures (forward, backward, and stepwise) offer two compelling advantages over the direct solution. The first of these is the advantage of economy. When the available predictors are highly correlated, they provide redundant information. Under these circumstances, a subset of the available predictors may explain nearly as much criterion variable variance as is explained by the entire set of predictors. Often, little additional predictive power is gained after the first few predictors have been included in the regression equation. A stepwise solution enables us to include only those predictors that add significantly to predictive power. Stepwise solutions are particularly useful when the focus of our research is on developing an equation to predict the criterion variable from the smallest possible subset of predictors.

The second advantage of the stepwise methods is the solution they offer to the problem of **multicollinearity.** Multicollinearity is said to exist when predictor variables are strongly correlated with each other or with a linear combination of other predictor variables. When predictor variables are correlated in this way, they are redundant. It makes little sense to include redundant predictors in multiple correlation and regression analysis, because they add nothing to predictive power, detract from the statistical significance of R, and create computational problems that make it impossible to solve the equations necessary to finding an optimal set of regression weights. The stepwise solutions obviate this problem, since redundant variables will not be selected for inclusion in a stepwise procedure.

If we opt for a stepwise approach, a choice must still be made between the forward, backward, and stepwise solutions. All of these approaches will select a subset of the available predictor variables for inclusion in the regression equation, but the three solutions will not always select the same predictors or yield identical R^2 values. It is good practice, then, to examine the results of several different solutions in choosing that one which maximizes R^2 with the desired number of predictors.

Hierarchical Regression Analysis. Forward, backward, and stepwise solutions allow statistical considerations to control the entry and removal of predictor variables from the regression equation. In some cases, though, the researcher may wish to assume this control. This is accomplished using a **hierarchical regression analysis** in which the researcher determines at each step which predictor variable or set of predictors will be included in the equation. For example, if some predictors are less expensive than others, the researcher might direct that the least expensive predictor be entered first, followed by the second least expensive predictor next, the third least expensive variable next, and so on. In this way, it may be possible to construct an equation using several inexpensive variables that explains as much variance in Y as would a smaller subset of more expensive predictors.

A hierarchical solution is also useful when we wish to determine if a set of one or more predictors *adds* significantly to R^2 after one or more other predictors have already been included in the regression equation. For example, in a study of the variables related to length of treatment at Bubba's Mental Health Clinic, a researcher might want to know if a patient's insurance coverage adds significantly to predicted variance in length of treatment after severity and duration of the treated disorder have been taken into consideration. You may notice that this application of hierarchical regression analysis is equivalent to semipartial correlation analysis.

Quantifying Accuracy of Prediction

We have seen that the multiple regression equation meets a least-squares criterion in that errors of prediction are minimized and balanced. We will next consider measures of predictive error (and accuracy) in multiple regression analysis. The same measures examined in chapter 11 in the context of bivariate regression are found to be useful again in evaluating multiple regression equations.

The Coefficient of Determination. An accurate multiple regression equation is one that predicts a high proportion of the variance in the criterion variable. In Figure 13.1, when predictive accuracy is high, area *abc* will occupy a large portion of the total area of *Y*. Conversely, when predictive accuracy is low, area *abc* will occupy a smaller portion of the total area of *Y*. In multiple regression, as in bivariate regression, the ratio of predicted variance to total variance (i.e., the proportion of variance in *Y* that is predicted) is called the coefficient of determination and is equal to the squared multiple correlation (R^2).

The Coefficient of Nondetermination. If R^2 is the proportion of criterion variable variance that is predicted, $1 - R^2$, the coefficient of nondetermination, must be the proportion of variance that is not predicted. In other words, it is an index of predictive inaccuracy that is equal to the ratio of residual variance to total variance in *Y*.

Standard Error of the Estimate. More directly interpretable than residual variance is the standard error of the estimate, $s_{Y-Y'}$. In multiple regression, as in bivariate regression, the standard error of the estimate is equal to the square root of the residual variance, and gives an indication of the average absolute error of prediction.

Cross-Validation and Shrinkage. Values of the regression constant (a) and regression weights ($b_1 - b_k$) are computed to produce a linear combination of predictor variables having the highest possible correlation with the criterion variable. This is equivalent to saying that predicted variance in Y (R^2) is maximized. However, when the number of predictor variables in the equation is large relative to the number of cases analyzed, the computed values of the regression constant and regression weights may be "overfitted" to the idiosyncrasies of the sample data. That is, although the computed constant and regression weights maximize R for this specific sample, these values may differ considerably from those that would be optimal for some other sample. The problem of overfitting becomes particularly problematic in the case of a stepwise solution. Not only are the regression constant and regression weights fitted to sample idiosyncrasies, even the predictors that are selected for inclusion by a stepwise analysis may be overfitted to the sample at hand. In other words, the selected predictors may be best for this sample, but not for another sample.

In applying a regression equation developed using data from one sample in making predictions for a second sample, predictive accuracy will depend upon how well the regression constant and regression weights that form the equation generalize to the new sample. If the regression equation has been overfitted to the peculiarities of the sample on which it was developed, predictive accuracy will decline when that equation is applied to a new sample. This loss in predictive accuracy is called "shrinkage" and should always be evaluated in settings in which a regression equation is to be used in making predictions for cases other than those used in developing the equation.

The most effective and direct means of evaluating the shrinkage of a multiple regression equation is a **cross-validation** study. Here, an equation developed with one sample is used in making "predictions" for a second sample in which outcomes (i.e., values on the criterion variable) are already known. The squared correlation between obtained and predicted values of Y ($r^2_{YY'}$) computed for this cross-validation sample is compared directly to the value of R^2 obtained with the original sample to assess shrinkage.

Occasionally a cross-validation study will reveal the existence of a **moderator variable.** If a regression equation is highly predictive of job success in a sample of males, for example, but a cross-validation study using females shows considerable shrinkage of R^2, sex is a moderator variable. Moderator variables define the limitations or boundaries of regression equations. They force us to qualify our conclusions about the predictive utility of a regression equation in much the same way that interaction effects in analysis of variance require that descriptions of the effects of independent variables be stated in conditional terms.

As an alternative to cross-validation, the magnitude of shrinkage that we can expect to observe in a cross-validation study can be estimated according to Equation 13.2.

EQUATION 13.2

$$\hat{R}^2 = 1 - (1 - R^2)\left(\frac{N - 1}{N - k}\right)$$

where,

$\hat{R}^2$ = estimated value of R^2 in the cross-validation
R^2 = obtained value of R^2
N = sample size
k = number of predictor variables

Equation 13.2 is based upon the fact that the amount of shrinkage in R^2 will be inversely related to the size of the sample upon which the regression equation was developed and directly related to the number of predictor variables combined in the regression equation. With few cases and many predictors, the opportunity for overfitting is maximized and shrinkage will likely be substantial. For this reason, it is generally true that we should strive to collect data from a minimum of 10 cases per predictor variable in order to avoid excessive shrinkage in cross-validation. When stepwise methods are used, which capitalize even more on chance, an even higher ratio of cases to predictors is desirable. Of course, estimating shrinkage according to Equation 13.2 assumes that the cross-validation sample comes from the same population as the original sample. This equation will not provide a good estimate of the shrinkage that would occur if the equation were applied to a sample from some different population.

In addition to conducting multiple regression research with a sufficiently large sample size, shrinkage in R^2 can be reduced by intentionally adopting regression weights that are less than optimal. In a modification of a procedure known as **unit weighting** (Harris, 1985), predictor variables, expressed as standard scores, are all assigned regression weights of the same absolute value. The signs of these weights, positive or negative, are set to be consistent with the signs of the optimal weights they replace. Finally, the absolute values of the weights must sum to 1.0. This procedure, which predicts standardized values of the criterion variable, eliminates overfitting the regression equation to any particular sample, consequently eliminating the problem of shrinkage when the equation is applied to a new sample.

We might suspect that unit weighting would achieve this resistance to shrinkage only at the cost of dramatically lowering the predictive accuracy of the equation. In fact, though, when unit weighting is applied in those settings in which shrinkage is most likely to be a problem (i.e., a stepwise procedure including a small sample and a large number of predictors, with an attempt to generalize to a sample quite different from the one used in the development of the equation), predictive accuracy in the cross-validation sample is often superior for the unit-weighted equation than for an optimally-weighted equation.

Regression with Nominal Scale Predictors

Although all of the examples of multiple regression we have considered thus far used continuous (i.e., interval or ratio scale) variables, it is also possible to include nominal scale predictors in a regression equation. However, because the numbers which represent the categories of nominal variables have no quantitative meaning, these categorical variables cannot be used as predictor variables in their original form.

We saw in chapter 1, though, that any categorical variable may be converted to a series of dichotomously scored "dummy" variables in a process known as dummy variable coding. The number of dummy variables created is equal to the number of categories of the original variable and each case is scored 0 or 1 on each dummy variable. Scores of 0 typically are used to indicate lack of membership in the category represented by a dummy variable; scores of 1 show that a case is a member of that category.

Dummy variables have the advantage over multicategory nominal variables of being subject to meaningful mathematical manipulation. While a multicategory nominal variable cannot be used in its original form as a predictor in regression analysis, the dummy variables formed from this nominal variable can be so used. However, we cannot use all of the dummy variables derived from a nominal variable, since the kth dummy (where k = the number of levels of the multicategory nominal variable) can be completely predicted from the first $k - 1$ dummies. Entering all the dummy variables would create a situation of multicollinearity, which would make solving the regression equation impossible. This problem can be overcome by using a stepwise procedure or by excluding one of the dummy variables from the regression equation. This does not result in any real loss of information, since, as stated above, the kth dummy is completely determined by the preceding $k - 1$ dummies. Thus, the accuracy of predictions obtained with $k - 1$ dummies will be identical to what would be achieved with all k dummies included. An example of the use of dummy variables in multiple regression analysis is provided later in Box 13.3.

Power Transformations of Predictors: Polynomial Regression

Multiple regression, as presented thus far, is a method of describing linear relationships between predictor and criterion variables. With some relatively simple transformations of the predictor variables, however, the multiple regression equation can be used to describe and quantify nonlinear relationships as well. In what is called **polynomial regression,** a variety of nonlinear relationships may be quantified by including as predictors the original predictor variable (X) and successive powers of that variable. The polynomial regression equation follows.

EQUATION 13.3

$$Y' = a + b_1X + b_2X^2 + b_3X^3 + \ldots + b_kX^k$$

The number of powers to which we raise the predictor is determined by the suspected shape of the curve relating X to Y. Specifically, the predictor will be included in the equation one more time than there are "bends" in the curve. Look back at Figure 10.5 in chapter 10. In a perfectly linear relationship (Figure 10.5a) there are no bends and variable X need appear only once in order to describe the relationship between X and Y:

$$Y' = a + b_1X$$

When there is a single bend in a curve relating X to Y (Figure 10.5b or 10.5c), the relationship will be better described by including variable X twice in the equation, once in its original form, and once squared:

$$Y' = a + b_1X + b_2X^2$$

When there are two bends in the curve, forming an S-shaped curve, X will appear three times:

$$Y' = a + b_1X + b_2X^2 + b_3X^3$$

We will normally enter powers of X one at a time into a polynomial regression equation. This makes it possible to evaluate the significance of the increase in R^2 at each step using Equation 13.5, to be presented later.

Multiplicative Combinations of Predictors

A last type of predictor variable transformation to be examined here is the multiplicative combination of two or more predictors. These multiplicative combinations are used in situations in which two or more predictors are known (or suspected) to combine interactively, that is, multiplicatively, in determining the value of the criterion variable.

Take, for instance, the situation where we wish to predict job performance (Y) from a measure of ability (X_1) and a measure of motivation (X_2). At high levels of motivation, different levels of ability might be expected to have quite different effects on performance. At low levels of motivation, however, ability becomes irrelevant; that is, performance will be low regardless of ability level.

To predict performance from these interacting variables, it would be fruitful to include the multiplicative combination of ability and motivation as a third predictor in the regression equation.

For a two-variable predictive equation of this sort, the regression equation would be:

$$Y' = a + b_1X_1 + b_2X_2 + b_3X_1X_2$$

Of course, higher-order interactions may be included as well. When there are three predictors, for instance, the regression equation might include three two-way interaction terms and a three-way interaction term:

$$Y' = a + b_1X_1 + b_2X_2 + b_3X_3 + b_4X_1X_2 + b_5X_1X_3 + b_6X_2X_3 + b_7X_1X_2X_3$$

Needless to say, we should consider carefully how many multiplicative combinations of predictors are to be included in the regression equation. The increased predictive power that these combinations can provide can be more than offset by the increased overfitting that results from the inclusion of too many predictor terms.

SIGNIFICANCE TESTS FOR MULTIPLE CORRELATION AND REGRESSION

Three types of significance tests are commonly used with multiple correlation and regression. First, we may wish to know if the overall value of R is statistically significant. This significance test is a test of the null hypothesis that the value of R in the population is zero. The F statistic serves as the test statistic in accomplishing this test.

EQUATION 13.4

$$F = \frac{R^2(N - k - 1)}{(1 - R^2)\,k}$$

where,

R^2 = the squared multiple correlation being tested for significance
N = sample size
k = number of predictors in the equation

This F statistic is distributed with k and $N - k - 1$ degrees of freedom.

It is instructive to notice those factors that raise and lower the computed value of F in Equation 13.4. First, of course, is the value being tested for significance—the multiple correlation. In addition, though, as N decreases and/or k increases, F decreases. Thus, the smaller the sample and the more predictors used, the less likely it is that the multiple correlation will be found to be statistically significant.

The second type of significance test assesses the significance of the increase in R^2 that results from the addition of one or more predictors to those already included in the regression equation. This is a test of the null hypothesis that, in the population, the additional predictor(s) adds nothing to predictive accuracy.

BOX 13.2

FORWARD MULTIPLE REGRESSION ANALYSIS

We found in Box 13.1 that a substantial multiple correlation ($R = .87$) exists between duration of treatment received by patients at Bubba's Mental Health Clinic (Y) and severity of the treated disorder (X_1) and insurance coverage (X_2). On the basis of this multiple correlation, it should be possible to develop a multiple regression equation that predicts treatment duration from a linear combination of severity of disorder and insurance coverage. In this box we will use forward multiple regression analysis to accomplish this objective.

The forward multiple regression analysis selects at each step that predictor variable which explains the most additional variance in the criterion variable. Listed below for each step of the analysis are statistics pertaining to the predictive accuracy of the regression equation at that step: R, R^2, R^2 adjusted for shrinkage (Equation 13.2), and the standard error of the estimate. The statistical significance of R is also evaluated at each step using the F statistic (Equation 13.4). Raw score and standardized regression weights (b and β, respectively), as well as tests of the significance of the individual regression weights (Equation 13.6) are also listed at each step, along with the raw score regression constant (a). At step 2, the significance of the increase in R^2 is tested for significance (Equation 13.5).

Entered on Step 1:* *Insurance Coverage

R = .825
R^2 = .681 $F = 17.078$ Sig = .003
Adjusted R^2 = .641
Std. Error = 25.117

Variables in the Equation	b	β	t	sig. t
Insurance Coverage	.698	.825	4.133	.003
Constant (a)	31.763			

Entered on Step 2:* *Severity of Disorder

R = .862
R^2 = .744 $F = 10.15$ Sig = .0085
Adjusted R^2 = .670
Std. Error = 24.073

Variables in the Equation	b	β	t	sig. t
Insurance Coverage	.624	.737	3.635	.008
Severity of Disorder	5.215	.265	1.307	.233
Constant (a)	2.555			

Significance of Increase in R^2

$F = 1.723 \quad p > .05$

This test involves comparing R^2 with and without the additional predictor(s), again using the F statistic.

EQUATION 13.5

$$F = \frac{(N - p - m - 1)(R^2_{p+m} - R^2_p)}{m(1 - R^2_{p+m})}$$

where,

N = sample size
p = the number of original predictors
m = the number of additional predictors
R^2_{p+m} = R^2 with the original and additional predictors
R^2_p = R^2 with only the original predictors

BOX 13.2—*continued*

Insurance coverage was selected at the first step of the analysis because, of all available predictors, it shows the strongest correlation to treatment duration. Alone, this predictor explains a significant 68.1% of the variance in treatment duration. Added at the second step is severity of disorder. This additional predictor adds a nonsignificant 6.8% additional explained variance. We also see only a slight reduction in prediction error (standard error of the estimate) as we move from step 1 ($s_{Y-Y'} = 25.117$) to step 2 ($s_{Y-Y'} = 24.073$). Finally, notice that the test of significance of R at step 2 shows a lower value of F ($F = 10.15$) than was observed at step 1 ($F = 17.078$), even though R is higher at step 2. This has occurred because the F test is adjusted for the number of predictor variables included in the regression equation.

Given the results of this forward stepwise regression analysis, we would probably use the equation developed at step 1 in predicting treatment duration from insurance coverage. However, to illustrate the usage of a multiple regression equation, let us here use the two-predictor equation developed at step 2 in predicting treatment duration for a patient with $20,000 insurance coverage and a disorder rated as having a severity of 5. First, the raw score regression equation uses predictors in raw score form in predicting the criterion expressed in raw score form:

$$\begin{aligned} Y' &= a + b_1(\text{Insurance}) + b_2(\text{Severity}) \\ &= 2.555 + .624(20) + 5.215(5) \\ &= 41.11 \end{aligned}$$

Next, we will use the standard score regression equation with the same predictors expressed in z-score form:

$$\begin{aligned} Y'_z &= \beta_1(z_{\text{insurance}}) + \beta_2(z_{\text{severity}}) \\ &= .737(-.32) + .265(-.54) \\ &= -.38 \end{aligned}$$

This F statistic is distributed with m and $N - p - m - 1$ degrees of freedom.

The third type of significance test used in multiple regression analysis is a test of the significance of the individual regression weights. This test is useful in evaluating the relative importance of each predictor variable when combined with the other predictors in the equation. The null hypothesis in each test is that the regression weight in the population is zero. A significant regression weight means that the corresponding predictor variable adds appreciably to the predictive power that is provided by the other predictor variables in the equation. A nonsignificant regression weight indicates that the corresponding predictor variable adds little or no predictive power.

The t statistic serves as the test statistic in this test. The computation of t is tedious and generally unnecessary, since tests of the significance of individual predictors are included routinely in the output from computerized multiple regression analysis. For the first predictor, X_1, t is computed as in Equation 13.6.

BOX 13.3

MULTIPLE REGRESSION WITH A NOMINAL SCALE PREDICTOR

We have discovered in previous chapters that several continuous variables are related to canine halitosis, including dog size and dental hygiene. It is also likely that a dog's breed, a nominal scale variable, is related to halitosis. In this box, we will use forward multiple regression analysis to develop an equation to predict canine halitosis from dog size, dental hygiene, and breed.

Data pertinent to this analysis are shown in Table 13.3. Along with scores on the Whewie Canine Halitosis Scale (Y), scores are recorded for each of 20 dogs on the variables of size in pounds (X_1), dental hygiene (X_2), recorded as the number of tooth brushings in the last two-month period, and breed (X_3), where 1 = Sheltie, 2 = German Shepherd, and 3 = Boston Terrier.

In order to include the nominal scale variable of breed in the analysis, we must first recode this variable as a set of dummy variables (chapter 1), with one dummy variable for each category of the original multicategory nominal scale variable. The recoded data are in Table 13.4, where a score of 0 on a dummy variable means that a dog is not of the breed represented by that variable, and a score of 1 indicates that a dog is of that breed.

TABLE 13.3 **Scores on the Whewie Canine Halitosis Scale (Y), Size (X_1), Dental Hygiene (X_2), and Breed (X_3)**

Halitosis	Size	Hygiene	Breed
Y	X_1	X_2	X_3
8	25	3	1
2	15	6	3
6	40	1	2
5	45	0	2
7	28	3	1
2	10	5	3
4	7	6	3
8	20	3	1
6	30	3	1
10	50	2	2
7	35	3	2
3	12	4	3
7	32	2	1
4	15	6	3
6	45	3	2
5	52	1	2
3	22	5	3
8	28	3	1
9	25	3	1
5	50	0	2

EQUATION 13.6

$$t = \frac{b_1}{\sqrt{[(N-1)s^2_{X_1}][1 - R^2_{1.23\ldots k}]}}$$

where,

b_1 = regression weight corresponding to X_1
N = sample size
$s^2_{X_1}$ = variance of X_1
$R^2_{1.23\ldots k}$ = squared multiple correlation between X_1 and all of the remaining k predictor variables. (Notice that the original criterion variable, Y, is not used in computing this R^2 value.)

TABLE 13.4 Scores on the Whewie Canine Halitosis Scale (Y), Size (X_1), Dental Hygiene (X_2) and Breed, Coded as a Series of Dummy Variables: Sheltie (X_3), German Shepherd (X_4), and Boston Terrier (X_5). Scoring on the Dummy Variables is 0 = Nonmember, 1 = Member

Halitosis	Size	Hygiene	Sheltie	Shepherd	Terrier
Y	X_1	X_2	X_3	X_4	X_5
8	25	3	1	0	0
2	15	6	0	0	1
6	40	1	0	1	0
5	45	0	0	1	0
7	28	3	1	0	0
2	10	5	0	0	1
4	7	6	0	0	1
8	20	3	1	0	0
6	30	0	1	0	0
10	50	2	0	1	0
7	35	3	0	1	0
3	12	4	0	0	1
7	32	2	1	0	0
4	15	0	0	0	1
6	45	3	0	1	0
5	52	1	0	1	0
3	22	5	0	0	1
8	28	0	1	0	0
9	25	3	1	0	0
5	50	0	0	1	0

continued

In testing the second regression weight, b_2, this value would be substituted for b_1 in the numerator of Equation 13.6. In the denominator, $s^2_{X_2}$ and $R^2_{2.13 \ldots k}$ would be substituted for $S^2_{x'}$ and $R^2_{1.23 \ldots k}$. Similar substitutions would be made in testing remaining regression weights.

Examples of multiple regression analysis and related statistics are provided in Boxes 13.2 and 13.3. Box 13.2 describes a forward regression analysis in which all variables are measured along continuous scales. Box 13.3 illustrates how dummy variable coding can be used when predictor variables are measured at the nominal level.

BOX 13.3—*continued*

TABLE 13.5 Correlations between Predictor Variables: Halitosis, Size, Hygiene, Sheltie, Shepherd, and Terrier

	Halitosis	Size	Hygiene	Sheltie	Shepherd	Terrier
Halitosis	1.0					
Size	.44	1.0				
Hygiene	−.39	−.62	1.0			
Sheltie	.60	−.13	−.19	1.0		
Shepherd	.18	.85	−.40	−.54	1.0	
Terrier	−.81	−.75	.61	−.48	−.48	1.0

Since scores on one dummy variable can be predicted perfectly from scores on the other two dummy variables, a condition of multicollinearity exists between these dummy variables. In order to solve the equations of the multiple regression analysis, one of the dummy variables must be excluded from the analysis. We will allow the forward regression analysis to select the variable(s) to be excluded.

As we begin this analysis, it will be helpful to examine a matrix of the correlations between the variables being analyzed. These simple correlations are given in Table 13.5. From this table we can anticipate that the forward analysis will select the dummy variable of Terrier on the first step since, of all available predictors, this variable shows the strongest correlation to the criterion variable, halitosis. The negative sign of the correlation means that Boston Terriers (Terrier = 1) show relatively low halitosis scores and non-Boston Terriers (Terrier = 0) show relatively high halitosis scores. Which predictor variables will be selected on subsequent steps will depend not just on correlations to the criterion variable, but also on correlations between the predictors. The forward multiple regression analysis is summarized next.

Entered on Step 1: ***Terrier***

R = .806

R^2 = .650 F = 33.40 Sig = .0001

Adjusted R^2 = .630

Std. Error = 1.393

Variables in the Equation	**b**	β	t	**sig.** t
Terrier	−3.93	−.81	−5.780	.0001
Constant (a)	6.93			

SUMMARY

Multiple regression analysis forms a linear combination of two or more predictor variables ($X_1 - X_k$) in predicting values on a single criterion variable (Y). The proportion of variance in Y that is successfully predicted by this weighted combination of predictors is equal to R^2, the squared multiple correlation. Several methods of multiple regression analysis are available. A direct solution includes all available predictors in the regression equation and is particularly useful when we wish to quantify the relationship between an entire set of predictor variables and the criterion variable. Several varieties of stepwise solutions are also available, which select for inclusion in the equation a subset of nonredundant predictor variables. Stepwise solutions are often used when the focus of the research is on

BOX 13.3—*continued*

Entered on Step 2: Size

R = .845
R^2 = .715 $F = 21.29$ Sig = .0001
Adjusted R^2 = .681
Std. Error = 1.294

Variables in the Equation	b	β	t	sig. t
Terrier	−5.35	−1.10	−5.576	.0001
Size	− .06	− .39	−1.965	.066
Constant (a)	9.19			

Significance of Increase in R^2

$F = 3.88$ $p > .05$

Entered on Step 3: Dental Hygiene

R = .847
R^2 = .717 $F = 13.52$ Sig = .0001
Adjusted R^2 = .664
Std. Error = 1.328

Variables in the Equation	b	β	t	sig. t
Terrier	−5.45	−1.12	−5.321	.0001
Size	− .06	− .36	−1.706	.107
Hygiene	.07	.07	.373	.714
Constant (a)	8.92			

Significance of Increase in R^2

$F = .12$ $p > .05$

After selecting Terrier as the best available predictor in step 1, the analysis included size in step 2, thereby adding 6.5% explained variance. The test of significance for the increase in R^2 from step 1 to step 2 (as well as the test of the regression weight corresponding to the size variable added at step 2) shows that this increase failed to reach statistical significance. For purposes of illustrating the stepwise process, though, a third step has been taken, at which the variable of dental hygiene was included in the equation. Inclusion of this third predictor added a nonsignificant .2% explained variance. At this point there is clearly nothing to be gained by including additional predictors and the analysis is terminated.

prediction. Hierarchical regression analysis puts the researcher in control of entering predictors on each step. Multiple regression is most often accomplished using interval or ratio scale criterion and predictor variables. However, dichotomously scored nominal scale variables can be used as either the criterion variable or as predictors. By raising predictor variables to powers greater than one, it is possible to evaluate nonlinear relationships between the predictor and criterion variables. Multiplicative combinations of predictor variables can also be included in the regression equation to evaluate interaction effects. A variety of measures of predictive accuracy are available for use with multiple regression analysis, all of which are based on the multiple correlation, R. When a multiple regression equation developed with one sample is subsequently used in making predictions for a second sample, some loss in predictive accuracy can be expected. This shrinkage is a result of overfitting the regression equation to sample idiosyncrasies. Three types of significance tests are useful in evaluating the replicability of findings obtained in multiple correlation and regression analysis. First, the overall test of significance tests the obtained value of R against the null hypothesis that $R = 0$ in the population. Second, we can evaluate the significance of increases in R^2 that result from the addition of one or more predictor variables to the regression equation. Third, the significance of each individual predictor variable can be determined by testing corresponding regression weights.

NOTES

1. Causal relationships between two variables can only be established through a true experiment in which one variable is manipulated and a second variable is subsequently observed to vary. However, when certain assumptions are made about which variables might exert a causal influence over other variables and which variables cannot exert a causal influence, correlational analyses, including multiple regression, become useful in mapping out causal relationships between variables. This application of multiple regression analysis, called path analysis, is growing rapidly in popularity among social and behavioral scientists. Other techniques, like structural analysis and time-series analysis, also use a correlational approach to explore possible patterns of cause-and-effect. All of these methods are beyond the scope of this text, but the interested reader may refer to Asher (1976), Bentler (1980), and Shumway (1988).
2. Multiple regression analysis involving a dichotomously scored criterion (i.e., dependent) variable is mathematically equivalent to discriminant analysis, presented in chapter 14. Multiple regression analysis involving nominal scale predictor (i.e., independent) variables is mathematically equivalent to analysis of variance, presented in chapters 8 and 9.
3. See note 5 in chapter 12.
4. Equation 13.1 is called the raw score multiple regression equation because $X_1 - X_k$ refer to raw scores on the k predictor variables, and Y' refers to predicted raw scores on the criterion variable. When all variables are expressed in standard score form (i.e., z-scores), the multiple regression equation may be expressed more simply as

$$z_{Y'} = \beta_1 z_{X_1} + \beta_2 z_{X_2} + \ldots + \beta_k z_{X_k}$$

where,

$z_{Y'}$ = predicted values of Y expressed as z-scores
$\beta_1 - \beta_k$ = standardized regression coefficients, also called beta weights
$z_{X_1} - z_{X_k}$ = predictor variables $X_1 - X_k$, expressed as z-scores

CHAPTER 14

DISCRIMINANT ANALYSIS

Discriminant analysis is often described as a multivariate extension of the one-way ANOVA discussed in chapter 8. Like ANOVA, discriminant analysis enables us to examine differences between two or more groups. These groups may have been exposed to different treatments in an experimental research design (e.g., psychotherapy group vs. waiting list control group) or they may be naturally existing groups (e.g., males vs. females). As with ANOVA, discriminant analysis provides a method of testing the statistical significance of differences observed between the groups. Unlike ANOVA, though, which examines only one dependent variable at a time, discriminant analysis considers several variables simultaneously. These discriminating variables (sometimes called dependent variables) will generally be continuous (i.e., interval or ratio scale) variables, although it is possible to include dichotomously scored nominal scale variables.

Discriminant analysis also differs from ANOVA by providing a method through which differences between groups can be described in simple terms. For example, schizophrenics, paranoids, and depressives may be shown to differ significantly on a dozen or more variables, but these variables are undoubtedly intercorrelated, and thus, measure some common underlying characteristics. Describing the differences between these groups by referring to *all* of the discriminating variables, then, would be redundant and nonparsimonious. Discriminant analysis provides a mechanism for eliminating these dependent variable redundancies in describing between-group differences.

Finally, discriminant analysis is often used in classifying cases to groups when their group memberships are unknown. The Internal Revenue Service, for example, has used discriminant analysis to summarize the differences that exist between the tax returns of honest and dishonest taxpayers. Knowing the nature of these differences enables the IRS each year to classify any given taxpayer's return to one of these categories or the other.

DISCRIMINANT ANALYSIS AS A SIGNIFICANT DIFFERENCE TEST

We saw in chapter 8 that one-way ANOVA assesses the statistical significance of between-group differences on a single dependent variable. To review quickly, this is accomplished by comparing the groups' between-group variance to their within-group variance using the F statistic:

$$F = \frac{\text{between-group variance on the dependent variable}}{\text{within-group variance on the dependent variable}}$$

Within-group variance is the variability found within any single group's distribution of scores and results from individual differences and measurement error. Between-group variance refers to variability between the means of the groups and results from individual differences, measurement error, *and treatment effects.* If there is no treatment effect, or if the groups are essentially equivalent, between-group variance will equal within-group variance and F will equal 1. As treatment effects grow more powerful, though, between-group variance will increase and F will increase as well. Thus, the F statistic is used in assessing the strength of treatment effects as reflected in between-group differences.

The Discriminant Function

Discriminant analysis, like one-way ANOVA, provides a method of testing the statistical significance of differences between two or more groups, but examines several dependent variables simultaneously. This is accomplished by constructing a linear combination of these variables, forming a single composite variable called a **discriminant function.**

The discriminant function takes the form given in Equation 14.1.

EQUATION 14.1

$$D = a + w_1V_1 + w_2V_2 + \ldots + w_pV_p$$

where,

D = scores on the discriminant function
a = the discriminant function constant
$w_1 - w_p$ = discriminant function weighting coefficients for each of p dependent variables
$V_1 - V_p$ = scores on the original p variables

The discriminant function constant (a) and weighting coefficients ($w_1 - w_p$) used in forming the discriminant function are selected to create a discriminant function that provides the greatest possible discriminating power. In other words, no other constant or weights would provide as much separation of group means on the discriminant function, while still maintaining as little within-group variability of scores on the discriminant function. To express this in yet another way, the discriminant function is formed so as to maximize F:

$$F = \frac{\text{between-group variance on } D}{\text{within-group variance on } D}$$

Discriminant Functions beyond the First

It may have occurred to you that the discriminant function that provides the best overall separation of groups (i.e., the highest possible value of F) is only one of an infinite number of possible combinations of the p original dependent variables. However, as will be made clear in a moment, p (the number of original variables) or $k - 1$ (where k = the number of groups being compared), whichever is smaller, is the maximum number of *useful* discriminant functions that can be constructed. These discriminant functions all combine the same set of p original variables, but each uses different values of the constant and weighting coefficients. Each discriminant function is formed to maximize the overall separation of groups (i.e., F is maximized) while still being **orthogonal** (i.e., uncorrelated) to preceding discriminant functions.

The first discriminant function always provides the best possible overall or average separation of groups. When we compare only two groups, there is no reason to examine other combinations of the original variables, since these other discriminant functions would necessarily be less powerful than the first. When

(a) Distributions on the first discriminant function.

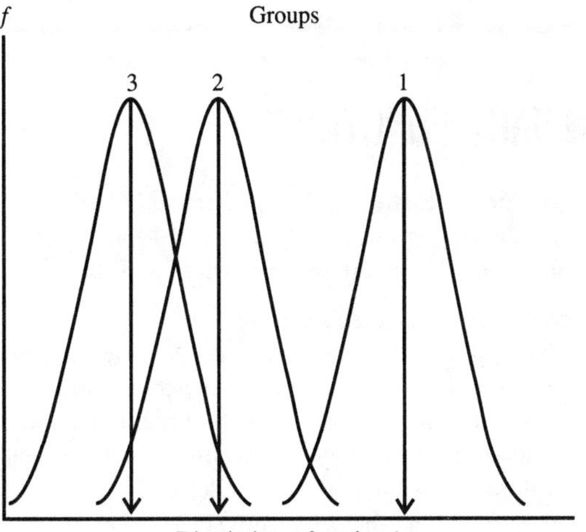

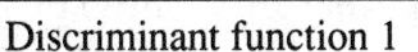

(b) Distributions on the second discriminant function.

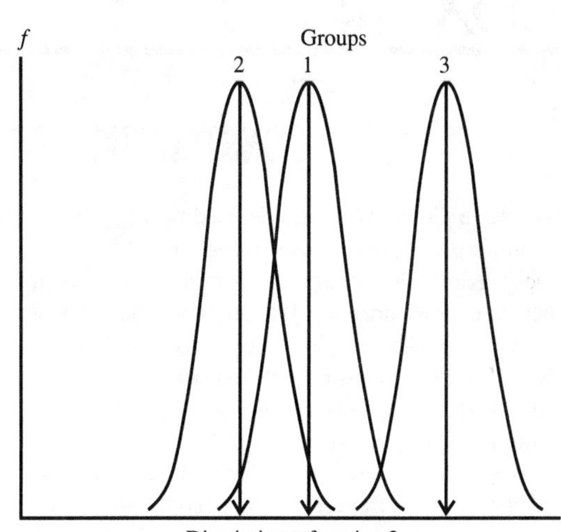

Figure 14.1
Distributions of three groups on two orthogonal discriminant functions.

three or more groups are being compared, though, additional orthogonal discriminant functions are possible and potentially useful. In the case of three groups, the first discriminant function will give the best overall separation of groups, but it may fail to provide appreciable separation of some groups. For example, the first, most powerful (overall) discriminant function may provide good separation of Group 1 from Groups 2 and 3 in a three-group problem, but may give little discrimination of these later two groups. A second discriminant function, orthogonal to the first, and thus, measuring something completely different than is measured by the first discriminant function, will necessarily provide less overall separation of the groups (since the first discriminant function was designed specifically to maximize overall separation), but it may discriminate between those groups that were not separated well by the first discriminant function. Figure 14.1 illustrates this situation.

Figure 14.1 shows three groups' distributions of scores on each of two discriminant functions. The first function (Figure 14.1a) has succeeded in separating Group 1 from Groups 2 and 3. That is, the mean of Group 1 on this first discriminant function differs substantially from the means of Groups 2 and 3. Groups 2 and 3, though, do not differ appreciably on the first discriminant function. A second function (Figure 14.1b), however, which is orthogonal to the first, does maximize the separation between Groups 2 and 3. Between the two discriminant functions, all of the groups have been separated. Additional discriminant functions would not be useful since these would only separate groups that have already been separated, and would do so less successfully than have the first two discriminant functions.

The computation of the discriminant function constant (a) and weighting coefficients ($w_1 - w_p$) is beyond the scope of this text (see Harris, 1985, Overall & Klett, 1972, or Tabachnick & Fidell, 1983). Let it suffice to say that computers are best equipped to handle the computational specifics of discriminant analysis. An example of discriminant analysis is provided in Box 14.1.

BOX 14.1

CONSTRUCTION OF DISCRIMINANT FUNCTIONS

Wegotchu Corporation has decided to begin manufacturing automobiles in the United States. Recognizing that public relations will be critical to the success of this endeavor, Wegotchu has decided to establish an in-house public relations department in their U.S. plant. This department will employ individuals in three occupational categories: liars, damn liars, and statisticians.

Wegotchu intends to use discriminant analysis in studying the differences between liars, damn liars, and statisticians at corporate headquarters. It is hoped that this will enable the company to more accurately identify individuals best suited to these positions in the U.S.

Data were collected from five liars, five damn liars, and five statisticians on each of three variables: The Nixon Veracity Scale, the LePew Personal Hygiene Profile, and Simon Legree's Measure of Moral Development. These data are presented in Table 14.1.

Creating Discriminant Functions

The first task in a discriminant analysis, which will be demonstrated in this box, is to create one or more orthogonal discriminant functions that maximize the separation of groups. Since the maximum number of useful functions will equal the smaller of $k - 1$ (where k = the number of groups) or p (where p = the number of discriminating variables), the number of functions in this problem will be limited to two, since $k - 1 = 2$. Computer-generated equations defining the first and second discriminant functions follow:

$$
\begin{aligned}
D_1 &= a + w_1V_1 + w_2V_2 + w_3V_3 \\
&= -5.97 + .28(\text{Veracity}) + .02(\text{Hygiene}) + 1.20(\text{Moral Development}) \\
D_2 &= a + w_1V_1 + w_2V_2 + w_3V_3 \\
&= -3.59 + .56(\text{Veracity}) + .08(\text{Hygiene}) - 1.00(\text{Moral Development})
\end{aligned}
$$

TABLE 14.1 Scores of Five Liars (Group 1), Five Damn Liars (Group 2), and Five Statisticians (Group 3) on the Nixon Veracity Scale, the LePew Personal Hygiene Profile, and Simon Legree's Measure of Moral Development

Group	Veracity	Hygiene	Moral Development
1	7	85	7
1	6	75	6
1	6	60	6
1	5	75	5
1	6	80	7
2	2	85	1
2	3	70	2
2	2	60	2
2	1	75	1
2	3	75	2
3	2	55	2
3	1	25	1
3	1	30	2
3	2	20	2
3	1	35	1

BOX 14.1—*continued*

Computing Discriminant Function Scores

It is instructive to examine the discriminant function scores of the 15 cases forming the three groups being examined in this problem. These scores are computed for each case by weighting and combining that case's values on the variables of Veracity, Hygiene, and Moral Development using the constants and weighting coefficients provided above. Discriminant function scores are listed in Table 14.2.[1] Means and standard deviations for each group on each discriminant function are in Table 14.3.

TABLE 14.2 Discriminant Function Scores for Five Liars (Group 1), Five Damn Liars (Group 2), and Five Statisticians (Group 3)

Group	D_1	D_2
1	6.24	.30
1	4.54	− .08
1	4.21	−1.30
1	3.06	.35
1	5.85	− .67
2	−2.36	3.45
2	−1.21	1.80
2	−1.70	.43
2	−2.85	2.08
2	−1.10	2.21
3	−1.81	.02
3	−3.95	−1.99
3	−2.64	−2.58
3	−2.58	−2.83
3	−3.73	−1.18

TABLE 14.3 Means and Standard Deviation for Each Occupational Group on Each Discriminant Function

	D_1		D_2	
	$\bar{X}$	s	$\bar{X}$	s
Group 1: Liars	4.78	1.15	− .28	.63
Group 2: Damn Liars	−1.84	.70	1.99	.97
Group 3: Statisticians	−2.94	.79	−1.71	1.04

Examining these means, we can see that the first discriminant function has achieved greater overall separation of the groups than has the second function. Notice that the average between-group difference on the first function is 5.15, compared to an average between-group difference on the second function of 2.47. We can also see from Table 14.3 that the first discriminant function has mostly discriminated between Group 1 vs. Groups 2 and 3. The second function mostly separates Groups 2 and 3, which were not well discriminated by the first function.

We can next compute a correlation between scores on the two discriminant functions to verify that they are indeed orthogonal. The Pearson correlation between D_1 and D_2 is $r = .009$, a value that differs from 0 only slightly because of rounding error. The two functions are essentially uncorrelated, and thus, measure two entirely different traits.

Testing the Significance of Discriminant Functions

Since each discriminant function is orthogonal to the others, each tells us something unique about the differences between the groups being compared. However, successive discriminant functions become less and less powerful. Consequently, we will frequently find that fewer than the maximum possible number of orthogonal discriminant functions are needed to achieve satisfactory between-group discrimination. We will generally examine only those functions that provide statistically significant separation of groups. We will look next at how the statistical significance of discriminant functions is assessed.

Any given discriminant function may be evaluated for significance using the *F* statistic, or some related statistic, which compares between-group variance on the discriminant function against within-group variance on that function. However, when many variables are combined to form a discriminant function, there is some danger that the variables may be weighted and combined in a fashion that capitalizes on the idiosyncrasies of the data at hand. The more variables being weighted and combined, the greater the opportunity to inflate *F* by capitalizing on these chance factors, particularly when the samples being examined are small. This being the case, test statistics for discriminant functions are adjusted for number of variables and sample sizes.

When three or more groups are being compared, such that two or more discriminant functions have been computed, we seldom evaluate the statistical significance of each function considered singly. Instead, the significance of the additional discriminating power provided by successive functions is assessed.

Let us consider the situation in which there are three discriminant functions. In the first step of significance testing, the between-group separation achieved with all three functions is evaluated, often using **Wilks' Lambda** (symbolized Λ), or the related χ^2 or *F* statistics. Wilks' Lambda is a commonly reported statistic that is inversely related to the overall separation of groups. Wilks' Lambda can range in value from 0 to 1. A value of $\Lambda = 1$ indicates no separation of groups; lower values represent progressively greater amounts of separation. If there is no significant separation at this first step of significance testing, we know that none of the individual discriminant functions provides significant separation. If significant separation is found at the first step, we look at the results of the second step.

At the second step of significance testing, the between-group separation provided by the first function is removed from the total, and the separation that remains, attributable to functions 2 and 3, is evaluated for significance. If there is no significant separation with function 1 removed, we know that the significance at the first step can be attributed to the first function. If there is significant separation at the second step, we look at the third step.

At the third step of significance testing, the between-group separation provided by the first and second functions is removed from the total, and the separation that remains, attributable to function 3, is evaluated for significance. If there is no significant separation with functions 1 and 2 removed, we know that the third function is nonsignificant. Too, we know that the significance seen at the second step (with function 1 removed) can be attributed to function 2. If significant separation is retained at the third step, we know that all three discriminant functions are significant.

Other Indicators of a Discriminant Function's Power

In addition to these tests of statistical significance, the discriminating power of discriminant functions can be described in other ways. The **canonical correlation** associated with a given discriminant function describes the discriminating power of that function as the correlation between scores on the function and scores on the variable that defines group membership. The canonical correlation varies from 0 to 1, never taking on negative values. The squared canonical correlation indicates the proportion of the total variance in the discriminant function that is explained by group membership, or conversely, the proportion of variance in group membership that is explained by the discriminant function.

The discriminating power of each discriminant function may also be measured by the **eigenvalue** associated with that discriminant function. The relative sizes of these eigenvalues reflect the proportion of the total between-group separation that is contributed by each discriminant function. Thus, eigenvalues associated with early discriminant functions are larger than those associated with less powerful, later functions. More easily interpreted than an eigenvalue, though, is a direct expression of the proportion of between-group separation that is provided by each discriminant function. This proportion is computed by dividing the eigenvalue for a given discriminant function by the sum of the eigenvalues for all of the discriminant functions.

Significance testing of discriminant functions and measures of discriminant function strength are illustrated in Box 14.2.

INTERPRETING BETWEEN-GROUP DIFFERENCES

Significance tests of discriminant functions can reveal that groups differ in one or more independent ways, but it is still necessary to uncover the nature of these differences. Often, in fact, discriminate analysis is not used so much to determine whether between-group differences exist, since the groups are already known to differ, but to provide a means of describing how the groups differ. Using discriminant analysis to describe between-group differences is largely a matter of interpreting the discriminant functions that separate the groups. What do these functions measure? Box 14.3 provides a concrete example of the interpretation of discriminant functions to accompany the more general discussion that follows.

Univariate *F* Tests

Once one or more significant discriminant functions have been identified, it is common practice to use a series of univariate ANOVAs to see which of the original variables forming the discriminant function(s) show significance. The results of these univariate tests help to determine how the groups differ.

However, multiple ANOVAs do not alone provide for a complete understanding of between-group differences in the multivariate situation. For one thing, it is possible that even though none of the original variables provides significant

BOX 14.2

ASSESSING THE STRENGTH OF DISCRIMINANT FUNCTIONS

The two discriminant functions constructed in Box 14.1 are evaluated here for their discriminating power. Table 14.4 presents several descriptors of the discriminating power of the two functions.

Eigenvalues give an indication of the relative amount of between-group separation that is provided by each discriminant function. Thus, we see in this example that the first discriminant function, with its eigenvalue of 14.54, gives about five times as much discriminating power as does the second function, with its eigenvalue of 2.91. Dividing the eigenvalue of the first function (14.54) by the sum of the two eigenvalues ($14.54 + 2.91 = 17.45$), we find that the first function accounts for 83.32% of the between-group variance (i.e., separation). Similarly, dividing the eigenvalue of the second function by the sum of the two eigenvalues, we see that this second function accounts for 16.68% of the total separation achieved.

Canonical correlations also measure the between-group separation provided by each discriminant function. Analogous to the omega-square (ω^2) statistic described in conjunction with *t*-tests and ANOVA, the canonical correlation corresponding to a given discriminant function measures the strength of association between group membership and scores on that discriminant function. The canonical correlations listed in Table 14.4 show that both functions are strongly related to group differences. Squaring the canonical correlations we find that group membership explains 94% of the variance in the first discriminant function ($.97^2 = .94$) and 74% of the variance in the second function ($.86^2 = .74$).

TABLE 14.4 Indices of the Discriminating Power of Two Discriminant Functions

Discriminant Function	Eigenvalues	Percent of Variance	Canonical Correlation
1	14.54	83.32	.97
2	2.91	16.68	.86

discrimination, a discriminant function formed from these variables will yield significance. Conversely, particularly when samples are small, we may find one or more significant univariate comparison and not find a significant discriminant function.

In addition, the correlations among the original variables make interpreting the pattern of univariate significance tests difficult or impossible. Say, for instance, that two groups have been found to differ significantly on two correlated dependent variables. We know that these two variables measure the same underlying construct to the degree that they are correlated, and that they measure different constructs to the degree that they are uncorrelated. The question now becomes whether the groups that have been shown to differ on the two variables really differ in two ways, or if they differ in only one way. That is, did the variables both yield significance because they measure a single common trait on which the groups differ, or do the groups actually differ in two different respects, one as measured by the first variable, and a second as measured by the second variable?

BOX 14.2—*continued*

TABLE 14.5 Tests of the Significance of the Two Discriminant Functions

After Function	Wilks' Lambda	Chi-Square	df	Significance
0	.016	45.17	6	.0000
1	.256	14.99	2	.0006

Table 14.5 summarizes the outcomes of tests of the statistical significance of the discrimination achieved in this analysis. The row of Table 14.5 labeled "After Function: 0" describes the overall separation of groups after no (0) discriminant functions have been removed; i.e., using both discriminant functions. The very small value of Wilks' Lambda in this first row ($\Lambda = .016$) indicates excellent separation of groups using both discriminant functions. The χ^2 test of Wilks' Lambda ($\chi^2 = 45.17$) shows that the overall separation of groups achieved using both discriminant functions is highly significant.

The row labeled "After Function: 1" describes the amount of between-group separation that remains after that portion contributed by the first function has been removed. Wilks' Lambda is now larger ($\Lambda = .256$), indicating less overall group separation following removal of the first function. The χ^2 test of significance ($\chi^2 = 14.99$), though, is still significant. We know from this that the second function provides significant separation of groups. Too, because the first function is always stronger than the second, it must also be significant.

Identification of Discriminated Groups

A second approach to the description of between-group differences involves determining which groups are discriminated by each discriminant function. For instance, if a discriminant function separates patients with psychotic disorders from those with personality disorders, the discriminant function may be measuring severity of dysfunction.

Correlations between Discriminant Functions and Original Variables

Correlations (sometimes called "loadings") between discriminant functions and the original variables provide a valuable indication of what is being measured by each discriminant function. The rationale behind this approach to the interpretation of discriminant functions is one that has been presented on many previous occasions; that is, two variables (or a variable and a discriminant function) measure the same thing to the degree that they are correlated. If a discriminant function is found to be highly correlated with a particular subset of the original variables, that discriminant function can be interpreted as measuring whatever the subset of original variables is known to measure.

Scatterplots in the Interpretation of Discriminant Functions

As we have seen throughout this book, graphs are very useful in summarizing the characteristics of our data. This is true again in the context of discriminant analysis where graphs can be used to clarify the nature of the between-group differences identified through the analysis.

Graphs used in displaying the results of a discriminant analysis are simply scatterplots in which each axis represents a discriminant function (see Figure 14.2 in Box 14.3). The horizontal axis represents the first discriminant function and the vertical axis represents the second function. In those cases in which there are more than two discriminant functions, a series of scatterplots can be used in presenting all possible pairs of discriminant functions. It should be remembered, though, that a plot of the first two functions is especially enlightening since the initial discriminant functions are more powerful than are subsequent functions.

The first step in graphing the results of a discriminant analysis is to compute discriminant function scores for each case in the analysis. This process, illustrated in Box 14.1, is accomplished by simply substituting each case's scores on variables $V_1 - V_p$ into Equation 14.1, along with values of the discriminant function constant (a) and weighting coefficients ($w_1 - w_p$). Next, each case's discriminant function scores are used as coordinates in locating that case in the scatterplot.

The resulting scatterpoint will depict each of the groups being examined as a cluster of points. These clusters will be distinct and separated to the degree that the discriminant functions have successfully discriminated between the groups; they will be diffuse and overlapping to the extent that the discriminant functions have failed to discriminate. We will also observe that the groups' clusters will show the most overall separation along the horizontal axis (the first discriminant function) with less separation seen on the vertical axis (the second function). In addition, each axis will provide better separation of some groups than of others. Finally, most computer programs will print a **centroid** for each group. A group centroid is simply a point in the scatterplot located at the group's mean on each of the discriminant functions. This point is called a centroid because, as a measure of central tendency, it tends to be located in the center of the cluster of points that represents a group.

DISCRIMINANT ANALYSIS VS. MULTIPLE ONE-WAY ANOVAS

Discriminant analysis presents certain advantages over the alternative approach to analyzing multiple dependent variables, that is, computing a separate univariate ANOVA for each variable. However, discriminant analysis carries disadvantages of its own.

BOX 14.3

INTERPRETING DISCRIMINANT FUNCTIONS

The two discriminant functions developed in Box 14.1 and evaluated for significance in Box 14.2 are interpreted here. The question being asked is "*How* do liars, damn liars, and statisticians differ?"

Table 14.6 summarizes the univariate differences between the three groups and shows that the groups differ significantly on all three of the original discriminating variables. However, the intercorrelations between these variables shown in Table 14.7 (especially between Veracity and Moral Development) make it difficult to determine whether or not the groups really differ in three distinctly different ways. The fact that the groups differ significantly on two orthogonal discriminant functions, though, assures us that these groups can be differentiated in two respects. Describing these differences requires that we interpret the discriminant functions along which the groups differ.

One of the best ways of doing this is to examine the correlations between scores on the discriminant functions and the original variables as shown in Table 14.8. The first function is almost equally represented by Veracity and Moral Development and we may therefore label this first function "truthfulness" (or "honesty" or any other term that seems to fit this combination of traits). The second function mostly measures Hygiene. Consequently, its interpretation is quite straightforward—"personal hygiene."

TABLE 14.6 Means, Standard Deviations, and Univariate Tests of Difference between Liars, Damn Liars, and Statisticians on Three Discriminating Variables

	Group 1: Liars		Group 2: Damn Liars		Group 3: Statisticians			
Variables	$\bar{X}$	s	$\bar{X}$	s	$\bar{X}$	s	F	df
Veracity	6.00	.71	2.20	.84	1.40	.55	60.40	2, 12 ($p. < .001$)
Hygiene	75.00	9.35	73.00	9.08	33.00	13.51	23.89	2, 12 ($p. < .001$)
Moral Development	6.20	.84	1.60	.55	1.60	.55	81.38	2, 12 ($p. < .001$)

TABLE 14.7 Correlations between Veracity, Personal Hygiene, and Moral Development

	Veracity	Personal Hygiene	Moral Development
Veracity	1.0		
Hygiene	.17	1.0	
Moral Development	.75	.08	1.0

continued

TABLE 14.8 Correlations between Two Discriminant Functions and Three Original Discriminating Variables

Variables	D_1	D_2
Veracity	.83	.06
Hygiene	.34	.90
Moral Development	.96	−.28

The scatterplot of the discriminant function scores shown in Figure 14.2 will also assist in describing the differences between liars, damn liars, and statisticians. Using what we already know about the traits being measured by the two discriminant functions along with the relative positions of the three groups on these functions shown in Figure 14.2, we can draw the following additional conclusions. Liars, damn liars, and statisticians are marked by progressively lower levels of truthfulness (Discriminant Function 1), with statisticians and damn liars displaying approximately the same low levels of truthfulness. Statisticians can be distinguished from damn liars primarily by the lower levels of personal hygiene (Discriminant Function 2) seen among statisticians, a problem not so apparent in damn liars.

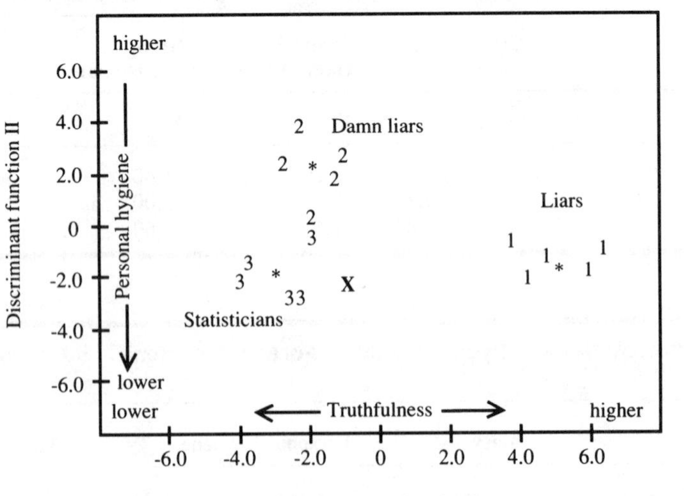

Figure 14.2

Scatterplot of discriminant analysis of liars (Group 1), damn liars (Group 2), and statisticians (Group 3). Asterisks mark group centroids. *X* marks location of job applicant discussed in Box 14.4.

Advantages of Discriminant Analysis

Multiple Dependent Variables. Groups being compared in the context of a discriminant analysis are unlikely to differ in only a single respect. To capture fully the nature of the differences between groups, it is necessary to examine several potential discriminating variables. This is a task for which discriminant analysis is uniquely suited.

Reduced Error Rates. Although between-group differences on the original variables are routinely examined using univariate ANOVAs, these univariate comparisons do not provide a substitute for the discriminant analysis. Because each univariate test of significance carries its own Type I and Type II error probabilities, the more significance tests we perform, the more Type I and Type II errors we can anticipate. A long series of univariate comparisons will inevitably produce a relatively large number of these errors. Because there will typically be fewer discriminant functions to be tested for significance than there are original variables, discriminant analysis reduces the number of significance tests and the number of errors.

Compounding the problem of inflated error rates in multiple univariate comparisons is the fact that these comparisons are not statistically independent. The outcomes of a series of univariate significance tests performed on correlated variables are linked, just as the variables being analyzed are linked. Thus, if a Type I or Type II error occurs in one analysis, error probabilities in analyses of correlated variables will be affected. In contrast, discriminant analysis tests for significance only uncorrelated discriminant functions. Thus, the outcomes of the significance tests in a discriminant analysis are independent.

Easier Interpretation of Between-Group Differences. When several discriminant functions are found to be significant, we know that the groups being compared differ in as many different respects as there are significant discriminant functions. Each discriminant function measures something unique and different. In using discriminant analysis to compare groups, we avoid the problems of interpretation that arise when several correlated dependent variables are evaluated with separate univariate significance tests.

Disadvantages of Discriminant Analysis

Despite these advantages, discriminant analysis presents its own difficulties.

Interpretation of the Discriminant Function(s). It is easy enough to form a linear combination of variables that will provide the maximum separation of groups. It is often not a simple matter to determine what this linear combination measures. In such a situation, we know that the groups differ significantly on the discriminant function, but we cannot interpret the nature of this difference. Thus, if the discriminant functions are interpretable, they facilitate the description of between-group differences. But discriminant functions are not always interpretable.

The Assumptions of Discriminant Analysis. Every statistical procedure is based on certain assumptions about the nature of the data being analyzed and discriminant analysis is no different in this respect. However, the assumptions of discriminant analysis are often difficult to assess, let alone meet.

First, it is assumed that each discriminant function formed is distributed normally in each group being compared. Second, each discriminant function is assumed to show approximately equal variances in each group. Third, patterns of correlations between variables are assumed to be equivalent from one group to the next. Fourth, the relationships between variables are assumed to be linear in all groups. Fifth, no dependent variable may be perfectly correlated to a linear combination of the other variables. Such multicollinearity is surprisingly common, particularly when several highly correlated variables are entered into the analysis. Multicollinearity makes it impossible to solve the equations of the discriminant analysis and is remedied only by identifying and eliminating the offending variable(s). Finally, discriminant analysis is extremely sensitive to outliers. Eliminating these cases is not as simple as identifying outliers on the original variables. Any given case may show scores that are well within the normal range on all original variables, but still present as an outlier on one or more discriminant functions. Methods by which the assumptions of discriminant analysis may be assessed are beyond the scope of this text. The interested reader should refer to Tabachnick and Fidell (1983).

Fortunately, discriminant analysis is fairly robust with respect to violations of its assumptions, particularly when groups are fairly large and of equal sizes. It is suggested that we include a sufficient number of cases in the analysis so the size of the smallest group exceeds the number of variables being examined and the total sample includes at least 10 times as many cases as there are variables.

CLASSIFICATION OF CASES USING DISCRIMINANT ANALYSIS

Discriminant analysis is a very useful empirical diagnostic technique. That is, it is a method by which we can objectively classify cases to one of several groups on the basis of a previous quantitative examination of the characteristics of those groups. For example, once differences between several psychiatric diagnostic groups have been described through discriminant analysis of personality test subscale scores, we may use a given individual's scores on these subscales to assign him or her to the most likely diagnostic category or group. Or, if a personnel psychologist has distinguished between successful employees working in several occupational groups using discriminant analysis of several aptitude test scores, a job applicant's scores on these tests might be used for placing that applicant into the occupational group into which he or she is most compatible. Methods by which cases can be assigned to groups using discriminant analysis are discussed next. Box 14.4 provides a concrete example of these procedures.

Graphic Classifications

When the groups being considered are very different, assigning an unknown case to one of these groups is a very simple matter that can be accomplished graphically. Discriminant function scores for the to-be-assigned case are computed, a point for that case is plotted in the scatterplot of the discriminant analysis, and the case is assigned to the group to which it is nearest.

Classification through Re-analysis of the Data

Alternatively, a case of unknown group membership may be assigned by reanalyzing data from cases whose group memberships are known along with the case whose group membership is not known. In this analysis, of course, the to-be-assigned case's group membership code is left missing since it is unknown. Most discriminant analysis programs will print for each case, including the to-be-assigned case, the group in which that case's discriminant function scores are most likely to be found.

Classification Functions

Finally, the output of most discriminant analysis programs includes **classification function coefficients.** These weights and an accompanying constant are used to combine a case's scores on the original p variables in computing as many different classification function scores as there are groups. A case is assigned to the group with the largest classification function score.

We can understand the essentials of how these classification functions work. Say we have distributions of three groups' scores on a discriminant function, as shown in Figure 14.1a. Assume, moreover, that these distributions are all normal. We also have a case that is to be assigned to one of these three groups and a discriminant function score for that case. Three separate standard scores can be computed for the to-be-assigned case, each based on a different group's mean and standard deviation on the discriminant function. These z-scores will indicate the relative likelihood that the to-be-assigned case's discriminant function score would occur in each of the three groups (see chapter 4). The case can then be assigned to the group in which its score is most likely.

When there is more than a single discriminant function, this procedure is repeated for each discriminant function. Sometimes the correct classification is straightforward; the case's standard scores on all discriminant functions place it in the same group. Other times, though, the case's standard scores on one discriminant function will suggest assignment to one group, while the standard scores on another discriminant function will call for an assignment to a different group. When this happens, the correct group assignment must be determined by looking at the relative abilities of the different discriminant functions to separate the groups between which the classification decision must be made. Say, for instance, that we are working with the discriminant functions depicted in Figure 14.1, and we have a to-be-assigned case whose score on the first discriminant function suggests an assignment to Group 2. The case's second function score, though, calls for assignment to Group 3. We must decide between assigning the case to Groups

2 or 3. Since the second discriminant function in this example better separates Groups 2 and 3 than does the first function, we would place greater weight on the assignment suggested by the second function and assign the case to Group 3.

To further complicate matters, a priori probabilities of group membership must be taken into consideration when cases are assigned to groups. If there are many more members of one group than another group, then this fact should be considered in assigning a case of unknown group membership. In other words, a priori probabilities of group membership are important in predicting group membership and must be considered along with discriminant function scores in making group assignments.

Clearly, the process of assigning cases to groups can become quite involved. It is generally a good idea to use program-provided classification function coefficients in making group assignments. These functions take all important factors into consideration.

Classification Accuracy and Misclassification

Accurate assignment of cases to groups requires that the groups differ significantly on one or more discriminant functions. However, we have seen in previous chapters that statistical significance and practical significance are not always the same thing. Statistical significance of discriminant functions is necessary, but not sufficient, to ensure that classifications will be made with acceptable levels of accuracy. In assessing the practical utility of the classifications provided by a discriminant analysis, then, we must examine more than statistical significance. We need to look directly at how many cases are assigned correctly and at how many are misclassified.

The Confusion Matrix. We may adopt a postdictive approach to assessing the adequacy of classification, just as postdictive accuracy is used to estimate the predictive accuracy of regression equations (chapters 11 and 13). The same cases that are analyzed to derive the discriminant function(s) are postdictively assigned to groups on the basis of their discriminant function scores, and these assignments are compared for accuracy against the cases' actual group memberships in a **confusion matrix.** Box 14.4 includes a confusion matrix as Table 14.12. A confusion matrix summarizes both overall accuracy of classification and the relative levels of various types of misclassification.

In most applications, some errors are more serious than others. In medical diagnosis, for example, it is often more serious to assign an abnormal blood sample to the normal category ("false negative") than it is to assign a normal blood sample to the abnormal category ("false positive"). The confusion matrix enables us to assess the relative frequency of occurrence of the various types of errors that may occur when a specified set of discriminant functions is used in assigning cases to groups.

Cross-Validation. We saw in chapter 13 that a multiple regression equation developed for one sample may provide considerably less predictive accuracy when it is applied to data from a new sample. This same kind of "shrinkage" occurs with discriminant functions. Especially when sample sizes are small and several discriminating variables are used, a discriminant function that gives good classification accuracy in the original sample may provide considerably less accuracy when applied to data from new cases. The culprit responsible for shrinkage in discriminant analysis is overfitting of the discriminant function constant and weighting coefficients to the idiosyncrasies of the sample on which the discriminant function was developed.

The most effective way of establishing the validity of a discriminant function is to cross-validate on a new sample. Discriminant functions developed using one sample are used in categorizing cases from a second sample where correct group memberships are again known. The confusion matrix summarizing the outcomes of these classifications gives an indication of the level of accuracy and inaccuracy that we can expect in future applications of the discriminant functions.

Cross-validation is the most satisfactory way of establishing the utility of a discriminant function, but it is also the most expensive. To perform a cross-validation, we must hold back one-half to one-third of the available cases of known group membership so that these cases can be used in the cross-validation. The discriminant analysis, then, is based on only part of the available data.

Jackknifing. An alternative to cross-validation that is nearly as effective in establishing the utility of a discriminant function and allows us to use all available cases in constructing the discriminant functions is **jackknifing.** The discriminant analysis is performed repeatedly, each time leaving out a different case in calculating the discriminant function(s), but classifying the leftover case in the classification phase of the analysis. The misclassifications of the leftover cases that occur throughout this series of analyses are a good indication of the kinds of misclassifications we will see when the discriminant functions are applied to new data. The obvious disadvantage of jackknifing is the expense of performing the analysis repeatedly. It is a procedure best reserved for those situations in which cases are too scarce to allow us to hold back a cross-validation sample.

METHODS OF DISCRIMINANT ANALYSIS

In chapter 13 we identified three general approaches to multiple regression analysis: the stepwise methods (including forward, backward, and a combination of these two approaches), direct regression, and hierarchical regression. Discriminant analysis can also be accomplished using any of these approaches.

Direct Analysis

Direct analysis, the approach we have studied thus far in this chapter, enters all p original variables into the analysis. Direct analysis is generally selected if there are relatively few original variables or if we have theoretical reasons for including

BOX 14.4

CLASSIFICATION USING DISCRIMINANT ANALYSIS

TABLE 14.9 Scores for One Job Applicant on Veracity, Hygiene, and Moral Development

Variables	Scores
Veracity	2
Hygiene	40
Moral Development	3

In previous boxes we constructed discriminant functions, evaluated their discriminating power, and used discriminant functions to describe the nature of between-group differences. Here we will see how discriminant analysis can be used to classify individuals to the occupational categories of liars, damn liars, and statisticians.

Wegotchu Corporation, having analyzed the differences between liars, damn liars, and statisticians, is ready to begin hiring individuals to fill these occupational categories in their U.S. plant. Applicants are all administered the Nixon Veracity Scale, the LePew Personal Hygiene Profile, and Simon Legree's Measure of Moral Development. Scores from one applicant are given in Table 14.9.

The Graphic Approach to Classification

In determining this applicant's most likely occupational group, we begin by computing scores for the individual on each of the two discriminant functions, using the constants and weights determined in Box 14.1:

$$\begin{aligned} D_1 &= a + w_1(\text{Veracity}) + w_2(\text{Hygiene}) + w_3(\text{Moral Development}) \\ &= -5.97 + .28(2) + .02(40) + 1.20(3) \\ &= -1.01 \\ D_2 &= a + w_1(\text{Veracity}) + w_2(\text{Hygiene}) + w_3(\text{Moral Development}) \\ &= -3.59 + .56(2) + .08(40) - 1.00(3) \\ &= -2.27 \end{aligned}$$

We can now locate this applicant in the discriminant analysis scatterplot (Figure 14.2) using the applicant's discriminant function scores as coordinates. These scores position the applicant as shown in Figure 14.2 nearer to Group 3 (statisticians) than to any other group. On this basis, we would assign this individual to Group 3.

Classification Using Classification Functions

Alternatively, classification function coefficients output from the discriminant analysis can be used to assign the applicant to the most likely group. Weights and constants for computing these classification functions are presented in Table 14.10.

all variables. The disadvantage of direct analysis, particularly when a large number of variables is involved, is the increased likelihood of overfitting the discriminant functions to sample peculiarities. In addition, direct analyses of many variables can make it difficult for the researcher to demonstrate the statistical significance of the discriminant functions that are formed, since tests of the significance of discriminant functions are adjusted for the number of variables combined.

BOX 14.4—*continued*

TABLE 14.10 Classification Function Weighting Coefficients and Constants

Variable	Group 1: Liars	Group 2: Damn Liars	Group 3: Statisticians
Veracity	2.37	1.82	−.57
Hygiene	.55	.59	.27
Moral Development	11.65	1.42	3.79
constant	−65.08	−25.90	−8.16

The applicant's classification function scores are thus:

$$\begin{aligned}
\text{Group 1} &= -65.08 + 2.37(\text{Veracity}) + .55(\text{Hygiene}) + 11.65\,(\text{Moral Development}) \\
&= -65.08 + 2.37(2) + .55(40) + 11.65(3) \\
&= -3.39 \\
\text{Group 2} &= -25.90 + 1.82(\text{Veracity}) + .59(\text{Hygiene}) + 1.42(\text{Moral Development}) \\
&= -25.90 + 1.82(2) + .59(40) + 1.42(3) \\
&= 5.60 \\
\text{Group 3} &= -8.16 - .57(\text{Veracity}) + .27(\text{Hygiene}) + 3.79(\text{Moral Development}) \\
&= -8.16 - .57(2) + .27(40) + 3.79(3) \\
&= 12.87
\end{aligned}$$

The classification function score for Group 3 (statisticians) is the highest of the three. This confirms our decision to assign the case to this occupational group.

It may be helpful to explore the conceptual basis of these classification functions. Means and standard deviations on the two discriminant functions were computed in Box 14.1 (Table 14.3). Our applicant's discriminant function scores ($D_1 = -1.01$, $D_2 = -2.27$) can be evaluated for their relative likelihood of occurrence in each of the three occupational groups under consideration by converting them to standard scores. These z-scores are given in Table 14.11. The three z-scores listed for the first discriminant function were computed using the three groups' means and standard deviations on the first discriminant function.

continued

Stepwise Analyses

The stepwise analyses share one thing in common. They are all selective in the inclusion of discriminating variables in the discriminant function(s). Where there are redundant variables (i.e., variables that are highly correlated), stepwise procedures will eliminate one or more of these overlapping variables before forming the discriminant function(s).

BOX 14.4—*continued*

TABLE 14.11 One Applicant's Standardized Discriminant Function Scores Computed Using Means and Standard Deviations for Each of the Three Occupational Groups

Group	D_1	D_2
1: Liars	−5.03	−3.16
2: Damn Liars	1.19	−4.39
3: Statisticians	2.44	− .54

Similarly, the three *z*-scores listed for the second discriminant function were computed using the three groups' means and standard deviations on the second function. These *z*-scores tell us how far from each group's centroid (mean) the applicant's discriminant function scores fall.

Looking first at *z*-scores on the first discriminant function, we see that the applicant's discriminant function score deviates least from the centroid of Group 2 ($z = 1.19$). If a classification were to be made solely on the basis of the first function, the applicant would be assigned to Group 2. However, we also have information pertaining to the second discriminant function. Standard scores on this function indicate that the applicant's discriminant function score deviates least from the centroid of Group 3 ($z = -.54$).

How are we to choose between Groups 2 and 3? Remember that the second discriminant function was found previously (Box 14.1) to discriminate better between Groups 2 and 3 than does the first discriminant function. Since we must choose between assigning the applicant to either Group 2 or Group 3, it makes sense to base the decision on the discriminant function that best discriminates between these groups—the second function. Thus, we assign the applicant to Group 3 (statisticians).

Forward analysis selects at each of several steps the variable for inclusion in the discriminant function(s) that will add the most to the overall separation of the groups. Backward analysis begins with all variables included and eliminates at each step the variable that will cause the smallest loss of group separation. Forward and backward selection can be combined so that, at each step, a variable is added and variables previously included are examined to see if excluding one of them would not result in too large a loss of discriminating power.

The advantages of stepwise discriminant analyses include increased economy through the elimination of discriminating variables that do not add appreciably to the power of the discriminant function(s). Too, stepwise analyses enhance the likelihood of finding the discriminant function(s) statistically significant by reducing the total number of variables combined in forming the discriminant function(s). However, stepwise procedures can exacerbate the overfitting and shrinkage problems discussed earlier. The variables selected for inclusion in forming the discriminant function(s) may be the most useful in one sample, but they may not be the most valuable discriminators in some other sample.

TABLE 14.12 Confusion Matrix Summarizing Classification Errors in Discriminant Analysis

		Assigned Groups		
		Liars	*Damn Liars*	*Statisticians*
Actual Groups	*Liars*	5 100%	0 0%	0 0%
	Damn Liars	0 0%	5 100%	0 0%
	Statisticians	0 0%	1 20%	4 80%

Overall Accuracy: 93.33%

Evaluating Classification Accuracy
Finally we can evaluate the adequacy of the classifications made using the two discriminant functions by examining the confusion matrix shown in Table 14.12. This table summarizes the pattern of correct classifications and misclassifications that occurred when cases were assigned to groups on the basis of their discriminant function scores. In this admittedly contrived analysis, only one misclassification has occurred—a statistician was mistaken for a damn liar!

Hierarchical Analysis

Hierarchical analysis is a stepwise analysis in which the researcher, not statistical considerations, controls the entry of variables. This approach is often used when we wish to develop discriminant functions that use the least expensive variables available. Rather than allowing statistical considerations to control the selection of variables, the researcher will specify that the least expensive variable be entered first, the second least expensive variable next, the third least expensive variable next, and so on. The hope, of course, is that a set of several inexpensive variables will provide adequate discriminating power to meet the demands of the situation.

Another situation calling for the use of hierarchical analysis is when we wish to determine whether a set of variables enhances group separation after one or more other variables have been considered. In a study comparing characteristics of successful and unsuccessful students, we might wish to first remove differences due to ability (e.g., intelligence) to focus on the importance of school variables (e.g., class size, average age of teachers) in discriminating the two types of students. Ability variables would be entered into the discriminant analysis first, followed by the school variables of interest. The focus of the analysis would be on whether school variables added significantly to the discriminating power provided by ability variables.

SUMMARY

Discriminant analysis is a multivariate extension of one-way ANOVA. It is a method of testing the significance of differences between two or more groups on several dependent variables. Discriminant analysis is based upon combining several original dependent variables to form one or more orthogonal linear combinations of these variables, each called a discriminant function. Between-group differences are evaluated using these combination variables, thus reducing the multivariate problem to a series of univariate comparisons—one for each discriminant function. Discriminant analysis is also useful in describing the nature of the differences between groups. This interpretative phase of the analysis requires determining what is being measured by the discriminant functions that best separate the groups. A number of approaches are available, including an examination of correlations (loadings) between the discriminant functions and the variables that form these functions. Finally, discriminant analysis provides a way of classifying cases to groups in situations in which group memberships are unknown. A case is classified to that group in which the case's combination of discriminant function scores is most likely. Classification accuracy depends upon the power of the discriminant functions to separate groups. Discriminant analysis can be approached in several ways. Direct analysis combines all original variables in forming the discriminant functions. Stepwise analyses select at each of several steps the variable that will add the most to the between-group separation of the discriminant functions. Hierarchical analysis enables the researcher to control the order in which variables are chosen for inclusion in the discriminant functions.

NOTE

1. Discriminant function scores computed by hand using the constants and weighting coefficients given previously will differ slightly from the values listed in Table 14.2. This is a consequence of rounding error. The values in Table 14.2 are correct.

CHAPTER 15

MULTIVARIATE ANALYSIS OF VARIANCE

Multivariate analysis of variance (MANOVA) procedures are multivariate extensions of the univariate ANOVAs seen in chapters 8 and 9. MANOVAs share one feature in common—they all involve the use of two or more dependent variables. This distinguishes MANOVA from ANOVA, which analyzes only a single dependent variable at a time.

Both ANOVA and MANOVA designs answer the same basic research question. Do groups that are exposed to two or more levels of one or more independent variables differ significantly? Thus, ANOVA and MANOVA designs differ only in the number of dependent variables that are examined.

As an example of the type of research that would call for MANOVA, suppose a researcher wished to examine the effects of chemotherapy and memory enhancement training on cognitive functioning in Alzheimers patients. The independent variables or "factors" in this research are chemotherapy (drug vs. no-drug) and memory training (training vs. no-training). Any number of dependent variables measuring cognitive functioning might be used: tests of reading comprehension and retention, memory for names and faces, ratings provided by family members, and so on. A series of univariate factorial ANOVAs could be used to analyze the data collected in this experiment (with one ANOVA for each dependent variable), or a single MANOVA might be used that would simultaneously consider all dependent variables. Regardless of the analytic approach taken, the basic question being addressed is the same. Are there differences between groups that are sufficiently large that we may conclude that the independent variables are reliably linked to the dependent variables?

Like ANOVA, MANOVA is most commonly used in laboratory research, where the experimenter can actively manipulate the independent variable(s) of interest. However, neither in ANOVA or MANOVA is this necessary. Independent variables can be manipulated experimentally or may vary naturally (e.g., the variables of sex, age, religious preference). Of course, only those independent variables that are experimentally manipulated can be concluded to have causal connections to the dependent variables under consideration. Significant effects associated with naturally varying independent variables support only the conclusion that the independent variables and dependent variables are correlated.

TYPES OF MANOVA

All of the design variations that we considered in examining univariate ANOVAs apply to MANOVA as well. First, we may distinguish between one-way and factorial MANOVA. The **one-way MANOVA** compares two or more groups that occupy two or more levels of a single independent variable. One-way MANOVA is traditionally called discriminant analysis and was the focus of the preceding chapter.[1] **Factorial MANOVA** compares groups exposed to two or more levels of two or more independent variables or "factors." This chapter will focus on factorial MANOVA.

We learned in chapter 9 that factorial ANOVAs come in many shapes and sizes. All of the design variations in that chapter apply to factorial MANOVAs too. Factorial MANOVAs come in completely randomized designs (each case is exposed to only one combination of the levels of the factors), randomized block designs (each case is exposed to all treatment combinations), and split-plot designs (with repeated measures on some factors, but not on other factors). The levels of the factors can represent all levels of interest (fixed effect models), may be randomly sampled from a broader range of levels of interest (random effects models), or there may be a mixture of these two approaches (mixed effects models). Theoretically at least, every univariate ANOVA design has a multivariate counterpart. Practically speaking, though, statistical software packages provide for most, but not all MANOVA design options.

In this chapter we will examine only the most basic factorial MANOVA design, the completely randomized, two-factor, fixed effects MANOVA. The reader who wishes to learn more about the other MANOVA designs should refer to Harris (1988).

FACTORIAL MANOVA

Factorial MANOVA combines concepts from factorial ANOVA and discriminant analysis. Factorial MANOVA accomplishes the task of examining the effects of several independent variables (including both main effects and interaction effects), as does univariate factorial ANOVA. These effects are examined, though, on several dependent variables that are combined to form one or more linear composites, as in discriminant analysis. Box 15.1 provides an example of a factorial MANOVA to accompany the more general discussion that follows.

Factor A Main Effect

The main effect of Factor A is evaluated by forming one or more orthogonal discriminant functions (sometimes called "roots" in the tradition of MANOVA), which provide the greatest possible separation of the groups representing the levels of Factor A. These discriminant functions are linear combinations of the original dependent variables and each takes the form:

$$D = a + w_1V_1 + w_2V_2 + \ldots + w_pV_p$$

where,

a	=	the discriminant function constant
$w_1 - w_p$	=	discriminant function weighting coefficients for each of p dependent variables
$V_1 - V_p$	=	the p dependent variables

This is the same equation used in describing the form of discriminant functions in the preceding chapter (Equation 14.1). The maximum number of discriminant functions useful in evaluating the Factor A main effect is the smaller of the two values, p or A − 1, where p = the number of dependent variables and A = the number of levels of Factor A.

Once the dependent variables have been combined to form one or more discriminant functions, the amount of separation between groups that has been achieved can be measured using a variety of statistics. Most commonly reported in factorial MANOVA is Wilks' Lambda, which varies inversely with the overall separation of groups achieved using all discriminant functions. Although the significance of Wilks' Lambda can be tested directly, it is more common to see it transformed to the related *F* statistic for this purpose. A statistically significant *F* means that the groups representing the levels of Factor A differ sufficiently on the discriminant function(s) that the difference can be considered reliable and attributable to Factor A, rather than to sampling error.

Factor B Main Effect

The main effect of Factor B is evaluated by combining the original dependent variables to form one or more orthogonal discriminant functions that maximize the separation of the groups representing the levels of Factor B. It is important to note that the discriminant functions created to assess Factor B will be different from those used in assessing Factor A. The linear combination of dependent variables that best separates the groups representing the levels of Factor A will not be likely to provide the best possible separation of groups representing the levels of Factor B. The maximum possible number of discriminant functions that can be formed in assessing differences between the levels of Factor B is the smaller of the two values, p or $B - 1$, where $p =$ the number of dependent variables and $B =$ the number of levels of Factor B. The separation of groups representing the levels of Factor B which is achieved using these discriminant functions is then assessed for significance as described above. Statistical significance indicates that the groups representing levels of Factor B differ sufficiently on the discriminant function(s) that the differences can be considered reliable and attributable to Factor B, rather than to sampling error.

The A × B Interaction Effect

Finally, the effect of treatment combinations, the A × B interaction effect, is assessed by forming one or more discriminant functions that maximize the separation of the cells of the factorial data matrix. These discriminant functions will undoubtedly differ from those used in assessing Factor A and Factor B main effects, since those functions will probably not maximize the separation of groups representing treatment combinations. The maximum number of discriminant functions that can be formed in assessing the A × B interaction effect will equal the smaller of the two values, p or $(A - 1)(B - 1)$, where $p =$ the number of dependent variables, $A =$ the number of levels of Factor A, and $B =$ the number of levels of Factor B. The between-group separation achieved with these discriminant functions is evaluated for significance as described earlier. Statistical significance indicates that the different treatment combinations are accompanied by reliable differences on the discriminant function(s); that is, there is an interaction effect.

When the factorial MANOVA identifies a significant interaction effect, the interpretation of main effects can be misleading. The interaction shows that the effects of each factor are conditional upon the level of the other factor, so any

BOX 15.1

FACTORIAL MANOVA

Dr. Yogi Zen is trying to decide how to go about testing students in his classes. Undergraduate students, in particular, seem to dislike Dr. Zen's objective tests, and he is not sure how graduate students feel about his exams. To assess the effects of his testing method on his graduate and undergraduate students, Dr. Zen has decided to use a factorial MANOVA to examine the effects of two factors, test type (essay vs. objective) and student type (undergraduate vs. graduate), on several dependent variables related to student performance and sentiment: semester grades, absenteeism, and student ratings of Dr. Zen's teaching effectiveness. Data collected from four classes, representing all combinations of the two independent variables, are shown in Table 15.1. The variable of grades represents semester grades recorded on a 4-point scale (0 = F, 1 = D, 2 = C, 3 = B, and 4 = A). The variable of absences refers to the number of absences accumulated during the semester. The variable of ratings represents student ratings of Dr. Zen's "overall quality of instruction" obtained on a 5-point rating scale (1 = poor, 3 = average, 5 = superior).

Assessing the Interaction Effect

The multivariate interaction effect is examined first, since, if it is significant, main effects can be misleading. Table 15.2 summarizes those portions of the MANOVA that pertain to the multivariate interaction between test type and student type.

Shown in Table 15.2a are discriminant function weighting coefficients used to combine raw scores on grades, absences, and ratings in forming the linear combination of these variables that maximizes the separation of cells. The maximum number of discriminant functions that can be formed in assessing

TABLE 15.1 Data on Semester Grades, Absenteeism, and Student Ratings of Teaching Effectiveness from Undergraduates and Graduate Students Exposed to Essay or Objective Tests

	Factor B: Student Type					
	B_1: Undergraduate			B_2: Graduate		
Factor A: Test Type	*Grades*	*Absences*	*Ratings*	*Grades*	*Absences*	*Ratings*
A_1: Objective	2	6	1	4	2	5
	3	4	2	3	1	5
	1	1	4	3	0	3
	1	7	2	4	3	4
	2	9	1	3	3	5
	0	6	1	2	5	3
A_2: Essay	4	1	5	4	0	5
	4	3	5	3	2	5
	3	4	3	3	0	5
	2	2	4	4	0	5
	3	0	3	4	1	4
	1	5	3	3	1	3

the interaction effect is the smaller of the values, p (the number of dependent variables) or $(A - 1)$ $B - 1)$, where A = the number of levels of factor A and B = the number of levels of factor B. In this example, the number of discriminant functions is 1.

Table 15.2b presents interaction effect discriminant function scores for each student in the data matrix, along with cell means on this discriminant function. The pattern of differences seen between cell means is consistent with an interaction effect. Graduate students show little difference in their reactions to essay vs. objective testing; undergraduate students show a stronger difference.

TABLE 15.2 Summary Statistics Pertaining to the Multivariate A × B Interaction Effect

a. Raw score discriminant function weighting coefficients for the interaction discriminant function

Variables	**Weights**
Grades	.41
Absences	.06
Ratings	.88

b. Interaction discriminant function scores and cell means (centroids)

	Factor B: Student Type	
Factor A: Test Type	B_1: Undergraduate	B_2: Graduate
A_1: Objective	2.06 3.23 3.99 2.59 2.24 1.24 $\overline{X}_{A_1B_1} = 2.56$	6.16 5.69 3.87 5.34 5.81 3.76 $\overline{X}_{A_1B_2} = 5.11$
A_2: Essay	6.10 6.22 4.11 4.46 3.87 3.35 $\overline{X}_{A_2B_1} = 4.69$	6.04 5.75 5.63 6.04 5.22 3.93 $\overline{X}_{A_2B_2} = 5.44$

c. Wilks' Lambda and the F test for the A × B multivariate interaction

Wilks' Lambda	**Approx. *F***	***df***	**Significance**
.807	1.43	3, 18	.267

continued

BOX 15.1—*continued*

Table 15.2c next presents the multivariate test of the interaction effect. This test is found to be nonsignificant ($p > .05$), indicating that differences observed between cell means are not sufficiently large that they can be attributed to the different treatment combinations represented by the cells. Instead, these differences should be attributed to sampling error.

Assessing the Factor A Main Effect

The multivariate main effect of Factor A (test type) is examined next. Table 15.3 summarizes those portions of the MANOVA that pertain to this multivariate main effect.

Shown first in Table 15.3a are discriminant function weighting coefficients used to combine raw scores on grades, absences, and ratings in forming the

TABLE 15.3 Summary Statistics Pertaining to the Multivariate Factor A Main Effect

a. Raw score discriminant function weighting coefficients for the Factor A main effect

Variables	Weights
Grades	.39
Absences	−.28
Ratings	.42

b. Factor A discriminant function scores and row means (centroids)

	Factor B: Student Type		
	B_1: Undergraduate	B_2: Graduate	
A_1: Objective	−.48 .89 1.79 −.73 −1.32 −1.26	3.10 2.99 2.43 2.40 2.43 .64	$\overline{X}_{A_1} = 1.07$
Factor A: Test Type			
A_2: Essay	3.38 2.82 1.31 1.90 2.43 .25	3.66 2.71 3.27 3.66 2.96 2.15	$\overline{X}_{A_2} = 2.54$

c. Wilks' Lambda and the *F* test for the Factor A main effect

Wilks' Lambda	Approx. F	*df*	Significance
.605	3.91	3, 18	.026

linear combination of these variables that maximizes the separation of the levels of Factor A: essay exams vs. objective exams. The maximum number of discriminant functions that can be formed in assessing a main effect is the smaller of the two values, p (the number of dependent variables) or one less than the number of levels of the factor being examined. In this example, only one discriminant function can be formed because there are only two levels of Factor A.

Table 15.3b gives Factor A discriminant function scores for each student in the data matrix, along with row means on this discriminant function. The two row means differ in a manner consistent with a main effect of test type.

Table 15.3c presents the multivariate test of the Factor A main effect. This test is found to be significant, meaning that the difference seen between the two row means is too large to attribute to sampling error. Instead, the row means probably differ because of differences in treatment (i.e., types of tests) received by students in the two rows of the matrix.

Assessing the Factor B Main Effect

The multivariate main effect of Factor B (student type) is examined last. This main effect is not of any particular importance in Dr. Zen's decision to use essay or objective tests (it was included because student type might interact with test type), but will be examined here for any insights that it may provide about the nature of multivariate significance testing. Table 15.4 summarizes those portions of the MANOVA that pertain to the multivariate significance of student type.

Presented in Table 15.4a are discriminant function weighting coefficients used to combine raw scores on grades, absences, and ratings in forming the linear combination of these variables that maximizes the separation of the levels of Factor B: undergraduate vs. graduate students. The maximum number of discriminant functions that can be formed in assessing a main effect is the smaller of the two values, p (the number of dependent variables) or one less than the number of levels of the factor being examined. In this example, where there are only two levels of the student type factor, only one discriminant function is possible.

Table 15.4b shows Factor B discriminant function scores for each student in the data matrix, along with column means on this discriminant function. The two column means differ in a manner that is consistent with a main effect of student type.

Table 15.4c presents the multivariate test of the Factor B main effect. This test is found to be significant, so that the difference seen between the two column means is too large to attribute easily to sampling error. Instead, the difference between the column means reflects a reliable relationship between student type (graduate vs. undergraduate) and the discriminant function.

continued

BOX 15.1—*continued*

TABLE 15.4 **Summary Statistics Pertaining to the Multivariate Factor B Main Effect**

a. Raw score discriminant function weighting coefficients for the Factor B main effect

Variables	**Weights**
Grades	.50
Absences	−.19
Ratings	.51

b. Factor B discriminant function scores and column means (centroids)

		Factor B: Student Type	
		B_1: Undergraduate	B_2: Graduate
Factor A: Test Type	A_1: Objective	.37 1.76 2.35 .19 − .20 − .63	4.17 3.86 3.03 3.47 3.48 1.58
	A_2: Essay	4.36 3.98 2.27 2.66 3.03 1.08	4.55 3.67 4.05 4.55 3.85 3.03
		$\overline{X}_{B_1} = 1.77$	$\overline{X}_{B_2} = 3.61$

c. Wilks' Lambda and the *F* test for the Factor B main effect

Wilks' Lambda	**Approx. F**	***df***	**Significance**
.501	5.97	3, 18	.005

statements made about main effects must be qualified. Interpreting a multivariate interaction effect is best accomplished in the same way that univariate interactions are interpreted. Plot the cell means on the discriminant function(s) that produced the interaction and follow up with post hoc comparisons as described in the next section.

INTERPRETING BETWEEN-GROUP DIFFERENCES IN MANOVA

When one or more of the effects evaluated in MANOVA is found to be significant, the problem remains of interpreting the meaning of that significant effect. This includes determining which specific groups differ significantly, a task accomplished with post hoc comparisons. Second, it is necessary to describe the nature of the between-group differences. This is accomplished by interpreting the significant discriminant function(s). Finally, it is important to learn if effects identified as statistically significant are also practically significant. These issues and procedures are discussed next. Box 15.2 gives an example of the interpretation of between-group differences identified using factorial MANOVA.

Post Hoc Comparisons

A significant MANOVA main effect indicates that at least two row or column means differ significantly. If there are only two levels of the factor yielding a significant main effect, determining which two levels differ is not a problem. However, if the significant factor includes three or more levels, post hoc comparisons are needed to find the source(s) of the significant main effect. In the case of a significant interaction effect, post hoc comparisons enable assessing differences between cell means or combinations of cell means to determine the source(s) of that effect.

The Scheffé procedure was described in chapters 8 and 9 (see Equations 8.8 through 8.10) as a flexible approach to post hoc data snooping in ANOVA. This procedure is recommended for the same purpose in MANOVA. In the case of MANOVA, though, the means being compared are means (or "centroids") on the discriminant function(s) created in evaluating the effect being explored. The Scheffé test uses the value of MS_{within} in computing $t_{observed}$ (Equation 8.9). Since MS_{within} is not generally provided as part of the MANOVA output, it must be computed. First, compute discriminant function scores for each case in the data matrix. Next compute SS_{within} according to Equation 9.2 of chapter 9. Finally, compute MS_{within} by dividing SS_{within} by $df_{within} = N - (A)(B)$, where N = the total number of cases, A = the number of levels of Factor A, and B = the number of levels of Factor B.

Interpreting the Discriminant Functions

After post hoc comparisons have determined which groups differ, the second step in interpreting a significant MANOVA effect is to determine how the groups differ. This requires interpreting the discriminant function(s) created for the effect being examined. The interpretation of discriminant functions was described fully in the preceding chapter. To reiterate briefly here, though, the interpretation generally begins with a series of univariate tests to determine which of the original dependent variables have contributed to the overall significance of the discriminant function(s). Next, a discriminant function can be interpreted by determining which groups it best separates. Finally, correlations between a discriminant function and the original dependent variables can reveal what conceptual variable the discriminant function represents.

Evaluating the Strength of Effects in MANOVA

Effects uncovered using univariate ANOVA can be assessed for strength using the statistic omega-square. You may recall from chapters 8 and 9 that this statistic describes the strength of the association between an independent variable and a dependent variable by indicating the proportion of variability in the dependent variable that can be attributed to the different levels of the significant independent variable.

A similar index of strength of association is available in MANOVA. In assessing the strength of any given effect, Wilks' Lambda (Λ) reflects the ratio of within-group variance across all discriminant functions to total variance across all discriminant functions. Thus, Λ is the proportion of the total variance across all discriminant functions associated with any particular effect that is not explained by the different levels of the treatment. The value $1 - \Lambda$, then, represents the proportion of the total variance across all discriminant functions that is explained by the levels of that treatment. The value $1 - \Lambda$ can be computed for each effect in the MANOVA. In the case of each main effect, $1 - \Lambda$ measures the strength of association between an independent variable and the discriminant functions formed to assess that independent variable's effects. In the case of the interaction effect, $1 - \Lambda$ measures the strength of association between the different treatment combinations and the discriminant functions formed to assess the interaction effect.

FACTORIAL MANOVA VS. MULTIPLE FACTORIAL ANOVAS

Having examined factorial MANOVA, we can now assess the relative strengths and weaknesses of this analytic approach.

Advantages of Factorial MANOVA

As an extension of univariate factorial ANOVA to a multivariate situation, factorial MANOVA carries all of the advantages that accrue to univariate factorial ANOVA. As an extension of discriminant analysis to factorial data, factorial MANOVA carries the advantages of discriminant analysis. These advantages are discussed next.

BOX 15.2

INTERPRETING MANOVA RESULTS

The factorial MANOVA in Box 15.1 revealed main effects of Factor A (test type) and Factor B (student type) on multivariate combinations of measures of student performance and sentiment. The multivariate interaction effect was nonsignificant. In this box we will interpret the nature of the between-group differences revealed by the multivariate significance tests.

Interpreting the Interaction Effect
Since the multivariate test of significance of the interaction effect was nonsignificant, there is, strictly speaking, no interaction effect to interpret. Let us go through the steps that would be followed, though, if the multivariate test had yielded significance.

First, in order to know which of the original dependent variables contributed to the interaction, we examine the univariate significance tests summarized in Table 15.5a. Each of these tests assesses the significance of the interaction between test type and student type on one of the original dependent variables. Although neither grades nor absences approach significance, the interaction effect comes very close to significance ($p = .055$) on the variable of student ratings. How can there be a nearly significant univariate interaction and a nonsignificant multivariate interaction? Remember that the F test of the multivariate test of significance adjusts for the number of variables combined in forming the discriminant function(s). The more variables being examined, the greater the separation there must be in order for significance to be reached. Particularly when sample sizes are small and/or a large number of variables are combined, it can happen that a univariate test will reach significance when the multivariate test does not.

The second step in interpreting the between-group differences associated with the nonsignificant interaction effect includes interpreting the discriminant function that separates the treatment combinations. This is most readily accomplished by examining the correlations between the discriminant function and the original dependent variables. These correlations are given in Table 15.5b. The interaction effect discriminant function mostly reflects student ratings, which explain 86% of the variance in the discriminant function ($.93^2 = .86$). Grades are the second most important contributor to the discriminant function explaining 37% of the variance ($.61^2 = .37$), and absences are least important, explaining only 15% of the variance ($-.39^2 = .15$). The signs of these correlations tell us that grades and ratings are directly

TABLE 15.5 Statistics Pertaining to the Interpretation of the Multivariate A × B Interaction Effect

a. Univariate *F* Tests

Variable	$SS_{between}$	SS_{within}	$MS_{between}$	MS_{within}	F	Significance
Grades	1.50	16.67	1.50	.83	1.80	.195
Absences	2.67	73.67	2.67	3.68	.72	.405
Ratings	4.17	20.00	4.17	1.00	4.17	.055

b. Correlations between interaction effect discriminant function and original variables

Variable	Disc. Function
Grades	.61
Absences	−.39
Ratings	.93

continued

related to scores on the discriminant function and absences are inversely related to discriminant function scores. This pattern of correlations suggests that the interaction effect discriminant function may be interpreted as a measure of general "positivity" of student responses. That is, discriminant function scores increase as positive outcomes increase (high grades, low absenteeism, and high student ratings); discriminant function scores decrease as negative outcomes increase (low grades, high absenteeism, and low student ratings). Looking at the cell means in Table 15.2, then, we can conclude that there is a tendency for undergraduates to react more positively to essay tests than to objective tests, a tendency not seen among graduate students, who react equally well to both types of tests.

Finally, we may use Wilks' Lambda (Λ) and $1 - \Lambda$ as measures of the strength of the interaction effect. Since $\Lambda = .81$ (Table 15.2c) represents the proportion of variance in the interaction effect discriminant function that is not explained by the different treatment combinations, $1 - \Lambda = .19$ is the proportion of variance that is explained by these combinations. Relatively little of the variability in the interaction effect discriminant function is linked to differences in treatment combinations from one cell to the next.

Interpreting the Factor A Main Effect

Factor A (test type) was found to have a significant multivariate effect on a composite measure of grades, absences, and ratings. Table 15.6a gives results of the univariate significance tests of the Factor A main effect. Since all of these univariate tests are significant, we know that all of the original dependent variables contributed to the significance of the Factor A multivariate main effect.

Next, Table 15.6b presents correlations between the Factor A discriminant function and the original dependent variables. These correlations show that the Factor A discriminant function measures mostly absenteeism, which explains 67% ($-.82^2 = .67$) of the variance in the discriminant function, and student ratings, which explains 62% ($.79^2 = .62$) of the variance. The least important contributor to this discriminant function was the variable of grades, which accounted for only 38% ($.62^2 = .38$) of the variance. The signs of the correlations tell us that grades and ratings are directly related to the discriminant function and absences are inversely related. The Factor A discriminant function, like the interaction discriminant function, appears to provide a measure of general positivity of student responses. As student outcomes become more positive, scores on the discriminant function increase; as outcomes become more negative, scores on the discriminant function decrease. Looking at the row means in Table 15.3, then, we can conclude that students show a generally more positive response to essay tests than to objective tests.

Finally, the strength of the Factor A main effect may be evaluated using Wilks' Lambda (Λ) and $1 - \Lambda$. Since $\Lambda = .61$ (Table 15.3c) is the proportion of variance in the Factor A discriminant function that is *not* explained by test type, $1 - \Lambda = .39$ is the proportion of variance in the composite outcome measure that *is* explained by test type.

Interpreting the Factor B Main Effect

Factor B (student type) was also found to have a significant multivariate effect on a composite measure of grades, absences, and ratings. Table 15.7a shows results of the univariate significance tests of the Factor B main effect. Since all of these univariate tests are significant, we know that all of the original dependent variables contributed to the significance of the Factor B multivariate main effect.

Next, Table 15.7b presents correlations between the Factor B discriminant function and the original dependent variables. These correlations mean that the Factor B discriminant function is most influenced by student ratings, which account for 67% ($.82^2 = .67$) of the variance in the discriminant function. The variable of absences is second most important, accounting for 52% ($-.72^2 = .52$) of the variance.

BOX 15.2—*continued*

Grades are least important, explaining 49% ($.70^2 = .49$) of the variance. The signs of the correlation show that grades and ratings are again positivity related to discriminant function scores and absenteeism is inversely related. Thus, the Factor B discriminant function, like the two functions interpreted previously, provides a measure of general positivity of student responses. Looking at the column means in Table 15.4, then, we can conclude that graduate students show a significantly more positive overall reaction to Dr. Zen's classes than do undergraduate students.

Finally, the strength of the Factor B main effect is reflected in the values of Λ and $1 - \Lambda$. Since $\Lambda = .50$ (Table 15.4c) and $1 - \Lambda = .50$ for the main effect of student type, half of the variance in the Factor B discriminant function is explained by student type and half is left unexplained.

TABLE 15.6 Statistics Pertaining to the Interpretation of the Multivariate Factor A Main Effect

a. Univariate *F* Tests

Variable	$SS_{between}$	SS_{within}	$MS_{between}$	MS_{within}	F	Significance
Grades	4.17	16.67	4.17	.83	5.00	.037
Absences	32.67	73.67	32.67	3.68	8.87	.007
Ratings	8.17	20.00	8.17	1.00	8.17	.010

b. Correlations between Factor A discriminant function and original variables

Variables	Disc. Function
Grades	.62
Absences	−.82
Ratings	.79

TABLE 15.7 Statistics Pertaining to the Interpretation of the Multivariate Factor B Main Effect

a. Univariate *F* Tests

Variable	$SS_{between}$	SS_{within}	$MS_{between}$	MS_{within}	F	Significance
Grades	8.17	16.67	8.17	.83	9.80	.005
Absences	37.50	73.67	37.50	3.68	10.18	.005
Ratings	13.50	20.00	13.50	1.00	13.50	.002

b. Correlations between Factor B discriminant function and original variables

Variables	Disc. Function
Grades	.70
Absences	−.72
Ratings	.82

Independent Evaluations of Main and Interaction Effects. Factorial MANOVA provides tests of the effects of several independent variables and the effects of treatment combinations within a single analysis. Tests of the significance of main and interaction effects are statistically independent, provided sample sizes are equal.

The Power of Convergence. No single operationally defined dependent variable is likely to capture perfectly the conceptual variable of interest to a researcher. By using several dependent variables in a MANOVA design, though, the problem of measurement is attacked from several angles. This is the power of convergence and is made possible by MANOVA.

Assessment of Multiple Effects. Independent variables of interest to the researcher are likely to affect a variety of different conceptual variables. For example, an organization's new no-smoking policy will affect satisfaction, productivity, absenteeism, health insurance claims, and a variety of other variables. In order to better examine the breadth of effects of the independent variables, it makes sense to include several dependent variables in a multivariate analysis.

Increased Power. Especially when sample sizes are large, MANOVA can provide a more powerful test of significance than is available using univariate ANOVA. A discriminant function constructed specifically to maximize F may yield significance when none of the original dependent variables reach significance.

Reduced Error Rate. MANOVA also provides the advantage of reducing error rates, relative to those that occur in a series of univariate ANOVAs. By combining several dependent variables into a reduced set of discriminant functions, MANOVA reduces the number of significance tests required, and thus, reduces the number of Type I and Type II errors. Moreover, by testing only orthogonal discriminant functions for significance, it is guaranteed that the significance tests computed in a MANOVA will be statistically independent. Univariate ANOVAs, which analyze a set of correlated dependent variables, are not independent, and an error in one test can produce errors in other tests.

Interpretive Advantages. Finally, MANOVA can offer an interpretive advantage over a series of univariate ANOVAs. As we saw in the previous chapter, correlations between dependent variables make it difficult or impossible to interpret a series of significant ANOVAs. In contrast, discriminant functions used in examining any given effect in a factorial MANOVA are orthogonal to each other. Thus, groups are known to differ in as many different ways as there are discriminant functions.

Disadvantages of Factorial MANOVA

Despite these potential advantages, factorial MANOVA seems as often to frustrate as to illuminate. This has led Tabachnick and Fidell (1983) to express a sentiment shared by many others who have worked with factorial MANOVA. "Because of the increase in complexity and ambiguity of results with MANOVA, one of the best overall recommendations is: Avoid it if you can" (p. 230). Before taking on a MANOVA, be sure that this is really the best approach to data analysis. Here are some of the potential drawbacks to factorial MANOVA.

Interpretive Disadvantages. We learned in the preceding chapter that discriminant functions are not always easy to interpret. They are designed to separate groups, not to make conceptual sense. Compounding the interpretation problem in factorial MANOVA is the fact that each effect evaluated for significance uses different discriminant functions. Factor A may be found to influence a combination of variables totally different from the combination most affected by Factor B or the interaction between Factors A and B.

Assumptions. A further disadvantage of factorial MANOVA is that this method is based upon the same numerous assumptions that are required by discriminant analysis. As we saw in the last chapter, these assumptions are difficult to assess and to meet.

First, it is assumed that each discriminant function in factorial MANOVA is normally distributed in each group being compared on that function. Second, discriminant functions are assumed to show approximately equal variances across groups. Third, patterns of intercorrelation between the dependent variables are assumed to be equivalent within each group. Fourth, the relationships among dependent variables are assumed to be linear within each group. Fifth, multicollinearity prevents solving the equations of the MANOVA, and the offending variable(s) must be identified and eliminated. Finally, MANOVA is extremely sensitive to multivariate outliers, which must be identified and eliminated.

Alternatives to Factorial MANOVA

Given the potential pitfalls of factorial MANOVA, it is wise to consider analytic alternatives. One obvious possibility is to eliminate the need for multivariate analysis by combining and/or eliminating dependent variables so that only one variable need be analyzed, presumably using a univariate factorial ANOVA. Can the several dependent variables be logically combined, perhaps by adding scores across variables to form a total?

Another approach that can be recommended is the analysis of orthogonal factor variates (see chapter 16) using several factorial ANOVAs, one ANOVA for each factor variate. Factor analysis enables forming a reduced set of orthogonal linear combinations of the original variables. These linear combinations, called factor variates, have one clear advantage over discriminant functions. Factor variates are formed to be conceptually meaningful and easily interpreted. This means that a series of ANOVAs computed using factor variates as dependent variables will be more likely to yield interpretable results than will a factorial MANOVA. That factor variates, like discriminant functions, are orthogonal, means that each univariate ANOVA will be statistically independent of the others.

There are disadvantages to this approach, though. First, multiple ANOVAs mean increased error. However, since there are fewer factor variates than there are original dependent variables, this problem is minimal. Second, factor scores are formed to make conceptual sense, not to maximize group separation. Thus, the univariate analysis of factor variates is less powerful than is MANOVA.

SUMMARY

Multivariate analysis of variance (MANOVA) is the multivariate extension of univariate ANOVA. One-way MANOVA, traditionally called discriminant analysis, was the focus of the preceding chapter. Factorial MANOVA was examined in this chapter. Factorial MANOVA enables us to assess the main and interaction effects of two or more independent variables on a linear combination of two or more dependent variables. Put simply, the several dependent variables examined in factorial MANOVA are reduced to a single composite variable, the discriminant function, which is then analyzed through univariate factorial ANOVA. The Factor A main effect analyzes the linear combination(s) of dependent variables which provides for the greatest separation of groups representing the levels of Factor A. Factor B is assessed using the linear combination(s) that best separates the groups representing levels of Factor B. The interaction effect analyzes the linear combination(s) which best separates the cells of the factorial data matrix (i.e., treatment combinations). Once one or more treatment effects is found to be significant, the task begins of interpreting the nature of the between-group differences. Determining which groups differ is accomplished with post hoc comparisons. Determining how the groups differ is accomplished by interpreting the discriminant function(s) on which those differences occur. Although factorial MANOVA can offer some advantages over a series of univariate factorial ANOVAs, it presents some difficulties as well, not the least of which is interpreting the nature of significant between-group differences. Discriminant functions formed in the factorial MANOVA are designed to maximize between-group separation, not to be conceptually meaningful.

NOTE

1. Although discriminant analysis and one-way MANOVA are mathematically identical procedures, they are usually accomplished with different computer programs. Since the traditional focus of discriminant analysis is on the description of between-group differences and the subsequent classification of cases to groups, the discriminant analysis output will generally emphasize information pertinent to these applications (e.g., classification function coefficients, scatterplots of cases in the discriminant function space, confusion matrices). One-way MANOVA is traditionally used to test the significance of treatment effects by assessing differences between groups exposed to different treatments. Thus, output from MANOVA programs is heavy on tests of significance. MANOVA programs also differ from discriminant analysis programs in providing more of the design flexibility that is useful in assessing treatment effects. MANOVA programs, for example, include factorial and repeated measures designs that are unavailable in discriminant analysis programs.

CHAPTER 16

FACTOR ANALYSIS

Significance Tests in Factor Analysis
- Stability of Factor Structure
- Comparing Factor Structures

Principal Components Analysis vs. Factor Analysis

Summary

Notes

Much research in the social and behavioral sciences focuses on grouping elements into relatively homogeneous categories on the basis of similarities between those elements. The elements may be variables, as in factor analysis, or cases or stimuli, as in cluster analysis. Although factor and cluster analysis both examine similarities between elements, these analyses proceed in rather different fashions. Consequently, factor analysis will be treated in this chapter, and cluster analysis will be examined in chapter 17.

Factor analysis refers to a large family of related techniques, all of which examine the correlations between a set of variables to identify those groups of variables that are relatively homogeneous (i.e., highly correlated).[1] These groups of variables are said to represent **factors.** The most straightforward type of factor analysis, both conceptually and mathematically, is **principal components analysis.** Although purists argue that principal components analysis is not a "true" factor analysis at all, only rarely will principal components analysis lead us to draw conclusions different from what would follow from a true factor analysis. This being the case, principal components analysis will be presented here as a model to all forms of factor analysis, and we will use a common parlance in describing all forms of factor analysis, including principal components analysis.

APPLICATIONS OF FACTOR ANALYSIS

By identifying groups of highly intercorrelated variables, factor analysis enables us to determine how many underlying factors are measured by a set of *p* original variables. In other words, factor analysis is used to uncover the **factor structure** of a set of variables. Several purposes may thus be served, as discussed next.

Theory Development

First, there may be theoretical reasons for examining the factor structure of a collection of variables. A researcher in psychological testing, for example, might find it theoretically useful to know that a dozen tests of apparently different cognitive abilities group themselves into only three sets of highly correlated tests. The original tests, then, do not tap 12 different abilities, but only three underlying factors. As another example, research into family dynamics may have shown that functional and dysfunctional families differ significantly on 20 different variables. Given the correlations that surely exist between these variables, though, it would be foolish, not to mention nonparsimonious, to conclude that the families differ in 20 different ways. A factor analysis of the 20 variables would undoubtedly reveal a reduced set of factors that would provide a more parsimonious description of the fundamental differences between the two types of families. In sum, factor analysis is a means by which we can group variables in achieving explanatory parsimony.

Data Simplification

Data simplification is a second goal of factor analysis. A factor analysis will generally reveal that a collection of variables represents a considerably smaller number of underlying factors, each of which is represented by several variables. Once those variables have been identified that represent a factor, our research may be simplified considerably by eliminating some of these redundant variables from further consideration.

Data simplification also occurs when we use factor analysis to form **factor scores.** Once a reduced set of factors has been identified, scores on the original variables can be weighted and combined so as to form composite variables called **factor variates.** A factor variate measures a fundamental characteristic or trait (i.e., a factor) that is measured in common by the variables that are combined in forming the factor variate. It is certainly simpler to work with a reduced set of factor variates than to deal with scores on all of the original variables.

Not only are there fewer factor variates than original variables, these factor variates can be created to be completely orthogonal. Although the original variables present a complex mixture of unique and shared variance, factor variates are "simple" in the sense that each measures a unique trait or characteristic.

Factor Analysis as a Precursor to Other Analyses

The statistical independence of factor variates makes factor analysis useful as a precursor to other kinds of statistical analysis. For one thing, factor analysis can offer a solution to the problem of multicollinearity. We have seen that highly correlated predictor variables can prevent the solution of the necessary equations in multiple regression analysis. Similarly, highly correlated dependent variables can short-circuit a discriminant analysis or multivariate analysis of variance. Solutions already offered to the problem of multicollinearity included the elimination of one or more variables from the analysis or the use of a stepwise procedure to remove redundant variables. A third solution is offered by factor analysis. Instead of using correlated original variables as predictors or dependent variables, these variables can first be factor analyzed and orthogonal factor variates can be entered into subsequent analyses. Factor variates, being uncorrelated, preclude the problem of multicollinearity.

Factor analysis can also precede univariate significant difference tests in accomplishing many of the same goals that are achieved with multivariate significant difference tests. Both discriminant analysis and multivariate analysis of variance were described previously as providing an alternative to multiple univariate analyses of correlated dependent variables. In the simplest case, this is accomplished by combining several correlated dependent variables to form a single discriminant function that provides the best possible separation of groups. Where more than one discriminant function is needed, these functions are orthogonal, thus ensuring the statistical independence of the significance tests of those discriminant functions. The problem with discriminant functions is that they are formed to maximize group separation, not to be conceptually meaningful. Consequently, it is often difficult or impossible to interpret a discriminant function in order to determine how the groups being compared differ.

As an alternative, a set of correlated dependent variables may be factor analyzed to create a reduced set of orthogonal factor variates. Each factor variate can then be analyzed in a separate univariate analysis. The orthogonality of the factor variates ensures the statistical independence of the multiple univariate analyses. Moreover, as we shall see later in this chapter, factor variates are generally formed with ease of interpretation in mind. Thus, if groups are found to differ on one or more factor variates, the nature of the between-group differences will usually be pretty clear.

FACTOR EXTRACTION

Factor analysis can be conceived of as a method of examining a matrix of correlations in search of groups of highly intercorrelated variables. To illustrate this notion, look at the matrix of correlations between five variables, V_1 through V_5, shown in Table 16.1. Some of the correlations in this matrix are quite high (.80 to .90), while others are low (.05 to .20). Let us assume, as we have by now become accustomed to doing, that two or more variables measure the same underlying trait or characteristic (i.e., factor) to the degree that they are correlated. This being the case, two factors can be identified in Table 16.1, one consisting of variables V_1, V_2, and V_3, and the second consisting of variables V_4 and V_5. Notice that the variables within each of these factors show relatively high intercorrelations. Notice too that the correlations between variables representing different factors are quite low. Notice, finally, that although we can "eyeball" the factor structure in this small correlation matrix, some more objective procedure is needed for use with larger matrices or where correlations are not so obviously low or high. The mathematics that provide this objectivity will be considered next.

Extracting the First Factor Variate

We have seen in previous chapters that the key to much of multivariate analysis is the formation of linear combinations of variables that meet one or more predetermined criteria. In the case of multiple regression analysis, a linear combination of predictor variables is constructed to maximize the correlation (R) between this composite variable and a criterion variable. In discriminant analysis and multivariate analysis of variance, several dependent variables are combined to maximize group separation on one or more orthogonal composite variables, the discriminant functions. In principal components analysis, a linear combination of p original variables is created that gives the largest possible sum of squared

TABLE 16.1 Correlations between Variables V_1 through V_5 Showing Two Underlying Factors

	V_1	V_2	V_3	V_4	V_5
V_1	1.00				
V_2	.80	1.00			
V_3	.90	.88	1.00		
V_4	.20	.15	.20	1.00	
V_5	.10	.05	.10	.90	1.00

correlations to the original variables.[2] Each of these correlations is called a **factor loading** and the sum of the squared loadings that is maximized is called an **eigenvalue.** The composite variable thus formed is referred to as the first factor variate (or, more accurately, the first **principal component**) and takes the form given in Equation 16.1.

EQUATION 16.1

$$F_1 = w_1 z_1 + w_2 z_2 + \ . \ . \ . + w_p z_p$$

where,

F_1 = scores on the first factor variate
$z_1 - z_p$ = standardized scores on the p original variables
$w_1 - w_p$ = factor score weighting coefficients for the p standardized variables

The mathematics through which weighting coefficients $w_1 - w_p$ are determined is beyond the scope of this text. The interested reader should refer to Harris (1985) or Overall and Klett (1972). Let it suffice to say here that the matrix of correlations between the p original variables contains all of the information necessary to find these values.

Consider what the first factor variate represents. Since it has been formed from the original variables, we know it measures something that is measured by these variables. Since the first factor variate has been formed to maximize the sum of the squared correlations to the original variables, we know that it provides the best possible measure of what the original variables measure. In other words, the first factor variate measures the underlying factor that is most strongly reflected in the set of p original variables.

Extracting the Second and Subsequent Factor Variates

The first factor variate is only one of a multitude of possible combinations of the p original variables. At the second step in the analysis, a second linear combination is formed, called the second factor variate, by selecting new values of $w_1 - w_p$ in Equation 16.1. These weights are chosen to meet two criteria. First, the second factor variate must be orthogonal to the first. Second, within this constraint of orthogonality, the second factor variate is formed to maximize the sum of squared correlations between the second factor variate and the p original variables. In other words, the second factor variate is formed so as to maximize its associated eigenvalue while being uncorrelated to the first factor variate.

The fact that the second factor variate is formed from a linear combination of the p original variables tells us that it, like the first factor variate, taps some trait or characteristic that was measured by the p original variables. The fact that the second factor variate is orthogonal to the first tells us that the second factor variate measures a trait different from the one tapped by the first factor variate. Finally, the fact that the second factor variate is formed to maximize its associated eigenvalue tells us that this factor variate, of all the possible combinations that could have been formed, provides the best possible measure of this second characteristic as it is contained within the p original variables.

At the third and subsequent steps of the analysis, third and subsequent factor variates are extracted in a similar manner, each orthogonal to preceding factor variates, and each showing the highest possible eigenvalue. Each factor variate thus measures a trait that is measured by the original p variables, each measures a uniquely different trait, and successive factor variates tap factors that are less and less strongly represented in the original variables.

How Many Factors?

The maximum number of orthogonal factors that can be extracted from p original variables is equal to p. However, we are seldom interested in more than a subset of these factors, since, after the first few factors have been extracted, subsequent factors generally show only weak correlations to the original variables. Remember, the first factor variate shows the largest possible sum of squared correlations to the original variables. The second factor variate will therefore necessarily show a smaller sum of squared correlations to the original variables. Similarly, the third and subsequent factor variates will show successively smaller sums of squared correlations to the original variables. At some point before all possible factors have been extracted, we will generally find a factor variate that shows only a very small sum of squared correlations to the original variables. This is a factor variate that measures a trait or characteristic represented in only a minor way in the original variables. Since the purpose of factor analysis is to find which distinctively different traits, characteristics, or factors are measured by a set of p variables, we can reasonably stop extracting factors when they no longer strongly represent characteristics measured by the variables being analyzed. Next we will see how to decide how many factors the p original variables "really" represent.

Eigenvalues. As defined earlier, an eigenvalue is the sum of the squared correlations between a factor variate and the p original variables. As such, a factor's eigenvalue reflects the overall strength of relationship between that factor and the original variables. We saw earlier that successive factors will yield progressively lower eigenvalues. Since there is little point in extracting factors that show only a weak relationship to the variables being analyzed, factor extraction can be stopped when factors begin to yield low eigenvalues. In practice, only factors with eigenvalues of 1.0 or greater are considered to be stable (i.e., replicable). In most instances, the number of factors with eigenvalues of 1.0 or greater represents the maximum number of factors that can be considered stable. When a large number of variables are being factor analyzed, many unimportant factors will be associated with eigenvalues as large as 1.0, making it especially important to consider other indicators of the "correct" solution.

Given the importance of the eigenvalue in determining the number of factors to be extracted, let us examine this statistic a bit more closely. We have seen before that a squared correlation indicates the proportion of variance in one variable that is explained by another variable. In the context of factor analysis, then, each squared factor loading gives the proportion of variance in an original variable that is explained by a given factor variate. Since the largest possible squared factor loading will equal 1.0, it follows that the largest possible eigenvalue in any factor analysis will equal $p \times 1.0 = p$. The obtained eigenvalue for a factor must be evaluated relative to this upper limit. Dividing a factor's eigenvalue by p gives the proportion of variance in the set of p original variables explained by that factor. Factors with eigenvalues of 1.0 or greater thus explain at least as much variability in the set of original variables as is found in one of those variables. Since a major purpose of factor analysis is data simplification, it makes little sense to study factor variates that explain less variance than is found in one of the original variables. This is why factor extraction generally ceases when eigenvalues fall below 1.0.

Explained Variance and the Scree Curve. Successive factors explain progressively less of the variance of the original variables, but because each factor is orthogonal to the others, each explains a unique portion of the total variance. Thus, as factors are extracted, the cumulative explained variance increases, rapidly at first, and more slowly as more factors are extracted. A good factor solution is one that explains the most variance with the fewest factors. Determining the correct number of factors, then, is a matter of balancing comprehensiveness against parsimony. In practice, we are usually happy with a factor solution that explains 50–75% of the variance in the original variables with one-quarter to one-third as many factors as there are variables.

The **scree curve** is a graph that depicts the percentage of variance in p original variables that is explained by each factor of a p-factor solution. An example is shown in Figure 16.1. To use the scree curve in selecting a factor solution, look for that point along the curve where the extraction of an additional factor fails to add appreciably to the cumulative explained variance. This point may occasionally appear as a definite "elbow" in the curve. The optimal factor solution is one factor less than the solution corresponding to this elbow. In Figure 16.1, solutions of three or more factors seem not to add appreciably to cumulative variance explained by the two-factor solution. This being the case, the two-factor solution would appear to be optimal.

Communalities. Instead of summing the squared loadings for a given factor to find the factor's eigenvalue, we can instead sum the squared loadings for a given variable across factors to find the variable's **communality.** This value represents the proportion of variance in a variable which is explained by the set of extracted factor variates. If all variables show high communalities (the maximum communality, of course, is 1.0), the factors that have been extracted can

Figure 16.1

A scree curve depicting the percentage of variance in p original variables explained by each of p factors. The "correct" solution is one fewer factors than the solution corresponding to the elbow of the scree curve.

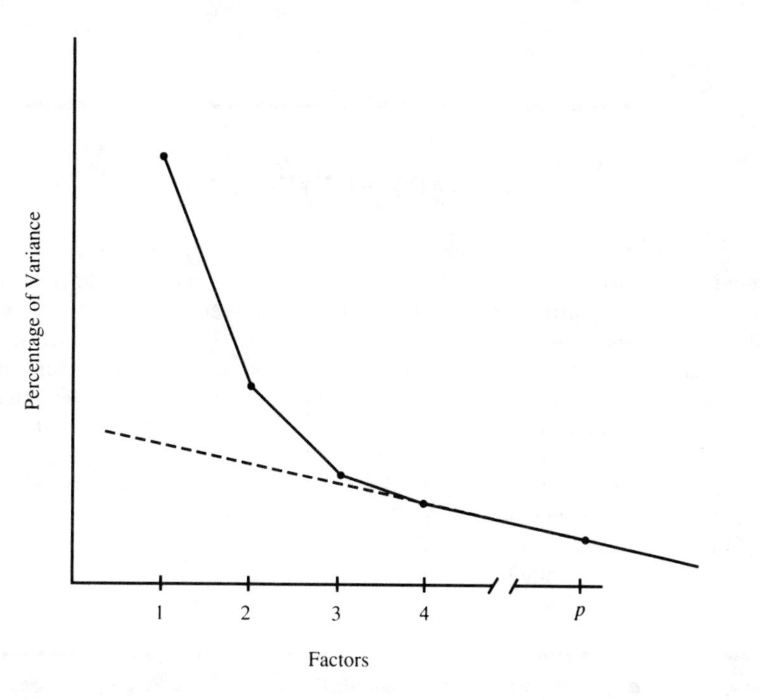

be understood to have explained most of the variance in the variables being analyzed. On the other hand, the presence of low communalities means that the variables showing these low communalities still contain variance unexplained by the factors that have been extracted. This suggests that more factors might profitably be extracted. As long as several variables display low communalities, there may be a need to extract additional factors.

Interpretability. A final consideration in determining how many factors to extract, and arguably the most important, is the interpretability of the factors. Unless we can determine what characteristic or trait a given factor variate measures, it is seldom wise to study that factor. If it makes theoretical (or practical) sense for a group of p variables to yield two, but not three factors, then we should lean strongly toward the two-factor solution. If the three-factor solution makes more sense, that solution is to be preferred.

We will consider in the next section how factors are interpreted, but let us pause here to recall what has been covered thus far. The first phase of factor analysis involves the extraction of factors. This phase of the analysis yields factor score weighting coefficients, factor loadings, eigenvalues, and communalities for the chosen factor solution. Box 16.1 provides an example of the extraction phase of factor analysis. This box also demonstrates the computation of factor scores from each case's scores on the original variables.

BOX 16.1

FACTOR EXTRACTION

Practitioners at Bubba's Mental Health Clinic routinely administer five psychological inventories at intake to patients who are admitted with complaints of depression: the Jeff and Abdul Depression Inventory, the Kierkegaard Existential Angst Inventory, the LaPew Personal Hygiene Scale, the Midas Greed Scale, and Wundt's Inventory of Introvertive Inclination. Dr. Bubba, hoping to cut costs associated with administering all of these tests, has requested a factor analytic study of the five measures. It is his hope that this study will identify redundancies between the tests, leading to the elimination of some of them.

Data for the analysis are presented (in standard score form) in Table 16.2. A matrix of correlations between the five tests follows in Table 16.3. It is clear from Table 16.3 that Dr. Bubba's suspicion is correct—there are redundancies in the measures. An eyeball analysis suggests that Depression and Greed form one factor and that the remaining variables form a second factor. A principal components analysis follows, which will confirm this hypothesis.

TABLE 16.2 Standardized Scores for Ten Patients on Five Tests: the Jeff and Abdul Depression Inventory, the Kierkegaard Existential Angst Inventory, the LaPew Personal Hygiene Scale, the Midas Greed Scale, and Wundt's Inventory of Introvertive Inclination

Case	Depression	Angst	Hygiene	Greed	Introversion
1	−1.62	.04	−.30	−.32	.11
2	−.44	−1.16	1.22	−1.39	−1.00
3	.15	1.24	−1.17	.75	1.59
4	.88	1.04	−1.17	.75	.85
5	−.15	−1.36	.13	−.32	−1.37
6	.59	−.56	−1.17	1.10	−.63
7	1.33	.24	.35	−.68	.11
8	−1.03	.64	1.43	−1.39	.11
9	−.88	1.04	−.30	.04	1.23
10	1.18	−1.16	1.00	1.46	−1.00

TABLE 16.3 Correlations between the Jeff and Abdul Depression Inventory, the Kierkegaard Existential Angst Inventory, the LaPew Personal Hygiene Scale, the Midas Greed Scale, and Wundt's Inventory of Introvertive Inclination

	Depression	Angst	Hygiene	Greed	Introversion
Depression	1.00				
Angst	−.13	1.00			
Hygiene	−.17	−.45	1.00		
Greed	.54	.05	−.61	1.00	
Introversion	−.13	.97	−.52	.14	1.00

Extracting the First Factor Variate
The first factor variate is formed by determining values of $w_1 - w_p$ in Equation 16.1 that will maximize the sum of the squared correlations between the first factor variate and the five original variables. These factor score weighting coefficients are listed in Table 16.4, along with factor loadings, eigenvalue, and communalities.

The eigenvalue of 2.45 associated with the first factor means that this factor accounts for about two and one-half times as much variance in the set of five variables as any single variable. Dividing this eigenvalue by $p = 5$, we find that the first factor explains about 49% of the variance in the set of five variables. The communalities listed in Table 16.4 indicate that Factor I explains most of the variance in Angst, Hygiene, and Introversion, but explains little of the variance in Depression and Greed. This suggests that a second factor should be extracted.

Extracting the Second Factor Variate
A second factor variate is formed next that is orthogonal to the first and that shows the maximum possible sum of squared loadings (i.e., eigenvalue). Factor score weighting coefficients for the first two factors are given in Table 16.5, along with factor loadings, eigenvalues, and communalities.

Table 16.4 Factor Score Weighting Coefficients, Factor Loadings, Eigenvalue, and Communalities for the One-Factor Solution

Variables	Weights for Factor I	Loadings for Factor I	Communalities
Depression	.05	.12	.01
Angst	.35	.85	.72
Hygiene	−.33	−.81	.66
Greed	.20	.50	.25
Introversion	.37	.90	.81
Eigenvalue		2.45	
Percent Variance		49%	

TABLE 16.5 Factor Score Weighting Coefficients, Factor Loadings, Eigenvalues, and Communalities for the Two-Factor Solution

Variables	Weights for Factor I	Weights for Factor II	Loadings for Factor I	Loadings for Factor II	Communalities
Depression	.05	.48	.12	.82	.69
Angst	.35	−.26	.85	−.44	.92
Hygiene	−.33	−.17	−.81	−.30	.75
Greed	.20	.46	.50	.77	.84
Introversion	.37	−.23	.90	−.38	.95
Eigenvalues			2.45	1.69	
Percent Variance			49%	34%	

continued

BOX 16.1—*continued*

The eigenvalue of 1.69 for Factor II means that this factor explains more variance than is found in any one of the original variables considered singly. Thus, the factor meets the minimum criterion for inclusion in the final solution. An eigenvalue of 1.69 indicates that Factor II explains about 34% of the variance in the original variables considered as a set. Thus, Factors I and II together explain 83% of the variance in the five variables. Communalities listed in Table 16.5 show that most of the variance in all of the variables has been explained by the first two factors. Nonetheless, a third factor may be extracted.

Extracting the Third Factor Variate

Factor III is extracted by weighting the five original variables to form a factor variate that is orthogonal to the first two and again shows the highest possible eigenvalue. Factor score weighting coefficients, factor loadings, eigenvalues, and communalities for the three-factor solution are in Table 16.6.

The eigenvalue associated with Factor III is less than 1.0, indicating that this factor accounts for less variance than is found in any one of the original variables. Such a factor does not contribute to a parsimonious description of the factor structure underlying the five variables and should not be included in the final solution. Too, none of the variables shows a particularly strong loading on the third factor, meaning that it will be difficult to interpret. All things considered, the two-factor solution is optimal.

Computing Factor Scores

The factor score weighting coefficients for the two-factor solution can be used in computing two factor scores for each case. These factor scores are computed by applying the weights listed in Table 16.5 to each case's standardized scores on the original variables according to Equation 16.1. For example, the first case's score on Factor I would be computed as:

TABLE 16.6 Factor Score Weighting Coefficients, Factor Loadings, Eigenvalues, and Communalities for the Three-Factor Solution

Variables	Weights for Factor I	Weights for Factor II	Weights for Factor III	Loadings for Factor I	Loadings for Factor II	Loadings for Factor III	Communalities
Depression	.05	.48	.94	.12	.82	.54	.98
Angst	.35	−.26	.42	.85	−.44	.24	.97
Hygiene	−.33	−.17	.69	−.81	−.30	.40	.91
Greed	.20	.46	−.35	.50	.77	−.20	.88
Introversion	.37	−.23	.28	.90	−.38	.16	.98
Eigenvalues				2.45	1.69	.57	
Percent Variance				49%	34%	11%	

BOX 16.1 —*continued*

$$\begin{aligned} FI &= w_1(\text{Depression}) + w_2(\text{Angst}) + \ldots + w_5(\text{Introversion}) \\ &= .05(-1.62) + .35(.04) - .33(-.30) + .20(-.32) + .37(.11) \\ &= .01 \end{aligned}$$

The first case's score on Factor II is computed as:

$$\begin{aligned} FII &= w_1(\text{Depression}) + w_2(\text{Angst}) + \ldots + w_5\,(\text{Introversion}) \\ &= .48(-1.62) - .26(.04) - .17(-.30) + .46(-.32) - .23(.11) \\ &= -.90 \end{aligned}$$

Factor scores for other cases may be computed in a similar manner and are listed in Table 16.7.

TABLE 16.7 Factor Scores Based on the Two-Factor Solution

	Factor Scores	
Case	*Factor I*	*Factor II*
1	.01	−.91
2	−1.48	−.53
3	1.57	−.07
4	1.26	.50
5	−1.10	.43
6	.21	1.28
7	−.06	.18
8	−.54	−1.57
9	.88	−.91
10	−.75	1.60

Two features of these factor scores may be noted. First, the correlation computed between the two sets of factor scores is equal to zero (within rounding error), showing that the factor variates measure completely different characteristics or traits. (Just what these characteristics are will be found by interpreting the factors in Box 16.2.) Second, the reader may wish to verify that correlations between the factor scores and scores on the original variables match the factor loadings presented in Table 16.5 (again, allowing for rounding error).

FACTOR INTERPRETATION: FACTOR ROTATION

We can learn what trait or characteristic a given factor measures by examining the factor loadings associated with that factor. This method of factor interpretation is directly analogous to the interpretation of discriminant functions by examining correlations between those functions and the original discriminating variables. If a factor and a variable are strongly correlated (i.e., the variable shows a strong loading on that factor), we can assume that the factor and the variable measure the same thing. Conversely, a low correlation between a factor and a variable shows that the factor does not measure what that variable measures. Thus, by examining the pattern of high and low loadings on each factor, we can often determine what a factor does and does not measure. In general, loadings of ±.40 or greater are considered "high"; weaker loadings are considered "low".

The interpretation of factors by examining factor loadings can be enhanced by including in the analysis several **marker variables.** These are variables that measure known characteristics. For example, if several marker variables that measure verbal reasoning all load strongly on the same factor, we can be fairly confident that all of the other variables that load strongly on this factor also measure verbal reasoning. Similarly, if several marker variables known to measure spatial reasoning load strongly on a second factor, this factor may be interpreted accordingly, and all other variables that load strongly on that factor may be assumed to reflect spatial reasoning too. The inclusion of too many marker variables, though, can be misleading, since these marker variables will force the appearance of factors that correspond to the markers. Other variables in the analysis will necessarily load on one or another of these forced factors, but may not really be particularly good measures of the factors on which they load. The analysis of the same variables with a different set of marker variables might lead to very different conclusions about what the variables being examined really measure.

The collection of factor loadings output from a factor analysis is called the **factor structure matrix.** Factor structure is most interpretable when several conditions are met: (1) each variable loads strongly on one and only one factor; (2) each factor shows two or more strong loadings; and (3) most loadings are either high or low, with few of intermediate value. Collectively, these characteristics of a factor structure lead us to label that factor structure as "simple."

Unfortunately, we seldom see a simple factor structure following the initial factor extraction phase of factor analysis. Instead, all variables will tend to load strongly on the first factor and many variables will load equally on two or more factors. The factors extracted in the initial phase of factor analysis are defined by weighting coefficients $w_1 - w_p$ so that each factor is orthogonal to the others and so that each factor explains as much variance in the p original variables as possible. Interpretability of the factors is not a criterion in the extraction phase. In order to achieve a simpler factor structure, one that is more interpretable, it is usually necessary to redefine the factors in a second phase of factor analysis, **factor rotation.**

TABLE 16.8 Unrotated Factor Structure Matrix for a Two-Factor Solution

Variables	Loadings for Factor I	Loadings for Factor II	Communalities
A	.73	.54	.82
B	.82	.49	.91
C	.72	.69	.99
D	.77	−.43	.78
E	.84	−.44	.90
Eigenvalues	3.02	1.39	
Percent Variance	60.4%	27.8%	

There are two basic types of factor rotation. **Orthogonal rotations** substitute new factor score weighting coefficients ($w_1 - w_p$ in Equation 16.1), but keep the factor variates orthogonal. While the original factor variates are defined in such a way that each explains the greatest possible variance, the rotated factors are defined to provide the simplest possible factor structure. **Oblique rotations** also redefine the original factor variates for increased ease of interpretation, but allow the rotated factor variates to be correlated.

Orthogonal Rotations

Although orthogonal rotations are normally accomplished mathematically, they were originally done manually using graphs and can still best be understood when approached graphically. First, examine the unrotated factor structure matrix presented in Table 16.8. This factor structure matrix provides little insight into how variables A through E are grouped. All of the variables show strong loadings on Factor I and moderate loadings on Factor II. This is far from a simple structure as defined previously.

Next, this unrotated factor structure is represented graphically in Figure 16.2a. This graph depicts Factor I as the horizontal axis, and Factor II as the vertical axis. Variables A through E are represented as points, located using their loadings on Factors I and II as coordinates. Given that variables are located in this "factor space" by their factor loadings, and given that highly correlated variables will load similarly, it follows that these highly correlated variables will form clusters in the factor space. Variables that are less strongly correlated will be located further apart.

Factor rotation involves literally rotating the factor axes either clockwise or counterclockwise around the origin to better position the factor axes through, or at least nearer to, clusters of highly correlated variables. The perpendicularity

Figure 16.2

Factor rotations involve rotating the factor axes around the origin so as to place them through or as near as possible to clusters of highly correlated variables.

(a) The unrotated factor space showing loadings on Factors I and II.

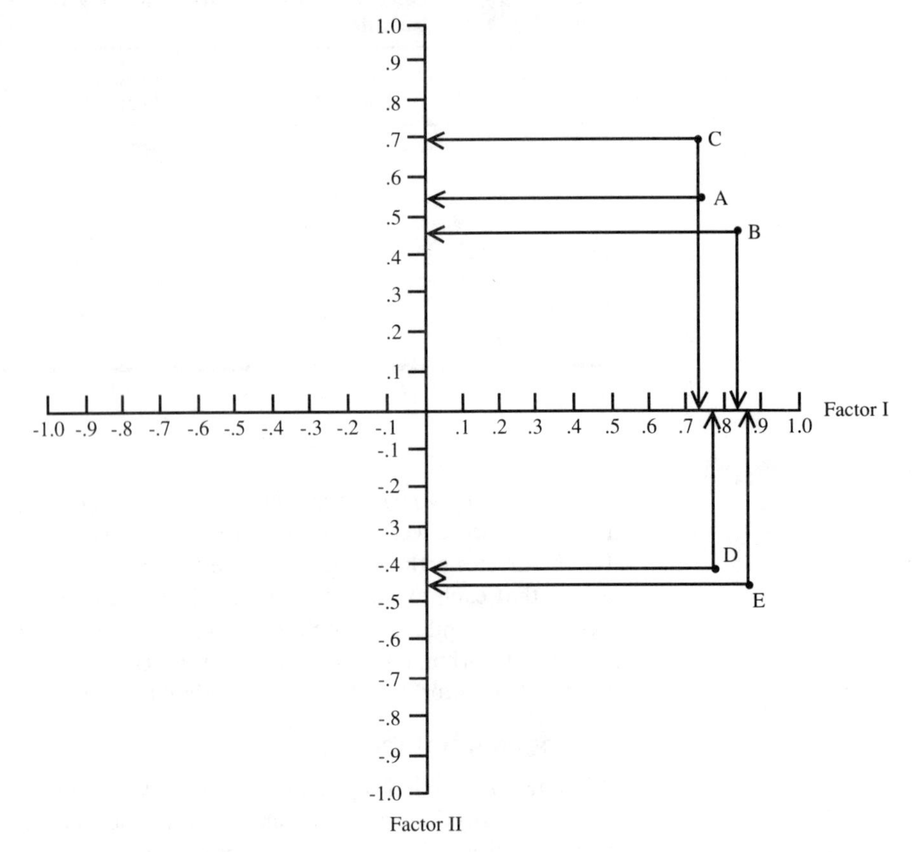

of factor axes is maintained throughout an orthogonal rotation. Figure 16.2b shows the orthogonally rotated factor axes. Rotated Factor I, labeled Factor I-R, is located to pass nearer to the cluster of variables consisting of D and E. The rotation has also repositioned Factor II, now labeled Factor II-R, nearer to the second cluster of variables, A, B, and C. The coordinates of the variables on the rotated factor axes may be read to determine a new set of factor loadings, the **rotated factor structure,** in Table 16.9.

Two characteristics typical of all orthogonal rotations can be seen in the rotated factor loadings of Table 16.9. First, the rotated factors explain the same total variance as do the unrotated factors, but this explained variance is redistributed. In the present example, both the original and rotated solutions explain about 88% of the variance in the five variables, but the rotated solution distributes the explained variance differently between the factors. Too, although the total variance explained by the two solutions is the same, the proportion of variance of individual variables that is explained is different, as shown by the changed communalities listed in Table 16.9.

Figure 16.2— *continued*

(b) An orthogonal rotation showing loadings on rotated Factors I – R and II – R.

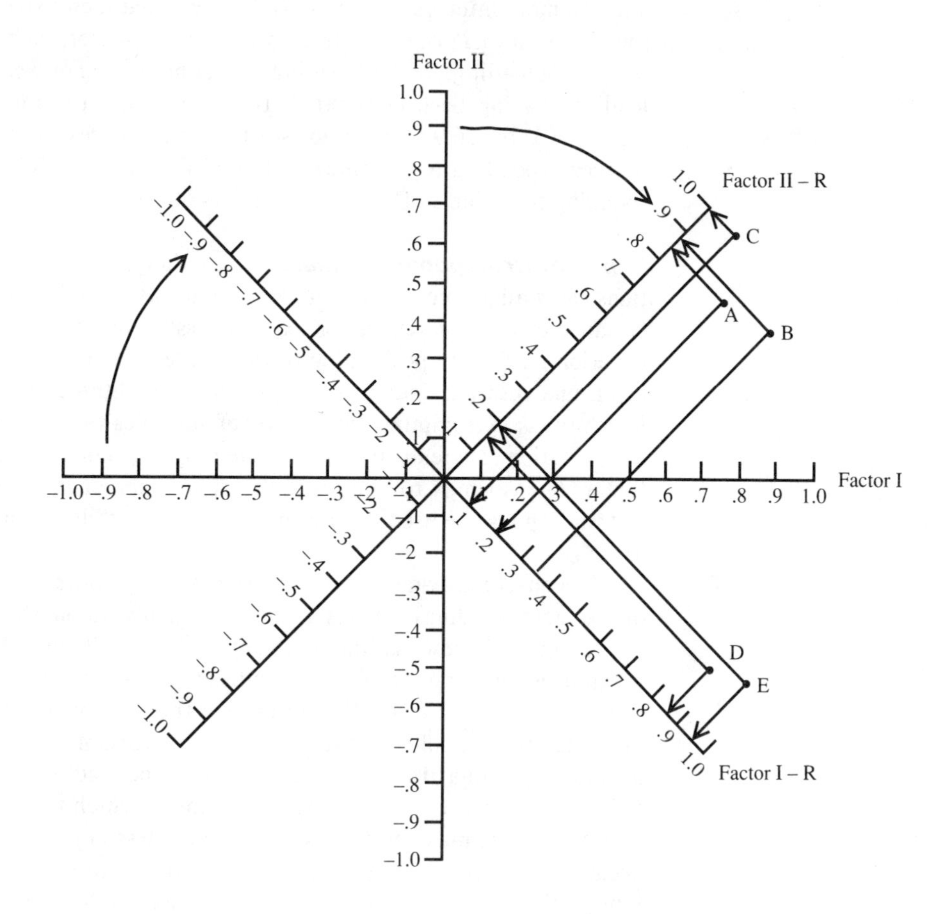

TABLE 16.9	**Orthogonally Rotated Factor Structure Matrix for a Two-Factor Solution**		
Variables	**Loadings for Factor I-R**	**Loadings for Factor II-R**	**Communalities**
A	.19	.87	.79
B	.33	.90	.92
C	.11	.97	.95
D	.87	.17	.79
E	.96	.19	.96
Eigenvalues	1.84	2.57	
Percent Variance	36.8%	51.4%	

Second, the rotated factor structure is considerably simpler, and consequently, more interpretable, than is the unrotated factor structure. In the rotated solution each variable loads strongly on only one factor, each factor shows at least two strong loadings, and all loadings are either strong or weak, with intermediate loadings having been eliminated. It is clear from the rotated factor structure matrix of Table 16.9 that variables A through E represent two underlying factors, one corresponding to variables A, B, and C (Factor II-R), and the other corresponding to variables D and E (Factor I-R).

Types of Orthogonal Rotation. Another way of stating that rotated solutions show all strong or weak loadings is to say that the rotation maximizes the variance of the squared factor loadings associated with each factor. When this criterion guides the positioning of the rotated factor axes, the rotation is called a **varimax rotation.** Factor interpretation is facilitated by the varimax rotation, which tends to minimize the number of variables that load strongly on a factor. This rotation also tends to equalize the proportion of variance explained by each factor. The varimax rotation is the most common orthogonal rotation, but other criteria can also be used to determine the "correct" location of the rotated factor axes.

In a **quartimax rotation,** the criterion is the minimization of the cross-products of the factor loadings. This is achieved if each variable shows a high loading on one factor and a low loading on the other factors. Thus, while varimax rotation maximizes the variance of the columns of the factor structure matrix, the quartimax rotation maximizes the variance of the rows of the matrix. Quartimax rotation tends to simplify the interpretation of variables rather than factors. This is because the quartimax rotated loadings associated with each variable all tend to be either high or low, making it easy to see which factors are related to each variable. Quartimax rotation is considerably less popular than varimax rotation because researchers are usually more interested in interpreting factors than in interpreting variables. The quartimax rotation tends to produce a **general factor,** that is, a factor on which all of the variables show fairly strong loadings. General factors are often very difficult to interpret. Indeed, it is the presence of a general factor in the unrotated solution that often indicates the need for rotation.

Equimax rotation aims at achieving a compromise between the varimax and quartimax solutions. This rotation attempts to enhance the interpretability both of the factors and of the variables. Many argue that the equimax rotation fails, though, to achieve this goal in many situations and the technique is used only occasionally.

Oblique Rotation

Factors that are produced by rotations like varimax are desirable from a statistical point of view because they are orthogonal. However, orthogonal factors may not provide a fully accurate depiction of a reality in which the underlying factors are probably somewhat correlated. An orthogonal rotation forces statistical independence onto a reality in which factors are statistically dependent. An oblique rotation has the advantage of enhancing the interpretability of factors (relative to unrotated solutions) without imposing orthogonality on those factors.

Oblique rotation, like orthogonal rotation, is normally accomplished mathematically, but can better be understood pictorially. Look back at the graphed factor structure of Figure 16.2a. No orthogonal rotation can capture completely the true structure of the variables plotted in this graph, since no rotation of perpendicular (i.e., orthogonal) factor axes can place both axes directly through the variable clusters. An oblique rotation though, like the one depicted in Figure 16.2c, provides greater flexibility in positioning factor axes by relaxing the requirement that the factors be orthogonal (i.e., perpendicular). By positioning factor axes directly through clusters of highly correlated variables, an oblique rotation maximizes the correlations (i.e., loadings) between the variables in each cluster and one of the factors. In general, oblique rotations create factors that more strongly represent clusters of highly correlated variables than do orthogonal rotations.

Figure 16.2— *continued*

(c) An oblique rotation showing loadings on rotated Factors I – R and II – R.

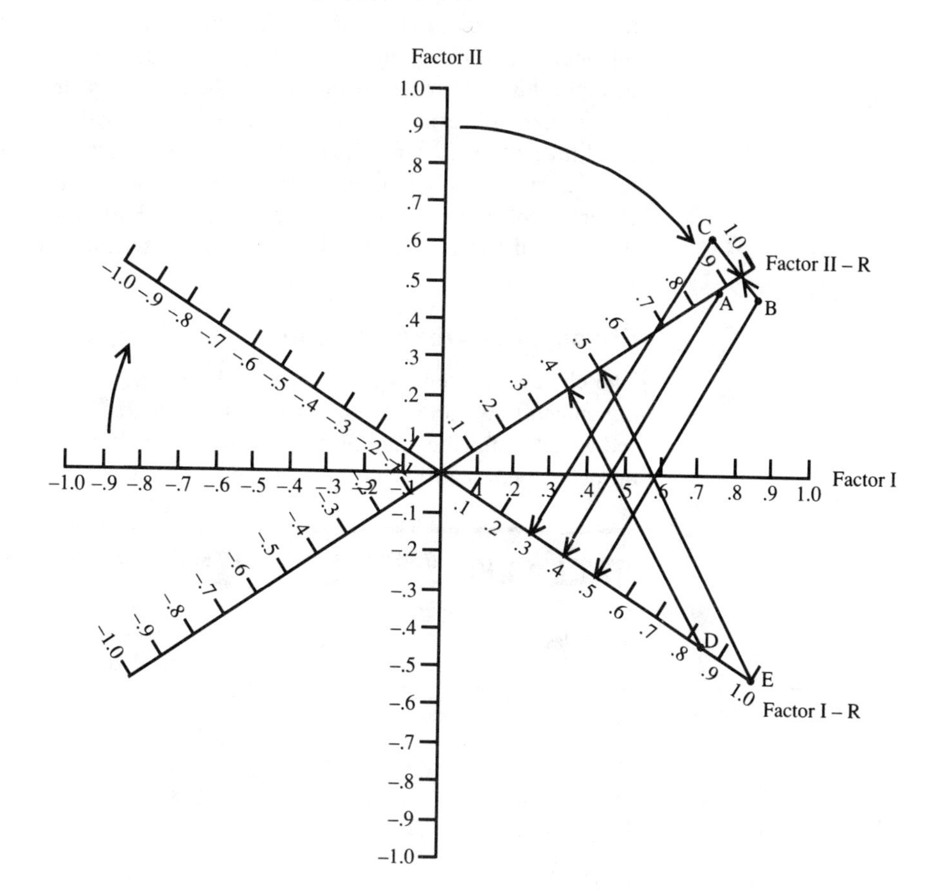

Oblique factors, though, are correlated to the degree indicated by the cosine of the angle formed between the two rotated factor axes. In Figure 16.2c, this angle is approximately 65 degrees, such that the correlation between Factor I-R and Factor II-R is cosine (65°) = .42.

Both advantages and disadvantages of oblique rotations can be seen in Table 16.10, the factor structure matrix captured by the oblique rotation depicted in Figure 16.2c.[3] Consider first the advantages. Compared to the orthogonal rotation (Table 16.9), the oblique rotation creates factors more strongly correlated to the variables that most define those factors. Thus, variables D and E, which most represent Factor I, show slightly stronger loadings to the obliquely rotated Factor I than to the orthogonally rotated Factor I. Similarly, variables A, B, and C, which most represent Factor II, show generally stronger loadings on the obliquely rotated Factor II than on the orthogonally rotated Factor II. Second, the oblique rotation captures the reality that the two factors underlying variables A through E are correlated, and not independent as is suggested by the orthogonal rotation.

However, oblique rotations generally present one disadvantage relative to orthogonal rotations; that is, oblique rotations can be more difficult to interpret. To the degree that obliquely rotated factors are correlated, all loadings will tend to be high, thus obscuring the factor structure of the variables. This is seen in Table 16.10 where all variables show moderate to high loadings on both oblique factors. Facilitating the interpretation of oblique solutions is the **pattern matrix.** The pattern matrix is a standard part of the output from most factor analysis programs. It can be considered to be equivalent to a factor structure matrix, except that the influence of the correlations between factors on the sizes of the factor loadings is eliminated.

Choosing between Orthogonal and Oblique Rotations

The choice between an orthogonal and an oblique rotation must be made with our purpose in mind. If the whole purpose of the factor analysis is to create a reduced set of orthogonal factor variates that will be entered into other analyses, an orthogonal solution is the obvious choice. On the other hand, if the factor

TABLE 16.10 Obliquely Rotated Factor Structure Matrix for a Two-Factor Solution

Variables	Loadings for Factor I-R	Loadings for Factor II-R
A	.40	.90
B	.50	.95
C	.30	.96
D	.88	.40
E	1.00	.48
Eigenvalues	2.27	3.02
Percent Variance	45.4%	60.4%

analysis is being used to uncover the factor structure underlying a set of variables, an oblique rotation may be appropriate, and the choice between orthogonal and oblique solutions is usually made after trying both. If an oblique rotation suggests that the factors show a correlation of $\pm.30$ or higher or if we have sound theoretical reasons to expect correlated factors, we are probably better off using the oblique solution. If the oblique solution suggests that the factors have a correlation of less than $\pm.30$, and if the orthogonal solution is readily interpretable, it is a good idea to stick with the mathematically simpler orthogonal solution. Box 16.2 gives an example of both orthogonal and oblique factor rotation.

Computing Rotated Factor Scores

A factor structure matrix, be it the end result of the initial factor extraction, an orthogonal rotation, or an oblique rotation, lists correlations between a set of factor variates and a set of p original variables. These correlations provide all of the information that is necessary to "work backwards" in computing the factor score weighting coefficients that define the factor variates. Factor score weighting coefficients are a standard part of the output from any factor analysis program and can be used in computing factor scores according to Equation 16.1.

SIGNIFICANCE TESTS IN FACTOR ANALYSIS

Tests of statistical significance all address the issue of the reliability of findings. In the case of factor analysis, significance tests assess either the stability of a factor structure obtained from one sample or the similarity between factor structures obtained from two samples.

Stability of Factor Structure

A statistically significant factor structure is one we would expect to observe again in other samples drawn from the same population. It is a factor structure that can be presumed to reflect the structure of variables in the population from which the observed sample was drawn. Unfortunately, relatively few significance tests have been developed for use in assessing the stability of factor structure. The existent tests assume very large samples, and are all mathematically beyond the scope of this text (see Harris, 1985 or Morrison, 1967).

However, it is not difficult to assess indirectly the stability of a factor solution. First, realize that a factor analysis is no better than the correlations upon which it is based. A factor analysis of almost any set of variables will find factors even when the correlations between those variables are minuscule, but these factors will be meaningless. Remember, a factor is defined by a set of highly intercorrelated variables. If the variables being examined lack these high correlations, there are no factors, regardless of the output from the factor analysis. Unless several of the variables being analyzed show correlations of at least $\pm.30$, there is little point in a factor analysis.

In evaluating the stability of a factor solution, it is also wise to examine the correlations between variables that represent each extracted factor. What is the

BOX 16.2

FACTOR ROTATION: INTERPRETING FACTORS

It was determined in Box 16.1 that five measures administered to depressed patients at Bubba's Mental Health Clinic represent two strong underlying factors. Here we will interpret the two-factor solution in order to learn exactly what these two factors represent.

First, consider the unrotated factor structure matrix given in Table 16.11. The first thing we notice about this factor structure is that it deviates from our definition of a "simple" structure. A couple of variables (Angst and Greed) show substantial loadings on both factors and there are a fair number of moderate strength factor loadings throughout the matrix. Despite this, the factor structure represented in Table 16.11 is interpretable. Factor I shows its strongest positive correlations (loadings) to Angst and Introversion, and shows a strong negative relationship to Hygiene. Thus, Factor I might be interpreted as existential angst of the sort that accompanies the excessive ruminations of the very introverted. High levels of existential angst appear to be accompanied by neglect of one's personal hygiene. Factor II is most strongly represented by Depression and Greed. The characteristic measured by this factor, then, seems to be a somewhat more worldly form of depression that is linked to insatiable greed.

The fact that two orthogonal factors have been extracted from the five original variables supports two conclusions. First, these five measures represent only two strong underlying factors. Second, because redundancies exist among the five original variables, it should be possible to eliminate some of the redundant tests, particularly if one or two good measures of each factor are retained.

Orthogonal Factor Rotation

Although both factors are interpretable without rotation, a simpler factor structure can be achieved with rotation. We will look first at an orthogonal rotation.

The original factor solution is depicted graphically in Figure 16.3a, where each axis represents a factor and variables are positioned using their loadings as coordinates. Figure 16.3b shows the orthogonal rotation (varimax) of the original factors. The perpendicularity of factor axes is maintained throughout the rotation, which places factor axes nearer to the two most obvious variable clusters. Reading the new coordinates of the five variables on these rotated axes, we have the rotated factor structure matrix presented in Table 16.12.

Several characteristics of this rotated factor structure matrix can be noted. First, the varimax rotation has indeed maximized the variances of the squared loadings on each factor. These variances for the unrotated solution (Table 16.11) are .09 and .06 for Factors I and II, respectively. For the rotated solution, the variances are .17 and .11 for Factors I and II. Second, the rotated factor structure matrix is

TABLE 16.11 **Unrotated Factor Structure Matrix for the Two-Factor Solution**

Variables	Loadings for Factor I	Loadings for Factor II	Communalities
Depression	.12	.82	.69
Angst	.85	−.44	.92
Hygiene	−.81	−.30	.75
Greed	.50	.77	.84
Introversion	.90	−.38	.95
Eigenvalues	2.45	1.69	
Percent Variance	49%	34%	

BOX 16.2 —*continued*

Figure 16.3

Rotating the two-factor solution of Depression, Angst, Hygiene, Greed, and Introversion.

(a) The unrotated two-factor solution showing loadings on Factors I and II.

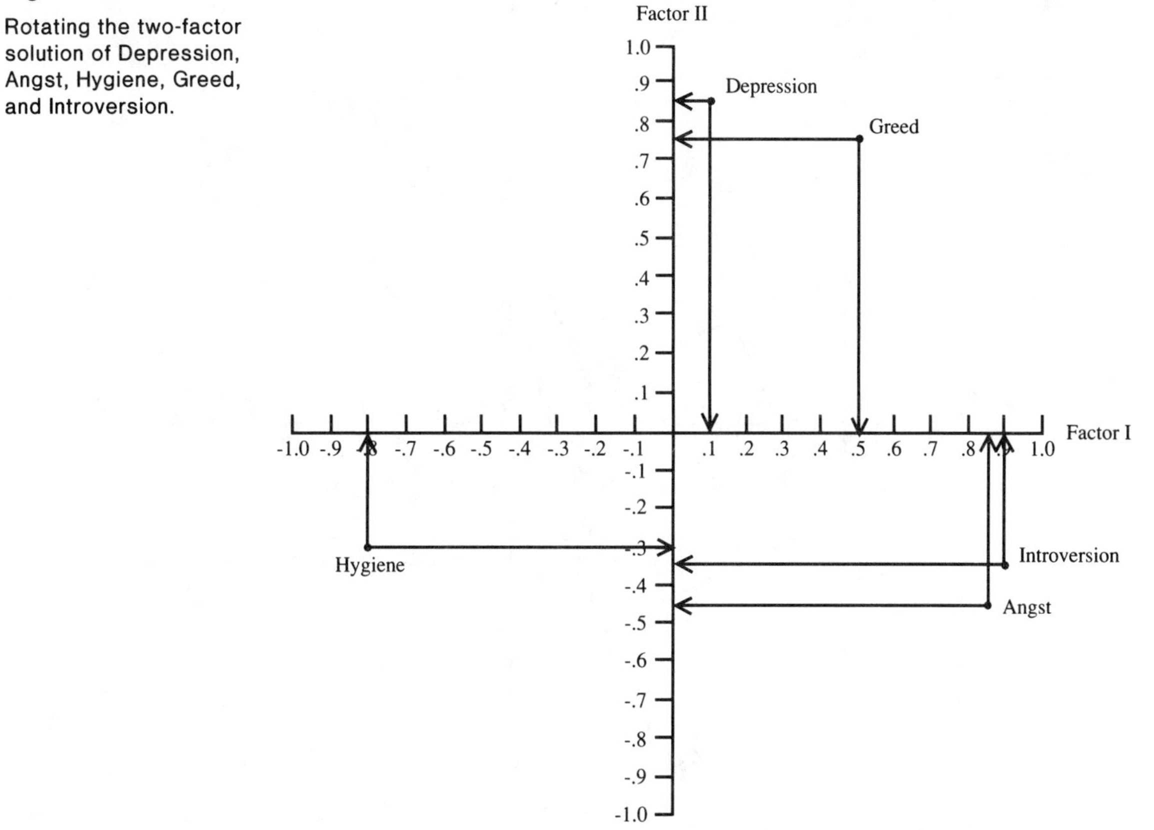

TABLE 16.12 Varimax Rotated Factor Structure Matrix for the Two-Factor Solution

Variables	Loadings for Factor I-R	Loadings for Factor II-R	Communalities
Depression	−.21	.80	.68
Angst	.96	−.07	.93
Hygiene	−.63	−.59	.75
Greed	.15	.91	.85
Introversion	.98	.00	.96
Eigenvalues	2.35	1.82	
Percent Variance	47%	36%	

continued

BOX 16.2 —*continued*

Figure 16.3— *continued*

(b) An orthogonal rotation showing loadings on Factors I – R and II – R.

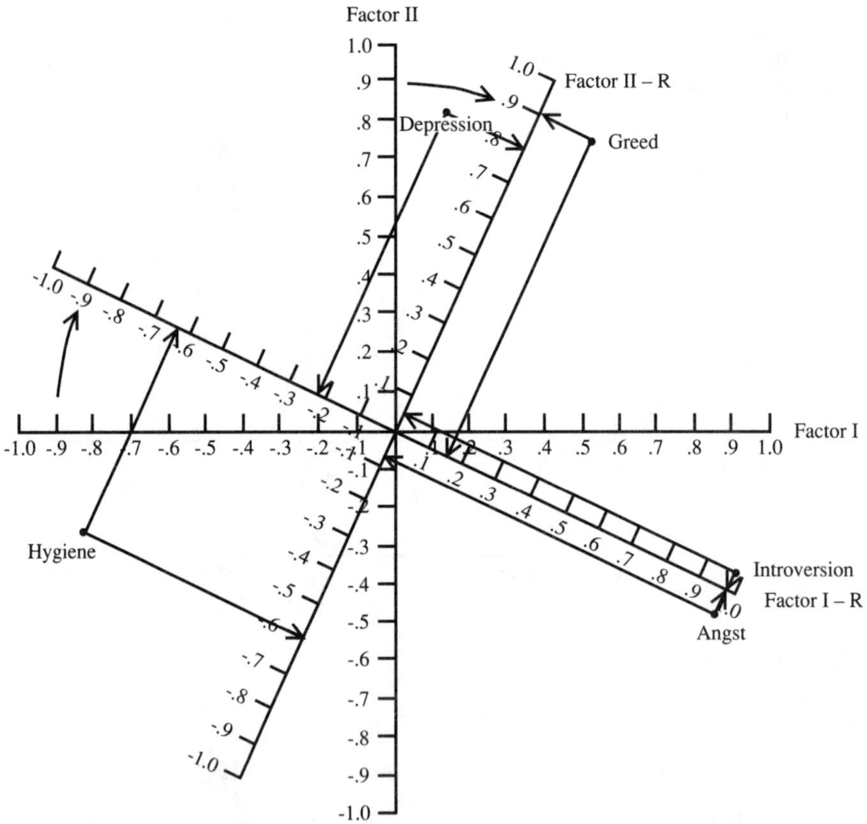

considerably simpler than the unrotated factor structure. Loadings are all either high or low, both factors show at least two large loadings, and, with the exception of the variable Hygiene, all variables load on only one factor. Third, the rotated factors account for the same total variance as did the unrotated factors, but this variance has been redistributed slightly between the factors. Too, the communalities have changed slightly from the original to the rotated solution, indicating that the rotated factors explain slightly different proportions of the variance in the individual original variables.

Although the unrotated factor structure was interpretable, the simpler, rotated structure lends itself even more readily to interpretation. Indeed, this is the only reason to rotate factors. Factor I, as before, seems to represent existential angst. Factor II, also as before, represents depression linked to greed. One noteworthy

TABLE 16.13 Factor Score Weighting Coefficients for the Varimax Rotated Two-Factor Solution

Variables	Weights for Factor I-R	Weights for Factor II-R
Depression	−.14	.46
Angst	.42	−.10
Hygiene	−.24	−.29
Greed	.01	.50
Introversion	.42	−.06

change from the unrotated solution concerns the variable of Hygiene, which now shows approximately equal negative loadings on both factors.

Factor scores for the orthogonally rotated factors may be computed according to Equation 16.1 using the factor score weighting coefficients given in Table 16.13 for the orthogonally rotated factor variates. Rotated factor scores are presented in Table 16.14 for each of the ten original cases. The interested reader may confirm that, allowing for rounding error, these two rotated factor variates are orthogonal and are correlated to the five original variables as reflected in the rotated factor loadings.

Oblique Rotation

A visual inspection of Figure 16.3b suggests that orthogonal factors provide a very good description of the structure of the five variables being analyzed in this example. Nonetheless, an oblique rotation will be presented here for instructional purposes. This oblique rotation is shown in Figure 16.3c and the factor loadings captured in this rotation are listed in Table 16.15. The two oblique factor axes show an angle of about 78 degrees. The cosine of this angle gives the correlation between Factor I-R and Factor II-R: .21. This is quite a low correlation, but suggests that the two factors identified in this example are not completely independent. As existential angst (Factor I) increases, there is a slight tendency for levels of materialistic depression (Factor II) to increase as well. Given the very low correlation between the factors, though, and the good interpretability of the orthogonal rotation, we would be advised to accept the orthogonal rotation as the optimal solution.

TABLE 16.14 Factor Scores Based on the Varimax Rotated Two-Factor Solution

	Factor Scores	
Case	*Factor I-R*	*Factor II-R*
1	.36	− .83
2	−1.14	−1.08
3	1.44	.56
4	.95	.96
5	−1.16	− .05
6	− .30	1.25
7	− .13	.14
8	.12	−1.65
9	1.15	− .48
10	−1.29	1.16

TABLE 16.15 Obliquely Rotated Factor Structure Matrix for the Two-Factor Solution

Variables	Loadings for Factor I-R	Loadings for Factor II-R
Depression	−.25	.70
Angst	1.00	.19
Hygiene	−.58	−.77
Greed	.10	.90
Introversion	.99	.24
Eigenvalues	2.39	1.99
Percent Variance	47.8%	39.8%

continued

BOX 16.2 —*continued*

Figure 16.3— *continued*

(c) An oblique rotation showing loadings on Factors I – R and II – R.

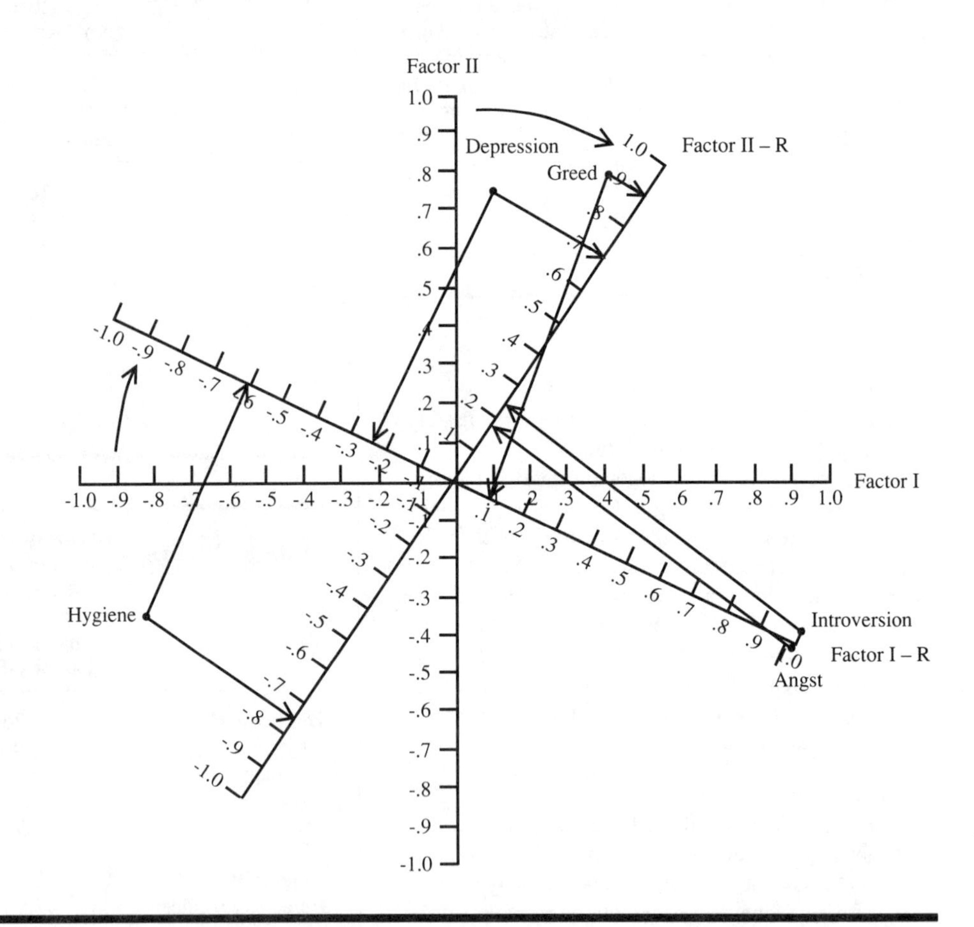

average squared correlation between the variables that load strongly on each factor? How does this value compare to the average of the squared correlations between variables that load on different factors?

The stability of a factor solution is also dependent on sample size. In general, a minimum of 10 cases per variable is recommended, with a minimum of 100 cases when fewer than 10 variables are being analyzed. We can make do with fewer cases, though, if there are large correlations between variables and relatively few factors are extracted.

Finally, if a factor structure holds up across several different methods of factor extraction and factor rotation, we can be more confident in the stability of the solution. When the data are sound, it makes remarkably little difference how they are analyzed.

Comparing Factor Structures

A number of procedures are available for comparing factor structures obtained from two samples. Some of these techniques involve comparing two entire factor structure matrices (Levine, 1977) and are beyond the scope of this text.

It is also possible to compare pairs of factors from two solutions. Sometimes variables will show such similar loadings on the two factors being compared that it is obvious these two factors are the same. The interpretation given to one factor could be used equally well in defining the other factor.

More formally, pairs of factors may be compared for similarity using a Pearson product-moment correlation computed between loadings on the factors being compared. Correlations computed in this manner must be interpreted cautiously, though, since they tend to run high. This is because many variables will show similarly low loadings on both factors being compared. Thus, two factors can give a high correlation by virtue of the similarity in the loadings of variables that do not even define those factors!

A related method of comparing factors involves computing pairs of factor scores for one sample using that sample's factor score weighting coefficients and also using the second sample's factor score weighting coefficients. The factor scores generated in this way may be compared for similarity using the Pearson correlation.

Regardless of which method is chosen for comparing pairs of factors, we must determine which factors to compare. For example, the first sample's Factor I may be the second sample's Factor II. The inclusion of marker variables in both analyses can assist us in identifying corresponding factors.

PRINCIPAL COMPONENTS ANALYSIS VS. FACTOR ANALYSIS

Principal components analysis has been presented in this chapter as a model for all factor analytic procedures because of its conceptual and mathematical simplicity. Indeed, much factor analytic research begins with a principal components analysis as a precursor to further examinations of the data using one or more of the other factor analytic procedures. Principal components analysis, though, differs from other forms of factor analysis in one important way. These other types of factor analysis, most commonly principal axes factor analysis, image factor analysis, and maximum likelihood analysis, begin by removing from each variable variance that which is unique to that variable, (i.e., variance that is not shared with one or more of the other variables in the analysis). In other words, these methods look only at the common variance of the variables being analyzed. Variables are sorted into factors on the basis of how they share this common variance. Different factor analytic techniques use different approaches to estimating how much of the total variance in a set of p variables is common variance and how much is unique.

Choosing between principal components analysis and "true" factor analysis is mostly a matter of following tradition. According to this tradition, principal components analysis is usually used when our intent is to develop a reduced set of factor variates (principal components) for use in other analyses. Factor analysis is more commonly used when our focus is on uncovering the structure of a set of p original variables. As stated previously, though, we will seldom see substantial differences in the solutions obtained using these different procedures. When differences are seen, we should question the stability of the obtained solutions.

SUMMARY

Factor analysis is a family of procedures. Principal components analysis, one type of factor analysis, is the focus of this chapter. Factor analysis examines correlations among a set of p original variables in order to identify clusters of highly correlated variables. These clusters represent factors that underlie the original variables. Knowing the factor structure of a set of variables is often useful for theoretical reasons. In addition, because there are generally fewer factors than original variables, factor analysis achieves data simplification. Factor analysis proceeds in two stages, factor extraction, and factor rotation. In the extraction phase, the first factor is the linear combination of the p original variables that shows the greatest possible sum of squared correlations to the original variables. The second and subsequent factors are linear combinations of the p original variables which are orthogonal to preceding factors and again maximize the sum of squared correlations to the original variables. Thus, each successive factor represents a unique trait measured by the set of p original variables. Successive factors explain less and less of the variance in the original variables such that fewer than p factors are needed in order to explain most of the variance in those variables. Factors are interpreted by examining their correlations, called loadings, to the p original variables. This interpretation is often facilitated by factor rotation, the second stage of factor analysis, in which the original factors are redefined. Orthogonal rotations keep the factors uncorrelated. Oblique rotations relax the requirement of orthogonality and allow the redefined factors to be correlated. Relatively few significance tests have been developed for use in factor analysis. However, the stability of a factor solution can be assessed indirectly. Techniques are also available that enable comparing factor solutions obtained from two different samples.

NOTES

1. Although factor analysis is usually performed on a matrix of Pearson product-moment correlations, Ferguson and Takane (1989) have suggested that other measures of association may be factor analyzed.
2. The first factor variate (or more accurately, the first principal component) is sometimes described as that weighted combination of the original variables which shows the greatest possible variance. This is the same linear combination that yields the highest sum of squared correlations to the original variables.
3. Communalities are not presented in Table 16.10 because the correlation between oblique factors means that the factors do not explain unique components of the variance in the variables being analyzed. This makes it inappropriate to sum the squared factor loadings across factors to find the total variance explained in any given variable. Eigenvalues are shown in Table 16.10, which, as always, reflect the variance in the set of original variables explained by each factor. Again, though, since the factors are correlated, they do not explain unique components of this total variance, and thus, cannot be summed to obtain cumulative explained variance.

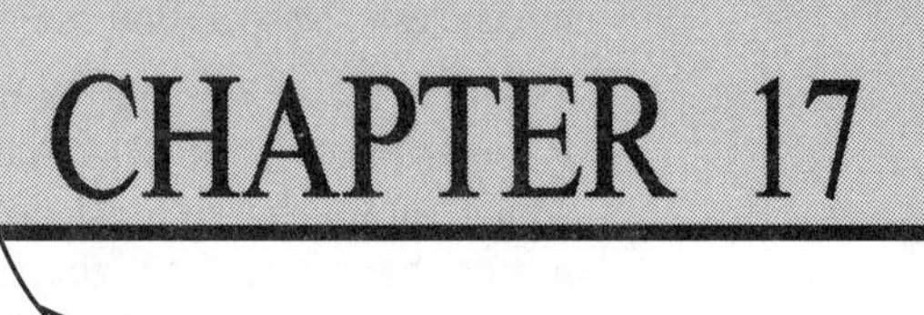

CHAPTER 17

CLUSTER ANALYSIS

The early stages of research in any area are usually marked by an emphasis on the development of typologies. Psychologists may wish to know more about the categories of mental disorders, sociologists may seek to determine how many distinctly different types of cities exist, and marketing researchers may want to establish a taxonomy of cola drinks. **Cluster analysis** provides a method that assists in these endeavors. It is a method by which relatively discrete, homogeneous groups or **clusters** of elements may be identified. These elements may be people, cities, colas, or any other collection of elements of interest to the researcher.

CLUSTER VS. FACTOR ANALYSIS

Cluster analysis is similar in many respects to factor analysis (chapter 16), but the two methods are usually applied to different types of problems. Factor analysis is traditionally used to uncover the underlying structure of a set of variables by identifying groups of homogeneous (i.e., highly correlated) variables. Cluster analysis is traditionally used to uncover the underlying structure of a set of cases (be these animate or inanimate) by identifying groups of homogeneous cases. Too, factor analysis is generally limited to the analysis of correlations; cluster analysis is a more flexible technique in that many different indices of similarity (or dissimilarity) are acceptable as input.

The similarities between factor and cluster analysis, though, are more enlightening than are the differences, and it is worth exploring them further. In the usual data matrix, rows represent cases, and columns represent variables that describe those cases. Correlations computed between columns of the data matrix describe relationships between variables, and a factor analysis of these correlations identifies groups of highly intercorrelated variables. Correlations may also be computed between the rows of the data matrix, though. These correlations describe similarities between cases, and a factor analysis of these correlations identifies relatively homogeneous groups of cases, referred to as clusters.

Factor analyzing correlations between cases, rather than variables, is called ***Q*-type factor analysis** (in contrast to ***R*-type factor analysis,** which refers to the traditional analysis of variables), and was a precursor to modern methods of cluster analysis. Box 17.1 provides an example of a Q-type factor analysis.

Although factor and cluster analysis share the common goal of identifying groups of relatively similar elements, we seldom find one method of analysis used within the traditional domain of the other method. Factor analysis is almost always reserved for the analysis of the structure of variables; cluster analysis is used in the search for clusters of elements other than variables.

THE DATA FOR CLUSTER ANALYSIS

Cluster analysis accepts as input a matrix of **proximities,** numerical values that reflect interelement similarity or dissimilarity. Similar elements are often described as "proximate;" dissimilar elements are described as "distant." These synonyms will be used freely in the discussion that follows.

BOX 17.1

Q-TYPE FACTOR ANALYSIS

The marketing firm of Conem, Dupem, and Lie has been hired to market a new product, Burpee Cola. In order to prepare an advertising campaign for this new cola, the company wants to know how consumers perceive cola drinks in general and Burpee in particular. How are colas categorized by consumers? Into which category do they place Burpee? Knowing this will give Conem, Dupem, and Lie the foundation for preparing an effective marketing campaign.

Taste testers have collected data on 10 colas, including Burpee Cola, on five measures: carbonation, sweetness, darkness, burpability, and viscosity. These data are presented in Table 17.1.

In order to determine empirically how many subtypes of cola drinks exist, these data will be analyzed using a *Q*-type factor analysis. The first step in this analysis is the computation of correlations between rows (colas) of the data matrix. These correlations are presented in Table 17.2 and serve to quantify similarities between colas.

Table 17.3 shows the varimax rotated factor structure matrix resulting from a principal components analysis of these correlations. Two factors with eigenvalues of 1.0 or greater were extracted, accounting for 86.3% and 11.7% of the variance in the cases. The factor loadings in the rotated solution reveal that the Colas 1 through 5 represent the first factor or cluster and that Colas 6 through 10 represent the second group of colas. It appears, then, that the taste testers grouped colas into two categories, with Burpee Cola included in the second group. Interpreting these clusters is a task saved for Box 17.2.

TABLE 17.1 Scores of Colas on Five Descriptor Variables: Carbonation, Sweetness, Darkness, Burpability, and Viscosity

Cola	Carbonation	Sweetness	Darkness	Burpability	Viscosity
1 Sludge	20	60	60	4	7
2 Same Old Soda	25	70	40	4	8
3 Old Brown	25	73	45	3	8
4 Thick 'n Sweet	23	60	50	3	7
5 Sweet One	15	80	65	2	9
6 Burpee Cola	33	35	60	8	3
7 Econocola	34	40	45	9	4
8 Tickle	35	40	50	9	5
9 Zippy	28	30	80	7	3
10 Belcher	32	32	70	8	4

TABLE 17.2 Correlations Between 10 Colas Based on Five Descriptor Variables

	Cola 1	Cola 2	Cola 3	Cola 4	Cola 5	Cola 6	Cola 7	Cola 8	Cola 9	Cola 10
Cola 1	1.0									
Cola 2	.91	1.0								
Cola 3	.94	.99	1.0							
Cola 4	.99	.96	.98	1.0						
Cola 5	.98	.95	.96	.98	1.0					
Cola 6	.86	.66	.70	.82	.76	1.0				
Cola 7	.89	.82	.83	.90	.82	.95	1.0			
Cola 8	.89	.78	.80	.89	.81	.97	.99	1.0		
Cola 9	.80	.52	.56	.72	.69	.96	.84	.88	1.0	
Cola 10	.82	.57	.61	.76	.71	.99	.89	.93	.99	1.0

TABLE 17.3 Factor Structure Matrix Following a Varimax Rotation of a Principal Components Analysis of Correlations Between 10 Colas

Colas	Loadings on Factor I-R	Loadings on Factor II-R
1	.80	.59
2	.96	.28
3	.95	.32
4	.86	.50
5	.88	.43
6	.43	.90
7	.62	.75
8	.57	.80
9	.28	.95
10	.33	.94
Eigenvalues	8.63	1.17
Percent Variance	86.3%	11.7%

Proximities are sometimes generated directly. For instance, subjects might be instructed to use a 1–10 scale in judging directly the overall similarity between all possible pairs of colas. A cluster analysis of these proximities would identify groups of colas perceived by subjects to be relatively similar.

Alternatively, proximities can be computed or "derived" from a matrix of descriptive data. For example, each of several colas might be measured (objectively or subjectively) for level of carbonation, sweetness, viscosity, darkness of coloration, and so forth. The proximity between any two colas would be derived by comparing the two colas across the set of descriptor variables. The two most common derived proximities are the correlation and squared Euclidean distance, each discussed below.

The Correlation as a Measure of Proximity

The correlation between two elements across a set of descriptors provides a measure of proximity that reflects profile similarity, but which is insensitive to score levels on the descriptor variables. In other words, the correlation between values listed for two elements on p descriptor variables will reflect the degree to which the two elements show similar patterns of high and low scores across the p descriptors, but score levels on the descriptors are not reflected in this correlation. Thus, the values listed for two elements on p descriptor variables might be very different and still produce a perfect correlation as long as the profiles of the two elements are identical.

To illustrate this point, examine the data in Table 17.4. This matrix lists values on each of four descriptor variables for two colas, A and B. We see in this table that the colas are not identical, yet the correlation computed between the two colas (columns) is perfect, $r = 1.0$. This perfect correlation is a consequence of the identical profiles of the two colas across the four descriptors, as shown in Figure 17.1. For every "peak" in the profile of Cola A, there is a corresponding peak for Cola B. For every "valley" in the profile of Cola A, there is a corresponding valley for Cola B.

Squared Euclidean Distance as a Measure of Proximity

The **squared Euclidean distance** between two elements is computed as the sum of the squared differences between those elements across a series of p descriptor variables as shown in Equation 17.1.

TABLE 17.4 Data for Two Colas, A and B, on Four Raw Score Descriptor Variables

Variables	Cola A	Cola B
Carbonation	70	40
Sweetness	8	5
Viscosity	5	2
Darkness	6	3

Figure 17.1

Profiles of two colas, A and B, across four descriptor variables. The profiles match even though the score levels differ.

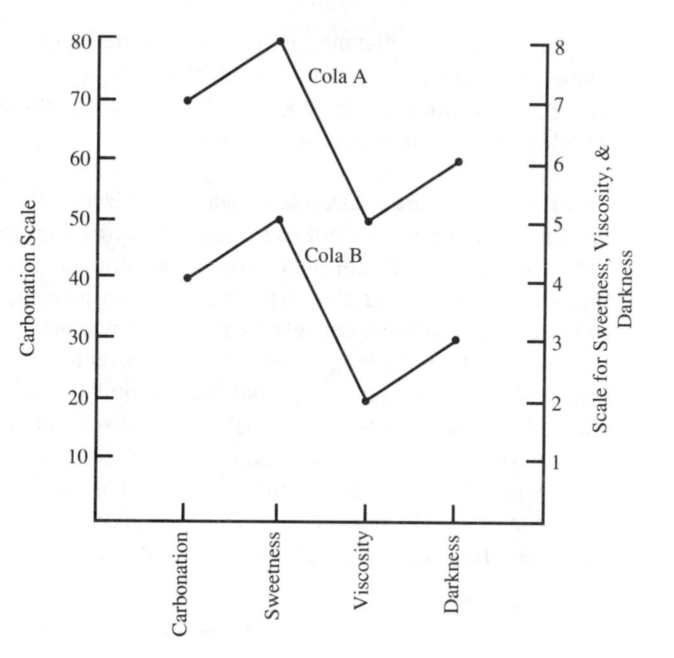

EQUATION 17.1

$$d^2_{AB} = \sum_{i=1}^{p} (A_i - B_i)^2$$

where,

d^2_{AB} = the squared Euclidean distance between elements A and B
p = the number of descriptor variables on which the elements are being compared
A = values on the p descriptor variables for element A
B = values on the p descriptor variables for element B

The squared Euclidean distance is sensitive both to profile differences and to level differences. The squared Euclidean distance between Colas A and B described in Table 17.4 may be computed according to Equation 17.1 as:

$$\begin{aligned} d^2_{AB} &= \sum_{i=1}^{p} (A_i - B_i)^2 \\ &= (70 - 40)^2 + (8 - 5)^2 + (5 - 2)^2 + (6 - 3)^2 \\ &= 900 + 9 + 9 + 9 \\ &= 927 \end{aligned}$$

Squared Euclidean distance is inversely related to the similarity between elements, and takes a value of 0 when two elements are identical. The value of $d^2_{AB} = 927$ computed above shows that the elements being compared are different, despite their identical profiles.

Computing Squared Euclidean Distance Using Standard Scores. The careful reader may have noticed in the preceding example that the squared Euclidean distance is susceptible to distortion from magnitude differences that exist from one descriptor variable to the next. The value computed above, $d^2_{AB} = 927$, was determined almost entirely by the difference between the colas on one variable, carbonation. As long as all variables present scores that are of comparable magnitude, each variable will contribute equally to d^2. However, variables associated with large score values will have a disproportionate effect on d^2.

To overcome this problem, squared Euclidean distance is usually computed after standardizing the descriptor variables. Table 17.5 shows standardized values corresponding to the raw score values listed previously in Table 17.4. The squared Euclidean distance computed using these standardized values is

$$\begin{aligned} d^2_{AB} &= (A_i - B_i)^2 \\ &= (1 + 1)^2 + (1 + 1)^2 + (1 + 1)^2 + (1 + 1)^2 \\ &= \quad 4 \quad + \quad 4 \quad + \quad 4 \quad + \quad 4 \\ &= 16 \end{aligned}$$

By standardizing descriptor variables prior to computing d^2, the influence of score magnitude is eliminated.

FORMING CLUSTERS

Once interelement proximities are obtained, they may be analyzed using cluster analysis. The process of forming clusters occurs in a stepwise or "hierarchical" fashion, to use the terminology of cluster analysis.

Divisive clustering begins with all elements grouped into a single, large, heterogeneous cluster. At each successive stage or step of the analysis, this cluster is divided into progressively smaller clusters, each of increasing homogeneity. At the last stage, there are as many clusters as there are elements.

TABLE 17.5 Data for Two Colas, A and B, on Four Standardized Descriptor Variables

Variables	Cola A	Cola B
Carbonation	1	−1
Sweetness	1	−1
Viscosity	1	−1
Darkness	1	−1

More common is **agglomerative clustering.** This procedure begins with each element considered as a separate "cluster." At each stage of the agglomerative procedure, elements are combined to create fewer, larger, more heterogeneous clusters. At the last stage, agglomerative procedures form a single cluster consisting of all the elements. The agglomerative approach will be examined in more detail here, since it is the more commonly used procedure. The discussion that follows is illustrated by an example in Box 17.2.

At each step or stage of the agglomerative cluster analysis, the critical decision to be made concerns which elements or clusters to combine. The general principle guiding this decision is that the most similar elements or clusters should be combined at each stage.

Selecting elements to combine at the first stage is straightforward. Those two elements are combined that show the greatest proximity (i.e., highest positive correlation, lowest squared Euclidean distance, or highest direct proximity rating). At the second stage, either two other elements will be combined to form a second cluster, or an element may be added to the cluster formed at the first stage. At the third and subsequent stages, either two elements will be combined to form a new cluster, or an element may be added to a previously formed cluster, or two clusters may be combined.

To decide which of these actions to take at each stage depends upon a comparison of three distances: (1) the distance between the two most similar ungrouped elements; (2) the distance between an existing cluster and the most similar ungrouped element; and (3) the distance between the two most similar existing clusters. A new cluster is formed if the first of these distances is smallest. An element is added to an existing cluster if the second distance is smallest. Finally, two existing clusters will be combined if the third distance is smallest.

Several agglomerative clustering methods are available that differ primarily in how distances affecting clusters are measured. We will consider some of the options next.

Single Linkage Method

In the **single linkage method,** also called the "nearest neighbor" method, the distance between an element and a cluster is computed using as representative of the entire cluster that one element contained within it that is most similar to the element being considered for inclusion. The distance between two clusters is equal to the distance between the most similar individual elements contained within those two clusters.

Complete Linkage Method

The **complete linkage method,** also called the "furthest neighbor" method, uses the opposite approach. The distance between an element and a cluster is set equal to the distance between the element and the most distant (i.e., least similar) member of the existing cluster. The distance between two clusters is set equal to the distance between the most dissimilar members of the two clusters.

Average Linkage Method

The **average linkage method** defines the distance between an individual element and a cluster as the average of all the distances between that element and members of the cluster. The distance between two clusters is the average of all of the distances between all members of the two clusters. Because the average linkage method uses more of the available information than either single linkage or complete linkage, it is generally preferred over these methods.

Other Clustering Methods

Other agglomerative methods have been developed that are considerably more complicated than those described here. Let it suffice to say that all methods attempt to combine elements and clusters at each stage so that the two most similar elements or clusters not already combined will be combined. We will generally find only relatively subtle differences between the solutions produced using different clustering methods. It is a good idea, though, to analyze data using several methods and to compare the results. Demonstrating a common solution from several clustering procedures lends support to the stability of the solution.

DEPICTING THE CLUSTER SOLUTION

The basic output from a cluster analysis is a summary of actions taken at each stage of the analysis. What elements or clusters were combined at each stage? More importantly, which elements are members of the various clusters that exist at each stage? This information is often presented in tabular form. **Icicle plots** (see Figure 17.2 in Box 17.2) provide the same information in graphic form.

Another important part of the output from a cluster analysis is the **agglomeration schedule.** This schedule records at each stage the distance between the elements and/or clusters that were combined at that stage of the analysis. At the initial stages, where highly similar elements and/or clusters are being combined, these distances will be quite small. At subsequent stages, distances will grow progressively larger. In the later stages, after all of the relatively similar elements and clusters have already been grouped, the distances recorded can become quite large.

SELECTING A CLUSTER SOLUTION

Each stage of the agglomerative procedure presents a different cluster solution. Selecting the "right" solution is the greatest challenge facing the researcher using cluster analysis. The following suggestions can be offered.

Using the Agglomeration Schedule

The agglomeration schedule can give one clue to the "true" structure of the elements being clustered. As the distances listed in this schedule become progressively larger from stage to stage, there will often occur a point at which the distance shows a sudden, exceptionally large increase. At this stage, the analysis has grouped elements together that are really quite dissimilar. The "correct" solution, then, is the one depicted at the preceding stage where the elements combined were still relatively similar.

Interpretability of the Cluster Solution

Theory and interpretability should also guide our choice of cluster solutions. If it makes more theoretical sense for the elements being clustered to form three clusters than four, use the three-cluster solution. If no theory exists to guide our selection of a solution, but five clusters are more interpretable than four, go with the more interpretable solution. More will be said later about interpreting cluster solutions.

Parsimony

Finally, it should be remembered in selecting a cluster solution that a major purpose of cluster analysis is to reduce the complexity of the data by grouping elements into a reduced number of homogeneous categories. If two solutions are equally acceptable from all other standpoints, the solution containing the smaller number of clusters (i.e., the more parsimonious solution) is to be preferred.

INTERPRETING CLUSTERS

Simply knowing that there are two distinct types or clusters of cola drinks, six types of cities, or four types of depression is not especially useful. We also need to be able to describe each of the clusters and the differences that distinguish them. This is the problem of cluster interpretation.

Cluster interpretation begins with an examination of the members of each cluster. Sometimes labels for the clusters will emerge directly from an inspection of cluster membership. Take the example of a cluster analysis of cities. If a two-cluster solution grouped New York, Los Angeles, Chicago, and Philadelphia into one cluster and Wahoo (Texas), Prairie Village (Nebraska), Desolation (Utah), and Earth's End (Montana) into the second cluster, we might reasonably conclude that the two city clusters are distinguished primarily by population.

In situations in which proximities have been derived from p descriptor variables, means can be computed for each cluster on each descriptor. The profiles created in this way can also assist in defining the clusters.

Significant difference tests may also be used to evaluate differences between the clusters. Univariate comparisons between clusters on each of the p descriptor variables are one possibility. The reader is aware by now, though, of the pitfalls associated with multiple univariate tests involving correlated variables. When there is a sufficient number of elements to support it, a discriminant analysis (chapter 14) is a useful alternative to multiple univariate comparisons. A discriminant analysis can help both in describing the nature of the differences between clusters and in testing those differences for significance.

BOX 17.2

HIERARCHICAL AGGLOMERATIVE CLUSTER ANALYSIS

This box provides an example of hierarchical agglomerative cluster analysis. Shown in Table 17.6 are data for the same 10 colas examined in Box 17.1, expressed now in z-score form. The question being addressed again in this box is this. How many distinctly different types of colas are there and how is Burpee Cola positioned?

Computation of Proximities

First, proximities must be derived from the data in Table 17.6. For this analysis, squared Euclidean distances will be computed according to Equation 17.1. To illustrate the computation of d^2, two values have been computed. First is the distance between Colas 1 and 2:

$$
\begin{aligned}
d_{12}^2 &= \sum_{i=1}^{p} (\text{Cola 1} - \text{Cola 2})^2 \\
&= (-1.06 + .30)^2 + (.43 - .96)^2 + \ldots \\
&\quad + (.53 - .98)^2 \\
&= 3.5
\end{aligned}
$$

Next, the distance between Colas 3 and 5 is computed:

$$
\begin{aligned}
d_{35}^2 &= \sum_{i=1}^{p} (\text{Cola 3} - \text{Cola 5})^2 \\
&= (-.30 + 1.82)^2 + (1.12 - 1.50)^2 + \ldots \\
&\quad + (.98 - 1.42)^2 \\
&= 5.2
\end{aligned}
$$

In a similar manner, squared Euclidean distances may be computed for all other pairs of colas to generate the matrix of proximities in Table 17.7.

Clustering the Colas

The next step in the analysis is to form clusters. At the first stage, those two colas that are most similar (i.e., have the lowest squared Euclidean distance) will be grouped together. The smallest distance in Table 17.7 is .31, for Colas 2 and 3. Thus, these two colas form the first cluster.

At the second stage, proximities are examined again to enable combining those elements and/or clusters that are most similar. These proximities are

TABLE 17.6 Standardized Scores for 10 Colas on Five Descriptor Variables: Carbonation, Sweetness, Darkness, Burpability, and Viscosity

Cola	Carbonation	Sweetness	Darkness	Burpability	Viscosity
1 Sludge	−1.06	.43	.28	−.62	.53
2 Same Old Soda	−.30	.96	−1.30	−.62	.98
3 Old Brown	−.30	1.12	−.91	−.98	.98
4 Thick 'n Sweet	−.61	.43	−.51	−.98	.53
5 Sweet One	−1.82	1.50	.67	−1.35	1.42
6 Burpee Cola	.91	−.91	.28	.84	−1.24
7 Econocola	1.06	−.64	−.91	1.20	−.80
8 Tickle	1.21	−.64	−.51	1.20	−.36
9 Zippy	.15	−1.18	1.85	.47	−1.24
10 Belcher	.76	−1.07	1.06	.84	−.80

BOX 17.2—*continued*

the same as those used at stage 1, except that Colas 2 and 3, which were combined at stage 1, now form a cluster and distances to this cluster must be determined.

Distances to a cluster may be computed in several ways. The single linkage method computes the distance between an element and a cluster using as representative of the entire cluster that one element contained within it that is most similar to the element being considered for inclusion. The complete linkage method sets the distance between an element and a cluster equal to the distance between that element and the most distant member of the cluster. Finally, the average linkage method defines the distance between an element and a cluster as the average of all the distances between that element and members of the cluster. Distances computed in all three of these ways are presented for the data at hand in Table 17.8.

TABLE 17.7 Squared Euclidean Distances Between 10 Colas Based on Standardized Scores on Five Descriptor Variables

	Cola 1	Cola 2	Cola 3	Cola 4	Cola 5	Cola 6	Cola 7	Cola 8	Cola 9	Cola 10
Cola 1	0									
Cola 2	3.54	0								
Cola 3	2.78	.31	0							
Cola 4	.96	1.33	.93	0						
Cola 5	3.20	7.18	5.25	4.93	0					
Cola 6	10.95	14.52	15.25	11.18	25.27	0				
Cola 7	12.13	11.06	12.90	10.62	26.78	1.82	0			
Cola 8	11.03	10.58	12.11	10.00	24.81	1.71	.38	0		
Cola 9	10.88	20.85	20.16	14.01	22.86	3.26	9.43	8.31	0	
Cola 10	10.07	16.12	16.29	11.67	23.10	.87	4.28	3.20	1.33	0

TABLE 17.8 Squared Euclidean Distances Between Cluster I and Individual Colas Computed According to the Single Linkage, Complete Linkage, and Average Linkage Methods

	Cluster I				
Colas	**Distance to Cola 2**	**Distance to Cola 3**	**Single Linkage Distance**	**Complete Linkage Distance**	**Average Linkage Distance**
1	3.54	2.78	2.78	3.54	3.16
4	1.33	.96	.96	1.33	1.14
5	7.18	5.25	5.25	7.18	6.22
6	14.52	15.25	14.52	15.25	14.89
7	11.06	12.90	11.06	12.90	11.98
8	10.58	12.11	10.58	12.11	11.35
9	20.85	20.16	20.16	20.85	20.51
10	16.12	16.29	16.12	16.29	16.21

continued

Look at the top row of Table 17.8. We see first that the distance (d^2) between Cola 1 and Cola 2 (one of the members of Cluster I) is 3.54 and that the distance between Cola 1 and Cola 3 (the other member of Cluster I) is 2.78. The single linkage distance between Cola 1 and the cluster is equal to the distance between Cola 1 and the nearest member of the cluster: 2.78. The complete linkage distance is equal to the distance between Cola 1 and the furthest member of the cluster: 3.54. The average linkage distance is equal to the average (mean) distance between Cola 1 and the members of the cluster: $(3.54 + 2.78)/2 = 3.16$. Other distances in the table are computed in like manner.

For purposes of this analysis, let us use the average linkage distances. These are included in Table 17.9 along with distances between the individual elements (colas). The smallest distance in Table 17.9 is .38, between Colas 7 and 8. Consequently, at stage 2 we group these colas into a second cluster.

Stage 3 begins by computing distances between individual colas and each of the first two clusters, as well as the distance between the two clusters. At this stage, as always, the two most similar colas and/or clusters will be grouped. In this instance, Colas 6 and 10 will be grouped to form a third cluster.

The agglomerative process continues in this fashion until, at stage 9, all 10 colas have been grouped into a single, large cluster. The agglomeration schedule shown in Table 17.10 lists the smallest distance found at each stage of the analysis. Cluster membership at each stage of the analysis is listed in Table 17.11 and is also depicted with an icicle plot in Figure 17.2.

Consider first Table 17.11. The body of this table indicates cluster membership for each cola (listed by rows) in each cluster solution (listed by columns). To determine the cluster membership for any given solution, find the column corresponding to that solution and read the cluster number entries listed in that column. For example, in the four-cluster solution, Colas 1–4 are members of the first cluster, Cola 5 is the only member of the second cluster, Colas 6, 9, and 10 are members of the third cluster, and Colas 7 and 8 are members of the fourth cluster. Looking at the two-cluster solution, we find that Colas 1–5 are members of the first cluster and that Colas 6–10 are members of the second cluster.

TABLE 17.9 Proximities Matrix Input to Stage 2 of the Cluster Analysis

	Cluster I	Cola 1	Cola 4	Cola 5	Cola 6	Cola 7	Cola 8	Cola 9	Cola 10
Cluster I	0								
Cola 1	3.16	0							
Cola 4	2.29	.96	0						
Cola 5	6.22	3.20	4.93	0					
Cola 6	14.89	10.95	11.18	25.27	0				
Cola 7	11.98	12.13	10.62	26.78	1.82	0			
Cola 8	11.35	11.03	10.00	24.81	1.71	.38	0		
Cola 9	20.51	10.88	14.01	22.86	3.26	9.43	8.31	0	
Cola 10	16.21	10.07	11.67	23.10	.87	4.28	3.20	1.33	0

Figure 17.2

Icicle plot depicting cluster membership at each stage of the hierarchical cluster agglomerative analysis.

```
        Number of
Stage   Clusters                 Colas
                                  1
                     8  7  9  0  6  5  3  2  4  1
  9        1         xxxxxxxxxxxxxxxxxxxxxxxxxxxx
  8        2         xxxxxxxxxxxxx  xxxxxxxxxxxxx
  7        3         xxxxxxxxxxxxx  x  xxxxxxxxxx
  6        4         xxxx  xxxxxxx  x  xxxxxxxxxx
  5        5         xxxx  x  xxxx  x  xxxxxxxxxx
  4        6         xxxx  x  xxxx  x  xxxx  xxxx
  3        7         xxxx  x  xxxx  x  xxxx  x  x
  2        8         xxxx  x  x  x  x  xxxx  x  x
  1        9         x  x  x  x  x  x  xxxx  x  x
```

TABLE 17.10 Agglomeration Schedule of the Hierarchical Agglomerative Cluster Analysis of 10 Colas

Stage	No. of Clusters	Smallest Distance
1	9	.31
2	8	.38
3	7	.87
4	6	.96
5	5	2.14
6	4	2.29
7	3	4.79
8	2	5.14
9	1	15.41

Look next at the icicle plot in Figure 17.2. This plot provides the same information as Table 17.11, but in graphic form. Each level (row) of the icicle plot represents one stage in the analysis, or one possible cluster solution. The bottom row represents stage 1, where Colas 2 and 3 are clustered. Notice how this fact is depicted in the icicle plot by placing X's adjacent to each other. At stage 2, we see that Colas 7 and 8 are clustered. Again, adjacent X's indicate that the corresponding colas (listed across the top of the plot) are grouped together at this stage of the analysis.

TABLE 17.11 Cluster Membership at Each Stage of the Hierarchical Agglomerative Cluster Analysis of 10 Colas

	Number of Clusters								
Colas	*9*	*8*	*7*	*6*	*5*	*4*	*3*	*2*	*1*
1 Sludge	1	1	1	1	1	1	1	1	1
2 Same Old Soda	2	2	2	2	1	1	1	1	1
3 Old Brown	2	2	2	2	1	1	1	1	1
4 Thick 'n Sweet	3	3	3	1	1	1	1	1	1
5 Sweet One	4	4	4	3	2	2	2	1	1
6 Burpee Cola	5	5	5	4	3	3	3	2	1
7 Econocola	6	6	6	5	4	4	3	2	1
8 Tickle	7	6	6	5	4	4	3	2	1
9 Zippy	8	7	7	6	5	3	3	2	1
10 Belcher	9	8	5	4	3	3	3	2	1

Values in the table indicate the cluster membership of each cola for each of the nine cluster solutions.

continued

Moving up the icicle plot, colas are grouped into fewer and fewer clusters at each stage, until, at stage 9, all colas form a single cluster.

Selecting the Correct Cluster Solution
Each stage of the cluster analysis presents a potential solution. We will now select from among these solutions the one that is "correct."

The agglomeration schedule (Table 17.10) shows that, until stage 9, colas and/or clusters combined at each stage were relatively similar (i.e., the squared Euclidean distances recorded at stages 1–8 are relatively small). At stage 9, though, there occurs a sudden, large increase in distance. At this stage, clusters have been combined that are quite dissimilar. This supports the selection of the two-cluster solution created at stage 8, where the clusters combined are still relatively similar. The ease with which the two-cluster solution may be interpreted (discussed in the next section) also supports the choice of this solution.

Interpreting the Cluster Solution
Cluster interpretation begins with an examination of descriptive statistics for each cluster on each of the descriptor variables used in the analysis. These descriptive statistics, and *t*-test comparisons for statistical significance, are presented in Table 17.12.

The two clusters differ significantly on all descriptor variables except darkness. Cluster I colas may be described as thick and sweet, with low carbonation and low burpability. Cluster II colas, including Burpee Cola, are heavily carbonated, with high burpability, low sweetness, and low viscosity. Colas in the two clusters do not differ systematically in coloration.

TABLE 17.12 Cluster Profiles across Five Descriptor Variables for the Two-Cluster Solution

	Cluster I		Cluster II			
Variables	$\bar{X}$	s	$\bar{X}$	s	$t(df = 8)$	p
Carbonation	21.4	4.0	32.4	2.7	−5.06	.001
Sweetness	68.6	8.7	35.4	4.6	7.59	.0001
Darkness	52.0	10.4	61.0	14.3	−1.14	.29
Burpability	3.2	.8	8.2	.8	−9.45	.0001
Viscosity	7.8	.8	3.8	.8	7.56	.0001

SUMMARY

Cluster analysis is a method of analyzing numerical indices of proximity (similarity) between elements to identify relatively discrete, homogeneous groups or clusters of elements. Thus, cluster analysis is useful in uncovering the structure of a set of elements in much the same way that factor analysis uncovers the structure underlying a set of variables. In fact, one type of factor analysis, called *Q*-type factor analysis, was a precursor to modern approaches to cluster analysis. Agglomerative hierarchical clustering methods are used most often today. These methods begin with each element considered a cluster and, in a series of steps or stages, elements are combined to form larger clusters. Determining the "correct" number of clusters is not always easy, but clusters should contain fairly homogeneous elements, should be interpretable, and, all other things being equal, the goal of parsimony suggests that fewer clusters are better than more clusters. Identifying the members of each cluster will often suggest an interpretation of the cluster solution. Descriptive statistics for each cluster and comparisons between clusters are also useful in cluster interpretation.

CHAPTER 18

MULTIDIMENSIONAL SCALING

Although the discrete, hierarchically ordered categories generated by cluster analysis (chapter 17) give a logical descriptive structure for many objects and events in the world, some things are better described according to their positions along continuous dimensions. **Multidimensional scaling analysis** is a means by which the researcher may explore these dimensional aspects of the structure of a set of elements.

The marketing researcher who is studying consumer perceptions of colas may discover through cluster analysis that subjects group colas into several discrete categories. A multidimensional scaling analysis may reveal that these categories are ordered along such continuous dimensions as sweetness, level of carbonation, or cost. The industrial/organizational psychologist studying group dynamics in an organization may use cluster analysis to identify several discrete, homogeneous groups of employees; multidimensional scaling analysis may reveal that these groups differ along one or more continuous dimensions, such as income level, industriousness, ability level, and the like.

In short, like cluster analysis, multidimensional scaling analysis is a descriptive methodology that is often used in the initial stages of research when our focus is still on describing the problem under investigation. Our choice of cluster analysis or multidimensional scaling is generally dictated by the type of description being sought. Where the elements being examined are best described in terms of categories, groups, or types, cluster analysis will offer the clearest picture. When no such types exist, or when our interest is in identifying the continuous dimensions along which elements are perceived to vary, the method of choice is multidimensional scaling. Of course, as the preceding discussion has suggested, we may often wish to apply both types of analysis. It is a simple matter to examine any set of elements from the perspectives of both cluster analysis and multidimensional scaling analysis since both methods analyze proximity data.

Multidimensional scaling analysis progresses through three steps or stages. First, proximity data are generated for all possible pairs of elements being examined. Second, these proximities are used to map or "scale" the elements into one or more spatial dimensions. Third, the resulting solution is interpreted. These three steps are discussed in the sections that follow and an example is given later in Box 18.1.

THE DATA FOR MULTIDIMENSIONAL SCALING ANALYSIS

Multidimensional scaling analysis uncovers the dimensional structure of a set of elements by examining the proximities between those elements. Only a researcher's creativity limits the ways in which these proximities may be generated.

Direct Proximities

The proximity of any two elements is often assessed by asking one or more subjects to judge this proximity directly. For example, subjects might use a 1–10 scale in judging the "similarity" between two elements. Or, depending on the nature of our research, the elements might be judged for "degree of relationship," "similarity of meaning," "emotional closeness," or other instructions may be given to ensure that the appropriate type of psychological proximity between elements is assessed. Of course, depending on the instructions given to subjects, the outcomes of the multidimensional scaling analyses may be quite different. Two employees judged to be quite "similar," for instance, might easily be judged to be very "emotionally distant."

Direct proximities need not be obtained subjectively as the preceding examples might suggest. Indeed, there are many direct, objective measures of proximity. For example, the proximity between two street intersections might be assessed objectively by similarity in number of accidents, number of tickets given, or traffic volume. The emotional closeness of two employees might be measured objectively by the number of conversations that take place between those employees in a 24-hour period. The semantic relationship between two words might be measured as the amount of overlap between lists of free associates to those words.

Derived Proximities

Proximities between elements may also be derived, as described in chapter 17. Briefly, the proximity between any two elements is determined by comparing the elements across several descriptor variables. The correlation between two elements across several discriptor variables gives one measure of derived proximity. Squared Euclidean distance (Equation 17.1) is also commonly used to measure proximity. Derived proximities can be based on objective descriptors, subjective ratings, or a combination of both.

Choosing between Direct and Derived Proximities

The choice between direct and derived proximities often seems to be directed more by habit than by reason. Traditionally, derived proximities have been emphasized in cluster analysis. In contrast, researchers using multidimensional scaling have frequently been quite vocal in calling for the use of direct proximities and have criticized the use of derived proximities.

Critics of derived proximities point out that the usual purpose of multidimensional scaling is to identify those dimensions which subjects use spontaneously in ordering the world around them. When proximities between elements are derived by comparing elements across a series of experimenter-selected descriptor variables, subjects' spontaneous perceptions are not being tapped. Only when subjects are permitted to define "proximity" for themselves will the proximity ratings (and the resulting multidimensional scaling solution) reflect subjects' free, spontaneous, self-chosen perceptual dimensions.

On the other hand, there are legitimate arguments for the use of derived proximities. First, some stimulus elements are so complex that subjects may be unable to give reliable direct judgments of psychological proximity. Judging similarities between people is a case in point. People are incredibly complex stimuli, and to ask a subject to simultaneously consider two people and judge their "similarity" may overtax even the most facile mind. At the very least, we can easily understand that these judgments would tend to display low inter-judge reliability, and even intra-judge reliability would be expected to be weak. When dealing with highly complex stimuli, then, it may be necessary to define more clearly the subject's task by asking for ratings on a series of specific scales from which proximities can then be derived. In this manner, subjects are asked only to consider one stimulus element at a time on only one attribute at a time, substantially reducing the information processing load.

Another circumstance that calls for the use of derived proximities is that in which no single subject is sufficiently familiar with all elements to judge all pairs of elements for proximity. As an example, a researcher might wish to use multidimensional scaling to study the dimensions along which 100 cities vary, but no single subject knows all 100 cities well enough to judge directly the proximities between them. What we might do is ask each of several subjects to describe, using a series of rating scales, the few cities with which he or she is familiar and then derive proximities from this collection of ratings.

Whether we use direct or derived ratings may not be a truly critical issue, since Wish (1976) has demonstrated that multidimensional scaling solutions based on direct and derived similarities are very similar when derived similarities are based on a large number of intuitively reasonable descriptor variables. Also, as we shall see in a later section, even if multidimensional scaling analysis is performed on direct proximities, the interpretation of the resulting solutions often depends heavily on subjects' ratings of the stimulus elements on a set of researcher-selected attribute scales. This fact further diminishes the apparent advantage of using direct proximity judgments for multidimensional scaling analysis.

SCALING STIMULUS ELEMENTS USING PROXIMITIES

Once proximities have been generated for all pairs of stimulus elements being examined, we are ready to analyze these proximities through multidimensional scaling analysis. The mathematical complexities of multidimensional scaling are beyond the scope of this text, but we can easily understand the fundamentals of this method of analysis by considering some simple examples.

Say there are three stimulus elements, A, B, and C, which have been judged for proximity using a 1–7 scale, where 1 = very proximate (i.e., similar, emotionally close, etc.), and 7 = very distant. These proximities are listed in Table 18.1. Let us begin the scaling of the elements by representing stimulus element A as a point anywhere in open space as depicted in Figure 18.1a. Now, assuming that 1 unit of psychological proximity equals 1 cm of physical distance between elements, we can represent stimulus element B as a point 4 cm distant from element A, as shown in Figure 18.1b. Of course, element B might have been located in any direction away from A. The only important feature of the **stimulus map** being created is the relative positioning of points, that is, the whole configuration. Next, we must position element C. The proximities of Table 18.1 tell us that C is 2 cm distant from element B, but this could position C anywhere along the dotted circle in Figure 18.1c. To pinpoint its location, we must consider the last proximity: A–C = 6. In order for all proximities to be met by mapped distances, element C must be located as shown in Figure 18.1d.

(a) Element A is positioned anywhere in space.

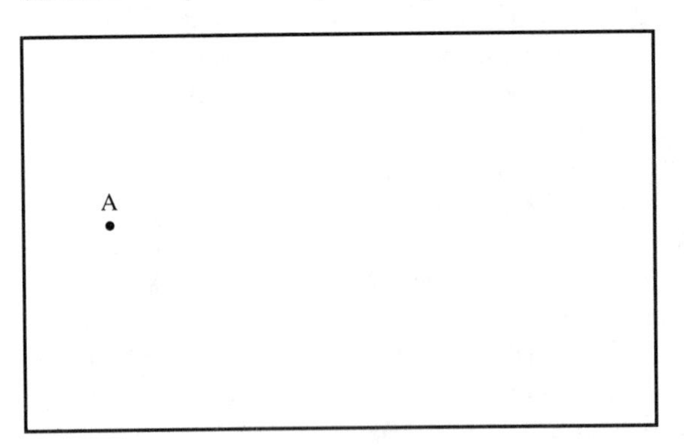

(b) Element B is positioned 4 cm from Element A.

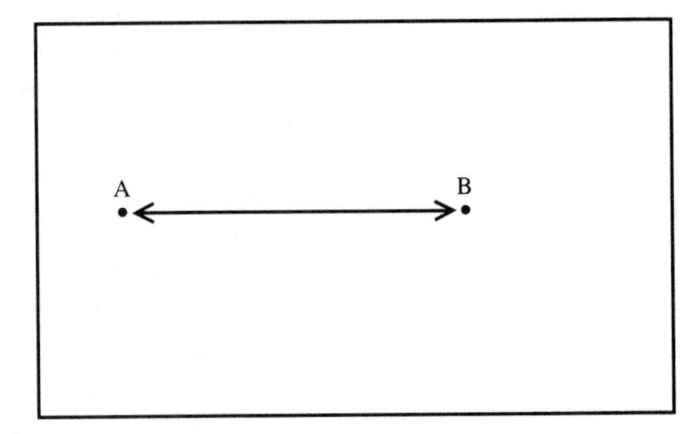

(c) Element C must be positioned somewhere 2 cm distant from Element B.

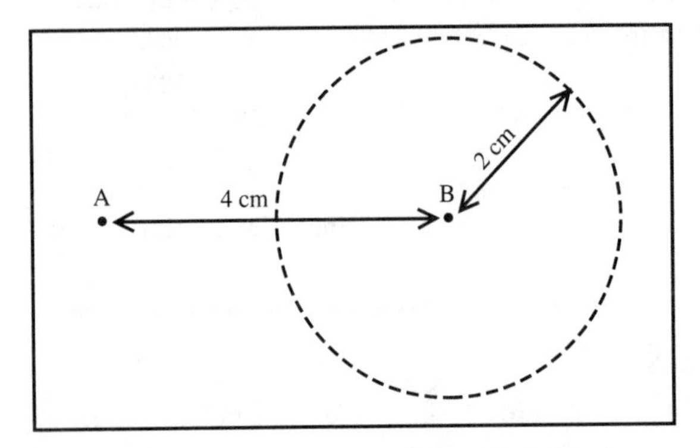

Figure 18.1
Multidimensional scaling solution for proximities presented in Table 18.1.

TABLE 18.1 Proximities for Three Stimulus Elements, A, B, and C

Stimulus Pairs	Proximities
A–B	4
B–C	2
A–C	6

Once the configuration of elements has been determined, we may overlay one or more coordinate axes to facilitate locating any given stimulus element in the map. The position of these axes is arbitrary and the coordinates themselves have no special meaning other than to locate the elements in the map. Thus, the coordinates of a multidimensional scaling solution are unlike the factor loadings (chapter 16) used as coordinates in graphing factor structure. These factor loadings are meaningful and interpretable correlations between individual variables

(d) Element C is positioned.

(e) Positioning the coordinate axes.

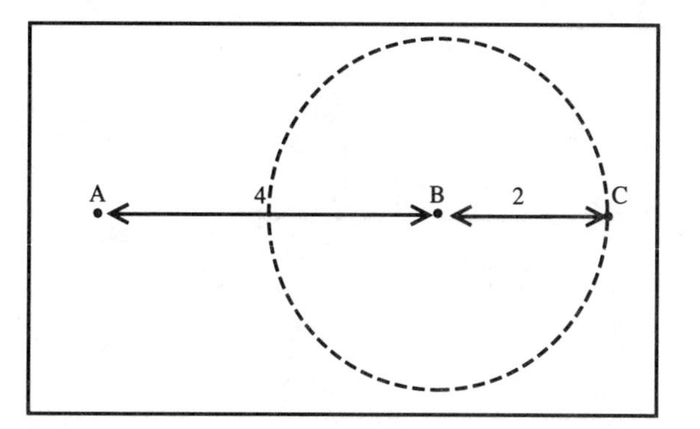

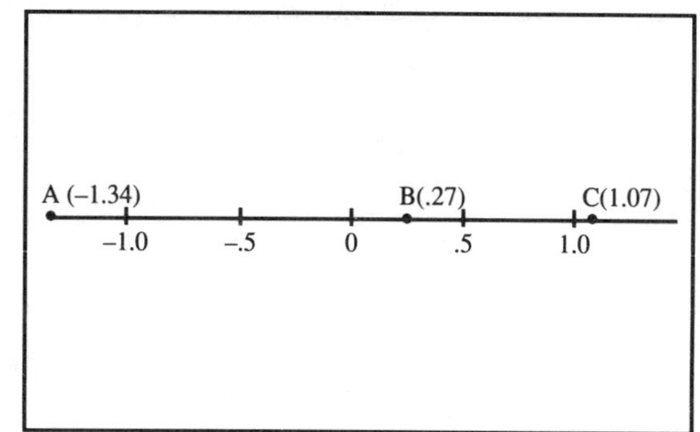

Figure 18.1— *continued*

and factor variates. Multidimensional scaling coordinates, in contrast, carry no meaning other than to describe the relative locations of points in the multidimensional scaling solution. In locating the coordinate axes in the multidimensional scaling map, though, it is customary to position the axes so that the coordinates are standardized to show a mean of zero across stimulus elements. Figure 18.1e shows a single coordinate axis positioned to meet this requirement. Only one axis is required because the points are configured along a single spatial dimension. Elements A, B, and C have coordinate values of -1.34, .27, and 1.07, respectively, along this coordinate axis. Consider how these coordinates were assigned. Element A falls 0 cm from the far left side of the dimension, B is 4 cm further to the right, and C is 6 cm to the far right. The mean of these values (0, 4, and 6) is 3.33 and the standard deviation is 2.49. Converting the original values to z-scores we have our standardized coordinates. For element A, $(0 - 3.33)/2.49 = -1.34$. For element B, $(4 - 3.33)/2.49 = .27$. For element C, $(6 - 3.33)/2.49 = 1.07$.

What does Figure 18.1e (or any multidimensional scaling solution) tell us about the mapped stimulus elements? First, the map captures, in a single picture, all of the information that was contained about stimulus proximities in the judgments that were used to generate the map. Second, Figure 18.1e shows that elements A, B, and C can be described as varying along a single dimension, with elements A and C occupying relatively extreme locations on opposite ends of this dimension and element B occupying a more moderate location. Determining what the dimension *is* along which the elements vary is a problem of interpretation we will save for later.

Consider next another simple example, again involving three stimulus elements A, B, and C showing the pattern of proximities given in Table 18.2. In Figure 18.2a we position element A anywhere in space. In Figure 18.2b, we position element B 4 cm distant from A. (As in the previous example, numerical proximities are assumed to correspond directly to physical distances, measured in centimeters.) Figure 18.2c indicates that element C may be located anywhere along the dotted circle which has a radius of 2 cm from B. In determining where

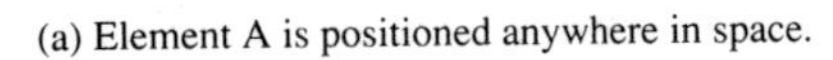
(a) Element A is positioned anywhere in space.

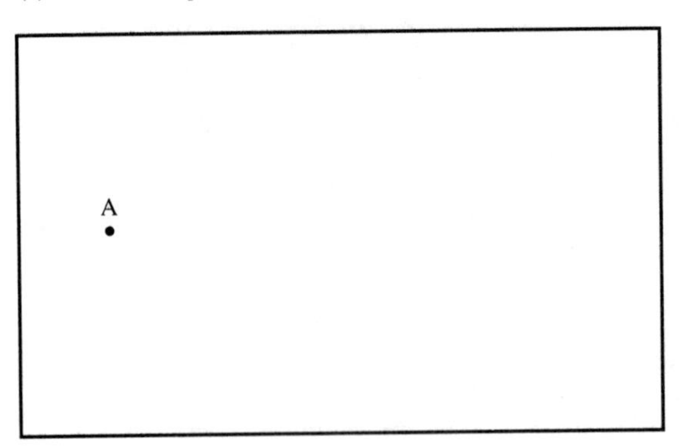

(b) Element B is positioned 4 cm from Element A.

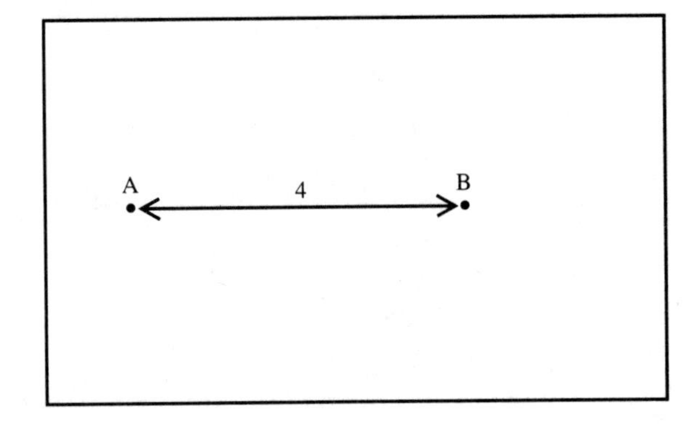

(c) Element C must be positioned somewhere 2 cm distant from Element B.

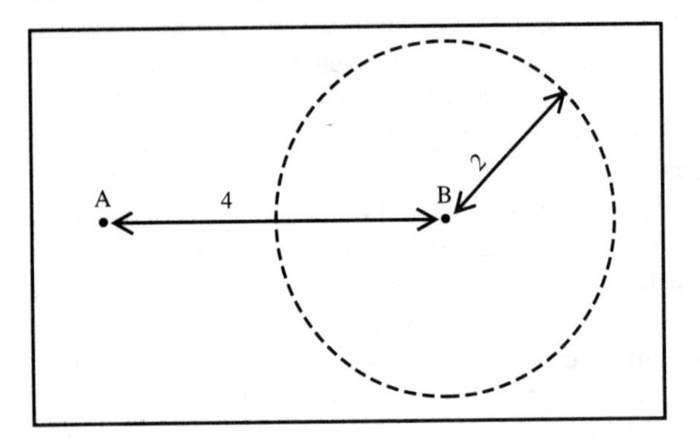

Figure 18.2

Multidimensional scaling solution for the proximities presented in Table 18.2.

along this circle to locate element C, we look at the last proximity in Table 18.2: A−C = 3. In order for all of the proximities in Table 18.2 to be matched by physical distances in the stimulus map, point C must be located as shown in Figure 18.2d. Finally, Figure 18.2e shows the placement of two coordinate axes (one for each of the two dimensions of the solution). Coordinates of the stimulus elements on the two dimensions are given in Table 18.3. As in the previous example, these coordinates are standardized to have a mean of zero, but have no meaning other than to provide a numerical description of the relative locations of elements A, B, and C in the two-dimensional solution.

The solution depicted in Figure 18.2e differs from that of Figure 18.1e because it has required that we use a second (vertical) dimension to capture graphically the whole pattern of proximities. The proximities that produced Figure 18.1e indicate that elements A, B, and C can be described as varying along a single dimension. The proximities that produced Figure 18.2e, though, indicate that elements A, B, and C vary along more than one dimension. As in the previous example, though, determining what those dimensions are depends upon our interpretive efforts, to be discussed later.

(d) Element C is positioned.

(e) Positioning the coordinate axes.

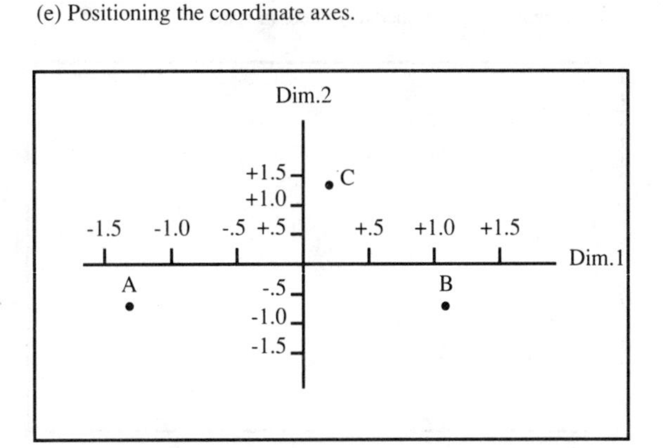

Figure 18.2— *continued*

TABLE 18.2 Proximities for Three Stimulus Elements, A, B, and C

Stimulus Pairs	Proximities
A–B	4
B–C	2
A–C	3

TABLE 18.3 Coordinates for the Two-Dimensional Solution Depicted in Figure 18.2

Stimulus Element	Dimension 1	Dimension 2
A	−1.32	−.70
B	1.11	−.70
C	.20	1.41

The reader can imagine for himself or herself that proximity patterns involving large numbers of stimulus elements can easily require that a third dimension (the dimension of depth) be used in mapping a solution. In fact, mathematics does not limit us to three dimensions. Multidimensional scaling solutions often require four or more dimensions.

Goodness-of-Fit

In both of the preceding examples we were able to achieve a perfect "fit" between the proximity data and the distances between elements in the stimulus maps. In Figure 18.1e the physical distances between graphed stimulus points match exactly the proximities upon which the map was based. Similarly, the configuration of Figure 18.2e gives an exact match between the input proximities and the physical distances between the mapped stimulus points.

(a) Element A is positioned anywhere in space.

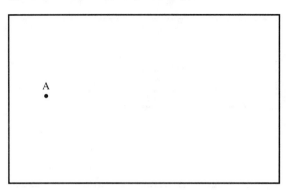

(b) Element B is positioned 4 cm from A.

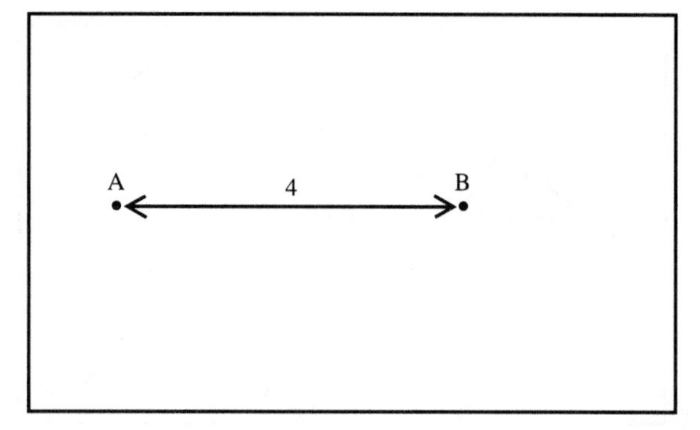

(c) Positioning Element C with the constraint that the solution be one-dimensional.

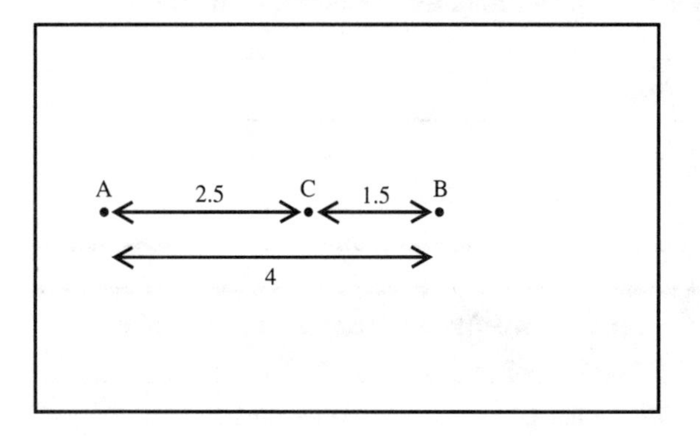

Figure 18.3

A one-dimensional solution for the proximities given in Table 18.2.

We generally do not see such a close fit between proximities and physical distances, however. Instead, a multidimensional scaling solution will generally present a certain amount of **stress,** that is, a deviation between the proximities input to the analysis and the physical distances displayed in the stimulus map. Let us explore further the concept of stress.

Using the proximities of Table 18.2 (the same proximities that are fit perfectly by the two-dimensional map of Figure 18.2e), let us "force" a one-dimensional solution as shown in Figure 18.3. In Figure 18.3a, we begin by positioning stimulus element A anywhere in space. In Figure 18.3b, we locate element B 4 cm away from element A. Next, we must position element C, with the constraint that our solution be one-dimensional. Under these circumstances, element C is positioned between A and B as shown in Figure 18.3c. In this location, element C is not quite 2 full cm from element B as the proximities would require, nor is it a full 3 cm distant from element A, as required by the proximities. In other words, there is a deviation between the proximities and the physical distances in the multidimensional scaling solution (i.e., stress). This stress is unavoidable if we insist on mapping the proximities of Table 18.2 into a one-dimensional space.

TABLE 18.4 Proximities and Mapped Distances for Stimulus Elements Depicted in Figure 18.3

Stimulus Pairs	Proximities	Mapped Distances
A–B	4	4 cm
B–C	2	1.5 cm
A–C	3	2.5 cm

The amount of stress in this one-dimensional solution, or in any multidimensional scaling solution, may be measured in a variety of ways. Perhaps the most straightforward measure is the squared correlation between proximities and mapped distances. Proximities and mapped distances for the example in Figure 18.3 are given in Table 18.4. In this example, the squared correlation between proximities and mapped distances is $r^2 = .99$, indicating a close, but less than perfect fit between proximities and mapped distances in the one-dimensional solution.

Another commonly used measure of stress is **Kruskal's stress.** Strictly speaking, this statistic measures "badness-of-fit" since the value of stress increases as the match between proximities and mapped distances decreases. Values of Kruskal's stress are commonly reported in the output of multidimensional scaling programs and can range from 0, indicating a perfect fit, to 1.

Selecting the Correct Dimensionality

We can always achieve a perfect fit ($r^2 = 1$, stress $= 0$) by mapping k elements into a $k - 1$ dimensional space (where $k =$ the number of stimulus elements being mapped). However, this would be a most nonparsimonious practice. How many dimensions, then, should our multidimensional scaling solution contain? As in selecting the "correct" number of factors or clusters, choosing the "correct" dimensionality of a multidimensional scaling solution is a subjective process. Nonetheless, some guidelines exist to guide the decision.

Goodness-of-Fit. First, as a set of k elements are mapped into one, two, three, and higher dimensional spaces, measures of stress will indicate better and better fit between the proximities and the mapped distances between stimulus elements. Typically, though, this improved goodness-of-fit will show a point of diminishing returns. That is, after a certain dimensionality has been reached, we see only minor further reductions in stress at higher dimensionalities. All other things being equal, a dimensionality that yields a value of $r^2 \geq .90$ or a Kruskal's stress of .15 or lower can be considered to provide an adequate fit between proximities and mapped distances.

Number of Stimulus Elements. A second guideline for selecting the "correct" dimensionality involves considering the number of elements being mapped. Kruskal and Wish (1978) have recommended that the maximum dimensionality, D, is given by Equation 18.1:

EQUATION 18.1

$$D \leq \frac{k-1}{4}$$

where,

D = the maximum number of dimensions in the multidimensional scaling solution
k = the number of stimulus elements being mapped

Thus, for 10 elements, the maximum number of dimensions would be 2, since $2 \leq (10 - 1)/4$; for 20 elements, the maximum dimensionality is 4, since $4 \leq (20 - 1)/4$. Solutions using more dimensions than given by Equation 18.1 capitalize on idiosyncrasies in the proximities data and tend to be unreliable.

Interpretability. Finally, we select a dimensionality with an eye toward the importance of each dimension in the interpretation of the solution. We will examine the problem of interpreting multidimensional scaling solutions in the next section. In simple terms, though, there is little point in moving to a solution having a higher dimensionality if the extra dimension(s) does not facilitate our interpretation of the solution.

INTERPRETING THE MULTIDIMENSIONAL SCALING SOLUTION

The basic output from multidimensional scaling analysis is a map of stimulus elements plotted as points in a space of one or more dimensions. The configuration of the elements in this map summarizes the interelement proximities. In this stimulus map, the closer two elements are located to each other, the more psychologically "proximate" these elements can be assumed to be, however "proximate" may have been defined in the particular research setting. Thus, the stimulus map summarizes graphically an immense quantity of information about how subjects perceived the elements being examined. These perceptions are captured numerically by the coordinates that locate the stimulus elements in the map. Once the stimulus map has been obtained, though, we must still make some sense of it. This is the problem of interpretation.

The Neighborhood Approach to Interpretation

In interpreting a multidimensional scaling solution, we may be interested primarily in determining which elements are seen as generally similar (proximate) and which are seen as different. This is referred to as the neighborhood approach to interpretation because it consists of identifying groups of elements located in the same "neighborhood" of the stimulus map.

We can often gain considerable insight into how a subject has organized his or her perceptions of a set of elements by identifying the neighborhoods represented in the stimulus map. If, for example, a multidimensional scaling solution of cities showed Dallas, Chicago, and New York in one neighborhood and Wahoo

(Texas), Prairie Home (Minnesota), and Smokestack (New Jersey) in a second neighborhood, it might be reasonable to conclude that city size was an important determinant of judgments of city similarity. If, though, one neighborhood contained New York and Smokestack, a second contained Chicago and Prairie Home, and a third included Dallas and Wahoo, it would be reasonable to conclude that perceptions of city similarity were based on geographical proximity.

Dimensional Interpretation: The Regression Approach

Neighborhood interpretations, while often useful, focus on identifying discrete, separate groups of elements. Often, though, elements will not form groups, but will be distributed evenly along one or more continuous dimensions. Identifying these continuous dimensions can be accomplished using multiple regression.

The dimensional interpretation of a multidimensional scaling solution using regression analysis requires that we obtain, in addition to the proximities from which the solution is generated, measures of each stimulus element on each of several descriptive scales. These measures may be obtained subjectively or objectively. The descriptive scales used in this interpretive phase of the analysis should have some reasonable chance of being salient in subjects' perceptions of the stimulus elements being examined. Thus, in studying perceptions of colas, ratings might be obtained on sweetness, carbonation level, price, and other attributes of potential importance to subjects' perceptions of colas. In a multidimensional scaling study of psychotherapists, very different attribute scales would be more appropriate, such as ratings of empathy, friendliness, acceptance, and so forth.

The regression approach to interpreting the multidimensional scaling solution uses the coordinates of the stimulus map as independent variables in a series of multiple regression analyses, with one analysis to predict scores on each of the descriptive scales. In the terminology of regression analysis, each descriptive scale is regressed on the coordinates of the multidimensional scaling stimulus map. The stimulus map coordinates reflect the arrangement of elements in the stimulus map and ratings of the stimulus elements on any given attribute scale reflect subjects' perceptions of the stimulus elements along that one attribute. If the squared multiple correlation (R^2) between coordinates and ratings on an attribute is high, it means that the positioning of elements in the stimulus map is strongly related to the positioning of the elements along the attribute dimension. Conversely, if R^2 is low, it means that that particular attribute scale was less salient in subjects' perceptions as captured in the stimulus map. Through a series of regression analyses, then, we can determine the degree to which various attributes are related to subjects' perceptions of the elements, as depicted by the multidimensional scaling solution.

Positioning Attribute Vectors in the Solution. Once one or more salient attributes have been identified (generally speaking, those attributes with which the multidimensional scaling map coordinates show a statistically significant value of R^2), Schiffman, Reynolds, and Young (1981) have described a simple procedure through which the attributes can be represented as vectors (i.e., lines) drawn into the stimulus map. In a solution having two dimensions, a multiple regression equation that yields a significant R^2 value for some attribute will include two standardized regression weights or "beta" weights (chapter 13), one for each of the dimensions. To represent this attribute as a vector in the multidimensional scaling solution, plot a point in the map using as coordinates the beta weights for Dimension 1 and Dimension 2. This is called the "beta point." Next, draw a line through the beta point and the origin of the map. Finally, put an arrow on the end of the line nearest the beta point to indicate the direction in which levels of the attribute represented by the vector increase. This procedure is repeated to represent each salient attribute in the multidimensional scaling solution. Where the multidimensional scaling solution includes three or more dimensions, there will be several stimulus maps, one for each pair of dimensions. Positioning attribute vectors in each of these maps involves using as coordinates for the beta point those beta weights that correspond to whichever dimensions are represented in any particular map. Thus, the coordinates for the beta point in a map representing Dimensions 2 and 3 would be the beta weights for these dimensions. Figure 18.4 in Box 18.1 provides an example of attributes represented as vectors in a two-dimensional scaling solution.

Attribute vectors in the multidimensional scaling solution enable us to see where each mapped element falls along each of the attributes that were most perceptually salient to subjects. In addition, the vectors divide the multidimensional scaling map into regions in a manner that may make neighborhood interpretations easier.

Box 18.1 gives a concrete example of multidimensional scaling analysis, including the regression interpretation of the stimulus map.

VARIETIES OF MULTIDIMENSIONAL SCALING

Multidimensional scaling analysis is a family of related procedures. It is beyond the scope of this book to describe in detail the many alternatives available to users of multidimensional scaling, but some of the options will be mentioned here. Multidimensional scaling techniques differ most importantly by: (1) what level of measurement is assumed to exist in the proximity data; and (2) whether the analysis is based on data from one proximity matrix or several.

Level of Measurement in Multidimensional Scaling

It has been most convenient in this chapter to attribute ratio scale properties to proximity data. That is, a proximity rating of 4 in Table 18.1 became a mapped distance of 4 cm in Figure 18.1. A proximity of 2 was represented by a mapped distance of 2 cm. A proximity of 0 would have translated to a mapped distance of 0 cm. Although multidimensional scaling analysis can be performed with the assumption of ratio scale data, it is much more common to assume only that

BOX 18.1

MULTIDIMENSIONAL SCALING ANALYSIS

There have long been personality conflicts within the Division of Metaphysical Sciences at Rocky Bottom State University. Lately, though, these conflicts have disrupted the effective functioning of the Division. Division Head, Professor Yogi Zen, has decided to examine the social structure of the Division as a preliminary to taking some action to improve the situation. Multidimensional scaling has been selected as a tool through which this goal might be achieved.

Obtaining Proximities between Stimulus Elements
Professor Zen's first task is to obtain a matrix of proximities between all members of the faculty of the Division. He has used a 1–9 scale in rating the "similarity" between all of the nine faculty members (where 1 = highly similar; 10 = highly dissimilar) as shown in Table 18.5.

Scaling the Proximities
Next, these proximities are analyzed using multidimensional scaling analysis. One- through three-dimensional solutions are generated yielding Kruskal stress values of .31, .13, and .04, respectively. Squared correlations between proximities and mapped distances for the one- through three-dimensional solutions are .75, .92, and .99. On the basis of these indicators of stress, and based on the number of elements being mapped (Equation 18.1), the two-dimensional solution is adopted for further consideration. This solution is presented in Figure 18.4.

Each faculty member is represented by number in this stimulus map. Those judged by Professor Zen to be quite similar (e.g., faculty members 3 and 4) are located fairly close together; those judged to be less similar (e.g., faculty members 7 and 5) are more distant. The map summarizes graphically Professor Zen's original similarity judgments in a manner that makes these judgments more useful in helping us to understand his perceptions of the social structure of the Division.

Interpreting the Solution
Using a neighborhood approach to interpreting the map, we see that five faculty members (1, 2, 3, 4, and 7) form a fairly homogeneous cluster (clique?). Based on his personal knowledge, Dr. Zen might notice that these faculty members share in common active

TABLE 18.5 Ratings of Similarity Between Nine Members of the Faculty of the Division of Metaphysical Sciences (1 = Highly Similar; 10 = Highly Dissimilar)

Faculty Members	Faculty Members: 1	2	3	4	5	6	7	8	9
1	—								
2	4	—							
3	3	4	—						
4	2	4	2	—					
5	8	8	9	9	—				
6	6	8	8	8	7	—			
7	3	3	3	3	8	9	—		
8	7	6	8	8	5	2	7	—	
9	8	6	6	7	6	5	8	8	—

continued

BOX 18.1—*continued*

Figure 18.4

Two-dimensional multidimensional scaling solution for the proximity data presented in Table 18.5. Faculty members are represented by their numbers. Included are vectors representing the attributes Clinical-Experimental and Humanistic-Behavioristic.

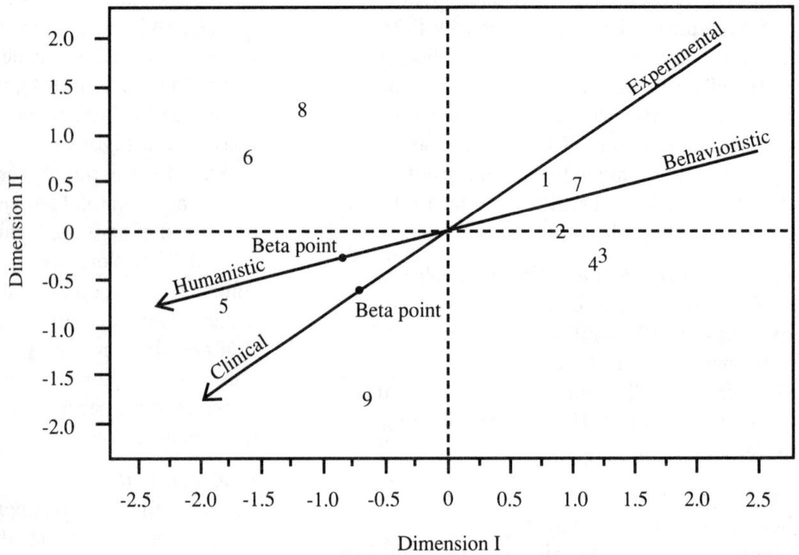

research interests. Other faculty members (5, 6, 8, and 9) are relatively unique, nonmembers of this cluster. Dr. Zen might recall that these faculty members do not engage in much research activity.

In order to explore the continuous dimensions along which the faculty vary, Professor Zen has rated each of the nine members of the faculty on each of 10 7-point bipolar attribute scales. These ratings and coordinates for each faculty member in the stimulus map are given in Table 18.6.

Using the data of Table 18.6, a series of 10 multiple regression analyses are performed next. In each analysis, ratings on one attribute scale are regressed on the stimulus map coordinates. Thus, in the first regression analysis, ratings on the first attribute scale (Tall–Short) serve as the dependent (criterion) variable and the Dimension I and Dimension II coordinates serve as independent (predictor) variables. The second regression analysis treats ratings on the second attribute scale (Young–Old) as the dependent variable, with dimension coordinates again serving as the independent variables. In a similar manner, all attributes are analyzed in a series of 10 multiple regression analyses. The results of these analyses are summarized in Table 18.7.

Ratings on two attribute scales (Behavioristic–Humanistic and Experimental–Clinical) are significantly correlated ($p < .05$) with the positioning of faculty members in the multidimensional scaling solution. Thus, it may be concluded that, of the 10 attributes examined, these two attributes figured most prominently in Professor Zen's judgments of the "similarity" of faculty members.

These two salient attributes are next positioned as vectors in Figure 18.4 using the procedure described by Schiffman, Reynolds, and Young (1981). The beta point for the attribute dimension Behavioristic–Humanistic is located using, as coordinates, the beta

TABLE 18.6 Coordinates of Nine Faculty Members in the Two-Dimensional Stimulus Map Depicted in Figure 18.4 and Ratings of These Faculty Members on 10 Bipolar Attribute Scales

Faculty	Dim. 1	Dim. 2	Tall–Short	Young–Old	Loud–Soft	Strong–Weak	Friendly–Unfriendly	Behaviorist–Humanist	Experimental–Clinical	Calm–Agitated	Good–Bad	Deep–Shallow
1	.78	.65	2	2	2	3	3	3	3	2	4	2
2	.96	.00	3	3	2	2	4	3	3	3	3	5
3	1.10	− .36	2	3	2	4	6	2	3	2	5	3
4	1.10	− .36	3	4	3	3	4	3	3	2	3	3
5	−1.69	− .79	7	4	2	3	3	7	5	7	6	4
6	−1.55	.73	3	6	6	5	5	5	6	3	1	6
7	1.04	.48	3	4	4	5	5	3	3	3	4	2
8	−1.08	1.24	3	4	2	2	5	5	3	2	2	6
9	− .65	−1.58	2	6	5	5	2	6	7	2	4	4

TABLE 18.7 Summary of Results of 10 Multiple Regression Analyses Used in Interpreting the Dimensional Characteristics of the Multidimensional Scaling Solution Depicted in Figure 18.4

Attribute Scales	R^2	F	p	$Beta_1$	$Beta_2$
Tall–Short	.31	1.36	.32	−.53	−.17
Young–Old	.46	2.60	.15	−.62	−.28
Loud–Soft	.12	.42	.68	−.33	−.11
Strong–Weak	.08	.27	.77	−.09	−.27
Friendly–Unfriendly	.37	1.76	.25	.22	.56
Behaviorist–Humanist	.90	28.55	.0009	−.91	−.26
Experimental–Clinical	.74	8.36	.0184	−.68	−.51
Calm–Agitated	.31	1.38	.32	−.51	−.24
Good–Bad	.38	1.85	.24	−.59	.18
Deep–Shallow	.51	3.15	.12	−.68	.23

continued

weights for the first and second dimensions (−.91 and −.26, respectively). A line drawn through this beta point and the origin of the map represents the attribute. An arrowhead placed on the end of the line nearest the beta point shows the directionality of the attribute through the space. Faculty members at this end of the vector received higher numerical ratings on the attribute Behavioristic–Humanistic; they are perceived as more humanistic. Faculty members at the opposite end of the attribute vector received lower scores on the attribute; they are perceived as more behavioristic. A vector representing the attribute Experimental–Clinical is positioned in a similar fashion. Coordinates for this vector's beta point again correspond to the beta weights for dimensions 1 and 2 from the multiple regression equation: −.68 on Dimension 1 and −.51 on Dimension 2. A line through this point and the origin of the map represents the attribute, and an arrow on the end of the line nearest the beta point shows that faculty members toward this end of the attribute vector are more clinical in orientation, while faculty at the opposite end of the vector are more experimental.

In addition to identifying the salient dimensions that organize Professor Zen's perception of his Division, the attribute vectors help to define the neighborhoods of the multidimensional scaling solution. As is seen too often in the metaphysical sciences, there is a schism in Professor Zen's Division between clinical humanists (located toward the left of the map) and behavioristic experimentalists (located toward the right side of the map).

proximities possess the characteristics of ordinal scale data. This approach is sometimes called **nonmetric scaling** and was used in Box 18.1. Multidimensional scaling programs typically allow the user to specify which scale of measurement is assumed to exist in the proximities.

Number of "Ways"

It has also been convenient in this chapter to describe how multidimensional scaling analysis transforms a single matrix of interelement proximities into a spatial configuration of points. This single proximities matrix may be generated by one subject or may be based on averaged judgments from several subjects, but the multidimensional scaling solution represents just one matrix. The analysis of a single proximities matrix is called a "two-way" analysis, the first "way" referring to the rows of the matrix, and the second "way" referring to the columns of the matrix.

Some multidimensional scaling analyses, called **individual differences multidimensional scaling analyses,** provide for a "three-way" analysis. In this type of analysis, each of several subjects provides a separate proximities matrix. The third "way" then, refers to subjects. A three-way analysis produces both a map of stimulus elements, based on the averaged interelement proximities from the several subjects, and a **subject map.** In this subject map, subjects are represented as points and the similarities between their proximity matrices are transformed into distances between points, such that subjects whose judgments are similar will be located near each other in the subject map and subjects whose judgments are dissimilar will be located further apart. The third "way" in three-way multidimensional scaling analysis may also correspond to occasions, as, for example, when proximities data are obtained on two or more occasions. In this situation, of course, the "subject map" describes changes in perception across occasions.

SUMMARY

Multidimensional scaling analysis, like cluster analysis, is a technique for analyzing interelement proximity data. However, while cluster analysis identifies discrete sets of relatively homogeneous elements, multidimensional scaling identifies the continuous dimensions along which elements vary. The basic output of multidimensional scaling analysis is a stimulus map in which elements are depicted as points and the distances between these points reflect the proximities of the input data. Thus, multidimensional scaling analysis is a descriptive method useful in depicting graphically what would otherwise be an indigestibly large amount of numerical information. Multidimensional scaling solutions can take on any specified dimensionality and determining the "correct" dimensionality of the solution is often more art than science. However, measures of the goodness-of-fit between interelement distances in the multidimensional scaling map and the original interelement proximities can be used in selecting the "correct" solution. The interpretability of solutions also plays a key role in selecting a solution. Interpreting the multidimensional scaling solution may be approached using the neighborhood and/or regression methods. The neighborhood approach identifies groups or clusters of similar elements in the stimulus map and seeks to label these groups. The regression approach identifies attribute dimensions which are strongly related to the positioning of elements in the stimulus map. Multidimensional scaling analyses can be distinguished on the basis of the level of measurement that is assumed to exist in the interelement proximities and according to how many proximity matrices are analyzed.

APPENDIX A

TABLE OF AREAS UNDER THE NORMAL CURVE

(A) z	(B) area between mean and z	(C) area beyond z	(A) z	(B) area between mean and z	(C) area beyond z	(A) z	(B) area between mean and z	(C) area beyond z
0.00	.0000	.5000	0.55	.2088	.2912	1.10	.3643	.1357
0.01	.0040	.4960	0.56	.2123	.2877	1.11	.3665	.1335
0.02	.0080	.4920	0.57	.2157	.2843	1.12	.3686	.1314
0.03	.0120	.4880	0.58	.2190	.2810	1.13	.3708	.1292
0.04	.0160	.4840	0.59	.2224	.2776	1.14	.3729	.1271
0.05	.0199	.4801	0.60	.2257	.2743	1.15	.3749	.1251
0.06	.0239	.4761	0.61	.2291	.2709	1.16	.3770	.1230
0.07	.0279	.4721	0.62	.2324	.2676	1.17	.3790	.1210
0.08	.0319	.4681	0.63	.2357	.2643	1.18	.3810	.1190
0.09	.0359	.4641	0.64	.2389	.2611	1.19	.3830	.1170
0.10	.0398	.4602	0.65	.2422	.2578	1.20	.3849	.1151
0.11	.0438	.4562	0.66	.2454	.2546	1.21	.3869	.1131
0.12	.0478	.4522	0.67	.2486	.2514	1.22	.3888	.1112
0.13	.0517	.4483	0.68	.2517	.2483	1.23	.3907	.1093
0.14	.0557	.4443	0.69	.2549	.2451	1.24	.3925	.1075
0.15	.0596	.4404	0.70	.2580	.2420	1.25	.3944	.1056
0.16	.0636	.4364	0.71	.2611	.2389	1.26	.3962	.1038
0.17	.0675	.4325	0.72	.2642	.2358	1.27	.3980	.1020
0.18	.0714	.4286	0.73	.2673	.2327	1.28	.3997	.1003
0.19	.0753	.4247	0.74	.2704	.2296	1.29	.4015	.0985
0.20	.0793	.4207	0.75	.2734	.2266	1.30	.4032	.0968
0.21	.0832	.4168	0.76	.2764	.2236	1.31	.4049	.0951
0.22	.0871	.4129	0.77	.2794	.2206	1.32	.4066	.0934
0.23	.0910	.4090	0.78	.2823	.2177	1.33	.4082	.0918
0.24	.0948	.4052	0.79	.2852	.2148	1.34	.4099	.0901
0.25	.0987	.4013	0.80	.2881	.2119	1.35	.4115	.0885
0.26	.1026	.3974	0.81	.2910	.2090	1.36	.4131	.0869
0.27	.1064	.3936	0.82	.2939	.2061	1.37	.4147	.0853
0.28	.1103	.3897	0.83	.2967	.2033	1.38	.4162	.0838
0.29	.1141	.3859	0.84	.2995	.2005	1.39	.4177	.0823
0.30	.1179	.3821	0.85	.3023	.1977	1.40	.4192	.0808
0.31	.1217	.3783	0.86	.3051	.1949	1.41	.4207	.0793
0.32	.1255	.3745	0.87	.3078	.1922	1.42	.4222	.0778
0.33	.1293	.3707	0.88	.3106	.1894	1.43	.4236	.0764
0.34	.1331	.3669	0.89	.3133	.1867	1.44	.4251	.0749
0.35	.1368	.3632	0.90	.3159	.1841	1.45	.4265	.0735
0.36	.1406	.3594	0.91	.3186	.1814	1.46	.4279	.0721
0.37	.1443	.3557	0.92	.3212	.1788	1.47	.4292	.0708
0.38	.1480	.3520	0.93	.3238	.1762	1.48	.4306	.0694
0.39	.1517	.3483	0.94	.3264	.1736	1.49	.4319	.0681
0.40	.1554	.3446	0.95	.3289	.1711	1.50	.4332	.0668
0.41	.1591	.3409	0.96	.3315	.1685	1.51	.4345	.0655
0.42	.1628	.3372	0.97	.3340	.1660	1.52	.4357	.0643
0.43	.1664	.3336	0.98	.3365	.1635	1.53	.4370	.0630
0.44	.1700	.3300	0.99	.3389	.1611	1.54	.4382	.0618
0.45	.1736	.3264	1.00	.3413	.1587	1.55	.4394	.0606
0.46	.1772	.3228	1.01	.3438	.1562	1.56	.4406	.0594
0.47	.1808	.3192	1.02	.3461	.1539	1.57	.4418	.0582
0.48	.1844	.3156	1.03	.3485	.1515	1.58	.4429	.0571
0.49	.1879	.3121	1.04	.3508	.1492	1.59	.4441	.0559
0.50	.1915	.3085	1.05	.3531	.1469	1.60	.4452	.0548
0.51	.1950	.3050	1.06	.3554	.1446	1.61	.4463	.0537
0.52	.1985	.3015	1.07	.3577	.1423	1.62	.4474	.0526
0.53	.2019	.2981	1.08	.3599	.1401	1.63	.4484	.0516
0.54	.2054	.2946	1.09	.3621	.1379	1.64	.4495	.0505

Appendix A *continued*

(A) z	(B) area between mean and z	(C) area beyond z
1.65	.4505	.0495
1.66	.4515	.0485
1.67	.4525	.0475
1.68	.4535	.0465
1.69	.4545	.0455
1.70	.4554	.0446
1.71	.4564	.0436
1.72	.4573	.0427
1.73	.4582	.0418
1.74	.4591	.0409
1.75	.4599	.0401
1.76	.4608	.0392
1.77	.4616	.0384
1.78	.4625	.0375
1.79	.4633	.0367
1.80	.4641	.0359
1.81	.4649	.0351
1.82	.4656	.0344
1.83	.4664	.0336
1.84	.4671	.0329
1.85	.4678	.0322
1.86	.4686	.0314
1.87	.4693	.0307
1.88	.4699	.0301
1.89	.4706	.0294
1.90	.4713	.0287
1.91	.4719	.0281
1.92	.4726	.0274
1.93	.4732	.0268
1.94	.4738	.0262
1.95	.4744	.0256
1.96	.4750	.0250
1.97	.4756	.0244
1.98	.4761	.0239
1.99	.4767	.0233
2.00	.4772	.0228
2.01	.4778	.0222
2.02	.4783	.0217
2.03	.4788	.0212
2.04	.4793	.0207
2.05	.4798	.0202
2.06	.4803	.0197
2.07	.4808	.0192
2.08	.4812	.0188
2.09	.4817	.0183
2.10	.4821	.0179
2.11	.4826	.0174
2.12	.4830	.0170
2.13	.4834	.0166
2.14	.4838	.0162
2.15	.4842	.0158
2.16	.4846	.0154
2.17	.4850	.0150
2.18	.4854	.0146
2.19	.4857	.0143
2.20	.4861	.0139
2.21	.4864	.0136
2.22	.4868	.0132
2.23	.4871	.0129
2.24	.4875	.0125
2.25	.4878	.0122
2.26	.4881	.0119
2.27	.4884	.0116
2.28	.4887	.0113
2.29	.4890	.0110
2.30	.4893	.0107
2.31	.4896	.0104
2.32	.4898	.0102
2.33	.4901	.0099
2.34	.4904	.0096
2.35	.4906	.0094
2.36	.4909	.0091
2.37	.4911	.0089
2.38	.4913	.0087
2.39	.4916	.0084
2.40	.4918	.0082
2.41	.4920	.0080
2.42	.4922	.0078
2.43	.4925	.0075
2.44	.4927	.0073
2.45	.4929	.0071
2.46	.4931	.0069
2.47	.4932	.0068
2.48	.4934	.0066
2.49	.4936	.0064
2.50	.4938	.0062
2.51	.4940	.0060
2.52	.4941	.0059
2.53	.4943	.0057
2.54	.4945	.0055
2.55	.4946	.0054
2.56	.4948	.0052
2.57	.4949	.0051
2.58	.4951	.0049
2.59	.4952	.0048
2.60	.4953	.0047
2.61	.4955	.0045
2.62	.4956	.0044
2.63	.4957	.0043
2.64	.4959	.0041
2.65	.4960	.0040
2.66	.4961	.0039
2.67	.4962	.0038
2.68	.4963	.0037
2.69	.4964	.0036
2.70	.4965	.0035
2.71	.4966	.0034
2.72	.4967	.0033
2.73	.4968	.0032
2.74	.4969	.0031
2.75	.4970	.0030
2.76	.4971	.0029
2.77	.4972	.0028
2.78	.4973	.0027
2.79	.4974	.0026
2.80	.4974	.0026
2.81	.4975	.0025
2.82	.4976	.0024
2.83	.4977	.0023
2.84	.4977	.0023
2.85	.4978	.0022
2.86	.4979	.0021
2.87	.4979	.0021
2.88	.4980	.0020
2.89	.4981	.0019
2.90	.4981	.0019
2.91	.4982	.0018
2.92	.4982	.0018
2.93	.4983	.0017
2.94	.4984	.0016
2.95	.4984	.0016
2.96	.4985	.0015
2.97	.4985	.0015
2.98	.4986	.0014
2.99	.4986	.0014
3.00	.4987	.0013
3.01	.4987	.0013
3.02	.4987	.0013
3.03	.4988	.0012
3.04	.4988	.0012
3.05	.4989	.0011
3.06	.4989	.0011
3.07	.4989	.0011
3.08	.4990	.0010
3.09	.4990	.0010
3.10	.4990	.0010
3.11	.4991	.0009
3.12	.4991	.0009
3.13	.4991	.0009
3.14	.4992	.0008
3.15	.4992	.0008
3.16	.4992	.0008
3.17	.4992	.0008
3.18	.4993	.0007
3.19	.4993	.0007
3.20	.4993	.0007
3.21	.4993	.0007
3.22	.4994	.0006
3.23	.4994	.0006
3.24	.4994	.0006
3.25	.4994	.0006
3.30	.4995	.0005
3.35	.4996	.0004
3.40	.4997	.0003
3.45	.4997	.0003
3.50	.4998	.0002
3.60	.4998	.0002
3.70	.4999	.0001
3.80	.4999	.0001
3.90	.49995	.00005
4.00	.49997	.00003

Source: Taken from Table A (pp. 459–60) of R. P. Runyon & A. Haber, *Fundamentals of Behavioral Statistics*, 6th ed. Published by McGraw-Hill, New York. Reprinted by permission.

APPENDIX B

CRITICAL VALUES OF t

df	Level of significance for one-tailed test					
	.10	.05	.025	.01	.005	.0005
	Level of significance for two-tailed test					
	.20	.10	.05	.02	.01	.001
1	3.078	6.314	12.706	31.821	63.657	636.619
2	1.886	2.920	4.303	6.965	9.925	31.598
3	1.638	2.353	3.182	4.541	5.841	12.941
4	1.533	2.132	2.776	3.747	4.604	8.610
5	1.476	2.015	2.571	3.365	4.032	6.859
6	1.440	1.943	2.447	3.143	3.707	5.959
7	1.415	1.895	2.365	2.998	3.499	5.405
8	1.397	1.860	2.306	2.896	3.355	5.041
9	1.383	1.833	2.262	2.821	3.250	4.781
10	1.372	1.812	2.228	2.764	3.169	4.587
11	1.363	1.796	2.201	2.718	3.106	4.437
12	1.356	1.782	2.179	2.681	3.055	4.318
13	1.350	1.771	2.160	2.650	3.012	4.221
14	1.345	1.761	2.145	2.624	2.977	4.140
15	1.341	1.753	2.131	2.602	2.947	4.073
16	1.337	1.746	2.120	2.583	2.921	4.015
17	1.333	1.740	2.110	2.567	2.898	3.965
18	1.330	1.734	2.101	2.552	2.878	3.922
19	1.328	1.729	2.093	2.539	2.861	3.883
20	1.325	1.725	2.086	2.528	2.845	3.850
21	1.323	1.721	2.080	2.518	2.831	3.819
22	1.321	1.717	2.074	2.508	2.819	3.792
23	1.319	1.714	2.069	2.500	2.807	3.767
24	1.318	1.711	2.064	2.492	2.797	3.745
25	1.316	1.708	2.060	2.485	2.787	3.725
26	1.315	1.706	2.056	2.479	2.779	3.707
27	1.314	1.703	2.052	2.473	2.771	3.690
28	1.313	1.701	2.048	2.467	2.763	3.674
29	1.311	1.699	2.045	2.462	2.756	3.659
30	1.310	1.697	2.042	2.457	2.750	3.646
40	1.303	1.684	2.021	2.423	2.704	3.551
60	1.296	1.671	2.000	2.390	2.660	3.460
120	1.289	1.658	1.980	2.358	2.617	3.373
∞	1.282	1.645	1.960	2.326	2.576	3.291

Source: "Appendix B is taken from Table III of Fisher & Yates': *Statistical Tables for Biological, Agricultural, and Medical Research* published by Longman Group UK Ltd. London (previously published by Oliver and Boyd Ltd, Edinburgh) and by permission of the authors and publishers."

APPENDIX C

CRITICAL VALUES OF CHI-SQUARE

Level of Significance

Degrees of freedom df	.10	.05	.02	.01
1	2.706	3.841	5.412	6.635
2	4.605	5.991	7.824	9.210
3	6.251	7.815	9.837	11.341
4	7.779	9.488	11.668	13.277
5	9.236	11.070	13.388	15.086
6	10.645	12.592	15.033	16.812
7	12.017	14.067	16.622	18.475
8	13.362	15.507	18.168	20.090
9	14.684	16.919	19.679	21.666
10	15.987	18.307	21.161	23.209
11	17.275	19.675	22.618	24.725
12	18.549	21.026	24.054	26.217
13	19.812	22.362	25.472	27.688
14	21.064	23.685	26.873	29.141
15	22.307	24.996	28.259	30.578
16	23.542	26.296	29.633	32.000
17	24.769	27.587	30.995	33.409
18	25.989	28.869	32.346	34.805
19	27.204	30.144	33.687	36.191
20	28.412	31.410	35.020	37.566
21	29.615	32.671	36.343	38.932
22	30.813	33.924	37.659	40.289
23	32.007	35.172	38.968	41.638
24	33.196	36.415	40.270	42.980
25	34.382	37.652	41.566	44.314
26	35.563	38.885	42.856	45.642
27	36.741	40.113	44.140	46.963
28	37.916	41.337	45.419	48.278
29	39.087	42.557	46.693	49.588
30	40.256	43.773	47.962	50.892

Source: Taken from Table B (p. 461) of R. P. Runyon & A. Haber, *Fundamentals of Behavioral Statistics*, 6th ed. Published by McGraw-Hill, New York. Reprinted by permission.

APPENDIX D

CRITICAL VALUES OF *A*

	Level of significance for one-tailed test					
	.05	.025	.01	.005	.0005	
	Level of significance for two-tailed test					
$N-1$*	.10	.05	.02	.01	.001	$N-1$*
1	0.5125	0.5031	0.50049	0.50012	0.5000012	1
2	0.412	0.369	0.347	0.340	0.334	2
3	0.385	0.324	0.286	0.272	0.254	3
4	0.376	0.304	0.257	0.238	0.211	4
5	0.372	0.293	0.240	0.218	0.184	5
6	0.370	0.286	0.230	0.205	0.167	6
7	0.369	0.281	0.222	0.196	0.155	7
8	0.368	0.278	0.217	0.190	0.146	8
9	0.368	0.276	0.213	0.185	0.139	9
10	0.368	0.274	0.210	0.181	0.134	10
11	0.368	0.273	0.207	0.178	0.130	11
12	0.368	0.271	0.205	0.176	0.126	12
13	0.368	0.270	0.204	0.174	0.124	13
14	0.368	0.270	0.202	0.172	0.121	14
15	0.368	0.269	0.201	0.170	0.119	15
16	0.368	0.268	0.200	0.169	0.117	16
17	0.368	0.268	0.199	0.168	0.116	17
18	0.368	0.267	0.198	0.167	0.114	18
19	0.368	0.267	0.197	0.166	0.113	19
20	0.368	0.266	0.197	0.165	0.112	20
21	0.368	0.266	0.196	0.165	0.111	21
22	0.368	0.266	0.196	0.164	0.110	22
23	0.368	0.266	0.195	0.163	0.109	23
24	0.368	0.265	0.195	0.163	0.108	24
25	0.368	0.265	0.194	0.162	0.108	25
26	0.368	0.265	0.194	0.162	0.107	26
27	0.368	0.265	0.193	0.161	0.107	27
28	0.368	0.265	0.193	0.161	0.106	28
29	0.368	0.264	0.193	0.161	0.106	29
30	0.368	0.264	0.193	0.160	0.105	30
40	0.368	0.263	0.191	0.158	0.102	40
60	0.369	0.262	0.189	0.155	0.099	60
120	0.369	0.261	0.187	0.153	0.095	120
∞	0.370	0.260	0.185	0.151	0.092	∞

*N = number of pairs

Source: Taken from Table E (p. 468) of R. P. Runyon & A. Haber, *Fundamentals of Behavioral Statistics*, 6th ed. Published by McGraw-Hill, New York. Reprinted by permission.

APPENDIX E

CRITICAL VALUES OF *U*

Critical values for a one-tail test at .05 significance level or two-tail test at .10 significance level.

N_2 \ N_1	1	2	3	4	5	6	7	8	9	10	11	12	13	14	15	16	17	18	19	20
1	--	--	--	--	--	--	--	--	--	--	--	--	--	--	--	--	--	--	0 19	0 20
2	--	--	--	--	0 10	0 12	0 14	1 15	1 17	1 19	1 21	2 22	2 24	2 26	3 27	3 29	3 31	4 32	4 34	4 36
3	--	--	0 9	0 12	1 14	2 16	2 19	3 21	3 24	4 26	5 28	5 31	6 33	7 35	7 38	8 40	9 42	9 45	10 47	11 49
4	--	--	0 12	1 15	2 18	3 21	4 24	5 27	6 30	7 33	8 36	9 39	10 42	11 45	12 48	14 50	15 53	16 56	17 59	18 62
5	--	0 10	1 14	2 18	4 21	5 25	6 29	8 32	9 36	11 39	12 43	13 47	15 50	16 54	18 57	19 61	20 65	22 68	23 72	25 75
6	--	0 12	2 16	3 21	5 25	7 29	8 34	10 38	12 42	14 46	16 50	17 55	19 59	21 63	23 67	25 71	26 76	28 80	30 84	32 88
7	--	0 14	2 19	4 24	6 29	8 34	11 38	13 43	15 48	17 53	19 58	21 63	24 67	26 72	28 77	30 82	33 86	35 91	37 96	39 101
8	--	1 15	3 21	5 27	8 32	10 38	13 43	15 49	18 54	20 60	23 65	26 70	28 76	31 81	33 87	36 92	39 97	41 103	44 108	47 113
9	--	1 17	3 24	6 30	9 36	12 42	15 48	18 54	21 60	24 66	27 72	30 78	33 84	36 90	39 96	42 102	45 108	48 114	51 120	54 126
10	--	1 19	4 26	7 33	11 39	14 46	17 53	20 60	24 66	27 73	31 79	34 86	37 93	41 99	44 106	48 112	51 119	55 125	58 132	62 138
11	--	1 21	5 28	8 36	12 43	16 50	19 58	23 65	27 72	31 79	34 87	38 94	42 101	46 108	50 115	54 122	57 130	61 137	65 144	69 151
12	--	2 22	5 31	9 39	13 47	17 55	21 63	26 70	30 78	34 86	38 94	42 102	47 109	51 117	55 125	60 132	64 140	68 148	72 156	77 163
13	--	2 24	6 33	10 42	15 50	19 59	24 67	28 76	33 84	37 93	42 101	47 109	51 118	56 126	61 134	65 143	70 151	75 159	80 167	84 176
14	--	2 26	7 35	11 45	16 54	21 63	26 72	31 81	36 90	41 99	46 108	51 117	56 126	61 135	66 144	71 153	77 161	82 170	87 179	92 188
15	--	3 27	7 38	12 48	18 57	23 67	28 77	33 87	39 96	44 106	50 115	55 125	61 134	66 144	72 153	77 163	83 172	88 182	94 191	100 200
16	--	3 29	8 40	14 50	19 61	25 71	30 82	36 92	42 102	48 112	54 122	60 132	65 143	71 153	77 163	83 173	89 183	95 193	101 203	107 213
17	--	3 31	9 42	15 53	20 65	26 76	33 86	39 97	45 108	51 119	57 130	64 140	70 151	77 161	83 172	89 183	96 193	102 204	109 214	115 225
18	--	4 32	9 45	16 56	22 68	28 80	35 91	41 103	48 114	55 123	61 137	68 148	75 159	82 170	88 182	95 193	102 204	109 215	116 226	123 237
19	0 19	4 34	10 47	17 59	23 72	30 84	37 96	44 108	51 120	58 132	65 144	72 156	80 167	87 179	94 191	101 203	109 214	116 226	123 238	130 250
20	0 20	4 36	11 49	18 62	25 75	32 88	39 101	47 113	54 126	62 138	69 151	77 163	84 176	92 188	100 200	107 213	115 225	123 237	130 250	138 262

(Dashes in the body of the table indicate that no decision is possible at the stated level of significance.)

Source: Taken from Table I (pp. 473–76) of R. P. Runyon & A. Haber, *Fundamentals of Behavioral Staistics*, 6th ed. Published by McGraw-Hill, New York. Reprinted by permission.

Critical values for a one-tail test at .025 significance level or two-tail test at .05 significance level.

N_2 \ N_1	1	2	3	4	5	6	7	8	9	10	11	12	13	14	15	16	17	18	19	20
1	--	--	--	--	--	--	--	--	--	--	--	--	--	--	--	--	--	--	--	--
2	--	--	--	--	--	--	--	0 / 16	0 / 18	0 / 20	0 / 22	1 / 23	1 / 25	1 / 27	1 / 29	1 / 31	2 / 32	2 / 34	2 / 36	2 / 38
3	--	--	--	--	0 / 15	1 / 17	1 / 20	2 / 22	2 / 25	3 / 27	3 / 30	4 / 32	4 / 35	5 / 37	5 / 40	6 / 42	6 / 45	7 / 47	7 / 50	8 / 52
4	--	--	--	0 / 16	1 / 19	2 / 22	3 / 25	4 / 28	4 / 32	5 / 35	6 / 38	7 / 41	8 / 44	9 / 47	10 / 50	11 / 53	11 / 57	12 / 60	13 / 63	13 / 67
5	--	--	0 / 15	1 / 19	2 / 23	3 / 27	5 / 30	6 / 34	7 / 38	8 / 42	9 / 46	11 / 49	12 / 53	13 / 57	14 / 61	15 / 65	17 / 68	18 / 72	19 / 76	20 / 80
6	--	--	1 / 17	2 / 22	3 / 27	5 / 31	6 / 36	8 / 40	10 / 44	11 / 49	13 / 53	14 / 58	16 / 62	17 / 67	19 / 71	21 / 75	22 / 80	24 / 84	25 / 89	27 / 93
7	--	--	1 / 20	3 / 25	5 / 30	6 / 36	8 / 41	10 / 46	12 / 51	14 / 56	16 / 61	18 / 66	20 / 71	22 / 76	24 / 81	26 / 86	28 / 91	30 / 96	32 / 101	34 / 106
8	--	0 / 16	2 / 22	4 / 28	6 / 34	8 / 40	10 / 46	13 / 51	15 / 57	17 / 63	19 / 69	22 / 74	24 / 80	26 / 86	29 / 91	31 / 97	34 / 102	36 / 108	38 / 111	41 / 119
9	--	0 / 18	2 / 25	4 / 32	7 / 38	10 / 44	12 / 51	15 / 57	17 / 64	20 / 70	23 / 76	26 / 82	28 / 89	31 / 95	34 / 101	37 / 107	39 / 114	42 / 120	45 / 126	48 / 132
10	--	0 / 20	3 / 27	5 / 35	8 / 42	11 / 49	14 / 56	17 / 63	20 / 70	23 / 77	26 / 84	29 / 91	33 / 97	36 / 104	39 / 111	42 / 118	45 / 125	48 / 132	52 / 138	55 / 145
11	--	0 / 22	3 / 30	6 / 38	9 / 46	13 / 53	16 / 61	19 / 69	23 / 76	26 / 84	30 / 91	33 / 99	37 / 106	40 / 114	44 / 121	47 / 129	51 / 136	55 / 143	58 / 151	62 / 158
12	--	1 / 23	4 / 32	7 / 41	11 / 49	14 / 58	18 / 66	22 / 74	26 / 82	29 / 91	33 / 99	37 / 107	41 / 115	45 / 123	49 / 131	53 / 139	57 / 147	61 / 155	65 / 163	69 / 171
13	--	1 / 25	4 / 35	8 / 44	12 / 53	16 / 62	20 / 71	24 / 80	28 / 89	33 / 97	37 / 106	41 / 115	45 / 124	50 / 132	54 / 141	59 / 149	63 / 158	67 / 167	72 / 175	76 / 184
14	--	1 / 27	5 / 37	9 / 47	13 / 51	17 / 67	22 / 76	26 / 86	31 / 95	36 / 104	40 / 114	45 / 123	50 / 132	55 / 141	59 / 151	64 / 160	67 / 171	74 / 178	78 / 188	83 / 197
15	--	1 / 29	5 / 40	10 / 50	14 / 61	19 / 71	24 / 81	29 / 91	34 / 101	39 / 111	44 / 121	49 / 131	54 / 141	59 / 151	64 / 161	70 / 170	75 / 180	80 / 190	85 / 200	90 / 210
16	--	1 / 31	6 / 42	11 / 53	15 / 65	21 / 75	26 / 86	31 / 97	37 / 107	42 / 118	47 / 129	53 / 139	59 / 149	64 / 160	70 / 170	75 / 181	81 / 191	86 / 202	92 / 212	98 / 222
17	--	2 / 32	6 / 45	11 / 57	17 / 68	22 / 80	28 / 91	34 / 102	39 / 114	45 / 125	51 / 136	57 / 147	63 / 158	67 / 171	75 / 180	81 / 191	87 / 202	93 / 213	99 / 224	105 / 235
18	--	2 / 34	7 / 47	12 / 60	18 / 72	24 / 84	30 / 96	36 / 108	42 / 120	48 / 132	55 / 143	61 / 155	67 / 167	74 / 178	80 / 190	86 / 202	93 / 213	99 / 225	106 / 236	112 / 248
19	--	2 / 36	7 / 50	13 / 63	19 / 76	25 / 89	32 / 101	38 / 114	45 / 126	52 / 138	58 / 151	65 / 163	72 / 175	78 / 188	85 / 200	92 / 212	99 / 224	106 / 236	113 / 248	119 / 261
20	--	2 / 38	8 / 52	13 / 67	20 / 80	27 / 93	34 / 106	41 / 119	48 / 132	55 / 145	62 / 158	69 / 171	76 / 184	83 / 197	90 / 210	98 / 222	105 / 235	112 / 248	119 / 261	127 / 273

(Dashes in the body of the table indicate that no decision is possible at the stated level of significance.)

Appendix E *continued*

Critical values for a one-tail test at .01 significance level or two-tail test at .02 significance level.

N_2 \ N_1	1	2	3	4	5	6	7	8	9	10	11	12	13	14	15	16	17	18	19	20
1	--	--	--	--	--	--	--	--	--	--	--	--	--	--	--	--	--	--	--	--
2	--	--	--	--	--	--	--	--	--	--	--	--	0 26	0 28	0 30	0 32	0 34	0 36	1 37	1 39
3	--	--	--	--	--	--	0 21	0 24	1 26	1 29	1 32	2 34	2 37	2 40	3 42	3 45	4 47	4 50	4 52	5 55
4	--	--	--	--	0 20	1 23	1 27	2 30	3 33	3 37	4 40	5 43	5 47	6 50	7 53	7 57	8 60	9 63	9 67	10 70
5	--	--	--	0 20	1 24	2 28	3 32	4 36	5 40	6 44	7 48	8 52	9 56	10 60	11 64	12 68	13 72	14 76	15 80	16 84
6	--	--	--	1 23	2 28	3 33	4 38	6 42	7 47	8 52	9 57	11 61	12 66	13 71	15 75	16 80	18 84	19 89	20 94	22 98
7	--	--	0 21	1 27	3 32	4 38	6 43	7 49	9 54	11 59	12 65	14 70	16 75	17 81	19 86	21 91	23 96	24 102	26 107	28 112
8	--	--	0 24	2 30	4 36	6 42	7 49	9 55	11 61	13 67	15 73	17 79	20 84	22 90	24 96	26 102	28 108	30 114	32 120	34 126
9	--	--	1 26	3 33	5 40	7 47	9 54	11 61	14 67	16 74	18 81	21 87	23 94	26 100	28 107	31 113	33 120	36 126	38 133	40 140
10	--	--	1 29	3 37	6 44	8 52	11 59	13 67	16 74	19 81	22 88	24 96	27 103	30 110	33 117	36 124	38 132	41 139	44 146	47 153
11	--	--	1 32	4 40	7 48	9 57	12 65	15 73	18 81	22 88	25 96	28 104	31 112	34 120	37 128	41 135	44 143	47 151	50 159	53 167
12	--	--	2 34	5 43	8 52	11 61	14 70	17 79	21 87	24 96	28 104	31 113	35 121	38 130	42 138	46 146	49 155	53 163	56 172	60 180
13	--	0 26	2 37	5 47	9 56	12 66	16 75	20 84	23 94	27 103	31 112	35 121	39 130	43 139	47 148	51 157	55 166	59 175	63 184	67 193
14	--	0 28	2 40	6 50	10 60	13 71	17 81	22 90	26 100	30 110	34 120	38 130	43 139	47 149	51 159	56 168	60 178	65 187	69 197	73 207
15	--	0 30	3 42	7 53	11 64	15 75	19 86	24 96	28 107	33 117	37 128	42 138	47 148	51 159	56 169	61 179	66 189	70 200	75 210	80 220
16	--	0 32	3 45	7 57	12 68	16 80	21 91	26 102	31 113	36 124	41 135	46 146	51 157	56 168	61 179	66 190	71 201	76 212	82 222	87 233
17	--	0 34	4 47	8 60	13 72	18 84	23 96	28 108	33 120	38 132	44 143	49 155	55 166	60 178	66 189	71 201	77 212	82 224	88 234	93 247
18	--	0 36	4 50	9 63	14 76	19 89	24 102	30 114	36 126	41 139	47 151	53 163	59 175	65 187	70 200	76 212	82 224	88 236	94 248	100 260
19	--	1 37	4 53	9 67	15 80	20 94	26 107	32 120	38 133	44 146	50 159	56 172	63 184	69 197	75 210	82 222	88 235	94 248	101 260	107 273
20	--	1 39	5 55	10 70	16 84	22 98	28 112	34 126	40 140	47 153	53 167	60 180	67 193	73 207	80 220	87 233	93 247	100 260	107 273	114 286

(Dashes in the body of the table indicate that no decision is possible at the stated level of significance.)

Appendix E *continued*

Critical values for a one-tail test at .005 significance level or two-tail test at .01 significance level.

N_2 \ N_1	1	2	3	4	5	6	7	8	9	10	11	12	13	14	15	16	17	18	19	20
1	--	--	--	--	--	--	--	--	--	--	--	--	--	--	--	--	--	--	--	--
2	--	--	--	--	--	--	--	--	--	--	--	--	--	--	--	--	--	--	0 38	0 40
3	--	--	--	--	--	--	--	--	0 27	0 30	0 33	1 35	1 38	1 41	2 43	2 46	2 49	2 52	3 54	3 57
4	--	--	--	--	--	0 24	0 28	1 31	1 35	2 38	2 42	3 45	3 49	4 52	5 55	5 59	6 62	6 66	7 69	8 72
5	--	--	--	--	0 25	1 29	1 34	2 38	3 42	4 46	5 50	6 54	7 58	7 63	8 67	9 71	10 75	11 79	12 83	13 87
6	--	--	--	0 24	1 29	2 34	3 39	4 44	5 49	6 54	7 59	9 63	10 68	11 73	12 78	13 83	15 87	16 92	17 97	18 102
7	--	--	--	0 28	1 34	3 39	4 45	6 50	7 56	9 61	10 67	12 72	13 78	15 83	16 89	18 94	19 100	21 105	22 111	24 116
8	--	--	--	1 31	2 38	4 44	6 50	7 57	9 63	11 69	13 75	15 81	17 87	18 94	20 100	22 106	24 112	26 118	28 124	30 130
9	--	--	0 27	1 35	3 42	5 49	7 56	9 63	11 70	13 77	16 83	18 90	20 97	22 104	24 111	27 117	29 124	31 131	33 138	36 144
10	--	--	0 30	2 38	4 46	6 54	9 61	11 69	13 77	16 84	18 92	21 99	24 106	26 114	29 121	31 129	34 136	37 143	39 151	42 158
11	--	--	0 33	2 42	5 50	7 59	10 67	13 75	16 83	18 92	21 100	24 108	27 116	30 124	33 132	36 140	39 148	42 156	45 164	48 172
12	--	--	1 35	3 45	6 54	9 63	12 72	15 81	18 90	21 99	24 108	27 117	31 125	34 134	37 143	41 151	44 160	47 169	51 177	54 186
13	--	--	1 38	3 49	7 58	10 68	13 78	17 87	20 97	24 106	27 116	31 125	34 125	38 144	42 153	45 163	49 172	53 181	56 191	60 200
14	--	--	1 41	4 52	7 63	11 73	15 83	18 94	22 104	26 114	30 124	34 134	38 144	42 154	46 164	50 174	54 184	58 194	63 203	67 213
15	--	--	2 43	5 55	8 67	12 78	16 89	20 100	24 111	29 121	33 132	37 143	42 153	46 164	51 174	55 185	60 195	64 206	69 216	73 227
16	--	--	2 46	5 59	9 71	13 83	18 94	22 106	27 117	31 129	36 140	41 151	45 163	50 174	55 185	60 196	65 207	70 218	74 230	79 241
17	--	--	2 49	6 62	10 75	15 87	19 100	24 112	29 124	34 148	39 148	44 160	49 172	54 184	60 195	65 207	70 219	75 231	81 242	86 254
18	--	--	2 52	6 66	11 79	16 92	21 105	26 118	31 131	37 143	42 156	47 169	53 181	58 194	64 206	70 218	75 231	81 243	87 255	92 268
19	--	0 38	3 54	7 69	12 83	17 97	22 111	28 124	33 138	39 151	45 164	51 177	56 191	63 203	69 216	74 230	81 242	87 255	93 268	99 281
20	--	0 40	3 57	8 72	13 87	18 102	24 116	30 130	36 144	42 158	48 172	54 186	60 200	67 213	73 227	79 241	86 254	92 268	99 281	105 295

(Dashes in the body of the table indicate that no decision is possible at the stated level of significance.)

APPENDIX F

CRITICAL VALUES OF T

	Level of significance for one-tailed test			
	.05	.025	.01	.005
	Level of significance for two-tailed test			
N	.10	.05	.02	.01
5	0	--	--	--
6	2	0	--	--
7	3	2	0	--
8	5	3	1	0
9	8	5	3	1
10	10	8	5	3
11	13	10	7	5
12	17	13	9	7
13	21	17	12	9
14	25	21	15	12
15	30	25	19	15
16	35	29	23	19
17	41	34	27	23
18	47	40	32	27
19	53	46	37	32
20	60	52	43	37
21	67	58	49	42
22	75	65	55	48
23	83	73	62	54
24	91	81	69	61
25	100	89	76	68
26	110	98	84	75
27	119	107	92	83
28	130	116	101	91
29	140	126	110	100
30	151	137	120	109
31	163	147	130	118
32	175	159	140	128
33	187	170	151	138
34	200	182	162	148
35	213	195	173	159
36	227	208	185	171
37	241	221	198	182
38	256	235	211	194
39	271	249	224	207
40	286	264	238	220
41	302	279	252	233
42	319	294	266	247
43	336	310	281	261
44	353	327	296	276
45	371	343	312	291
46	389	361	328	307
47	407	378	345	322
48	426	396	362	339
49	446	415	379	355
50	466	434	397	373

Source: Taken from Table J (p. 477) of R. P. Runyon & A. Haber, *Fundamentals of Behavioral Statistics*, 6th ed. Published by McGraw-Hill, New York. Reprinted by permission.

APPENDIX G

CRITICAL VALUES OF *F*

Degrees of freedom for denominator	Degrees of freedom for numerator																							
	1	2	3	4	5	6	7	8	9	10	11	12	14	16	20	24	30	40	50	75	100	200	500	∞
1	161 **4052**	200 **4999**	216 **5403**	225 **5625**	230 **5764**	234 **5859**	237 **5928**	239 **5981**	241 **6022**	242 **6056**	243 **6082**	244 **6106**	245 **6142**	246 **6169**	248 **6208**	249 **6234**	250 **6258**	251 **6286**	252 **6302**	253 **6323**	253 **6334**	254 **6352**	254 **6361**	254 **6366**
2	18.51 **98.49**	19.00 **99.01**	19.16 **99.17**	19.25 **99.25**	19.30 **99.30**	19.33 **99.33**	19.36 **99.34**	19.37 **99.36**	19.38 **99.38**	19.39 **99.40**	19.40 **99.41**	19.41 **99.42**	19.42 **99.43**	19.43 **99.44**	19.44 **99.45**	19.45 **99.46**	19.46 **99.47**	19.47 **99.48**	19.47 **99.48**	19.48 **99.49**	19.49 **99.49**	19.49 **99.49**	19.50 **99.50**	19.50 **99.50**
3	10.13 **34.12**	9.55 **30.81**	9.28 **29.46**	9.12 **28.71**	9.01 **28.24**	8.94 **27.91**	8.88 **27.67**	8.84 **27.49**	8.81 **27.34**	8.78 **27.23**	8.76 **27.13**	8.74 **27.05**	8.71 **26.92**	8.69 **26.83**	8.66 **26.69**	8.64 **26.60**	8.62 **26.50**	8.60 **26.41**	8.58 **26.30**	8.57 **26.27**	8.56 **26.23**	8.54 **26.18**	8.54 **26.14**	8.53 **26.12**
4	7.71 **21.20**	6.94 **18.00**	6.59 **16.69**	6.39 **15.98**	6.26 **15.52**	6.16 **15.21**	6.09 **14.98**	6.04 **14.80**	6.00 **14.66**	5.96 **14.54**	5.93 **14.45**	5.91 **14.37**	5.87 **14.24**	5.84 **14.15**	5.80 **14.02**	5.77 **13.93**	5.74 **13.83**	5.71 **13.74**	5.70 **13.69**	5.68 **13.61**	5.66 **13.57**	5.65 **13.52**	5.64 **13.48**	5.63 **13.46**
5	6.61 **16.26**	5.79 **13.27**	5.41 **12.06**	5.19 **11.39**	5.05 **10.97**	4.95 **10.67**	4.88 **10.45**	4.82 **10.27**	4.78 **10.15**	4.74 **10.05**	4.70 **9.96**	4.68 **9.89**	4.64 **9.77**	4.60 **9.68**	4.56 **9.55**	4.53 **9.47**	4.50 **9.38**	4.46 **9.29**	4.44 **9.24**	4.42 **9.17**	4.40 **9.13**	4.38 **9.07**	4.37 **9.04**	4.36 **9.02**
6	5.99 **13.74**	5.14 **10.92**	4.76 **9.78**	4.53 **9.15**	4.39 **8.75**	4.28 **8.47**	4.21 **8.26**	4.15 **8.10**	4.10 **7.98**	4.06 **7.87**	4.03 **7.79**	4.00 **7.72**	3.96 **7.60**	3.92 **7.52**	3.87 **7.39**	3.84 **7.31**	3.81 **7.23**	3.77 **7.14**	3.75 **7.09**	3.72 **7.02**	3.71 **6.99**	3.69 **6.94**	3.68 **6.90**	3.67 **6.88**
7	5.59 **12.25**	4.74 **9.55**	4.35 **8.45**	4.12 **7.85**	3.97 **7.46**	3.87 **7.19**	3.79 **7.00**	3.73 **6.84**	3.68 **6.71**	3.63 **6.62**	3.60 **6.54**	3.57 **6.47**	3.52 **6.35**	3.49 **6.27**	3.44 **6.15**	3.41 **6.07**	3.38 **5.98**	3.34 **5.90**	3.32 **5.85**	3.29 **5.78**	3.28 **5.75**	3.25 **5.70**	3.24 **5.67**	3.23 **5.65**
8	5.32 **11.26**	4.46 **8.65**	4.07 **7.59**	3.84 **7.01**	3.69 **6.63**	3.58 **6.37**	3.50 **6.19**	3.44 **6.03**	3.39 **5.91**	3.34 **5.82**	3.31 **5.74**	3.28 **5.67**	3.23 **5.56**	3.20 **5.48**	3.15 **5.36**	3.12 **5.28**	3.08 **5.20**	3.05 **5.11**	3.03 **5.06**	3.00 **5.00**	2.98 **4.96**	2.96 **4.91**	2.94 **4.88**	2.93 **4.86**
9	5.12 **10.56**	4.26 **8.02**	3.86 **6.99**	3.63 **6.42**	3.48 **6.06**	3.37 **5.80**	3.29 **5.62**	3.23 **5.47**	3.18 **5.35**	3.13 **5.26**	3.10 **5.18**	3.07 **5.11**	3.02 **5.00**	2.98 **4.92**	2.93 **4.80**	2.90 **4.73**	2.86 **4.64**	2.82 **4.56**	2.80 **4.51**	2.77 **4.45**	2.76 **4.41**	2.73 **4.36**	2.72 **4.33**	2.71 **4.31**
10	4.96 **10.04**	4.10 **7.56**	3.71 **6.55**	3.48 **5.99**	3.33 **5.64**	3.22 **5.39**	3.14 **5.21**	3.07 **5.06**	3.02 **4.95**	2.97 **4.85**	2.94 **4.78**	2.91 **4.71**	2.86 **4.60**	2.82 **4.52**	2.77 **4.41**	2.74 **4.33**	2.70 **4.25**	2.67 **4.17**	2.64 **4.12**	2.61 **4.05**	2.59 **4.01**	2.56 **3.96**	2.55 **3.93**	2.54 **3.91**
11	4.84 **9.65**	3.98 **7.20**	3.59 **6.22**	3.36 **5.67**	3.20 **5.32**	3.09 **5.07**	3.01 **4.88**	2.95 **4.74**	2.90 **4.63**	2.86 **4.54**	2.82 **4.46**	2.79 **4.40**	2.74 **4.29**	2.70 **4.21**	2.65 **4.10**	2.61 **4.02**	2.57 **3.94**	2.53 **3.86**	2.50 **3.80**	2.47 **3.74**	2.45 **3.70**	2.42 **3.66**	2.41 **3.62**	2.40 **3.60**
12	4.75 **9.33**	3.88 **6.93**	3.49 **5.95**	3.26 **5.41**	3.11 **5.06**	3.00 **4.82**	2.92 **4.65**	2.85 **4.50**	2.80 **4.39**	2.76 **4.30**	2.72 **4.22**	2.69 **4.16**	2.64 **4.05**	2.60 **3.98**	2.54 **3.86**	2.50 **3.78**	2.46 **3.70**	2.42 **3.61**	2.40 **3.56**	2.36 **3.49**	2.35 **3.46**	2.32 **3.41**	2.31 **3.38**	2.30 **3.36**
13	4.67 **9.07**	3.80 **6.70**	3.41 **5.74**	3.18 **5.20**	3.02 **4.86**	2.92 **4.62**	2.84 **4.44**	2.77 **4.30**	2.72 **4.19**	2.67 **4.10**	2.63 **4.02**	2.60 **3.96**	2.55 **3.85**	2.51 **3.78**	2.46 **3.67**	2.42 **3.59**	2.38 **3.51**	2.34 **3.42**	2.32 **3.37**	2.28 **3.30**	2.26 **3.27**	2.24 **3.21**	2.22 **3.18**	2.21 **3.16**
14	4.60 **8.86**	3.74 **6.51**	3.34 **5.56**	3.11 **5.03**	2.96 **4.69**	2.85 **4.46**	2.77 **4.28**	2.70 **4.14**	2.65 **4.03**	2.60 **3.94**	2.56 **3.86**	2.53 **3.80**	2.48 **3.70**	2.44 **3.62**	2.39 **3.51**	2.35 **3.43**	2.31 **3.34**	2.27 **3.26**	2.24 **3.21**	2.21 **3.14**	2.19 **3.11**	2.16 **3.06**	2.14 **3.02**	2.13 **3.00**
15	4.54 **8.68**	3.68 **6.36**	3.29 **5.42**	3.06 **4.89**	2.90 **4.56**	2.79 **4.32**	2.70 **4.14**	2.64 **4.00**	2.59 **3.89**	2.55 **3.80**	2.51 **3.73**	2.48 **3.67**	2.43 **3.56**	2.39 **3.48**	2.33 **3.36**	2.29 **3.29**	2.25 **3.20**	2.21 **3.12**	2.18 **3.07**	2.15 **3.00**	2.12 **2.97**	2.10 **2.92**	2.08 **2.89**	2.07 **2.87**

Source: Taken from Table D (pp. 463–65) of R. P. Runyon & A. Haber, *Fundamentals of Behavioral Statistics,* 6th ed. Published by McGraw-Hill, New York. Reprinted by permission.

Appendix G *continued*

Degrees of freedom for denominator	Degrees of freedom for numerator																							
	1	2	3	4	5	6	7	8	9	10	11	12	14	16	20	24	30	40	50	75	100	200	500	∞
16	4.49 8.53	3.63 6.23	3.24 5.29	3.01 4.77	2.85 4.44	2.74 4.20	2.66 4.03	2.59 3.89	2.54 3.78	2.49 3.69	2.45 3.61	2.42 3.55	2.37 3.45	2.33 3.37	2.28 3.25	2.24 3.18	2.20 3.10	2.16 3.01	2.13 2.96	2.09 2.89	2.07 2.86	2.04 2.80	2.02 2.77	2.01 2.75
17	4.45 8.40	3.59 6.11	3.20 5.18	2.96 4.67	2.81 4.34	2.70 4.10	2.62 3.93	2.55 3.79	2.50 3.68	2.45 3.59	2.41 3.52	2.38 3.45	2.33 3.35	2.29 3.27	2.23 3.16	2.19 3.08	2.15 3.00	2.11 2.92	2.08 2.86	2.04 2.79	2.02 2.76	1.99 2.70	1.97 2.67	1.96 2.65
18	4.41 8.28	3.55 6.01	3.16 5.09	2.93 4.58	2.77 4.25	2.66 4.01	2.58 3.85	2.51 3.71	2.46 3.60	2.41 3.51	2.37 3.44	2.34 3.37	2.29 3.27	2.25 3.19	2.19 3.07	2.15 3.00	2.11 2.91	2.07 2.83	2.04 2.78	2.00 2.71	1.98 2.68	1.95 2.62	1.93 2.59	1.92 2.57
19	4.38 8.18	3.52 5.93	3.13 5.01	2.90 4.50	2.74 4.17	2.63 3.94	2.55 3.77	2.48 3.63	2.43 3.52	2.38 3.43	2.34 3.36	2.31 3.30	2.26 3.19	2.21 3.12	2.15 3.00	2.11 2.92	2.07 2.84	2.02 2.76	2.00 2.70	1.96 2.63	1.94 2.60	1.91 2.54	1.90 2.51	1.88 2.49
20	4.35 8.10	3.49 5.85	3.10 4.94	2.87 4.43	2.71 4.10	2.60 3.87	2.52 3.71	2.45 3.56	2.40 3.45	2.35 3.37	2.31 3.30	2.28 3.23	2.23 3.13	2.18 3.05	2.12 2.94	2.08 2.86	2.04 2.77	1.99 2.69	1.96 2.63	1.92 2.56	1.90 2.53	1.87 2.47	1.85 2.44	1.84 2.42
21	4.32 8.02	3.47 5.78	3.07 4.87	2.84 4.37	2.68 4.04	2.57 3.81	2.49 3.65	2.42 3.51	2.37 3.40	2.32 3.31	2.28 3.24	2.25 3.17	2.20 3.07	2.15 2.99	2.09 2.88	2.05 2.80	2.00 2.72	1.96 2.63	1.93 2.58	1.80 2.51	1.87 2.47	1.84 2.42	1.82 2.38	1.81 2.36
22	4.30 7.94	3.44 5.72	3.05 4.82	2.82 4.31	2.66 3.99	2.55 3.76	2.47 3.59	2.40 3.45	2.35 3.35	2.30 3.26	2.26 3.18	2.23 3.12	2.18 3.02	2.13 2.94	2.07 2.83	2.03 2.75	1.98 2.67	1.93 2.58	1.91 2.53	1.87 2.46	1.84 2.42	1.81 2.37	1.80 2.33	1.78 2.31
23	4.28 7.88	3.42 5.66	3.03 4.76	2.80 4.26	2.64 3.94	2.53 3.71	2.45 3.54	2.38 3.41	2.32 3.30	2.28 3.21	2.24 3.14	2.20 3.07	2.14 2.97	2.10 2.89	2.04 2.78	2.00 2.70	1.96 2.62	1.91 2.53	1.88 2.48	1.84 2.41	1.82 2.37	1.79 2.32	1.77 2.28	1.76 2.26
24	4.26 7.82	3.40 5.61	3.01 4.72	2.78 4.22	2.62 3.90	2.51 3.67	2.43 3.50	2.36 3.36	2.30 3.25	2.26 3.17	2.22 3.09	2.18 3.03	2.13 2.93	2.09 2.85	2.02 2.74	1.98 2.66	1.94 2.58	1.89 2.49	1.86 2.44	1.82 2.36	1.80 2.33	1.76 2.27	1.74 2.23	1.73 2.21
25	4.24 7.77	3.38 5.57	2.99 4.68	2.76 4.18	2.60 3.86	2.49 3.63	2.41 3.46	2.34 3.32	2.28 3.21	2.24 3.13	2.20 3.05	2.16 2.99	2.11 2.89	2.06 2.81	2.00 2.70	1.96 2.62	1.92 2.54	1.87 2.45	1.84 2.40	1.80 2.32	1.77 2.29	1.74 2.23	1.72 2.19	1.71 2.17
26	4.22 7.72	3.37 5.53	2.89 4.64	2.74 4.14	2.59 3.82	2.47 3.59	2.39 3.42	2.32 3.29	2.27 3.17	2.22 3.09	2.18 3.02	2.15 2.96	2.10 2.86	2.05 2.77	1.99 2.66	1.95 2.58	1.90 2.50	1.85 2.41	1.82 2.36	1.78 2.28	1.76 2.25	1.72 2.19	1.70 2.15	1.69 2.13
27	4.21 7.68	3.35 5.49	2.96 4.60	2.73 4.11	2.57 3.79	2.46 3.56	2.37 3.39	2.30 3.26	2.25 3.14	2.20 3.06	2.16 2.98	2.13 2.93	2.08 2.83	2.03 2.74	1.97 2.63	1.93 2.55	1.88 2.47	1.84 2.38	1.80 2.33	1.76 2.25	1.74 2.21	1.71 2.16	1.68 2.12	1.67 2.10
28	4.20 7.64	3.34 5.45	2.95 4.57	2.71 4.07	2.56 3.76	2.44 3.53	2.36 3.36	2.29 3.23	3.24 3.11	2.19 3.03	2.15 2.95	2.12 2.90	2.06 2.80	2.02 2.71	1.96 2.60	1.91 2.52	1.87 2.44	1.81 2.35	1.78 2.30	1.75 2.22	1.72 2.18	1.69 2.13	1.67 2.09	1.65 2.06
29	4.18 7.60	3.33 5.52	2.93 4.54	2.70 4.04	2.54 3.73	2.43 3.50	2.35 3.32	2.28 3.20	2.22 3.08	2.18 3.00	2.14 2.92	2.10 2.87	2.05 2.77	2.00 2.68	1.94 2.57	1.90 2.49	1.85 2.41	1.80 2.32	1.77 2.27	1.73 2.19	1.71 2.15	1.68 2.10	1.65 2.06	1.64 2.03
30	4.17 7.56	3.32 5.39	2.92 4.51	2.69 4.02	2.53 3.70	2.42 3.47	2.34 3.30	2.27 3.17	2.21 3.06	2.16 2.98	2.12 2.90	2.09 2.84	2.04 2.74	1.99 2.66	1.93 2.55	1.89 2.47	1.84 2.38	1.79 2.29	1.76 2.24	1.72 2.16	1.69 2.13	1.66 2.07	1.64 2.03	1.62 2.01
32	4.15 7.50	3.30 5.34	2.90 4.46	2.67 3.97	2.51 3.66	2.40 3.42	2.32 3.25	2.25 3.12	2.19 3.01	2.14 2.94	2.10 2.86	2.07 2.80	2.02 2.70	1.97 2.62	1.91 2.51	1.86 2.42	1.82 2.34	1.76 2.25	1.74 2.20	1.69 2.12	1.67 2.08	1.64 2.02	1.61 1.98	1.59 1.96
34	4.13 7.44	3.28 5.29	2.88 4.42	2.65 3.93	2.49 3.61	2.38 3.38	2.30 3.21	2.23 3.08	2.17 2.97	2.12 2.89	2.08 2.82	2.05 2.76	2.00 2.66	1.95 2.58	1.89 2.47	1.84 2.38	1.80 2.30	1.74 2.21	1.71 2.15	1.67 2.08	1.64 2.04	1.61 1.98	1.59 1.94	1.57 1.91

Appendix G *continued*

Degrees of freedom for denominator																								
36	4.11 7.39	3.26 5.25	2.86 4.38	2.63 3.89	2.48 3.58	2.36 3.35	2.28 3.18	2.21 3.04	2.15 2.94	2.10 2.86	2.06 2.78	2.03 2.72	1.89 2.62	1.93 2.54	1.87 2.43	1.82 2.35	1.78 2.26	1.72 2.17	1.69 2.12	1.65 2.04	1.62 2.00	1.59 1.94	1.56 1.90	1.55 1.87
38	4.10 7.35	3.25 5.21	2.85 4.34	2.62 3.86	2.46 3.54	2.35 3.32	2.26 3.15	2.19 3.02	2.14 2.91	2.09 2.82	2.05 2.75	2.02 2.69	1.96 2.59	1.92 2.51	1.85 2.40	1.80 2.32	1.76 2.22	1.71 2.14	1.67 2.08	1.63 2.00	1.60 1.97	1.57 1.90	1.54 1.86	1.53 1.84
40	4.08 7.31	3.23 5.18	2.84 4.31	2.61 3.83	2.45 3.51	2.34 3.29	2.25 3.12	2.18 2.99	2.12 2.88	2.07 2.80	2.04 2.73	2.00 2.66	1.95 2.56	1.90 2.49	1.84 2.37	1.79 2.29	1.74 2.20	1.69 2.11	1.66 2.05	1.61 1.97	1.59 1.94	1.55 1.88	1.53 1.84	1.51 1.81
42	4.07 7.27	3.22 5.15	2.83 4.29	2.59 3.80	2.44 3.49	2.32 3.26	2.24 3.10	2.17 2.96	2.11 2.86	2.06 2.77	2.02 2.70	1.90 2.64	1.94 2.54	1.89 2.46	1.82 2.35	1.78 2.26	1.73 2.17	1.68 2.08	1.64 2.02	1.60 1.94	1.57 1.91	1.54 1.85	1.51 1.80	1.49 1.78
44	4.06 7.24	3.21 5.12	2.82 4.26	2.58 3.78	2.43 3.46	2.31 3.24	2.23 3.07	2.16 2.94	2.10 2.84	2.05 2.75	2.01 2.68	1.98 2.62	1.92 2.52	1.88 2.44	1.81 2.32	1.76 2.24	1.72 2.15	1.66 2.06	1.63 2.09	1.58 1.92	1.56 1.88	1.52 1.82	1.50 1.78	1.48 1.75
46	4.05 7.21	3.20 5.10	2.81 4.24	2.57 3.76	2.42 3.44	2.30 3.22	2.22 3.05	2.14 2.92	2.09 2.82	2.04 2.73	2.00 2.66	1.97 2.60	1.91 2.50	1.87 2.42	1.80 2.30	1.75 2.22	1.71 2.13	1.65 2.04	1.62 1.98	1.57 1.90	1.54 1.86	1.51 1.80	1.48 1.76	1.46 1.72
48	4.04 7.19	3.19 5.08	2.80 4.22	2.56 3.74	2.41 3.42	2.30 3.20	2.21 3.04	2.14 2.90	2.08 2.80	2.03 2.71	1.99 2.64	1.96 2.58	1.90 2.48	1.86 2.40	1.79 2.28	1.74 2.20	1.70 2.11	1.64 2.02	1.61 1.96	1.56 1.88	1.53 1.84	1.50 1.78	1.47 1.73	1.45 1.70
50	4.03 7.17	3.18 5.06	2.79 4.20	2.56 3.72	2.40 3.41	2.29 3.18	2.20 3.02	2.13 2.88	2.07 2.78	2.02 2.70	1.98 2.62	1.95 2.56	1.90 2.46	1.85 2.39	1.78 2.26	1.74 2.18	1.69 2.10	1.63 2.00	1.60 1.94	1.55 1.86	1.52 1.82	1.48 1.76	1.46 1.71	1.44 1.68
55	4.02 7.12	3.17 5.01	2.78 4.16	2.54 3.68	2.38 3.37	2.27 3.15	2.18 2.98	2.11 2.85	2.05 2.75	2.00 2.66	1.97 2.59	1.93 2.53	1.88 2.43	1.83 2.35	1.76 2.23	1.72 2.15	1.67 2.06	1.61 1.96	1.58 1.90	1.52 1.82	1.50 1.78	1.46 1.71	1.43 1.66	1.41 1.64
60	4.00 7.08	3.15 4.98	2.76 4.13	2.52 3.65	2.37 3.34	2.25 3.12	2.17 2.95	2.10 2.82	2.04 2.72	1.99 2.63	1.95 2.56	1.92 2.50	1.86 2.40	1.81 2.32	1.75 2.20	1.70 2.12	1.65 2.03	1.59 1.93	1.56 1.87	1.50 1.79	1.48 1.74	1.44 1.68	1.41 1.63	1.39 1.60
65	3.99 7.04	3.14 4.95	2.75 4.10	2.51 3.62	2.36 3.31	2.24 3.09	2.15 2.93	2.08 2.79	2.02 2.70	1.98 2.61	1.94 2.54	1.90 2.47	1.85 2.37	1.80 2.30	1.73 2.18	1.68 2.09	1.63 2.00	1.57 1.90	1.54 1.84	1.49 1.76	1.46 1.71	1.42 1.64	1.39 1.60	1.37 1.56
70	3.98 7.01	3.13 4.92	2.74 4.08	2.50 3.60	2.35 3.29	2.32 3.07	2.14 2.91	2.07 2.77	2.01 2.67	1.97 2.59	1.93 2.51	1.89 2.45	1.84 2.35	1.79 2.28	1.72 2.15	1.67 2.07	1.62 1.98	1.56 1.88	1.53 1.82	1.47 1.74	1.45 1.69	1.40 1.62	1.37 1.56	1.35 1.53
80	3.96 6.96	3.11 4.88	2.72 4.04	2.48 3.56	2.33 3.25	2.21 3.04	2.12 2.87	2.05 2.74	1.99 2.64	1.95 2.55	1.91 2.48	1.88 2.41	1.82 2.32	1.77 2.24	1.70 2.11	1.65 2.03	1.60 1.94	1.54 1.84	1.51 1.78	1.45 1.70	1.42 1.65	1.38 1.57	1.35 1.52	1.32 1.49
100	3.94 6.90	3.09 4.82	2.70 3.98	2.46 3.51	2.30 3.20	2.19 2.99	2.10 2.82	2.03 2.69	1.97 2.59	1.92 2.51	1.88 2.43	1.85 2.36	1.79 2.26	1.75 2.19	1.68 2.06	1.63 1.98	1.57 1.89	1.51 1.79	1.48 1.73	1.42 1.64	1.39 1.59	1.34 1.51	1.30 1.46	1.28 1.43
125	3.92 6.84	3.07 4.78	2.68 3.94	2.44 3.47	2.29 3.17	2.17 2.95	2.08 2.79	2.01 2.65	1.95 2.56	1.90 2.47	1.86 2.40	1.83 2.33	1.77 2.23	1.72 2.15	1.65 2.03	1.60 1.94	1.55 1.85	1.49 1.75	1.45 1.68	1.39 1.59	1.36 1.54	1.31 1.46	1.27 1.40	1.25 1.37
150	3.91 6.81	3.06 4.75	2.67 3.91	2.43 3.44	2.27 3.13	2.16 2.92	2.07 2.76	2.00 2.62	1.94 2.53	1.89 2.44	1.85 2.37	1.82 2.30	1.76 2.20	1.71 2.12	1.64 2.00	1.59 1.91	1.54 1.83	1.47 1.72	1.44 1.66	1.37 1.56	1.34 1.51	1.29 1.43	1.25 1.37	1.22 1.33
200	3.89 6.76	3.04 4.71	2.65 3.38	2.41 3.41	2.26 3.11	2.14 2.90	2.05 2.73	1.98 2.60	1.92 2.50	1.87 2.41	1.83 2.34	1.80 2.28	1.74 1.17	1.69 2.09	1.62 1.97	1.57 1.88	1.52 1.79	1.45 1.69	1.42 1.62	1.35 1.53	1.32 1.48	1.26 1.39	1.22 1.33	1.19 1.28
400	3.86 6.70	3.02 4.66	2.62 3.83	2.39 3.36	2.23 3.06	2.12 2.85	2.03 2.69	1.96 2.55	1.90 2.46	1.85 2.37	1.81 2.29	1.78 2.23	1.72 2.12	1.67 2.04	1.60 1.92	1.54 1.84	1.49 1.74	1.42 1.64	1.38 1.57	1.32 1.47	1.28 1.42	1.22 1.32	1.16 1.24	1.13 1.19
1000	3.85 6.66	3.00 4.62	2.61 3.80	2.38 3.34	2.22 3.04	2.10 2.82	2.02 2.66	1.95 2.53	1.89 2.43	1.84 2.34	1.80 2.26	1.76 2.20	1.70 2.09	1.65 2.01	1.58 1.89	1.53 1.81	1.47 1.71	1.41 1.61	1.36 1.54	1.30 1.44	1.26 1.38	1.19 1.28	1.13 1.19	1.08 1.11
∞	3.84 6.64	2.99 4.60	2.60 3.78	2.37 3.32	2.21 3.02	2.09 2.80	2.01 2.64	1.94 2.51	1.88 2.41	1.83 2.32	1.79 2.24	1.75 2.18	1.69 2.07	1.64 1.99	1.57 1.87	1.52 1.79	1.46 1.69	1.40 1.59	1.35 1.52	1.28 1.41	1.24 1.36	1.17 1.25	1.11 1.15	1.00 1.00

APPENDIX H

PERCENTAGE POINTS OF THE STUDENTIZED RANGE

Error df	α	*k* = *number of means or number of steps between ordered means*									
		2	3	4	5	6	7	8	9	10	11
5	.05	3.64	4.60	5.22	5.67	6.03	6.33	6.58	6.80	6.99	7.17
	.01	5.70	6.98	7.80	8.42	8.91	9.32	9.67	9.97	10.24	10.48
6	.05	3.46	4.34	4.90	5.30	5.63	5.90	6.12	6.32	6.49	6.65
	.01	5.24	6.33	7.03	7.56	7.97	8.32	8.61	8.87	9.10	9.30
7	.05	3.34	4.16	4.68	5.06	5.36	5.61	5.82	6.00	6.16	6.30
	.01	4.95	5.92	6.54	7.01	7.37	7.68	7.94	8.17	8.37	8.55
8	.05	3.26	4.04	4.53	4.89	5.17	5.40	5.60	5.77	5.92	6.05
	.01	4.75	5.64	6.20	6.62	6.96	7.24	7.47	7.68	7.86	8.03
9	.05	3.20	3.95	4.41	4.76	5.02	5.24	5.43	5.59	5.74	5.87
	.01	4.60	5.43	5.96	6.35	6.66	6.91	7.13	7.33	7.49	7.65
10	.05	3.15	3.88	4.33	4.65	4.91	5.12	5.30	5.46	5.60	5.72
	.01	4.48	5.27	5.77	6.14	6.43	6.67	6.87	7.05	7.21	7.36
11	.05	3.11	3.82	4.26	4.57	4.82	5.03	5.20	5.35	5.49	5.61
	.01	4.39	5.15	5.62	5.97	6.25	6.48	6.67	6.84	6.99	7.13
12	.05	3.08	3.77	4.20	4.51	4.75	4.95	5.12	5.27	5.39	5.51
	.01	4.32	5.05	5.50	5.84	6.10	6.32	6.51	6.67	6.81	6.94
13	.05	3.06	3.73	4.15	4.45	4.69	4.88	5.05	5.19	5.32	5.43
	.01	4.26	4.96	5.40	5.73	5.98	6.19	6.37	6.53	6.67	6.79
14	.05	3.03	3.70	4.11	4.41	4.64	4.83	4.99	5.13	5.25	5.36
	.01	4.21	4.89	5.32	5.63	5.88	6.08	6.26	6.41	6.54	6.66
15	.05	3.01	3.67	4.08	4.37	4.59	4.78	4.94	5.08	5.20	5.31
	.01	4.17	4.84	5.25	5.56	5.80	5.99	6.16	6.31	6.44	6.55
16	.05	3.00	3.65	4.05	4.33	4.56	4.74	4.90	5.03	5.15	5.26
	.01	4.13	4.79	5.19	5.49	5.72	5.92	6.08	6.22	6.35	6.46
17	.05	2.98	3.63	4.02	4.30	4.52	4.70	4.86	4.99	5.11	5.21
	.01	4.10	4.74	5.14	5.43	5.66	5.85	6.01	6.15	6.27	6.38
18	.05	2.97	3.61	4.00	4.28	4.49	4.67	4.82	4.96	5.07	5.17
	.01	4.07	4.70	5.09	5.38	5.60	5.79	5.94	6.08	6.20	6.31
19	.05	2.96	3.59	3.98	4.25	4.47	4.65	4.79	4.92	5.04	5.14
	.01	4.05	4.67	5.05	5.33	5.55	5.73	5.89	6.02	6.14	6.25
20	.05	2.95	3.58	3.96	4.23	4.45	4.62	4.77	4.90	5.01	5.11
	.01	4.02	4.64	5.02	5.29	5.51	5.69	5.84	5.97	6.09	6.19
24	.05	2.92	3.53	3.90	4.17	4.37	4.54	4.68	4.81	4.92	5.01
	.01	3.96	4.55	4.91	5.17	5.37	5.54	5.69	5.81	5.92	6.02
30	.05	2.89	3.49	3.85	4.10	4.30	4.46	4.60	4.72	4.82	4.92
	.01	3.89	4.45	4.80	5.05	5.24	5.40	5.54	5.65	5.76	5.85
40	.05	2.86	3.44	3.79	4.04	4.23	4.39	4.52	4.63	4.73	4.82
	.01	3.82	4.37	4.70	4.93	5.11	5.26	5.39	5.50	5.60	5.69
60	.05	2.83	3.40	3.74	3.98	4.16	4.31	4.44	4.55	4.65	4.73
	.01	3.76	4.28	4.59	4.82	4.99	5.13	5.25	5.36	5.45	5.53
120	.05	2.80	3.36	3.68	3.92	4.10	4.24	4.36	4.47	4.56	4.64
	.01	3.70	4.20	4.50	4.71	4.87	5.01	5.12	5.21	5.30	5.37
∞	.05	2.77	3.31	3.63	3.86	4.03	4.17	4.29	4.39	4.47	4.55
	.01	3.64	4.12	4.40	4.60	4.76	4.88	4.99	5.08	5.16	5.23

Source: Taken from Table O (p. 486) of R. P. Runyon & A. Haber, *Fundamentals of Behavioral Statistics*, 6th ed. Published by McGraw-Hill, New York. Reprinted by permission.

APPENDIX I

CRITICAL VALUES OF THE PEARSON PRODUCT-MOMENT CORRELATION

	Level of significance for a directional (one-tailed) test				
	.05	.025	.01	.005	.0005
	Level of significance for a non-directional (two-tailed) test				
$df = N-2$	.10	.05	.02	.01	.001
1	.9877	.9969	.9995	.9999	1.0000
2	.9000	.9500	.9800	.9900	.9990
3	.8054	.8783	.9343	.9587	.9912
4	.7293	.8114	.8822	.9172	.9741
5	.6694	.7545	.8329	.8745	.9507
6	.6215	.7067	.7887	.8343	.9249
7	.5822	.6664	.7498	.7977	.8982
8	.5494	.6319	.7155	.7646	.8721
9	.5214	.6021	.6851	.7348	.8471
10	.4973	.5760	.6581	.7079	.8233
11	.4762	.5529	.6339	.6835	.8010
12	.4575	.5324	.6120	.6614	.7800
13	.4409	.5139	.5923	.6411	.7603
14	.4259	.4973	.5742	.6226	.7420
15	.4124	.4821	.5577	.6055	.7246
16	.4000	.4683	.5425	.5897	.7084
17	.3887	.4555	.5285	.5751	.6932
18	.3783	.4438	.5155	.5614	.6787
19	.3687	.4329	.5034	.5487	.6652
20	.3598	.4227	.4921	.5368	.6524
25	.3233	.3809	.4451	.4869	.5974
30	.2960	.3494	.4093	.4487	.5541
35	.2746	.3246	.3810	.4182	.5189
40	.2573	.3044	.3578	.3932	.4896
45	.2428	.2875	.3384	.3721	.4648
50	.2306	.2732	.3218	.3541	.4433
60	.2108	.2500	.2948	.3248	.4078
70	.1954	.2319	.2737	.3017	.3799
80	.1829	.2172	.2565	.2830	.3568
90	.1726	.2050	.2422	.2673	.3375
100	.1638	.1946	.2301	.2540	.3211

Source: "Appendix I is taken from Table VIII of Fisher & Yates': *Statistical Tables for Biological, Agricultural, and Medical Research* published by Longman Group UK Ltd. London (previously published by Oliver and Boyd Ltd, Edinburgh) and by permission of the authors and publishers."

REFERENCES AND RECOMMENDED READINGS

Chapter 1

Anderson, N. H. (1981). Scales and statistics: Parametric and nonparametric. *Psychological Bulletin, 58,* 305–316.

Gardner, P. L. (1975). Scales and statistics. *Review of Educational Research, 45,* 43–57.

Michell, J. (1986). Measurement scales and statistics: A clash of paradigm. *Psychological Bulletin, 100,* 398–407.

Nunnally, J. (1978). *Psychometric theory.* New York: McGraw-Hill.

Townsend, J. T., & Ashby, F. G. (1984). Measurement scales and statistics: The misconception misconceived. *Psychological Bulletin, 96,* 394–401.

Wolf, G., & Cartwright, B. (1974). Rules for coding dummy variables. *Psychological Bulletin, 81,* 173–179.

Chapter 2

Anscombe, F. J. (1973). Graphs in statistical analysis. *American Statistician, 27,* 17–21.

Chapter 3

Shavelson, R. J. (1988). *Statistical reasoning for the behavioral sciences* (2nd ed.). Boston: Allyn and Bacon.

Chapter 4

Anastasi, A. (1988). *Psychological testing* (6th ed.). New York: Macmillan.

Ghiselli, E. E., Campbell, J. P., & Zedeck, S. (1981). *Measurement theory for the behavioral sciences.* San Francisco: W. H. Freeman.

Chapter 5

Comrey, A. L., Bott, P. A., & Lee, H. B. (1989). *Elementary statistics: A problem-solving approach* (2nd ed.). Dubuque, Iowa: Wm. C. Brown.

Hinkle, D. E., & Oliver, J. D. (1983). How large should the sample be? A question with no simple answer? Or. . . ? *Educational and Psychological Measurement, 43,* 1051–1060.

Hinkle, D. E., Oliver, J. D., & Hinkle, C. A. (1985). How large should the sample be? Part II—The one-sample case for survey research. *Educational and Psychological Measurement, 45,* 271–280.

Runyon, R. P., & Haber, A. (1988). *Fundamentals of behavioral statistics* (6th ed.). New York: Random House.

Shavelson, R. J. (1988). *Statistical reasoning for the behavioral sciences* (2nd ed.). Boston: Allyn and Bacon.

Chapter 6

Chase, L. T., & Tucker, R. K. (1976). Statistical power: Derivation, development, and data-analytic implication. *The Psychological Record, 26,* 472–486.

Cohen, J. (1969). *Statistical power analysis for the behavioral sciences.* New York: Academic Press.

Lipsey, M. W. (1989). *Design sensitivity: Statistical power for experimental research.* Newbury Park, CA: Sage Publications.

Nelson, N., Rosenthal, R., & Rosnow, R. L. (1986). Interpretation of significance levels and effect sizes by psychological researchers. *American Psychologist, 41,* 1299–1301.

Runyon, R. P., & Haber, A. (1988). *Fundamentals of behavioral statistics* (6th ed.). New York: Random House.

Siegel, S., & Castellan, N. J. (1988). *Nonparametric statistics for the behavioral sciences* (2nd ed.). New York: McGraw-Hill.

Chapter 7

Blair, R. C., & Higgins, J. J. (1985). Comparison of the power of the paired samples t test to that of Wilcoxon's signed-ranks test under various population shapes. *Psychological Bulletin, 97,* 119–128.

Blair, R. C., Higgins, J. J., & Smitley, W. D. S. (1980). On the relative power of the U and t tests. *British Journal of Mathematical and Statistical Psychology, 33,* 114–120.

Bradley, D. R., Bradley, T. D., McGrath, S. G., & Cutcomb, S. D. (1979). Type I error rate of the chi-square test of independence in R × C tables that have small expected frequencies. *Psychological Bulletin, 86,* 1290–1297.

Camilli, G., & Hopkins, K. D. (1978). Applicability of chi-square to 2 × 2 contingency tables with small expected cell frequencies. *Psychological Bulletin, 85,* 163–167.

Chase, L. J., & Tucker, R. K. (1976). Statistical power: Derivation, development, and data-analytic implication. *The Psychological Record, 26,* 472–486.

Cochran, W. G. (1954). Some methods for strengthening the common chi-square tests. *Biometrics, 10,* 417–451.

Cohen, J. (1969). *Statistical power analysis for the behavioral sciences.* New York: Academic Press.

Daniel, W. W. (1978). *Applied nonparametric statistics.* Boston: Houghton-Mifflin.

Friedman, H. (1982). Simplified determinations of statistical power, magnitude of effect and research sample sizes. *Educational and Psychological Measurement, 42,* 521–526.
Kirk, R. E. (1968). *Experimental design: Procedures for the behavioral sciences.* Belmont, CA: Brooks/Cole.
Liebetrau, A. M. (1983). *Measures of association.* Beverly Hills, CA: Sage Publications.
Maxwell, S. E., Camp, C. J., & Avery, R. D. (1981). Measures of strength of association: A comparative examination. *Journal of Applied Psychology, 66,* 525–534.
Nelson, N., Rosenthal, R., & Rosnow, R. L. (1986). Interpretation of significance levels and effect sizes by psychological researchers. *American Psychologist, 41,* 1299–1301.
Nicewander, W. A., & Price, J. M. (1983). Reliability of means and the power of statistical tests: Some new results. *Psychological Bulletin, 95,* 524–533.
Overall, J. E. (1980). Power of chi-square tests for 2 × 2 contingency tables with small expected frequencies. *Psychological Bulletin, 87,* 132–135.
Siegel, S., & Castellan, N. J. (1988). *Nonparametric statistics for the behavioral sciences* (2nd ed.). New York: McGraw-Hill.

Chapter 8

Cohen, J. (1969). *Statistical power analysis for the behavioral sciences.* New York: Academic Press.
Daniel, W. W. (1978). *Applied nonparametric statistics.* Boston: Houghton-Mifflin.
Keppel, G. (1982). *Design and analysis: A researcher's handbook* (2nd ed.). Englewood Cliffs, NJ: Prentice-Hall.
Kirk, R. E. (1968). *Experimental design: Procedures for the behavioral sciences.* Belmont, CA: Brooks/Cole.
Levin, J. R. (1975). Determining sample size for planned and post hoc analysis of variance comparisons. *Journal of Educational Measurement, 12,* 99–108.
Liebetrau, A. M. (1983). *Measures of association.* Beverly Hills, CA: Sage Publications.
Lindman, H. R. (1974). *Analysis of variance in complex experimental designs.* San Francisco: W. H. Freeman.
Maxwell, S. E., Camp, C. J., & Avery, R. D. (1981). Measures of strength of association: A comparative examination. *Journal of Applied Psychology, 66,* 525–534.
Nelson, N., Rosenthal, R., & Rosnow, R. L. (1986). Interpretation of significance levels and effect sizes by psychological researchers. *American Psychologist, 41,* 1299–1301.
Siegel, S., & Castellan, J. J. (1988). *Nonparametric statistics for the behavioral sciences* (2nd ed.). New York: McGraw-Hill.
Smith, R. A. (1971). The effect of unequal group size on Tukey's HSD procedure. *Psychometrika, 36,* 31–34.
Stoline, M. R. (1981). The status of multiple comparisons: Simultaneous estimation of all pairwise comparisons in one-way ANOVA designs. *American Statistician, 35,* 134–141.

Chapter 9

Cohen, J. (1969). *Statistical power analysis for the behavioral sciences.* New York: Academic Press.
Keppel, G. (1982). *Design and analysis: A researcher's handbook* (2nd ed.). Englewood Cliffs, NJ: Prentice-Hall.
Kirk, R. E. (1968). *Experimental design: Procedures for the behavioral sciences.* Belmont, CA: Brooks/Cole.
Levin, J. R. (1975). Determining sample size for planned and post hoc analysis of variance comparisons. *Journal of Educational Measurement, 12,* 99–108.
Liebetrau, A. M. (1983). *Measures of association.* Beverly Hills, CA: Sage Publications.
Lindman, H. R. (1974). *Analysis of variance in complex experimental designs.* San Francisco: W. H. Freeman.
Maxwell, S. E., Camp, C. J., & Avery, R. D. (1981). Measures of strength of association: A comparative examination. *Journal of Applied Psychology, 66,* 525–534.
Nelson, N., Rosenthal, R., & Rosnow, R. L. (1986). Interpretation of significance levels and effect sizes by psychological researchers. *American Psychologist, 41,* 1299–1301.
Smith, R. A. (1971). The effect of unequal group size on Tukey's HSD procedure. *Psychometrika, 36,* 31–34.

Chapter 10

Blalock, H. M. (1964). *Causal inferences in non-experimental research.* Chapel Hill: University of North Carolina Press.
Blalock, H. M. (Ed.) (1971). *Causal models in the social sciences.* Chicago: Aldine.
Bradley, D. R., Bradley, T. D., McGrath, S. G., & Cutcomb, S. D. (1979). Type I error rate of the chi-square test of independence in R × C tables that have small expected frequencies. *Psychological Bulletin, 86,* 1290–1297.
Camilli, G., & Hopkins, K. D. (1978). Applicability of chi-square to 2 × 2 contingency tables with small expected cell frequencies. *Psychological Bulletin, 85,* 163–167.
Carroll, J. B. (1961). The nature of data, or how to choose a correlation coefficient. *Psychometrika, 26,* 347–372.
Cochran, W. G. (1954). Some methods for strengthening the common chi-square tests. *Biometrics, 10,* 417–451.
Hinkle, D. E., Wiersma, W., and Jurs, S. G. (1988). *Applied statistics for the behavioral sciences* (2nd ed.). Boston: Houghton-Mifflin.
Kenny, D. A. (1979). *Correlation and causality.* Toronto: Wiley.
Overall, J. E. (1980). Power of chi-square tests for 2 × 2 contingency tables with small expected frequencies. *Psychological Bulletin, 87,* 132–135.

Chapter 11

Edwards, A. L. (1984). *An introduction to linear regression and correlation* (2nd ed.). New York: W. H. Freeman.

Chapter 12

Edwards, A. L. (1984). *An introduction to linear regression and correlation* (2nd ed.). New York: W. H. Freeman.
Elashoff, J. D. (1969). Analysis of covariance: A delicate instrument. *American Educational Research Journal, 6,* 383–401.
Huitema, B. E. (1980). *The analysis of covariance.* New York: Wiley.
Keppel, G. (1982). *Design and analysis: A researcher's handbook* (2nd ed.). Englewood Cliffs, NJ: Prentice-Hall.
Kirk, R. E. (1968). *Experimental design: Procedures for the behavioral sciences.* Belmont, CA: Brooks/Cole.

Lindeman, R. H., Merenda, P. F., & Gold, R. Z. (1980). *Introduction to bivariate and multivariate analysis.* Glenview, IL: Scott, Foresman and Co.

Chapter 13

Asher, H. B. (1976). *Causal modeling.* Sage University Paper Series on Quantitative Applications in the Social Sciences, Series No. 07–003. Beverly Hills and London: Sage Publications.

Bentler, P. M. (1980). Multivariate analysis with latent variables: Causal modeling. *Annual Review of Psychology, 31,* 419–456.

Blalock, H. M. (1964). *Causal inferences in non-experimental research.* Chapel Hill: University of North Carolina Press.

Blalock, H. M. (Ed.) (1971). *Causal models in the social sciences.* Chicago: Aldine.

Darlington, R. B. (1968). Multiple regression in psychological research and practice. *Psychological Bulletin, 79,* 161–182.

Draper, N. R., & Smith, H. (1981). *Applied regression analysis.* New York: Wiley.

Drasgow, F., & Dorans, N. J. (1982). Robustness of estimators of the squared multiple correlation and squared cross-validity coefficient to violations of multivariate normality. *Applied Psychological Mesurement, 6,* 185–200.

Edwards, A. L. (1984). *An introduction to linear regression and correlation* (2nd ed.). New York: W. H. Freeman and Co.

Harris, R. J. (1985). *A primer of multivariate statistics* (2nd ed.). Orlando, FL: Academic Press.

Johnson, R. A., & Wichern, D. W. (1988). *Applied multivariate statistical analysis* (2nd ed.). New York: Prentice-Hall.

Kenny, D. A. (1979). *Correlation and causality.* Toronto: Wiley.

Kerlinger, F. N., & Pedhazur, E. J. (1973). *Multiple regression in behavior research.* New York: Holt, Rinehart, and Winston.

Lindeman, R. H., Merenda, P. F., & Gold, R. Z. (1980). *Introduction to bivariate and multivariate analysis.* Glenview, IL: Scott, Foresman and Co.

Nunnally, J. (1978). *Psychometric theory.* New York: McGraw-Hill.

Pedhazur, E. J. (1982). *Multiple regression in behavioral research.* New York: Holt.

Schmidt, F. L. (1971). The relative efficiency of regression in simple unit predictor weights in applied differential psychology. *Educational and Psychological Measurement, 31,* 699–714.

Shumway, R. H. (1988). *Applied statistical time-series analysis.* Englewood Cliffs, NJ: Prentice-Hall.

Tabachnick, B. G., & Fidell, L. S. (1983). *Using multivariate statistics.* New York: Harper and Row.

Wainer, H., & Thissen, D. (1976). Three steps toward robust regression. *Psychometrika, 41,* 9–34.

Wilkinson, L. (1979). Tests of significance in stepwise regression. *Psychological Bulletin, 86,* 168–174.

Chapter 14

Bock, R. D. (1975). *Multivariate statistical methods in behavioral research.* New York: McGraw-Hill.

Harris, R. J. (1985). *A primer of multivariate statistics* (2nd ed.). Orlando, FL: Academic Press.

Huberty, C. J. (1975). Discriminant analysis. *Review of Educational Research, 45,* 543–598.

Huberty, C. J. (1984). Issues in the use and interpretation of discriminant analysis. *Psychological Bulletin, 95,* 156–171.

Johnson, R. A., & Wichern, D. W. (1988). *Applied multivariate statistical analysis* (2nd ed.). New York: Prentice-Hall.

Lindeman, R. H., Merenda, P. F., & Gold, R. Z. (1980). *Introduction to bivariate and multivariate analysis.* Glenview, IL: Scott, Foresman and Co.

Mardia, K. V. (1971). The effect of nonnormality on some multivariate tests and robustness to nonnormality in the linear model. *Biometrika, 58,* 105–121.

Nunnally, J. (1978). *Psychometric theory.* New York: McGraw-Hill.

Overall, J. E., & Klett, C. J. (1972). *Applied multivariate analysis.* New York: McGraw-Hill.

Tabachnick, B. G., & Fidell, L. S. (1983). *Using multivariate statistics.* New York: Harper and Row.

Chapter 15

Bird, K. D. (1975). Simultaneous contrast testing procedures for multivariate experiments. *Multivariate Behavioral Research, 10,* 343–351.

Bird, K. D., & Hadzi-Pavlovic, D. (1983). Simultaneous test procedures and the choice of a test statistic in MANOVA. *Psychological Bulletin, 93,* 167–178.

Bock, R. D. (1975). *Multivariate statistical methods in behavioral research.* New York: McGraw-Hill.

Harris, R. J. (1985). *A primer of multivariate statistics* (2nd ed.). Orlando, FL: Academic Press.

Lindeman, R. H., Merenda, P. F., & Gold, R. Z. (1980). *Introduction to bivariate and multivariate analysis.* Glenview, IL: Scott, Foresman and Co.

Mardia, K. V. (1971). The effect of nonnormality on some multivariate tests and robustness to nonnormality in the linear model. *Biometrika, 58,* 105–121.

Olson, C. L. (1976). On choosing a test statistic in multivariate analysis of variance. *Psychological Bulletin, 83,* 579–586.

Tabachnick, B. G., & Fidell, L. S. (1983). *Using multivariate statistics.* New York: Harper and Row.

Chapter 16

Cattell, R. B. (1966). The scree test for the number of factors. *Multivariate Behavioral Research, 1,* 245–276.

Cattell, R. B., & Baggaley, A. R. (1960). The salient variable similarity index for factor matching. *British Journal for Statistical Psychology, 13,* 33–46.

Cattell, R. B., Balcar, K. R., Horn, J. L., & Nesselroade, J. R. (1969). Factor matching procedures: An improvement of the *s* index; with tables. *Educational and Psychological Mesurement, 29,* 781–792.

Cattell, R. B., & Vogelman, S. (1977). A comprehensive trial of the scree and KG criteria for determining the number of factors. *Multivariate Behavioral Research, 12,* 289–325.

Ferguson, G. A., & Takane, Y. (1989). *Statistical analysis in psychology and education* (6th ed.). New York: McGraw-Hill.

Gorsuch, R. L. (1983). *Factor analysis* (2nd ed.). Hillsdale, NJ: Erlbaum.

Harris, R. J. (1985). *A primer of multivariate statistics* (2nd ed.). Orlando, FL: Academic Press.
Johnson, R. A., & Wichern, D. W. (1988). *Applied multivariate statistical analysis* (2nd ed.). New York: Prentice-Hall.
Levine, M. S. (1977). *Canonical analysis and factor comparison.* Sage University Paper Series in Quantitative Applications in the Social Sciences, Series No. 07–006. Beverly Hills and London: Sage Publications.
Lindeman, R. H., Merenda, P. F., & Gold, R. Z. (1980). *Introduction to bivariate and multivariate analysis.* Glenview, IL: Scott, Foresman and Co.
Morrison, D. F. (1967). *Multivariate statistical methods.* New York: McGraw-Hill.
Nunnally, J. (1978). *Psychometric theory.* New York: McGraw-Hill.
Overall, J. E., & Klett, C. J. (1972). *Applied multivariate analysis.* New York: McGraw-Hill.

Chapter 17

Borgen, F. H., & Barnett, D. C. (1987). Applying cluster analysis in counseling psychology research. *Journal of Counseling Psychology, 34,* 456–468.
Everitt, B. S., & Dunn, G. (1983). *Advanced methods of data exploration and modelling.* London: Heinemann Educational Books.
Spath, H. (1980). *Cluster analysis algorithms.* New York: Wiley.
Tryon, R. C., & Bailey, D. E. (1970). *Cluster analysis.* New York: McGraw-Hill.

Chapter 18

Everitt, B. S., & Dunn, G. (1983). *Advanced methods of data exploration and modelling.* London: Heinemann Educational Books.
Kruskal, J. B., & Wish, M. (1978). *Multidimensional scaling.* Sage University Paper Series on Quantitative Applications in the Social Sciences, Series No. 07–011. Beverly Hills and London: Sage.
Nunnally, J. (1978). *Psychometric theory.* New York: McGraw-Hill.
Schiffman, S. S., Reynolds, M. L., & Young, F. W. (1981). *Introduction to multidimensional scaling: Theory, methods, and applications.* New York: Academic Press.
Wish, M. (1976). Comparisons among multidimensional structures of interpersonal relations. *Multivariate Behavioral Research, 11,* 297–324.

INDEX

E

F

G

H

T

U

V

W

X

Y

Z